Advance Praise for Alvin S. Felzenberg's *Governor Tom Kean: His Journey from the New Jersey Statehouse to the 9–11 Commission*

"Tom Kean has devoted his life to serving his state and country as one of the most popular and productive governors in New Jersey history and as president of Drew University, where he continued his efforts to foster excellence in and access to education. Tom's demonstrated commitment to bipartisanship and fact-finding uniquely qualified him to chair the 9/11 Commission, a task he carried out with his customary fairness and effectiveness. It has been an honor for me to work with Tom, both when we were governors and when I named him to chair our campaign against teen pregnancy and to serve on the board of the initiative to build One America. He is a wonderful man and a genuine patriot, and I am grateful Al Felzenberg's fine biography does justice to Governor Kean's outstanding legacy."

—President William Jefferson Clinton

"Al Felzenberg has brought forth a suburb biography of a man who was ahead of his time in many ways. As a governor, Tom Kean was working on education and welfare reform before it was politically safe or even fashionable to do so. For many years, his was but a lone voice calling for Republicans to reach out to African Americans. The American people received a brief glimpse of Tom Kean's unique style of leadership when he chaired the 9–11 Commission. In retracing Kean's steps from the New Jersey Statehouse to the 9–11 Commission, Felzenberg shows how Kean, in his understated way, was so often able to persuade presidents, Congresses, and his fellow governors to move in the direction he envisioned for New Jersey and our whole nation. It is a fascinating story and a delightful read of a great American statesman."

—Jack Kemp, former member of Congress (R-NY), former secretary of HUD, and Republican vice presidential candidate in 1996

"Fascinating. This is a thorough yet fun biography. An ambitious, yet caring flesh-and-blood American political leader comes alive in Felzenberg's biography of Tom Kean. Reagan, Clinton, race relations, and terrorism all intersect for a compelling political tale."

—Juan Williams, author of *Eyes on the Prize*

"The story of Tom Kean in many ways is that of a man without a party. He was often too liberal for the Republicans and too incorruptible to succeed as a Democrat in New Jersey. But party politics, as his role leading the 9–11 Commission showed once again, is not what Kean has been about. If the phrase 'fair-minded statesman' has meaning anymore, it applies to him. Al Felzenberg understands Kean inside out, and captures him well in this insightful book."

—David Maraniss, author of *First in His Class: A Biography of Bill Clinton*

"Al Felzenberg has written a first-class biography of a first-class public servant. Tom Kean has contributed his entire professional career to public life but perhaps his greatest accomplishment is his latest. With grace, wisdom, and purpose, he led the bipartisan 9–11 Commission to produce a report of such force and clarity that it surely will be viewed by history as a major contribution to the security of the American people."

—Senator Joseph Lieberman (D-CT)

"It is the very good fortune of Thomas Kean that his biography is written by fellow Princetonian Al Felzenberg. No one is more widely experienced than Felzenberg at every level. And Kean is an insufficiently regarded political figure, a star of twenty years of Republican politics. *How did he do it?* How did the extraordinarily successful governor of the State of New Jersey manage to win 62 percent of the African American vote? Governor Kean was in many respects an exemplar of Republican independence. Courted and admired by Presidents Nixon and Reagan, but always, as author Felzenberg describes, maintaining just the remove from partisan politics required to make him a national figure, keynoter at a Republican Convention and, finally, president of Drew University. It is all told here, with intelligence and insight, supremely informed, supremely readable."

—William F. Buckley, Jr., Editor-at-Large, *National Review*

"Many of the great changes in public policy over the last quarter-century have been produced not in Washington but in the states. Thomas Kean, as governor of New Jersey in the 1980s, was one of those who produced great changes. Later, as chairman of the 9–11 Commission, Kean was a major shaper of national intelligence policy as well. Al Felzenberg, who knows Kean well, vividly tells the fascinating story of this patrician politician, whose career has ramifications far beyond New Jersey."

—Michael Barone, *U.S. News & World Report* and coauthor of
The Almanac of American Politics

"Tom Kean has lived a life in politics—in the best sense of the word. A politics rooted in service and civility. No one knows that story better than Al Felzenberg, and he tells it with grace—and a deep sense of how rare a politician Tom Kean turned out to be."

—George Stephanopoulos, host of WABC's *This Week* and
author of *All Too Human*

"Tom Kean is one of the valuable and rare politicians who can rise above partisanship to lead based on values. Al Felzenberg, in this carefully researched and vividly written biography, shows how as New Jersey's governor, Kean was able to forge an enlightened consensus on issues such as education and the environment. It was a mix of vision and wisdom that served him, and the world, so well when he was tapped to chair the 9–11 Commission."

—Walter Isaacson, author of *Benjamin Franklin: An American Life* and
coauthor of *The Wise Men: Six Friends and the World They Made*

"As a society, we pay too much attention to presidents, too little attention to some other public servants, who do enormous good in their careers. Tom Kean is one such statesman and Al Felzenberg has done a bang-up job of illuminating the career of a superb governor or New Jersey, university president, and chairman of the 9–11 Commission. During the 9–11 hearings and afterward, the nation came to know what the Garden State has long recognized—Tom Kean is a man of great integrity, courageous leadership, and sensible forthrightness. Before we can produce more leaders like Kean, we first must understand how they came to be, and Felzenberg beautifully traces the character and career of this extraordinary man. This is a book that students, biography-lovers, and good citizens everywhere will enjoy reading from cover to cover."

—Larry J. Sabato, director of the Center for Politics, University of Virginia

"This is a landmark work, an insider's account of the take-no-prisoners world of New Jersey politics. It's the story of a gentleman—highborn but unassuming—who tamed the political beast. This is must-reading for anyone who wants to know how politics really works."

—Martin Tolchin, coauthor of *To the Victors*

"I really enjoyed reading *Governor Tom Kean: His Journey from the New Jersey Statehouse to the 9–11 Commission.* I learned lots I did not know and solidly confirmed my opinion formed years ago when I met Tom: that he is an extraordinarily gifted and likable human being."

—Edward I. Koch, former mayor of New York City

Governor Tom Kean

*To Brad Graves —
With best wishes —*

GOVERNOR TOM KEAN

From the New Jersey Statehouse to the 9–11 Commission

Alvin S. Felzenberg

December 10, 2006

Rivergate Books
An imprint of Rutgers University Press
New Brunswick, New Jersey, and London

Library of Congress Cataloging-in-Publication Data

Felzenberg, Alvin S.
Governor Tom Kean : from the statehouse to the 9–11 Commission /
Alvin S. Felzenberg.
p. cm.
Includes bibliographical references and index.
ISBN-13: 978-0-8135-3799-3 (hardcover : alk. paper)
1. Kean, Thomas H.   2. Legislators—United States—Biography.
3. United States. Congress. House—Biography.   4. National Commission
on Terrorist Attacks upon the United States.   5. Governors—New Jersey—
Biography.   6. Legislators—New Jersey—Biography.   7. New Jersey—
Politics and government—1951–   8. Drew University—
Presidents—Biography.   I. Title.
E840.8.K33F45   2006
974.9′043092—dc22
2005024908

British Cataloging-in-Publication information for this book is available
from the British Library.

The publication of this volume has been made possible, in part,
by gifts from Maurice Lee Jr., Susan N. Wilson,
and the Schumann Fund for New Jersey.

Manufactured in the United States of America

To the memory of my parents,
Lillian Ritter Felzenberg (1917–1993),
who liked Tom Kean, and
Joseph Felzenberg (1912–1964),
who would have

Contents

Preface

Like its subject, this book has had a long history. Long before I began my research, I had thought that Thomas Howard Kean's journey from a shy and withdrawn child with a rebellious streak to an effective state legislator, a transformational governor, and, certainly, one of the most significant actors on the New Jersey political stage during the second half of the twentieth century would make for an interesting book. Yet I held off. When Tom Kean stepped down as New Jersey's forty-eighth governor in 1990 at the age of fifty-four, I, like so many who had observed his career, believed that his public career had not drawn to a close, but that he had merely ended a chapter. Subscribing to the prevailing conventional wisdom—readers will discover that the conventional wisdom was more often wrong than right when it concerned Tom Kean—I assumed that it was only a matter of time before he would return to elective politics. Barring that, I presumed he was certain to accept a high government post, before settling in as one of that rapidly disappearing breed of retired statesmen who frequent Washington, and are often referred to as "wise men."[1] The time to write his biography, I reasoned, would be then.

Ten years later, with Kean still serving as president of Drew University, having passed up three opportunities to run for the U.S. Senate (he would decline two more) and having cast aside entreaties from two presidents that he join their Cabinet, I began to reconsider. One day, I received an e-mail from Marlie Wasserman of Rutgers University Press. Picking up on a prior conversation, she wanted to know whether I had any topics in mind for a book that might interest her readers. "What about a book about Tom Kean?" I asked. I thought that Kean's efforts to reform education and welfare policy, preserve much of the state's natural environment, improve the quality of life in New Jersey, and instill pride among its residents deserved recognition. I also believed that his particular style of leadership would prove instructive to those interested in how public figures got things done. New Jerseyans like to say, or at least they once did, that theirs is the most powerful governorship in the nation. As students of the state's political system know, New Jersey's 1947 constitution grants more formal powers to the governor than any other state constitution does. Several strong personalities have served as New Jersey's governor. Yet, after they left office, most, save for Woodrow Wilson, who is remembered for other reasons, were quickly forgotten—at least by the general public. The dearth of literature about them pales by comparison to that about political figures of other states, even when one excludes national figures with presidential ambitions. I did not want this to happen to Tom Kean.

As a state legislator and as a governor, Kean displayed a style of leadership that has become all too rare in the modern era: that of the citizen politician marshaling resources at his command to resolve important and potentially divisive problems through persuasion, consensus, and bipartisanship. How he developed this method of leading, what he achieved through it, and what lessons other officeholders and those who study them might draw from Kean's example, I thought, merited exploration as well.

Marlie asked me to write a book proposal, which she could take to her editorial board. I prepared one, and we signed a contract several months later, in late June 2001. Weeks later came the attacks of September 11. Little did I know when I held my first interviews with Kean (our second took place September 10, 2001) and hit the shelves and microfilm reels at the Library of Congress and other libraries that Kean would play a major role in investigating those attacks and recommending ways to reduce the likelihood of their reoccurrence. That would be another fifteen months away. Kean's appointment as chairman of the National Commission on Terrorist Attacks upon the United States (9–11 Commission) in December 2002 proved the original conventional wisdom correct, but in ways neither he nor I had anticipated.

No, Kean was not going to Washington as a U.S. senator or a Cabinet secretary. Yet in heading the most extensive investigation of the U.S. government in its history, he would have an opportunity to shape national policy that few senators and Cabinet secretaries ever receive. I kept that thought in the back of my mind as I worked on the early sections of this book and as the commission conducted its investigation. By the time both the book and the commission's deliberations neared completion, I realized that I was writing about a figure of national as well as of state significance.

Readers should find Tom Kean's public career of interest because of what it tells about how government performed in the turbulent times in which he served and how he used the three principal posts he occupied (legislator, governor, and commission chairman) to shape public policy. Given that political leaders reflect their times as much as they help shape them, Kean's public career, which spanned over four decades, can serve as a focal point for a better understanding of what transpired in New Jersey and in American society in the years in which he was politically active. Kean was elected to the New Jersey Assembly three months after the Newark riots of 1967, a cataclysmic event that lingered in the minds of New Jersey policymakers for decades. He took his seat in the first legislature to be elected after federal and state courts mandated that state legislatures be apportioned according to the "one man, one vote" principle. That change, coupled with the implementation of the state's first permanent, broadbased tax, two years before Kean first sought public office, forever changed the relationship between New Jersey residents and their state government.

During the time Kean served as a state legislator and as governor, state governments assumed responsibilities that had once been the exclusive preserve of counties and municipalities. It was then when they began to consume larger portions of the total amount of spending on goods and services in most states. The effects of such spending were seen in the emergence of state transit systems (New Jersey Transit), statewide systems of higher education (replete with community colleges, four-year state colleges, and an expanded state university), and increased state spending on public education, with a greater emphasis on equal spending per pupil (*Robinson v. Cahill*, *Abbott v. Burke*). Also during this time, the states played more of a role in reducing urban ills and reversing environmental degradation than ever before in U.S. history.

A generation after the New Jersey Constitution of 1947 strengthened the executive branch and streamlined the judicial branch of state government, the state legislature began to increase its capacity to meet growing public demands for services. As a member of the assembly's leadership for most of the time he spent in that chamber, Kean played a central role in making the legislature a full partner with the other branches as New Jersey's state government began to address problems that were becoming statewide in nature.

The nature of those problems, the state's demographic makeup, and the political equilibrium of the two parties often determined that policymaking would be rooted more in pragmatism than in ideology. As a legislator, Kean often took a "third way" approach, occupying ground between liberal, urban-oriented Democrats and conservative, rural-based Republicans, with his fellow suburbanites tipping the balance. His successful employment of this strategy facilitated his rise through the ranks of the majority party's leadership. Because he had been elected Speaker during a time when his party did not control a majority of seats in the chamber, Kean acted more as the spokesman for the assembly than as the principal spokesman for his party. Elected with the help of Democratic votes, Kean, the Republican Speaker, acted more as an executive than as a legislative leader. The manner in which he comported himself allowed for smooth passage of legislation he favored in a closely divided chamber. As minority leader, he kept his troops cohesive, exploited divisions within the majority party, and worked to increase substantially the number of seats his party held. With the two parties not that far apart ideologically, he put his party behind government reform. In advocating procedures that were ideologically neutral, such as ethics codes and financial disclosure by public officials, he entered into coalitions, sometimes simultaneously, with reform Democrats and conservative Republicans.

Kean became governor at a time when demands for state services remained strong, but when revenues were shrinking, owing to a national recession and federal cutbacks. Kean and his fellow governors had to decide whether and how to fund programs. Some, like Kean, who considered infrastructure, education, the arts, and the environment "investments," acted to fill the gap, appropriating additional state funds and forging partnerships with other levels of government and the private sector, thereby expanding their administrations' reach. In good times, as well as in bad, they also needed to decide how they would use the increased responsibilities the federal government had thrust upon them. For much of his time in office, Kean walked a delicate line between a national Republican administration, wanting to cut back on programs, and a state legislature, with one or both houses controlled by the Democrats, wanting to increase levels of taxes and spending.

Kean and other centrist governors also maneuvered between a Republican administration and a Democratic Congress to influence national welfare and education policies. Increasingly, they came to be regarded more as pragmatists and problem solvers than as partisans. By reaching across the aisle to each other and by working both party caucuses in both houses of Congress and the White House, they helped produce agreement between two mutually suspicious branches of government controlled by opposite parties.

Kean represented a "new breed" of state chief executives who were accomplishing things in state capitals when Washington seemed to be hopelessly "gridlocked." Finding common ground with his fellow governors of both parties and seen at home as an exponent of the political consensus that he had helped build in New Jersey, Kean found himself increasingly at odds with the electoral base of his national party. Simply stated, he was perceived as too moderate and accommodating on the "social issues" (i.e., abortion, gun control, and school prayer) to land a place on a national Republican party ticket. Nevertheless, his style of campaigning and governing could serve as a blueprint for how Republicans can win elections in "blue states."

From the outset of his service on the 9–11 Commission, Kean strove to ensure that its recommendations were enacted. He had witnessed several commissions make worthy recommendations, only to see them shelved after their mandates had expired. As the commission's chairman, he drew heavily on his experiences as an assembly leader and governor. He achieved unanimity on a panel of five Democrats and five Republicans, all appointed by national spokesmen of their respective parties, by employing the "third way" approach that had served him well in the past, by forging close relationships with his peers, by safeguarding the commission's independence, and by maintaining its integrity.

Kean succeeded in persuading an administration protective of its prerogatives to grant the commission access to more documents than had ever before been shared with anyone outside the executive branch. Then, after building public support for the commission's recommendations through the "bully pulpit" he established and commanded as its chairman, he prodded Congress and the president to enact its most important recommendations. From the island of bipartisanship Kean established in a heavily contentious and divided Washington, he made possible passage of the most significant change in the nation's intelligence-gathering apparatus in a half century.

In telling Tom Kean's story, I drew not only on my research, but on the perspective I developed as a participant in and as an observer of some of the events I describe. I worked on most of Tom Kean's campaigns. While he served in the assembly, I sometimes accompanied him to Trenton to observe proceedings in the legislature. When he held the posts of majority leader and as Speaker, I would, while working as an intern in the office of Governor William T. Cahill, listen to legislative debates on bills Kean had sponsored. During Kean's two terms as governor, I served as New Jersey's assistant secretary of state. My portfolio included overseeing cultural agencies housed within the Department of State and initiatives such as the establishment of the New Jersey Center for the Performing Arts in Newark.

Years later, when Kean became chairman of the National Commission on Terrorist Attacks upon the United States, I served as its principal spokesman, a task I continued to perform for its successor nonprofit organization, the 9–11 Public Discourse Project.

I make this disclaimer so that readers may take my activities and associations into account in assessing my analyses and conclusions. Obviously, I have opinions about episodes in which I participated and do not claim to have approached them with complete disinterest. I have, however, tried to be both authoritative and objective in my presentation of events and in my interpretation of them. On occasion, I have been able to supplement primary and secondary accounts of events I recount by offering my personal observations of them. As my major sources, I relied on interviews with well over one hundred people who interacted with Tom Kean, press accounts, and public records. I also relied on books and periodicals that, while they make no mention of Kean, cover eras in which he and his forebears were politically active. In addition, I consulted specialized publications devoted to areas of policy in which Kean worked (education, the environment, etc.). Where possible, so as not to disrupt the narrative, I included some of the most significant supplementary material in the endnotes.

Although he graciously consented to many hours of in-depth interviews, granted me access to personal and private papers, and encouraged his associates to share their candid reminiscences with me, this is not an authorized biography of Tom Kean. Nor is it an attempt to depict the major events of his public career from his point of view. The opinions it offers and the conclusions it reaches are mine alone. What follows is a political biography of Kean by someone who knows him well. While favorably disposed to my subject, I do not shy away from recounting his failures as well as his successes, his weaknesses as well as his strengths. For me, the researching and recording of Tom Kean's life and his contributions to his state and nation have been both exhilarating and revelatory. If those who read this book come away with an enhanced understanding of an extraordinary individual who rendered extraordinary public service in several arenas and of how he did it, I will have succeeded in my task.

Acknowledgments

When I began researching this biography, I already knew that writing could be a lonely task. Because of the encouragement and assistance of many people, the journey to completion proved both less desolate and less arduous than I expected.

First and foremost, I want to express my gratitude to former New Jersey governor Thomas H. Kean. From the instant I expressed an interest in writing his biography he cooperated fully in every possible way. He sat for more than one dozen interviews and always made himself available for follow-up questions. He opened his personal files to me and requested that his present and former associates, colleagues, and members of his family be of whatever assistance they could in the event I contacted them. For all this I thank him.

I want to thank Anthony Cicatiello for believing in this project from the outset and for his assistance throughout. I especially thank him for introducing me to Dale Feeney. Were it not for her readiness to check sources and facts at several libraries and in many newspapers and periodicals and her thoroughness, this book would have taken much longer to produce. I also thank the following people at Drew University for assistance they provided me in multiple ways over the past few years: Barbara Grove, Tom Evans, Tom Harris, Erin Hennessy, Peggi Howard, and Debra Meyers.

I thank the staffs at the Drew University, Princeton University, and Rutgers University libraries; the Newark, East Orange, Irvington, and Livingston libraries; the Library of Congress; the Historical Society of Petersborough, New Hampshire; and the Franklin D. Roosevelt, Harry S. Truman, Dwight D. Eisenhower, Gerald R. Ford, Ronald Reagan, George H. W. Bush, and William J. Clinton presidential libraries and the Richard Nixon Library and Birthplace for allowing me access to their collections, responding to my inquiries, and providing me with much needed information. Special thanks go to Bob Clark, Cynthia Koch, and Raymond Richman at the Franklin D. Roosevelt Presidential Library; Kelly D. Barton and Shelly Jacobs at the Ronald Reagan Presidential Library; Nealon DeVore at the William J. Clinton Foundation; David Goldberg, office of former president William J. Clinton; Bill Weeks at Fiduciary Trust International; and Rafael Medoff, director of the David S. Wyman Institute for Holocaust Studies for going out of their way to help me obtain materials. My heartfelt appreciation also goes to Rich Klein, Mack McLarty, Art Maurice, and Fran Wood, who did the same, and to Bill Schroh of Liberty Hall who repeatedly took time away from his other chores to comply with my requests for information contained in the files of the late U.S. Senator Hamilton Fish Kean and the late U.S. Representative Robert W. Kean. I thank former *Star-Ledger* cartoonist Bill Canfield for sending me clippings of all of his cartoons featuring Tom Kean. I also want to express my appreciation to Dr. Frederick M. Herrmann of the Election Law Enforcement Commission and David A. Miller of the New Jersey State Council on the Arts, New Jersey Department of State, for retrieving archived materials from their respective agencies' files for my use. I also thank Dr. Karl J. Niederer of the New Jersey Department of State's Archives and Records Management Division and his staff for their assistance.

I especially want to thank Hamilton Fish Kean II for lending me books, articles, and photographs from his personal collection and for patiently answering my many questions about Kean family history and genealogy. Several people read all or parts of this book in various stages of its evolution and provided suggestions and valuable criticism. My deepest appreciation goes to Michael Barone, William F. Buckley Jr., Larry Butler, Gail Chaddock, Richard E. Cohen, Saul Cooperman, Peter Hannaford, David Keene, Adam Klein, Chris Kojm, David Maraniss, Rick Mills, Robert P. O'Quinn, Norman Ornstein, Charles Peters, Richard Peterson, Alan Rosenthal, Larry Sabato, Scott Stossel, Martin Tolchin, Paul Trachtenberg, Grant Ujifusa, John Weingart, and Elizabeth Wood.

I express my deepest appreciation to Albert Armstrong and his able staff at the University Club of Washington, D.C., for allowing me to camp out after hours and on weekends in its wonderful business center, where much of this book was written. I especially thank Kimberly Blue and Tanya Moore for their good cheer, words of encouragement, and for looking in on me. I also thank Richard Peterson and Seyed M. Mirkhani for pulling me through multiple computer difficulties.

I remain grateful to John R. Marshall Jr. for escorting me to St. Mark's School and to Brantwood Camp, to Richard E. Noble for his insights into both institutions, and to St. Mark's Headmasters Elsa and Tony Hill and to Nikky De Louchry, Cindy Howe, and Mary Pettus, also at St. Mark's, for providing me with access to the school's archives and records. I thank all the individuals listed in the back of this book, who shared with me their recollections of Tom Kean. I especially thank former presidents Gerald R. Ford and Bill Clinton for taking time from their busy schedules to speak with me.

I want to acknowledge the generosity the Schumann Fund of New Jersey, Professor Maurice Lee Jr., and Susan N. Wilson extended to Rutgers University Press to assist in the publication of this work. Finally, I thank Marlie Wasserman and her staff at Rutgers University Press for guiding me and this project over numerous hurdles over several years. From the moment of its inception, Marlie understood how a book such as this might contribute to a better understanding of Tom Kean and of the extraordinary things he achieved for the people of New Jersey and the United States.

Governor Tom Kean

Prologue

April 8, 2004, was hardly an atypical day for Thomas H. Kean, chairman of the National Commission on Terrorist Attacks upon the United States (commonly known as the 9–11 Commission). George W. Bush's national security adviser, Condoleezza Rice, testified before the commission in open public session and under oath. For months, the Bush administration had resisted Kean's requests that Rice appear in such a format. It reversed its position after Richard Clarke, former antiterrorism adviser to Presidents Bill Clinton and George W. Bush, stated in a number of forums that Bush did not award a high priority to combating and counteracting terrorism in the days preceding the attacks of 9–11. As a result of the controversy that preceded her appearance, Rice's acceptance of Kean's invitation attracted considerable interest. Network as well as cable television and C-SPAN covered the hearing live.

Kean rose at 5:00 a.m. At 5:45, I met him at his hotel and we drove to the U.S. Capitol, where Kean joined the commission's vice chairman, former Indiana Democratic representative Lee H. Hamilton, for a series of interviews with major morning television shows. On his way to breakfast with commission staff in the Capitol's public cafeteria, Kean encountered members of Congress with whom he had worked on other issues in the past. Senator Lamar Alexander (R-TN), who had worked closely with Kean on education when both men served as governors, congratulated Kean on his work with the commission. Congressman Sherwood Boehlert (R-NY) reminisced with Kean about efforts the two had made to arrest the spread of acid rain in the 1980s.

At 8:45, Kean, carrying his briefcase over his shoulder and a binder in each arm, made his way past hundreds of people who hoped to gain admission to the hearing. Some had been standing in line for hours in the long corridor leading to Room 216 of the Hart Senate Office Building. As Kean entered the chamber, he bid hello to families of victims of the September 11 attacks, with whom he had been working closely for the previous sixteen months. He exchanged greetings with some familiar faces—New Jersey reporters who had covered him during his days in the New Jersey statehouse. He also stopped to chat with others who had more recently become part of his world—the Washington press corps.

After placing his materials on the dais, Kean and his fellow commissioners retreated to a private room to greet the hearing's sole witness, who would testify for three hours. With camera crews from media affiliates from all over the world standing six deep, their lenses focused on Rice, Kean swore in the witness. Rice read a twenty-minute opening statement. After she finished, Kean asked only three questions before deferring to his colleagues. As the tone of the questioning grew particularly combative, bursts of applause and occasional expressions of disapproval erupted in various quarters of the room. Some came from family members of those who had perished in the attacks of 9–11. "Accountability, ma'am, accountability," one called out.[1] Kean made feeble attempts to maintain order. It was not his way either to gavel down colleagues or to attempt to silence those who had suffered great losses and had waited for more than two years to observe public officials being cross-examined.

As he adjourned the hearing, Kean, not for the first time, made news of his own. In his matter-of-fact way, he noted that many of the questions put to Rice centered on the contents of a classified intelligence brief Bush had received on August 6, 2001. "We feel it is important that the American people get a chance to see it," he said, as he requested that the government declassify the document.[2] The next day, the administration complied.

That was neither the first time, nor the last, when powerful forces gave way to Tom Kean's demands. The story of the how this soft-spoken gentleman from New Jersey with the calm disposition, easy ways, and ready smile proved so apt at getting powerful figures to bend to his will began long before the 9–11 Commission came into being. It started nearly seven decades prior to the April day on which Rice testified.

chapter 1

The Early Years

The Boy in the Photograph

In the parlor of a stately home in Greenwich, Connecticut, rests an album of photographs. They record the wedding reception of Elizabeth Stuyvesant Kean and Edward L. Hicks III, on October 29, 1942. One picture depicts a group of bridesmaids. Standing among them is a small boy in knickers. He is Thomas Howard Kean, age seven, brother of the bride. Family friends remembered him as Beth Kean's "bratty little brother," the mischievous little boy with a knack for crawling under dining tables and biting guests on the ankles. "Oh, he could be a pest," Beth Hicks recalled. "And he knew how to get my mother's goat."[1] Tom Kean fully shared that opinion. "The only way they could ever get me to quiet down was to cram me into a suit," he would say sixty years later, reflecting back on his sister's wedding.[2]

Beth Hicks had not planned for her brother to appear in this photograph. Nor could she have stopped him. Tom had been standing in a corner, watching as the photographer fussed with his equipment. Just as he prepared to snap the shutter, Tom ran across the room and joined the group. Though Tom Kean would gain plenty of attention in the course of a public career that would span five decades, at this stage of his life, he was still struggling to command it in a family with five other children, in a household headed by a congressman, and at a time when all the adults in his life were preoccupied with news from a world at war.

As a child, Tom Kean exhibited none of the easy manner and poise he would demonstrate as an adult. "I was shy, often lonely, and generally unsure of my place in the world," he wrote.[3] The story of how such a child grew into a man so comfortable in front of a camera or behind a podium, whom total strangers would come to know as their "friend Tom," took many turns. It began in New York City on April 21, 1935, at 11 East Seventy-fourth Street. It was there that Thomas Howard Kean was born. He would later joke that his mother might have ended his political career before it even began had she followed up on an idea she had to dub him "Bunny."[4] (He was born on Easter Sunday.) Other relatives came to his rescue when they assigned him a more suitable nickname, "Tommy."

A Distinguished Lineage

The instant he drew his first breath, Tom Kean became part of several of the most distinguished families in American history. One newspaper, announcing the wedding engagement of his parents, lamented that it lacked the space to list all of his father's illustrious forebears.[5] Any chronology of the Kean family reads like a history of the United States seen through the lens of a family that helped shape the nation's destiny, with each ensuing generation adding a chapter of its own. Tom's father served for twenty years in the House of Representatives. His grandfather and great-uncle had both been U.S. senators. Among his ancestors were five colonial governors.[6] The signatures of Kean forebears adorn the nation's founding documents. Through ties of kinship or marriage, the Keans are related to some of the nation's most notable dynasties, such as the Livingstons, the Winthrops, the Fishes, the Morrises, the Alsops, and the Roosevelts.

The story of the Keans in North America began with the arrival of British mariner turned merchant James Kean, in Charleston, South Carolina, in the 1750s. James's son John Kean, born in 1756, was the first of Tom Kean's ancestors to be born in what would become the United States. A merchant by trade, John Kean was a partner in the firm of Lavien & Co. (One of the principals, Peter Lavien, was a half brother of Alexander Hamilton, who would himself have close ties to the Keans.) An early supporter of American independence, John Kean engaged in revolutionary activities that led to his imprisonment aboard a British warship during the seizure of Charleston Harbor.

Kean was elected to the South Carolina Assembly in 1781 and to the Continental Congress four years later. His casting the decisive vote on a committee that recommended banning slavery from the Northwest Territory remains a source of Kean family pride. John Kean married Susan Livingston, niece of New Jersey's first constitutional governor, William Livingston, in 1786.[7] President George Washington appointed John Kean the first cashier of the Bank of the United States.[8] John Kean died in 1795 in Philadelphia, at the age of thirty-nine. His widow returned to New Jersey with her young son, Peter. She purchased William Livingston's home, "Liberty Hall," in Union Township. It would remain the Kean family seat for generations.

If walls could talk, Liberty Hall would keep historians well occupied. The young Alexander Hamilton took up residence there while he prepared for his college entrance examinations at Francis Barber's school in nearby Elizabeth—courtesy of a clergyman acquaintance of both Livingston and Barber. In its parlor, future chief justice of the United States and governor of New York John Jay wed Livingston's daughter Sarah. Out of one of its windows another of Livingston's daughters eloped with a young army officer named William Henry Harrison. In the early days of the Republic, a row of presidents beginning with George Washington frequented Liberty Hall. Martha Washington took rest there en route to her husband's inauguration as the first president in New York City.

From the time James Kean arrived in South Carolina, the Keans took pains to retain the proper pronunciation of their name, which rhymes with *rain* rather than with *green*. Tom Kean's grandfather, U.S. senator Hamilton Fish Kean, refused to have a mountain peak named in his honor in the Canadian Rockies lest passersby mispronounce it.[9] In his capacity as executor of Hamilton Fish Kean's estate, Tom Kean's father, Robert W. Kean, granted permission to Newark State Teachers College, which relocated on the late U.S. senator's property, to change its name to Kean College upon the condition that its trustees retain the traditional pronunciation.[10]

The Keans had reason for concern. In 1884, after congressman and future U.S. senator John Kean, Tom Kean's great-uncle, obtained a post office for a growing Monmouth County community in his district, the village named itself Keansburg in his honor. By the time it incorporated as a borough in 1917, local residents had taken to pronouncing it *Keensburg*. Family lore holds that the Kean name and its pronunciation originated in northwestern Scotland. Robert W. Kean observed that well into the twentieth century the area north of Glasgow contained Keans who pronounced their name *Kane*.[11] After Tom Kean had been elected governor, a genealogist in the employ of the Irish Tourist Board provided him with evidence that his family name may have had Irish origins. The researcher found that families who spelled their name *Kean* and pronounced it *Kane* hailed from Counties Derry, Galway, and Waterford.[12]

Tom Kean could trace his long-standing interest in history to the influence of his father, who often related the narratives of the Kean family and of the United States as if they were one and the same. They often were. Born in 1893 in Elberon, New Jersey, where his mother's family retained a summer home, Robert Winthrop Kean was the second son of future U.S. senator Hamilton Fish Kean and the former Katharine Winthrop, a direct descendant of the first governor of the Massachusetts Bay Colony, John Winthrop. His parents named him in honor of his maternal grandfather, Robert Winthrop, a sometime associate of J. P. Morgan. Robert Winthrop had married the daughter of Moses Taylor, one of the richest Americans of the nineteenth century. Taylor helped finance the Civil War and later served as president of City Bank. Thanks to his mother's fortune, Robert W. Kean and his descendants became beneficiaries of sizable trusts, which contributed substantially to their incomes.[13]

Through his Kean forebears, Robert W. Kean could lay claim to partial ownership of two New Jersey utility companies founded by his grandfather, Colonel John Kean (son of Peter Kean and grandson of the Revolutionary War patriot), the Elizabethtown Gas Company and the Elizabethtown Water Company, and more than one bank. Colonel John Kean served as an officer of several railroad companies that maintained operations in central New Jersey (as would several of his heirs) and as president of the National Bank of Elizabeth, which his father, Peter Kean, established.[14] Active in Whig politics, Colonel John Kean was an ardent supporter of Henry Clay for president. Once, he presided over a large New Jersey gathering which a highly inebriated Daniel Webster addressed.[15] Through the Kean side of his family, Robert W. Kean inherited sizable landholdings. He would give two hundred acres to the town of Livingston. Saint Barnabas Hospital currently sits on land once owned by Robert.

As Elizabeth ("Elsa") Stuyvesant Howard's middle name connotes, her forebears had been in the New World long enough to have regarded the early Keans as pesky immigrants. Her ancestor Peter Stuyvesant presided over the transfer of ownership of Niew Amsterdam from the Dutch to the British government, which promptly renamed it New York. Like the Keans, the Howards spent much of the year in New York City. During the summers, they took up residence in Hyde Park, where Elsa's mother, the former Rose Post, and her great-aunt, Mrs. Frederick Vanderbilt, occupied positions at the summit of what one society editor called the Hudson River valley's "highbrow coterie."[16] Among Mrs. Vanderbilt's social circle was her neighbor, Sara Delano Roosevelt, whose son, Franklin, would be the cause of much discussion, annoyance, and aggravation in Robert W. Kean's household. Sara Roosevelt and Rose Howard belonged to the same Manhattan sewing circle, a group of socially prominent women who met in each other's homes to make clothes for needy children as they exchanged gossip.

Elsa found Sara Delano Roosevelt to be anything but the cold, domineering, and dictatorial figure historians made her out to be.[17] Robert W. Kean, who knew Sara as a friend of his maternal grandmother, shared these sentiments.[18] While they held similar opinions of Sara, Robert and Elsa differed in the regard in which they held her daughter-in-law. Elsa considered Eleanor Roosevelt a neighbor and clubwoman, attempting good works. Robert W. Kean objected to Eleanor's outspokenness. He conveyed those sentiments to his son Tom in the form of a campaign button he passed along to him. It read, "We don't want Eleanor either." Tom's sister Rose Lansbury attributed her father's aversion to Eleanor more to partisanship than to male chauvinism.[19] She noted, for instance, that although her father professed to dislike opinionated women, he greatly admired Republican congresswoman Clare Boothe Luce, who was known for having a tart tongue.

Robert was also an admirer of Theodore Roosevelt and a distant relation though an aunt who married a first cousin of TR.[20] Growing up, he joined his Roosevelt cousins for summers at Oyster Bay and social events in Washington and New York, as did Eleanor and Franklin, his contemporaries in age. It was not until the 1920s that clashing political ambitions led to fissures in family relationships. In 1920, Theodore Roosevelt Jr., campaigning for the GOP, referred to Franklin, then running for vice president on the Democratic ticket, as a renegade. Four years later, Eleanor, anxious that her husband remain politically viable after he contracted polio in 1921, vigorously campaigned for the reelection of New York governor Al Smith, whose Republican opponent was Theodore Roosevelt Jr. Most of the Oyster Bay Roosevelt clan, of which Robert W. Kean considered himself a member, thought Eleanor had crossed a line when she alleged that as assistant secretary of the navy, Theodore Jr. had been implicated in the Teapot Dome scandal.[21]

A Father in Politics

When Tom Kean was three years old, his father won election to the U.S. House of Representatives. Robert W. Kean's decision to change careers, forsaking the life of investment banker for that of a congressman, heavily influenced how his youngest son would grow up. In the twenty years prior to his election to Congress, Robert W. Kean had led a relatively quiet existence as a partner in Kean-Taylor, a Wall Street investment company that his father had founded. That vocation had allowed him ample time for family life and recreation. As a junior congressman during the Great Depression and in the years preceding and during World War II, Robert W. Kean had little time for much outside of his work.

Home movies taken in the 1920s show a youthful, athletic Robert W. Kean swimming with his older children in the Atlantic Ocean at Elberon or at the family swimming pool in Livingston, pursuing winter sports at various locations, and playing tennis. Those taken after the births of his younger children primarily depict him at family get-togethers. Because of the nature of his father's responsibilities and the seriousness with which Robert W. Kean took them, Tom Kean found himself a witness to great events as a child, but with few companions with whom he could contemplate or discuss their significance.

Robert W. Kean had grown up surrounded by politicians. As a boy, he became fascinated by what he observed and by the tales he heard old-timers tell. When he was six, the New Jersey Legislature named his father's brother, John Kean (the oldest son of the colonel), to the U.S. Senate.[22] Through his friendships with Republican senators Nelson Aldrich of Rhode Island, Murray Crane of Massachusetts, and Joseph Foraker of Ohio, John Kean quickly became a Senate insider. He served on the Foreign Affairs and Interstate Commerce committees. He usually followed the powerful Aldrich's lead in opposing efforts to reduce tariffs and increase regulation of corporations. Foraker remembered Senator John Kean for his vigilance in seeing that "nothing improper was enacted."[23]

While John Kean was in Washington, his brother Hamilton Fish Kean (father of Robert W. Kean) looked out for the senator's political interests back home. As a child, Robert W. Kean accompanied his father on his political rounds. He would always remember one particularly active Civil War veteran, who had lost an arm in battle, Major Carl Lenz, then chairman of the Essex County Republican organization.[24] Patriotism and reverence for the sacrifices Americans made during the nation's wars were values each generation of Keans instilled in the next. Upon the United States' entry into the First World War, Hamilton Fish Kean delivered a passionate address about the war's aims at Liberty Hall as he presented the American and New Jersey flags to the New Jersey National Guard.[25] Robert W. Kean's daughter Rose said that the Fourth of July was more important to her father than Christmas.[26] Every year, on that day, he would recite the Declaration of Independence aloud to his children from the text printed in the *New York Times*. Afterward, he would take them with him to the center of Livingston, where he delivered an annual address. On the way back home, he habitually declared that he had "made the eagle scream."[27]

In addition to his father, uncle, and Civil War veterans turned politicians, Robert W. Kean took his inspiration from Theodore Roosevelt. During the Spanish-American War, when he was five years old, Robert W. Kean was presented with a portrait of the Rough Rider by Howard Chandler Christy. When he was ten, while at a gathering at the Roosevelt homestead at Oyster Bay, Robert caught the president's eye. After a religious service on the battleship *Kearsage,* TR grabbed Robert's arm and, over the boy's mother's protests, marched him off to a stag luncheon. A year later in 1905, Kean's uncle, the U.S. senator, arranged for Robert to serve as a Senate page for one day so that he could observe Roosevelt's inauguration at close range. He and his Roosevelt cousins sat behind the president on the reviewing stand throughout the inaugural parade.[28]

Under the watchful eye of his uncle's private secretary, Donald H. McLean, Robert W. Kean attended the 1912 Republican convention.[29] There he got a close glimpse into the raw-fisted tactics that forces close to incumbent president William Howard Taft used to squash ex-president Theodore Roosevelt's hopes of wresting the party's nomination away from Taft. Roosevelt won all nine nonbinding presidential primaries—including New Jersey's—that year. Robert W. Kean believed that the former president's demonstrated popular support entitled him to the nomination. His elders disagreed. Once among TR's most ardent backers, John and Hamilton Fish Kean disapproved of Roosevelt's "trust busting" and of his attempts to curtail corporate power.[30]

After graduating from Harvard in 1915, Kean, in the tradition of Roosevelt, went out West in pursuit of big game. Upon his return, he accepted employment with First National Bank of Roosevelt in Carteret, where his father was a stockholder.[31] In 1916, Robert W. Kean, in response to President Woodrow Wilson's call for recruits to pursue Pancho Villa back into Mexico (after Villa had led a raid across the border, killing several Americans), joined the National Guard, serving under General John J. Pershing. He would serve again under Pershing's command after the United States entered World War I.

With college-educated junior officers at a premium, Robert W. Kean entered the U.S. Army as a second lieutenant. The Second Division, to which he was assigned, participated in some of the heaviest fighting of the war. Its officers suffered particularly high casualties.[32] Robert W. Kean received the Distinguished Service Cross and the Silver Star for "extraordinary heroism in action" around Vierzy, France. While Kean was away, his mother and his future wife kept him abreast of news from the home front. His mother kept him up to date on political developments. Katharine Winthrop Kean made no effort to conceal the contempt she felt for her son's commander in chief,

Woodrow Wilson. Wilson had angered her when, after having declared "politics adjourned" for the duration of the war, he urged the election of a Democratic Congress days before the 1918 congressional elections. After the returns became known, she wrote her son that the Republicans had taken control of Congress "in spite of Mr. Wilson's meddling."[33]

After his discharge from military service in 1919, Robert W. Kean began his affiliation with Kean-Taylor. The following year, he and Elizabeth Stuyvesant Howard were wed. After returning from their honeymoon, Robert and Elsa Kean took up residence at 28 East Thirty-eighth Street in Manhattan in a house that they rented from Robert's mother's family. Two years into his marriage, Robert inherited a 300-acre estate in Livingston, New Jersey, from his uncle, Alexander Kean, his father's youngest brother. On its grounds at 395 Mount Pleasant Avenue stood a three-story Tudor revival mansion his uncle, an architect, had designed. After spending two years making renovations, Robert, Elsa, and their two children moved there in 1924. They would eventually add two wings to the house, along with a garage, a squash court, a swimming pool, a caretaker's cottage, a playhouse, and a greenhouse.

Though he would maintain a rented house in New York City while he remained at Kean-Taylor, Robert W. Kean gradually made Livingston his permanent residence and established himself as a pillar in a community that then numbered no more than 3,000. He became a vestryman at St. Peter's Episcopal Church, another structure his uncle had designed, founded Livingston's first American Legion Post and its first Boy Scout troop, and supported the Livingston free public library. In 1927, Robert W. Kean organized the Livingston National Bank. (He served as its president for a quarter century.) He also performed political chores for his father while the older man served on the Republican National Committee from 1919 to 1928 and during his three campaigns for the U.S. Senate.[34]

In 1929, Robert W. Kean sought his first political office when he ran for the Republican County Committee in a newly created precinct in Livingston. His loss caused the town newspaper to lament the voters' shortsightedness in passing over the war-hero son of the recently elected U.S. senator from New Jersey.[35] At the time, his father, along with Camden County Republican leader David Baird and Governor Morgan Larson, constituted the triumvirate that controlled the New Jersey GOP and much of the state. In his single term in the U.S. Senate, Hamilton Fish Kean generally voted the conservative line, but always with an eye toward what he believed to be in the best interest of his constituents. Having opposed nearly all of Franklin Roosevelt's New Deal initiatives, he strenuously supported the Roebling Company of Trenton when it sought the contract to supply the cable for the Golden Gate Bridge, a project of the Works Progress Administration.

Hamilton Fish Kean pressed for continued protection of the petrochemical industry, a primary New Jersey employer. Noting the strength of the industry's German competitors, Kean declared that his primary interest was "to help the Germans in the United States, not the Germans in Germany."[36] Kean won wide editorial support when he proposed appointing a member of the Canadian government to the Federal Reserve Board as a means of stabilizing Canadian currency on par with that of the United States.[37] Like his grandson Tom, who would have little memory of his grandfather, save for watching the older man fish off a pier in Elberon, Hamilton Fish Kean exerted considerable energy battling ocean pollution and protecting the state's beaches. While a candidate for U.S. senator in 1928, Kean accepted an appointment from President Calvin Coolidge to an advisory board studying the effect of oil pollution on the fishing industry. When he sought reelection in 1934, Kean took credit for forcing New York City to cease dumping garbage into the ocean and to construct disposal plants.[38] Hamilton Fish Kean sponsored legislation to allow the U.S. Army to lease its site at Sandy Hook to the state and to permit bathing facilities at Fort Hancock.[39]

As would his son and grandson, Hamilton Fish Kean ardently supported civil rights for African Americans. Born in 1862, at the height of the Civil War, he had become politically active at a time when African Americans were strongly represented among the Civil War veterans who ran the state and national Republican parties. During the run-up to the 1924 Republican National Convention, in his capacity as Republican national committeeman from New Jersey, he successfully resisted a credentials challenge an all-white slate of delegates posed to the integrated Georgia delegation.[40] In the decades following Reconstruction, African Americans comprised much of what remained of the Republican Party in the South. In recognition of the role that African American–dominated southern delegations played in the nominating process, Republican presidents often distributed federal patronage to their members. It was not an unusual occurrence for African Americans to serve as postmasters, customs inspectors, and other federal posts in states that had denied the franchise to members of their race.

Presumably at National Committeeman Kean's urging, Calvin Coolidge's handlers selected George F. Cannon of Jersey City, an African American known for his efforts to make lynching a federal crime, to deliver one of the seconding speeches in favor of the president's nomination. After his election to the U.S. Senate, Kean became a lead sponsor of antilynching measures. In 1934, he boasted in a brochure intended for general audiences that he had worked "shoulder to shoulder" with Oscar De Priest (R-IL), the first African American elected to Congress from a northern state, in this effort.[41] Kean antagonized the national leadership of the NAACP, however, when he voted in favor of North Carolinian John J. Parker's nomination to the Supreme Court. In recognition of the jurist's work to elect him in 1928 and hoping to attract support among southern whites in 1932, President Herbert Hoover nominated Parker, a segregationist, for the post. Kean, along with most party stalwarts, voted to confirm him. The nomination was defeated 41 to 39, with 10 Republicans voting against it.[42]

After Hamilton Fish Kean lost his bid for re-election in 1934, his son Robert affiliated with Arthur T. Vanderbilt's "Clean Government" Republican association. Vanderbilt's forces had recently taken control of the county party machinery, supplanting Jesse R. Salmon's regular Republican organization. Adept at public relations, Vanderbilt's insurgents had taken to bestowing the moniker "Clean Government" beneath the names of their designated candidates on ballots. The label, Robert W. Kean noted, became the "guiding star" for most suburban Republicans.[43] Vanderbilt financed his political operation in part by requiring officeholders he helped elect to pay an assessment of 10 percent of their salaries. Kean, whatever his private misgivings about the practice, found it preferable to Salmon's custom of funding party operations with money extorted from bootleggers.[44]

In 1936, Robert W. Kean, with Vanderbilt's backing, won election as an Alf Landon delegate to that year's Republican National Convention. With President Franklin Delano Roosevelt piling up a record landslide against Landon, Democrat Frank Towey, riding Roosevelt's coattails, defeated twenty-two-year veteran Essex County congressman Republican Frederick R. Lehlbach. In 1938, with Roosevelt not on the ballot, his attempt to "pack the Supreme Court" unpopular, and the economy worsening, Towey appeared particularly vulnerable in a seat still considered to be primarily Republican. Kean decided to run for it. Although Vanderbilt supported him, the leader's hold over the party nominating machinery was not yet strong enough to commandeer the nomination of a protégé.[45] Once "Clean Government" Republican Dallas Townsend of Montclair entered the race, Kean found himself running as an "insurgent" on his opponent's home turf and as an "organization" man every place else.

To hold down Townsend's "hometown" vote, Robert W. Kean engaged in tactics he found both amusing and embarrassing. In one ward, two Italian American brothers simultaneously served as Democratic and Republican leaders. They were said to collude to determine how the ward would go in primary and general elections. The

Republican assured Kean that for five hundred dollars he could deliver him one particular precinct 158 to 49. Kean paid and won it by that exact margin. (In the general election, Kean lost the same precinct 69 to 526.) Kean won the primary by 712 votes. He was particularly proud that the *New York Tribune,* then the voice of the so-called eastern Republican establishment, saw his nomination as a victory for "younger elements" within the party.[46]

To ensure victory in the general election, Kean embarked on a strategy his son Tom would later repeat. He pushed for heavy vote turnout in Republican areas, while he peeled away from the Democrats votes from members of groups not known to favor Republican candidates. A principal base of Kean's support was his fellow World War I veterans, operating informally through the network of American Legion and Veterans of Foreign Wars posts that had sprung up in his district and all across the country. Kean had been cultivating their support and tending to their concerns for years prior to his declaration of candidacy.[47]

Kean campaigned heavily in Jewish and Italian American precincts in Newark and in Polish American wards in Irvington. As his father had before him and his son would after him, Robert Winthrop Kean actively sought support from African Americans. At a late-night rally the night before the election, Kean brought to Montclair High School Colonel Arthur Little, who had commanded the all-black 369th Infantry during the War to End All Wars.[48] As he asked for their votes, Robert W. Kean offered a succinct explanation for his support of programs that benefited African Americans: "Most of my ancestors came over here because they wanted to. Many of yours came over under compulsion. Therefore, I feel that we owe a duty to your people to give them every opportunity for advancement and education through public funds."[49] Aware that this once most dependable of Republican constituencies was abandoning the party of Abraham Lincoln for that of Franklin Roosevelt, enticed by the promise of federal assistance and jobs, Kean told his listeners that no one would know for whom they had voted.[50]

After his election, Kean took to receiving his African American constituents at his home in Washington, D.C., a city then still in the grasp of racial segregation. The frequency of these occurrences led his son Tom to wonder whether his father had any white constituents, because the only ones he had encountered at home were black.[51] Robert W. Kean's hold on the votes of middle-class African Americans in Montclair tightened after he successfully stopped the New Jersey National Guard from building an armory smack in the middle of one of their neighborhoods.

Kean defeated Towey by 12,000 votes. His was among the 75 seats the Republicans gained, increasing their strength from 89 to 164 in the House of Representatives in 1938. On January 5, 1939, the *Newark Star-Eagle* ran a photograph of Kean and his family on their way to his swearing-in. Two-year-old Tommy was pictured prominently in the center holding his parents' hands. According to family lore, Robert W. Kean's standing within his party's caucus plummeted after he attended his first White House reception as a congressman. As he made his way through the receiving line to shake the president's hand, Franklin D. Roosevelt bellowed, "Winthrop, you don't know how good it is to see a friendly face."[52]

Only family members and close friends addressed Robert Winthrop Kean as "Winthrop" or "Win." The warm greeting Roosevelt had given him caused Kean to worry that the president's display of familiarity with the freshman Republican congressman would cost him a coveted committee assignment. Robert W. Kean wound up on the Banking Committee. Five years later, he moved over to Ways and Means. With Elsa expecting their sixth child, Kean delayed moving his family to Washington. He temporarily took rooms at the Shoreham Hotel. After daughter Katharine was born, the Keans rented a home at 2201 R Street, N.W.

A Lonely Childhood

Robert W. Kean's election to Congress meant that he and his family would continue to maintain two residences, but that their commute between them would be longer. When Kean worked at Kean-Taylor, the family spent the late fall and winter months in New York. From early spring to the autumn, they resided in Livingston with Robert commuting to the city, usually by train, while his children were chauffeured to and from New York day schools. After Robert W. Kean's election to Congress, the Keans stayed in Washington, with Robert commuting back to his district on weekends. When Congress was in recess, the younger children traveled from Livingston to Washington, where they attended school, every Monday. They returned to New Jersey on weekends.

The change in their parents' living arrangements did little to inconvenience the Keans' three older children. Beth (born in 1921), Robert Jr. (born in 1922), and Hamilton (born in 1925) were well into their teens by the time their father won election to Congress. Beth was leading an active social life in Washington and New York and would be wed within three years. Bob and Ham were away at boarding school. Robert W. and Elsa Kean's three younger children—Rose (born in 1931), Tom (born in 1935), and Katharine (born in 1939)—grew up as their parents' second family. Sandwiched between two girls, one four years older and the other four years younger, and bereft of male companions close to his own age, Tom grew up more as an only child than as one of six. His oldest brother, Bob, twelve years his senior, was Tom's godfather.

Tom's childhood differed from the early years of his older siblings in other respects. He had come along at a time when his parents had less time and energy to devote to him. Once, Tom asked his mother why, unlike the four older children, neither he nor his younger sister had to take piano lessons. "When the first four children said they didn't want to go to piano lessons," his mother explained, "your father and I forced them to go because we thought it was good for them. By the time you came along, we were a little older and a little more tired. When you said you didn't want to take piano lessons, we said 'fine.'"[53]

Tom grew up very much aware that his father was somewhat older than the parents of his classmates. They had fathers serving in the Second World War. His had fought in the First. He remembered engaging in fewer activities with his father than had his older siblings. "Mostly," Tom recalled, "he [Robert W. Kean] talked about things he had done."[54]

"My father was an 'old Roman,'" Tom explained, conveying in a single phrase both Robert W. Kean's sense of civic responsibility and his stern demeanor. "He had a certain way of doing things," Tom said, recalling that parenting was often hard on his father.[55] The product of a strict upbringing, Robert W. Kean, Tom remembered, found it "hard to show emotion." Reflecting on his own formative years, Tom's father wrote that he had conducted his life in a manner consistent with what his own father had expected. Though he deeply respected and admired Hamilton Fish Kean, Robert felt closer to his mother, Katharine Winthrop Kean, who he said had done more to influence his character than had anyone else.[56] Tom's brother Hamilton remembered Katharine as a woman of zest as well as generosity.[57] His sister Beth recalled that she had been better able to relate to children than had their grandfather the senator.

The pattern of a mother who openly expressed affection and a more reserved, standard-setting father was repeated in Robert W. Kean's household. Of his own mother, Tom Kean would say that Elsa was "totally devoted to family." "You knew," he recalled, "that she had no other interest than your welfare."[58] One of Tom's friends remembered her as a "very lovable, sweet person." "Gentleness came from her," he said.[59] Elsa filled the Kean household with music, laughter, and song. According to her children she had a keen sense of humor and considerable tact. They also recall her acting as a "go-between" to their father.

While family remained Elsa's highest priority, her husband's change in occupation meant that the burdens on her time also increased. She had to run two households. She also had to meet the demands that Washington society placed on wives of junior members of Congress. Most began their Washington sojourns by dropping off calling cards at the homes of Cabinet officers, federal officials, senators, and congressmen and waiting for the women of these respective households to arrange to meet with them. One historian described the ritual that a new arrival into Washington society, the wife of the assistant secretary of the navy in 1913, performed: "Each day she set out in a carriage with a card case and made between twenty and thirty stops—Monday on the wives of Supreme Court Justices; Tuesday, congressional wives; Thursday, Cabinet members; Friday, Diplomats. . . . On Wednesdays, she received at home, never able to predict who or how many her visitors would be."[60] The routine Elsa followed in 1939 was not much different from the one Eleanor Roosevelt had endured a quarter century earlier, except that Elsa made her rounds by automobile. Typically, younger women received intense briefings on how to comport themselves at such stops and during first meetings with more established Washington hostesses from an older woman in their family who was well versed in this tribal custom. Katharine Winthrop Kean carefully instructed Elsa in this art.[61]

The omnipresence of the war added to the demands on Tom's parents' time while he was growing up. The war, Tom Kean would later say, was all people talked about. Reminders of the war were a daily presence. Tom would long remember regularly scheduled blackouts as well as the rationing of sugar, gasoline, and other goods. "People saved everything because there were so many shortages," he recalled. "We saved bottle caps, string, and rubber bands." He also remembered his mother wrapping "Bundles for Britain" and knitting socks and sweaters to be sent to Allied children.[62] The Keans' two older sons saw combat in Europe. Their son-in-law did battle in Asia. Every day, Elsa penned a letter to each, as she had two decades earlier to her beau, Robert W. Kean. She also resumed another prior activity when she joined the Gray Ladies, a group of volunteers that assisted nurses at Washington hospitals.[63]

With her husband away, Beth Hicks and her infant son, Ted, moved in with the Keans in Washington. After enduring a miscarriage, Beth contracted scarlet fever and suffered a series of infections, which resulted in the amputation of a leg. Her illnesses added to her family's worries. At Tom's school seldom did a day pass without hearing news that a father or an uncle or a brother of a classmate had been injured or killed in battle. When word came that Tom's brother Hamilton had been seriously wounded in the Battle of the Bulge, the atmosphere in the Kean household grew particularly tense. All the while Tom was growing up, circumstances conspired to ensure that his parents had more on their minds than how best to keep their youngest son amused.

When it was time for Tom to start school, his family enrolled him in the Potomac School. When he reached the fourth grade, he entered St. Albans, a prestigious school for boys affiliated with the National Cathedral. If his commuting pattern meant that Tom would be unable to spend time with children his own age in Washington over the weekends, the nature of wartime Washington further impeded his ability to draw close to whatever friends he had been able to make. Most of his classmates were sons of diplomats, military personnel, or refugees. Few stayed in the nation's capital for extended periods.

Tom took to amusing himself by exploring the city, either on foot or by trolley. Indulging what would become a lifetime fascination with history, he learned to identify each of the city's statues memorializing historical figures. Years later, while in a car or in a taxi, he would show friends landmarks where he had played hide-and-seek or learned to roller skate. He referred to July and August, when he was back in Livingston, as "the longest months."[64] Knowing no children his age in the area, Tom spent hours by himself in the woods, learning to distinguish among varieties of trees and birds. All his life, he would continue to seek solace in the stillness of forests.

Unlike other families of wealth, privilege, and social standing, the Keans did not frequent country clubs. Nor did they entertain much. They pursued most of their recreation and entertainment within the confines of their well-contained estate—replete with five live-in servants, a groundskeeper, and gardeners. During the summers, Tom's parents arranged for a college student to stay at their Livingston home as a tutor to Tom. He began to play tennis regularly with one, cultivating his skills at the sport that became one of his lifetime passions.

All the Kean children came to regard the time they spent in Livingston as stifling. "I always though it unfortunate that my [great-] uncle chose to build there," Rose confided.[65] Beth confessed that as she grew older, she grew more impatient and bored with life in Livingston and could not wait to get back to New York or Washington.[66] Hamilton recalled feeling isolated in Livingston: "We didn't know anybody." Family tradition and social mores forbade the children to associate with other youngsters unless both sets of parents were well acquainted. "My mother would not dream of visiting people across the road," Hamilton said.[67] Occasionally the Keans would arrange for children of their friends to play with their children or keep them company. Few friendships formed.

When in his parents' company, Tom sought to get their attention in ways that often got him into trouble. Sometimes to quiet him, they yielded to his demands. On certain evenings, he would sneak out of bed and hide behind the railing above the front hall at his Livingston home and strain to listen to his parents' phonograph or radio. He grew especially fond of the recordings of Irish tenor John McCormack. He looked forward to Sunday nights, when comedian Jack Benny would be on the radio.

Whether in Livingston or in Washington, Tom returned the affection of the few companions he did acquire during his childhood— dogs. They became constants in his life. His earliest memory was sitting on a blanket, close to a dog that belonged to his sister Rose.[68] The first family photograph to include Tom shows him seated not far from the family's German shepherd Adolf. Elsa had named the pet for "that funny-looking man in Germany, who barked when he talked."[69] Tom later recalled that the shepherd was particularly protective of him as an infant and as a small child, following him around, not allowing strangers to approach him. He was also prone to kill birds, chickens, and other small animals and drop his prey at Robert W. Kean's feet. The dog eventually succumbed to poison put out by a local farmer determined to protect his chickens. Tom received his first dog, a brown cocker spaniel, when he reached the age of twelve. He named it Pepsi in honor of his favorite beverage and proved a conscientious master. Tom, like the young Theodore Roosevelt, took on other pets, turning the Livingston grounds into his own private zoo. He had a pet mouse and several pet chickens.[70]

Tom devoured every book about dogs he could find. He grew especially fond of Albert Payson Terhune's fictional accounts of the adventures of collies. *Lad of Sunnybank* was among his favorites. Tom became a devotee of L. Frank Baum's *Wizard of Oz* and of J. M. Barrie's *Peter Pan*. His interest in reading awakened, he took to searching out stories in which, as he once put it, "the younger son did things."[71] Most adventure stories of the era had cast the older sons in heroic roles. Before long, he would be acquiring new role models.

"That Man" Roosevelt

While Tom was too young to absorb the full magnitude of the issues that weighed heavily on his father's mind prior to and during the war, he did pick up some of the congressman's politics by sheer osmosis. When asked the identity of his boyhood heroes, Tom Kean suggested that to have offered up the name Roosevelt in his household would have been problematic.[72] Robert W. Kean admonished his children to remember that they were related to the *Oyster Bay* Roosevelts.[73] That he made such a distinction was understandable, given the partisan strains that crept into the relationship between the Keans and the Hyde Park Roosevelts. Under ordinary circumstances and in earlier times, Eleanor and Franklin Roosevelt would have made it onto any list of prospective guests at a Kean wedding. Yet, Robert and Elsa did not invite them to Beth's. They mailed the first couple an announcement of the pending nuptials instead. In reply, the Roosevelts sent the newlyweds a silver bowl, engraved with the initials of the bride and groom and inscribed, "from the President and Mrs. Roosevelt."[74] It rests in Mrs. Hicks's parlor in Greenwich, not far from the photo album containing the picture of Tom and her bridesmaids.

For young Tom, British prime minister Winston Churchill and the Federal Bureau of Investigation's director J. Edgar Hoover were "safer" choices as role models than was FDR. Churchill's appearance before the U.S. Congress had been among the events Tom's parents declared beneficial for him to observe. In the late 1930s and early 1940s, Hoover became a hero to American youths partly because of the FBI's much publicized successes in catching German spies, infiltrating pro-Nazi "front groups," and preempting would-be saboteurs.[75] Hollywood documented Hoover's achievements in films such as *Confessions of a Nazi Spy* (1939), which featured Edward G. Robinson in the role of a Hoover-like figure. Tom caught occasional glimpses of the FBI director at the Allied Inn, where Hoover customarily ate lunch and where Elsa would occasionally take Tom as a reward for good behavior.

In his unpublished memoir, Robert W. Kean suggested that his true opinion of the man who called him Winthrop was more complicated than he let on. Of Roosevelt's first one hundred days as president, Congressman Kean wrote: "Roosevelt seemed like a breath of fresh air. He acted strongly, closed all the banks, proposed new and radical legislation and in dulcet tones announced 'there is nothing to fear but fear itself.'"[76]

Though he had as a candidate railed against waste and corruption in New Deal programs such as the WPA, Robert W. Kean could not bring himself to oppose all Roosevelt's efforts to provide public assistance to the needy. Although he criticized the Social Security system Roosevelt put into place, his objections were of a different kind than those that other Republicans made. Robert W. Kean lamented that the system did not cover domestic servants and agricultural workers, many of whom were African American.[77] In recognition of his decades-long efforts to extend Social Security's reach to include more Americans and his expertise on its workings, Kean's colleagues and a good many of his constituents took to referring to him as "Mr. Social Security."[78]

With regard to Roosevelt, Robert W. Kean proved equally ambiguous when it came to foreign policy. When Hitler's foreign office launched a bitter personal attack on Roosevelt, Kean predicted that such comments would stiffen Americans' resolve to stand behind their president. "Criticism of the President," he stated, was a "privilege Americans reserved to themselves."[79] He need not have added the phrase "and especially within the Republican caucus or in the Kean household." Save for the times when the president came under attack by foreigners, anything that smacked of the name Roosevelt remained "problematic" for the Keans.

War in Europe

The son of one of the preeminent public figures in his region and an aspiring politician in his own right who had fought in World War I, Robert W. Kean was certain to have followed events in Europe and how they were influencing the political climate in Essex County and New Jersey prior to his election to Congress. In the years preceding America's entry into World War II, Robert W. Kean, like many of his fellow veterans and much, if not most of the country, opposed measures that he believed would increase the odds of the United States becoming embroiled in another war in Europe. A Gallup Poll taken after he entered Congress reported that most Americans felt that too little good had resulted from U.S. participation in the previous war to have justified the sacrifices. Yet the junior congressman from Essex County kept his distance from those who, while professing neutrality, either professed to see little difference between the belligerents or seemed resigned to a German victory. Much as Kean respected Charles Lindbergh for the sincerity of his convictions, he considered the aviator hero's failure to acknowledge that a British victory was in the interest of the United States a fatal "blind spot."[80]

Robert W. Kean carved out a position that put him in favor of all measures to defend the United States and assist Great Britain short of bringing the United States into the war. His record shows a deliberate effort on his part to maintain a balanced position between intervention and isolationism. (His son Tom would later maneuver in a similar fashion, striking out positions between two opposite ideological poles.)

In 1939, Congressman Kean voted to repeal the embargo Congress had placed on the sale of arms to the combatants, arguing, as had Roosevelt, that the Neutrality Act of 1935 worked in favor of Hitler by preventing U.S. sales of munitions to Britain. He was one of only six Republicans to support the provision that allowed nations to pay for materials and transport them to their destinations on a cash-and-carry basis. (The measure passed.) Kean took his stand after consulting its architect, Bernard Baruch, whom the congressman respected for his able administration of the War Mobilization Board during World War I.[81] Displaying another characteristic that others would detect in his son Tom, Robert W. Kean, once he had made up his mind on an issue, would not let critics deter him. He reminisced that he took his stand knowing that some would brand him a "tool of war munitions manufacturers."[82]

Kean would later oppose arming U.S. merchant vessels and allowing them to travel into combat zones.[83] He voted to reinstate the draft on September 3, 1940, as a defense measure. Yet he opposed its extension in August 1941 because he felt it placed unfair burdens on initial draftees, who would have their stays extended.[84] (The bill passed by one vote.) Kean opposed in principle Roosevelt's Lend-Lease plan because, in his view, it gave the president too much discretion over what equipment the United States would make available to countries resisting the Axis aggression.[85] While he had no reservations about helping Britain, he was cautious, even skeptical, about the wisdom of assisting the Soviet Union. Yet he voted for final passage of an amended bill on March 11, 1941, and a week later for a $7 billion aid appropriation to Britain.[86]

Robert W. Kean and the Holocaust

Robert W. Kean entered electoral politics at a time when the Nazi persecution of Jews was on the rise. During 1938, the year Kean ran for Congress, Hitler achieved his goal of uniting Germany and Austria (in March) and the Munich Pact, which yielded half of Czechoslovakia to Germany, was signed (in September). Kristallnacht, the Nazi-instigated destruction of Jewish-owned businesses, homes, and synagogues, and the deportation of some Jews and the wide-scale murder of others occurred days after Kean's election. During his first year in office, 1939, Hitler occupied the remainder of Czechoslovakia and invaded Poland.

Prior to the outbreak of the war in Europe, in New Jersey and elsewhere, groups advocating American censure of Hitler actively made their case, while Nazi front organizations met with increased resistance. Jewish leaders and their allies organized boycotts of German-made goods and pressed for relief for Hitler's victims and for the easing of immigration restrictions. Jewish vigilantes associated with the crime boss Abner "Longie" Zwillman disrupted pro-Nazi rallies in Newark and Irvington. In 1935, the New Jersey legislature passed a law prohibiting the spread of propaganda, incitement of racial hatred, and knowingly leasing space to groups advocating such practices.[87] A year before Kean won election to Congress, federal, state, and local officials investigated Camp Nordland, an operation of the pro-Hitler American Bund. Less than a month before the attack on Pearl Harbor, America First (the most prominent isolationist organization) staged a rally at the Newark Mosque.[88]

Robert W. Kean often expressed sympathy for victims of anti-Semitism both in the United States and in Europe. Jewish voters comprised one of the largest voting blocs in Kean's congressional district. They were "friendly [politically] most of the time," he observed, "but, on Election Day, their liberal interests, their admiration for Franklin Roosevelt, and their desire that the U.S. enter the war against Germany, caused many to vote the straight Democratic ticket." This truism notwithstanding, Congressman Kean took an active interest in issues of concern to his Jewish constituents. Through the press, personal contacts, and especially his principal political strategist, Edward Gaulkin, who was well known to the Jewish community, Kean kept Jewish residents in his district informed of his activities.[89]

Kean took note of anti-Semitic incidents he witnessed. One made such an impression on him that he mentioned it in a memoir he penned forty years after it took place. On June 4, 1941, Representative John Rankin (D-MI), known for his dislike of African Americans, immigrants, and Jews, took to the floor of the House and denounced "Wall Street and a little group of our international Jewish brethren" for "attempting to harass the President . . . and the Congress . . . into plunging the United States into war" unprepared.[90] Representative Morris Michael Edelstein (D-NY) replied that the number of Jewish bankers was infinitesimally small and cautioned his colleague against seeking scapegoats. Moments later, Edelstein collapsed and died of a heart attack. Kean noted in disgust that "the day after Edelstein's death, he [Rankin] was back on the floor . . . arguing about his pet legislation, the Tombigbee Inland Waterway."[91]

Four months later, Kean raised his voice in protest when another public official cast aspersions on an entire group of Americans. At a House Banking Committee hearing, Georgia commissioner of agriculture Tom Linder declared that the only thing that was keeping FDR's price administrator, Leon Henderson, a New Jersey native, in his job was the official's closeness to "Baruch, Morgenthau, Straus, Ginsberg and the Guggenheim interests." Linder asserted that he represented farmers, whom he termed "100 percent American." Kean inquired whether Linder considered himself "100 percent American."

When the witness answered in the affirmative, Kean replied, "When you come in with such un-American statements, as far as I am concerned, your whole testimony has no weight. Further, I resent the attempt to arouse racial intolerance and antagonism."[92]

In his approach to the substance of Henderson's price-controls proposals, Robert W. Kean applied tactics his son Tom would later employ when considering unpopular measures he deemed necessary. Believing the administration's measure unfair because it exempted large parts of the economy from its reach, Kean voted for it only after trying to pass alternatives closer to his liking. He especially liked the proposal advanced by his colleague on the Banking Committee, Representative Al Gore Sr. (D-TN).[93]

As Robert W. Kean confronted verbal anti-Semitism, his son Tom witnessed its more violent forms. One day, after a classmate of Tom's, the son of a rabbi, stepped off a school bus on the way home from St. Albans, he was assaulted by a group of children, who taunted him with anti-Semitic epithets. The next day, Tom and his friends huddled to figure out what they might do to help their companion fend off another attack. They contemplated getting off at their friend's stop but abandoned the idea after someone asked how they would find their way home.[94]

For the rest of his life, Robert W. Kean believed that, but for the Japanese attack upon Pearl Harbor, the United States might have been able to stay out of the war and that it would have been in its best interest to have done so. Had history taken this course, he argued, the Soviet Union would have emerged from the war too weak to threaten Western democracies. Germany, he acknowledged, would have remained a major power under Nazi rule. The principal losers, he conceded, would have been European Jews. "We in the United States did not know of the terrible treatment of the German Jews," he said, "though they themselves [American Jews] seemed to know something about it . . . they sensed something dreadful was going on with respect to their relatives and compatriots."[95] Jewish leaders in Robert W. Kean's district, Tom recalled, did know about Hitler's plans to annihilate the Jews of Europe and passed along what they had learned to the congressman.[96]

Whether at their behest or on his own initiative, Robert W. Kean was one of the few in Congress to call upon the Roosevelt administration to undertake vigorous efforts to rescue Jews in Hitler-occupied Europe from certain death. On March 19, 1943, Kean took the floor of the House. "Mr. Speaker," he began, "we in the United States cannot but have the deepest sympathy for the plight of the Jewish population in Nazi-dominated Europe. Our State Department has suggested to the British Government that a meeting be held in Ottawa to consider means for alleviating the situation of these helpless people, to which a favorable reply has been received. I call upon our Government and the British Government for speed in their study of this serious problem. Those who are murdered in the immediate future cannot be brought back to life."[97]

The timing of Kean's remarks was just as significant as what he said. Days before he delivered them, both houses of Congress passed resolutions that "condemned atrocities" inflicted upon the civilian population in Nazi-occupied countries and "especially the mass murder of Jewish men, women, and children." The resolutions, while they vowed that the guilty would be held accountable, said nothing about rescuing Jews facing imminent death. The Joint Emergency Committee, an umbrella organization comprising several Jewish leaders and organizations, had pressed to no avail for language calling upon the U.S. government to do more to save European Jews.[98] In calling for more direct action than most of his peers were willing to advocate, Robert W. Kean clearly intended to force Roosevelt's hand. His effort may well have been a part of a coordinated strategy entered into with critics of U.S. policy not only outside the administration, but also within it.

On November 24, 1942, four months before Kean delivered his remarks, the United States confirmed that it had evidence that Hitler intended to murder all Jews in Europe as part of the "final solution" to what he and his historical antecedents had termed the "Jewish problem." It reported that two million persons had already perished in Nazi-run death camps. Months prior to this official announcement, Gerhard Riegner, the World Jewish Congress's representative in Switzerland, acting on information he had received from a German industrialist, passed along identical information to the State Department, to Secretary of the Treasury Henry S. Morgenthau Jr., and to Rabbi Steven S. Wise.[99] Upon receiving the news, Morgenthau asked his staff to prepare a report, documenting American efforts to rescue Jews in Hitler-occupied Europe.

In the aftermath of Kristallnacht, the state-sanctioned violence against Jews in Germany that occurred in November 1938, Morgenthau began pressing the State Department to increase the number of Jewish and other refugees from central and eastern Europe admitted to the United States. Existing quotas, already reduced in the 1920s from what they had previously been, had gone 99 percent unfilled.[100] Morgenthau's principal antagonist within the administration had been Assistant Secretary of State Breckenridge Long, who had ordered consular officials to postpone and postpone and postpone the granting of visas.[101] After the United States entered the war, Roosevelt's public position remained that the most effective way to come to the aid of Hitler's Jewish victims was by winning the war as quickly as possible.

After the State Department confirmed what Hitler's true intentions toward the Jews actually were, several organizations began pressing the administration to do more to save them. On March 1, 1943, a few weeks before Kean raised the matter on the House floor, mainstream Jewish organizations, in a show of support for Roosevelt's official policy, held a "Stop Hitler Now" rally at New York's Madison Square Garden. Prominent speakers included New York City mayor Fiorello La Guardia, New York governor Thomas E. Dewey, and clergy of all major faiths. At the same site eight days later and ten days before Robert W. Kean made his remarks, Jewish activists led by a Zionist activist from British Mandate Palestine who went by the name of Peter Bergson and the playwright Ben Hecht presented a pageant, titled "We Will Never Die," before an audience of 40,000. A month later, the group repeated the performance in Washington's Constitution Hall with Eleanor Roosevelt, several Supreme Court justices, Cabinet secretaries, and 250 congressmen and 49 senators in attendance.[102]

Bergson and his compatriots sought the creation of an agency, run under international auspices, to work actively to rescue Jews in areas under Nazi control. Prior to and after the mounting of the "We Will Never Die" pageant, Bergson and Hecht walked the corridors of congressional office buildings beseeching senators and congressmen to introduce resolutions on behalf of the establishment of such an entity. Morgenthau raised the matter directly with Roosevelt. On January 13, 1944, he presented the president with the report he had asked his assistants at the Treasury Department to prepare. Its title, *Report to the Secretary on the Acquiescence of This Government in the Murder of the Jews,* summarized its findings.

Nine days later, Roosevelt, by executive order, created the War Refugee Board. Operating out of Canada and funded by the American Joint Distribution Committee, the WRB sent officials from neutral countries to attempt to rescue Jews from certain slaughter. Under its auspices, Swedish banker Raoul Wallenberg journeyed to Hungary, where he established safe havens for most of the remaining 120,000 Jews. WRB's files, located at the Franklin D. Roosevelt Presidential Library, contain correspondence from Robert W. Kean in which he made inquiries on behalf of constituents.

The extent to which Kean and Morgenthau collaborated on efforts to force Roosevelt's hand remains unclear. Kean, through his activities on the Banking and Ways and Means committees, had ample occasions to interact with the treasury secretary. Congressman Kean had defended Morgenthau, Baruch, and other Jews against

Linder's anti-Semitic tirade. The Morgenthaus, like the Roosevelts, the Howards, and the Vanderbilts, hailed from Hyde Park. Although Kean and Morgenthau were not close friends, their daughters were.[103] Historians attribute Roosevelt's quick response to Morgenthau's entreaties to the latter's warning that Congress planned to hold hearings on the indifference the administration had shown to the plight of European Jewry. Preparing to seek reelection to a fourth term, Roosevelt was eager to deny his critics the opportunity to embarrass him.

Long after the war ended, Robert W. Kean continued to support causes of concern to his Jewish constituents. He was an early proponent of the establishment of the state of Israel, which he proclaimed "a strategically important ally of the United States."[104] Tom recalled that his parents recoiled at Washington dinner parties when State Department officials and CIA operatives, expressing the "Arabist" point of view, referred to the Jewish state as the "Zionist entity," rather than by its real name.[105]

As the war in Europe entered its final phases, the man around whom much of the political discussions in the Kean household had centered, Franklin Roosevelt, died suddenly. Tom broke the news to his family after hearing it on the radio. He would long remember Arthur Godfrey's description of the funeral cortege's journey from the White House to Union Station in Washington. Their politics notwithstanding, he said, the Keans, like the rest of the nation, respected Roosevelt's qualities as a war leader and mourned his passing.[106]

The end of World War II served as the occasion for the Keans to focus on Tom's poor performance in school. "I was unsuccessful at almost everything I tried," he later wrote.[107] Not only did he receive bad grades and seem in need of discipline, but he appeared to have a learning disorder, later diagnosed as dyslexia. He also had a stutter, which grew more pronounced whenever he was called on in class. Tom's plight occasioned a family summit at which Robert and Elsa Kean decided that the time had come to send him to boarding school. He was to attend St. Mark's, the alma mater of his father and two older brothers.

chapter 2

Kean Comes of Age

St. Mark's School

St. Mark's School, situated in Southborough, Massachusetts, twenty-seven miles west of Boston, was the second boarding school in the United States to be modeled on the English public schools.[1] Founded in 1865 and affiliated with the Episcopal Church, the school took as its mission the education of sons of the nation's socially prominent families. It remained an all-male school until the last quarter of the twentieth century. St. Mark's founders expected its graduates to take their places among the country's ruling elite and to put into practice the ideals they had acquired at the school to the benefit of society.

As did its brother schools, St. Mark's sought to instill the values of its leadership ethic through a curriculum that emphasized a "muscular Christianity," acquired through rigorous athletic competition, church attendance, Spartan living conditions, and an education grounded in the classics.[2] Also like them, St. Mark's took as its organizing principle the admonition in the Gospel of St. Luke that "to whom much is given, much is expected." As a soldier, scholar, and statesman, Theodore Roosevelt epitomized the kind of graduate that schools such as St. Mark's hoped to produce. The scion of a leading American family, he served as a role model for many of its alumni, including two generations of Keans.

Tom Kean entered St. Mark's first form at the age of eleven in the fall of 1946. His brother Ham feared that, given his brother's poor academic record, disciplinary problems, unkempt appearance, and insistence on getting his own way, Tom would find the transition to boarding school particularly difficult. Ham wrote St. Mark's assistant headmaster, Edward J. ("Ned") Hall, of his concerns and asked the educator to keep an eye on Tom. Years later while Thomas Kean was serving as New Jersey's governor, Hall wrote Elsa of his delight in seeing one of his former charges rise to such heights. "And I *did* look out for him," he added, letting the family know that he had taken Ham's admonition to heart.[3]

Ham Kean's initial anxieties had been warranted. Unlike Robert W. Kean and Ham, both of whom had older brothers at St. Mark's at the time they arrived, Tom showed up not knowing a soul. Corporal punishment and hazing, meted out by upperclassmen, were still prevalent. More than fifty years later, Tom would vividly recall the fear that passed through his living quarters as students waited to be summoned down the hall after lights-out to be punished for some in- fraction.[4] (Tom's would be the last class to experience paddling.)[5] "The seniors [or sixth formers] generally ran the place," he recalled.[6] Most of the hazing consisted of older students sending younger ones to run errands. One of the more dreaded rituals was called Bloody Sunday. On that day, new students struggled to avoid detection and possible capture by upperclassmen. Tom took refuge in a practice he had developed during his summers in New Jersey: hiding in the woods. He escaped detection but contracted poison ivy.

St. Mark's proved a stiff challenge for Tom. He accumulated de- merits for tardiness and came to believe he had set a record for the number of times he had been dressed down for leaving his room un- tidy.[7] Punishments included shoveling coal and copying passages from the *Congressional Record* by hand. Though he experienced dif- ficulty adjusting to his new surroundings, Tom did find relief from the harshness of his daily routine in the person of a teacher who would exert great influence over him, William Gaccon. A graduate of St. John's College at Cambridge University, Gaccon taught Latin and occasionally Greek. He began teaching at St. Mark's in 1931, joined the British navy during World War II, and returned to St. Mark's after the war. The year Tom arrived, Gaccon was serving as housemaster in charge of all dormitories. In his history of St. Mark's, Ned Hall wrote of Gaccon's "quiet, but effective supervision," both of students and of staff, and spoke of the teacher's apartment as the school's "nerve center." Many an alumnus would find Hall's description of Gaccon's operation familiar: "Little boys creep into the warmth of his [Gaccon's] living room early in the morning to study; prefects drop in during the later evening to report on local conditions."[8]

Tom became one of the many who flocked to Gaccon's rooms seeking shelter and companionship. "[Gaccon] practically adopted me," he said more than fifty years later. "He paid attention to me."[9] Tom was free to go to Gaccon's quarters at almost any time. He spent countless afternoons talking to the teacher about whatever happened to be on his mind. "He helped me work out my problems by giving me a sense of self-confidence and convincing me that I had something to contribute not only to my classes but to a greater good as well," Tom would say of the man he considered his mentor. Gaccon, he noted, was the most respected person on campus. He found that the attention Gaccon bestowed upon him caused his fellow students and other faculty members to regard him in a different light. "They probably figured," Tom opined, "that if Gaccon thought I was okay, they might find that I was okay too."[10] For the first time in his life, Tom began making permanent friends.

Under Gaccon's tutelage, Tom's stutter lessened. Eventually, it all but disappeared, returning occasionally during moments of fright, anxiety, or fatigue. Gaccon's influence was also seen in Tom's acquisition of one of his most discernable characteristics: an accent reflecting both Gaccon's British intonations and those of the surrounding New Englanders. When asked what was the first thing he noticed about Kean, former president Bill Clinton said without hesitation that "he [Kean] did not sound like he was from New Jersey."[11]

Another teacher who made an indelible impression on Tom was the cantankerous William Begg, whom Tom would remember as one of the school's great characters.[12] A native of Brooklyn (who never lost his Brooklyn accent), with a Ph.D. from Columbia, Begg shared Robert W. Kean's politics. He liked to say that Harry Truman was his second favorite among the living ex-presidents.[13] (The only other living ex-president at the time was Herbert Hoover.) Along with Gaccon's tutelage and Begg's wisecracks, Elsa's daily letters became another staple in Tom's life at St. Mark's. He recalled that she had a special knack for making the ordinary sound interesting as she filled him in on what was transpiring at home, interlacing the news with humorous tidbits.

Though Gaccon would help raise Tom's confidence, and Begg would sharpen Tom's sense of humor, neither succeeded in turning him into much of a student. Transcripts of Tom's grades at St. Mark's during his first four years show a monotonous string of 50s and 60s, interrupted by a strong set of 80s in religion and eventually history. In later years, Kean's advisers and audiences alike would marvel at his ready command of scripture. He did not consider it much of an achievement. "I went, after all, to a religious school," he would protest. "We had it drummed into us."[14] Maybe so, but however Tom came to them, his early acquaintance with Cranmer's Book of Common Prayer and the King James Bible instilled in him a lifelong appreciation for the English language and of how its cadences can inspire audiences. As a public speaker later in life, he would cite scripture often. Eventually, he would add to his ready repertoire of quotations lines from Shakespeare, Lincoln, Churchill, and Kennedy.

A Growing Interest in History and Public Affairs

The stories, lessons, and parables that Tom found in the Bible stirred his imagination. His sustained study of history did the same. He developed a fondness for the ancient world, the Italian Renaissance, and Elizabethan England and began to show an interest in the history of his family and of the United States. Throughout his life, Tom liked to say that his father at age ten sat on Teddy Roosevelt's lap and that Roosevelt, at roughly the same age, observed Lincoln's funeral cortege from his bedroom window. He would enthuse that only a few generations separated him and his contemporaries from the nation's founding era.[15] Tom delighted in telling listeners that when his grandparents were young, old-timers who wished to insult people referred to them as Hessians. When an elderly servant caught Tom's grandfather, Hamilton Fish Kean, at the age of eight with his head in a barrel of molasses, she blurted out, "You Hessian," before she disciplined him.[16]

Kean recalled that from the moment he first studied history, he wanted to be a history teacher, no matter how poorly he performed or whatever the quality may have been of particular instructors.[17] Of all his history teachers, he considered his father superior to most of his lecturers: "My father was very much interested in history and in family history particularly. He would tell us some of the stories; and when we visited Liberty Hall, of course, we'd hear the stories about the house; and we'd get to see people at family weddings and so on. People would come to Liberty Hall and start talking about how they were related to you and why we were going to a Roosevelt wedding, or a Winthrop wedding, or what have you."[18] An accomplished historian and genealogist, Robert W. Kean did not have to look any further than the lives of his forebears in order to keep his children amused. Two of his great-aunts, one the wife of future secretary of state Hamilton Fish, dined with Abraham Lincoln at the White House. His grandmother, while serving as hostess to her son, Senator John Kean, a bachelor, edited written opinions of Supreme Court justices, at their request. Robert W. Kean also had at his command stories about the greats, the not-so-greats, and the ne'er-do-wells who paid calls on his uncle and father when they served in the Senate. He was well armed with tales about Winthrops after he had exhausted his repertoire about the Keans.

Through his reading as well as by listening to the stories his father would tell, Tom acquired two historical heroes: Abraham Lincoln and Theodore Roosevelt. He admired Lincoln because of the manner in which the sixteenth president "redefined the Declaration of Independence" by extending its universal principles about equality of opportunity to African Americans. He confided that during his own career he sought to define himself by reading (and "getting right with") Lincoln. Tom also acquired a deep respect for the way in which Lincoln used language to express his ideas, describing complex notions in the simplest of terms. Lincoln's phraseology, he would say, shed additional insight into his special genius.[19]

Tom cited Roosevelt's commitment to conservation, willingness to cross swords with the titans of his day, and occasional gestures to African Americans, such as his dining with Booker T. Washington at the White House, as characteristics he admired. He also had high regard for Roosevelt's proclivity to keep "his integrity intact, even on occasions when his actions contradicted his rhetoric."[20] Because of the kinship between the Keans and the Oyster Bay Roosevelts, Tom grew up regarding Roosevelt's legacy as part of his political inheritance. Portraits of Lincoln and Roosevelt hang on the wall in Tom Kean's home opposite the front door, welcoming all arrivals.

During Tom's final two years at St. Mark's, his grades began to improve. Though still hardly a model student, he no longer placed at the bottom of his class. He finished the sixth form twenty-second out of thirty-eight. During the first form, he had placed thirteenth out of fifteen. He had also become somewhat of a person of standing on campus. How high Tom rose in the esteem of his peers became manifest when they designated him, with faculty concurrence, a monitor during his final year at St. Mark's, an honor that had also been bestowed on his father and two brothers. In his junior and senior years, Tom was elected to the student council. He joined the debating team, French club, and dramatic club, and helped found the Society of St. Andrew, a religious organization.[21] Through the influence of a classmate, Lee Berthelsen, the son of a musician, he also acquired a taste for opera. Before their graduation, Tom, Lee, and a friend treated St. Mark's French club to a parody of a scene from Bizet's *Carmen*.[22]

Tom played football, which was compulsory at St. Mark's. Required to participate in three other sports, he went out for tennis, soccer, and wrestling. Though he would excel only in tennis, Coach William E. Gaccon found something in his "adopted son's" soccer playing to praise: "The fullbacks were at times known to mis-kick (Kean's speed was an advantage on such occasions), but they worked tire-lessly and despite the loss of Haskings during the latter half of the season, they provided Berthelsen, who played an excellent game in goal, with sound protection."[23]

Although Tom began to follow current events at St. Mark's, his interest in them did not come voluntarily. *Time* magazine was re-quired reading at the school, and students would routinely be exam-ined on its contents. Tom discovered that on those occasions when his father's name appeared in the periodical, there would be a ques-tion about Congressman Kean on the test. Not surprisingly, he began paying closer attention to his father's activities. While Tom was at St. Mark's (and later while he was at Princeton), his father's influ-ence in Washington was growing. With the Republicans in control of the House from 1947 to 1949, and again from 1953 to 1955, Robert W. Kean made the most of his increased seniority and expertise. He con-tinually pressed to extend Social Security's reach to more Americans, including the self-employed. By the time he retired in 1959, the pro-gram covered 90 percent of Americans.

While on the Ways and Means Committee, Kean forged close bonds with Representative Wilbur Mills (D-AK), and with Wilbur Cohen, the principal author of the Social Security Act of 1935, who oversaw the administration of the program for decades afterward.[24] After Mills became chairman of the committee during what would be Kean's last term in the House, he sought Kean's advice on legisla-tion.[25] Robert W. Kean called his experiences as chairman of a House subcommittee that investigated wrongdoing at the Internal Revenue Service the most interesting of his experiences in Congress.[26] The work of the "Kean Committee" resulted in the streamlining of the agency, the removal from office of IRS officials, and the conviction of several cronies of former president Truman on corruption charges.

Younger members of the House regarded Robert W. Kean as their lodestar when it came to taxation and Social Security. Future presi-dent Gerald R. Ford, elected to Congress ten years after Kean, re-called that whenever Kean rose to speak, junior members rushed to the floor because they knew that "whatever Bob Kean had to say—and it would usually pertain to Social Security—would be of impor-tance to the people of their districts." Ford compared the atmosphere Kean produced in the House on such occasions to that depicted in a once-popular television commercial for the financial brokerage firm E. F. Hutton. "When Bob Kean spoke," Ford recalled, "everyone listened." Younger congressmen, Ford remembered, held the elder Kean in awe.[27] Kean, in turn, was among the first in his party to re-gard Ford as a comer. On the eve of Richard Nixon's nomination for president, Robert W. Kean told a former colleague, Frances Bolton of Ohio, that Ford would make an excellent vice presidential nominee.[28]

One Republican Kean did not like very much was Wisconsin senator Joseph McCarthy. In an issue of his newsletter, *Kean Comments,* which was mailed to residents of his district, the congressman referred to the senator as a "loud, shouting demagogue."[29] Tom remembered sorting the hate mail this issue generated.[30] Kean attracted national attention when he, along with eighteen other Members of the House, including Ford, wrote NATO commander Dwight D. Eisenhower, suggesting that he run for president. Ike's handwritten reply became one of his most prized possessions. During each of the years Eisenhower was president, he invited the group to the White House for lunch.

While at St. Mark's, Tom had occasion to observe his father's political activities up close. Along with his sister Rose, Tom, then thirteen years of age, attended the 1948 Republican National Convention in Philadelphia. He remembers being attracted to Senator Robert Taft's campaign, primarily because of the Ohioan's campaign song, which set new lyrics to the tune "I'm Looking Over a Four-Leaf Clover." His sister, because of her friendship with the daughters of California governor Earl Warren, the eventual vice presidential nominee and future chief justice of the United States, had a different favorite. Their father, while he considered Taft the best-informed U.S. senator, supported the eventual nominee and almost president, Thomas E. Dewey.[31]

The Newspaper Columnist

His interest in current events and national politics awakened, Tom began writing a political column for the student newspaper, the *Saint Marker.* He called it "Sound and Fury." It ran every other week. Not surprisingly, the opinions Tom advanced bore a close resemblance to those that his father espoused in Washington. Yet Tom's pieces differed from those his father might have written in the manner in which he justified his point of view. Usually, Tom summarized two distinct positions before volunteering his own, which usually fell between the two. Most of the time, the seventeen-year-old commentator would offer up alternatives that neither side had considered. Often, he would take the conservative side of the argument, but would clothe his stand in language usually associated with liberals. After he became an elected official, he would just as readily take liberal positions, and defend them with rhetoric that resonated well among conservatives.

In a piece he penned about his father's nemesis, Joseph McCarthy, Tom wrote that the U.S. senator from Wisconsin had properly identified diplomat John Service and Professor Owen Lattimore as Communists (or at least as Communist sympathizers) but had falsely accused others, such as General George C. Marshall, of being the same. In his endeavor to suggest ways in which to improve upon McCarthy's performance, which he said had been to "hit one Communist for every four men he accuses," Tom recommended that voters clean up "the mess in Washington" by replacing an administration headed by Harry Truman, who had tolerated both security risks and corruption, with one led by (Kean family favorite) Dwight D. Eisenhower.[32]

In contemplating whether convicted spies Julius and Ethel Rosenberg should be executed for passing along atomic secrets to the Soviet Union, Tom advocated a course of action different from the two options available to the sentencing judge; administration of the death penalty or a thirty-year prison sentence with the possibility of parole after ten years. Tom recommended that President Eisenhower commute the Rosenbergs' death sentence to life imprisonment. Such action, he suggested, would deprive the Communists of new martyrs they could use in their ongoing propaganda offensive against the West, while ensuring that the convicted felons rendered no additional harm to society. Tom dismissed one Rosenberg sympathizer who urged clemency, Pablo Picasso, as a "Communist artist, whose latest pictures feature the Russian dove of peace."[33]

Turning his attention to Asia, Tom praised Republican Senate leader Robert Taft for condemning European nations that refused to support the United States during the Korean War.[34] He wrote admiringly of General Douglas MacArthur's suggestion that the United States remove its Seventh Fleet from the Formosa coast, thereby enabling Chiang Kai-shek's 500,000-man army to attack the Chinese mainland. Such a diversion, Tom argued, would compel China to remove its troops from the Korean peninsula, thereby ending the Korean War.[35] As would his fellow anti-Communist, Richard Nixon, whom he defended in his columns, Tom would come to favor rapprochement and increased trade with the People's Republic of China.[36]

During his final year at St. Mark's, Tom's classmates got the chance to hear from the progenitor of many of the opinions they had been reading. Robert W. Kean visited his alma mater. The *Saint Marker* observed, "There are not many speakers who can keep an audience on their toes for three and a half hours, but that is exactly what Representative Robert W. Kean of New Jersey did a week ago when he spoke to the Sixth Form in Mr. Barber's study."[37]

In addition to his other activities at St. Mark's, Tom Kean served as advertising manager of his class yearbook, *The Lion*. Along with the many ads he sold was a half-page ad to Kean-Taylor. Whether in deference to his increasing interest in public affairs, in anticipation of his political career, or in recognition of the manner in which he related to his peers, the editors of the school's yearbook placed the following inscription beneath Tom's photograph: "A politician is a walrus who can sit on a fence and yet keep both ears to the ground."[38] Accompanying it was a caricature of a walrus tossing currency in the air.

Brantwood Camp

For prestigious boarding schools that took as their mission the preparation of the nation's elite for lives of service, maintaining summer programs for the underprivileged was common practice. While a student at Endicott Peabody's Groton, Franklin Roosevelt had twice put in two-week stints as a counselor at a camp the school operated on New Hampshire's Lake Asquam. His biographers cite this experience as his first encounter with children with backgrounds less well off than his own. Groton publications announced that the camp's purpose was to "bring a little sunshine and pleasure" into the campers' lives and to combat snobbery among Groton boys while instilling in them a sense of service.[39]

Performing charitable works had long been a custom of the Keans. When Robert W. Kean was at St. Mark's, he belonged to the Missionary Society, which raised funds for poor whites in Appalachia.[40] Tom Kean recalled that both of his parents made it their practice to help people of lesser means. Sometimes they would support people they knew who had fallen on hard times, as when Elsa gave financial assistance to the widow of a local minister.[41] Robert W. Kean would often, and anonymously, pay the costs of sending deserving young people, whom he either knew personally or had heard about, to college.[42] Both made anonymous donations of food, clothing, and goods to Livingston neighbors who were struggling during the Great Depression.

At the height of the economic downturn of the 1930s, Senator Hamilton Fish Kean allowed local children who had no other place to swim to use the pond on his estate. When neighbors complained of noise, rowdy behavior, and foul language, the township of Union ordered it closed. Senator Kean protested the decision and offered to pay the costs of a local policeman to ensure that the children both behaved and continued to "enjoy the recreation" in very hot weather.[43] Fearful that the senator would prevail, a local official urged that the town enforce its ruling in haste.[44] After losing his final appeal, the senator showed up on the last day the pond remained open to observe the children at play. Some of them spotted him, as he attempted to hide in the woods, vicariously enjoying what would be their last group swim on his property.

The idea of St. Mark's operating a "fresh air" camp originated with Headmaster William G. Thayer, who had been headmaster when Robert W. Kean was at St. Mark's and who officiated at the future congressman's wedding. Like his counterparts at Groton, Thayer believed such an undertaking would provide solace to impoverished youths, while enabling St. Markers to develop leadership skills. He had his eye on a piece of land in Peterborough, New Hampshire. Because of the striking resemblance it bore to John Ruskin's home in the English Lake District, it was given the same name as the celebrated critic's estate, Brantwood. A camp had operated on the site from 1904 to 1914 but had closed during World War I. St. Mark's acquired the deed in 1920 from Mrs. W. H. Scofield, whose son had been a member of St. Mark's class of 1916. Eventually, the camp would acquire another property along Silver Lake for canoeing, swimming, and overnight campouts.[45]

Each summer, between twenty and twenty-five St. Markers in the fifth and sixth forms (the last two years) would serve as counselors to seventy boys, who came for a two-week stay. There would be three such stays each summer. Counselors lived in shacks with up to a dozen campers. Alumni of St. Mark's administered the camp. Tom's brother Ham had been a counselor years earlier. Toward the end of Tom's fourth form (his sophomore year), Assistant Headmaster Ned Hall, who was also Brantwood's director, still "looking out" for Tom, requested his help. Hall explained that he would be shorthanded that summer and inquired whether Tom would consider working as a counselor. Tom was reluctant at first. At sixteen, he would be only six months older than some campers he would be supervising. Nevertheless, he found Hall, and presumably Ham, quite persuasive. Besides, spending the summer at a place where there would be at least some people he knew was preferable to passing the time in Livingston, where he still had few acquaintances his own age.

Once he overcame his initial panic after one of his charges ran away and eventually returned, Tom took quickly to his new responsibilities. Among his early duties was that of swimming instructor. "They didn't have one, so I pitched in," he remembered. Tom came to value the time he spent at Brantwood both for what he was able to achieve and for what the experience taught him about himself. "I was forced into a leadership position," he said. "When you are in charge of twelve- to fifteen-year olds," he observed, "you are forced to make decisions every few minutes." Tom found he enjoyed making those decisions and came to believe he was capable of making the right ones. He greatly enjoyed working with children. Knowing they depended on him caused him to take his responsibilities seriously. Tom's self-esteem and his self-confidence grew, he recalled, when the leadership of the camp made a point of saying he had done well.[46] That affirmation, plus his joy in working with younger people, made him want to contribute to the camp even more.

Tom would return as a counselor for his final two summers at St. Mark's and during each of his four summers as a college student, when he would serve as assistant director and eventually as associate director. While he was at college, he hired Brantwood's chef, its cooks, and its doctor and planned the camp's activities. Two letters in Brantwood's files, both written during his final year at St. Mark's, attest to the diligence with which he performed his duties. In the first, the secretary to the headmaster wrote Peter Freeman, the camp's director, that she had grown tired of waiting for the counselors to come for materials they needed. "Since up to yesterday no one had appeared I sent for Tommy Kean, and he took the sheets and was going to distribute them at a Brantwood meeting yesterday afternoon," she wrote. "I hope this is all right," she added.[47] That she had sought out Tom gives testimony to the confidence that others had in him.

The second letter, also to Freeman, was from Tom. Written in pencil and on stationery he had borrowed from the *The Lion,* St. Mark's yearbook, it provides a glimpse of his leadership style as well as his ability to evaluate others: "Scott informs me he cannot make it for the 4th term, but could, if you could squeeze him in for the 3rd term bunch. See if you can, he's better than most of the third term bunch. I have recruited Porter for the 4th term, and have asked him to write you."[48]

Like St. Mark's, Brantwood tried to instill "muscular Christian" values through education and competition. Campers quickly learned that they were at Brantwood for self-fulfillment rather than primarily for recreation. New arrivals received tests to see how well and how fast they learned their fellow campers' names. They competed against one another in athletics. Shacks were inspected for neatness and cleanliness, with cabins and campers receiving grades. Campers were encouraged to take pride in their respective shacks and in their camp. Badges and merit awards were routinely bestowed. The most coveted award a camper could win was a "stay over" for two additional weeks. Counselors conferred and selected recipients. They announced the names of their secret designees during the last night.

During his service at Brantwood, Tom for the first time confronted societal issues with which he would deal for the rest of his life. He encountered children who had received no dental care; most had never worn new clothes. "At Brantwood," he found, "you couldn't get involved with the kids without understanding their families and their problems." Prior to his involvement with these children, Tom reflected, "social problems had been abstractions. Now they came home," he said. He derived great pleasure in knowing that he was able to make a difference in some campers' lives. "Although it was only for a few weeks a year, we could give them a life of values," he said. "For many, especially the ones who stayed longer, we made a real difference."[49]

Brantwood drew its campers from Episcopalian parishes in New York and Boston. It extended its reach to poor children of Jersey City as a result of the friendship Hall enjoyed with future New York bishop Paul Moore, whose first parish had been Grace Church Van Vorst, in one of the city's toughest neighborhoods. About 20 percent of the campers were African American. Through his association with Brantwood and its charges, Tom began to display characteristics he would exhibit throughout his time in public service. It was there that he developed the capacity to listen intently to what people told him. At Brantwood, he began to show empathy for younger counselors and campers and became genuinely interested in their problems. "You always felt that he understood, and you knew that he cared," recalled John Marshall, a former camper, who at fifteen served as junior counselor to the sixteen-year-old Tom.[50]

Campers in whom Tom took a special interest became known as "Kean boys." Largely, they were of two varieties: natural athletes and those who conveyed signs of emotional hurt. Tom retained vivid memories of one boy who fell into the latter category. "He was clearly a car kleptomaniac," he remembered. "One day, he got out and stole the camp truck." Asked how he handled that situation, Tom replied, "I had to get him out of the Peterborough jail to start with." Tom refused to give up on the fellow, who, under his tutelage, wound up winning Brantwood's "most improved camper" prize as well as a "stay over."[51] Tom brought the troubled youth around not by disciplining him but by reasoning with him. At Brantwood, Tom began a lifetime practice of delegating vast responsibility to younger people. Just as others had bestowed it on him before he thought he was ready, Tom would, in turn, entrust younger aides with the power to make decisions. He would also back them up.

When Tom would argue a point, those who knew him from those years recalled, he had a way of making others want to be on his side. "[Tom] was always on the right side," Marshall said, "and you always wanted to be on whatever side he was on."[52] Fellow St. Marker and Brantwood trustee Linzee Coolidge spoke of Tom's special "presence."[53] "When he said something, you believed him," he recalled. Tom's classmate Albert Beveridge noticed a certain gravitas in Tom when he was in the second form at St. Mark's. "He projected a sense of self, high moral values and standards, and seriousness of purpose," Beveridge remembered.[54]

Tom also became somewhat of a magnet for those in need of a shoulder to lean on. Asked whether he was aware of just how approachable he was, Tom replied, "I could be standing by myself at a reception and people I had never met, usually after they had had a little too much to drink, would walk up to me and tell me their life's story."[55] Noting this quality in him, the Keans' pastor at St. John's Church on Lafayette Square in Washington, Leslie Glenn, suggested that Tom consider entering the ministry.[56] For his part, Tom found it flattering that, of all the people on whom they could unburden themselves, so many selected him. (Those who later campaigned with him observed that Kean would rather start conversations with the shyest person in the room than talk to dignitaries. When they called this preference to his attention, candidate Kean joked that he found it a better way to pick up votes.)

Rather than attempt to lead by issuing commands, Tom made his points through inference and by asking questions. "[Tom] would not always say precisely what he wanted," Coolidge explained, "but somehow, you always knew."[57] (State legislators, gubernatorial aides, state cabinet officers, and his fellow 9–11 commissioners would echo those sentiments decades later.) Seldom, if ever, did Tom confide his inner thoughts to associates. "He could build a brick wall around himself," John Marshall said.[58] Someone who knew him from childhood attributed the origins of this trait to Tom's being one of six children: "Growing up in such an environment, you quickly find that once you say something, you have opened up a waterfall." The same held true of environments such as those of St. Mark's and Brantwood, where adolescents lived in close proximity to one another and with minimal privacy.

It was at Brantwood that Tom first displayed a characteristic that became apparent to all who spent time in his company over the next several decades: his distinctive sense of humor. Marshall captured its essence in two words: *that grin.* "There would be this grin," Coolidge would say of Tom.[59] Peter Freeman, who was with Tom at both St. Mark's and Brantwood and would serve as best man at his wedding, knew "something was up" whenever Tom flashed that "toothy grin."[60] Jay Engel, who forged a friendship with Tom while both were teaching at St. Mark's, spoke of a "mischievous twinkle in Kean's eye."[61] Tom's associates came to regard the appearance of "that grin" as a sign that he believed himself about to win an argument, score a point, or crack a joke.

To convey real or feigned displeasure at having to perform a task he disliked, Tom developed another gesture: the snarl. Marshall first witnessed "the snarl" when he scored his first point against Tom in a Ping-Pong game. As governor, Kean would use his snarl to indicate he didn't want to attend a meeting or conduct business with certain individuals. It became his way of suggesting to a subordinate that he knew the underling had acted in his best interests, even if he found the task before him not to his liking.

Tom forged a lifelong bond with Brantwood. After he was elected governor, he resigned from all boards on which he served except for Brantwood's. The board's minutes show that, whatever his other commitments, he rarely missed a meeting. He visited the camp at least once a year. In 1985, in the midst of his campaign for reelection, he returned for Alumni Day. A former camper, then in his early forties, approached Kean, reminded him of their prior association, and thanked him for making a difference in his life. "Everyone [else] from my old neighborhood is either dead or in jail," the man told him, but he had become a successful entrepreneur. "I came back today to say thanks to you and this place."[62]

Through his network of contacts and knowledge of real estate, Kean helped the camp acquire its lakeside property. He also established a scholarship program to enable former campers to serve as counselors. Most needed to work in order to help pay their college expenses. Believing they made the best possible role models for the kind of campers Brantwood served, Kean often telephoned likely donors to say: "Look, we both think this would be good for Brantwood and for Johnny. We have so much money on hand already. Now, what can we do together to come closer to making this happen?" Most found him hard to resist. Kean headed a committee that worked to increase the numbers of African American "stay overs," counselors, and campers (of certain ages). In typical Kean fashion, he achieved his objectives not by violating the camp's traditions but by working through them. He reinstated a Brantwood tradition that had fallen into disuse: the "hang over." Through this device, students of promise, who had not "yet learned the Brantwood system," could remain for an additional two weeks. "We both sat on the board together; and he spoke up more about black considerations than I did," Marshall, an African American, remembered.[63]

After he had stepped down as associate director of Brantwood, Tom and a colleague established the Kean-Munroe Cup. It was awarded each summer to the camper who had profited from his association with Brantwood by "exhibiting conspicuous qualities of cheerful enthusiasm, unselfishness, and helpfulness to others."[64] "There were so many other things given to those who had already won things," Kean later said. "I wanted there to be something for the really nice kids."[65]

Kean's Princeton Experience

Throughout his teenage years, Tom spent more time at St. Mark's and Brantwood than he did at home. Reluctant to change his routine, he procrastinated when it came to deciding where he wanted to go to college. He settled on Princeton primarily because his two brothers had gone there and because he admired the halfback of its football team, Dick Kazmaier, who had won the Heisman Trophy by the largest margin in history.[66] By the time Tom got around to inquiring about other universities, St. Mark's headmaster, Bill Barber, himself a Princeton alumnus, cut him off. "But I've already told Princeton you were coming," Barber told him.[67] Rather than press the point, Tom went along.

At Princeton, Tom stayed in close contact with his fellow St. Markers on campus. During his freshman and sophomore years, he roomed in Reunion Hall (demolished in the 1960s) with Lee Berthelsen and Richard Doughton. During his last two years, he shared a quadrangle suite with Frederick Deming, Bud Canaday, and Joel McCrea in Blair Arch, a popular location smack in the center of campus. College life did little to improve Tom's housekeeping practices. Nor did it dampen his sense of humor. Tom's roommates joked about his soiled laundry, standing unattended in closets and in the middle of rooms. "Tom, when are you going to wash that pile of socks?" Deming once asked him. "I don't know," Tom answered, shrugging his shoulders. "What will you do when you get down to your last pair?" Tom's inquisitor persisted. "Buy new ones, I guess," he replied, while trying to suppress "that grin."[68]

Tom's siblings and friends recall his being anything but the "big man on campus." To do that at Princeton in the 1950s, according to Al Beveridge, who had been at both St. Mark's and Princeton with Tom, "you had to distinguish yourself in one of three ways: athletics, academics, or the club system."[69] Although good at tennis, Tom played primarily with friends; he did not go out for the team. As far as academics went, Tom did well in subjects that interested him, such as history, but did little more than "get by" in the natural and social sciences. With regard to the clubs, Tom wanted as little to do with them as possible. In the opening days of the twentieth century, "eating clubs" began springing up on campus, replacing fraternities, which the university administration had abolished. Woodrow Wilson, while president of Princeton, disapproved of the club system that was emerging because it tended to accentuate social differences among undergraduates. His failure to curb its growth, plus his insistence that the graduate college be built on the main campus, rather

than on the nearby golf links, hastened his departure from the university (and into New Jersey politics).

F. Scott Fitzgerald's depiction of the eating clubs held true for
several decades: "Ivy, detached and breathlessly aristocratic; Cottage,
an impressive mélange of brilliant adventurers and well-dressed
philanderers; Tiger Inn, broad shouldered and athletic, vitalized by
honest elaboration of prep-school standards; Cap and Gown, anti-
alcoholic, faintly religious and faintly powerful; flamboyant Colonial;
literary Quadrangle; and the dozen others varying in age and position."[70] After going briefly into eclipse during World War II, the clubs
were resurgent during the so-called quiet 1950s, when Tom was a
Princeton undergraduate. At a time when conformity was said to
have trumped individualism on college campuses, the club system
represented the pinnacle of such conformity. The week of Tom's
graduation, *Life* magazine captured the spirit of the era when it proclaimed that year's college graduates part of a "silent generation."[71]

Both of Tom's brothers had belonged to Ivy Club. Beveridge
affiliated with Tiger Inn. Tom made his way into Campus, which he
termed a collection of "quiet, nice kids."[72] What Tom disliked most
about the club system was the way the clubs selected their members.
Club representatives would call upon prospective members in their
rooms. Through the questions they asked and the expressions they
showed, recruiters made clear whether they approved or disapproved
of a potential member's family pedigree, religion, ethnic origins, or
father's occupation. Often they would interview roommates at the
same time. If they lost interest in one of them, they would ask him to
leave and the other to remain.

In the decades prior to Tom's arrival at Princeton, students who
received no invitation to join a club took their meals at the Commons,
where they dined with underclassmen. Often they sat alone and in
silence.[73] By Tom's time on campus, the university mandated that
every student be granted an invitation to at least one club. The system that emerged became known the "100 percent" rule. If a student
interviewed with every club, one had to take him. Club officers would
confer at the end of the "bicker" process to divide the "rejects" among
them. Tom found this "reform" a poor improvement over what had
preceded it because "everyone knew who they [the ones deemed less
desirable] were."[74]

Given Tom's success as a columnist while at St. Mark's, he might
have been expected to have joined the *Daily Princetonian,* where future celebrity journalists like R. W. Apple and Robert Caro, both classmates of Tom's, were making their mark. Having already decided that
he wanted to be a teacher rather than a journalist, Tom shied away
from activities that would consume so much of his free time. Instead,

he poured whatever extra hours he had into Brantwood. As others competed for letters and prizes and engulfed themselves in Princeton traditions, Tom ordered camp supplies and hired staff. He persuaded at least one of his Princeton companions, engineering student Art Merritt, to become a counselor.[75]

For recreation, Tom learned to play bridge and retained the fondness for all-night Ping-Pong marathons he had developed at St. Mark's. He made use of the campus's close proximity to New York City, an hour away by train, to indulge his passion for opera. By then, his interest in opera had extended beyond the music. He grew increasingly curious about the lives and careers of singers, the strengths of various conductors, and how opera companies were managed. "Lee [Berthelsen] used to follow singers and castings in the way others followed baseball players and battling averages," Tom explained. "I found it interesting and began doing it too."[76] The two began arguing over the quality of various singers, performances, and recordings. Aware that Berthelsen was a Mario Lanza enthusiast, Tom would deliberately express doubt as to whether the young truck driver from Philadelphia turned tenor was actually any good. Berthelsen could always tell whether Tom was saying what he actually believed or was arguing the opposite just to provoke a reaction.[77] His periodic failures to suppress "that grin" gave him away whenever he was kidding.

At Princeton, Tom's interest in public affairs continued to grow. Periodically, he attended forums sponsored by the Whig-Cliosophic Society, the oldest college debating society in the country. He remembered with disdain the title of one particular debate, "Resolved: That Integration Would Be Harmful to the Negro."[78] Controversy arose while Tom was a student over whether Alger Hiss, an alleged Soviet spy who had gone to prison on a perjury conviction, should be allowed to speak on campus. Unlike many liberals, Tom thought Hiss had been guilty. Unlike many conservatives, he believed that the former official should be allowed to speak. As it turned out, Hiss, Tom recalled, delivered one of the most boring presentations he had ever heard.

In conversations with friends in the wee hours of the morning, Tom would drop occasional hints of someday running for public office. Displaying sentiments that he may have heard at home, Tom suggested to Deming that the post of U.S. senator was particularly desirable because an incumbent did not have to run every two years, as did a representative.[79] During a discussion in which they compared the pros and cons of various occupations, Merritt asked Tom why anyone would want to run for public office, given the tedious chores politicians had to perform. He recalled that Tom uttered in reply, and in a strong voice, "Service."[80] Deming found Tom particularly liberal "for a Republican," caring more about people and their problems than many liberal Democrats he knew. Beveridge doubted that Tom would eventually seek elective office. Tom's self-effacing nature, deference to others, and ability to suborn his ego in his relationships, he said, were not characteristics common among politicians.[81]

Each day, Tom poured over the *Newark Evening News,* still the voice of what remained of Arthur Vanderbilt's "Clean Government Republicanism," and the *New York Herald Tribune,* the echo chamber of what was once known as the "eastern Republican establishment." Robert W. Kean was still receiving ample coverage in both. Princeton's proximity to Livingston allowed Tom to spend time at home. He would visit with his parents several times a month. Often, Tom brought friends to Sunday dinner. His interest in current events increasing, he found he could relate to his father in new ways. Whereas his elder brothers had bonded with their father earlier in their lives, either through their common pursuit of sports and business or through their sharing of wartime recollections, decades apart, Tom and Robert W. Kean drew closer through their mutual attraction to the political game.

The elder Kean lifted the curtain for Tom on how policy was made in Eisenhower's Washington. Robert W. Kean was personally acquainted with many prominent figures of the era, including his Harvard classmate Christian Herter, then deputy secretary of state (and eventually John Foster Dulles's successor as secretary). At Herter's behest, Robert W. Kean added reciprocal trade to his portfolio of policy concerns. After winning reelection to his tenth consecutive term in 1956, Robert W. Kean showed interest in following in his father's and uncle's footsteps by running for the U.S. Senate. Tom listened intently to family discussions on this subject.

Through his work with Brantwood, excursions to New York, visits with his family in Livingston and Washington, and bull sessions, bridge games, and Ping-Pong matches with close friends, Tom carved out a pleasant existence for himself independent of the social scene at Princeton. Although he had not become a star in athletics, academics, or club life, he was playing the lead in a world he had created for himself. Of all Princeton had to offer him, nothing had greater appeal to Tom than its history department. He savored the time he spent in class listening to the likes of modern American historian Eric F. Goldman, medievalist Joseph Strayer, colonial expert Paul Craven, Renaissance scholar E. H. Harbison, and European history luminary Gordon Craig, who treated his classes to satirical impersonations of Adolf Hitler.

In order to qualify for graduation, every Princeton student was required to write a senior thesis that constituted an original contribution to an academic discipline. Kean prepared an account of Polish nobleman Count Julian Ursin Niemcewicz, who, inspired by the American Revolution, attempted to establish a constitutional republic in his native land. In his preface, Tom confessed that his interest in his subject went "beyond historical curiosity."[82] During the period between his two efforts to participate in the creation of a free, democratic Polish state, Niemcewicz made his way to the United States, where he wed Susan Kean, the first John Kean's widow. In his honor, his stepson, Peter Kean, subsequently renamed Liberty Hall Ursino, in commemoration of the count's birthplace.

After he returned to Poland to accept a position in the Grand Duchy of Warsaw, the entity Napoleon established in 1807, Niemcewicz wrote his wife some two hundred letters in which he recorded his experiences. Future generations of Keans dutifully preserved them, along with Niemcewicz's diaries, notebooks, poems, and plays. Tom's interest in Susan Livingston Kean's second husband peaked as he discovered the extent of Niemcewicz's political, literary, and musical connections. The Polish nobleman counted among his friends the first three presidents of the United States and the first secretary of the treasury, Alexander Hamilton. Niemcewicz's description of slave life at Mount Vernon was the first contemporary account to make its way into print.[83] The Mount Vernon Ladies Association drew heavily upon his descriptions of Mount Vernon's interiors in their restoration of the mansion. Tom could barely conceal his amusement as he described the pains Niemcewicz took to avoid taking sides between Jefferson and Hamilton in their bitter political disputes, as he shuttled back and forth between these feuding partisans, while retaining the confidence of each.[84] (Tom would later display a similar quality.) Tom also dutifully recorded the Polish count's success in getting the ever discreet and taciturn George Washington to render an opinion on how his successor was performing as president.

Some of the quotations Tom included from Niemcewicz's writings bore too close a relation to what were then contemporary events for his inclusion of them to have been completely coincidental. Writing in the aftermath of the 1956 Hungarian uprising against Soviet rule and of the USSR's previous attempts to crush independence movements within countries it considered satellites, Tom made note of Russia's duplicity and its suppression of Polish independence in the eighteenth century. He cited in detail Niemcewicz's account of the Russian army's especially cruel treatment of Jews as it made its way through conquered territories. "They were tortured until they told where their money was hidden, or if they had no money, until they died," Tom quoted from the count. On beholding a hummingbird for the first time, Niemcewicz, Tom informed his readers, observed, "How happy for hummingbirds that they are not born in Russia."[85]

Niemcewicz's readiness to mentor young people also caught Tom's attention. Citing Franz Liszt as his source, Tom relayed that Niemcewicz was an early patron of Frederick Chopin.[86]

Tom, the budding historian, included a five-page bibliography in which he offered his opinions of works he had consulted. One book he found "thoroughly unreliable for any kind of factual data"; another he dismissed as "almost useless" to historians.[87]

Tom's thesis adviser, R. R. Palmer, considered Tom's thesis a major contribution to historical research. In the opening pages of his classic *Age of Democratic Revolution,* Palmer credited Tom with enhancing the quality of his professor's research.[88] When it came time for Tom to depart "Ole Nassau" for the last time as an undergraduate, he did so with a sense of true accomplishment.

Taking Pity on the Army

Attending Princeton at a time of universal conscription, Tom affiliated with the ROTC. His war-hero father noted with pride that so many As appeared on Tom's report card in the category reserved for ROTC. Tom never informed the congressman that the markings connoted absences from drills and other obligations. Upon his graduation, Tom joined the New Jersey National Guard's Fiftieth Armored Division. He completed his basic training at Fort Dix and went on active duty each summer at Camp Drum, in Watertown, New York, not far from the Canadian border. Having been warned by army veterans never to volunteer for anything while in uniform, Tom pretended not to hear when a drill sergeant asked all in the unit who had graduated from college to raise their hands. He was most content when those who did were marched off to KP.[89] Another memory of military life he carried with him was that of a classics instructor from Stanford in his unit, who posted a different quotation from Plato each day on the base's bulletin board. One day, as the troops were "falling into line" at 4:30 a.m., Tom's squad leader barked, "Okay, which of you guys has been signing your name 'Plato'?"[90]

At Camp Drum, Tom formed a friendship with fellow guardsman Gary Stein, with whom he shared an interest in history and world affairs. The two later joked about the hours they spent protecting the nation's security by picking up cigarette butts at Camp Drum and depositing them into buckets. Stein remembered that military life did little to improve either Tom's housekeeping practices or his attire: "He was not the picture of a spiffy, dashing soldier in his rumpled fatigues." Tom, he recalled, had been the only person at Camp Drum to have combat boots with zippers.[91] He made this acquisition so that he could squeeze in several extra minutes of sleep while his companions struggled with buckles and laces in preparation for their first formation.

Looking back on his days in the military, Tom would joke that his period of service proved hard on the army.[92] One particular torture he put it through was the exercise known as "keeping abreast of Tom Kean's whereabouts." Each time Tom would relocate to his parents' homes in Livingston or in Washington, or to Brantwood, or the town in which he was teaching, he informed the National Guard. With each change of residence, he would be transferred to a different unit. Eventually, Tom recalled, the army lost touch with him completely. Before it had completely given up on him, duty of a different nature summoned Tom Kean home.

chapter 3

In the Service of His Father

A Call to Duty

Less than a year after his graduation from Princeton, Tom Kean found himself working in his first political campaign. U.S. senator H. Alexander Smith had announced his plans to retire in 1958. Robert W. Kean hoped to succeed him. The entire Kean family became part of his effort to do so. Tom's participation had not been entirely voluntary. "There really was no choice," he said. "It was what you did."[1] The sense of obligation he felt had not been communicated to him verbally. But the expectation had been there. Helping the family patriarch achieve his ambition was what Keans did.

In rallying to their father's side, Tom and his siblings were filling a role that Robert W. Kean had himself played a generation earlier when his father, Hamilton Fish Kean, sought reelection to the U.S. Senate in 1934. His managers prevailed upon the candidate's youngest son, Robert, to make his father's case before his fellow veterans of the Great War. In a speech he titled "A Veteran's View of the New Deal," which the campaign published and heavily distributed, Lieutenant Robert W. Kean, after castigating several of FDR's policies, ended his remarks with a personal testimonial to his father.

Robert W. Kean found, as would his son Tom a quarter century later, that he enjoyed himself on the stump. He interpreted the enthusiastic receptions he had received in Jersey City and Bayonne as signs that his father would fare better in Democratic Hudson County than the campaign's managers feared.[2] He would be proved wrong. Hamilton Fish Kean lost Hudson by 133,942 votes and the election by

231,488 votes. His challenger, former governor A. Harry Moore, won a healthy plurality through the efforts of Jersey City mayor and Democratic boss Frank Hague.[3] Also working against Hamilton Fish Kean was his opposition to most of Franklin Roosevelt's New Deal at a time when FDR's popularity was at its peak. The off-year election of 1934 was one of the few in which the president's party picked up seats in Congress. In the Senate, Democrats gained nine, Kean's included.

In 1958, Robert W. Kean would also fail to buck a national trend running against his party. With a Republican in the White House and the nation in recession, the Democrats picked up ten Senate seats. Again, New Jersey's was among them.

Opening Moves

Robert W. Kean announced his candidacy for U.S. senator late in January 1958 on the eve of the New Jersey Chamber of Commerce's annual train trip to Washington.[4] He had several reasons for wanting to enter the race. As the fourth-ranking Republican on the Ways and Means Committee, he knew that his prospects of becoming its ranking member, let alone its chairman, should the Republicans regain control of the House, were slim. Having served in the House for twenty years, he had grown tired of having to campaign for reelection every two years. The election of 1958 provided him with an opportunity to serve in a post both his father and uncle had occupied. At the age of sixty-four, it might be his last chance to "move up."

As the justification for his campaign, Kean offered his record of increasing Social Security benefits and expanding the number of Americans the system reached, his support for President Eisenhower's defense and cold-war policies, and his advocacy of free trade. With his announcement, Kean became the instant front-runner.[5] Democrats considered him the most experienced and the most popular candidate the Republicans could field. He appeared to command a sizable electoral base in the state's largest county and had a history of attracting support from Democrats and independents. Just two years earlier, when he won reelection to his tenth term in the House, Kean polled 5,000 votes ahead of the greatly popular President Dwight D. Eisenhower. Observers opined that Kean's Democratic opponent would be whichever candidate the recently reelected governor, Robert B. Meyner, deemed the strongest.

Meyner had much riding on this election. Unexpectedly elected governor in 1953, the first Democrat elected in a decade, and reelected handily over magazine publisher Malcolm Forbes four years later, he had become a topic of conversation among national Democrats surveying the field for possible dark-horse presidential or vice presidential candidates in 1960. To his record of low taxes, high-caliber appointments, and sound administration, he hoped to add the election of a U.S. senator to demonstrate his skills in casting a statewide Democratic Party in his image. As his choice for the Democratic senatorial nomination in 1958, Meyner settled on Harrison A. Williams, a former one-term congressman from Union County.

Williams had been elected to Congress by a narrow margin. He had won his seat—considered a safe Republican seat—in a special election held in 1953 to fill the vacancy that occurred when Representative Clifford P. Case became a U.S. senator. Williams won reelection in 1954 but lost by 4,000 votes to Florence Dwyer in 1956, the year Eisenhower won reelection by a landslide. Williams's ability to run strong in Republican areas caught Meyner's attention. Once Williams expressed interest in running, Meyner staffed the hopeful's campaign with veteran operatives from his recent reelection campaign. One obstacle standing in Meyner and Williams's way within the Democratic Party was Hudson Democratic boss John V. Kenny, who opposed Meyner's choice. Angered that Meyner had shown him insufficient deference after having won the governorship in 1957 with Kenny's help, the leader set out to demonstrate that no Democrat could win a state primary without Hudson's support. To make his point, Kenny fielded Hoboken mayor John J. Grogan against Williams. Joseph McLean, a renegade Meyner appointee, also announced for the seat.

As Meyner and Kenny waged war through surrogates, Robert W. Kean worked to fend off two primary challengers: Bernard M. Shanley and Robert Morris. Shanley, as President Eisenhower's special counsel and appointments secretary, had used his powers over patronage appointments to befriend several county party leaders. He entered the race with the support of state senators Walter Jones of Bergen County and Hap Farley of Atlantic, both of whom presided over their respective county organizations. Morris, as a result of his service on the staff of the Senate Internal Security Subcommittee, was a favorite among conservatives.

All in the Family

Because Robert W. Kean's legislative duties prevented him from campaigning on most weeknights, his campaign sent stand-ins to represent him at events. With both of his brothers serving in this capacity, Tom performed other tasks for his father's operation. He found that he liked campaign work. He especially liked the people.[6] To manage his campaign, Robert W. Kean turned to Joseph Harrison of Montclair, who had run his two previous congressional campaigns. Harrison had served in past Republican state administrations and in 1958 was editing the *New Jersey Law Journal.* Like Ed Gaulkin, who had managed Congressman Kean's earlier campaigns before becoming Essex County prosecutor and a state appellate court judge, Harrison had deep roots in the Jewish community.

Assisting Harrison was Paul Williams, whom Tom remembered as an "old party war horse."[7] A former adviser to Senator Hamilton Fish Kean, Williams cast his lot with Vanderbilt's "Clean Government Republicanism" in 1934, spearheading its "outreach" efforts to Italian Americans. (He had changed his name to Williams from Di Guglielmo). Joseph Sullivan, a former newspaperman then serving as Kean's principal congressional aide, oversaw day-to-day operations. Alfred Beadleston, a Monmouth assemblyman and future state senate president, came on board after the primary as the campaign's chairman.

The campaign's top command stirred Tom's imagination with tales of campaigns past, filling him in on their colorful characters and acquainting him with the origins of ancient feuds that still determined political alliances and, often, electoral outcomes. Tom grew particularly close to the young man who headed his father's speakers' bureau, Herb Roemmele of Maplewood. Closer to Tom in age than the triumvirate of Harrison, Williams, and Sullivan, the genial Roemmele was a 1953 graduate of Lehigh, a stockbroker, and a protégé of Robert W. Kean. One day the campaign learned that the person it had scheduled to appear at a gathering in Fanwood had canceled. Roemmele asked Tom to fill in.

At first, Tom felt terrified at the prospect. When it came time for him to speak, he resolved to "strap himself in mentally and mumble" his way through.[8] He found that once he succeeded in directing his attention away from his nervousness and toward the substance of what he had to say, he actually enjoyed speaking before this group. The following day, several of the event's organizers called his father's headquarters to say that the congressman's youngest son had done exceptionally well. They asked that he be sent out more often to speak on his father's behalf. Betty Arthur (considered by most to be the alter ego of Congresswoman Florence Dwyer) had been especially taken with Tom's presentation, as was the wife of Fanwood's mayor.

Tom proved particularly effective in speaking before groups of women and young voters. His family took notice of how well he had taken to his new role. His sister Beth remarked that "it was apparent to most observers that Tom was really enjoying it."[9] His brother Hamilton recalled that he spoke loudly and forcefully.[10] On the strength of a heavy vote in his native Essex County, Robert W. Kean prevailed in the primary, placing 24,000 votes ahead of Shanley, with Morris a distant third. On the Democratic side, Williams placed ahead of Grogan by 15,000 votes statewide. In Hudson County, Williams received a mere 10,000 votes to Grogan's 70,000. In spite of Williams's poor showing in the Democrats' banner county, Meyner had achieved his first objective.

A Study in Contrasts

From the outset, the contest between Kean and Williams was a study in contrasts. Kean, with his gray hair and mustache and courtly mien, appeared the embodiment of the Republican establishment. Williams, thirty-eight, symbolized the transfer of power to a new generation that had grown up during the Great Depression, fought in World War II, and populated the growing suburbs. He projected the image Meyner sought to create of a state Democratic Party shorn of the vestiges of boss rule and political corruption. That was not what the Kean campaign had counted on. Since the 1930s, Vanderbilt's "Clean Government Republicans" had been the only ones seen to address the issue of bossism.

During the general election campaign, Williams stressed his partisan affiliation, while Kean emphasized his moderate to progressive record and his political independence. At first, Williams, in an attempt to appeal for votes among his fellow veterans, criticized Kean for his past opposition to Lend-Lease and the extension of selective service. Eventually, he ceased trying to paint the decorated World War I hero and proven internationalist as an isolationist. Instead, he focused on the economy, an issue that worked in the Democrats' favor during an economic downturn. Running as a New Deal and Fair Deal Democrat, Williams favored increased federal spending as the best antidote to recession. Kean proposed tax cuts and accelerated construction of the interstate highway system. Unlike the across-the-board tax cuts future Republicans would propose, Kean called for a 10 percent cut for lower-income Americans, a 7 percent cut for middle-income Americans, and a 5 percent cut for Americans in higher income brackets. He also wanted to cut taxes on businesses and capital gains.[11]

Going on the offense, Kean charged that Williams had accelerated the exodus of jobs from New Jersey to the Sunbelt by voting to finance electrical power systems and water reclamation projects in southern and western states, where unions were weaker and wages were lower than in New Jersey.[12] In the aftermath of the Soviets' launch of *Sputnik,* Kean suggested that the United States create a federal academy of science to serve as a "continuing reservoir" of scientists and engineers in vital fields. He advocated providing free professional training to high-achieving college and graduate students who agreed to spend four years in service to the government. Kean's bill, which the Democratic majority refused to bring to a vote, closely resembled the National Defense Education Act, which passed that same year under Democratic sponsorship. Meyner, acting as Williams's stand-in, suggested that Kean, nearing retirement age, would not be in the Senate long enough to attain the seniority and the political clout necessary to benefit the state. Years later, Robert W. Kean conceded the validity of that argument.[13]

Modernized Campaign Techniques

During the 1958 New Jersey campaign for senator, both sides pioneered techniques that would become commonplace in future campaigns and elections. By prearrangement, President Eisenhower telephoned Mrs. James W. Khalaf Jr. at her Maplewood home on his birthday, October 14, to ask her to vote for his "good friend Bob Kean." With press on hand to cover the event, Ike said he hoped New Jersey women would make 2 million "chain calls" before Election Day.[14] Eisenhower's telephone call anticipated the computerized messages voters would later find on their answering machines and voice mails from national party celebrities. For Kean's campaign, Ike's single telephone call produced several days of positive press coverage.[15]

Willing as Robert W. Kean was to use Eisenhower to attract attention to his campaign, he failed to press the president to campaign with him. "I am running on my record and expect to win without taking up the valuable time of some very busy people," Rep. Kean said.[16] His stance contrasted sharply with that of New York gubernatorial hopeful Nelson Rockefeller, who made maximum use of Eisenhower as he campaigned to unseat incumbent governor W. Averill Harriman. While Kean's campaign made much of the five-minute meeting Kean had with Ike in New York City, it stopped short—perhaps with its eye on national polls—of urging his election as a means of furnishing another vote for the president's policies. In addition to the recession and the launch of *Sputnik,* which harmed U.S. prestige, Eisenhower suffered political damage when his chief of staff, Sherman Adams, resigned amid allegations of conflict of interest and personal misconduct. Democrats harped on all three issues.[17] If Kean's campaign's contradictory actions with regard to the national administration bespoke its indecision, Williams displayed no similar compunctions in rallying known national Democrats to his side. The 1960 presidential hopefuls Hubert H. Humphrey and John F. Kennedy both campaigned for him.

As Republicans grasped for ways to attract free publicity, Democrats spent lavishly, broadcasting their message on a new medium that could reach the widest possible audience—television. In the final days of the campaign, Williams mounted a twelve-hour telethon on a Newark television station, while Kean stepped up his touring schedule. Tom Kean vividly described what a typical campaign day was like for his parents: "They would begin their day around 6:00 a.m. Between 7:00 a.m. and 8:00 a.m. a car would come to collect them. In it would be a young man, Bill Kohm, on leave from his full time position as aide to [Bergen County state senator] Walter Jones, with a schedule of the day's events. Until midnight, the three would then make dozens of stops, crisscrossing the length and width of the state. They would turn in sometime between 12:00 midnight and 1:00 a.m., only to repeat this routine again in a few hours."[18]

Elsa Kean never spoke at the countless meetings and rallies she attended. Nor did she display signs of boredom upon hearing her husband deliver the same speech for the twelfth time in a single day. "She was the perfect campaign wife," Tom Kean said.[19] Never did she consider skipping a day. In Kean parlance, "That was not something you did."

Comparing press coverage of his father's final campaign to that of his own political races, Tom Kean voiced disappointment at the frivolous attitude the state press displayed toward candidates and issues in 1958. One night, he remembered, "one journalist walked up to my father to inquire whether he was going to say anything different at an evening appearance from what he had said in the afternoon." Robert W. Kean replied that he did not expect that to be the case. "Good," blurted out the reporter, "because we are all planning to go out to dinner." "Imagine," Tom Kean recalled in disgust, "what if my father had in response to an unanticipated question put forth a proposal he had been saving for just such an occasion? Who would have known about it?"[20]

On the stump, Robert W. Kean appeared stilted and overconfident. While willing to appear at prearranged "coffees" at the homes of people he knew, Kean was reluctant to knock on doors of strangers and ask for their support.[21] In a televised debate with Wiliams, Kean referred condescendingly to his opponent as "a rather nice young man."[22] To a crowd of supporters in Monmouth County, Kean went so far as to say that the "election was in the bag," provided party workers did what was expected of them.[23] Few of the state's newspapers disagreed with Kean's assertion that his record was his strongest suit.

All but the most partisan in their Democratic leanings endorsed him.[24] Democratic strategists advised Williams not to attack Kean's record but to direct his fire at controversial national Republicans, such as Vice President Richard Nixon.[25]

On those occasions when the Democrat strayed from their advice, Kean was ready with a strong reply. When Williams questioned Kean's commitment to making Social Security coverage universal, Kean provided the press with quotations from Democratic congressmen, attesting to the validity of his claims.[26] As he had for twenty years, Kean campaigned heavily in African American neighborhoods. He took pride in his vote for Representative Adam Clayton Powell's amendment to bar federal aid for school construction in segregated areas. Williams had opposed it.[27] The immediate past president of the NAACP endorsed Kean on the grounds that an increase in northern Democrats in Congress would mean the perpetuation of the "blockade" southern committee chairmen had erected against civil rights legislation.[28]

As the campaign drew to a close, Democrats remained optimistic that Williams, buoyed by an army of patronage workers Meyner had put at his disposal, and the depressed state of the economy, would win. Republicans voiced forebodings. Stoics among them suggested that the pace of Rockefeller's incessant campaigning in New York would prompt New Jersey Republicans and independents who commuted to New York, to turn out for Kean.[29]

Election night began with a quiet family dinner at the Kean household. As was his custom, Robert W. Kean ventured to his polling place to see how he had done. He carried it 516 to 390.[30] He returned home to gather his family for what he expected to be a long evening. With Tom driving, Robert and Elsa Kean and their youngest daughter, Katharine, headed to the Military Park Hotel in Newark to await the returns. When the counting was over, Kean had lost by 85,000 votes. He had carried his native county of Essex, but only by 4,000 votes. He had hoped to win it by 25,000.[31] Results were similar in other parts of the state. Kean carried Bergen, but by a smaller margin than had prior statewide Republican candidates. In Atlantic, in spite of Farley's boast that Kean would lead by 12,000 votes, the Republican placed only 8,000 votes ahead of Williams.[32] In spite of the feud between Kenny and Meyner, Hudson County gave Williams a majority of 73,000, twice the amount it had given Meyner the previous year. Some in Kean's camp had hoped to hold the Democrat's edge in Hudson down to 50,000.[33]

Pundits and politicians alike attributed Kean's loss to the campaign's meager spending. Beadleston called Kean's budget the thriftiest on record.[34] Finishing without a debt, the campaign spent a total of $175,000, $325,000 less than Clifford Case's narrowly successful senatorial effort four years earlier, and $625,000 less than Malcolm Forbes's failed gubernatorial run the year before. More money, all sides agreed, might have added to his margin in Atlantic. Roemmele estimated that an additional $50,000 might have helped Republicans hold Williams's margin down in Hudson.[35]

Kean family tradition holds that Robert W. Kean, having financed his own campaign during the primary, expected the state party to cover most of his general election expenses.[36] Kean contributed $60,000 to his primary effort, of which his campaign spent $34,000.[37] In his later years, he lamented having had to spend funds in the primary he might have been able to use in the general election.[38] As Tom remembered, wealthy candidates like his father found it difficult to persuade people of lesser means to contribute to their campaigns during a recession, especially when, on the other side of the Hudson River, Rockefeller and Harriman were digging into their personal fortunes to finance their campaigns.[39] Robert W. Kean may have had his reasons for shying away from their example. If so, they were as personal as they were political.

Ghosts of Campaigns Past

Prior to his election to the U.S. Senate in 1928, Hamilton Fish Kean had for decades contributed generously to local and county Republican organizations. His son, Robert W. Kean, had occasion to observe his practices and methods. "I could realize that a great deal of money was going into the primary to politicians who, I am sure, pocketed half of it," he reflected.[40] Elsewhere, he expressed his misgivings: "I grew to have a horror of seeing so much hard earned money going down the drain and hated the thought of overspending. . . . Also my father's opponent kept attacking him for trying to buy the election. This hurt me for I knew there was some slight truth in the allegation."[41]

An example of how Hamilton F. Kean invested his personal funds in his and his party's future success was his purported contribution of $35,000 to Hoboken saloonkeeper William P. Verdon in 1920 in the hope of turning out a strong vote for the party's presidential candidate, Warren Harding, in Hudson County.[42] Harding carried Hudson by a wide margin, as he did the rest of New Jersey. After the election, people in both parties questioned whether Verdon had used Kean's money for the purposes the national committeeman had intended. Kean years later told investigators that he had always found Verdon "straightforward."[43] At first glance, the alliance between Verdon the saloonkeeper and Kean the patrician, professing to support prohibition, seemed an odd pairing. The glue that held it together was a mutual aversion to the leading Republican figure in New Jersey at the time, Walter E. Edge. An early supporter of Edge's gubernatorial campaign in 1915, Verdon broke with the newly elected governor when Edge denied the Hudson leader the patronage he felt was his due. At the time Kean and Verdon forged their alliance, Kean was planning to oppose Edge in the 1924 senatorial primary.

Running as a "dry" in 1924, Kean fell 60,000 votes short in the primary. Four years later, running as a "wet," he won the nomination, placing first in a field of five, edging out former U.S. senator Joseph Frelinghuysen and former governor Edward Stokes. After the election, the Senate, perhaps at the instigation of Kean's general election opponent, Democrat Edward Edwards, who had accused Kean of seeking to "buy the seat" with a "bag of boodle," with a likely assist from Senator Walter E. Edge, conducted an inquiry into Kean's spending practices. Its investigators were particularly interested in allegations that Kean had given $200,000 to Atlantic County boss "Nucky" Johnson in exchange for political support.[44] He allegedly bestowed his largesse on two other leaders as well: John McCutcheon, of Passaic County, and David Baird of Camden. The three produced substantial margins for Kean in their domains, resulting in his eking out a primary victory of 14,371 votes.[45]

The U.S. Senate investigation found no evidence that Kean had spent in excess of the $50,000 maximum the law allowed on his senatorial primary.[46] His manager, John H. Scott, supplied evidence that Kean wrote his campaign two personal checks of $25,000 each and spent a total of $49,366.33.[47] A *Newark Evening News* editorial found that Kean's team had kept records "with the exactness of a broker trained to remember the eighths."[48] Investigators never established that Kean had intended the largesse he bestowed upon Republican county organizations years in advance of his candidacy to assist his subsequent campaign. At the hearing, Kean maintained that his accusers had attacked him out of jealousy and envy. "A lot of people," he said, "became sour" because he hadn't "come up with money promised them."[49]

When he sought political office, Robert W. Kean found that his Democratic opponents seldom passed up the opportunity to charge that Keans tried to buy elections. Evoking ghosts of earlier eras, future congressman Edward Patten, while campaigning for Williams, told a Democratic rally in Middlesex County that the Kean family had for years used their personal fortune to defeat Democratic candidates.[50] If Patten's purpose had been to preempt a Republican, known to be able to self-finance his campaign, from using every weapon at his disposal to win the election, he may have succeeded.

The Elder Statesman

Although Robert W. Kean would rarely discuss the disappointment he felt upon failing to follow both his father and uncle to the U.S. Senate, his children shared in his sense of loss. Tom Kean referred to his father's defeat as "one of the world's great injustices." "He had worked so hard for so long, and now his career was over," he said.[51]

In 1959, Robert W. Kean took over the reins of the Essex County Republican organization and remained its chairman for two additional one-year terms. During his three years of service, Robert W. Kean worked to make the party's ticket more reflective of the county's changing demographics. At his insistence, the party put on its ticket for assembly Herbert W. Tate, an African American. When the delegation he helped elect balked at naming Tate its leader, Chairman Kean drove to Trenton to remind them who really ran the Essex Republican Party.[52] Tate was selected.

Robert W. Kean remained active in national and party affairs, lending a hand to Richard Nixon's 1960 presidential campaign, Nelson Rockefeller's attempts to win the 1968 nomination, and Gerald Ford's efforts to remain president in 1976. In 1960, President Eisenhower named the former congressman chairman of the National Advisory Committee for the White House Conference on Aging. Eventually, Robert W. Kean confined his political activities to helping advance the ambitions of his son Tom. He would participate wholeheartedly in the younger man's campaigns, privately advising on strategy, providing insights into people and issues, and occasionally writing checks. As Tom ascended the ladder of the New Jersey political hierarchy, his father delighted in his successes.

Bob and Elsa traveled the world. They remained in touch with friends they had made in Washington. When Congress was in session, the Keans could be found at their Washington home, 2435 Kalorama Road, which they had purchased after the war. They also spent time with their many grandchildren. The home in which Tom and Debby Kean raised their three children sat on land adjoining Robert W. Kean's estate. Ranking high among Tom's children's memories were walks they took in the woods with their father and grandfather, accompanied by the ex-congressman's cocker spaniel, Taffy. Afterward they would flock to the refrigerator in their grandparents' kitchen, which Elsa kept well stocked with Coca-Cola.

Increasingly, Robert W. Kean invested more of his energies into four lifelong pursuits: St. Barnabas Hospital, family genealogy, gardening, and managing the family trusts. He also served on the boards of directors of family-controlled companies, the Elizabethtown Water

Company, the Elizabethtown Gas Company, the Livingston National Bank, and the National State Bank of Elizabeth.

In retirement, Robert W. Kean maintained a voluminous correspondence on family and New Jersey history with his brother's widow, Mary Alice Kean, an accomplished preservationist and amateur historian.[53] He privately published two volumes of memoirs: *Dear Marianne,* an account of his military service in World War I, and *Four Score Years,* recollections of his youth, interspersed with family history. The latter's dedication evolved into a creed for subsequent generations: "To my descendants, present and future: With the hope that they will find our ancestors and their families worthy to emulate, and that they will remember that the important thing is 'not so much whether you are proud of your forebears, but would they be proud of you.'"[54] He was working on a memoir of his years in Congress at the time of his death in 1980 at the age of eighty-six.

Lessons Learned

Through participation in his father's final campaign, Tom learned several lessons he would put to use during his subsequent career in elective politics. Having watched his father shield himself from Democrats' charges that Republicans favor the rich, Tom Kean, as governor, made sure that the bulk of refunds his administration sent to taxpayers went to people of middle and lower incomes. He would, also like his father, favor using incentives to encourage individuals to act in ways beneficial to themselves and society, be it enticing young adults into teaching or prodding people off the welfare rolls.

Unlike his father, Tom Kean would use television heavily, both as a candidate to carry his message to voters and as an elected official to build support for his programs. Whereas his father showed reluctance to draw upon party celebrities to draw attention to his campaign and to mobilize his party's base, Tom was always glad to appear with presidents of his own party, whatever their standing in the polls. "On balance," he would say, "a president . . . can only help you through the increased visibility his appearing with you attracts to your campaign."[55] Another lesson Tom learned from what he observed of his father in 1958 was to always campaign as if he were the underdog, no matter how certain he may have been of his pending victory.

In his father's campaign, Tom discovered that he enjoyed speaking before groups. In his friendly debates with Robert Morris, he came to appreciate the increasing role conservatives were beginning to play within the GOP and what issues they deemed especially important. Finally, while Tom Kean would never self-finance his statewide campaigns, he did not shy away from investing personal funds on his own behalf when he believed it would affect the outcome of an election or spur on likely donors. Late during his 1981 campaign at a summit he convened of his top fund-raisers, Kean asked his backers to make one final push. When someone asked whether he would be willing to do the same, Kean replied in the affirmative. Given his reputation for frugality, Kean's decisive answer convinced skeptics that he actually believed he would win the election. Reassured, they departed determined to do what he asked of them.

chapter 4

Kean Finds His Calling

From Bored Broker to Budding Academic

Upon the conclusion of his unsuccessful campaign, Robert W. Kean suggested that Tom follow yet another family tradition by spending at least a year at Kean-Taylor, the investment firm Hamilton Fish Kean had founded and where Robert W. Kean had spent two decades prior to his election to Congress, and in which he still maintained a controlling interest. "My father believed that in order to be a good citizen or to do well in public service, you had to have an understanding of how the financial system of the country worked," Tom explained.[1] Tom found that he enjoyed financial research. He would later find his ability to read financial statements useful as an elected official, university president, and corporate board member.

Yet, after the pace to which he had grown accustomed in a political campaign and the fun he had had working with memorable characters such as Joe Sullivan, Joe Harrison, and Paul Williams, Tom found life cloistered away among middle-aged men wearing green eyeshades nothing but drudgery.[2] In November 1959, Tom received a telephone call from the headmaster of St. Mark's informing him that a beloved faculty member had died. He wanted to know if Tom would be interested in returning to his alma mater to teach history. Tom leaped at the chance. "This is the first time we lost anyone to a God damn school," an officer at Kean-Taylor proclaimed upon hearing the news.[3]

Tom began his new duties immediately after Thanksgiving. By February of the following year, a profile on him in the *Saint Marker* captured Tom Kean in full enjoyment of his new pursuits: "A person walking down the corridor of North Two, sometime after the end of evening study hour, is likely to be startled by a booming laugh which seemingly emits from everywhere. The laughter stops and a deep voice, says, 'Oh, the Washington Senators; they are my despair.'"[4] Tom immersed himself totally in the school. He proved a popular teacher and a much sought-after adviser. He coached wrestling, soccer, and baseball; advised the student newspaper, student council, and senior class; and helped students launch a photography magazine. In 1962, the year he departed, the graduating class dedicated its yearbook, *The Lion,* to Tom Kean, citing his "unceasing friendship and patient advice."[5]

While at St. Mark's, he introduced several innovations into its curriculum. One was a semester-long course devoted to the *Iliad* in translation.[6] In addition to reading the core text, students, under Tom's watchful eye, studied the history of the period in which Homer's epic had taken place. He took a similar cross-disciplinary approach to the works of Dickens. Together with English instructor Jay Engel, Tom founded a discussion group they titled "Labyrinth." They limited its size to five or six boys of "high academic standing, who competed to gain entry."[7] At its meetings, students debated ideas of the great philosophers. The concept of "Kean boys," well known at Brantwood, was now much in evidence at St. Mark's.[8]

Political Apostasy

Tom Kean committed his first act of political apostasy at St. Mark's when he agreed to serve as faculty adviser to the Kennedy for President Club. While following John F. Kennedy's emergence on the national scene, he had became enthralled with the eloquence of the Massachusetts senator's speeches and the idealism that he aroused in his listeners. He was much taken with Kennedy's buoyancy, the breath of fresh air he injected into politics, and the sense he projected that anything was possible.[9] In subsequent years, Kean would refer to the aura that surrounded Kennedy as magical.[10] Many of the speeches Kean would deliver in the course of his political career conveyed the Kennedy can-do spirit. Kean later admitted that when he first considered running for the state legislature, he envisioned himself as a "young John Kennedy, enthralling voters with impassioned speeches."[11]

A budding historian, Tom could hardly have helped but notice similarities between Kennedy's background and his own. Both had been born into political families, had attended exclusive preparatory schools and Ivy League universities, and had gravitated to the study of history and literature. Observing that Kennedy had become something of a role model for Tom, one of his colleagues tried to divest this would-be Kennedy of illusions. "The only difference between Kennedy and Nixon," his acquaintance scoffed, "was that one had a Harvard education."[12] Tom was not dissuaded. His enthusiasm for Kennedy caused consternation not only at St. Mark's but also in Livingston.

Robert W. Kean, both an alumnus and a trustee of St. Mark's, learned about his son's defection from the partisan fold. "My father liked Nixon," Kean explained; "he had served with him in the House." Nixon, then vice president, knew Tom as "Bob Kean's son." Years later, Tom attributed his decision to back the Democrat for president in 1960 not to any personal aversion to Nixon but to his "being so taken with Kennedy." Asked how his father took the news, Tom offered the four-word reply: "He was not pleased."[13]

As the Essex County party chairman, Robert W. Kean worked hard to elect Nixon president in 1960. In October, he presented Nixon to a rally of ten thousand people he assembled at the West Orange Armory. Nixon's press secretary, Herb Klein, declared it one of the three largest and most enthusiastic receptions Nixon received during the campaign.[14] The local newspaper recounted the precision with which Robert W. Kean's organization had tended to the smallest detail.

> An indication of the extensive spade work done by the Essex GOP organization appeared as the caravan left the Garden State Parkway and turned into 15th Avenue, Newark. Residents, forewarned by Republican loudspeakers, turned out in fair numbers in this solidly Democratic area.
>
> The evening affair, at which Nixon arrived about 9 [:00 p.m.], was tumultuous. The Essex Republicans hired 60 buses to bring enthusiasts from all sections of the county. They ran a shuttle bus service to the armory along Pleasant Valley Way, where parked cars were lined up for what seemed like miles. A band, a drum and bugle corps and singing kept the crowd happy. Torchlight parade was ruled out, however, as a fire hazard.[15]

Consistent with an old Kean custom of campaigning hard in Democratic strongholds, former congressman Kean had arranged for Nixon to address en route to the rally a gathering of more than two thousand African Americans at a public housing project in Newark. To introduce the vice president, Kean produced none other than baseball great and civil rights hero Jackie Robinson.[16]

Whenever Nixon or his running mate, Henry Cabot Lodge, campaigned in New Jersey, each, seeking to benefit from Robert W. Kean's continued popularity in his region, made mention of the former congressman.[17] If the elder Kean could not persuade his son Tom to toe the party line, he could take some solace in knowing that his progeny was carrying out his rebellion outside New Jersey.[18] Although displeased with his son's heresy, Robert W. Kean had done something similar almost fifty years earlier. During the 1912 presidential campaign, with his own father, Hamilton Fish Kean, and his uncle, former U.S. senator John Kean, working to reelect incumbent Republican president William Howard Taft, Tom's father showed up at a rally for the Progressive Party ("Bull Moose") candidate, former president Theodore Roosevelt. Spotting the nineteen-year-old Robert W. Kean in the crowd, the Rough Rider cried out, "I won't tell the family you were here."[19]

Witness to History

Tom Kean completed the 1959–60 academic year at St. Mark's and stayed on for another two. He spent the summers traveling. The first summer, he visited Greece with fellow instructors. The second, he went to Japan by himself. The third, he traveled around the world, stopping in Egypt, Lebanon, India, Burma, Thailand, and Cambodia. Content as he was with life at St. Mark's, Tom realized that he "had to get out." The thought came to him after he had to decline an invitation to dinner with a group of friends who were visiting from Boston. Tom had agreed to help students put the next issue of the school newspaper to bed. It dawned on him that, had they invited him to join them on any of the next six consecutive evenings, similar commitments would stand in his way. "Twenty years could pass by very quickly," he remembered thinking, "and I was not qualified to teach anyplace other than where I was."[20] In order to teach in a public school, he had to have a teaching certificate from a state board of education. To teach at a college or university, he would need to obtain a graduate degree. Tom decided to broaden his options.

He won acceptance to Columbia University's Teachers College. Though his actual degree would be a master's in the teaching of history, Tom was much more interested in the substance of history. He spent most of his time attending seminars led by Columbia's leading historians: eighteenth-century American expert Richard Morris; Progressive Era specialist Richard P. Hofstadter; New Deal scholar William Leuchtenburg; educational historian Jacques Barzun; Renaissance luminary Garritt T. Mattingly; and a young political scientist, Richard E. Neustadt, who catapulted to fame when photographers spotted a copy of his trailblazing book, *Presidential Power*, on John F.

Kennedy's desk. Tom did well enough in his studies to gain admission into Columbia's Ph.D. program. He passed the qualifying examinations but did not complete his dissertation.

Much as he enjoyed researching historical questions, Tom detested the educational methodology courses he had to take in order to qualify for a New York State teacher's certificate. Decades after he left Columbia, he would still proclaim this part of his graduate education "dreadful." He remembered handing in one paper in which he dismissed a widely hailed educational experiment as "worthless." To his surprise, not only did he receive an A on the paper, but his instructor had written on it that Tom's was the best one he had seen on that subject.[21]

With civil rights emerging as the dominant domestic issue at the time, Tom considered writing his doctoral dissertation on Woodrow Wilson's record in that area. Impressed with a study by Leonard Levy titled *Thomas Jefferson and Civil Liberties: The Darker Side,* he planned to explore the contradictions in Wilson's advocacy of "self-determination" for the peoples of Europe and of racial segregation at home. He had planned to title his dissertation *Woodrow Wilson and Civil Rights: The Darker Side.* Had he written it, he would have been certain to have contrasted Wilson's racial attitudes with those of his Kean forebears.

Tom did not confine his concern for civil rights to the classroom. While at Columbia, he opened the first northern office of the Southern Christian Leadership Conference, the organization Martin Luther King Jr. founded, and volunteered his services. By the time of the 1963 March on Washington, King had joined Kennedy in Tom's growing pantheon of heroes. "Then, in the early 1960s," he explained, "there was a sense that there was a right and a wrong. What King advocated was right—and he wanted to achieve it in the right way, through nonviolence."[22] Although Tom would attend marches and rallies at which King spoke, he did not consider himself part of a movement. He noted that none of the civil rights organizations of the time had large staffs. "You would write King a letter," he said, "and King would write you back personally."[23]

While at Columbia, Tom witnessed another cultural phenomenon: how the presence of arts institutions can transform neighborhoods. Then living on Manhattan's West Side in an apartment building called Lincoln Towers, he saw what would become the Lincoln Center for the Performing Arts take form. Prior to its construction, he remembered, the area the complex would occupy consisted of fleabag hotels, one decent restaurant, and a drug hangout known as "Needle Park."[24] Tom had joined preservationists in their attempt to rescue from the wreckers the old Metropolitan Opera House, where he spent countless hours in the standing-room section. He would retain a piece of the old Met's curtain as a souvenir. But after the Met reopened in its new location at Lincoln Center, he went to the opera with even greater frequency.

Living in New York provided Tom with ample opportunity to keep up with his fellow St. Markers, who were making their ways in their chosen fields. Those who knew him then remember a sensitive young man, anxious to make his mark and scornful of anything he considered pompous. A friend recalled having a drink with Tom at the Knickerbocker Club one St. Patrick's Day, when an elderly member of the club looked up from his newspaper, gazed out the window, and asked Tom, "Is that Bobby Kennedy out there marching?" "Why yes," Tom replied. "Well, he needs a haircut," Tom's questioner shot back.[25] For years, Kean would delight in telling this story to friends, impersonating the old codger and flashing "that grin." His listeners could detect a not-so-concealed admiration for Kennedy's willingness to confront the sensibilities of people of a certain generation and social standing.

While Tom was studying at Columbia in the early 1960s, there occurred a series of cataclysmic events that would change the United States in profound ways. Tom immediately grasped their significance. The Cuban missile crisis made the prospect of nuclear war appear a reality to him for the first time. Tom recalled observing families evacuate New York, convinced that the city was about to be attacked. Then, in 1963, while the erstwhile organizer of the St. Mark's Kennedy for President Club was walking across Central Park on his way to class, he learned of John F. Kennedy's assassination. He observed New York residents, hardly known for their informality, stopping total strangers to inquire whether they had heard the news. Tom headed back to his apartment on Seventy-second Street and Broadway, where, like the rest of the nation, he remained glued to the television set for the next three days, witnessing the murder of Kennedy's accused assassin and watching Kennedy's funeral. He would subsequently attribute his decision to enter public service to Kennedy's example and to a series of events that transpired in the aftermath of his first role model's passing.

Of these, the most significant were Lyndon Johnson's vigorous pursuit of Kennedy's long-stalled civil rights legislation and the manner in which the national Republicans responded. As the son and grandson of Republican officeholders who had worked to extend civil rights to African Americans, Tom burst with pride when a higher percentage of Republicans than Democrats in Congress supported the 1964 civil rights bill, which Johnson signed into law July 2. None had been more instrumental to its passage than one of his father's former

House colleagues, Senate minority leader Everett Dirksen, who ended his impassioned speech on the measure's behalf by paraphrasing Victor Hugo. "No army is stronger," Dirksen proclaimed, "than an idea whose time has come."[26]

Yet, Tom was dismayed that the front-runner for his party's presidential nomination, Barry Goldwater, voted against the legislation. Unlike southern segregationists in whose company Goldwater's vote had placed him, the Arizonan opposed the measure not because he favored segregation but because he feared the effects of federal intrusion into areas he considered preserves of the states. Goldwater especially opposed the public accommodations and fair employment provisions of the bill, which he prophesied would necessitate the emergence of a federal police state to enforce.[27] Goldwater's critics saw his vote as part of a political strategy calculated to attract votes from southern whites and northerners who opposed integration.[28] With party strategists and commentators proclaiming Goldwater's nomination unstoppable, Tom Kean suddenly had a cause.

Scranton's Youth Coordinator

Having completed his master's degree and passed his Ph.D. qualifying examinations, Tom decided to take a break from his studies. He had read that Pennsylvania governor William W. Scranton was about to declare his candidacy for the 1964 presidential nomination in a last-minute attempt to block Goldwater's nomination. On June 2, a week before the civil rights bill came to a vote, Goldwater defeated New York governor Nelson A. Rockefeller in the winner-take-all (of the delegates) California primary by 68,350 votes, carrying 51.67 percent of the vote. With Rockefeller's defeat, observers considered Goldwater's nomination a certainty. Scranton had considered entering the race earlier in the year but had demurred. He changed his mind after Goldwater declared himself against the civil rights bill.

Tom liked what he had heard about Scranton. Smart, clean-cut, and earnest, Scranton, a product of Hotchkiss and Yale (both the college and the law school), had served as special assistant to Secretary of State Christian Herter before winning a seat in the House of Representatives in 1960. Two years later, Scranton was elected governor of Pennsylvania. Many considered the youthful Scranton the Republican equivalent of John F. Kennedy in both style and outlook. That suited the twenty-nine-year-old Tom Kean just fine. Like Kean's, Scranton's family had been active in Republican politics for generations. The Pennsylvania governor's mother was equally known for her activities on behalf of civil rights as for her years of service on the

Republican National Committee. In the two years Scranton had been governor, he had reformed his state's civil service, doubled spending on education, stood down party conservatives by raising the sales tax, and embarked on a strategy of economic development.[29] A generation later, Kean would build a similar, but not identical, record as governor of New Jersey.

As he pondered Scranton's late-hour and uphill campaign, Tom recalled what a young instructor at Princeton, who had volunteered on behalf of Averill Harriman's ill-fated attempt to wrest the 1956 Democratic nomination away from Adlai Stevenson, had told him. The instructor found that, having signed on with the perceived underdog, he had better access to Harriman's immediate entourage than his counterparts, assisting the then front-runner, had to Adlai Stevenson's. Tom asked his father how he might be of help to Scranton. He received word to contact Warren Sinsheimer, a young lawyer in New York, who was heading Scranton's campaign committee. Sinsheimer had taken as his model the "Draft Willkie" effort of a generation earlier, which had, through a combination of grassroots organization, establishment support, and media savvy, managed to catapult the lesser-known Willkie into the 1940 presidential nomination over a field of better-known candidates.[30]

At that convention, Orin Root Jr., a nephew of Theodore Roosevelt's secretary of war, Elihu Root, and his cohorts had filled the galleries with young people, future president Gerald R. Ford among them, shouting "We want Willkie."[31] Prompted by the clamor they heard over the radio and buoyed by local Willkie committees, citizens flooded their delegations with telegrams demanding that Willkie be nominated. A couple of lucky breaks, which put Willkie forces in command of convention machinery, and a well-made deal by the candidate helped smooth Willkie's path. On the sixth ballot, delegates deserted more entrenched candidates, and favorite sons withdrew, releasing their delegates, and Willkie was nominated.

Sinsheimer and his forces faced a steeper challenge than the one the Willkieites had confronted a generation earlier. For four years, Goldwater's operatives had successfully worked to take over local and state Republican Party organizations in several states. Many of those they controlled were in the South, where Goldwater's vote against the civil rights bill had been especially popular, and in the Midwest and the Southwest, where his rugged individualist creed and militant anticommunism had wide appeal. At a time when a majority of delegates were selected not in primaries but through party conventions and caucuses, organizations that Goldwaterites controlled, as expected, named pro-Goldwater delegations. For Scranton to be nominated, he had to pick up the support of every uncommitted delegate and persuade at least two hundred others who had already committed to Goldwater or were leaning his way to abandon him.[32]

Sinsheimer instructed Tom to open a "Scranton for President" office in New Jersey. Tom did. Scranton's man next asked Kean if he could pay his own way to the Republican National Convention in San Francisco. When Kean said he could, Sinsheimer told him, "Fine, you are now the national coordinator for 'Youth for Scranton.'"[33] Among the precocious and politically ambitious young people rallying to Scranton's banner and technically working under Kean, were future New York Knick and U.S. senator Bill Bradley, a former intern in Scranton's congressional office; future congressman Rodney Frelinghuysen, whose father, Peter H. B., brought Scranton's foreign policy and defense proposals before the convention's platform committee; and future governor Christine Todd Whitman, daughter of New Jersey state chairman Webster B. Todd, who was attending the convention as a page.[34]

Tom's job as youth coordinator entailed mobilizing armies of young people and party moderates to make Scranton's case to delegates. He was not entirely without resources. Officially out of the race, Rockefeller turned his entire campaign organization over to Scranton. Overnight, the newly sprung Scranton campaign was blessed with a headquarters at the Fairmont Hotel and the services of California's leading political consulting firm, Spencer Roberts.[35] Its principal, Stuart Spencer, had managed Rockefeller's primary campaign against Goldwater in California. In 1966, he would help Ronald Reagan become governor of California. Seeking to create the impression of a stampede for Scranton, much as Root had for Willkie, Tom organized a series of publicity stunts to command the attention of the media. He hoped that through increased positive press coverage, he and his compatriots could create the impression that a groundswell of support existed for his candidate.

He recorded one such endeavor: "For one thing, we arranged to have the public address system at the airport announce repeatedly that all television cameras and personnel were to proceed to Gate 6 to cover the arrival of Governor Scranton. A few cameras went to Gate 6, of course, but so did everyone else at the San Francisco airport with time on their hands. After the governor stepped off the plane into a throng of people, the media dutifully reported Scranton's surprisingly large airport crowd on the evening news."[36] In addition to inspiring such spontaneous confusion, Scranton's campaign mailed engraved invitations to every registered Republican in the greater San Francisco area, requesting their presence at a reception with

Scranton. Thousands showed up, creating a mob scene. Reporters, elbowing their way through the throng, muttered to one another that they had not observed comparable turnouts for Goldwater.[37]

As Scranton's youth coordinator, Tom produced the convention's second most memorable event, the so-called lockout of Scranton demonstrators. It was surpassed in media coverage only by delegates' booing of Nelson Rockefeller as he spoke in support of a platform plank condemning "extremism," a euphemism Goldwater detractors used when referring to the John Birch Society and other right-wing organizations said to be supporting Goldwater's candidacy. Aware of their candidate's antipathy to certain unions, Goldwater's handlers had ordered that all the convention's printing go to nonunion printers. One retained to print convention tickets and credentials turned out to be one of Scranton's leading California supporters. Before long, Scranton's youth coordinator had at his disposal an inexhaustible supply of tickets to the convention. Tom ordered tables set up at the University of California at Berkeley, Stanford, and other nearby colleges, where Scranton volunteers provided passes to students who were willing to demonstrate on the Pennsylvanian's behalf. One writer described what transpired as Kean's "guests" attempted to enter the convention hall:

> In the Cow Palace parking lot, all was chaos. Fifteen hundred screaming ticket holders and credential wielders were outside. The fire department had barred the doors because the hall was already thousands past capacity. Soon police had seized thousands of forged tickets, all entitling the bearer to Seat 4 in Row G of Section A. Some had been bought from scalpers; some had unwittingly been distributed by congressmen. But the lion's share were held by Scranton ringers, some recruited outside Scranton's downtown headquarters, most from a table set up on Berkeley's Bancroft Way, just off campus, the traditional spot for student politicking. [Advocating partisan causes on university grounds was banned.][38]

Viewers watching the chaos on television received the impression that Goldwater's minions had barred Scranton supporters. Enjoying the frenzy, Tom showed up with an ample supply of tickets. Each time a Goldwater marshal ordered him removed, Tom would slip into the nearest entrance, flashing his "credentials."[39] William Knowland, a former U.S. senator and publisher of the *Oakland Tribune*, became so enraged at Scranton's tactics that he pressured Berkeley officials to prohibit all political recruiting on Berkeley's Bancroft Way.[40] Their decision helped trigger the rebellion known to history as Berkeley's free-speech movement. Tom would long boast that it was he rather than political leftist Mario Savio who had ignited it.[41]

As had Kennedy's, Scranton's campaign became the vehicle through which Tom could engage his postadolescent penchant for rebellion. This time, he chose to do it inside rather than outside the political party in which he had been reared. It did his political future in New Jersey no harm because so much of the state's political establishment—including Republican state chairman Webster B. Todd, Atlantic County state senator and party boss Hap Farley, U.S. senator Clifford P. Case, and, of course, former congressman Robert W. Kean—all supported Scranton. It would be some time before they and their counterparts in the Northeast would realize that the Goldwater phenomenon they considered an aberration was in actuality a harbinger of a long-lasting shift in the party's ideological center of gravity away from the *noblesse oblige* Republicanism commonplace in their region toward a more libertarian, individualistic conservatism of the Southwest and a social conservatism of the South and elsewhere.

In the interest of party unity, the New Jersey delegation cast half of its 40 votes for Scranton and half for Goldwater. After Goldwater was nominated, Case, along with former Essex County freeholder Leslie Blau, refused to vote to make the convention's decision unanimous.[42] Just how far the Republican Party had moved away from its roots was evidenced in the composition of the Georgia delegation. For the first time since it began sending delegates to Republican conventions, Georgia sent an all-white delegation. In order to make the GOP more competitive in the South, its local and national leaders cast aside the aspirations of its one-time African American supporters in favor of all-white delegations largely opposed to civil rights legislation. What Hamilton Fish Kean had resisted in 1924 had become the order of the day in 1964. One African American alternate delegate from New Jersey, George Fleming, walked out of the convention, charging that southern delegates wearing Goldwater badges spat on him, called him names, and tried to put lit cigarettes in his pockets. He said that he witnessed another Goldwater supporter attempt to singe the coat of an African American delegate with a cigarette lighter.[43] For years to come, Tom would recount Fleming's recollections to audiences as part of his attempt to persuade the national Republican Party to be more welcoming to minorities. Although he carried five states in the once solid Democratic South, Goldwater carried only 6 percent of the votes cast by African Americans, down from Nixon's 32 percent four years earlier.

Although his first foray into national politics ended in defeat for his candidate, Tom came away from the convention with a sense of accomplishment. He had participated in political theatrics on the grandest possible scale. He had seen at close range how the media might be used to convey messages and create impressions. He came to find that he liked the gamesmanship and the drama that characterized so much of politics. "I learned that I really enjoyed the process," Kean recalled.[44] Sinsheimer remembered him as a "terrific young man, who was able and enthusiastic about all he did."[45]

Rat Finks and Exterminators

Tom returned from San Francisco determined to continue his efforts to further civil rights and assist the disadvantaged but, this time, in New Jersey. After campaigning for moderate Republicans in the fall election, he, along with Sinsheimer, with backing from civic-minded businessmen, such as Blau, opened up a storefront in Newark, where local residents could obtain access to attorneys, public housing, and government benefits. Their operation was part of the "Committee of Sixty-eight," an effort by the Republican National Committee to reestablish lines of communication between the GOP and African American communities that had been severed during the 1964 presidential campaign. Their effort fizzled in three months.[46] Tom also became executive vice president of the Realty Transfer Company, a family land development and real-estate investment firm, headquartered at the Elizabethtown Water Company Building in Elizabeth.

Tom's early ventures into presidential and state politics persuaded him that solutions to problems that interested him were more likely to emerge at the state level of government than in Washington, D.C. State governments, he concluded, were less bureaucratic and less remote from people's daily concerns than the federal government, a view most conservatives, and some liberals, at the national level would come to share. They also commanded more resources to invest in solving problems in cities than most municipalities. When he mentioned his interest in becoming active in state politics to Webster Todd, the state party chairman suggested that Tom work for him in a similar capacity as he had for Sinsheimer.[47]

Tom would always look upon Todd as both an early mentor and the embodiment of selfless service to the party. Todd served two stints as state party chairman, from 1961 to 1969 and, again, from 1973 to 1977. His primary contribution to the health of the state party was his holding of its structure together, often with his own resources, after it suffered some of its worst setbacks at the polls in the post–World War II era.[48] Todd's chairmanship coincided with the GOP's loss of three gubernatorial elections (1961, 1965, and 1973) and landslide defeats in congressional and county elections in the aftermath of Goldwater's nomination in 1964 and the Watergate scandal and cover-up, which resulted in Nixon's resignation as president in 1974, two years after winning reelection by the widest margin in history. Bright spots in Todd's tenure included the GOP's taking control of the state legislature in 1963 and 1967. Nixon's victories in 1968 and 1972 were more the result of national trends and Democratic disarray than of efforts by the Republican State Committee.[49] Kean was the principal architect of campaigns that doubled the size of the assembly minority in 1975 and enabled Gerald Ford to place ahead of Jimmy Carter in New Jersey in 1976.

After adding Tom to his operation, Todd asked his new youth coordinator to monitor a growing controversy that had erupted inside the state Young Republicans. As part of the strategy Goldwater operative F. Clifton White had put in place to win the 1964 presidential nomination for his candidate, conservatives attempted to install one of their own as chairman of the national Young Republicans at its convention in 1963. Although they controlled of a majority of state chapters, a series of parliamentary maneuvers, credentials disputes, and floor fights prevented the long-awaited transfer of power from taking place. During the boisterous proceedings, some moderates within the New Jersey delegation waved their fingers at a group of conservatives within their midst and proclaimed them "nothing but a bunch of Rat Finks." Their conservative opponents responded by calling their accusers Exterminators.[50]

What had begun as a friendly rivalry among competing factions soon took a bitter turn. In 1965, after attending a New Jersey YR convention in Wildwood, a visitor from Idaho, seeking election to a post in the national organization, complained to the Anti-Defamation League of the B'nai Brith that she overheard several New Jersey Young Republicans singing anti-Semitic and racist lyrics set to the tune of popular songs. Both the Republican national and state committees began looking into the charges. Todd resolved to investigate them after the 1965 election.[51] The state chairman asked William F. Tomkins, former deputy attorney general in the Eisenhower administration, to head the state committee's investigation.[52] In a series of hearings, witnesses testified that they had heard at least ten persons affiliated with the Rat Finks sing songs with the offensive lyrics. Todd demanded that the state YRs purge bigots from its rolls by June 1966. He also threatened to withdraw state party recognition of the group if it failed to comply.

In response, the national YRs suggested that it would suspend the state chapter if it agreed to Todd's demands.[53] Some saw behind its action the hand of Richard Plechner, the reputed head of the

Rat Finks, who served as vice chairman of the national organization. Todd would eventually prevail, but not without the help of other party leaders who, as Tom remembered, employed some rather unconventional practices. The *New York Times* reported an incident that ensued at an Atlantic City conclave when a perceived troublemaker refused to obey a ruling from the chair: "When he [Plechner] refused to return to his seat, three armed guards threw him to the floor. His glasses were slapped aside and he suffered a small gash on the chin."[54] Tom, who was at the meeting, said the guards had been retained by Atlantic County Republican Party chairman and state senator Frank S. (Hap) Farley. More a pragmatist than an ideologue, Farley sided with Todd as much out of self-interest as out of personal loyalty. For more than a century, African Americans who worked in the tourist industry comprised one of the mainstays of the resort city's county Republican machine. Often, they produced half of the votes Republicans received in Atlantic County.[55] Years after African Americans elsewhere began drifting away from the party of Lincoln, African Americans in Atlantic County stayed loyal to the local Republican organization. Farley worked hard to keep things that way.

Once, after a party function at an Atlantic City Hotel, Farley allowed Tom a glimpse into but one of the ways in which the local boss rewarded the party faithful. Taking Tom by the elbow, Farley headed into the kitchen and began making the rounds among the cooks, clean-up crew, and other workers. As he exchanged pleasantries, the county chairman pressed crisp twenty-, fifty-, and one-hundred-dollar bills into waiting palms.[56] After the fate that befell the GOP in 1964, Farley was not about to allow the Democrats to tag Republican candidates as either racists or extremists. At some point such charges might impact on his ability to elect his handpicked tickets locally.

Within days of the tumultuous Atlantic City meeting, Todd ordered state YRs to suspend six county chapters that the Rat Finks dominated.[57] He assigned Tom the task of recruiting new slates of officers who would petition for the reinstatement of reconstituted chapters. Some conservatives feared Tom would use this power to purge the organization of conservatives known for their aversion to liberal Republican U.S. senator Clifford P. Case. Instead, he took an even-handed approach. He lectured moderates that if they wanted to control the party machinery, they needed to be as willing as conservatives to take on unglamorous tasks of party building. He prodded their ideological rivals to demonstrate that conservatism was not, as their critics charged, a smokescreen for intolerance but a political philosophy that might contain solutions to some of the state's most pressing problems. He told both sides he preferred large chapters that had contentious meetings to small ones that remained bereft of debate and were of no value to candidates.

Meanwhile in Washington, Republican national chairman Ray Bliss brokered a compromise through which Plechner relinquished his national post in exchange for a statement by the party that it found no evidence he was either anti-Semitic or racist. Decades later, Kean tried to add perspective to the situation that had confronted him: "Look, a bunch of people got a little drunk one night and said and did some things they should not have. They knew what they had done was wrong. But they were proud and turned the derogatory name that others bestowed upon them into a 'badge of honor.' They would be damned if they would let themselves be pushed around."[58] He had approached the entire episode like the camp counselor he once was, taking the most unruly campers to task, while offering the others an opportunity to gain his confidence. Late during his tenure as governor, he startled some veterans of the Rat Fink affair by naming Plechner to the state superior court. When some state senators challenged the wisdom of the appointment, citing Plechner's alleged controversial past activities, Kean responded that all that had happened "a long time ago and that Plechner had been an exemplary citizen since."[59] Both the state and county bar associations supported the appointment, as would the state senate.

A Good Time to Be a Republican (Candidate)

Tom's next opportunity to demonstrate his skills as a go-between for Todd occurred within his native Essex County. After Robert W. Kean turned the reins of the Essex County Republican organization over to his assistant Bill Yeomans, party donors, skeptical about Yeomans's capacity to handle money, took their complaints to Todd. The state chairman and Joe Intile, Yeomans's deputy, whom many considered the real power in the Essex party, suggested that Tom be placed in charge of Essex party finances. One of his principal roles would be starting each Election Day with sixty thousand dollars in cash on hand and overseeing its distribution, in amounts of twenty and thirty dollars, to precinct workers. He would also cosign all checks the party issued to cover the costs of advertising, rent, and other campaign expenses.

In 1966, the Garden State GOP shared in a rising Republican tide in which the GOP picked up three seats in the U.S. Senate and forty-seven in the House of Representatives. Among the new GOP stars were Charles A. Percy of Illinois and Edward W. Brooke of Massachusetts, the first African American to serve in the Senate since the end of Reconstruction. Reelected in landslides were two potential 1968 presidential nominees: Nelson A. Rockefeller of New York and George Romney of Michigan. Among the eight new Republican governors elected were future vice president Spiro T. Agnew in Maryland and a former film actor turned television host, Ronald Reagan, in California. In New Jersey, incumbent U.S. senator Clifford Case was returned to office, winning 62 percent of the vote against Warren Wilentz, son of the famous Middlesex County chairman and party boss. Case won Essex County by 5,000 votes. Elected on his coattails were three new Republican freeholders.

After Tom toiled in the political vineyards for two years at Todd's behest, a series of circumstances coalesced in 1967 to turn Tom Kean from a political operative into a candidate. Several factors worked in his favor. As a result of court-ordered reapportionment, the legislature New Jersey voters elected that year would be substantially larger. The state senate increased from twenty-one to forty seats and the assembly from sixty to eighty.[60] The sudden availability of new open seats, primarily in the suburbs, and the dearth of seasoned Republicans in the heavily Democratic legislature that had been elected in 1965, provided ample opportunities for well-educated, politically connected, highly motivated, and ambitious young people interested in breaking into elective politics—people such as Tom Kean. He was further assisted by both his well-known name and his past service to the party organization.

The off-year election of 1967 augured to be another banner year for Republicans in New Jersey. President Lyndon Johnson's popularity was sagging as a result of his handling of the Vietnam War; his insistence on pursuing a "guns and butter" economic policy, which portended higher taxes, inflation, or a combination of the two; and increased urban unrest and civil strife in cities such as Los Angeles, Detroit, and, especially, Newark. Phrases such as "liberal excesses," "soft on crime," and "law and order" entered the political lexicon. At Todd's urging, the state party adopted a slogan that encompassed all these sentiments: "Why wait till 68?"[61] In addition to these national woes, factors unique to New Jersey accounted for the public dissatisfaction with the Democratic Party. One was higher taxes. After failing to enact an income tax in 1966, Democratic governor Richard J. Hughes steered to passage a 3 percent sales tax.

However unpopular it may have been with voters, the sales tax, the first permanent broad-based tax in New Jersey's history, forever changed the relationship between state government and its citizens. Prior to 1966, New Jersey funded its entire budget through excise taxes on gasoline, liquor, and tobacco; corporate taxes; and motor vehicle registration fees. The state did not subsidize its municipalities or primary and secondary schools. The twenty-one counties and the 567 municipalities, rather than the state, dispensed social welfare. Local property taxes funded public education and welfare. Acting in a manner reminiscent of Lyndon Johnson a year earlier, Hughes, upon his reelection in 1965, embarked on a liberal, activist agenda, and at record speed. His mini-version of the Great Society included three new cabinet departments (higher education, transportation, and community affairs), a network of new community colleges, and renovated institutions for the mentally ill and the infirm. All of these actions ensured that the legislature that was elected in 1967 would exert greater impact over what transpired in the state than any that had preceded it.

In addition to higher taxes, another issue working against the Democrats was the legislature's passing, with Hughes's acquiescence, "S-400," a law awarding benefits to striking workers. Due to take effect in 1968, the legislation ignited storms of protest across the state. Editorial writers railed against it. Republicans said that the measure would be an incentive for workers to strike. Some termed it a subsidy to strikers. "Good government" groups decried the measure as nothing more than an attempt to buy union support in the 1967 elections.

Additional issues working in the Republicans' favor were increased crime and white backlash, both perceived to be direct results of the Newark riots, which erupted the July preceding the election. The disturbances left in their wake twenty-six dead and a thousand injured. Another weight the Democrats had to carry was the prospect of busing schoolchildren across district lines to achieve racial balance. Carl T. Marburger, Hughes's education commissioner, raised this possibility shortly after the riots.

Riffs in the Party

In order for the New Jersey Republicans to benefit from Democratic disarray in both Washington and Trenton, they first needed to nominate candidates. This proved no easy task in Tom Kean's Essex County, where the Republican organization faced a strong internal challenge. Although they called themselves Reform Republicans, the dissidents never stated precisely what they wished to reform. And although they castigated the existing party apparatus as boss-ridden, the "reformers" appeared to march in lockstep with commands of two bosses of their own: Dr. Virginius Mattia, Chairman of Hoffman LaRoche, and Walter Weller, the company's president. Well funded, the "reformers" mounted the first modern public relations campaign in New Jersey history, replete with huge bulletin boards, radio ads, and the retention of a professional public relations firm.

The Essex County GOP had not experienced this kind of a challenge since Arthur T. Vanderbilt's "Clean Government Republicans"
wrested control from the corrupt Salmon machine three decades before. On that earlier occasion, however, the dissidents offered both
a program and a style of governing that differed substantially from
those of their opponents. The *Newark News*, once the voice of the
Vanderbilt forces, pondered the predicament that confounded the
Essex party and its possible effect on the statewide election: "For no
visible reason, Clean Government organization candidates are being
opposed by a rival slate. . . . The newcomers advertise themselves as
reform Republicans, which at the least seems an infringement on the
Clean Government copyright. . . . But then, the Republicans have
habitually been the greatest source of hope, encouragement, and aid
to the Democratic Party in its time of deepest trouble."[62]

Bereft of issues and unable to criticize the organization's ability to
win elections, given its impressive track record in 1966, "reformers"
aimed their fire at what both sides considered the organization's
weakest link: Essex County chairman Bill Yeomans. A product of
Newark ward politics, Yeomans represented a dying breed of clubhouse politicians who eked out livelihoods by receiving city and
county patronage in exchange for helping to elect officials. With
suburban professionals believed to comprise a majority of Essex Republican primary voters, "reformers" hoped to topple what they considered an anachronistic leadership.

Unable to fend off a primary fight, party regulars sought candidates with names well known to voters. They began courting Tom
Kean as a means of ensuring that the newly created, heavily suburban 11-F assembly district was in friendly hands. The district included
the "safe" Republican towns of Caldwell, Essex Fells, Maplewood,
Millburn–Short Hills, South Orange, Roseland, and Livingston. It also
contained heavily Democratic Irvington, which comprised 40 percent
of it. "I thought it would be fun to run," Kean said, reflecting back on
his entry into elective politics. "I thought it would be something interesting to do for a couple of years."[63]

New Partnerships

Upon learning that the steering committee had approved his nomination, Tom delivered a short acceptance speech and subsequently
asked Herb Roemmele, his father's former campaign adviser, to
manage his campaign.[64] Well known and well liked, Roemmele epitomized the new breed of suburban businesspeople who were making
their presence felt in Essex County politics. Active in their own ca-

reers, these men and women regarded politics more as a hobby than as a vocation. Whatever rewards they derived from political activity came from opportunities it afforded them to forge friendships, make professional contacts, or derive satisfaction in knowing that they had elected high-caliber candidates.

The certainty of Tom Kean's nomination set off a scramble for the other assembly seat in the newly established district. Millburn attorney Philip D. Kaltenbacher, who served as an officer in his family's business, the Seton Leather Company, won the steering committee's nod by one vote over fellow Millburn resident Larry Miller. Two years younger than Kean, Kaltenbacher also came from a family that had long been prominent in New Jersey business and political circles. On his mother's side of his family, Kaltenbacher was related to several past local and state politicians.[65] Kaltenbacher's paternal grandfather, a German Jewish immigrant, founded the Seton Leather Company in the late nineteenth century. Educated at the Newark Academy, Yale University, and its law school, Kaltenbacher, like Kean, believed people of his background had an obligation to give something back to their community. "We owe those around us more than just making a living," he recalled his mother telling him. Also like Kean, Kaltenbacher had been a youthful admirer of John F. Kennedy. Kaltenbacher could recall in vivid detail a speech Kennedy had delivered on the Yale Green in 1959 and students' reactions to it.[66]

After returning to New Jersey in 1962, Kaltenbacher joined the Newark law firm of Hannoch Weisman and began dabbling in local politics. He assisted assembly hopeful Irwin Kimmelman, a lawyer with his firm, and, afterward, served as Kimmelman's legislative aide. Both Kean and Kaltenbacher came to their nominations more conversant with state issues than with local ones. Kean would later say of the local Republican organization in Livingston, "Most of them did not know me; they may have felt they were being asked to vote for me just because I was the son of someone they liked. Some may have resented that."[67] Kimmelman cautioned Kaltenbacher, who had stayed out of Millburn affairs, that he would fare better "coming in from the side," having established his credentials outside of politics, than had he first "slugged it out in municipal politics, where all you get are enemies."[68]

The pairing of Tom Kean and Phil Kaltenbacher produced one of the most successful and enduring political alliances and personal friendships in modern New Jersey history. No sooner did this partnership begin than Tom made a match of a different kind.

He first encountered Deborah Bye at a party in New York City, when he was studying at Columbia. Although he had gone with another date, Tom spent much of the evening talking with Debby.[69] A graduate of Bennett College, Debby was the only child of a socially prominent family in Wilmington, Delaware, where her father was an insurance executive. At the time she met Tom Kean, Debby was working at Tiffany's. He was instantly smitten with her radiant smile, easy laugh, and irreverent sense of humor. Peter Freeman, Tom's former New York City roommate, observed the Kean-Bye romance as it blossomed. "It was obvious from the first that he was crazy in love with her," Freeman reminisced.[70]

Nearly forty years later, Kean's face would still brighten whenever an aide announced that Debby was on the phone. Years after leaving the governorship, he would credit Debby with helping him retain his humility. Upon seeing him return home with the latest plaque he had been presented, she would ask him, "How many great men are there in the world?" As Kean would plead ignorance, she would answer her own question with the words "One less than you think."

She and Tom dated a few times before she returned to Wilmington. Tom mentioned to his godmother, Ruth (Mrs. Henry F.) Dupont, a cousin of his mother's, that he had made the acquaintance of the Wilmington beauty and suggested he would like to see her again. "Oh, I know Debby," the older woman said. She arranged to have Tom and Debby over to her home at Wintherthur for dinner. The only problem, as Kean remembered it, was that the wrong Debby showed up. Realizing her mistake, Mrs. Dupont produced the "right Debby" the next day at brunch.[71]

For the next several months, Tom steadily traveled the length of the New Jersey Turnpike to and from Wilmington. The couple wed June 3, 1967, in Old Drawyers Church in Odessa, Delaware. Asked what Debby thought of the career he was planning to enter, Tom replied, "She knew I was not a nine-to-five kind of guy." "She probably thought I wouldn't work very hard," he added.[72] Debby got her first inkling that her life with Tom Kean would be anything but conventional at her wedding reception, when Joe Intile took Tom aside so that he could cosign a stack of county party checks.[73]

Running Hard

After a three-week honeymoon in Ireland, Tom returned to New Jersey for the primary campaign. The lateness in which the legislative districts had been drawn necessitated that the primary be held in September, rather than in June, as was the custom. From the outset, Kean and Kaltenbacher campaigned as a team. They enjoyed each other's company on the stump and engaged in more than a casual amount of good-natured ribbing. Kaltenbacher regaled audiences with tales of Kean's alleged stinginess. Taking the bait, Kean announced that the candidates had agreed to split the costs of their signs. Rather than dividing the expenses on a fifty-fifty basis, he deadpanned that each would be assessed according to the number of letters in their surnames. Both later estimated that they each spent a total of between two and five thousand dollars on their campaign.

True to the prevailing practice in New Jersey politics at the time, the GOP organization ballot on which Kean and Kaltenbacher appeared had a distinctive ethnic flavor. In the last year in which state senate candidates would run countywide, appearing beside the assembly candidates were six senate hopefuls with names easily recognizable to Italian American, Irish American, WASP, Jewish, and African American voters. To the young Tom Kean's disgust, those who called themselves "reformers" circulated brochures bearing the likeness of J. Harry Smith, the sole African American on either ticket, along with the phrase "left-wing dominated."[74] Opposite Kean and Kaltenbacher in 11-F district, the reformers pitted Livingston attorney and former assemblyman Donald J. Fitzmaurice and Mrs. Vivian Tompkins Lange, an officeholder in the New Jersey Federation of Republican Women and the sister of a well-known attorney active in GOP circles.

Initially, Robert W. Kean had not been enthusiastic about his son's foray into state politics. He had made his career in Congress at a time when the federal government had taken on increased responsibilities and the states descended into bastions of parochialism, corruption, and, in the South, racial segregation. The former congressman hoped that any progeny of his who followed in his path would set his sights on Washington rather than Trenton. He consoled himself with the thought that Tom would one day carry on the family tradition in the national legislature, after he had acquired some political experience. The instant his son declared his candidacy, the old warrior cast aside his misgivings and went into full combat mode. Robert W. Kean revived the family practice of opening his home to Kean supporters to rally the faithful and cultivate enthusiasm. In his manner of entertaining, Robert W. Kean proved much more constrained than his father, who routinely hosted state party events.

In 1931, Hamilton Fish Kean had bused thousands from all across the state to a barbecue at Green Lane Farm, his Union County estate, on behalf of gubernatorial candidate David Baird Jr. Billed as a "Veterans' Barbecue," the event featured boxing matches, a cockfight, hot dogs, hamburgers, and barrels of beer.[75] To a crowd of ten thousand veterans chanting, "We want beer," Baird and Kean committed to its legalization.[76] Critics focused on Kean's open flaunting of Prohibition and his violation of the Sabbath.[77] Baird lost the race to the even "wetter" former governor A. Harry Moore by 230,053 votes.

Guests to Robert W. Kean's estate found Tom's father all too willing to guide them through the museum he had assembled of Kean-related political Americana. There, carefully framed, were his mother's penned recollections of President James A. Garfield's death in Long Branch, months after he had been shot by an assassin. Also on display was the sheepskin copy of the Declaration of Independence John Quincy Adams had sent to close friends. Not far away was the loving cup Hamilton Fish Kean presented to his mother-in-law in gratitude for having loaned him sufficient securities to keep his investment firm afloat during the panic of 1907.[78] In a gazebo rested a maquette of the statue of Abraham Lincoln that Daniel Chester French designed for the Lincoln Memorial. The artist had given it as a gift to the congressman's uncle, Grenville Winthrop, who made his home not far from French's studio in Stockbridge, Massachusetts.[79]

Weeks before the primary, Robert W. Kean telephoned Herb Roemmele to say the campaign might profit from an additional mailing.[80] Having learned the lesson of 1958, the elder Kean paid the postage and printing costs himself. Roemmele believed that that last bit of effort helped determine the final outcome of Tom Kean's first primary.[81] At Roemmele's suggestion, Kean and Kaltenbacher had opened their own headquarters in a part of the district where they expected the most resistance in the general election. Located at 1300 Springfield Avenue in Irvington, it quickly became a place for party activists to meet, socialize, and stuff envelopes. One young homemaker and mother of two, Karla Squier, was among the many to make the Irvington site a second home. Squier became Kean's self-appointed second set of eyes and ears, riding herd over his volunteers by day; standing guard against would-be sign stealers by night.

As they had with each other, Kean and Kaltenbacher bonded deeply with Roemmele. Four years older than Kean and six years Kaltenbacher's senior, Roemmele took on the roles of coach, cheerleader, alter ego, and older brother. He reveled in their successes and grimaced (in private, of course) at their mistakes. Rather than refer to them as candidates or by name, he simply spoke of "the boys." "The boys will be over by five p.m.," he would say to a jittery hostess, preparing to introduce Kean and Kaltenbacher to her neighbors. When the primary results were counted, Kean and Kaltenbacher easily prevailed. In a field of four, Kean polled 6,337, Kaltenbacher 5,949, Fitzmaurice 4,089, and Lange, 3,949.

Other organization candidates were less successful. In a turnout of 20 percent, the reformers had nominated five of the six candidates they had run for state senator. Reformers were nominated for county sheriff and for two of three freeholder posts up for election. Yeomans estimated that the reformers spent more than twice the organization's seventy-five-thousand-dollar expenditure. With regard to the party structure, the primary had settled nothing. Bolstered by the votes of Newark's county committee, which he still controlled, Yeomans won reelection as chairman. Weller remained campaign manager for the candidates he had helped nominate. Again, Kean and Kaltenbacher set out on their own.

The Home Stretch

Though confident that they would win in what was supposed to be a safe Republican district, Kean and Kaltenbacher concluded that the only way they could lose was by failing to hold their own in heavily Democratic Irvington, and turnout there in the off-year election was high. They set as their highest priority meeting as many of the sixty thousand residents of Irvington as possible. The candidates made their way through the ethnic wards, knocking on doors of people they did not know, sampling mysterious foods, dodging ferocious pets, and befriending children. Old-time party workers, who had campaigned for Kean's father, such as Phil Heymann, escorted the well-heeled Ivy Leaguers to the heavily Democratic, Jewish, and working-class Marshall Street apartments. Kean and Kaltenbacher spoke at the Polish hall, visited the Ukrainian Catholic Church, attended Italian American festivals, and showed up at block parties and civic associations, always with a local resident escorting them. As had Robert W. Kean three decades earlier, Tom Kean found it particularly advantageous to remind parishioners that one of his forebears had wed a Polish count.

They named C. Stewart Hausmann, a longtime Irvington resident, businessman, and recently elected Essex County freeholder, their Irvington campaign chairman and picked up the endorsement of popular former mayor William Lovell, a Republican, who had repeatedly won nonpartisan elections. Kean and Kaltenbacher rented sound trucks, mounted literature drops, and transformed offices of friendly stockbrokers and lawyers into evening telephone banks. Though they did not hide their partisan affiliation, the candidates dubbed their official campaign operation "Citizens for Kean and Kaltenbacher," so that Democrats and independents would feel more comfortable supporting them. Under Roemmele's supervision, their campaign assembled committees of doctors, lawyers, teenagers, carpenters, college students, and veterans—all for Kean and Kaltenbacher.

Every town in the district and each ward in Irvington had its own designated chair, many with their own block captains. Pictures of the candidates posing with different local luminaries appeared each week in suburban newspapers. The candidates took to stopping by at editorial boards of all newspapers that circulated in the district, sometimes in advance of invitations. Every Sunday night, Roemmele and the boys would talk by telephone or in person to go over the events of the past week and to plan events for the next one.[82]

To oppose Kean and Kaltenbacher in the November election, the Democrats nominated Bernard A. Kuttner, a former Irvington corporate counsel, and South Orange resident and New Jersey Bell executive Eugene McNany. Kuttner, a Dartmouth graduate and Seton Hall Law School alumnus, was well known throughout the district as a result of his long association with the Jaycees, state and county bar associations, and the Anti-Defamation League of B'nai Brith. He was expected to carry Irvington and run well among Jewish voters districtwide. McNany, most thought, would fare similarly among Catholics.

Kean and Kaltenbacher took well to their new roles as candidates. They delighted when friendly locals with influence would "give the sign" to blue-collar Democrats that it was okay for them to cross party lines to support the two young Republicans. One, Father Fronczak of the Polish Catholic Church of the Sacred Heart on Grove Street, would invite the candidates to select winning bingo numbers. They found out afterward that he only bestowed such honors on candidates he wanted his parishioners to support.

Some voters tried to test their mettle in unconventional ways. "You look like a nice fellow, have one of these," said a diner at Millburn's Casa Columbo restaurant. Not knowing what he had been presented, Kaltenbacher bit into some very hot peppers.[83] "There are lots of voters in the room way in the back. Go in and say hello." another told Kean, pointing the way. Unsuspecting, the candidate stumbled into a bachelor party. Before he could make his exit, a naked woman popped out of a cake and began draping parts of her anatomy over the blushing candidate's shoulder.[84] (Kean would later learn how to shield himself from such embarrassments. The weekend before his reelection as governor, while attending a Greek festival, Kean carefully kept his distance from a belly dancer who seemed determined to sit on his lap.)

When on the stump or in joint appearances with their opponents, Kean and Kaltenbacher stuck to the overall themes of their campaign: repeal of S-400, preservation of the neighborhood schools, increased law enforcement, and use of state aid to hold down local property taxes. Kean's demeanor made an impression on his listeners as did his words. "He had a certain aura about him," Hausmann remembered. "He had more on the ball than everyone else, and it showed. You could see Princeton, New England schooling, and all that sophistication. But he carried it well. He was always friendly, never arrogant.[85] "Tom always ran a hard, clean campaign. That was the first thing I noticed about him," reflected John Miller, Irvington Democratic chairman and clerk to the assembly.[86]

Kean also displayed a feisty competitiveness and a love of the political game, a trait reporters quickly noticed. Showing himself to be the "happy warrior" on the stump, he would chide Democrats to "come out of hiding" and explain where they stood on strikers' benefits. "They [the Democrats] got us into this mess," he would say. "Now they won't explain how to get us out of it," he bellowed. He warned that the law would produce "prolonged strikes, heavier tax burdens, mass exodus of industry and homeowners, and have a crippling effect on New Jersey's economic growth for years to come."[87]

In his first try for elective office, Kean learned how to work divisions within Democratic ranks to his advantage. In an attempt to shield Democrats from voters' backlash in the aftermath of State Education Commissioner Marburger's remarks on the possibility of busing schoolchildren to achieve racial balance, Governor Hughes declared that as long as he remained governor, the state would never compel students to be bused across district or municipal lines in order to achieve integration.[88] While he was campaigning for Democratic candidates, someone handed the governor a leaflet that undermined his credibility. Advocating the election of one of Kean and Kaltenbacher's opponents, the flier read: "Protect the Maplewood and South Orange school system. Help [Democrat] Gene [E. McNany] fight State Education Commissioner Carl L. Marburger's plan of forced introduction of Newark pupils into our school system and the forced busing of our children into the city. Our communities need Gene to represent us in the state legislature to fight this plan to alter our district boundaries."[89] McNany maintained that he had raised the busing issue before the Republicans had, and that if his opponents voiced opposition to Marburger's proposal, they were just following his lead.[90] Sensing an opportunity to foment mischief, Kean and Kaltenbacher charged that the Democrats were "deliberately and maliciously" trying to mislead voters into believing that the Republicans favored the controversial Marburger plan, which Hughes continued to insist did not exist. They invited the governor to "direct the same invective and name calling he aimed at Republicans at members of his own party."[91]

As the campaign drew to a close, Kean and Kaltenbacher were getting indications that they would indeed run well in Irvington. The *Irvington Herald* endorsed only Kuttner.[92] Districtwide, Kean and

Kaltenbacher outpolled their opponents by a two-to-one margin. (Kean received 32,675 votes, Kaltenbacher 32,825, Kuttner 17,964, and McNany, 16,702.) Only in Irvington had it been close. There, Kuttner placed first with 7,825 votes. Kaltenbacher followed with 7,251. Kean received 7,112, and McNany, 6,870. Their next time out, both would carry the town, with Kean placing first.

Countywide, all six Essex Republican candidates for the state senate won, as did five other Republican assembly candidates and five Democratic assembly candidates. Republicans won control of both houses of the legislature by wide margins, shifting partisan control from a two-to-one Democratic majority to three-to-one Republican majority. One of Hughes's assistants, angered at the outcome, pronounced the results "a reaction against President Johnson, against last summer's riots, against Negroes in the cities, against the war in Vietnam, against taxes, against anyone who was in office, against anything you can name."[93] Hughes was more sanguine. Noting that only two years earlier Democrats had captured control of both houses of the legislature for the first time in fifty-three years, he attributed the shift in partisan control to a natural rotation in party fortunes.[94] The governor denied that the results reflected a repudiation of his program and predicted they would not impede his ability to implement it. Little could he foresee that much of what he would achieve would come through the efforts of a newly elected freshman Republican assemblyman from Essex who talked with a New England accent.

chapter 5

The Precocious Freshman

An Agenda Shaped by Outside Forces

Kean's first year in the New Jersey Assembly, 1968, was one of the most tumultuous in American and world history.[1] As he was learning the legislative ropes, the Tet Offensive, though militarily a defeat for the Viet Cong, would cause Lyndon Johnson to reassess Vietnam War strategy. That, plus antiwar candidate Eugene McCarthy's unexpectedly strong showing in the New Hampshire presidential primary and the even more serious challenge to his renomination posed by Robert Kennedy, contributed to Johnson's decision not to seek reelection. Civil rights leader Martin Luther King Jr. and Robert F. Kennedy would both be assassinated in the spring. In the summer, Soviet troops invaded Czechoslovakia, ending the seemingly eternal "Prague Spring." Clashes between antiwar protesters and Mayor Richard Daley's Chicago police during the Democratic National Convention put additional strains on a "new deal" coalition that had begun to unravel with the racial disturbances of the previous year. Alabama governor George C. Wallace's third-party candidacy threatened to uncouple northern, working-class voters from their traditional Democratic allegiances. Running on a promise of "bringing the nation together," Richard Nixon won election by a narrow margin in a three-way contest to become the thirty-seventh president.

Nascent environmental, feminist, consumer, and other movements were coming into their own, with their leaders adopting the tactics their predecessors in the civil rights struggle had so skillfully employed. Slower to catch hold, but no less significant, was a more

politically mature and more confident conservatism than the kind
Kean had encountered at the Cow Palace in San Francisco in 1964.
Taking their inspiration from William F. Buckley Jr. (founding editor
of *National Review,* syndicated newspaper columnist, and television
personality) and Ronald Reagan (the recently elected governor of
California), these conservatives would come to play an increasingly
important role in state party primaries. Kean was among the first
New Jersey elected officials both to take them seriously and recognize their increasing strength. He would come to borrow ideas from
this "movement," just as he would from most of the others.

Of the many pressures on the legislature when Kean entered it,
none seemed more immediate to its members than what commentators had called the "the urban crisis" and its accompanying racial
divisions. The summer before Kean won his first election, the Newark
riots wreaked havoc on the state's largest city. Similar disturbances
erupted in Plainfield and other cities. Businesses, residents, and jobs
began leaving New Jersey cities at an accelerated pace. What were
once thriving downtowns became ghost towns after dark and often
through much of the day. Analysts added the term *white flight* to the
growing list of phenomena associated with the growing crisis.

Liberals saw the urban crisis as an opportunity for the nation to
address long-neglected social ills. Moderates feared that unless the
underlying causes of urban unrest were addressed and the perceived
anger of inner-city residents' assuaged, violence would recur and
spread to nearby suburbs. Conservatives pressed for stronger anticrime measures, longer prison sentences, and restoration of the death
penalty. As he took his seat in a newly constituted legislature, Kean
identified the urban crisis as his highest priority. In his first interview
after being sworn in, he said, "We've got to find funds for Newark, a
city in trouble."[2] How many dollars should be spent and toward what
ends would remain high on the state's agenda for the rest of Kean's
days in public service.

First Rung of the Ladder

Shortly after the 1967 election, the seven newly elected Republican
assemblymen from Essex County unanimously elected Kean leader
of their county delegation. He appeared the natural choice. He was
friendly, knowledgeable, and personable. He also exuded earnestness,
idealism, and sincerity. Nearly four decades later, in 2003, when
C. Stewart Hausmann was asked to explain Kean's appeal, he said,
"You could not help but like him."[3]Former president Bill Clinton,
when asked what accounted for Kean's emergence as a spokesman

for his fellow governors, responded in a similar way: "He kind of grew on you."[4]

Assured that he could rely on a bloc of seven Essex votes, Kean could enter into negotiations with other delegation leaders with considerable standing. Before long, he and his Essex compatriots realized that if they entered into an alliance with their ten counterparts from Bergen County, they could determine the flow and content of legislation.[5] Kean held the coalition of the two counties' assemblymen together through the easy rapport he established with Bergen's Richard Vander Platt and Richard De Korte. Legislators from each county signaled their voting alliance to the rest of the chamber by moving bills of importance to their sister county. Herb Rinaldi of Essex, for instance, sponsored a bill to develop the Hackensack Meadowlands, in Bergen County, while Vander Platt and his Bergen colleagues introduced legislation to assist Newark, a subject foremost on the minds of Kean and his peers from Essex. When likeminded suburban legislators from neighboring Monmouth, Morris, Union, Somerset, and Union counties joined the Kean–Vander Platt group, a legislative majority that reflected the views of a majority of the state's residents could be achieved, just as advocates of reapportionment had intended. All that stood in their way was what they saw as an archaic legislative leadership. It did not take them long to come up with a way to challenge it.

A week into his first term, Kean introduced his first bill. At the request of a lobbyist for the Mutual Benefit Insurance Company, he offered legislation to extend tax abatements offered under the "Fox-Lance" amendment to the tax code to entice businesses to build in Newark. All his colleagues seemed to be for the measure. Unfamiliar with the tax code, Kean tried to read his way through it so that he could appear more knowledgeable than he was. Terrified that he would be asked to comment when it came to the floor, he mumbled brief remarks. To his surprise and amusement, his bill passed unanimously.[6]

Taking on His Elders

By custom and prearrangement, party bosses determined who would lead both houses of the legislature, just as they decided who in their respective jurisdictions would run for legislative office. Democratic bosses tended to be mayors of large cities or party chairs of urban counties, who influenced what transpired in legislative caucuses from their home bases. Republican leaders operated from positions of power within the rurally dominated state senate. The then-prevalent practice of annual rotation of legislative leaders worked to keep power not in the hands of legislative party caucuses, which technically elected the leadership of the two parties, but in those of the county party chieftains. By mutual agreements, the bosses cobbled together legislative leadership arrangements that advanced their interests and reflected the geographic balance.

The year Kean took office the assembly Speaker was Al Smith of Atlantic County, who, Kean remembered, "cried publicly" when one of his bills failed to pass.[7] Smith had been the handpicked choice of Atlantic County senator "Hap" Farley. To balance Farley's pick, Peter Moraites of Bergen County, which sent the assembly a delegation of ten Republicans, became majority leader.[8] Assemblyman Bill Dickey of Camden County, who, in white linen suits, Kean said, resembled the Good Humor man, served as assistant majority leader.[9] As Kean and his peers saw it, no one had bothered to tell the old guard that a majority of the majority caucus represented suburban rather than rural districts. The young Turks resolved that they would.

Kean and a group of his fellow freshmen in the assembly decided during an outing at Monmouth Racetrack that they would use their collective votes to break the hold the bosses exerted on the internal workings of the legislature. They concluded that the best way to achieve their ends was to throw their collective weight behind a more senior member who, with help from the freshmen, could defeat the bosses' choice for one of the leadership posts. In exchange for their support, they expected the person they had assisted to be receptive to having one of their own make it onto the leadership ladder during the next leadership election. They agreed to give their support for assistant majority leader to Barry Parker of Burlington County.[10] The following January, the affable Parker prevailed against the leaders' agreed-upon choice, Doug Gimson of Hunterdon County.

Kean's "Third Way"

As they waited their turn to run the assembly, Kean and his colleagues pursued their urban agenda. In order to enact it, Kean took on a role to which he would revert many times during his public career. He carved out for himself a niche on the ideological spectrum that was somewhat to the left of the more rural, "stand pat," conservative Republican leadership and slightly to the right of liberal and reform-leaning Democrats aligned with Governor Richard J. Hughes. As the leader of a vocal brand of suburban moderates, Kean helped produce a majority of votes for many of Hughes's urban initiatives. At the same time, he exerted with his Essex and Bergen colleagues leverage to steer state resources not only to big cities, which elected Democrats, but also to suburban enclaves, which Republicans largely represented. He would also use his influence to assist towns such as Irvington, which was neither a city nor a suburb, and while remaining a Democratic bastion, had a history of embracing Republicans who tended to its needs.

Twenty-five years before Bill Clinton proclaimed himself a "new Democrat," Tony Blair talked of a "third way," or George W. Bush coined the phrase "compassionate conservatism," Kean was practicing the kind of governance all three came to espouse. It entailed holding the majority of one's own party together, while embracing the rhetoric and sometimes the substance advanced by the other party, in order to forge a centrist majority. As governor, Kean steered a middle course between the Reagan administration, which wanted to curtail increases in domestic spending, and a Democratic legislature, which wanted to raise taxes to a higher level than that acceptable to Kean. Together with his fellow governors, he bridged divides between Republican presidents and Democratic Congresses. He would find middle ground once again on the 9–11 Commission, which consisted of five Republicans and five Democrats. From his earliest days in the legislature, Kean would cast himself as a problem solver rather than as an ideologue. This image would serve him well.

Toward an Urban Policy

On February 11, 1968, the blue-ribbon commission Hughes had named to probe the causes of the previous summer's disturbances issued its report. It recommended that the state increase its commitment to better housing, welfare, job training, health care, and education. Hughes immediately embraced the panel's proposals. The Republican legislature named a select commission, which included Kean, to assess them. Support for what the Governor's Commission on Civil Disorders (also known as the Lilley Commission, in honor of its chair, New Jersey Bell president Robert D. Lilley) had recommended grew after its national counterpart, the President's Advisory Commission on Civil Disorders (also called the Kerner Commission for its chairman, Illinois governor Otto Kerner), issued its report on March 1. The Kerner Commission's report had cited white racism as the primary cause of disturbances that had erupted in Detroit, Newark, and elsewhere. It warned that the nation was "moving toward two societies, one black, one white—separate and unequal," and that economic and social disparities would worsen unless immediate action was taken "on a scale equal to the dimensions of the problems."[11]

In response to the two reports, Hughes proposed that the state absorb county and municipal welfare costs and provide massive infusions of state aid to the cities. Kean played a pivotal role in re-fashioning Hughes's proposals to make them more palatable to the Republican legislature. That proved no easy task at first, given that the Republican assembly leadership appeared more interested in reversing Hughes's past initiatives than in enacting his new ones. After a measure to abolish the recently established Department of Community Affairs cleared committee with Kaltenbacher's the only dissenting vote, Kean declared that the assembly leadership could not count on Essex's seven Republicans to override an expected veto by Hughes.[12] The department survived.

As a substitute for Hughes's 100 percent welfare takeover pro-posal, Kean and a friendly Republican state senator, Alexander Mat-turi, introduced identical bills that required the state to assume up to 75 percent of county welfare costs in four categorical programs: Assistance to Families with Dependent Children, Medicaid, disability assistance, and aid to the blind. Too shrewd a politician to turn down three-fourths of the loaf the two Republicans wanted to hand him, Hughes accepted their offer. When his Republican colleagues in the assembly hinted that they might not go along, Kean fought hard for his proposal in the party caucus. "We took the tack that if the Repub-lican legislature doesn't take an interest in critical urban problems, then they can't count on Essex votes for other types of legislation," he told reporters afterward.[13] To pick up support for his proposal, Kean agreed to a 50 percent state expenditure on disability costs, as op-posed to the 75 percent he initially recommended, in exchange for his colleagues' acceptance of the rest of his plan. He subsequently steered the entire welfare package to passage, producing the first urban aid package in the state's history.

Dire events that were then unfolding outside the legislative chamber undoubtedly produced additional pressure for its passage. Three days after Kean delivered his ultimatum to the GOP caucus, Martin Luther King Jr. was slain in Memphis. His assassination, to-gether with the racial disturbances that followed it, created a sense of urgency in many state capitals and in Congress. Days before King's murder, the civil rights leader had visited Newark, showing up at a public housing project and at South Side High School, to drum up support for the poor people's march he was planning to hold in Wash-ington.[14] Days after King's killing, the Newark business, clerical, and philanthropic communities established the Greater Newark Urban Coalition. It took as its first task lobbying for enactment of the Lilley Commission's recommendations.[15] Sporting buttons proclaiming "I Care" in white letters on a black background, Kean and other officials participated in the "walk for understanding" that United Community Corporation President Timothy Still organized the weekend after King's assassination.[16]

On April 25, Hughes, in a special message to the legislature, called upon the state to make a moral commitment to address urban ills. He requested $126 million in additional aid to the cities, passage of Kean's 75 percent state assumption of welfare spending, enhanced law enforcement, $25 million in emergency school aid, the establishment of a school lunch program, and the creation of neighborhood education centers.[17] Kean became the prime sponsor of all of these measures. After the Republicans passed an alternative package to Hughes's, costing $90 million, the governor signed it. He returned the following year for the remainder of the funds he had initially sought.[18] Adhering to their "third way" course, Kean and his fellow centrists provided the necessary margin of votes to pass the aid package. This story repeated itself when the parties haggled over how large a bond issue to present to the voters in 1968. Hughes wanted to borrow $1.9 billion; the Republicans, $890 million. They compromised at $990 million, a figure $220 million higher than the bond issue voters had rejected five years earlier.[19] Again, Hughes pressed for the rest of his plan the following year, and the Republicans acquiesced.

As the Democratic governor and the Republican legislature wrangled over spending proposals, Kean and his faction functioned as the fulcrum in a perpetual see-saw over how to allocate the spending increases. When the rurally oriented legislative leadership tried to restrict state aid to towns that received only the minimal amount of assistance, the Kean group again threatened to sustain Hughes's expected veto.[20] When Hughes vetoed what he called giveaways to the wealthy suburbs, Kean and his colleagues returned to the GOP fold, voting with the "stand patters" to press for a return of some state revenues to their districts.

With regard to urban aid, Kean's second year was very much a repeat of the first, with a couple of added wrinkles. Early in 1969, the City of Newark, on the verge of bankruptcy, threatened to close the Newark Library and Museum. Kean assembled a coalition of suburban legislators to provide $2.8 million in operating funds to the two institutions. When municipal officials shuttered the facilities before Kean could put his plan to a vote, the young legislator termed the closings "a stupid, malicious act."[21] Whether his choice of words was the result of losing his temper or a calculated demonstration of annoyance, it foretold the emergence of a political style in which Kean would raise the volume of his rhetoric shortly before striking a deal.

In addition to guiding Hughes's urban aid package to passage, by the end of his first term Kean had secured the adoption of a $16-million urban aid appropriation that allocated $12 million to schools, $2 million to reimburse towns that had incurred additional public safety expenses as a result of unanticipated disturbances, with the remainder going to promote "black capitalism," an idea Richard Nixon had floated during his 1968 presidential campaign.[22]

The Educational Opportunity Fund

Among several measures that Hughes signed into law in the aftermath of the assassinations of Martin Luther King Jr. and Robert F. Kennedy was a bill that Kean had sponsored to help students from disadvantaged backgrounds attend college. Though this bill encountered less resistance and less press attention than Kean's urban aid initiatives, his efforts to establish the Educational Opportunity Fund had an equally complicated history. Shortly after his election to the assembly, Kean asked each of the Essex organization's defeated 1967 Republican legislative contenders whether they had any special projects they would like him to advance in Trenton. J. Harry Smith, who would later serve as president of Essex County College, voiced concern at the low number of inner-city youths that were going to college. Although tuition costs at county colleges were minimal, they were still higher than most poor students could afford. Smith maintained that access to higher education was a right that should be available to all citizens of the state.[23]

Smith did not have to press too hard in order to make his case. Kean had spent years at Brantwood trying to assist the very kind of students that Smith was seeking to help. He quickly introduced a bill to increase the amount of funds the state made available to needy students attending college. Kean subsequently learned that Hughes's chancellor of higher education, Ralph A. Dungan, had a proposal of his own which he had been pressing upon legislators. He approached Dungan to see if their bills might be combined. Dungan told Kean that additional funds by themselves would not solve the problem Smith had identified. Graduates of urban high schools, he explained, were leaving school so ill-prepared for college that they were bound to flunk out. Merely providing students with money to pay tuition, he said, would not suffice. Dungan wanted state colleges to help educationally disadvantaged students to succeed in college.[24]

Kean rewrote his bill. The new version reflected the concerns of its three promulgators. It had the state fund most of the educational costs of students from poor backgrounds enrolled in colleges and universities in New Jersey (Smith's primary objective). It required these institutions to establish compensatory educational programs for underprepared students and provided them with funds to do so (as Dungan had proposed). It also mandated that colleges and universities provide mentors to counsel students as they made the transition to college life and to assist them with problems they encountered on and off campus (Kean's idea). Kean introduced his Educational Opportunity Fund proposal in May. The measure (A-767, popularly known as the "Kean bill") cleared the assembly. But when it failed to reach the state senate floor as quickly as he desired, Kean, though still a political novice, tried his hand at some political logrolling. Kean's counterpart in the senate, William T. Hiering (R-Ocean), introduced a bill allowing for state aid to independent colleges. When the bill reached the assembly's Education Committee, Kean put a hold on it. Hiering inquired as to the reason, and Kean mentioned the E.O.F. legislation. Not surprisingly, both bills cleared the respective houses.[25] Hughes signed Kean's bill into law on July 12.

Kean would consider the measure his greatest achievement of his ten years in the assembly. In his subsequent career as a university president, Kean would participate in the program he had created, advising Trenton officials periodically on ways to strengthen it. Of Kean's efforts as a freshman legislator to bring his proposal to fruition, Dungan would say more than thirty years later: "Our relations were always excellent. He was above all a trustworthy, straight-shooter with a strong and intelligent interest in higher education. Having a sensitive social conscience and an awareness of the deeply flawed performance of NJ public schools in that era, he undoubtedly was a strong supporter of the EOF program—our effort to pick up the educational slack."[26]

The Camp Counselor and the Student Radicals

Seven months after Hughes had signed the Educational Opportunity Fund into law, a long-simmering dispute between Rutgers University administrators and African American students on its Newark campus erupted into a crisis. On February 24, 1969, a group calling itself the Black Organization of Students (BOS) occupied Conklin Hall, the major building on the Rutgers–Newark campus.[27] Among several demands they made was that the university agree to accept the top 50 percent of all African American graduates of Newark high schools.[28]

The takeover immediately polarized the university, its surrounding community, and much of the legislature. Members of the radical Students for a Democratic Society and the conservative Young Americans for Freedom clashed with each other outside the building.[29] Angry white vigilantes, associated with Newark councilman

Anthony Imperiale, whom the press described as a "tough talking, wise-cracking, pistol-toting, former Marine," rushed the doors of the building carrying a telephone pole.[30] Imperiale had burst onto the state political scene during the Newark riots when he sought to block people he deemed troublemakers from making their way into Italian American neighborhoods.[31] Hughes had termed Imperiale and his cohorts "brownshirts."[32] Imperiale won election to the city council in the spring of 1968. Months later he would chair Alabama governor George C. Wallace's presidential campaign in New Jersey. His presence on the scene increased tensions on campus and off.

Three days after the students had barricaded themselves inside Conklin Hall, the protesters evacuated the building.[33] Soon afterward they and university officials offered differing accounts of the agreement they had reached that broke the stalemate. The students insisted that the university had acceded to their demands. Rutgers president Mason W. Gross maintained that his signature on a transcript of negotiations in which he participated with the students merely attested to the accuracy of what he had said.[34] Kean, now chairman of the assembly Education Committee, announced that he would hold hearings on several matters pertaining to the university. He also said that he would ask Dungan to investigate the validity of the student complaints that Rutgers had been sluggish in its efforts to recruit minority students.[35]

Kean's reliance on Dungan as an investigator and arbiter pleased the students and their supporters.[36] From the time he first joined Hughes's administration, after serving as an adviser to John F. Kennedy and as Lyndon Johnson's ambassador to Chile, Dungan had prodded state colleges and universities to increase their enrollments of minority students.[37] His standing in the African American community rose when he brokered an agreement between local activists and officials at the then-yet-to-be-built Newark College of Medicine and Dentistry that allowed community participation in its governance and its teaching hospital to provide health care to the surrounding neighborhoods.[38]

As he emerged from a closed-door meeting with leaders of the Black Organization of Students in Trenton, Kean related that the students told him that Rutgers had undertaken virtually no effort to recruit African American students from Newark high schools. He said that if that was indeed the case, "someone had fallen down on the job." He promised that Dungan would ascertain the facts. Kean also announced that he and members of his committee would meet with students again the following Saturday on the Rutgers-Newark campus.[39]

Once on the site, Kean brought to bear skills he had acquired in the years he had spent advising, teaching, and counseling young people. When the students began making demands, Kean calmly replied, "You don't have to demand anything. I am here to talk to you."[40] When a student asked that if the conversation could be recorded, Kean said, "Fine."[41] He also agreed to see them without a university administrator present. Years later, Kean tried to recapture the atmosphere that surrounded such meetings between student protesters, university officials, and policy makers of the late 1960s: "Students did not feel they had to talk much in those days. They 'confronted.' Those Rutgers academics, good 1950s liberals, just did not know how to talk to them. And half their [the students'] grievances were legitimate."[42]

Kean baffled Rutgers administrators when he described the student protesters, who had caused them so much worry, as nice kids; some he called "rather charming."[43] Having created enough havoc of his own outside the Cow Palace five years earlier and within the assembly majority caucus more recently, he may have even admired their spunk. Based on their prior dealings with Kean, the students went into the meeting prepared to trust him. Former student spokesman Vicki Donaldson remembered that Kean listened intently as the students documented their grievances against the university. "I think we convinced him that we were not rabble-rousers from the projects," she said.[44]

After hearing the students out, Kean told them that their demands, whatever their merits, would be unattainable without a mechanism in place to implement them.[45] He told them he was prepared to fight to make more funds available to admit more minority students to the university, but only as part of a comprehensive plan. Within minutes, Kean had turned a potentially adversarial proceeding into a discussion in which he and the students were on the same side, working together to resolve what all in the room agreed was an important problem.

In his report, Dungan faulted Rutgers officials for not addressing enrollment and recruitment issues before student frustrations had reached the boiling point.[46] Over the next several weeks, the chancellor and university officials offered competing plans designed to increase minority enrollments. The Rutgers Board of Governors went so far as to approve a plan that went beyond what the protesters had demanded, offering to admit all disadvantaged high school graduates in the three cities where the university maintained campuses.[47]

Kean, meanwhile, subtly shifted legislative discussions away from the disruptions and toward how the Rutgers proposals would work.[48] Declaring that the public was "vitally concerned with its state University," Kean convened the hearings.[49] Their purpose, he said, would be to find out how many students would be enrolled under the new Rutgers plan, how any adopted changes would impact on Rutgers's operations, and what kind of remedial and developmental programs the university would initiate to equip students to handle college work.[50]

Kean also broadened the hearings' scope, extending the investigation beyond questions of minority enrollments to how Rutgers allocated funds it received through state bond issues to its three campuses.[51] Of the $63 million Rutgers took in through the most recently enacted higher education bond issue, it planned to spend only $6.1 million on its Newark campus.[52] The intra-university debate over how its central administration distributed these and other monies had been almost as protracted, divisive, and bitter as had that over minority admissions. In his capacity as chairman of the Education Committee, Kean had paid several visits, some unannounced, to the Newark campus to inspect its physical plant, library, athletic facilities, and student center. In convening the hearings, Kean made mention of other issues he knew to be on his colleagues' minds, including the wisdom of "open admissions," whether students who had occupied Conklin Hall should be subject to disciplinary action, and whether Rutgers should expand its outreach to minority applicants beyond the three cities where it maintained campuses.[53]

During a ten-hour hearing conducted by the education committees of the assembly and the senate, Kean allowed his conservative colleagues to air their grievances over the manner in which Gross had handled the disturbances. Several considered Gross too lenient. Eventually, Kean seized on a statement Gross made at the hearing as a means of resolving the immediate issue, while allowing his colleagues an opportunity both to record their disapproval of the university's administration and to discipline it.

In response to a question on how he intended to fund the new Urban University program through which Rutgers would admit disadvantaged students from urban areas and prepare them for college work, Gross said that the university had sufficient funds to finance the program for one semester. After that, he volunteered, he would seek to continue its operations either through a supplemental appropriation from the legislature or with funds allocated to other university accounts.[54] Several of Kean's colleagues interpreted the educator's remarks either as an attempt to blackmail them into funding a policy they had not approved or as evidence of a cavalier attitude toward legislative directives, reflected in previous budgeting allocations to the university. Kean also established at the hearing that Gross intended to spend $2 million on a program that would serve 800 students, while the recently established Educational Opportunity Fund was reaching 1,700 students at a cost of $2.5 million.

When Gross went ahead with his plan to request supplemental funding to continue the Urban University program, Kean, rather than work to defeat the measure, had it amended to transfer the newly appropriated funds and jurisdiction over the program from Rutgers to the Department of Higher Education, which subsequently consolidated Gross's program into the state EOF.[55] He also joined with those seeking to forbid the transfer of funds between accounts in the manner in which Gross was contemplating in the absence of legislative approval. By casting the legislature's dispute with the university in terms of accountability, Kean had given his colleagues a way to record their disapproval of university policy, while addressing the substance of the students' concerns. There would be other times in Kean's career when he would clothe liberal objectives in conservative garb and vice versa, giving something to both sides, as he worked to achieve a consensus.

Saving Sunfish Pond

While he was establishing a reputation as a problem solver and consensus builder on matters pertaining to education and urban affairs, Kean just as quickly earned his bona fides as a maverick when the subject at hand was conservation. Whatever their many disagreements, disparate elements within the state's power structure had by 1968 come to accept that the urban crisis needed to be addressed. They had also agreed as to the means. Although he had encountered obstacles as he sought to enact his proposals, Kean had been able to operate within a prevailing consensus as he juxtaposed himself between rurally based, conservative Republicans and urban-oriented, liberal Democrats. When it came to conservation, there had developed a consensus within the state power structure, but of a different kind. As he tried to achieve his goals, Kean repeatedly found himself bumping against it. In the late 1960s, business, labor, and government, when faced with a choice between conservation and economic development, frequently came down on the same side, which they termed "progress." It would be decades before all three realized that unhampered development could impact adversely on both the public health and the state of the economy.

Early in his legislative tenure, Kean leaned that a consortium of power companies planned to incorporate a forty-four-acre glacial lake in the northwest corner of New Jersey, the last of its kind in the state, into a pumped storage reservoir. They proposed pumping water from the Delaware River up the mountain at night, storing it in an enlarged pond, and running it back down during the day, harnessing its electrical power potential by forcing the return flow through specially constructed conduits. The plan was to have been part of the proposed Tocks Island Dam project at the foot of the Delaware, where a thirty-seven-mile man-made lake would be created. The site they sought to use as the first reservoir was at the top of a mountain in the Worthington State Forest, bordering the Appalachian Mountains at the Delaware Water Gap, and was known as Sunfish Pond. It sat within 715 acres of the Worthington tract the state had sold to the Jersey Central Power and Light Company (JCP&L) in 1961. In addition to the power companies, the plan had the support of business, labor, the Army Corps of Engineers, and the governors of the four surrounding states.[56]

For a time, it appeared that the only group that thought the lake was worth salvaging was a small group of conservationists who comprised the Lenni Lenape League. For several years, they had been staging annual "Save Sunfish Pond" public programs and events. What it lacked in funds and political clout, the group made up for in media savvy. In 1967, at its invitation, Supreme Court justice William O. Douglas, savior of the towpath that runs beside the Chesapeake and Ohio Canal, led a much-publicized hike there.[57] Former interior secretary Stewart Udall had spoken of the area's special beauty. Yet no one with the power to spare Sunfish Pond was prepared to intervene on its behalf. That remained the case until Tom Kean came on the scene.

After reading about the power companies' plans in the press, Kean telephoned local conservationists and asked to tour the site. Its pristine beauty immediately impressed the former camp counselor, who had spent much of his childhood in the Livingston woods. He also became quite taken with Casey Kays, the principal spokesman for the Lenni Lenape League. Decades later, Kean recalled Kays as "one of those people who make America wonderful."[58] Kays was neither wealthy nor prominent. A factory worker by day, he had a flair for coining a phrase and a knack for attracting attention. He spoke with particular eloquence whenever the subject turned to his favorite topic. "I don't have a lot of money," he would say, "and I don't have a backyard. The state park system is my backyard, and I won't let anyone destroy it."[59]

Kean introduced a bill authorizing the state to reacquire 390 acres of the 715-acre tract it had sold to the power company. "The legislators will have to decide whether they will go with the special interest groups on this or not," he proclaimed upon introducing the measure.[60] Kean would steer the bill through the assembly four times in four consecutive years, each time with a larger number of cosponsors than the last, only to see it die in the senate.[61]

Initially, Kean was stung at the intensity of the opposition his measure aroused and by the tactics those who favored the plan used to thwart him. Essex County Democratic assemblyman Paul Policastro announced on the assembly floor that the people of Kean's district had sent a bird watcher to Trenton.[62] Industry and labor spokesmen cited the need for additional electricity, predicting brownouts if the project did not go forward. One Hudson County Democratic legislator—and an employee of Public Service Electric and Gas—said that unless the power companies expanded their existing pumped storage facilities along the Delaware, they would have no alternative other than to "lead New Jersey down the road to darkness."[63] Utility lobbyists swirled around Kean to "explain" the project to him. "They kept thinking I didn't understand [the proposal]," he said years later.[64] After they had concluded that he had, they assumed Kean was trying to hold up the project as a means of extracting concessions from colleagues on another piece of legislation.[65] Upon learning that that was not the case, they charged that Kean was acting to protect his family's interests.[66] After he told them that the utility companies his family owned and operated favored the project, they began referring to him as a traitor to business as they advanced various psychological theories that might account for his apostasy.[67]

When Kean showed up for a meeting with industry lobbyists, wearing a bandage on his arm, one inquired into the cause of his injury. "A bee sting," Kean replied. "It should have gone right to your heart," the lobbyist blurted out, only half in jest.[68] Soon major Republican donors were calling Kean to explain that his actions would mean the ruination of the party. "They kept thinking I didn't understand," he recalled. "And the more they opposed me, the madder I got. . . . I just got my teeth into it, and I wouldn't let go."[69]

Kean pushed on many fronts. He worked the press. ("It was a wonderful issue to talk about," he said.)[70] Though still a freshman legislator, he began to apply some of the media savvy he had observed in others while toiling on Bill Scranton's behalf four years earlier. "They were destroying something that had been there from the ice age," Kean would say decades later.[71] Such lines, especially when uttered with the earnest intensity that Kean exuded, attracted much ink. He took the battle beyond New Jersey borders, surprising his adversaries when he persuaded U.S. senator Clifford P. Case to withhold support for a utility-initiated rider to a Senate Rivers and Harbors bill that would have authorized the project.[72]

After a hastily convened summit, which included both of the state's U.S. senators, Hughes, the executive director of the Delaware River Basin Commission (a consortium of the state governments of Delaware, New Jersey, New York, and Pennsylvania), industry representatives, conservationists, and Kean, the companies modified their proposal. Instead of developing Sunfish Pond, they offered to relocate the pump storage facility to an alternative site. To make their plan work, they would draw water one thousand feet up the mountain and construct a gigantic dike.

Kean and the conservationists refused the compromise, arguing that seepage from the pumped Delaware River water would introduce algae into Sunfish Pond, destroying its pristine quality.[73] They also worried about damage the shift would cause to the surrounding watershed and maintained that the project would deface the top of the Kittatiny mountain range. "Nobody can argue against cheap power," Kean said in a prepared statement to a U.S. Senate committee, "but at what price? The loss of natural assets that can never be replaced."[74] Back home, Kean complained of being subjected to "one of the most intense lobbying efforts" he had ever seen.[75] The coalition in favor of the project included the two largest power companies in the state (JCP&L and Public Service Electric and Gas), the Chamber of Commerce, the Delaware River Basin Commission, four sitting governors, and the state AFL-CIO. Former governor Robert B. Meyner, whose administration had both purchased the Worthington tract and made the decision to sell part of it to the utilities, and Conrad L. Wirth, former National Parks Service director, served as advisers to the power companies.[76]

For Kean, Kays, and their allies, victory ultimately came in 1972 when Governor William T. Cahill, citing excessive costs, risks of overdevelopment, and environmental concerns, withdrew New Jersey's support for the entire Tocks Island Dam project.[77] The thread on which Kean had been pulling while a freshman assemblyman and continued to tug as he rose through the assembly's ranks had, by the time he became its Speaker, unraveled an entire tapestry that had been years in the making. With information supplied by friends in the conservation movement and others, Kean discovered that agricultural runoffs from dairy and poultry farms in New York State containing pesticides threatened to pollute the entire man-made lake the Army Corps of Engineers prepared to create through its construction of the Tocks Island Dam. To prevent the runoff and its contents from seeping into tributaries flowing into the reservoir, New York State would have had to control the use of pesticides or construct sewage treatment plants, at a cost of billions of dollars, to remove the pollutants. Unwilling to confront this dilemma, New York governor Nelson A. Rockefeller, once the dam's most enthusiastic backer, suddenly lost interest in the project.[78] Kean described his efforts to save Sunfish Pond as the "mouse that slew the [Tocks Island] mountain."[79]

"They [the corporate lobbyists] forced me to look at the whole project," Kean said years later. "A beautiful part of the state would have been under water. It just did not make any sense. The benefits were not there. The whole thing was not what it was cracked up to be."[80] He would come to regard the battle to save Sunfish Pond as the catalyst that sparked the emergence of the environmental movement in New Jersey. He explained: "What started out as a little bill turned into a major bill. That was a process leading up to all the efforts to preserve the wetlands and the creation of the Department of Environmental Protection. For all those other bills I put through, this was sort of the lead. And in the middle of the fight, Earth Day was passed nationally. Rachel Carson's *Silent Spring* [had] become very popular."[81]

Kean was just as vigorous in his efforts to increase the regulation of pesticides as he was in protecting the glacial lake. He sparred repeatedly with the agricultural school at Rutgers University, which leased space to the Pesticide Association of New Jersey. When the organization began lobbying against his bill, Kean lambasted the university for encouraging the continued use of "hard pesticides," when it should have been "pressing for a cleaner environment."[82] At one point, he accused it of parroting chemical companies that were inflicting damage to groundwater.[83]

"Nixon's the One"

On the same day that Robert Kennedy won the 1968 California presidential primary and was felled by an assassin's bullet, New Jersey held its presidential primary. By a prior arrangement brokered by state Republican chairman Webster Todd, neither of the two major contenders for the Republican presidential nomination—former vice president Richard Nixon and New York governor Nelson A. Rockefeller—fielded a slate of delegates in the primary. The uncontested slate of delegates the state party put on the ballot declared itself uncommitted to any candidate. Most expected it to vote for New Jersey's favorite son, U.S. senator Clifford P. Case, on the first ballot.

Tom Kean ran as an alternate delegate. Just four years after attending his second Republican National Convention as Bill Scranton's youth coordinator, Kean would serve as a decision maker at his third. A *Newark Evening News* photographer captured Kean's transition from the back bench to the front row when he snapped a picture of Kean and Scranton conferring on the floor of the 1968 convention, not as a candidate and aide, but as fellow delegates from neighboring states.[84] Kean's inclusion in the delegation during his first year in the assembly signified his emergence as a force in state politics. It was also his reward for his efforts on Todd's behalf to expand the party's base. Even after he had become an elected official in his own right, Kean was still pitching in as Todd's—now unofficial—youth coordinator.

He was serving in that capacity the first time I had the occasion to meet with him. I was then a freshman at Rutgers–Newark. One winter day, on my way to class, I ran into Dominick Mazzagetti, a junior, who headed the campus College Republicans. He had been urging me to join the group. I had demurred. Both my parents had been registered Democrats. My mother occasionally pitched in as a Democratic election board worker on Election Day. Kean's previous opponent, Bernard Kuttner, was my mother's personal attorney. "Hey do me a favor," Dominick said. "The Republican National Committee is holding a workshop on campus this winter. I need help. Can you have lunch with me and Assemblyman Kean this Saturday?" Although I had not met Kean, I had observed him campaign in Irvington the previous fall and had heard good things about him since.

The idea of holding workshops in areas where the Republicans had fared poorly originated with Ray Bliss, the Ohio political operative who became chairman of the Republican National Committee shortly after Goldwater's defeat. Bliss, like Todd, with whom he worked to resolve the Rat Fink fiasco, placed more of a premium on nuts-and-bolts party building than on ideology.[85] I was studying political science and thought that attending one of Bliss's workshops might be interesting. I agreed to accompany Dominick to the Newarker Restaurant at the Newark airport to join Kean for lunch.

Twenty minutes into the meeting, Kean had put the entire program together and had delegated much of its implementation to me. "Look," he began,

we Republicans are supposed to be the party of local and state government, and the Democrats, the party of increased federal control. To demonstrate that we have better solutions to domestic problems, we plan to showcase speakers from every level of government. Since New Jersey does not have a Republican governor right now, Rhode Island governor John Chafee will talk about the influence one can exert from that role. I will speak about what the Republican majority is doing in the legislature. Case will cover Congress. My friend Henry Patterson, mayor of Princeton, and a couple of others will talk about local government. I have invited some freeholders and a couple of county chairmen.

Kean then turned his attention to the potential audience:

How many students can we accommodate and how many do you think would come? How should we attract them? How many can you personally bring? How should we structure the afternoon program so the students will want to return after lunch? Students we invite don't all have to be from Republican families, by the way. It would be better if they weren't. Where should we hold the event? Which of the things we discussed can you handle? What can we do to help make this event a success?

I discovered, as many had before me and many more would after me, how hard it was to turn Tom Kean down. He seemed so committed to what he was doing. He also seemed as if he would be fun to work with. In his navy blazer, gray slacks, and penny loafers, Kean could easily have passed for the graduate student he had been just four years earlier. In his manner of speech, demeanor, and appearance, he bore no resemblance to the kind of politician I had grown accustomed to seeing. He seemed more like a Republican version of John F. Kennedy than the potbellied, cigar-chomping, back-slapping Essex County Democratic politicians I had encountered primarily on Election Day. And unlike them, Kean appeared genuinely interested in what I had to say.

Over lunch, Kean peppered the conversation with questions about me. He wanted to know where I lived, what high school I had attended, and what I was studying in class. When I would mention a book with which he was familiar, he would offer good-natured comments indicating his approval or disdain. "Are they still assigning that antiquated thing?" he would ask. "You are supposed to be attending a modern university. Maybe we ought to look into that down in Trenton." Kean had a special way of getting others to want to help him. I recall thinking as I departed, "This project has to work. Kean really is a nice fellow. He has invested much of his time and effort trying to pull this off. He has taken some risk, persuading all these party figures to appear. He would be terribly embarrassed if nobody showed up to hear them. We cannot let that happen." I not only signed on to help but wound up a member of Dominick's organization too.

As the convention neared, Tom and Debby Kean boarded a train for Miami Beach to join the rest of the delegation. Although Todd professed neutrality between Nixon and Rockefeller, all knew that the favorite-son strategy, in New Jersey and elsewhere, was part of an effort among party moderates to deprive Nixon of a first-ballot victory. If things went according to plan, favorite sons would release their delegates on subsequent ballots, with most of them drifting toward Rockefeller. Prior to the balloting, word spread that Nixon might not actually have the necessary votes to ensure a first-ballot nomination. Sensing an opportunity to be king makers, Atlantic County senator Hap Farley, a longtime Nixon ally, and Bergen County chairman Nelson Gross, a onetime Case protégé, peeled eighteen votes away from Case to Nixon, splitting the delegation in open public view 22 to 18.[86] An associate of Gross maintained that the Bergen leaders reasoned that, in the event Nixon stumbled, the party would turn not to Rockefeller, as Case believed, but to the recently elected governor of California and late entry into the presidential race, Ronald Reagan, and that Reagan would fare no better in New Jersey in 1968 than had Goldwater four years earlier.[87]

For the rest of the 1968 campaign, Kean functioned primarily as a surrogate speaker on Nixon's behalf before college audiences. He found it preferable to blame the Democrats for starting the Vietnam War than to explain Nixon's admittedly ambiguous plan to bring the war to an end. Kean, the former history teacher, predicted that just as Eisenhower had ended the conflict in Korea after taking office in 1953, Nixon, who had served as Ike's understudy for eight years, would likewise find a way out of Vietnam. He also cited the beatings of student demonstrators at the hands of Chicago mayor Daley's police at the 1968 Democratic National Convention as evidence that the Democrats were less tolerant of opposing views within their party than were Republicans. Many of his young listeners found the messenger more appealing than his message.

Save for such appearances and obligatory campaigning for local candidates, Kean spent the remainder of the campaign and the year adapting to a new role, that of a father. On September 21, 1968, Debby Kean gave birth to fraternal twin boys: Thomas Howard Kean Jr. and Reed Stuyvesant Kean. Tales of the twins and their latest escapades— with particular emphasis on their unbounded capacity to get themselves into mischief—quickly became staples in Kean's expanding repertoire of stories.

Home-Style Campaigning

With the gubernatorial election of 1969 fast approaching, Kean made two significant announcements, both characteristic of the political style he was developing. He said that although conservative Cape May congressman Charles W. Sandman would not have been his choice for governor, he would go along with the decision of the Essex County organization and support Sandman in the primary. Kean's stand did not sit well with many of his fellow moderates, who were backing other candidates, primarily Camden County congressman William T. Cahill. "Tom always stayed with the organization no matter how much he and they may have disagreed and that worked to his favor," C. Stewart Hausmann noted.[88] Kean made his second announcement in the form of an ultimatum to the very organization to which he had just pledged fealty. Having heard that party leaders wanted to replace Kaltenbacher with another assembly candidate, Kean declared that he would be running in the primary with Kaltenbacher as his running mate, whether on the organization's line or off.[89] Kaltenbacher remained on the ticket.

Their second campaign proved much a replay of the first, with a few embellishments. More coordinators representing more groups posed for pictures with the candidates and hosted events on their behalf. As Kean and Kaltenbacher's recently designated youth coordinator, I was now among them. Robert W. Kean once again threw open his home to his son's supporters. Roemmele, Squier, Father Fronczak, and Phil Heymann were all back at their posts. One new recruit, my grandmother Bertha Felzenberg, then in her late seventies, started having the candidates to her home on certain Saturday mornings to meet her neighbors. As the candidates answered voters' questions, Grandmother Felzenberg would keep the assemblage well supplied with pastries, coffee, tea, and Kaltenbacher's favorite, crème de cacao.

By the time they sought reelection, Kean and Kaltenbacher had established an all but constant presence in Democratic Irvington. As incumbents, they had reason to forge strong relationships with the town's elected officials. Many, including Mayor Harry Stevenson, suspecting that Kean and Kaltenbacher would continue in their Trenton posts, constrained their public enthusiasm for their Democratic opponents. Kean established an easy rapport with Councilman Henry F. Skirbst, a fellow Republican and history teacher. Skirbst sent an open letter to his constituents in which he described how Kean and Kaltenbacher had helped hold down local property taxes by directing state aid Irvington's way.[90]

On another occasion, when Kean's news from Trenton was less positive, the assemblyman, acting through the councilman, broke the news himself and offered to work with the community to find a solution to an unanticipated problem. After discovering that a change in the state's urban aid formula meant that the town would receive less funding than previously anticipated, Skirbst, in an open letter to the school board, published in the *Irvington Herald*, wrote, "Assemblyman Kean asked that I contact him and advise him of what revisions might be made in the formula that would be of benefit to Irvington"[91]

By raising the issue himself and having a popular local official act as his intermediary, Kean had made himself not just a bearer of bad news but part of the solution to a problem. (As governor, he would use this approach again whether the problem concerned radon, dioxin, asbestos, polluted beaches, or budgetary shortfalls—these times without intermediaries.)

With Kaltenbacher at his side, Kean visited with editorial boards of every newspaper that circulated in his district, paying special attention to the weeklies. He made it his practice to return between elections, leaving a lasting impression on Verne Blake, editor of the *Irvington Herald,* known for her encyclopedic knowledge of the town, special fondness for young candidates, and reputation for the tough grillings she gave would-be officeholders. With Bernie Kuttner not on the ballot in 1969, the newspaper abandoned any pretense of neutrality: "We warmly back the incumbent team of Tom Kean and Philip Kaltenbacher who have proved so sensitive to Irvington's problems during their first-term 'warming period' in Trenton. Young, bright, and alert, they have won the respect of a broad spectrum of local citizens whom they have taken the time to meet and discuss problems with."[92]

Bill Cahill's Issues Director

Cahill's capture of the 1969 Republican gubernatorial nomination presaged good things for Kean. The Camden County congressman's nomination and subsequent election ended temporarily the internal squabbling that had long characterized Essex County Republican politics.[93] After finding a state post for the embattled Yeomans, Cahill commandeered George M. Walhauser Jr., son of a former congressional colleague, as Essex party chairman. Walhauser's designation of Roemmele as his principal deputy meant that Kean could now devote more time to state matters without having to look over his shoulder to see what was transpiring at home.

Optimistic about his chances of reelection, Kean offered his services to Cahill's campaign. The candidate's youthful staff, many of them from Washington, began seeking Kean's advice on state issues.[94] Kean began to suggest positions he felt were in Cahill's best interest to take. He was especially anxious that Cahill come out strongly in favor of environmental protection. To help make that happen, Kean took to performing several roles at once. First, he suggested to groups concerned that candidates were not addressing their areas of interest that they send Cahill and Meyner questionnaires, inquiring where they stood on certain issues. He would then help write the questions.

When the forms showed up at Cahill headquarters, aides, aware of Kean's expertise on the subject, asked that he complete them on Cahill's behalf. After they had been returned, Kean suggested that the recipients publicize the results.[95]

Cahill's campaign's willingness to delegate so much to Kean, especially on environmental matters, made for some embarrassing moments for Cahill after he had become governor. Months into his term, the legislature passed a bill Kean had sponsored establishing the Department of Environmental Protection. Cahill was not certain that he wanted to sign it. Kean reminded him that he had pledged to do so in his campaign. When a skeptical Cahill inquired where he had made that promise, Kean, flashing "that grin," took from his pocket a copy of a questionnaire Cahill had purportedly filled out during the campaign.[96] Cahill signed the bill establishing the new department on the first Earth Day, April 22, 1970.[97] Later that year, Kean would guide to passage the Wetlands Protection Act of 1970, the first such statute of its kind in the nation.

Soon, Cahill advisers began using Kean to undermine the credibility of Cahill's Democratic opponent, former governor Robert B. Meyner. After an eight-year absence from the statehouse, Meyner was still much admired for the high ethical standards he maintained in office, the caliber of his appointments, and his skills as an administrator. He was also more widely known across the state than Cahill. All that seemed to stand in the way of his easy return to Trenton was the refusal of Hudson County Democratic boss John V. Kenny—still angry at what he considered the insufficient deference Meyner had shown him—to endorse Meyner. Kean made it his business to put other obstacles in Meyner's way.

In a debate with Cahill, Meyner boasted that he had named six of the seven judges who were then currently sitting on the state supreme court. As chairman of the legislature's Joint Committee on Ethical Standards, Kean days later introduced legislation to bar former governors from appearing before judges and regulators they had appointed. "This happens to be the same court that Meyner's law firm is now appearing before to argue for a rate increase in auto insurance premiums," Kean said.[98] Not surprisingly, Cahill quickly endorsed Kean's bill.[99] At Kean's suggestion, Cahill, with the press in tow, visited Sunfish Pond. His appearance, announced ahead of time, gave Republican operatives ample time to plant stories about the role Meyner had played in acquiring the site while he was governor, selling it to the power companies, and after he left office, advising the industry, for a fee, as to how to defeat efforts to protect an environmentally sensitive site.[100]

Kean also went after Meyner's other postgubernatorial activities.

Following the surgeon general's 1964 finding that tobacco was a primary cause of lung cancer, regulators required tobacco companies to retain an outside counsel to oversee and approve tobacco advertisements. It was widely suspected in political circles that President Lyndon B. Johnson arranged for Meyner to be appointed administrator of the Cigarette Advertising Code as a reward for his efforts on LBJ's behalf at the 1960 Democratic National Convention. (Meyner, attending as a favorite son, refused to release his delegates on the first ballot. Most of them wanted to support the then front-runner and eventual nominee, John F. Kennedy. Johnson had been Kennedy's principal opponent.) Kean challenged Meyner to detail the circumstances that led to his appointment. He also challenged the former governor's assertion that he had gotten tough with the industry. Kean described Meyner as "a self-styled $100,000 a-year czar of cigarette advertising," who was too busy with his legal practice to stand up for the public interest.[101] While on the stump, Kean appeared to relish tearing into the former governor. Had he been looking for an occasion to settle a score with the governor, who had helped block Robert W. Kean's anticipated election to the U.S. Senate in 1958, the gubernatorial election a little more than a decade later proved the perfect opportunity.

Cahill defeated Meyner by more than 500,000 votes. The size of his margin had been inflated by instructions John V. Kenny gave his organization to vote the straight Democratic ticket, except at the top.[102] Returned to power with Cahill's election was the three-to-one Republican legislature. Republicans added one seat to their majority in the assembly. In District 11-F, Kean received 38,680 votes, Kaltenbacher 38,218, and their opponents 21,437 and 21,407 respectively. Both Republicans took Irvington handily.

Entry into the Leadership

Days after the election, a story ran in the *Newark Evening News* under the headline, "Jockeying Begins for GOP Leader Jobs." It reported that Barry Parker's elevation to majority leader had made the post he was vacating, that of assistant majority leader, an object of contention among three assemblymen, one of them Kean. The story cited Kean's advantages: his representation of a county that had seven other Republicans in its assembly delegation and his reputation as "one of the more thoughtful assemblymen to come on the scene lately."[103] Though the story did not run under a byline, Kean recognized it as the work of Peter Carter. He later recalled that it got him thinking about pursuing the position.[104] Prior to its publication, conventional wisdom in Trenton held that Union County's Peter Mc-

Donough, who had entered the assembly four years ahead of Kean, would be elevated to the post.

By the time the caucus had convened, McDonough had withdrawn and Kean, having worked the telephones and visited with his colleagues, prevailed over Union County assemblyman Charles J. Irwin by a considerable margin, more, Kean said, than what he had expected. Speaker designate Bill Dickey, of Camden County, proclaimed the newest member of the leadership team "able, competent, and conscientious" and promised to give him more responsibilities than previous occupants of the junior leadership post had exercised. Perhaps spotting "that grin" that many by now had come to recognize, a *Star-Ledger* reporter recorded that Kean was "elated" at his selection. Anxious to run as far as he could with the ball Dickey had tossed his way, Kean said he would work to strengthen the assembly's committee system. "My personal feeling is that the party conference is used far too much," he said. For the next two years he would work to weaken the hold it exerted on the flow of legislation.[105]

chapter 6

The Institutional Reformer

The Insider as Outsider

With the Republican Party in control of both the executive and legislative branches of New Jersey government, Kean no longer needed to chart a "third way" between conservative Republicans and liberal Democrats. The election of William T. Cahill, a liberal Republican, as governor in 1969 reduced the influence of the "stand patters" and shifted the center of gravity within the Republican Party decidedly to the left. As assistant majority leader in 1970 and majority leader in 1971, Kean had two main responsibilities: directing the flow of legislation to the assembly floor and enacting Cahill's legislative program. He did not find those tasks particularly onerous, given that he and Cahill shared many priorities.

In the four years Cahill served as governor, he raised the sales tax from 3 to 5 percent, prodded the Port of New York and New Jersey Authority to award mass transit a greater priority, repeatedly attempted to lower the voting age from twenty-one to eighteen, tried to enact a state income tax, stopped the Tocks Island Dam project, and secured an agreement from the New York Giants to play in a yet-to-be-constructed football stadium in the Hackensack Meadowlands.[1] Kean was heavily involved in each of these episodes. Nevertheless, he found that serving as point man for a governor as institutionally strong as New Jersey's and with a personality as hard-charging as Cahill's was not without challenges. In those instances where the two were not of one mind, Kean found that he could use his leadership position to prod Cahill in his direction. As he explained: "Sometimes, I was not above telling Bill Cahill, 'You've got a bill here and I'm going to make some political sacrifices to get it through. It's not popular in our caucus. I'm going to have to bang some heads, and the public may not like it either. I'll go to work for you, but, you know, I've got a bill that I am trying to get through to your desk, and I know it's not your favorite bill, but I'd like you to sign it.'"[2] Kean's willingness to use such access to advance measures of his colleagues as well as his own helped him consolidate his hold on the assembly leadership.

As he rose through the assembly's ranks, Kean made the environment and education his special concerns. Gradually, he expanded his policy portfolio to include consumer protection, ethics reform, and tenants' rights. As he had in the case of Sunfish Pond, Kean worked with citizen activists who operated primarily outside the realm of conventional party politics. Sometimes, he would take it upon himself to build such bases of support. He would often repeat advice that he had given budding environmentalists to their counterparts trying to advance other issues:

It's clear that people are more concerned about pollution and other environmental problems than they were only a year ago. But they should be aware that . . . [when] an environmental bill comes up for action the interests which stand to be affected show up in Trenton with strong and well-financed lobbies. If you tackle the Sunfish Pond problem, it's the electric companies; if it's protecting wetlands, it's the shore developers, and so on. Well-meaning legislators have a fight on their hands; when they attempt such legislation without evidence of public support, it's that much tougher.[3]

Whatever issue or cause he happened to be pursuing at any given time, Kean attempted to convince his colleagues, often through the press, that *silent* majorities—a term he borrowed from President Nixon—were prepared to assert themselves on Election Day if those in public office disregarded their concerns. After he had introduced legislation to allow class-action suits against polluters, Kean had a group of Rutgers law students poll every legislator on how they felt about the issue and publicized the results.[4] When his bill to protect New Jersey's coastline stalled in Trenton, he suggested that citizens who favored the measure send clamshells to their state legislators.[5] The press ran photos of shells piled up outside legislative offices.

Modernizing an Old Legislature

Kean entered the legislative leadership at a time when state legislatures all across the country were revising their operations. A combination of factors—court-ordered reapportionment of state legislatures in accordance with the "one man, one vote" principle; citizen demands for greater accountability of elected officials; and proliferation of younger, well-educated political leaders in state capitals, buoyed by John F. Kennedy's inaugural challenge to enter public service—fueled demands for legislative reform in many states. High on the agendas of "good government" groups were longer terms for legislative leaders, stronger committees, professionalized staffs, improved facilities, upgraded technology, and the creation of legislative budget offices to function as a check on governors.[6]

In 1971, while Kean was serving as assembly majority leader, the Citizens Conference on State Legislatures, a nonprofit organization funded by foundations, published *The Sometime Governments*, a study that ranked state legislatures according to several criteria.[7] Its authors hoped that in states that had received poor grades, pressure from the public and the media would prompt legislatures to change how they conducted business. In overall performance, New Jersey's legislature placed thirty-second.[8] Kean took to citing the survey's results in speeches, when he would rhetorically ask his absent colleagues if they were proud of the grades national experts had awarded their branch of government.[9] For the rest of his time in the assembly, he pressed for a stronger committees system, increased and more professional staff, and an independent check on the budget.

When he became assistant majority leader, Kean broke precedent by presenting his party caucus with written rules that governed how it conducted its business.[10] After he became Speaker, committees began to meet at regularly scheduled times, took recorded votes, and maintained professional partisan staffs.[11] Another of his innovations was the Conference Committee.[12] Patterned in part after its counterpart in the U.S. House of Representatives, the Conference Committee had the power to move bills stalled in other committees to the floor if its sponsors supplied evidence that it had sufficient votes to pass. Consisting of the heads of each county's assembly delegation, the Conference Committee, because of the absence of a competitive two-party system in some counties, became the only committee in the lower chamber to operate on a truly bipartisan basis. In order to make the legislature more of a partner in setting state priorities, Kean secured passage of legislation creating the legislative Office of Fiscal Affairs and persuaded Cahill to sign it.[13]

To bring professional management to the assembly, Kean retained Joseph A. Gonzales, a future president of the New Jersey Business and Industry Council, as the first executive director of the assembly majority. He permitted the Democratic minority to retain its own partisan director. He established the assembly's first full-time communications operation, retaining as its press secretary Carl Golden, who had performed a similar role for Representative Peter H. B. Frelinghuysen. Golden had come to Kean's attention through Jim Staples, of the *Newark Evening News,* who had covered the Sunfish Pond controversy. Kean was impressed with Golden's knowledge of the statehouse press, his quick wit, and his ability to anticipate how various reporters would cover certain stories. To pay Golden's salary, Kean abolished three part-time positions and transferred the occupant of another to the Speaker's payroll.[14]

Soon, Golden was preparing weekly columns for Kean's signature on legislative matters and issuing regular press releases laden with Kean quotations and telephone numbers journalists could call for further information. Reporters discovered that they might get Kean on the line if they dialed one of two numbers provided.[15] Kean developed a reputation for returning all reporters' calls, regardless of how small a readership their publication reached. He took to walking statehouse corridors, anticipating that reporters would stop him to ask a question. He was prone to drop by reporters' offices in the statehouse to chat about legislative business, national politics, or sports. Kean liked the intellectual fencing inherent in press conferences and interviews with editorial boards.[16]

Reporters sensed that Kean enjoyed their company. They appreciated his informal style. Most found him distinctly different from the run-of-the-mill statehouse politicians they were used to covering. He was brighter, better educated, and came across as devoid of cynicism and genuinely interested in policy. Over time, reporters developed in their minds, and sometimes let slip into their copy, a certain caricature of Kean. Their take on him was that of a genial fellow, tight with a buck, in spite of his personal wealth, and totally unconcerned about his attire or appearance. Kean fed such impressions when he volunteered that he thought of himself more as frugal than as cheap and preferred comfortable to stylish apparel. Reporters found Kean's running mates more than willing to share tidbits about their friend Tom, reinforcing the image they had in mind.

Kaltenbacher told of the times Kean pretended to be asleep so that he would not be asked to pay the tolls as the two commuted to Trenton, with Kaltenbacher driving.[17] On the coldest of days, Kaltenbacher would say, Kean would leave his overcoat in his car so that he would not have to pay to check it. (Kean would maintain he had done so in order to save time.) Jane Burgio, who succeeded Kaltenbacher on Kean's ticket in 1973, recalled the time she and Kean handed out leaflets at a shopping mall. An elderly couple, who did not speak English, after giving Kean the once-over, handed him a quarter.[18] Trenton insiders would insist that they first learned that Kean intended to run for governor in 1977 when he showed up in the assembly sporting a new suit.[19] One reporter set to paper the collective image his colleagues had of Kean: "For years I have labored under the impression that the Kean family had a loyal retainer whose duty it was to wear tweeds and blue, button-down broadcloths until they were suitably frayed and shiny, whereupon they were turned over to Tom."[20] When engaged in policy discussions as he walked the corridors with colleagues, reporters, or lobbyists, Kean would appear oblivious to his surroundings, coming across more as the teacher he once was rather than as a politician.

One permanent change Kean brought to the legislature came about more through accident than by design. The Sunday before he was to be sworn in as majority leader, Kean slipped on the ice outside his home, while carrying his two-year-old son, Thomas H. Jr., and fractured his leg in three places.[21] His leg in a cast, Kean found it difficult hobbling back and forth from his seat to the Speaker's rostrum on crutches. He requested that a telephone be installed at his desk. Upon spotting it, the minority leader demanded one as well. Soon telephones appeared on all eighty assembly desks.

A Broader Constituency, an Election, and a Stalemate

The 1971 legislative campaign brought some changes to Kean's operation and presented him with new challenges. At its outset, Irvington councilman Joseph A. Galluzzi announced that he would oppose Kaltenbacher in the Republican primary. Both of Herb Roemmele's boys won easy renomination, but only after having worked hard to shore up Kaltenbacher's support. With Roemmele's attention focused primarily on county affairs, Kean and Kaltenbacher asked Dr. Charles Nadel, a popular orthopedic surgeon at Irvington General Hospital, and one of the town's most respected citizens, to manage their campaign. Through a minor change made to their district, a legislative reapportioning committee added two precincts in Newark's Central Ward to their terrain. Rather than write off these two predominantly African American and Democratic areas, Kean and Kaltenbacher campaigned hard in them. They also began to pay even greater attention to developments within the Central Ward.

Kean first met Mary Smith, executive director of Babyland, an organization devoted to the care of infants of working mothers, in 1969. Babyland had come into existence in the aftermath of the Newark riots. Funded through foundations and local businesses, Babyland was committed to reducing one of the social ills that both the Kerner and Lilley Commissions had identified as an underlying cause of the disturbances: high unemployment. With women heading 67 percent of all Newark households, reducing unemployment entailed not only helping single mothers find work but also making it possible for them to accept it. Smith knew from personal experience that women, anxious about how their children would be cared for in their absence, chose to remain on welfare. Most day-care facilities at that time did not provide care to children under three years of age. Smith intended her organization to fill this void.[22]

Soon she discovered that in order to qualify for federal assistance, entities such as hers first had to be receive accreditation from their state government. That proved to be no easy feat in New Jersey, which lacked licensing standards for providers of day care to children under three. Smith discussed her predicament with one of Kean's leading supporters, Karla Squier, who had been assisting Babyland as a volunteer. Squier brought Smith to see Kean.

Before long, Kean was pressing for the adoption of standards for providers of infant care with all the tenacity he had brought to bear in the battle to save Sunfish Pond. He wrote letters, pestered bureaucrats, and denounced the bureaucracy as callous and insensitive. It took him years, but by the time he had risen to the top of the assembly's ranks, the state complied with his demands and Smith received the necessary "certificate of need." Through his efforts on Smith's behalf, Kean commenced a decades-long relationship with her institution. His experiences would have a direct bearing on how he approached day-care funding and welfare reform as governor.

As expected, Kean and Kaltenbacher won easy reelection to their third term. When the votes were counted, Kean again placed first, receiving 28,728, and Kaltenbacher came in second with 22,323. Their Democratic opponents, Harry McEnroe Jr., who would subsequently win election to the assembly, and Gerald M. Simons, polled 16,403 and 13,240 votes, respectively. Elsewhere in the state, Republicans fared less well. They lost twenty seats in the assembly. Factors contributing to their poor showing included Nixon's decision to have U.S. forces invade Cambodia; protests that ensued in its aftermath, including one at Kent State University in which four student demonstrators were fatally shot; and a skittish national economy. Final returns showed the

Democrats controlling forty seats and the Republicans thirty-nine. The remaining seat would be held by Newark councilman Anthony Imperiale, who had won election as an independent.

The election left neither party able to organize the assembly on its own. Forty-one votes were required to elect a speaker. The day after the election, Cahill publicly urged assembly Republicans not to make common cause with Imperiale, whose campaign tactics and unflattering rhetoric about African Americans the governor found distasteful.[23] Some Republicans, who had been courting Imperiale, quietly resented Cahill's overt intrusion into what some regarded primarily as a legislative prerogative. By itself, Imperiale's vote would not have been sufficient to enable the Republicans to organize the assembly. Sensing an opportunity, Democratic state chairman Salvador Bontempo made overtures to Imperiale. He broke off the talks after three African American assemblymen vowed to withdraw from any caucus in which Imperiale participated.

When the two parties convened to determine whom they would support for Speaker, Republicans unanimously lined up behind Kean. The Democrats, however, refused to coalesce behind the incumbent minority leader, David Friedland of Hudson County, who aspired to be elevated to the Speaker's post. Months prior to the election, the state supreme court had suspended Friedland from practicing law in the state for six months, finding that he had acted improperly in the settling of a loan-sharking case. As part of his efforts to persuade the plaintiff to drop charges against his client, reported to be an associate of organized crime boss "Joe Bayonne" Zacarelli, Friedland had handed $6,500 to the plaintiff's attorney. After deducting a fee, the attorney presented $5,000 to the man who had initiated the suit, who, in turn, agreed to drop the charges against Friedland's client.[24]

After the court had issued its ruling, Speaker Barry Parker refused to call a special session to consider expelling the Democratic leader from the chamber, arguing that voters would decide Friedland's fate in the upcoming election. Not surprisingly, Friedland, his legal difficulties notwithstanding, won reelection in a district where Republican opposition was minimal. When Friedland declared his intention to run for Speaker, Essex County Democratic chairman Harry Lerner and several other prominent Democrats, considering Friedland too much of a political liability to hold a major party post, demanded that he step aside. When he offered to run again for the post of majority leader instead, the Democratic caucus refused to go along.[25]

To some observers, the Democrats' sudden interest in both Friedland's ethics and his outside legal activities seemed belated. His efforts on behalf of his notorious client had been much in the news at the time the Democrats elected Friedland as minority leader. In 1968, assistant New Jersey attorney general William J. Brennan III had named Friedland as one of a handful of legislators who were "too comfortable" with organized crime. The legislative leadership responded to his charges by naming a special committee to investigate. Kean was among its members.[26] Although the committee found that Friedland had violated no assembly rules, it deemed the charges surrounding his settling of the loan-sharking case to be of sufficient importance to refer to the Middlesex County grand jury, which, in turn, ruled against the legislator and referred the matter to the state supreme court. As their choice for Speaker, assembly Democrats settled on S. Howard Woodson (D-Mercer). Assemblyman John Horn (D-Camden) was their choice for majority leader. Woodson commanded thirty-four votes in the Democratic caucus, five votes short of enough to elect a Speaker. Friedland controlled the other six.

As the Democrats feuded in public, Kean, the unanimous choice of his party's caucus, took the high ground, focusing on the accomplishments of the previous legislature. He credited the outgoing assembly with strengthening its committee system and staffing its committees with full-time professionals. He noted that in 1971, 80 percent of bills that passed the assembly had cleared committees, a record for the lower chamber, and pointed out that most of the others either had been minor bills or were passed on an emergency basis.[27] Of the two thousand bills that passed, about two dozen made it to the floor through the Conference Committee Kean created. The image Kean projected of his party and of himself as unified champions of "good government" contrasted sharply with that of the Democrats as feuding machine-politicians, with their outgoing leader under an ethical cloud.

As the weeks passed, neither party seemed able to command sufficient votes to organize the chamber. The Democrats' continued squabbling caused the early January convening of the new legislature to be delayed, and Cahill's State of the State address, originally scheduled to be delivered in the morning, was postponed until 6:00 p.m.

The Makings of a Deal

On the morning of January 12, 1972, the *Star-Ledger* carried a banner headline summarizing the events of the preceding tumultuous day in the state capital: "Friedland Hands Assembly to GOP."[28] He had indeed. Along with three colleagues, Michael Esposito and David Wallace, both from Hudson, and Joseph Higgins of Union, the spurned

Democrat had provided Kean with the votes necessary to make the Essex legislator, at the age of thirty-six, the youngest Speaker of the assembly in the state's history. Two other Democrats, believed to be in Friedland's camp, abstained. While news that a deal had been in the works came as a shock to the press, its architects had been at work for several weeks. To their own surprise, all the participants had kept the details secret until the last possible moment.

Days after the election, Richard DeKorte (R-Bergen), then serving as assistant majority leader under Kean, asked Democrats of all persuasions whether they had any suggestions as to how the assembly might be organized.[29] Friedland began making proposals. According to one eyewitness, at the time he began negotiating with the Republicans, Friedland did not know which Republican he was helping to elect Speaker, DeKorte, Kean, or someone else.[30] Having delegated the negotiations to DeKorte, Kean did not become a direct participant in them until late in the process. When six Republicans expressed skepticism about some of Friedland's terms, Kean said that he would only agree to Friedland's terms if the entire Republican caucus went along.[31]

The talks continued, with negotiations spilling over onto the assembly floor. There, in full public view, Friedland dropped his demand that he be named president pro tempore of the assembly, a post that did not exist, and Kean agreed to the rest of the Democrat's terms.[32] Under the arrangement, Friedland would receive half the patronage at the Speaker's disposal, totaling $17,500 for pages, sergeants-at-arms, and bill clerks. Friedland would chair the bipartisan Conference Committee with each of the three other Democratic defectors receiving a committee chairmanship. Friedland subsequently suggested that increased state aid to Hudson County had also been part of the package, an assertion Cahill denied.[33]

"Good government" groups, self-proclaimed "reformers" in both parties, and editorial writers immediately attacked the Kean-Friedland arrangement as a backroom deal. Democratic assemblywoman Ann Klein, a former chair of the League of Women Voters, said the Republicans had taken as their "bedfellow the worst element of the Democratic Party," sentiments the then-freshman assemblyman James Florio would continue to share three decades later.[34] Assemblyman George Richardson saw the hand of racism at work in the blocking of the advance of Woodson, an African American, who would have become the first member of his race to serve as Speaker.[35] The *Bergen Record* proclaimed the Kean-Friedland arrangement "the Sellout."[36] The *Star-Ledger* saw it as "Cynical Expediency." For two successive Sundays, the *Star-Ledger* ran editorial cartoons denouncing the deal: one portrayed the Republicans rolling out a carpet of welcome for Friedland as he crossed the aisle between the two parties; the other depicted a youthful Kean struggling to extricate himself from a pool of mud, interspersed with quicksand.[37] Another newspaper ran one with a burning cigar, titled "El Stinko," with the words *Kean-Friedland Assembly Deal* on a cloud of smoke.[38]

For the first time in his career, Kean received stinging criticism. *Star-Ledger* columnist Franklin Gregory voiced opinions that were representative of much of the statehouse press corps: "What in heaven's name was a nice guy like Tom Kean doing in getting mixed up in a wheeler-dealer game which at the same time gave Dave Friedland the power to control the flow of legislation plus a big chunk of the Assembly's patronage? . . . Or was Tom Kean's personal ambition for the speakership too tempting?"[39] Another journalist, a Delaware native who had attended school with Debby Kean, began getting calls from startled relatives. "Boy, they really play rough up there in New Jersey," one told him. "How did that nice fellow Tommy Kean get involved in all of this?"[40]

On the surface, Kean and Friedland seemed an unlikely pair. Friedland was flamboyant and flashy; Kean was laid-back. Friedland epitomized the tainted clubhouse politician; Kean the "good government" reformer. Though both could bring the assembly to a stop with flashes of oratorical eloquence, Friedland came across as irreverent and cynical; Kean, sincere and earnest. Although Friedland could cite passages from Shakespeare from memory and wrote poetry in his spare time, his colleagues most remembered his suggestion that the Statue of Liberty be placed on a rotating pedestal so that she would not have her back to New Jersey all of the time and his call to make the catfish the state fish, because it could survive in the polluted waters of the Passaic River.[41] While most conceded Friedland's brilliance, evidenced by his successfully arguing (at the age of twenty-five) before the state supreme court that the New Jersey legislature be apportioned according to population, some who worked with him up close questioned the depth of his convictions.[42]

That Friedland would hold back votes he commanded in order to extract the best possible deal surprised neither his admirers nor his detractors. Because it appeared so out of character, Kean's willingness to accommodate his apparent opposite, however, startled many of his admirers. In his first days as Speaker, Kean found himself continually having to fend off charges that he had entered into some clandestine arrangement with his Hudson counterpart. Every time reporters and others asked him how he would respond to this criticism, Kean would patiently explain that he had made all the terms of the agreement public and that he had bestowed no positions upon Friedland and his crew to which their years of seniority had not otherwise entitled them. Not once did he voice in public any hint of regret over the terms of the agreement, no matter how heated the criticism of his actions became.

Most frequently, he tried to explain away the arrangement as the only means available to him and his colleagues to break a stalemate that was preventing the legislature from tending to the people's business, attempting to present the deal he had struck as a positive good. Taking a page out of the book of Friedland, Kean told an Essex County audience that he saw the arrangement as a means through which he could further benefit his home county. As Speaker, he would be in a stronger position to have the state assume control of the county's mental hospital, provide more school aid, and pass legislation that would allow for the reform of the county's government.[43]

Kean reminded one columnist that none of Friedland's alleged misdeeds resulted from his activities as a legislator.[44] While that was literally the case, Kean, acting in his legislative capacity, had thought the charges against his colleague important enough to have referred them to a grand jury. Kean's comments about Friedland's nonlegislative activities left open the question of what, in his view, one of his peers had to do outside of the assembly chamber in order to forfeit the right to have a say in the running of the institution. Kean, perhaps in an effort to convince himself further in the rightness of his action, even suggested that Friedland sought to wash off a stain on his record through outstanding performance in the assembly.[45] In attempting to compartmentalize in public between Friedland's legislative and professional dealings, Kean had demonstrated both how far he was willing to go in order to satisfy his ambitions and how skillfully he had approached the negotiations.

His selection as Speaker behind him, Kean moved swiftly to direct public attention away from the circumstance of his election and toward how he intended to run the institution he now commanded and the agenda he wished to pursue. Kean announced that he would recognize both groups of Democrats as if each were a political party unto itself. In a gesture of good faith, Kean appointed a Hudson Democrat, not affiliated with Friedland, to advise him as he fulfilled a constitutional power of his office, the power to approve state leases.[46] Once, when he referred to Friedland as "associate leader" and reporters asked what Friedland would be leading, Kean deadpanned, "A group of assemblymen, I guess."[47] While Kean made good on his promise to name Friedland and his three cohorts to committee chairmanships, he also named two other Hudson Democrats chairs of committees, thereby allowing both sides to take credit for Hudson's increased clout within the legislature.[48] Mindful of his own caucus, he also named many Republicans to committee chairs as well.

Looking forward to the legislative session that lay ahead, Kean predicted that how the legislature performed would determine whether what he and his colleagues had done was justified.[49] Kean's tenure as Speaker would mark two of the most productive legislative sessions in New Jersey history. Months into his term, few were still discussing what had become known as the "Kean-Friedland Deal." Comments Friedland made a year later suggest that Kean had been correct when he asserted that, appearances to the contrary, he had given away much less than his critics had suspected. In a conversation with a reporter, Friedland, while admitting that Kean had fulfilled the terms of the agreement, indicated that he believed his apostasy had been a mistake. He insisted that all he got for his efforts had been "peanuts."[50] Kean, on the other hand, had walked away with a great deal. Elected only five years earlier to the assembly, he was now in command of the third most powerful elective office in the state. He mounted the Speaker's rostrum fully prepared to make the most of the opportunity his caucus, and a few Hudson County Democrats, had given him.

A Most Eventful Speakership

Years after he had relinquished the Speaker's gavel, Kean recalled the atmosphere that awaited him the day he first wielded it.

> Yes, it was very, very partisan. . . . For the two weeks [preceding the Friedland accord] and three weeks or so after [it transpired], it was a poisonous atmosphere. Everybody was distrustful.
>
> But it didn't take long, I don't think . . . for them to find out that if I said I was going to do something, I did it. Then I gave them [the Democrats] partisan staff, and they saw that I was going to treat them fairly.
>
> It wasn't as if we were enemies. A lot of these people were friends of mine. So, it didn't take long for them to recognize that if they wanted to get something done—and most people run for office because they want to get something done, not just to be there—that we were going to [have to] work together. Two months into that session, we were starting to get things done, and that just increased over the next two years.[51]

Kean's memory was accurate. A month after the assembly convened, only 21 percent of those surveyed by the Eagleton Institute admitted any knowledge about the so-called Kean-Friedland Deal.[52] In the short term, it worked to Kean's advantage that the public failed to give the matter the same attention as had the press.

As the assembly's Speaker, Kean reverted back to the "third way" approach he had adopted as a freshman legislator, but with a different twist. This time, with his entire caucus behind him, he would cut a path not between liberal Democrats and conservative Republicans but between competing factions of Democrats, whose disagreements had been factional and personal, rather than ideological. Because of the circumstances of his election as Speaker, Kean functioned more as an executive than as a traditional legislative leader. As the assembly's Speaker, he came to personify the assembly as a whole. If he eschewed the role of spokesman for the legislative majority, it was because his party was not in the majority.

Kean spent much of his first year as Speaker making the assembly function and clearing much of its calendar to accommodate debate on Cahill's long-awaited tax reform package. In conformity with the recommendation of a commission he had appointed to study the state's tax structure, Cahill proposed the enactment of a state income tax, a statewide property tax, and other revisions in the state code to arrest the steady climb in state property taxes and, in anticipation of pending court decisions, to mandate more equal school spending per pupil. When Kean informed Cahill that his income tax proposal was in trouble, the governor insisted that it be brought to a vote, so that "each of those sons of bitches" would have to go on record.[53] His plan went down to defeat in a vote of 52 to 23.[54] Only nine of thirty-nine Republicans, including Kean, supported it.

In addition to the traditional opposition to broad-based taxes in New Jersey at the time, and especially within his own party, the influence Cahill had been able to exert upon the legislature began to diminish after his closest political operative, Paul Sherwin, was indicted on corruption charges two weeks prior to the vote. Sherwin's indictment not only deprived Cahill of his closest adviser and most effective surrogate but took a toll on his standing with the general public. At the time the assembly considered Cahill's income tax, the governor's approval rating stood at 40 percent.[55] Kean used the tax debate as an opportunity to air an idea he had quietly been considering: establishing a permanent source of funds to acquire and preserve open space. He suggested setting aside a portion of the income tax proceeds for this purpose.[56] Although the defeat of the tax plan prevented his idea from taking hold, as governor Kean would seek to achieve this end through alternate means.

Occasionally during Kean's tenure as Speaker, national issues intruded into state affairs. When Democrats introduced a resolution calling for an immediate end to the Vietnam War, Kean, after having it amended to omit specific criticism of President Nixon and language calling for a halt to the bombing of North Vietnam, claimed the measure as his own. Afterward, he was able to reassure Nixon supporters that the resolution merely reiterated what Nixon himself had said about wanting to see a speedy end to the war. To the war's opponents, he could truthfully boast that under his leadership, the assembly became the first legislative chamber in the country to pass an antiwar resolution. As Speaker, Kean threw his weight behind measures to lower the voting age from twenty-one to eighteen. He authored New Jersey's consumer protection statute and legislation establishing the state's Division of Consumer Affairs. He pushed through legislation increasing penalties for unauthorized development of riparian lands from one hundred to three thousand dollars a day and the law requiring candidates for public office to disclose campaign donations.[57]

When it came time to reorganize the assembly in 1973, Kean became the first person to serve two consecutive terms as Speaker in state history. Content with the way he had run the assembly and not eager to reopen wounds of the previous year, Democrats ran no one against him for Speaker. "I'm a known commodity," Kean said after winning reelection by default. He began his second year in the post intent on passing bills he awarded the highest priority. After a committee added amendments to weaken a bill he had introduced to allow citizens to file class-action suits against polluters, Kean took what one newspaper described as "the unusual step of relinquishing the speaker's rostrum to lead the four hour debate on the floor." He subsequently pulled forty-eight votes his way.[58]

One month into his second year as Speaker, Kean sponsored New Jersey's first rent stabilization bill.[59] His action came amid reports in the press that landlords had been charging excessive rents in parts of the state that were experiencing housing shortages. Kean had cosponsored bills to regulate rents in prior sessions but had not been able to get them to the floor for a vote. With Kean serving as Speaker and Friedland chairing the conference committee, the two were able to bypass the committee of jurisdiction and bring the measure to a vote.[60] To improve its chances of passing, Kean, after consulting with tenant leaders, had it changed to empower localities, rather than the state, to peg rent increases to the consumer price index in areas experiencing housing shortages.

The debate that followed marked the first public verbal exchange between Kean and his future gubernatorial opponent, James Florio, then a freshman assemblyman. Florio argued that Kean's amendments had so weakened the bill as to render it ineffective. "In order to defeat the bill, you say it is not strong enough," Kean shot back, reminding his listeners that Florio had said nothing on the subject prior to the vote.[61] After the state supreme court ruled that the state had the power to regulate rents, Kean offered amendments to the legislation, restoring prior provisions.[62]

Kean's crowning achievement as speaker was steering to passage the Coastal Area Facility Review Act, to prevent industries considered most likely to increase pollution from locating along the state's coastline. He introduced the measure after assessing the impact of a major oil spill off Santa Barbara, which had badly marred much of California's coastline.[63] He argued that environmental protection and economic development were compatible goals, insisting that the well-being of the state's tourism, recreation, and fishing industries hinged on the continuation of clean beaches, rivers, and waterways. Similar to his efforts to save Sunfish Pond and to provide for class-action suits, Kean worked the issue in the media. At Kean's request, Cahill had made coastal protection one of his major priorities and spoke to the issue in his State of the State address.

Kean's bill prohibited most construction in the vicinity of the Atlantic Ocean, the Raritan and Delaware bays, and the Delaware River, a total of 1,750 square miles, representing one-seventh of New Jersey's landmass, in the absence of approval from the state's Environmental Protection Department. For the better part of two years, he lobbied strenuously to persuade the state senate to pass it. A coalition of power companies, petrochemical companies, developers, organized labor, the New Jersey State Chamber of Commerce, and others stood opposed. In an unusual show of support for its Speaker, the assembly passed the measure by a vote of 50 to 8. When the senate weakened the bill with amendments before eventually voting it down, Kean attributed its action to its members' desires for campaign contributions that election year.[64] In response to his and others' continued public prodding, the senate passed an amended version a month later.

When the assembly returned after the 1973 primary election, Kean took to the floor to deliver the closing arguments of a two-hour debate on an assembly-senate compromise. He challenged critics who asserted the measure would cause businesses to leave the state to supply him with a list of companies that were considering departing.[65] The measure passed 56 to 14. Its enactment proved a bittersweet victory for both Cahill and Kean. Days earlier, Cahill lost the Republican gubernatorial primary to his 1969 primary opponent, Representative Charles W. Sandman. Cahill's liberal policies, especially his attempts to pass an income tax, and his aloofness from party affairs had put a strain on his relations with party leaders. When added to these difficulties, the indictments not only of Sherwin, but of party chairman Nelson Gross and state treasurer Joseph McCrane on similar charges, rendered his likely defeat all but inevitable. Compounding the Garden State GOP's problems was the unfolding Watergate scandal, which many expected would take its toll on all Republicans running for office.

A New District and a New Running Mate

The Democrats' candidate for governor in 1973, Brendan T. Byrne, appeared to be the perfect antidote to the ethical scandals that plagued both the state and national Republican administrations. A former executive secretary to Governor Robert B. Meyner, Byrne had served as Essex County prosecutor and on the state superior court. Revelations of a wiretapped conversation in which a mobster complained of Byrne having resisted a bribe provided the Democrats with what appeared to be the perfect slogan: "Byrne: The Man Who Could Not be Bought."[66] Byrne demonstrated a flair for the dramatic when he marched into Cahill's office, tendered his resignation from the bench, and declared his candidacy on the statehouse steps.

Although Kean's district was considered safe Republican territory, he realized that he might have a tough race on his hands when a longtime supporter pulled him aside to inform him that, while he approved of Kean's performance in Trenton, he would be voting against him because he wanted to "send Dick Nixon a message."[67] Kean's difficulties were compounded by his having to run in some unfamiliar territory. As a result of another round of redistricting, Democratic-leaning Irvington had been removed from his district. In its stead, legislative mapmakers had added the Republican towns of Wayne, in Passaic County, and the borough of Lincoln Park, in Morris County. Though Wayne was Republican in orientation, many if not most of its voters were more conservative than were Republicans in the Essex County suburbs that still constituted the rest of Kean's district. More than a few had not taken well to Kean's advocacy of Cahill's ill-fated income tax. What effect the unfolding Nixon and Cahill scandals would have on Democrats and independents who had previously voted for Kean was an open question.

Citing increased business demands, Kaltenbacher withdrew from the race after winning renomination in the primary. A hastily assembled convention of county committee members from all the municipalities in the district selected Essex County vice chairwoman Jane Grey Burgio to replace him. Like Kean's, Burgio's family had been active in Essex County politics for generations. Her grandfather, Abram Blum, had been the founding mayor of Nutley, New Jersey. One of her uncles served as a town commissioner, while another served as town clerk. As a child, Burgio became interested in the political discussions conducted in the back of the butcher shop her family owned.[68] Through their work in the Young Republicans, she and her sister Ruth began volunteering in Robert W. Kean's campaigns and had befriended his son Tom. Burgio commanded a sizable following in the western Essex County suburbs, especially among women. To that base, she had been able to add business contacts her husband maintained through his tire business and his network of ham radio enthusiasts.

While the Democrats appeared resigned to Kean's reelection, they mounted a spirited effort to defeat Burgio. Their nominees for the assembly were Nicholas Saleeby, who had gone so far as to proclaim the assembly Speaker "a decent man,"[69] and Thomas P. Giblin, son of a former state senator and popular union leader who would go on to serve as both Essex County and state Democratic chairman. Kean worked the new towns in his district with the same precision he had once focused on Irvington. Taking on roles that Hausmann, Heymann, and others had once performed, outgoing assemblyman Mike Horn and young political activist Stuart Weiss began to show Kean around his new terrain.

In the largest landslide election in state history up to that time, Brendan Byrne defeated Charles Sandman by 721,378 votes. Elected with him were four-to-one Democratic majorities in both houses. In the assembly, Republican strength fell from thirty-nine seats out of eighty to fourteen. Kean and Burgio were among them. In their district Kean came in first with 18,175 votes. Burgio finished second with 16,478, Giblin third with 15,224, and Saleeby way behind. Giblin's surprising showing in Kean's hometown of Livingston and in Lincoln Park, where he placed ahead of Burgio, suggested that Kean's early fears had been warranted.

A Party Feud

Before relinquishing the Speaker's gavel, Kean had to tend to some unfinished business in Trenton. A Cahill-initiated measure to replace the part-time Public Utilities Commission (PUC) with the full-time Board of Public Utilities (BPU) had passed the senate in the spring. After Kean announced that the legislature would take the matter up during a lame duck session, two of the three part-time regulators on the PUC—former state senate president William Ozzard and Essex County Republican chair George M. Walhauser Jr.—charged that the Speaker was taking this action in order to benefit the Elizabethtown Water Company, which his family owned, and of which his brother Robert was president. Noting that they had opposed granting a rate increase to the company, Ozzard and Walhauser indicated that, given the pressures of their businesses, they would be unable to remain on the regulatory body if their positions were made full-time. They suggested that their exit would pave the way for Elizabeth to raise its rates.[70]

Ozzard further asserted that language in the bill that forbade regulators to hold local office would require him to step down as counsel to Somerset County. He suggested that Kean had inserted the measure as an act of retribution for his having blocked the rate increase.[71] Kean responded to such attacks by levying charges of his own. "The only people who oppose making the Public Utilities Commission full-time are people who will lose their jobs," he said. He also noted that Ozzard stood to lose a "$20,000 a year no-show job."[72] Buoyed by the public's revulsion at political corruption and featherbedding, the measure passed. Cahill signed it into law a month before leaving office.

Byrne Thwarts Rockefeller's Revenge

From the instant Cahill announced his intention to build a football stadium for the New York Giants, New York officials and civic boosters tried to block it at every turn. Rumors circulated that Governor Nelson Rockefeller and his brother David, then chairman of the Chase Manhattan Bank, pressured New York financial institutions to shun bonds New Jersey intended to float to finance the stadium's construction. When Rockefeller announced that New York would build a new stadium in Queens, New Jersey recalled the bonds it had already sent to market. Cahill subsequently asked the legislature to issue a "moral pledge" that obligated the state to pick up the interest costs of carrying the bonds in the event the stadium failed to be self-supporting. He and its other advocates hoped revenues raised from a racetrack to be built near the stadium would be sufficient to finance operations for the entire sports complex.

Powerful New York interests had not been the only ones opposed to Cahill's plans to move the Giants. Within New Jersey, the politically powerful Wilentz family had been working to block this eventuality. Its patriarch, Middlesex County Democratic leader David Wilentz, and his family held a controlling financial interest in the Monmouth Park Jockey Club. They feared that the private track would be unable to compete with a publicly operated one close by. Wilentz's son-in-law Leon Hess, chairman of the Hess Oil Company, in addition to his involvement with the Monmouth track, owned the New York Jets. Unhappy with conditions at Shea Stadium, where the team was located, the last thing he wanted to see was his longtime rival, New York Giants' owner Wellington Mara, obtain a state-of-the-art facility, courtesy of the state government in which his in-laws had played such a dominant role.[73]

Wilentz's younger son Robert, who had served in the assembly with Kean and preceded him as chairman of the Education Committee, acted as counsel for his family's interests. A shrewd and accomplished attorney, the younger Wilentz waged battle on many fronts, including the New Jersey and U.S. supreme courts. After losing his legal cases, he forged alliances with environmental and antitax organizations to block Cahill's proposal in the legislature.[74] During the 1973 campaign, Brendan Byrne had kept silent as to whether the state should guarantee the bonds that would finance the stadium. As legislation to do so advanced after his election, its opponents and proponents strenuously lobbied the governor-elect. The Wilentzes sought to convince Byrne that the state had been overly optimistic in its revenue projections for the stadium.

Byrne had ample cause to take the Wilentzes' views into account. David Wilentz had been among the first New Jersey political leaders to support Byrne for governor. Byrne also knew that he could not yield to all their demands without antagonizing another powerful interest that had supported his candidacy: the *Newark Star-Ledger*, which had editorialized for years on the benefits of luring professional football to New Jersey. Although Byrne would support the pending legislation, he gave his endorsement to it only after he had the Giants' lease amended to remove the exclusivity clause that restricted the stadium's use to a single occupant.[75] This opened the door for the Hess's Jets to follow the Giants across the Hudson River, as they would eventually do during Kean's first term as governor. In an aside, Byrne said the eventual solution to the problems besetting the racing industry would be for the state to take over all the remaining tracks. This, too, would occur during Kean's administration.

After Byrne announced his support for the legislation, the Wilentz group mounted a strenuous lobbying effort before the assembly. For the first time in his legislative career, Kean was conspicuously noncommittal about a major piece of legislation. He complained that he had not had time to review the lease, was not sure about the exclusivity elimination, and did not particularly want to handle the sports matter through a special session of a lame-duck legislature. He went on to say that he supported both the stadium's construction and the "moral obligation" pledge. After a two-hour filibuster, and a three-and-a-half-hour debate, the measure passed 42 to 28, with Kean voting no. As the stadium's supporters drifted from the statehouse to their cars, one of them suggested that Kean had been trying to give the project's opponents the upper hand by allowing the discussion to drag on. "I thought generally it was a good debate even though it was a little windy," Kean said after the vote.[76]

Why had Kean the legislative activist suddenly taken on the role of spectator? Perhaps he had been persuaded by the strengths of the Wilentzes' case. Robert Wilentz, Kean observed, had been one of the few legislators who could actually persuade legislators to change their minds through the force of argument.[77] (Part of Wilentz's prediction did come to pass. Over time, the racetrack would prove insufficient to finance the stadium's construction and maintenance.) Wilentz had acted as Kean's mentor in the assembly. Kean often credited him with showing him the legislative ropes, especially on the Education Committee, which Wilentz had chaired. (Kean's decision to reappoint Wilentz chief justice of the state supreme court produced one of the greatest controversies of his second term. See chapter 18.)

Although Kean had told Cahill that he supported in principle the concept of the state taking on a moral obligation to guarantee the stadium's bonds, he came to have misgivings over the manner in which Cahill's team had selected the site. State treasurer Joe McCrane's father-in-law, Eugene Mori, was reported to have owned land near where the stadium would be built. McCrane's eventual conviction for money laundering may have reinforced Kean's skepticism. When Cahill pressed Kean to acquiesce to the proposal, as Golden later recalled, Kean responded that the people Cahill had entrusted to bring the plan into fruition were about to go to jail.[78]

As the legislative session drew to a close, the "old Tom Kean" returned to public view. He voiced delight when his successor as Speaker, S. Howard Woodson, announced that he would continue Kean's practice of allowing both parties to retain professional partisan staff.[79] Kean took the occasion of the assembly transition to remind the majority party that he intended to be part of future assembly deliberations. Few on either side of the aisle envisioned how much of a role this new leader of a minority of fourteen would play.

chapter 7

In the Minority But Not in the Wilderness

Reminding Them He "Was There"

As leader of fourteen Republicans in an assembly of eighty members, Kean recognized that the "third way" strategy he had tried twice before would not be enough to enable him and his caucus to influence the direction of state policy. Instead, he tried an approach that consisted of four components: (1) holding the majority accountable; (2) presenting the Republicans as the party of reform; (3) exploiting ideological, regional, and personal divisions among feuding Democrats; and (4) using his acquired mastery of assembly rules and procedures to extract concessions from the majority party leadership. Kean began his tenure as minority leader by castigating the Democrats for abandoning some internal reforms he had put in place during the past four years. He criticized their restoring the power of the caucus, which allowed the majority party caucus to determine the flow of legislation to the floor.

On occasion, Kean appeared more liberal than the Democrats. He introduced measures shifting county welfare costs to the state, furthering a process he helped begin while still a freshman legislator; moved to ban the sale and possession of Saturday night specials (a type of handgun, then readily available); and advocated increasing the number of minority members on the state panel that allocated funds raised through bond issues. When the Byrne administration was slow to disburse matching funds raised through the state's Green Acres program, Kean attempted to steer a plan of his own through the

132

assembly's Conference Committee. He nearly succeeded.[1] When Byrne delayed declaring a position on the Tocks Island Dam, Kean publicly pressured the Democratic governor to allow Cahill's veto of the project stand.[2] Low-interest loans to Vietnam veterans who started their own businesses became another Kean cause.[3] Twice he lent his name to efforts to prevent the introduction of casino gambling into New Jersey. "The contention that the location of casinos in Atlantic City will bring about a return to that city's past glories is, in my view, a fantasy," he argued, prophetically.[4]

Kean continued to press for legislation to allow class-action suits against polluters. After industry lobbyists persuaded the assembly to weaken the bill by attaching amendments that would permit litigation only against companies that had been proved to have already violated existing statutes, he voted against his own measure in protest. "You might as well take the bill and tear it up and throw it away," he said in an impassioned speech.[5] He also pushed to limit the state's discretion in settling pollution cases out of court. In justifying his position, Kean used language more akin to antigovernment conservatives and "good government" advocates than environmentalists. He labeled the state one of the worst polluters and suggested that, if left to its own devices, it would cede too much to industry. When other Republicans criticized Byrne and the Democrats for creating the Department of the Public Advocate, Kean was supportive. "What could be more conservative or more Republican than an entity charged with holding government to account?" he asked.[6]

Yet, when Democratic leaders named only two Republicans to a committee to consider Byrne's awaited tax reform proposals, Kean attacked the majority for taking a partisan approach to such an important issue. "I think in the future you may have reason to regret this effort," he warned them.[7] That moment came six months into Byrne's term when, to the anger of many in his own party, Byrne went back on a pledge most observers believed he had made not to seek to impose a state income tax. Running for governor in 1973, Byrne stated that New Jersey could get by without an income tax for the foreseeable future. After he had become governor, he maintained that the state did not need such a tax to balance the budget but to comply with court orders requiring that alternatives to the property tax be found to fund education.[8] Byrne's advocacy of an income tax took a toll both on his overall popularity and on his standing within the Democratic Party. Six months into his term, with Byrne at odds with much of his party and Kean making the most of his opportunities, pundits observed that the Democratic legislative majority existed in name only.[9]

A Congressional Diversion

As he was settling into his new role of minority leader, Kean received a telephone call from U.S. congressman Peter H. B. Frelinghuysen. The veteran Republican had decided to retire after twenty-two years in office. Frelinghuysen said that he and several party leaders believed Kean was the person most likely to hold the seat for the Republicans.[10] Though this seat was considered safely Republican, handicappers expected fallout from the still-unfolding Watergate scandal to take an even more serious toll on Republican candidates in 1974 than it had in 1973. Freylinghuysen was not eager for a rematch with his 1972 opponent, thirty-seven-year-old television executive Fred Bohen, who had run a strong race and was expected to run again.

Kean announced his candidacy on March 26.[11] At first, he appeared headed to an easy nomination in the June primary. That changed when his former assembly colleague Millicent Fenwick announced she too would be a candidate.[12] A pipe-smoking patrician with a flair for the dramatic, Fenwick had served three years in the assembly when Cahill named her director of the state's Division of Consumer Affairs. Like two of her counterparts serving elsewhere— Betty Furness, who held a similar post in the administrations of President Lyndon B. Johnson and New York governor Nelson A. Rockefeller, and former "Miss America," Bess Meyerson, who served as New York City commissioner of consumer affairs for Mayor John V. Lindsay—Fenwick showed a knack for attracting publicity.[13] When Brendan Byrne did not immediately replace her upon taking office, Fenwick all but assumed that she would remain in her post, giving a bipartisan coloration to the Democratic state administration. When Byrne deemed otherwise, Fenwick decided to run for Congress.[14]

Kean and Fenwick had been political allies when they served together in the assembly. While each did not welcome the prospect of opposing the other, neither showed a willingness to stand aside. "All my life," Fenwick told Kean, "I have deferred to others. I just cannot do that anymore." She added that this campaign, undertaken at the age of sixty-four, would be her last opportunity.[15] When asked what would ensue in the event she lost, Fenwick said, "We'd be blessed with such a representative as Tom Kean."[16] With both candidates coming from the moderate to liberal side of the party, theirs quickly became a contrast between two distinctive political styles and a test of their organizational strengths.

Evoking an argument Harrison Williams had used against his father in 1958, Kean, as would Bohen in the general election, hinted that Fenwick might not be in Congress long enough to attain the sen-

iority necessary to be effective. Fenwick countered by citing the public service Winston Churchill, Golda Meir, and W. Averill Harriman
had rendered when all were well into their seventies.[17] In one of their
debates, Kean noticed that he had lost the audience's attention while
he was speaking. Glancing to his side, he observed Fenwick lighting
her pipe and instantly realized that he would have a fight on his
hands.[18] Both candidates tried to distance themselves from Richard
Nixon and Watergate. Kean said that he hoped and prayed that the
president was not guilty of wrongdoing and urged that the impeach-
ment process go forward so that Nixon would be able to exonerate
himself. Assuming the guise of the historian he once was, he urged
that the president's actions be seen in the context of those that his
two immediate predecessors had taken while in office.[19] Fenwick suggested that Nixon resign.

Organizationally and geographically, Fenwick started the race
with a clear advantage. Her home county of Somerset comprised 40
percent of the Fifth Congressional District. Its party chairman, Luke
Gray, headed one of the last effective Republican machines in New
Jersey. Of the forty-two towns in the congressional district, Kean had
represented only two: Livingston and Millburn. Together, they comprised 5 percent of the district. To add to that small base, Kean hoped
he could count on fourteen towns in Morris County, running as the
designated heir to Morris County's favorite son, Frelinghuysen. The
district also included three towns in Mercer County (Princeton Borough, Princeton Township, and West Windsor) and two in Middlesex.

To make up for what he lacked in superior organizational strength,
Kean introduced techniques into his campaign that had not been previously employed in primary elections in New Jersey. He advertised
on television. He used direct mail to introduce himself to likely primary voters. His campaign sent every registered Republican in the
district a newspaperlike newsletter, recounting Kean's record and
his family's long tradition in public service.[20] He maintained paid
telephone canvassers.

Kean's pioneering devices proved insufficient to match Gray's
forces on the ground. Nevertheless, Kean nearly won. He lost to Fenwick by 86 votes and picked up another 10 in the recount that followed. With a stronger push in his home base, small though it was,
he might have prevailed. As expected, he won the two Essex towns
3,688 to 424. He won the Morris portion of the district 6,241 to 4,038
and Mercer's 694 to 591. Fenwick trounced him in Somerset 7,157 to
1,699. She also carried the Middlesex towns 299 to 104.[21]

Upon learning of her victory, Fenwick declared that her only regret was that "that nice young Tom Kean had to lose."[22] Kean was more
sanguine. He would later say that his "heart had never been fully into

the race."[23] With six-year-old twin sons at home and his wife expecting their third child, had Kean been elected to Congress, he would have had to spend part of the week away from his family, as had his father before him. He was not all that eager to subject his children to the disruptions and separation from family and friends he had experienced as a child. Kean's confidants believe he ran only at his father's urging. Still, as politically ambitious and competitive as Tom Kean was at this stage of his career, he must have felt disappointment at his loss.

One thing to survive Kean's brief congressional campaign was the friendship he formed with his campaign manager, Tony Cicatiello. A native of Youngstown, Ohio, Cicatiello first became aware of Kean when he addressed a conference Cicatiello attended in New Jersey two years earlier. At the time, the twenty-five-year-old Cicatiello had been reading David Halberstam's *The Best and the Brightest,* the best-selling study of the Ivy League advisers that President John F. Kennedy had brought to Washington. Cicatiello was surprised to behold a state legislator from New Jersey who in demeanor and bearing resembled some of the figures in Halberstam's book, and who actually *quoted* from the work.[24] A year later, Cicatiello's friend Mark Haroff persuaded him to assist a young candidate for Congress whom Haroff's firm was advising, promising that this would be an easy race. The candidate turned out to be Kean. Right after Cicatiello had signed on, Fenwick announced for the seat.

Brendan's "Bad Boy"

The pace of Kean's legislative duties did not afford him time to reflect on his loss. On June 13, 1974, one week after the primary, Governor Brendan T. Byrne stood before a special session of the legislature and proposed the enactment of a state income tax with rates graduated from 1.8 percent to 8 percent. Suddenly Kean, as minority leader, was embroiled in one of the major legislative battles in New Jersey's history. Upon entering the debate, Kean set down markers that would influence not only how he would vote on this and future tax proposals but also how he would approach the very closely related issue of how to fund public education, the court-generated controversy that sparked the income-tax debate.

Once again, Kean carved out a centrist, "third way" position, this time between pro- and antitax ideologues. First, he insisted that tax rates on businesses and individuals remain competitive with those of surrounding states. He maintained that large corporations and wealthy individuals were likely to leave the state if taxes rose above a certain point and that their exodus would place an increased tax burden on those that remained. Second, he looked upon the income tax primarily as a way to raise revenue, rather than as a substitute for other taxes or as a means of redistributing income or equalizing spending on education. Generally, Kean favored a flat income tax with few deductions to a progressive income tax. He argued that taxes that looked progressive often fell hardest on the middle class, the income group that paid the most taxes and generally were allowed fewer deductions than people in higher brackets. On the matter of school financing, Kean was skeptical that increased spending on poorly performing schools, as court decisions mandated, would, by itself, improve student performance. He would continually press for uniform standards all students would be expected to meet and for benchmarks to measure their performance.

As Democrats quarreled among themselves over taxes, education financing, and a host of other issues, Kean found ways to make them pay attention to the handful of Republicans in the chamber. Often he did so through parliamentary maneuvers. His stalling of a measure that would have allocated funds raised in a previously passed bond issue was a case in point. Wrote one observer: "Assembly Republicans, with the help of some Democrats who abstained or were absent, defeated an emergency resolution—which required 60 votes for passage—to allow the measure to be voted on . . . yesterday. Minority Leader Thomas H. Kean, who led the fight to defeat the resolution, charged it was not in the public interest to vote on a measure that had not been considered for more than three minutes in the Assembly."[25]

After Kean, backed by his thirteen cohorts, performed several similar feats, Democrats found it preferable to confer with him prior to taking action, rather than afterward. "I wanted to let them know I was still there," he would later say, flashing "that grin."[26] After publicly expressing doubt that Republicans would support a proposed bond issue, he changed course after the majority leadership offered a compromise package that increased aid to mass transit. Once, he threatened to withhold the necessary votes to pass a wiretap bill but relented when assured that the measure was necessary to combat organized crime. Through moves such as these, Kean, the leader of a small minority, appeared to exert almost as much influence as he had when his party was in the majority. Such an occurrence wreaked further havoc upon those who were supposed to be in control. According to one observer:

On six occasions, the GOP has made it a point to stress that even though the lower house has been in session for a longer period than any other legislature in recent memory, the accomplishments have been minimal. And the Republicans, whose position can be negated by the Democrats at will, find themselves in a position to push around the majority. In the recent legislature, though, the Republicans have managed to gain a major concession on the question of how to solve the complex school financing question, and by giving in to the GOP, the Democrats have planted the seeds of another rift in their ranks.[27]

Not all the rifts among Democrats that Kean was able to exploit were rooted in differences over policy. Some were the result of personal, cultural, and even class differences. One day, Kean was talking with the assembly majority leader, Joseph LeFante of Hudson County, when Byrne's counsel Lew Kaden approached. Acting as though LaFante were not even there, Kaden conducted his business with Kean and departed. "That man will never talk to me. He's talking to you because you went to Princeton," LeFante confided to Kean afterward.[28] Kean filed the fact away, while remaining on good terms with both Democrats.

Toward the end of his first year as minority leader, Kean was showing signs that he had come to relish his role as the Republican skunk at what was supposed to have been a Democratic garden party. He stalled a measure to expand the membership of the Garden State Parkway's governing board by saying, "Do you know a Mayor Frank Rodgers [of Harrison]? It's been stated that this bill is to guarantee a job for Frank Rodgers."[29] When the majority passed a bill prohibiting solicitation of campaign contributions from public employees, Kean asked whether the practice was not already illegal. Taunting the majority with ridicule, he offered an amendment making it a crime to "solicit" as well as "demand"; he insisted that any bill that did not expressly outlaw the passing around of envelopes would "perpetuate the current political dinners . . . that are mostly composed of county and municipal employees."[30]

Throughout his second year as minority leader, Kean did even more to cast Republicans as the party of government reform, consumer protection, and increased accountability. He introduced a constitutional amendment calling for an elected state attorney general and state treasurer to serve as a check on the governor within the executive branch.[31] He castigated the proliferation of "legislative study commissions," which he said Democrats used as a means of avoiding facing up to problems."[32] His low regard for these commissions did not, however, discourage him from assailing Democrats for their reluctance to empower one such commission to monitor spending practices of the executive. He was particularly critical when the Democratic leadership broadened the commission's scope to include the entire executive branch as opposed to the governor alone and of its failure to name Republicans to the panel.[33]

Kean made executive abuses of perks a favored theme. He demanded that the budget specify how much money allocated for the governor's personal use could be spent on partisan politics.[34] Citing Byrne's practice of hosting monthly breakfasts for Democratic county chairmen, Kean charged that the governor had turned the executive mansion into a political clubhouse. Kean railed against allowing cabinet officers to reside rent-free in state-owned properties, replete with gardeners and maids. A favorite target of his became Ann Klein, commissioner of the Department of Institutions and Agencies, who accepted such perquisites at a time when her department was requesting that more funds be spent on the needy. With Carl Golden turning out a steady supply of releases on each of these allegations, Kean continued to make headlines.

Meanwhile, he continued his guerrilla tactics on the assembly floor. Even when they failed to bring results, Kean made Democrats pay a price in the form of negative publicity for not including Republicans in their deliberations. One journalist noted: "A Republican attempt to force immediate action on a Democratic bill was beaten back handily by the Democratic majority, after the bill's sponsor refused to go along with the tactical move. . . . Kean noted that the [open public meetings] bill had 73 of 80 sponsors and yet had been in committee for close to a year. He said he suspected the 'secret caucus' in the assembly was trying to kill it. He asked for immediate reconsideration."[35] Kean lost in this attempt 39 to 17. Still, by forcing the issue, he had picked up three Democratic votes.[36]

Not surprisingly, as legislators wrapped up business and prepared to hit the campaign trail, Kean gave the legislature a poor grade: "The inability of the two houses of the Legislature to agree on a solution to the state's tax and budgetary problems, and the almost constant haggling with the executive during this period, served to preclude action."[37] His words appeared to be uttered tongue in cheek. Nowhere did the minority leader mention the role he had played in bringing about the outcome he deplored.

Increasing the Minority

As he worked to elect more Republicans to the assembly in 1975, Kean took a personal hand in recruiting GOP challengers to incumbents and in raising and distributing campaign funds. In a break with tradition, he insisted that money he had helped raise not go primarily to incumbents, but to candidates with a chance of ousting a Democrat from office. Kean formed one of the state's first legislative political action committees. To manage it, he turned to yet another young man to whom he delegated vast responsibility: Hendrix Niemann, a recent Princeton graduate and future founder of *New Jersey Monthly* magazine. Through the PAC, Kean placed generic advertisements on radio and in newspapers that made the case for why voters should elect Republicans. Print ads and mailings included political cartoons he had commissioned, extolling favored party themes such as government reform, fiscal responsibility, and opposition to tax hikes.

His eye fixed on the state campaign, Kean delegated much of his own reelection effort to Burgio. To make better use of his time and to maximize his capacity to raise funds closer to home, the two legislators tried a rather unconventional campaign gimmick: the "non-fund-raiser fund-raiser." They sent out invitations to potential donors, offering to spare them a night of boring speeches and rubber chicken in exchange for a contribution. Many, getting the joke, sent donations. In contrast to the 1973 campaign, Kean and Burgio faced only token opposition in 1975. Two years after Kean ceased representing Irvington, the *Irvington Herald* was still endorsing him: "May we urge local residents with friends in the new 25th Legislative District to pass on a warm recommendation for support of Tom Kean and his running mate, Jane Burgio. Tom served Irvington well during the years when he was our representative in the Assembly and has since distinguished himself on a statewide basis, one of the few Republicans to survive the Democratic tidal wave of two years ago in his new bailiwick." To make it easier for readers, editor Verne Blake listed all the towns in Kean's new district.[38]

In what proved fortunate for Kean, Republican state chairman Todd and Kean persuaded President Gerald R. Ford to attend a one-thousand-dollar-per-plate dinner on behalf of the Republican State Committee. In a gesture of party unity, Kean brokered a deal through which the financially strapped state committee would receive the first thirty thousand dollars of the proceeds, with assembly candidates and the state committee dividing the rest.[39] Proceeds from the sale of tickets in southern New Jersey counties would go to retire the gubernatorial campaign debt of the regional congressman, Charles W. Sandman. Ford's remarks attested to the extent to which Kean had briefed the president on the political situation in New Jersey. Ford proclaimed the survivors of the 1973 elections "people of quality" and pointed out that their "limited block" could achieve little until they had added new recruits to their ranks. His warning of future energy crises brought to mind memories of long lines at gas pumps at the time Byrne had become governor amid energy shortages.[40] Kean made a point to have Newark's first African American mayor, Kenneth Gibson, a Democrat, on hand to greet the president. Ford's praise of Gibson's style of governance contrasted sharply with his administration's bumpy relations with New York City mayor Abe Beame. Weeks later, Ford would turn down New York City's request for emergency aid as a means of avoiding bankruptcy, sparking the famous *Daily News* headline "Ford to City: Drop Dead."[41]

In the 1975 election, Republicans more than doubled the size of their minority, bringing it from fourteen to thirty-one. As expected, Kean and Burgio coasted to an easy victory over challengers Charles P. Cohen and Joseph C. Tucci. Kean proclaimed the state returns a "good base to build on." He also saw in them another opportunity to foment further discord within Democratic ranks. Asked whether Governor Byrne had been a factor in the campaign, Kean responded in the affirmative, noting that candidates "who ran furthest away from him [Byrne] scored the best."[42] Branding Kean unresponsive and the GOP minority little more than one-man rule, Frank McDermott, a former state senate president who had won election to the assembly, announced plans to oppose Kean for minority leader.[43] Kean emerged from a twenty-minute caucus meeting as the unanimous choice of its thirty-one members.[44]

Kean Becomes Ford's New Jersey Campaign Manager

On November 16, 1975, Howard "Bo" Callaway, President Gerald R. Ford's national campaign chairman, announced that Kean would head the president's campaign in New Jersey.[45] In designating Kean, Ford's advisers passed over several other New Jersey Republicans years Kean's senior in both age and experience. Their choice of Kean displeased state party chairman Webster Todd, who said that he had not been consulted.[46] Todd had recommended the White House select Somerset County state senator Raymond H. Bateman. Todd could understand why the White House had not gone with his preference, given that Bateman had all but announced that he would be a candidate for governor in 1977. What he could not comprehend was why it went with Kean, the only other Republican believed to be contemplating a candidacy. For the moment, all Todd could do was to hope that the White House was not seeking a way for Kean, buoyed by the increased visibility and contacts his new role would bring his way, to leapfrog over Bateman to the 1977 gubernatorial nomination.

New Jersey gubernatorial politics had nothing to do with the Ford campaign's decision. Ford and his advisers had had the occasion to observe Kean at close range during the 1975 legislative campaign. They could only have been impressed at the quality of the briefing Kean had given the president and with the favorable publicity Ford's New Jersey visit received. More important, Kean had succeeded in doubling the size of the assembly's minority. That was no small achievement given the back-to-back defeats the state party had suffered in 1973 and 1974. Kean came to Ford's campaign with a proven record of having managed what all considered to have been a successful statewide campaign. Kean had also demonstrated the capacity to inject new blood into a state party that was led by an aging power structure. Moreover, there was also a high comfort level between the president and his New Jersey manager. Ford, like Nixon, knew Tom Kean as "Bob Kean's son."

Although the White House had put Kean in charge of Ford's New Jersey campaign, others still called the shots when it came to selecting delegates to the 1976 Republican convention. Todd and Case, as they had done eight years earlier, cobbled together a slate and again decided that it would run uncommitted to any candidate. While they hoped to avoid a contested primary in the state, and again succeeded, the state's uncommitted status left it open to last-minute appeals for support. This is precisely what ensued when Ronald Reagan, after a weak start, mounted a serious challenge to Ford's nomination. As one shrewd observer of the New Jersey political scene noted: "The nation's fastest shrinking party started the campaign with an incumbent president who made up the one-man field and managed to produce a two-man war and placed their incumbent in danger of defeat even before he faces the Democrats. The New Jersey Republican establishment acknowledged none of that. At a time when there was still only one real candidate, President Ford, and the state had only one way to go, the GOP opted to run uncommitted."[47]

When New Jersey elected its delegates on the last day of the primary balloting, Ford was engaged in a highly contested battle for the Republican presidential nomination. It fell to Tom Kean, as Ford's New Jersey manager, to persuade delegates who took their uncommitted status seriously to declare for Ford and to stay with him. Decades later, Kean confided that had Ronald Reagan fielded a slate of delegates against Todd and Case's, the Californian might have won as many as a third of the delegates. Some former Reagan advisers attributed the Reagan campaign's decision not to contest for delegates in New Jersey to their having to choose where to place their money in the first election of the post-Watergate era governed by spending limits.[48] Their need to "live off the land" during the early primaries, they say, militated against heavy expenditures in late-deciding states. With the attention of Reagan's high command focused elsewhere, a group of New Jersey conservatives put together a slate of their own pledged to the "former governor of California." Most were unknown to the Reagan camp, which refused to allow them to run under his name.[49]

In a disappointing showing for a sitting president, Ford won the New Hampshire primary by only 1,317 votes. After this shaky start, he won handily in Florida, Vermont, Massachusetts, and Illinois and appeared well on his way to an easy nomination. Reagan scored his first victory on March 23 in North Carolina. Pundits credited his win to the firm stance he had taken against relinquishing American sovereignty over the Panama Canal and the strength of Jesse Helms's political organization. Reagan went on to win Texas, Alabama, Georgia, Indiana, and Nebraska. Ford rebounded in West Virginia and Michigan. As the June New Jersey primary approached, those running on the uncommitted slate began to weigh their options.

Kean found his newly obtained access to the White House a powerful lever. Upon his recommendation, wavering delegates received invitations to state dinners and the Kennedy Center. Those eager to rub elbows with party celebrities, entertainers, and sports figures had their wishes granted. Kean meticulously kept track of every delegate and of how they were leaning. "After we had a certain person to a state dinner honoring Egyptian president Anwar Sadat, that person was no longer 'uncommitted,'" he joked.[50] Occasionally, he used his acquired largesse to reward party workers who had assisted in his own campaigns. Karla Squier recalled going with Kean to the White House three times before the Kansas City convention.[51]

The day before the New Jersey primary, Kean brought Ford to Paterson to rededicate the Great Falls as a National Historic Site. Stopping off at two partisan receptions afterward, Ford used his venture into New Jersey to ensure that the delegates running on the uncommitted line would support him at the convention. With Reagan much on his mind, he urged them not to "turn in a reliable Ford for a flashier model."[52]

New Jersey Gets an Income Tax

With one eye on the contest for the Republican presidential nomination, Kean kept his other fixed on what was transpiring in Trenton. In the fall of 1975, he had vigorously objected when the legislature passed the Public Schools Education Act, allocating $380 million in school spending to certain school districts without providing a funding source. Kean offered an accompanying bill (A-1736) that established uniform minimal standards for all children in the state.[53] Included in the bill were financial incentives for local districts to improve student performance and accompanying measurements. The assembly passed this measure in a vote of 67 to 9. Satisfied that the school funding formula would reflect the guidelines he had inserted into his bill, Kean joined with four other Republicans in voting to fund them through a 2 to 4 percent state income tax.[54] The assembly approved the measure 43 to 33.[55]

Following the vote, party conservatives directed their wrath against Kean. Placard-carrying demonstrators appeared across the road from his driveway. After party activists hanged Kean in effigy at a meeting of the Wayne Republican Club, Kean appeared unannounced to explain his position. While he did not completely mollify his critics, most went away satisfied that Kean, however misguided his views, was sincere in his opinions and had taken the time to listen to theirs.

When the senate, bowing to pressure from the New Jersey Education Association, weakened the accountability provisions Kean had inserted into the legislation, he tried to be conciliatory. He suggested that he might accept the senate changes and introduce a separate bill to restore the provisions in his initial bill that had been eliminated. He also remained open to voting for an income tax. Eventually he withdrew his support for the tax when the version that came to the floor contained no accompanying property tax relief, which its sponsors had promised, and few of the accountability measures he favored.[56]

As the deadline approached which the state supreme court had set for the legislature to either pass a funding mechanism or see its schools closed, Kean, on behalf of the assembly minority, appealed to the federal courts to keep schools open. Arguing on behalf of the assembly Republicans, Jonathan Goldstein, a former U.S. attorney, argued that the state supreme court lacked the authority under the state constitution to close the schools because it objected to the way they were funded. Kean argued that if a state were to enact an income tax, it should do it through the people's duly elected representatives, who acted "unfettered by the coercive action of the judiciary."[57] The federal courts refused to intervene.

On July 1, 1976, the New Jersey Supreme Court ordered the state's schools closed. Six days later, the assembly passed a 2 to 2.5 percent graduated income tax in a vote of 41 to 36. (Kean voted no and only two Republicans voted yes.)[58] The next day, the senate approved the tax 22 to 18. Though he had voted against the bill, Kean had not done all he might have to block its passage. He not only declined to allow the Republican caucus to make the measure a "party vote" but protected the two Republicans who had voted for the tax when their colleagues sought to discipline them. One of them later said Kean had even encouraged him to vote for the tax. "He [Kean] reasoned that he intended to run for governor, knew that the income tax was unpopular, thought the stated needed it, and did not want the issue hanging around."[59]

The President and the Kiddie Korps

The end of the presidential primary season set off another round of scrambling by both Ford and Reagan for support among New Jersey's uncommitted delegates. As part of his continued effort to hold the state's delegation for Ford, Kean warned on television that a Reagan nomination presaged a rerun of the Goldwater defeat of 1964.[60] With the convention fast approaching, John Sears, who had made the decision not to have Reagan mount a strong challenge to Ford in New Jersey, telephoned Kean. Sears said that he recognized that New Jersey was Ford territory. He then explained that Reagan would be passing through New Jersey on August 5 en route to another destination and wondered whether "Ronnie might be able to say a few words to the delegates" while he was in the state.[61] In what he later recognized as a mistake, Kean agreed.[62] With Kean standing, as one observer put it, "bravely in the lobby of the hotel" in Elizabeth, not far from Newark airport, Reagan and his manager, John Sears, worked on the delegates. They emerged with three additional votes, plus the backing of an alternate delegate, who was attempting to cast his vote in the stead of a delegate who had died after the primary.[63]

Until the moment of the balloting, Kean did not let the still "uncommitted" (but presumably for Ford) delegates out of his sight. Every time a rumor spread of new defections, Kean had the delegation polled.[64] Each time, Reagan's tally remained at four. To head off defections of an additional three delegates, Kean arranged for Vice President Nelson Rockefeller to meet with four Middlesex delegates.[65] Functioning as one of fourteen regional whips working the floor for Ford, Kean attempted to fend off a Reagan-inspired test of Ford's strength.[66] Reagan's supporters proposed a change in convention rules to require presidential contenders to declare their vice presidential choice prior to their official selection as the party's presidential nominee.[67] Kean echoed Ford's message that such a change would result in candidates bartering away the second spot in exchange for support for their presidential nomination.[68]

Ford edged past Reagan by a mere 117 votes, but not before Reagan's four New Jersey supporters squashed Case's attempt to cast a unanimous delegation vote for Ford.[69] Afterward, Kean was invited to Ford's suite to partake in a discussion about potential vice presidential candidates. He was impressed when Nelson Rockefeller appeared in his stocking feet to discourage Ford from allowing the delegates to make such an important decision so soon after Ford had prevailed in a heavily contested battle.[70]

On September 1, another announcement came out of Washington. Ford's new campaign manager, James Baker, declared that Kean would direct the president's New Jersey efforts in the fall. Baker said he was confident that "Tom's organizational ability and political professionalism will be a key to victory in New Jersey in November."[71] Kean wasted little time assembling an effective Ford state organization. Cicatiello directed its day-to-day operations. As its press secretary, Kean selected Greg Stevens, then a political reporter for the *Woodbridge Tribune.* Having gotten word that Rockefeller would address the New Jersey delegation, Stevens had asked Kean for a ride to the meeting. After Kean informed him that he had no room in his car, Stevens jumped onto the trunk. The lengths to which Stevens had been willing to go to get a story impressed Kean.[72]

Once on board, Stevens detected Kean's willingness to delegate considerable responsibilities to young, inexperienced aides. "If he [Kean] saw some quality he admired [in you], he would take a chance on you," Stevens recalled. "If you were good enough," he added, "you survived."[73] Scores of other young men soon joined Cicatiello and Stevens as assistants, advance men, and coordinators. Future congressman John LeBoutlier, future assemblyman Ken LeFebre, Robert Stanley Jr., and Henry Patterson Jr. were all among the newest generation of "Kean boys." The press dubbed them the "Kiddie Korps."[74]

Ford's campaign placed its New Jersey operation completely in Kean's hands. Kean advised the president to remind voters at every stop of similarities between what Jimmy Carter was promising voters in 1976 and what Brendan Byrne had told them three years earlier. (Both had promised not to impose new taxes.)[75] Kean's hand could be seen in what Ford said to audiences in New Jersey. "Don't be Byrned again," Ford told a crowd of youthful enthusiasts in northern New Jersey.[76] In Atlantic City, he said that New Jerseyans "know how risky it is when a candidate says one thing in a campaign and then does something else when he gets in public office in reference to taxes."[77]

More than a quarter of a century later, Ford could still recall remarks he made about Byrne's record, and the confidence he had in Kean as both a manager and a strategist.[78] Only once, and to Ford's subsequent regret, did he deviate from Kean's script. With the question whether to approve casino gambling in New Jersey again on the ballot, Kean advised the president not to comment on it. After suggesting that it was not his practice to voice an opinion on state issues, Ford, while in Atlantic County, where sentiment ran high in support of the measure, volunteered that he had "reservations about legalized gambling."[79]

With New Jersey a major battleground, Ford visited the state three times. Members of his family and other surrogates appeared on a weekly basis.[80] As the campaign's director, Kean served as the official host to the president and visiting dignitaries, becoming the most visible Republican in the state. A prophetic reporter speculated that whatever came of his efforts on behalf of the president, Tom Kean would come out of the election a winner: "By all accounts, Kean is calling the shots for the GOP campaign in New Jersey, who as President Ford's man in the state turns up everywhere. Should Ford win in New Jersey, Democrats and Republicans alike agree it would be a big feather in Kean's cap. Even if Ford fails to carry the state, the campaign will provide excellent training for the loyal kiddie korps Kean has installed at Ford's headquarters."[81]

Although he lost the election, Ford carried New Jersey 51 to 48 percent, finishing 53,334 votes ahead of Carter. In the months that remained in Ford's presidency, Kean made good on a promise he had made when he thought Ford would win. He brought the entire Kiddie Korps to Washington to receive the thanks of an appreciative president. Years later, Stevens recounted what Kean's action had meant to them at the time: "Kean did not have to do that. He did not have to bring these kids to see the president. That's how he grew his team. We would have done anything for him and we did."[82]

Within a few months they would be at it again.

Reaching for the Ring

On January 13, 1977, Webster Todd's premonition—that the enhanced standing the White House had given Kean might complicate Bateman's hopes to become the 1977 gubernatorial nominee—came true. Thomas H. Kean, age forty-one, stood before the microphones at the Holiday Inn in Livingston, his wife and parents at his side, and announced that he would be a candidate for governor. "I am running for governor," Kean said, "because it is the office where we can best nurture the pride New Jersey citizens want to feel in their state."[83] Kean promised to restore voters' trust in government. He vowed to let the income tax itself expire in eighteen months, as the law required, and proposed that a tax convention be convened to consider how it might be replaced.

Years later, Kean confessed that, even though he had entered the race as the decided underdog, he very much wanted to run. He had served in the assembly for ten years, had held all its major leadership positions, and felt he had achieved all he possibly could in the legislature. "I thought that I might as well go out with a bang," he recalled.[84] As had been the case when he ran for Congress, the contest between the two major candidates was more a contrast in political styles and test of organizational strength than a deabate over ideology. A reporter who had covered both Bateman and Kean contemplated the reasons that led each to seek the office: "Bateman at 49 virtually concedes he views the governorship as a cap to a productive legislative and political career that has spanned more than 29 years. . . . Kean displays a decidedly more lean and hungry political look, and no one would accuse him of being ready to retire, win or lose, this year."[85]

As Kean anticipated prior to declaring his candidacy, many within the state Republican high command were already with Bateman. At first glance, Bateman appeared an older version of Tom Kean. Bateman had been in the legislature twenty years, as opposed to Kean's ten. He had served in the leadership of both legislative chambers, while Kean had done so in only one. While both worked to improve how the legislature functioned as an institution, Bateman took an even more active role in advancing legislative reform than did Kean. Both political moderates, Bateman and Kean led their respective chambers at the same time. Both became the first to continue in their posts beyond one year. Yet because Bateman had run the upper chamber, and had served in the legislature longer, county leaders and pundits considered the senator the senior candidate. In Republican Party parlance of the era, 1977 was "Bateman's turn."

In spite of the similarities in their careers, Bateman and Kean rose to the top of the leadership ranks in different ways. Bateman had risen steadily and patiently from freshman assemblyman through senate president. Not until he ran against Byrne had he encountered serious Democratic opposition. Kean had to win a primary to obtain his first nomination and had to campaign heavily in Democratic Irvington. He subsequently fought, cajoled, or bargained his way up the legislative ladder, first by organizing the freshmen to gain leverage over his assembly elders, and later by making a deal with Hudson Democratic legislators to become assembly Speaker. Kean was in a position to make the case that he might run better than his rival in a general election. Having come within less than one hundred votes of besting Millicent Fenwick, in spite of her superior organizational backing, Kean saw little to lose and much to gain by taking on a challenge on a wider scale.

If Bateman won both the primary and the general elections, Kean would be young enough either to run for governor again or to seek one of the state's two seats in the U.S. Senate. If Bateman defeated him in the primary but lost the general election, Kean, having competed for the nomination, might be able to position himself as the inevitable Republican standard-bearer four years hence. There was also the chance that Kean would win. Besides, courtesy of Ford's campaign, he already had in place a young and enthusiastic team to assist him. Cicatiello would again be Kean's campaign manager; Stevens, its press secretary. Future lobbyist Nancy Becker signed on as issues director. The rest of the Kiddie Korps returned to their posts.

As expected, Bateman entered the race the heavy favorite. By the time of the primary, he would command the support of sixteen of the state's twenty-one county organizations. Kean went into the primary with the support of only three: Essex, Union, and Ocean. Essex's line came his way by virtue of Kean's favorite-son status. He picked up organizational backing in the other two not through the dictates of their county chairmen but through his careful cultivation of delegates to party conventions. Believing Bateman likely to take the Ocean County organization's support for granted, Kean personally courted every delegate and walked away with the prize. He did the same in Union County. In a hotly contested primary, Kean's organizational support worked to his favor, but marginally. He carried Union County by 474 votes (receiving 12,049 to Bateman's 11,575) and Ocean by only 10 (polling 12,038 to Bateman's 12,028).

In what some Kean supporters regarded as a tactical mistake, Kean entered into a deal with Bateman not to compete for the official endorsement of the Bergen County Republican organization. Instead, they opted for an open primary in which candidates' names would appear on the ballot side by side, rather than at the head of a ticket that included candidates for legislative, county, and local offices. Kean declared the arrangement a victory of sorts, because it deprived Bateman of organizational support in the county with the largest number of registered Republicans. Others maintained Kean was gaining ground and could have joined a slate that included several popular local officials, all of whom won.[86] One factor fueling Kean's perceived growing momentum was Bergen County state senator Joseph A. Woodcock's decision to drop out of the gubernatorial race and to endorse Kean.[87] In the primary, Kean finished 2,084 votes behind Bateman in Bergen (receiving 22,535 votes to Bateman's 24,619).

Kean tried to counter Bateman's superior organizational strengths, as he had Fenwick's, with television advertising and direct mail. He opened his campaign with a five-minute biography produced by Bailey-Deardourff, the company which had created similar advertisements for Ford the year earlier.[88] It contained catchy puns designed to raise Kean's name recognition. Two favorites were "Raise Kean" and "Start a Kean Mutiny." Kean supporters began identifying themselves as "Kean-raisers," sporting buttons and T-shirts. Subsequent ads and mailings recycled the "Don't be Byrned again" theme of the 1976 New Jersey Ford campaign in the form of a question. "Byrned up?" an announcer would ask. "Raise Kean" would be the reply. Kean's early and repeated use of television suggested, at least during the campaign's early phase, that he, unlike his father in 1958, was willing to dip into his own personal funds to finance his campaigns.[89]

Bateman's massive buy of TV ads in the last two weeks of the campaign overwhelmed his opposition. Kean either had decided against matching his opponent dollar-for-dollar in spending or had made the decision to do so too late to purchase the necessary airtime. Robert W. Kean admitted he never thought his son could win that primary and confided that he had been against his making the race.[90] Family councils may have decided against spending additional funds on a campaign its patriarch believed could not be won.

In the primary campaign's final days, Kean and Bateman flooded the mails with "comparative" pieces, detailing differences in their voting records. Kean sent out one reminding voters he had voted against the state income tax. Bateman countered by sending out a column Kean once wrote in support of an earlier version of the tax. Kean informed voters that he had opposed the "thorough and efficient" education funding formula, while Bateman had not, and that he favored the death penalty, which Bateman opposed. In joint appearances, Bateman employed a strategy of either ignoring Kean or taking positions identical to those of his opponent.[91]

At an event sponsored by the *Passaic Herald News* in Clifton, a bastion of anti–income tax sentiment, Kean sought to differentiate his views in voters' minds from those of his opponent. After Kean stated his preference for a tax convention, he indicated that he might be open to an income tax if the convention considered it the best option available. Seeing a chance to get to Kean's right, and therefore be more acceptable to conservatives, Bateman declared that he was unalterably opposed to an income tax. Pundits later claimed that in taking this step in order to defeat Kean, Bateman allowed himself little room in which to maneuver in the general election after Byrne asked the Republican nominee how he would meet the state's obligations without an income tax and, alternatively, what services he intended to cut, once it was repealed, in order to balance the budget.

In the primary campaign's closing days, Kean's Kiddie Korps embroiled their candidate in a controversy not of his making. After former governor William T. Cahill endorsed Bateman, a spokesman for Kean released a statement saying that the "Cahill crowd" was precisely what Kean was running against. "We are not particularly interested in the support of [former secretary of state] Paul Sherwin, [former state party chair] Nelson, and Noel Gross and Tony Statile," it continued.[92] Bateman termed the statement "the first dirty tactic and low blow of the campaign."[93] The day after its release, Kean said that the statement had gone out without his approval, did not reflect his views, and that he respected the integrity of the former governor.[94]

Kean may have had this incident on his mind years later when, in his memoir, he observed: "Tony [Cicatiello] and Greg [Stevens] are the kind of young people who have the idealism and energy that every campaign needs. You take a chance when you hire them, but I'm willing to do that. Once in a while they make mistakes, which is to be expected."[95] One observer saw its handling of the Cahill incident as a window into the strengths and weaknesses of Kean's "loyal and eager" youthful team: "Some regular GOP pols who have to deal with the Kean headquarters contend the Kiddie Korps has matured into a band of young storm troopers, but that's a standard gripe whenever the old guard comes up against new blood. And heaven knows, the Republican party needs new blood."[96]

However Kean was faring elsewhere, the *Irvington Herald* remained in his corner, noting his decade-long efforts on the town's behalf and his "integrity and statesmanlike approach to government issues."[97]

Bateman defeated Kean in a vote of 172,911 to 112,561. Kean was gracious in his concession and, for the first time since he had entered public life, took an extended vacation. He spent an entire month on Fishers Island, New York, beginning an annual summer sojourn to one of his wife's favorite places. He reassured his twin sons that his loss did not mean that they would have to move away from their friends. (Tom Jr. and Reed had friends whose families departed the area when their fathers lost their jobs.) For the first time in a decade, Kean would be not traveling regularly to Trenton. Upon his return, he showed up at Bateman's headquarters and volunteered his services, commandeering an empty desk.[98]

Having won renomination with 33 percent in a field that included seven other Democrats, Byrne wasted no time tearing into his opponent. In response to Byrne's demands that he state how he would run the state without an income tax, Bateman released a budget, ostensibly prepared in consultation with former U.S. treasury secretary William E. Simon, laden with spending cuts and increases in taxes on tobacco, liquor, and gasoline, and higher fees on certain services. Suddenly, Byrne's unpopular tax appeared the lesser of two evils. On the eve of the election, the state mailed homeowners rebates on their property taxes, financed by the income tax. Byrne's signature appeared prominently on the checks. When the balloting had concluded, the incumbent governor, who not so long ago members of his own party had written off as "one-term Byrne," won reelection by over 300,000 votes.

Byrne's New Highway Commissioner

Now out of the legislature, Kean continued at Realty Transfer, of which he was now president. He also taught public administration at Rutgers–Newark. Although he had not decided whether he would again run for governor, he sought ways to preserve his option to run.[99] One way for him to stay in the public eye presented itself shortly after the election. Safely reelected, Byrne asked Kean whether he had an interest in serving on the New Jersey Highway Authority, the independent authority that managed the Garden State Parkway. Byrne explained that he thought it would be helpful to have someone from the other party serve as a check against possible wrongdoing. Kean would replace former Democratic state chairman Salvatore A. Bontempo, who had resigned.[100] A reformer by inclination within his own party, Byrne found himself in agreement with Kean's often-expressed contentions that state contracts should be let through competitive bidding and that public bodies be held accountable to the public. As to what political utility Kean's service on the authority might be, Byrne wryly noted he had thought that "it could be helpful."[101]

Kean approached his new responsibilities with all the enthusiasm he had exhibited when still a freshman assemblyman. He took a special interest in the Garden State Arts Center, which the highway authority administered. Dismayed that the arts center had lost eighty thousand dollars in one night on a production of *Aida* by a local opera company, Kean pressed it to schedule big-name performers, such as Frank Sinatra, Tony Bennett, Johnny Mathis, Judy Collins, Jackson Browne, and Barry Manilow, and major national and international orchestras. To its roster of young and up-and-coming singers, he added the name of a young tenor, Luciano Pavarotti.

Kean used stewardship over the arts center as a vehicle through which to maintain ties with political leaders, party officials, business leaders, former legislative colleagues, and veterans of his past campaigns. He would bring many to performances as his guests and made certain that they received choice seats when he could not join them. Ronald Reagan described how Kean had used his position as highway commissioner to play official host to candidates whose election he just happened to favor: "I met Tom last year at the Ukrainian Festival, during the campaign, and he proved he was resourceful. Because I was a candidate, and Nancy and I were there together, and naturally we couldn't be on the platform at a non-partisan function like that. But Tom just happened to recognize us out there in the audience and thought the people would be happy to see us if we'd stand and take a bow, which we did."[102] Kean came away from his experience as highway commissioner well-versed in how the Garden State Parkway functioned. He also enhanced his expertise on the full range of transportation issues.

The Political Pundit

In addition to his other obligations, Kean, together with former state treasurer Richard C. Leone, a Democrat, began doing political commentary on the fledgling New Jersey Network. Sometimes the two would debate each other. On other occasions, each would appear alone on alternative nights. Because of his success in keeping New Jersey in the Republican column in the 1976 presidential election, several contenders for the 1980 Republican presidential nomination asked Kean to head their upcoming efforts in the state. Kean indicated that Ford remained his favorite, should the former president seek a rematch with Carter.

In 1978, Ford, still pondering such a possibility, returned to New Jersey to help Kean retire the debt incurred in the 1977 gubernatorial primary. As he had when Ford was the star attraction at a fund-raiser for the state party in 1975, Kean billed the event as a "unity dinner." Cahill served as master of ceremonies with Case, Bateman, and Fenwick all at the head table. The event produced some internecine sparks when Cahill declared that he considered Case too old to seek reelection after Ford had expressed the opposite opinion. With Cicatiello serving as Case's campaign manager, Reagan adviser Jeffrey Bell, having recently taken up residence in the state, defeated Case in the 1978 Republican senatorial primary. The following year, Kean was back at his old post, trying to increase the number of Republicans elected to the state assembly. Not surprisingly, he took a special interest in young assembly candidates like future congressman Bob Franks of Union County and future senate president John Bennett of Monmouth.

Ford's decision not to run for president in 1980 set the stage for a spirited contest between Ronald Reagan, George H. W. Bush, and several other contenders. Though Kean leaned toward Bush, he stayed officially neutral. He declined offers from both men to head their New Jersey primary campaign, pleading that such a function conflicted with his obligations as a political commentator. His decision left him free to interview political operatives associated with each of the campaigns, forging new friends, acquaintances, and allies in the process.

Kean opted not to attend the 1980 Republican National Convention in Detroit as a delegate but went instead as a reporter. The former columnist for the *Saint Marker* delighted in showing friends his freshly laminated press card. His duties at the convention precluded his hosting a party, as was expected of aspiring gubernatorial contenders, leaving him free to attend those his potential rivals held. In the evenings, his reportorial chores completed for the day, Kean would invite political leaders to his room to discuss "the 1981 situation." After he returned home, Kean, now in his dual capacity as political commentator *and* Reagan surrogate, continued asking people's advice. He made mental notes of what they told him, especially about past mistakes he had made and how he could attract further support.

As Kean neared his fateful decision, he would have to proceed without the advice and encouragement of his most ardent supporter. Robert W. Kean died September 21, 1980, at the age of eighty-six. Though he had gradually retreated to the background, the former congressman reveled in his son's achievements. On election nights, he and Elsa had always been among the first to arrive at headquarters; Elsa sporting a "Kean" button from one of Robert W.'s prior races, and Robert taking from his pockets yellowed tabulations of how he had fared in precincts in which Tom was competing. Tom's parents had dashed to Trenton on a bitter cold day when it appeared he might be elected Speaker. For more than a decade, Robert W. Kean had cast an admiring eye on the impact his son was having on public policy, the agility he had come to display in his handling of the press, and his success in making the assembly work.

In its tribute to one of the region's best-known and most admired residents, the *West Essex Tribune* captured the essence of the former congressman:

> Mr. Kean represented a breed of public servant that is extremely rare. He was raised in a tradition of public service for the good of the people—not the politician. He tackled everything he did with a certain unselfishness. While he definitely represented the very upper economic strata of the nation, he

recognized the basic needs of the people on social security and worked hard to improve the system. . . . In politics he was a real rarity—a true gentleman in a game where few such people could survive.[103]

Four months after this tribute appeared, another gentleman named Kean embarked on a journey that would carry him to even greater political heights.

chapter **8**

The Making of
the Governor, 1981

Positioning for the Primary

The year 1981 marked the first time when public funds would help subsidize state primary campaigns. Because candidates had to raise just fifty thousand dollars in order to qualify for two-to-one state matching funds, there were an unusually high number of contenders. Eight Republicans and thirteen Democrats competed for the gubernatorial nomination of their respective parties. The proliferation of candidates and state law's failure to provide for a runoff meant that the two eventual major party standard-bearers could be nominated by an even smaller plurality than the 33 percent Brendan Byrne had received four years earlier.

Ordinarily, Kean's reasonably good showing in the 1977 primary and his decade of service in the assembly and as its Speaker would have led party leaders to consider him the natural front-runner. However, most of the county chairmen who had spurned him four years earlier had not warmed to Kean during the intervening years. Some still smarted at his past reluctance to "wait his turn." Others offered Kean's two previous primary losses (to Fenwick and Bateman) as evidence that he could not win. Such arguments were pretexts. Kean's environmental activism and past actions to tighten ethical standards and hold government bodies accountable suggested to party power brokers that, as governor, he might be less "reliable" than other candidates would be.

Most coalesced around Paterson mayor Lawrence F. "Pat" Kramer. A four-time winner of nonpartisan elections in a Democratic stronghold, Kramer had run well in minority and working-class wards.[1] Whether he could repeat those successes in a partisan election in which he would carry the Republican label remained untested. Equally unclear was whether a Republican with his demonstrated liberalism could still win a Republican primary, given voters' recent rejection of Cahill and Case. Kramer's backers touted his capacity to run well in non-Republican strongholds as his strongest asset. Between his second and third terms as mayor, Kramer, in his capacity as commissioner of community affairs under Cahill, had, through his ability to dispense federal and state funds to localities, developed ties with party leaders across the state. Kramer began his candidacy with the backing of seven Republican county organizations.[2] Several more were poised to endorse him at the appropriate time.

Primarily because of his ability to self-finance his campaign, businessman Joseph "Bo" Sullivan also appeared a strong contender for the nomination. Sullivan, who ran a family business, Bomont Industries, touted his outsider status, his business acumen, and his self-proclaimed attractiveness to Catholics, Reagan Democrats, and social conservatives as his major strengths. The rest of the field consisted of Anthony Imperiale, who, in the years since his election to the assembly as an independent, had joined the GOP and won election to the state senate; former prosecutor and judge Richard P. McGlynn; Burlington County state senator Barry Parker; Hamilton Township Mayor Jack Rafferty; and Essex County state senator James A. Wallwork. Imperiale drew the most attention at candidates' joint appearances for the comic relief he interjected into the proceedings. At a gathering in Princeton, the burly ex-marine inquired of a well-educated, well-dressed, and well-heeled audience whether they would feel safer walking to their cars at night in a high-crime neighborhood with him or with "any of these other guys running." When asked the first thing he would do if elected, Imperiale said that he would "arrest Brendan Byrne for impersonating a governor."[3]

Handicappers considered Kean's principal assets his legislative experience, the name recognition he had acquired through his prior run, his ability to raise funds, and his genial personality. To this list, they would add the strength of the justification he offered for his candidacy. Kean's message, carefully developed with the assistance of Washington-based consultant Roger Stone, appealed to party conservatives and in ways that did not antagonize moderates. Kean had made Stone's acquaintance the previous year when the political strategist coordinated Ronald Reagan's presidential campaign in the Northeast. Although Stone failed to persuade Kean to chair Reagan's primary campaign in New Jersey, Kean had been impressed by the younger man's persistence.[4]

Kean declared his candidacy for governor on January 27, 1981.[5] As he had in 1977, he did so in a five-minute paid television advertisement produced by the firm Bailey-Deardourff. In the days and weeks preceding his announcement, Kean's campaign mailed postcards to all registered Republicans, inviting them to tune in. That effort aroused enthusiasm among his supporters and attracted ample press attention to a commercial that would only be broadcast once. The day after it aired, Kean followed up by holding press conferences in Newark, Trenton, and Cherry Hill.

In his announcement, Kean said that as governor he would focus his attention on four goals: creating jobs, reducing crime, cleaning up toxic waste sites, and preserving home rule.[6] As his campaign progressed, he advanced proposals to address each of these. To attract jobs to a state that experts were predicting would see unemployment rise to 8 percent in a period of recession, he proposed a series of tax cuts. In the event that party conservatives failed to see the parallels between his ideas and those Reagan was advancing in Washington, Kean was all too happy to remind them. He predicted that the tax cuts he advocated would do for New Jersey what Reagan's would for the country. With regard to crime, Kean favored restoring the death penalty and mandatory minimum sentences. His stance toward hazardous wastes as well as other forms of pollution ran parallel to that which he had taken toward crime. He promised to send to jail anyone who willfully polluted the state's air, soil, rivers, or groundwater. Rather than retreat from his ten-year record as an environmentalist, he recast his environmental stands as part of his anticrime package. Under the rubric of preserving home rule, he promised to restore state aid to well-performing school districts and to abandon state practices that overrode local zoning and land-use decisions.

Building a Team

After settling on Stone as his political strategist, Kean selected Roger Bodman, Congressman James A. Courter's principal political operative, to manage his campaign. Bodman had cut his political teeth working against Kean. He had assisted both Fenwick in 1974 and Bateman in 1977. In 1978, Bodman had managed Courter's successful primary campaign against the much better known Mercer County state senator William E. Schluter and Courter's winning general election campaign against the even better known incumbent congresswoman and former New Jersey first lady Helen S. Meyner. Bodman joined Kean's team as part of a "package deal" the candidate had brokered with several rising political luminaries. Harboring statewide ambitions of his own, Courter appreciated how a political alliance with a potential governor might work to his benefit. With party heavy-weights backing Kramer, Courter, with Kean and Stone's prodding, concluded that he could command greater influence with Kean. Courter became the first officeholder outside Kean's native Essex County to endorse Kean. With Courter signing on as chairman of Kean's campaign, Bodman became its manager.[7]

Freshman assemblyman Robert A. Franks joined Kean's campaign at the same time as Bodman. Franks had first encountered Kean when the future gubernatorial candidate was serving as Webster Todd's youth coordinator. Kean had addressed a gathering of teenage Republicans the sixteen-year-old Franks had assembled. Franks liked the way in which Kean had handled a difficult audience and admired his efforts to increase the state party's outreach to young people. In 1977, Franks organized "People for Bateman," a grass-roots volunteer operation committed to winning the Somerset County state senator the gubernatorial nomination. Impressed by Franks's organizational ability, Kean made a mental note to bring Franks, who subsequently had won election to the assembly, into his campaign should he run again for governor.

Al Fasola, an Indiana native and fraternity brother of Franks at DePauw University, became the third member of the triumvirate that headed Kean's campaign. Fasola had once served as executive director of the Essex County Republican organization and had managed Cahill's ill-fated 1973 primary campaign. He had worked with Franks and Bodman on Bateman's behalf in 1977. In 1981, Fasola became Kean's finance director.

To augment his team of Stone, Bodman, Franks, and Fasola, Kean made room for old loyalists. He allowed and even encouraged clusters of advisers to form around him, each able to pass along different pieces of information and a perspective his top command may have lacked. Kean had in place a functioning kitchen cabinet that included Roemmele, Kaltenbacher, Burgio, and several other veterans of past Kean operations. Cicatiello functioned as Kean's second set of eyes and ears, looking out for his well-being, resolving problems, alerting the candidate to potential dangers. He also recruited individuals to serve in key campaign positions. Dave Murray left the staff of Pennsylvania U.S. senator John Heinz to become Kean's press secretary. Another Cicatiello find, Ken Merin, then executive assistant to New York congressman William Carney, became issues director.

I served as Merin's part-time assistant, writing speeches, helping with debate preparation, and completing, for the candidate's review, questionnaires from interest groups. Having worked with Kean longer than some of the others, I was familiar enough with his legislative record and manner of speaking to prepare first drafts of speeches and first "cuts" of answers to questionnaires. Kean took pleasure in knowing that I was moonlighting in a cause of which my employers at the First Fidelity Bank disapproved. Its senior management, like most of the Newark business community, supported Kramer. After word had gotten to him that a senior officer at the bank had told me that I was backing a three-time loser, Kean told me to inform the individual that he could attend Kean's inauguration just the same.

Merin and I soon discovered that, in effect, Kean was his own issues director. After casting thousands of votes during his ten years in the assembly, Kean was better versed on state policy than any of his rivals. Merin and I routinely supplied Kean with black, loose-leaf binders filled with articles and talking points about policies being introduced in other states and at the federal level that Kean might want to recommend for New Jersey. Kean studied those binders in his car as he was driven to events. A young aide and Kean acolyte from Livingston, Steve Wlodychak, updated them each day.

James Pindar, a Roman Catholic priest and professor of English, public speaking, and rhetoric at Seton Hall University, functioned as Kean's leading surrogate and occasional driver. Early in the campaign, Pindar volunteered to help Kean tone down his New England accent. Finding the enterprise frustrating to student and teacher alike, Pindar abandoned it. Kean subsequently rejected two other suggestions political consultants had made: that he have cosmetic dental surgery to fill a prominent gap between his two front teeth and that he change the pronunciation of his name to *Keen*.[8]

In addition to his hired guns, old friends, and kitchen cabinet, Kean received assistance from opinion leaders and citizen activists whom he had gotten to know while he was in the assembly. Many of them peppered him with knowledge about the internal dynamics of their respective organizations and movements. Kean would use the information they provided to pry loose pockets of support from entities thought to be supportive of either his primary opponents or the Democrats. Several of his advisers thought it a waste of Kean's time, for instance, to appear before environmental organizations at all—and especially during primaries. Believing such audiences hopelessly Democratic in their sympathies, Bodman would intentionally ignore invitations for Kean to address them. Aware that Kean had many supporters in the environmental movement and convinced that he could acquire many more, Helen Fenske, a citizen activist who had spearheaded the grassroots campaign that blocked construction of a jetport in Morris County's Great Swamp, took matters into her own hands. She recorded on cassettes dates of upcoming events that she thought Kean should attend, along with suggested talking points.

She then arranged for Pindar to play the tapes for Kean in his car. If Kean found Fenske's arguments persuasive, he would order such appearances added to his schedule.[9]

Kean's staff found that the candidate harbored several other "Fenskes" among his contacts. Some had ties to labor groups, others to civil rights organizations, more to ethnic associations, and more than a few to conservative networks. Over the next eight years and beyond, Kean's staff would often ask themselves how he so often managed to know more about a subject than did people whose job it was to brief him. Sometimes the answer lay in the reading that Kean did prior to a meeting. On other occasions, someone he happened to know made mention of a certain topic to him. One question less often voiced was what qualities so many others saw in Kean that prompted them to want to save him from decisions people he had placed in authority had made. Kean's capacity to convey a need for assistance to those best able to provide it brought many would-be helpers his way.

Making Headway with Conservatives

Throughout the primary campaign, Kean continually presented himself as a tax cutter in the Reagan mold. His tax-cutting proposals became a marker against which the press and conservative opinion leaders assessed not only his plan but also those of his opponents. Kean advocated cutting business taxes by 50 percent, reducing the sales tax by 20 percent, and eliminating the state corporate net-worth tax and the state estate tax over four years.[10] Unlike Reagan, Kean did not call for lowering personal income taxes. With the state income tax competitive with surrounding states, he maintained that businesses he sought to attract would respond more favorably to cuts in other taxes.

To acquaint conservatives with Kean's proposals, Stone persuaded *Newsweek* to make note of Kean's tax ideas in its "Periscope" column.[11] Kean's campaign subsequently mailed copies of the article to conservative activists in New Jersey. Congressman Jack Kemp, whose Kemp-Roth tax reduction proposal formed the basis for much of what Reagan subsequently advanced, came at Courter's request to New Jersey to endorse Kean's plan.[12] An added inducement to Kemp had been Kean's embrace of urban enterprise zones, an idea the Buffalo congressman had put forward to attract businesses to areas of high unemployment through tax incentives. Soon, Kean had picked up the endorsement of the New Jersey Conservative Union.[13] Alarmed that Kean might corner the conservative market, his opponents sought to undermine his "Reaganite" credentials, noting that Kean had not

once endorsed Reagan prior to his nomination in 1980 and had sided
with Ford against Reagan in 1976.[14] Their arguments failed to convince. Sullivan, through his right-to-life stand on abortion, hoped to
attract social conservatives. Many of these, however, gravitated to
Kean primarily because he had challenged in two previous primaries
two "establishment" figures from Somerset County: Fenwick and
Bateman. Kean's willingness to play the insurgent, coupled with his
prior record of running well in the diverse ethnic enclaves of Essex
County, made him appear in their eyes less elitist than his opponents. Wallwork tried to lay claim to the conservative mantle. None
of his opponents succeeded in putting a damper on Kean's appeal to
economic conservatives.

A Beer in Bayonne and County Conventions

In March, Sullivan aired what became the most memorable political
ad of the campaign. In a thirty-second spot, a carpool of voters discussed the primary. "I heard Tom Kean was running again," said one.
"I thought he was finished the last time," chimed in another. "Can
you imagine him having a beer in a bar in Bayonne?" added a third,
laughing.[15] Kean was stung at the personal nature of Sullivan's attack
and at the ad's not-so-subtle hint of class resentment and reverse
snobbery. "It's disappointing," he said, "but I don't know what to say.
That's the tack he's taking." He added, defensively, "I think I've been
for a beer in Bayonne. I do drink more than champagne."[16] Weeks
later, Kean was regarding Sullivan's tactics as a good omen, volunteering that he "thought it kind" that Sullivan had singled him out.[17]
Kean took this as evidence that Sullivan believed that Kean was leading the field.[18] Sullivan's strategists hoped that if they could drive
Kean's approval ratings down, they could make the race a contest between Sullivan and the more liberal Kramer.[19]

With Kramer enjoying the support of those county organizations
that awarded their endorsements through votes of their respective
executive committees, Kean went after the handful that awarded
them through conventions. Middlesex County became the first battleground. Buoyed by scores of conservatives, Kean placed ahead of
Sullivan 301 to 285, with Kramer placing a poor third.[20] At the Union
County convention a week later, Kean led on the early ballot, but fell
fifty-three votes short as rivals ganged up against him and Union
Township municipal leader Earl Henwood, after sitting out early
ballots, declared for Sullivan.[21] When Kramer appeared to be coming
on strong in Ocean County, Kean took to the floor to ask his supporters to cast their votes for their favorite son from south Jersey, Barry

Parker. They complied. With three conventions behind him, Kramer, the purported favorite, had not won any, a fact both Kean and Sullivan happily kept before the press.

In the interval between the Middlesex and Union conclaves, Kean played a card that, through the publicity and funds it generated, pushed momentum his way. On April 2, Gerald Ford traveled to the state and endorsed Kean. Asked why he had not acted similarly four years earlier, the ex-president said he not been asked for his endorsement, contradicting what Kean had said to reporters prior to Ford's arrival. Pressed on the matter, Ford replied that he did not recall being asked. "I'm here to make up for my mistakes in 1977," he added.[22] Pictures of Kean and the still-popular Ford appeared on the front pages of most newspapers in the state the following day.

A Boost from an Unlikely Source

Midway through the primary campaign, Governor Brendan Byrne, with U.S. senator Bill Bradley at his side, called a press conference to propose changes in the election law governing primaries. Byrne favored raising the fifty-thousand-dollar threshold, providing for a runoff election when no candidate received in excess of 40 percent of the vote, and barring county party organizations from indicating on the primary ballot their preference for governor. Weeks later, the legislature passed Byrne's third recommendation.[23] Most observers attributed Byrne's opposition to these endorsements to his desire to improve the prospects of his preferred Democratic candidate, Attorney General John Degnan, whose support among the Democratic county organizations had been weak. Although Byrne's signature on the legislation ultimately did little to improve Degnan's prospects, it administered a fatal blow to Kramer's campaign. Kramer had based his entire campaign strategy on his ability to commandeer support from county Republican leaders. Suddenly, their capacity to deliver had been substantially reduced.

In the last weeks of the primary campaign, Kean advertised heavily on television and radio and sent out 1.5 million pieces of direct mail.[24] If, as the press noted, Kean "rolled to a comparatively easy [primary] victory," he had done so because he had waged a nearly perfect campaign. He has assembled a superior team, raised sufficient funds, spent his resources on the right things, and advanced a message that not only was popular with the primary electorate but differentiated him from his opponents. By the time the governor and legislature stripped party organizations of some ability to influence state primary nominations, Kean was already in a position to profit from their action. Although he attracted fewer votes than he had four years earlier (118,692 as opposed to 130,000), Kean led the field in thirteen counties. He had prevailed in only three in 1977. He also placed far ahead of the other candidates. Kramer came in second with 79,652 votes, Sullivan third with 64,112, and the others trailed far behind.

The Rise of James J. Florio

As Kean battled his way to the Republican gubernatorial nomination, his eventual Democratic opponent, Congressman James J. Florio, was also making his second attempt to capture his party's nomination for the state's highest office. Much as they differed in background, demeanor, and philosophy of government, Florio and Kean were evenly matched in some respects. Both were bright, well-read, good on their feet, and young. Kean was forty-six; Florio, forty-four. Florio's rise in state politics had been more combative and less steady than Kean's. It consisted of a series of primary victories and general election defeats, followed by victories and short tenures in office.

Florio had grown up in the Red Hook section of Brooklyn, New York, the son of a shipbuilder at the Brooklyn Navy Yard. After dropping out of Erasmus High School, Florio joined the navy, from which he emerged as an accomplished middleweight boxer. He attended Trenton State College on the GI Bill and Columbia University Graduate School as a Woodrow Wilson Scholar. The future politician traced his decision to enter public service to the influence of a professor, Richard E. Neustadt, who had also made an impression upon Kean. A veteran of the Truman White House and an adviser to John F. Kennedy, Neustadt urged his students to make their careers in public service. Jim Florio became one of many who did. "Neustadt changed my life," Florio said.[25]

After obtaining his M.A. degree, Florio enrolled in Rutgers Law School in Camden and became active in local Democratic politics. The winner of a contested primary for nomination to the assembly, Florio lost the general election in the Cahill landslide of 1969. He ran again two years later and won. Florio took his seat the year Kean became Speaker. A year later, Florio came within 12,000 votes of defeating the incumbent Republican congressman John C. Hunt. Again he lost in a GOP landslide, this one the product of Richard Nixon's easy reelection triumph over George McGovern in 1972. Two years later, the year Kean lost a congressional primary to Fenwick, Florio, benefiting from the Watergate scandal, defeated Hunt. His victory was one of the forty-five seats the Democrats added to their majority in the House of Representatives in 1974. Profiting from internal House reforms the sizable freshman class imposed on their elders, Florio began his congressional career as the chairman of a subcommittee. He subsequently used his chairmanship of the House Commerce Committee's Subcommittee on Transportation and Commerce as a vehicle to broaden his statewide exposure.

Three years after his election to Congress, as Kean and Bateman were competing for the 1977 Republican gubernatorial nomination, Florio became one of seven Democrats trying to wrest the Democratic gubernatorial nomination away from incumbent Brendan Byrne. Florio finished fourth, receiving 87,000 votes. Seventy-five percent of his total came from southern New Jersey; approximately half of his votes came from his congressional district. The following year, with Camden mayor and Camden County leader Angelo Ehrichetti implicated in the Abscam scandal (an FBI sting operation designed to flush out bribe-taking officials), Florio ran a slate of candidates against the organizations. Its victory left Florio the dominant political force in the county. Back in Washington, Florio sponsored legislation creating Superfund, the mechanism by which the federal government financed cleanups of toxic sites through fines collected from companies found guilty of polluting. To demonstrate his knowledge of mass transit, the environment, and other issues, Florio began holding hearings of his subcommittee not only in Washington but in New Jersey, increasing his visibility and name recognition throughout the state.

In the 1981 Democratic primary, Florio led a field of thirteen candidates, receiving 164,179 votes. Congressman Robert Roe came in second, with 98,660, followed by Newark mayor Kenneth Gibson with 95,212 votes, and senate president Joseph P. Merlino with 70,910. Again, three-fourths of Florio's votes came from southern New Jersey counties. Florio won his party's nomination with 25 percent of the vote; Kean won his with 30 percent. Both would refer to their momentous and fateful square-off as New Jersey's last "high-minded campaign."[26]

Florio Runs against Reagan

In accepting his nomination, Kean immediately went on the offensive. He challenged Florio to debate and offered to meet him at any time or place. "If he wants to go tomorrow, I'm ready," Kean said.[27] "I'll chase him around the state" became a familiar Kean refrain, as Florio showed reticence about sharing a podium with his opponent.[28] Mindful that, given the conservative stands he had taken

during the primary, Democrats might try to portray him as too conservative for the state, Kean presented Florio as too liberal. "Unless
he's changed," Kean said of his rival, "the last thing he is —is 'middle
of the road.'"[29]

Upon winning his party's nomination, Florio made clear that
he intended to run not only against Kean's economic plan but also
against Reagan's. The Democrat suggested that with the state in
midst of the most severe economic downturn since the Great Depression, Kean's program would exacerbate an already bad situation.
In taking this stand, Florio wagered that New Jersey voters would,
come November, both agree with him that Reagan's policies had failed
and express their displeasure at the polls by voting against Kean. He
hoped, too, that he could help history repeat itself by making the
election a referendum on Kean's tax proposals, just as Byrne had done
four years earlier with Bateman's. Florio's strategy of "running against
Reagan" entailed risks. The previous year, Reagan had carried New
Jersey by nearly half a million votes. His popularity soared in the
state as it did elsewhere when, in the spring of 1981, with the primary
campaign in full swing, Reagan survived a shooting by a would-be
assassin. In May 1981, on the eve of the New Jersey primary, the
Eagleton Poll recorded that 76 percent of New Jerseyans approved of
Reagan's performance, while 19 percent disapproved.[30]

With Florio trying to present Kean as a Reagan clone, Kean acted
early to inoculate himself against any possible anti-Reagan fallout by
pointing out where he disagreed with the national administration.
Kean took issue with how Interior Secretary James Watt managed national parks and enforced legislation protecting endangered species.[31] He opposed the sale of AWACS (Airborne Warning and Control
Systems) airplanes to Saudi Arabia, which Reagan was pressing.[32] He
objected to the administration's reluctance to provide operating subsidies to mass transit.[33] When Reverend Jerry Falwell, a noted social
conservative, criticized Kean for opposing a right-to-life amendment
to the U.S. Constitution and prayer in the public schools, Kean cited
the preacher's comments as further evidence that Tom Kean was his
own man.[34]

Having defined where he differed from the national administration, Kean voiced support for the president's overall approach to
taxes, spending, and crime. Kean maintained that although times had
changed since he had entered the legislature and that he had grown
more conservative with them, he continued to believe in a positive
role for state government.[35] Kean proclaimed that he regarded some
of Reagan's anticipated spending cuts as an opportunity for states to
become more active in certain areas. Though he insisted that voters
would decide the election on state rather than national issues, Kean

suggested that he would be more likely to enlist the Reagan administration as a partner in his efforts to improve the state than would Florio, who criticized practically everything Reagan attempted.

Early Moves

The first decision awaiting both candidates after the primary was who they wanted to see at the head of their respective state party operations. Although this decision technically rested with the two state committees, each of which elected its state chairman to a four-year term, gubernatorial standard-bearers, by custom, saw their choices ratified. After twice winning the Democratic gubernatorial nomination, Brendan T. Byrne had recommended that the Democratic State Committee select as its chair the party leader whose organization had done the most to secure his nomination. Both times, he quickly found himself at loggerheads with the person he had selected.[36] Kean was determined not to put himself in a similar situation. He announced at the state committee's organizational meeting that his choice for state chairman was Kaltenbacher. "I want you because you are my best friend," Kean told him, "and you are so loyal."[37] Herb Roemmele's boys were a team once again.

In another fateful decision, Kean brought Carl Golden back into his operation as press secretary, shifting Murray to the campaign's field operation. Having left the employ of the assembly not long after Kean departed, Golden had gone to work for Barry Parker and he remained with Parker after the state senator entered the gubernatorial primary. After Kean won the nomination, Kean and Golden reunited and resumed their custom of calling reporters, visiting editorial boards, and making themselves available to the press at all hours. They had the campaign retain a four-seat helicopter so that two reporters could always accompany Kean and an aide while they traveled. Florio's campaign, by contrast, rented a two-seater and usually assigned the second seat to an aide.[38]

When he journeyed by car, Kean would invite reporters to ride with him. An aide would follow behind, driving the reporter's car. Of the two candidates' availability to the press, one journalist said that reporters had to "maneuver around Florio's staff" in order to question the candidate, while Kean maneuvered "around his staff to get to reporters."[39] Kean's accessibly to reporters and the ease he showed in their presence may have subliminally influenced the coverage of the campaign. In any event, they and their editors awarded the two candidates equal amounts of space.

Kean Runs against Byrne

As Florio fired away at the Reagan administration, Kean criticized the performance of the outgoing Democratic administration in Trenton. He said that Byrne's tax and regulatory policies had driven businesses from the state. He criticized the Democratic administration for allowing the state's transportation infrastructure to deteriorate and for not preparing for the drought-like conditions the state was experiencing. Running on a "change" theme against a party that had controlled both the legislative and executive branches for eight years, Kean challenged Florio to say how his administration would differ from Byrne's. Kean's decision to make Byrne's performance a major issue in the campaign was less risky and promised greater results than Florio's efforts to make the election into a referendum on Reagan's— and for two reasons.

First, Kean and Florio were seeking election to a state rather than to a national office. Recent electoral history suggested, assisted by the state's practice of holding state and national elections in different years, that state voters did not regard state elections as referendums on the performance of national administrations. Second, Byrne's ratings were considerably lower than Reagan's. In the fall of 1981, 73 percent of registered voters rated Byrne performance in office "only fair" or "poor"; just 23 percent rated it "excellent" or "good."[40] By focusing his attacks on the Byrne administration, Kean presented Florio with a dilemma. If the Democrat agreed with any of Kean's criticisms, he risked antagonizing Democratic activists, donors, and a state administration upon which he relied for expert knowledge and assistance. If he defended Byrne's record, he stood to inherit all the retiring governor's critics. Florio sidestepped the trap Kean had set for him by focusing on stylistic and managerial differences between himself and the man he hoped to succeed. He suggested that he would take a more more hands-on approach to state government than had Byrne. He promised to centralize state government and to conduct budgeting, planning, and regulatory review from the governor's office.[41]

Having repositioned himself from the "conservative" of the primary to the "moderate-conservative" in the general election, Kean set out to make himself acceptable to major components of the electorate. More than he had in the primary, he pointed to his record on the environment, consumer protection, tenants' protection, and help for the disadvantaged. By emphasizing improved educational standards, Kean discussed education in ways that appealed to parents.

Not insignificantly, he spoke of his economic proposals more in terms of the jobs they would help create than of the taxes he intended to cut. Companies that produced high-paying jobs, he argued, decided where to base their operations on a variety of factors: the quality of the schools, the state of the environment, the presence or absence of crime, the state of the roads, the presence of cultural amenities, and, of course, tax rates. He suggested ways to make the state more attractive to such business concerns in each of these areas.

As the nominee of the dominant political party in a state where Democrats enjoyed a two-to-one edge in voter registration over Republicans, Florio had less need to appeal to Republicans and independents than Kean did to reach out to independents and Democrats. Florio's strategy appeared more calculated to increase Democratic turnout than to win converts. Nevertheless, he made an effort to win over groups who had voted heavily for Reagan the previous year. One was the so-called Reagan Democrats, people of working-class backgrounds, often members of unions, primarily Roman Catholic in religion, and of Irish American, Italian American, or eastern European ancestry. In appealing for their support, Florio tapped into the unease he perceived such voters felt about the economic downturn. He also stressed his support for the death penalty. Gun owners were another group he targeted. At this point in his career, Florio ran with the support of the National Rifle Association, which provided his campaign with considerable assistance.[42] Finally, as the first major-party candidate for state office with an Italian surname, Florio generated support from voters belonging to one of the state's largest ethnic groups.

Competing Visions

In interviews after the primary, Kean and Florio provided glimpses into how they viewed the office they sought to fill. Kean spoke in broad themes. He spoke of the importance of the public having confidence in its leaders: "In a democracy, the people must respect their leaders even while disagreeing with them and believe leaders care about them and are trying to do what is right on their behalf." He cited Reagan as an example of such a leader, taking care to indicate that he put himself in the category of those who occasionally disagreed with the president. Foreshadowing what would become the hallmark of his administration, Kean said that he would use the governorship as a vehicle through which to restore state pride. Kean's interviewer recorded that the Republican nominee came across as a man who exuded self-confidence, conveyed a sense of caring, and exhibited a style of governing through which he made "everyone working around him an integral part of the project at hand."[43]

Reporters used words like *intense, driven, controlled,* and *loner* when describing Florio. His statements suggested that he conceived of the governorship primarily in terms of procedures that needed to be mastered. He spoke of "remodeling and streamlining government in creative ways to face a world of shrinking economic resources." "Things are complicated," he liked to say; "the process is as important as the substance."[44]

One reporter described the candidate's aversion to spontaneity:

> Mr. Florio was asked to discuss his opinion of whether some services were better handled at the local government level, and he answered, in part:
> "We have to try to maximize the opportunity for modification of service delivery mechanisms with local site needs and opportunities."
> A reporter who had difficulty keeping up with Mr. Florio's rapid delivery checked the quotation with him after the meeting, and the congressman repeated it without missing a beat.[45]

Florio's avoidance of specifics when discussing any issue other than Reagan's budget and Kean's tax proposals may have been deliberate. Polls showed him going into the general election with a twelve-point lead. He had little reason to propose complicated programs that Kean could probe for weaknesses, or to take controversial stands that Kean could easily attack. His evasions, however, furnished Kean with opportunities to present himself as the candidate of ideas. Late in the campaign, Florio did advance a philosophy of government when he said, "We are not electing a governor, we are spelling out our view of the society we want." He then denounced what he labeled the "social meanness" of the Reagan administration.[46]

As the campaign progressed, Florio made Kean's economic proposals the central theme of his campaign. By the Democrat's arithmetic, New Jersey stood to lose more than $1 billion in anticipated federal aid, which Florio said the state would have to make up. Kean's plan, he said, would reduce state revenues by an additional $400 million. He described Kean's proposals as an albatross and an anchor that would weigh his opponent down, should he get the opportunity to enact them. Kean countered that his program would cost only $100 million. He said that the state could easily make up for a shortfall of this size through budget cuts. Kean allowed that, should economic conditions worsen, he would postpone implementing parts of his program. The more flexible Kean appeared, the harder it became for his opponent to paint him as a right-wing extremist.

Celebrity Endorsements

As Kean continued to run on state issues and Florio on national themes, the candidates diverged in some surprising ways in the degree to which they were willing to avail themselves of the help and attention that national spokesmen for their respective parties might bring their way. After Kean won the Republican nomination, President Reagan appeared with him twice, Vice President Bush, three times, and former president Ford, once, with Kemp, Pennsylvania governor Dick Thornburgh, and Delaware governor Pierre Dupont making frequent visits. Ailing former New York Republican senator Jacob K. Javits, who had served with Robert W. Kean in the House, signed a letter of endorsement for Kean's campaign to circulate.

Save for an occasional appearance with U.S. senator Bill Bradley of New Jersey, Florio campaigned primarily alone. The one exception he made to what appeared to be a rule was when he brought Representative Claude Pepper of Florida, known for his work on Social Security legislation, to a senior citizens' home in Irvington. Florio's most significant celebrity endorsement came his way by surprise. At an appearance before the convention of the Building and Construction Trades of the AFL-CIO in Atlantic City, Senator Edward M. Kennedy referred to the Democratic gubernatorial nominee as "a young and dynamic Congressman" who would lead the state to "new and more glorious days."[47] "I knew Kennedy was going to be here," Florio said afterward, "but I didn't know he was going to endorse me."[48] His failure to coordinate with Kennedy deprived him of the free publicity a joint appearance would have brought his way. Kennedy's popularity remained high in the state. In the New Jersey presidential primary the previous year, Kennedy had trounced incumbent president Jimmy Carter by a margin of two to one.

In their endorsement of Florio, several Democratic-leaning interest groups, accustomed to working with Kean, followed the Democratic standard-bearer's lead in attacking Reagan. Charles Marciante, president of the New Jersey AFL-CIO, said in a prepared statement that his organization was prepared to "counter a flood of conservative Republican campaign funds" expected to "affirm Reagan administration policies." All he would say about Kean was that the Republican "was an advocate of those policies." The New Jersey Education Association stated that its decision to back Florio would have been more difficult to make six or eight years earlier, noting that Kean had voted in favor of Cahill's income tax and for an early version of Byrne's, while Florio had opposed them. It listed Kean's support of "Reaganomics" as its primary reason for opposing his election.[49]

On the Stump

Consistent with his philosophy that the best way to campaign is to go right into an opponent's base and "crack it," Kean, in August, launched a $1.5-million blitz on Philadelphia television stations.[50] Several of the thirty-second spots made reference to what Kean would do to improve conditions in southern Jersey, Florio's home region. Simultaneously, the Republican State Committee began supplementing the effort with $750,000 in "institutional" ads that urged voters to elect Republican legislative candidates. All summer long, Kean made good on his promise to "chase Florio around the state." In each appearance he demanded to know when his opponent would debate him. During one of his many forays into Camden, Kean startled office workers when he walked into Florio's congressional district office and said, "Hello, I'm Tom Kean and I'm running for governor."[51]

Kean and Florio held their first debate August 26 at Monmouth College. In the course of a ninety-minute exchange, sponsored by the *Asbury Park Press* and the *Red Bank Register,* both men stuck to their overall messages: Kean pledged a change in direction in Trenton; Florio predicted that Kean's tax proposals would wreak havoc on the state. An observer spoke of Florio's "staccato, stop-and-go delivery."[52] Kean, reporters said, came across "relaxed and spontaneous"; Florio, "machinelike" and "precise."[53] Kean become the most animated when he lambasted three of Byrne's cabinet officers: Fred Burke (education), Joann Finley (health), and James Sheerhan (insurance). In a refrain reminiscent of Franklin Roosevelt's 1940 castigation of three Republican leaders, "Martin, Barton, and Fish," Kean blamed these three Byrne appointees for problems the state was experiencing in areas under their jurisdictions. Having shown himself worthy of the "happy warrior" moniker, Kean produced wide laughter throughout his audience when he said that Nationwide, an insurance company, was not nationwide any longer because it had ceased operating in New Jersey.[54]

When Florio endorsed targeted tax cuts to ensure that businesses benefiting from tax relief actually stayed in the state, Kean derided the Democrat's approach as tinkering, calling the suggestion a throwback to failed industrial policies that had government pick winners and losers. When Kean criticized Florio for opposing Reagan's policies, the Democrat answered that he did not have to apologize for voting against a budget that hurt seniors and gave windfalls to oil companies. Both candidates spoke in favor of the death penalty, changes in the school funding formula, and Reagan's recent firing of striking air traffic controllers.[55]

In his closing remarks, Kean returned to his "time for a change" theme. "We disagree about the Byrne Administration," Kean proclaimed. "He's happy with it, I'm not."[56] The parallel between how Kean chose to conclude and the manner in which Reagan had ended his exchange with Jimmy Carter a year earlier was unmistakable and deliberate. Having drawn the opportunity to have the last word, Reagan had asked his audience to consider whether they were better off in 1980 than they had been four years earlier. He suggested that those who answered in the affirmative should vote for Carter. Kean, also speaking last, suggested that those who were satisfied with Byrne's performance should vote for Florio.

While most pundits considered the first Kean-Florio debate a draw, some gave Kean the edge for holding his own and on the strengths of his "time-for-a-change" theme.[57] Audiences inside the hall and on television saw a Republican nominee thoroughly enjoying himself. After the debate ended, Kean dashed across the stage to shake hands with his opponent.[58] As Florio darted out of the hall and off to his next appearance, Kean and Golden remained, mingling with voters, granting interviews to reporters. This scene would repeat itself many times before the ballots were counted. One reporter observed that if a state trooper had been assigned to follow the two candidates, he would have ticketed Florio for speeding and arrested Kean for loitering.[59]

Kean had gone into the debate confident that he could hold his own. Fearful of Florio's reputation as a debater "with the machete tongue," his staff disagreed. They arranged for a mock debate at his headquarters. One group of aides departed with Kean to a separate room, to help the candidate cram for the upcoming exchange. Another remained where they were and prepared questions for Kean to answer. Forty minutes later, a disheveled Kean reemerged and took his place behind a lectern to debate Assemblyman Cary Edwards, playing the part of Florio. Kean flubbed every answer. Twenty minutes into the debate, he congratulated Edwards on his victory and went home, leaving his staff feeling despondent.[60] It was not until they observed Kean's actual performance the next day that Kean's crew realized they had been had. They scheduled no more mock debates.

Early in September, the man Florio tried to make the preeminent issue in the campaign made his first joint appearance with Kean. En route to an appearance in New York City on Labor Day weekend, President Ronald Reagan made a brief appearance with Kean at Newark airport. Prior to his arrival, Reagan released a statement praising Kean for his plans "to bring real economic growth to New Jersey."[61] Kean and Reagan chatted for three minutes in the president's

'A picture's worth a thousand votes . . . or more, I hope!'

Fig 8.1. After much debate within both the Kean and Reagan camps, the two sides concluded that it was in both their interests to have President Ronald Reagan, whose approval ratings were sagging during the 1981 recession, campaign for Kean. Reagan followed up on his brief September stopover with a longer appearance and much fanfare a month later. (© 1981 *The Star-Ledger*. All rights reserved. Reprinted with permission.)

compartment on Air Force One before posing for pictures. The brief-
ness of their joint appearance had been by mutual agreement. The
Kean camp was uncertain as to how heavily it wanted to associate
Kean with Reagan, whose approval ratings had fallen from 73 percent in May to 49 percent in September.[62] Believing Florio likely to
win, Reagan's advisers were skittish about investing too much of
Reagan's prestige in what they believed to be a losing effort. Stone
wrote years later that the White House had threatened that Reagan
might not campaign for Kean unless he curtailed his criticisms of
Interior Secretary James Watt.[63] The two sides concluded that it was
in their mutual interest to be seen as cooperative with each another.
Unreported at the time was that during the three minutes in which
the two were said to have exchanged pleasantries, Reagan recorded
a thirty-second radio spot for Kean.

More Beers in Bayonne

Shortly after Reagan departed, Kean officially kicked off his fall campaign with a heavily publicized tour of twelve New Jersey cities. In
Newark, his first stop, Kean faulted the Byrne administration for doing
too little to relieve prison overcrowding.[64] After speaking to a crowd
at the Casa Stoia restaurant, Kean toured Italian American wards
with his former primary rival, Anthony Imperiale, played a round of
bocce ball in Branch Brook Park, and visited Portuguese and African
American neighborhoods by himself.

On September 15, Kean paid visits to McHugh's Tavern in Bayonne and Barrett's Tavern in Jersey City. Flanked by Bo Sullivan and
U.S. labor secretary Ray Donovan, a Hudson County native, Kean ordered a round of beer for the house.[65] Kean's appearance and the accompanying publicity blunted Democratic attempts to pick up on
Sullivan's assertion that Kean lacked the common touch. The Republicans' choice of Barrett's had not been accidental A year earlier, a
boisterous crowd had welcomed Reagan to the same location. "We not
only couldn't get in on the floor," Reagan remembered, "there were
people standing on the bar."[66] While in town, Kean paid a call on Democratic mayor Dennis Collins, who confessed surprise at the depth of
the Republican candidate's familiarity with urban problems.[67] Later in
the week, Kean took his urban tour to Elizabeth, where he conferred
on urban matters with Democratic mayor Thomas Dunn.[68] As Kean
made his rounds, Florio, with Congress still in session, denounced
the Reagan administration from the House floor.[69]

In a joint appearance before the New Jersey School Boards Association, Kean lured Florio into a heated exchange over the future

of state education commissioner Fred Burke. When Florio charged that Kean, by making Burke an issue in the campaign, had undermined the morale of professional educators, Kean shot back, "It's not as if the Byrne administration has been God's gift to education." Their presentations completed, Florio departed by helicopter, while Kean lingered for an hour, mingling with his hosts, and chiding his opponent for not agreeing to more debates. When a reporter later asked Florio why he had not yet consented to more debates, the congressman showed annoyance. "Evidently, Kean has nothing else to do, but with my work in Washington, I have trouble with my schedule," he proclaimed. Days later, with Vice President Bush at his side, Kean turned Florio's Washington remark against him. "I'm sick and tired," Kean said, "of trying to run against an opponent who believes the way to campaign is by press releases from Washington." As September gave way to October, Florio was leading Kean by eight points in the polls.[70]

Playing to a Strength

Also in early October, Kean seized upon an opportunity to make headway on an issue about which he was already an expert: education. Earlier in the year, when announcing that student scores on the state basic skills examinations had improved, Education Commissioner Fred Burke predicted that student performance on the Scholastic Aptitude Tests would also rise.[71] When average SAT scores for New Jersey continued to decline, Burke said that the two tests could not be compared because more underprepared students had taken the SAT in New Jersey than elsewhere.[72] Burke's critics charged that he had watered down the basic skills test to enable more children to pass it.

Such allegations gained credence when Gustavo Mellander, president of Passaic Community College, said that students at his institution were entering college as poorly prepared as previously. He cited results of a test the state administered to incoming freshman to substantiate his claims.[73] Entering into the fray, Kean spoke of a "certain inherent cruelty in lulling students and parents to believe" that students were performing better than they actually were.[74] He promised that, as governor, he would replace Burke.[75] Mellander, a lifelong Democrat, endorsed Kean, citing the testing controversy as his reason.

When discussing education, Kean came across as both better versed on this topic and more passionate about it than his opponent.

While Florio proposed making schools cost-effective, Kean talked about "bringing excitement back to learning." He urged parents to press educators to go beyond minimum standards of proficiency by supporting high standards for students to meet. As he spoke, Kean would hold out his hand, parallel to his waist, raising it to his shoulder as told his listeners that he wanted to "raise the bar just a bit higher" for every student in the public schools, whatever their current level of performance. He spoke of attracting the best college graduates into New Jersey classrooms and ensuring that teachers came to their positions better trained in the subjects they were to teach. Before gatherings of teachers and parents, he appeared more the teacher he once was than the politician asking for votes.[76]

Informed that Florio had told one audience that he could not guarantee continued minimal aid to all school districts and, later on, suggested the opposite in a press interview, Kean resorted to ridicule: "I realize, of course, that four full days elapsed between these inconsistent positions, but is it not asking too much that a candidate for governor have a firm position on a matter of such importance? . . . It changes from newspaper to newspaper, if not from edition to edition."[77] Obviously enjoying himself, Kean suggested that residents would have to subscribe to all the major dailies in the state in order to keep abreast of Florio's position on minimal aid. Its elimination, he predicted, would force property taxes to rise by $65 million, spread over two hundred communities.

Winning One for the Gipper

On October 15, Reagan returned to New Jersey to participate in two events on Kean's behalf. At a hotel near the Morris County Airport, Reagan filmed a thirty-second television commercial for Kean. Reagan's remarks to the faithful at the Birchwood Manor in Whippany revealed that Kean had not lost his knack for briefing presidents. "Let me clear the air on a misunderstanding that evidently exists with Tom Kean's opponent," Reagan began. "It's not true that I'm running for governor of New Jersey." He quipped that Florio was unaware of that fact. Reagan then took aim at a television commercial the Democrats were running: "It's not true that I was going to take the Social Security away from that little old lady on television. I'm just trying to keep the program from going bankrupt so she would get her check. But there's one thing about doing a political commercial—she won't get residuals."[78] Reagan's visit raised $520,000 for the Republican State Committee.[79]

A Booing Backfires

Three days after Reagan departed, Kean and Florio had the last of their three formal debates in the heart of Florio's congressional district at Glassboro State College. The *Gloucester County Times* and the South Jersey Chamber of Commerce were its sponsors. That this debate would differ in tenor and tone from those that preceded it was apparent at the outset. The audience received Florio with a standing ovation and greeted Kean with boos and catcalls. The debate was unusual in another respect. Its moderator, Dick Sheeran, of Philadelphia KYW News, made no attempt to maintain order.[80] At one juncture, he responded to the heckling of Kean with the remark: "Well, we certainly have a spirited group with us today."[81]

Nor did Florio caution his supporters to be courteous. During his opening remarks, Kean cited the deteriorated condition of the road he had just driven down as an example of the state's neglect of southern New Jersey. Mistakenly, he referred to the road as Delby Drive. When it was his turn to speak, Florio began with the statement, "First of all, when we leave here, we'll drive down D-e-l-s-e-y Drive." The audience erupted into thunderous applause.[82] After Florio charged that when combined, Reagan and Kean's policies would inflict immeasurable pain on the state, Kean suggested that Byrne's recent budget cuts had already inflicted hardships on the state. "Tom doesn't know what pain is," Florio retorted, his voice dripping with distain.[83]

When the Democrat charged that Kean's tax proposals would funnel funds to multinational corporations, Kean responded, to loud boos, "That's absolute nonsense, Jim, and you know it." At one point during their exchange, Florio supporters took to chanting "Tommy Reagan, Tommy Reagan." Faint cries of "Jimmy Byrne, Jimmy Byrne" from the handful of Republicans who had been able to gain admittance to the proceedings were quickly drowned out. When Kean suggested group living for senior citizens unable to care for themselves as an alternative to nursing homes, one spectator shouted out, "Senior citizen compounds." Another yelled, "Don't put Grandma in a dormitory."[84] Although he soldiered on, Kean and his team left the hall feeling despondent. Afterward, he discovered that the experience he had endured appeared differently to people watching the debate on television than it did to those in the hall. Calls and letters of encouragement flowed into his headquarters from viewers who thought that he had been treated unfairly.[85]

The Home Stretch

In the closing weeks of the campaign, Kean, acting on what he said was information he had received from friends in Trenton, charged that, should Florio win, the Democratic legislature planned to raise the income tax in a lame-duck session. Kean pledged that he would not raise the income tax in the next four years and challenged Florio to do the same. He compared Florio's refusal to rule out that option to Byrne's statement that New Jersey could get by without an income tax for the foreseeable future. Having brought Byrne's name back into the campaign, Kean suggested that he would ask the sports authority to reconsider its decision to name its newly opened arena in Byrne's honor.[86] Byrne's granting the state authority permission to put his name on the structure contributed to his low ratings in public opinion polls, especially in Bergen County. Playing to such sentiments, the Republican national and state committees ran commercials depicting Byrne at a bill signing with a photo of the arena behind him.[87]

Kean's exuberance remained on the upswing as his campaign drew to a close. After reciting a litany of instances where Florio either contradicted himself or refused to state a position, Kean would depart from his text, throw his head back, and blurt out to the crowd, "And some people say I talk funny."[88] His self-deprecatory remark about his patrician New England accent reminded his listeners of both John F. Kennedy and Ronald Reagan.[89] On yet another return visit to Camden, with Jack Kemp back at his side, Kean suggested that his opponent was partly responsible for the deterioration that characterized so much of the city Florio represented in Congress: "You've got to wonder about a congressman who represents Camden and says he will bring to New Jersey the kind of things he brought to Camden. Well, look around—what is so good about what has happened in Camden?"[90]

Kean picked up most of the newspaper endorsements. Nineteen of the state's twenty-one dailies backed his election. In its endorsement of Florio, the *Bergen Record*, reminiscent of the NJEA, said it had wanted to support Kean but found his economic proposals "unpalatable and unworkable."[91] The *New York Times*, though it preferred Florio's targeted tax cuts to Kean's "supply side" proposals, favored the "affable" Republican (with whom it occasionally took issue) over the "loner" of a Democrat (with whom it was more frequently in agreement).[92] The *Newark Star-Ledger* praised Kean's command of state issues and decried Florio's "defeatist reaction" to

Reagan's redefined relationship between the federal government and the states.[93]

The Friday before the election, polls showed Florio with a 4 percent lead among likely voters. By Sunday, Kean had cut Florio's lead down to 2 percent. While Florio attributed the shift to "pollsters trying to create a contest where there is no contest," Kean, not surprisingly, saw things differently: "The more people knew about the race," he said, "the better I did."[94] The night before the election, Kean ended his campaign in the city in which it officially began. Before a gathering at Biase's Restaurant in Newark, he brought together the humor, ridicule, exuberance, and idealism that had characterized so many of his speeches in his yearlong quest to attain his state's highest office:

> The winds of change will sweep across Trenton.
> I want to change the programs.
> I want to change the people.
> I want to change the administration.
> My opponent won't change anything.
> He won't even change the name of the arena.
> We're going to change the name.
> The centerpiece of our campaign is to bring more jobs to the state.
> We are going to turn it around.[95]

Before the polls closed, Bodman confided to a newspaperman that he expected election night to be a "real nail biter." He did not know how right he was.

chapter 9

A Truncated Transition

"Too Close to Call"

Early gatherers to what had been billed as Kean's victory celebration at the Livingston Holiday Inn knew they were in for a long night as soon as they arrived. At 6:00 p.m., two hours before the polls were to close, Channel 7, the New York affiliate of ABC, relying on exit polls, declared a "trend" in Florio's favor.[1] Bodman went into full battle mode. "These New York stations ignore us for 364 days a year and on the 365th they tell us, before the polls have even closed, who will be New Jersey's next governor," he said.[2] Concerned that the network's report would discourage Kean supporters from voting, Bodman demanded that the station rescind its announcement. At 7:00 p.m., Channel 4, New York's NBC affiliate, on the basis of exit polls, proclaimed the contest "too close to call"; at 8:03 p.m., Channel 2, New York's CBS affiliate, called the race for Florio.[3] Kean had been watching the early returns at home. When the second network had written him off, he gathered his family and departed for the Holiday Inn, intending to concede. "Let's get this thing over with," he said to his staff as he arrived.[4] Bodman asked him to hold off.[5]

In the few minutes it had taken Kean to travel the short distance from his home to the hotel, other "trends" suggested Kean might be in the lead. First, Kean was holding his own in the southern New Jersey counties outside Florio's district. His travels into the region and heavy advertising in the Philadelphia media market were paying off. Second, Florio was not running as well as expected in working-class and Italian American enclaves, especially in heavily Democratic

Essex County. Though Kean would lose the predominantly Democratic county by 37,000 votes, he was carrying towns such as Bloomfield and Nutley and narrowly losing Belleville. Third, thanks to the
field operation Bodman, Franks, and others had put in place, Kean
was rolling up sizable margins in Monmouth, Somerset, and Ocean
counties, three musts for any Republican candidate. Kean was also
bringing Bergen County (which Bateman had lost to Byrne by 43,000
votes) back into the Republican column. He eventually carried it by
28,000 votes.

Most surprising of all was what was transpiring in heavily Democratic Middlesex County. Byrne had ouperformed Bateman there by
32,000 votes. Florio would pull ahead of Kean by only 6,000. Many
factors had helped Kean cut his losses in this Democratic bastion. Because of his often stated sympathies for people living under Soviet
domination, Ronald Reagan had run well in Middlesex precincts with
high numbers of Polish, Ukrainian, Hungarian, and Slavic American
voters. Kean worked hard to build on Reagan's showing. Middlesex
County's Republican organization, while unable to elect candidates
countywide, had long been run by conservative activists, capable of
mounting strong "get-out-the-vote" efforts for state and national
candidates. To assist them, the Republican National Committee sent
twenty full-time workers to help get out the vote in precincts Reagan
had carried, especially in such towns as Edison and East Brunswick.
Kean made it a point to campaign in Middlesex several times a week.

As the returns continued to pour in, both candidates settled in for
the long wait. The crowd at Kean's headquarters burst into cheers
when WNBC-TV called the race for Kean at 11:00 p.m.; tension rose
when it retracted its prediction moments later.[6] By midnight, it was
apparent that New Jerseyans would not know who had actually won
the election for some time. Speaking at 1:45 a.m., Kean said to his
supporters, "It's going to be a cliffhanger up to the last minute. I think
I'm going to be the next Governor."[7] "Anybody can do it the easy way,"
Florio told backers at the Cherry Hill Inn. "So we decided to stretch it
out a little to keep this rowdy crowd off the streets."[8] He too predicted
victory.

After both had spoken, Governor Brendan T. Byrne ordered all
voting machines impounded and placed under twenty-four-hour
guard. Kean later recalled that he felt confident that Byrne's action
would prevent postelectoral tampering with machines in the event
of a recount. Byrne assigned state police protection to both prospective governors-elect. Meanwhile, New Jersey chief justice Robert N.
Wilentz named retired supreme court justice Mark Sullivan to preside over the continued counting of the votes and to hear anticipated
court challenges. "I didn't know it was going to be so hard to find a

successor," Byrne quipped to reporters standing six deep in his office later in the day. When asked whether President Reagan might draw a message from the New Jersey returns, Byrne deadpanned, "Yes, he should keep buying New Jersey newspapers."[9]

The next day, Kean and Florio reverted to familiar patterns. Florio stayed away from the press. His staff announced that he had gone to a movie, alone.[10] Kean held a news conference. When asked how he was bearing up, he was unintentionally self-revealing about his emotions: "Well, I could show you ulcers. No, no. An election itself is a terribly nerve wracking experience. So, to have this tacked on to the end of it is just an addition. . . . I'm not talking about what's going on in my mind. It's just that every time you pick up the phone, you have 100 or 200 votes one way or another. And you just, well, you're concerned, then you think you're all right, and then, you wonder whether the next numbers that come in will be different." In response to the question whether he would seek a recount, Kean, assuming the role of a teacher explaining basic civics to a slow student, said, "No, we're ahead. You don't ask for a recount when you're ahead." "But if a recount is asked for," he continued, reverting to the role of the partisan, "then we are ready to respond."[11] Under state law, a recount could not commence until after the twenty-one counties had reported their final tallies, which they were required to do one week after an election.

Charges and Countercharges

As they awaited the official county returns, both campaigns made charges and countercharges, as if in preparation to challenge the ultimate results in court. Republican state chairman Kaltenbacher demanded that Donald Lan, the secretary of state, and his assistant play no role in tallying returns.[12] Both had participated in Florio's campaign, and the secretary of state served as clerk to the Board of Canvassers that would certify the final results. Byrne said that Lan's role would be ministerial in nature. With the Lan controversy subsiding, Florio charged that the one hundred volunteers the Republicans had sent to inner-city precincts, ostensibly to caution voters against violating election laws, had intimidated citizens, many of them African American, from voting.[13] The Election Day activities Florio described had been part of a "ballot security program" the Republican National Committed had initiated.

The national party, under the auspices of Ronald Kaufman, a close adviser to Vice President George H. W. Bush, had mounted a seventy-five-thousand-dollar operation to guard against possible voter fraud.[14]

Prior to the election, Republican officials mailed letters to voters, primarily in Democratic precincts, asking them to volunteer for the GOP. Mail that was returned for incorrect or insufficient addresses they took to local election officials and requested that the addressees be removed from voting rolls. Between the primary and the general elections, county election officials deleted abut twenty-six thousand names from voting lists that the Republicans had identified in this manner.[15] Though Democrats saw sinister motives behind the mailing, no one questioned the legality of the operation. Contrary to boasts on the part of national party officials, the practice was hardly new. Robert W. Kean had employed it when he first ran for Congress in 1938.[16]

Reports soon surfaced that on Election Day volunteers, wearing armbands and claiming to be part of the National Ballot Security Task Force, descended on polling places in the inner cities. They posted signs that read: "Warning: This area is being policed by the National Ballot Security Task Force. It is a crime to falsify a ballot or to violate election laws. If you are not registered, you cannot vote. You must vote in your own name. You may only vote one time."[17] The signs urged citizens to report violations and included a telephone number for them to call to report fraudulent activities. The telephone number proved to be the toll-free number of the Republican State Committee. A court ordered the signs removed. Rumors circulated that the Ballot Security volunteers had instructed residents of public housing projects that they could not vote if they had had any problems with the law.[18]

Following up on Florio's assertions, Democrats charged that Republican operatives had carried firearms into polling places.[19] Republican spokesmen, including Golden, said the party availed itself of off-duty policemen, who volunteered to escort lawyers into polling places in "rough areas." These lawyers had been part of the thousand-member Lawyers for Kean that Essex County political activist Conrad Koch and Bergen County assemblyman Cary Edwards had assembled to stand guard against election law violations.

The controversy widened when Newark's North Ward councilman Anthony Carrino, a longtime rival of Anthony Imperiale, asserted that the "volunteers" had not been off-duty policemen, but employees of a security firm that Imperiale operated.[20] He charged that Imperiale's agents had rushed into polling places "like a Gestapo." Imperiale admitted that he had sent thirty-five employees to the polls, but denied that they had worn armbands. He subsequently pleaded guilty to the technical violation of not placing disclaimers on signs they posted.

Democrats never formally charged ballot security officials with legal wrongdoing. In order to have persuaded a court that Republican poll workers had intimidated voters, they would have had to produce sufficient numbers of affidavits signed by voters substantiating such claims. Kean accurately summarized the situation when he later said, "I have not heard yet, in spite of tremendous efforts by all sorts of political people, of any voter who was intimidated in any way."[21] Few voters filed complaints.[22] Asked what he knew about Imperiale's Election Day activities, Kean said, in what had to have been the greatest understatement of the political season, that Imperiale had been "helpful" to him, as had all his other primary opponents.[23] For the second time, it appeared that Kean's path to higher office had been cleared, in part, through the actions of a stylistic opposite. Like David Friedland before him, Imperiale rather than Kean attracted the bulk of the criticism.

The Appearance and Disappearance of Jack Kelly

With the Imperiale controversy still in the news, Democratic operatives and the media turned their attention to the campaign activities of a non–New Jerseyan who went by the name of Jack Kelly. Part of "Commitment '81," Kaufman's operation that brought workers from other states to New Jersey to organize rallies, run canvasses, distribute literature, and man telephone banks, Kelly showed up in New Jersey after Labor Day. Bodman had carefully divided GOP headquarters into two sections, delineating where Kean's operation left off and Kaufman's began. Attired in jeans, cowboy boots, and a ten-gallon hat, his feet propped upon desks, Kelly regaled youthful campaign aides with tales of the times he had spent palling about with the likes of none other than Ronald Reagan, former Texas governor John Connally, and others. Many assumed he was a Texan.

In the days preceding the election, Kelly visited county courthouses, demanding to inspect emergency ballots, paper ballots voters could use when machines malfunctioned. He identified himself as a lawyer sent by the White House. Claiming a background in law enforcement, he declared himself on official business. The press's interest in Kelly grew after some GOP operatives identified him as the person who had distributed the signs that had caused so much controversy. With the number of reporters and officials wanting to talk with him on the rise, Kelly mysteriously disappeared. "He took off like a big bird right after the election," one Kean aide said.[24] Neither Notre Dame, nor Fordham Universities, institutions he said he had attended, appeared to have any record of his having enrolled.[25] In the ensuing weeks, Kelly's true identity, his whereabouts, and what he had done on Election Day became questions asked almost as frequently as who had won the election.

Throughout these controversies, Kean maintained that he was unfamiliar with details of what exactly his helpers had attempted to achieve on his behalf. Given the frantic pace of the campaign he had waged in its final weeks, putting in between twelve- and sixteen-hour days, his assertion seems plausible, if not likely. "I gather there were people posting notices and wearing armbands," Kean said. "They weren't part of the Kean campaign—not that I know of." "In any campaign," he continued, "sometimes people go overboard."[26] Of Kelly, he said, "There are a lot of people who want to know more about Jack Kelly. I'm one of them."[27] Kean noted that he was under the impression the Republicans were trying to prevent a recurrence of voter fraud in the state. "We make jokes about graveyard voting," he said. Fearing possible fraud, he voiced concern that ballots might suddenly appear "in some basement hall in Jersey City or Camden."[28]

Kean's "Inevitability"

As the counties prepared to certify their tallies, Florio remained largely out of sight. Kean remained visible. At headquarters, Kean led reporters on a tour of his operation as party workers prepared for a possible recount. The next day, the *New York Times* ran on its front page a photograph of Kean, embraced in a bear hug with longtime supporter Karla Squier.[29] "Had it been anyone else," Debby Kean joked to Squier afterward, "Tommy would have been long out the door."[30] The Friday following the election, Reagan, again on his way to New York City, stopped at Newark airport to give Kean a moral boost. "Make sure those numbers hold up," the president cautioned his protégé.[31] Two days later, Kean showed up at a performance of the New Jersey State Opera. The press carried photographs the next day of Kean standing beside singer Birgit Nilsson.

Kean's public displays of optimism were part of a wider strategy he and his advisers had devised to convey the impression of Kean's "inevitability" as the state's next governor.[32] Six days after the election, certified results from the counties showed Kean leading by 1,677 votes.[33] As Kean huddled with his staff, contemplating how best to turn the news to their advantage, someone blurted out, "Why don't we just announce that we won?"[34] The day after the counties had reported, Kean stood in the assembly chamber and told hundreds of supporters that, to the best of his knowledge, every single vote had been counted and that he would be the next governor.[35]

Having declared himself governor-elect, Kean next announced

his transition team. He named as cochairman Lewis B. Thurston III (executive director of the election law enforcement commission and a former GOP state senate aide) and Nicholas Brady (chairman of the investment firm Dillon Read and a close friend of Vice President Bush). The names of the rest of the members read like a list of a potential cabinet, consisting of representatives from business and government, minorities, women, and all geographic regions.[36] Florio called Kean's announcement presumptuous.[37] Borrowing a line from Winston Churchill, the congressman, then planning to ask for a recount, proclaimed that "it ain't over until the fat lady sings."[38] Days later, Florio requested a recount of the entire state.[39]

"Curiouser and Curiouser"

The day before the recount was to begin, the state police appeared at Kean's headquarters and confiscated two voting machines Bodman had rented to train those who would participate in the recount. An employee of a lumber company situated next door to the headquarters had noticed the machines in the parking lot. Having heard that voting machines had been impounded, the employee became suspicious and telephoned the state police. Heated words ensued between campaign officials and the office of the attorney general, which oversees the state police. The press reported that throughout the incident, the only person at headquarters who appeared unruffled by the entire affair was Kean. "It gets curiouser and curiouser," the would-be governor said, shaking his head as the offending machines were being carted off. "Isn't what they said in *Alice in Wonderland?*" he inquired of no one in particular.[40]

The recount commenced November 18. As the candidates squabbled over minor procedures (Florio demanding minor party candidate totals be recounted; Kean, that computer cards be counted manually), media attention shifted back to Jack Kelly, who suddenly reappeared. Speaking through his attorney, Kelly told the Essex County prosecutor that he had been in charge of all Ballot Security Task Force activities on Election Day. He took responsibility for the disputed signs but denied violating laws or intimidating voters.[41] Kelly had spent the interval between his two ventures into New Jersey in Oklahoma. He had told certain RNC officials that he was working to elect Republican County officials and others that he was performing inquiries on behalf of the Drug Enforcement Administration.[42] The RNC suspended Kelly from his post with pay, pending resolution of an internal investigation into misstatements on his résumé. Kean said that from everything he had heard about him, Kelly was a "con man."[43]

He added that those who had been taken in the most by the mysterious visitor had been those in his campaign.[44]

On November 24, Kean, in another of his free-flowing discussions with reporters, resumed the posture of the "inevitable" governor. He complained that the slowness of the recount was impeding his ability to form an administration. He urged the lame-duck legislature not to pass major legislation without consulting him and voiced the hope that he and the Democratic legislature would be able to work together in a bipartisan manner.[45]

Days before the Board of Canvassers was to convene, Florio accepted the county certifications as valid and conceded defeat. He declared himself satisfied that Kean had indeed won the election and no longer hinted that he might file suit to overturn the election.[46] The recounts results revealed that Kean had won the election by 1,797 votes.[47]

On December 2, 1981, Kean returned to the assembly chamber and pledged an administration that "would bring pride and prestige to the state." He promised to cut corporate taxes, re-instate the death penalty, and "cut back the size of government" and said he would be flexible as to when he would introduce the rest of his economic proposals, depending on the economic condition of the state. Again, he pledged not to raise the state income tax in the course of his term.[48]

That evening, Kean and his supporters held their long-postponed victory party. In a reference to Florio's observation about a fat lady singing, Kean introduced a "large" special guest. In a dress stuffed with pillows, and donning a Wagnerian helmet, a Kean volunteer burst into song. To "The Battle Hymn of the Republic," she recited lyrics that parodied various episodes of the campaign. When she finished, Karla Squier presented Kean with a directional sign she had acquired in an antique shop. It bore the words *Tom's turn*. None of the party leaders at whom she had directed her message took issue with it. Tom Kean's turn to be governor of New Jersey had arrived.

The Troika

After being certified governor-elect, Kean made his first appointment. He announced that Lewis B. Thurston III, who was already cochairing Kean's transition effort, would be his chief of staff. The move took most of Kean's campaign staff by surprise. "All of a sudden, he just appeared," Bodman said of Thurston's joining Kean's entourage after the election.[49] During the campaign, Kean had quietly asked Thurston to brief him on issues coming before the legislature. He happened not to mention Thurston's assignment to his campaign team. Some saw Kean's choice of Thurston as evidence that he sought to shift his emphasis away from politics and toward governing.

Kean would be the first governor since Meyner in 1953 to take office with his party in control of neither house of the legislature. Elected with him was an assembly which the Democrats dominated (forty-four to thirty-six). Awaiting him was a Senate the Democrats controlled (twenty-two to eighteen). In order to succeed, he would have to forge alliances with Democrats. Thurston appeared perfectly cast to assist in this regard. As the nonpartisan executive director of the bipartisan Election Law Enforcement Commission, he had been barred by law from partisan political activity. In his years as a Republican senate staffer, he had not shown much of a partisan edge. The press reacted positively to Thurston's selection. He was a familiar face with a pleasant demeanor who was said to "know his way around Trenton." Less evident to most observers were Thurston's administrative deficiencies. Fifteen months into this term, Kean would replace him as chief of staff with Greg Stevens, his 1977 campaign press secretary.

Seasoned Kean watchers had expected the chief of staff post to go to Joe Gonzalez, who had all but functioned in a similar capacity to Kean during his days in the assembly leadership. Rumor had it that Kean passed over Gonzalez because of a falling-out he had had with Carl Golden after Kean had departed the legislature. Bringing Gonzales back into the picture, some speculated, would have introduced unwelcome strains into Kean's inner circle. Cicatiello, another obvious choice for the job, preferred building his business, CN Communications, to going into government. He would continue troubleshooting for Kean, but from the outside.

Under different circumstances—without the ballot security controversy and the ensuing recount and with the Republicans in command of at least one legislative chamber—Kean might have retained Bodman as his chief of staff. At twenty-nine, Bodman had again demonstrated his skills as a political operative, having executed the strategy that brought Kean, however narrowly, to victory. Yet Bodman lacked experience in state government. Wanting to avail himself of Bodman's skills, Kean designated his former campaign manager as his principal emissary to organized labor, then Jim Florio's most loyal constituency. As Kean's labor commissioner, Bodman put the state's unemployment compensation fund, once on the verge of bankruptcy, on sound financial footing; brought order to a department that had been wrecked by financial mismanagement; and helped Kean pass the transportation trust fund, one of the hallmarks of his administration. Later, as Kean's transportation commissioner, Bodman oversaw the implementation of programs he helped enact.

No sooner had he announced Thurston's appointment than Kean noted that his pick would function as part of a troika with two other senior advisers. They would be expected to operate as equals. He named Cary Edwards, recently elected to the assembly leadership, as his counsel and Gary Stein, Kean's friend from his National Guard days, as his director of policy and planning.[50] In introducing the troika system to his operation, Kean was adopting a practice Ronald Reagan had implemented with successful results.[51] Brendan Byrne had also put the troika model into place during his first term, but he eventually abandoned the idea in favor of a strong chief of staff, as would Reagan and, later, Kean.[52] Some observers and even participants found the troika arrangement more a source of confusion than clarity, with lobbyists and legislators shopping their wares among competing power centers in the hope of finding a sympathetic ear in at least one.[53]

Bright, gregarious, and ambitious, Edwards, thirty-seven, quickly established himself as Kean's point man with the legislature. Before long, he was using the foothold the counsel's job afforded him into the state budget, itself a piece of legislation, as the vehicle through which to shape priorities for cabinet departments. As he would later claim, Edwards had taken control of the budget before Kean had even named a state treasurer. Because the New Jersey governor must approve the minutes of independent authorities in order for them to operate, Edwards could also affect what they did through his capacity to recommend that Kean sign or veto them. To assist him, Edwards retained a staff of twenty-six assistant counsel. His predecessor had managed with only twelve.[54] Hard-charging and hardworking, Edwards and the mini–law firm that he had set up within Kean's operation brought a youthful enthusiasm into the governor's office. Officials wanting to get in a word about their budgetary requests or render a plea for gubernatorial support for a certain measure could find Edwards on most nights, after midnight, at the Princetonian Diner on Route 1, where he conducted late-night study groups and bull sessions with his youthful aides.

Stein, at forty-eight, was the member of Kean's inner circle who was the closest to him in age, had known him the longest, and was the most confident of his standing with him. Around the time Kean left Kean-Taylor to teach at St. Mark's, Stein began practicing law in Paramus and dabbled in Bergen County politics. Working with a yellow legal pad and a staff of never more than three, Stein did the spadework that helped produce three of Kean's major achievements during his first years in office: prison-overcrowding relief, the transportation trust fund, and the high-technology initiative.

Recruiting the Rest of the Team

With his troika and labor secretary in place, Kean set out to fill constitutional offices whose terms would run concurrent with his. To fill
the post of attorney general, Kean turned to Irwin Kimmelman, a former assemblyman and judge, who had vigorously stood guard over
Kean's interests during the recount.

As secretary of state, he named his second legislative running
mate, Jane Burgio. Kean's choice of Burgio suggested he had learned
yet another lesson from his predecessors' experiences. For years, governors habitually named their principal political operative secretary
of state. From that post, the person who had helped commandeer the
governor's election tended to party affairs and political patronage.
The indictments of three successive secretaries of state in the 1970s
on corruption charges suddenly brought the position, as well as much
of state government, into disrepute.

Kean wanted to fill the post with someone of strong integrity and
upon whom he could rely to advance his administration's goals. In
the eight years she served in the assembly, Burgio had gotten along
well with colleagues of both parties. The possessor of a ready smile
and an easy way with people, she proved a ready and effective surrogate for Kean, especially with women's and cultural organizations.
"I'm not out to change the world," Burgio said after her appointment
was announced." I just want to improve the part I live in."[55] In the
course of eight years, the parts of state government that would come
under her aegis would grow. By the end of Kean's time in office, Burgio's department, once a sleepy backwater, was functioning in all but
name as the state's department of cultural affairs.

With this handful of appointees poised to take their places by the
time of his inauguration, Kean said that he might not have the rest of
his team in place until at least six weeks after he had taken office. To
help him fill posts that called for special expertise, Kean turned to a
professional executive search firm. This marked the first time in state
history when a governor would seek such professional assistance
during a transition.[56] Working with Kean at cost, the Morristown firm
of Christenson and Montgomery located two individuals who, as cabinet officers, would help Kean make good on his promise to stimulate
the state's economy and attract new businesses to the state.[57] One of
them, Borden Putnam, senior vice president at American Cyanamid,
became the first commissioner of the recently created New Jersey
Department of Commerce. The other, Kenneth Biederman, an economist with the City Federal Bank, became Kean's state treasurer.
Kean's appointment of Biederman, a registered Democrat, who had

voted in the previous year's Democratic primary, proved particularly controversial within Republican Party circles. Mercer County party officials found it especially irksome that Biederman's wife was serving as a member on the Democratic County Committee of Pennington at a time when they were scurrying to produce as many votes for Kean as possible during the 1981 campaign.

Kean selected Leonard Coleman, head of the Urban League, as energy commissioner; Michael Horn, the former assemblyman who had once guided Kean through the thickets of the town of Wayne, as banking commissioner; Robert Hughey, a former college instructor and professional planner, as commissioner of environmental protection; Gloucester County Republican chairman Eugene McCaffrey as president of the Civil Service Commission; Dr. Shirley Mayer as health commissioner; Essex County chairman John Renna as commissioner of community affairs; and Joseph Rodriquez as public advocate.

Byrne holdovers who reported not directly to the governor but to supervisory boards remained at the Departments of Agriculture and Higher Education. Upon the advice of criminologists, jurists, and organizations representing prison guards, Kean retained Byrne's commissioner of corrections, William Fauver.

Upon Cicatiello's recommendation, Kean picked Union County administrator George Albanese, thirty-seven, to serve as commissioner of human services. Albanese would run the department that had the biggest budget, largest number of employees, and that administered and provided programs for the indigent, disabled, mentally ill, children, and others in need of help.

Ironically, Kean encountered the most difficulty finding the person who would head the department whose mission most interested him: education. It would take him six months to place the right person at its helm.

As he relied on multiple advisers within his "official family," Kean continued to draw upon networks of people whose input he had come to value in the course of his career. Some were personal friends; others, politicians; and many, recognized experts in certain fields. Just as he had depended on environmental activist Helen Fenske to provide him with information he was not getting through conventional channels, Kean made sure that several people he respected were strategically placed within or on the peripheries of his administration in either full-time or voluntary posts where they could take stock of certain issues and keep him apprised of what was transpiring in certain state agencies. He developed the practice of appointing at least one personal friend or longtime acquaintance to important boards and commissions. Even if these contacts did not use the access they had to him to talk shop, the presence of Kean confidants in such posts served as a check on bureaucratic inertia or inattention.

Kean named his first campaign manager, Herb Roemmele, chairman of the governing board of the University of Medicine and Dentistry; his first running mate, Phil Kaltenbacher, chairman of the Port Authority of New York and New Jersey; campaign fund-raiser Jon Hanson chairman of the Sports and Exposition Authority; his long-time friend Cicatiello to the Rutgers University Board of Governors; his boyhood friend from St. Alban's School Bob Neff to the state racing commission; and a close friend of him and his wife, Margot Codey, to an advisory board on missing persons. And so it went. (In the months prior to my appointment as assistant secretary of state, Kean asked me to serve on a panel to advise him on how federal block grants earmarked for education might best be spent.)

A Smooth Transition

Weeks before his inauguration, Kean—perhaps in deference to the narrowness of his win and the prospect of divided government, with a Republican governor and a Democratic legislature—announced that he would take a "go slow" approach in the making of policy recommendations and suggested that he would work with the leadership of both parties to develop a legislative program. Such an approach was entirely consistent with the one he had taken when he became assembly Speaker, also by the narrowest of margins. Kean entered office assuming that he would have an easier time working with the legislature than had his three predecessors, none of whom had much legislative experience.[58] Having held every senior post in the assembly, where he retained many friendships, Kean hoped that the personal bonds he had established would help him transcend partisan and institutional differences between the two branches of government. Predisposed to govern by consensus, he assumed that his counterparts would respond positively to his overtures. When his early optimism proved unwarranted, he developed ways to circumvent the legislature where he could and to bring pressure to bear on it from the outside on behalf of his agenda when he could not.

The easy rapport Kean enjoyed with Byrne made for a smooth transition. Byrne promised to consult with Kean on major decisions and pledged not to sign into law measures Kean opposed. He also guided through the legislature salary raises for the cabinet officers as a means of enabling Kean to attract top-notch people to key posts.[59] When assembly Speaker Christopher Jackman made passage of the pay raises conditional upon Kean's acquiescence to a measure that exempted interest on savings from state income taxes, Kean declared himself a convert to Jackman's views.[60] Byrne further accommodated Kean by naming the governor-elect's designee, Jon Hanson, as one of his two final appointments to the sports authority. "And I gave [Kean] the better car," Byrne later joked.[61]

A New Spirit of Government

At Kean's direction, his inaugural committee organized a series of preinaugural concerts and galas showcasing New Jersey cultural institutions. "New Jersey has never accepted its proper responsibilities in cultural affairs," he proclaimed.[62] His inaugural committee became the first to distribute a share of its proceeds to cultural institutions. Inaugural events included performances by the New Jersey Opera, Symphony, and Ballet, in addition to name entertainers such as Bill Cosby and Tony Bennett. Events took place in Atlantic City, Newark, and Trenton.

In fashioning his inaugural address, Kean turned to an old friend from his days as a volunteer for Bill Scranton: James Humes, a former Pennsylvania state legislator and presidential speechwriter.[63] Kean took as his theme the need to redefine the state's relationship with the federal government, in an era when the national administration wished to turn more powers over to the states and reduce the growth of domestic spending. Kean called for bipartisan solutions to problems ranging from crime to those associated with transportation, the environment, urban areas, and education. Echoing earlier times in American history when the nation confronted similar challenges, Kean—reminiscent of Wilson, Roosevelt, and Kennedy—called for a "new spirit" of government that would define New Jersey's relationship with the federal government in the Reagan era. "Let us prove that a region is built not by what it takes from Washington but by what it makes on its own," Kean declared.[64]

Almost as an afterthought, Humes had tacked onto the speech a prayer that William Livingston had penned two centuries earlier, which seemed to fit the times in which his collateral descendant, Tom Kean, was taking office: "Our father, smile on the Governor, may he walk in uprightness and his ways please the Lord. Teach our legislators wisdom, let them be reasonable men such as that fear God, men of truth hating covetousness, so that justice may run as a mighty stream and righteousness as a river, and peace be within our borders and in our dwellings. Amen."[65]

During Kean's first months in office, he and his team would come to lament that, however reasonable legislators may have been in Livingston's day, their leaders proved particularly obstinate in Kean's.

chapter 10

Kean Settles In

By his own account, Tom Kean's first year in office was hardly his happiest.[1] Three of his appointees to major posts either had to withdraw from consideration or vacate their posts because of misstated or insufficient credentials. A fourth, his health commissioner, resigned after nine months in office. Kean and his wife became embroiled in a dispute with the New Jersey Historical Society over its purchase of furnishings for the official governor's residence. Kean decided to replace his chief of staff. (See chapter 16.) Six months into his term, sudden and acute back pain forced Kean into the hospital, where he underwent traction for the better part of a month. None of these setbacks proved as frustrating to Kean as his inability to find common ground with the Democratic legislative leadership, especially in the assembly, in order to pass his first budget. All through his first term, Kean faced Democratic majorities in both legislative houses.

A Change of Assembly Speakers

Kean had come into office aware that he would be inheriting a budgetary shortfall. Optimistic projections forecast a deficit of $130 million at the end of the fiscal year, which expired at the end of June. As he had indicated in the campaign, Kean believed he could close a gap of this size through hiring freezes, spending cuts, and layoffs.[2] During his first months in office, budget projections changed almost daily, with forecasted shortfalls increasingly higher for both the current and future fiscal years. By the time Kean delivered his much-awaited budget address, the estimated shortfall stood at $527 million. The projected deficit would top $700 million by the time Kean and the legislative leadership agreed on a plan to bring the budget into balance.

Three factors peculiar to the early 1980s contributed to the increasingly pessimistic budgetary projections that faced Kean and his fellow governors of the era. First, back-to-back recessions in 1980 and 1982 produced shortages of revenue, especially from state income taxes. Anticipated cutbacks in federal aid compounded the problems state budgeters faced as policy makers wrestled over how much of this shortfall they would make up with state-generated funds. In addition, an unexpected and sudden drop in the inflation rate, fueled by the Federal Reserve's tightening of credit, caused state budget analysts to pair down previously projected revenue estimates even further. Although Kean would make limited adjustments to it, the budget he submitted for fiscal year 1983 had been assembled, for the most part, by the previous administration.

As he made his final changes to the budget, evidence mounted that the legislative leadership, especially in the lower house, where all money bills originated, was not as prepared to work with him on a bipartisan basis as he had hoped. Democratic recalcitrance, especially in the assembly, could be attributed to a change in Speakers. Weeks before Kean took office, Alan Karcher (D-Middlesex), age thirty-eight, defeated incumbent Speaker Christopher Jackman (D-Hudson) by five votes. Jackman, a full-time union official, had been seeking an unprecedented third term as Speaker. The state AFL-CIO had not taken kindly to his defeat.[3] Jackman and Kean had gotten along well when they served together in the assembly. During the Byrne-Kean transition, Jackman had helped move legislation Kean favored. He would be in a position to assist Kean again, but not right away, and not with the full powers of the speakership at his disposal.

A lawyer by profession, Karcher came from a long line of Middlesex County politicians. Both his father and great-uncle had served in the assembly. Karcher was working as executive secretary to Governor Richard J. Hughes when Kean first entered the assembly in 1968. He won election to the assembly in 1973, the year that Brendan Byrne was elected governor in a landslide and, with the Republicans losing control of the assembly, Kean went from Speaker to minority leader. Although Karcher would long be remembered as one of his party's leading liberals, he had begun his legislative career as one of the most conservative Democrats in his party's caucus.[4] Unlike Kean, who had voted for the first of several income tax proposals Byrne put forward, Karcher had opposed them all.

Whereas Jackman had been known as a conciliator, Karcher's reputation had been that of a partisan brawler. "Given a choice between a wise compromise and a good public scrap," Kean wrote, "[Karcher] will take the scrap every time."[5] After he had become Speaker, Karcher, while moving decidedly to the left in his political philosophy, did not alter his political style. He quickly put Kean on notice that, should the governor attempt to enact the economic plan he had advanced during the campaign, he, as Speaker, would "hold the line" against it as firmly as his counterpart in the U.S. House of Representatives, Speaker Tip O'Neill (D-MA), had, with some success, resisted some of Reagan's budget proposals.[6] At its core, Karcher's strategy was to force Kean, by whatever means, to go back on his pledge not to raise the income tax during his first four years as governor. He hoped that any success he achieved in that area would erode Kean's credibility, thereby weakening his chances of reelection.

Karcher's stance suggested that he, like Florio before him, underestimated both Kean and Reagan. In adopting it, he assumed that the economic slump in which the state found itself when Kean took office would continue at least through Kean's term. The Speaker also failed to anticipate how Kean might either maneuver around him, or, as he had while a legislator, pick up the votes of enough Democrats to

Fig 10.1. Kean spent much of his first term at loggerheads with the Speaker of the assembly, Alan Karcher, over spending and other priorities. The governor came to outmaneuver his antagonist by circumventing the legislature, where possible, and by applying outside pressure on it when he could not. (© 1983 *The Star-Ledger*. All rights reserved. Reprinted with permission.)

pass his program. In an assembly where Democrats enjoyed a six-member majority, if Kean established an informal arrangement with Jackman, who controlled six votes from Hudson County, he might exercise effective control of the lower chamber, where the Republicans held thirty-seven seats.[7] For that to ensue, however, Kean first had to get his program to the floor. And that was something Karcher was determined to prevent.

Upon his election as Speaker, Karcher told Kean through the press that "if he [the governor] is talking about bi-partisanship" he would have to "deal with the Democratic Party as a whole."[8] What he meant was through its elected leadership. It soon became apparent that the two men's definition of *bipartisanship* differed considerably. To Kean, the term conveyed compromise. To Karcher, it implied capitulation. "We will work with the Governor," he said, "as long as his programs mesh with ours."[9] When Karcher's counterpart, senate president Carmen Orechio (D-Essex), exhibited a greater willingness to work with Kean, Karcher set out to make himself the preeminent spokesman for Democrats in both houses.[10] As Kean prepared the final changes to his budget, Karcher told him to expect a "short honeymoon."[11] That is precisely what he gave him.

The Battle of the Budget: Round One

In the run-up to his budget address in March, delayed a month so that Kean could digest the rapidly changing budgetary estimates, he made several symbolic gestures to demonstrate that he was doing what he could to cut state spending as a means of bringing the budget into balance. He announced hiring freezes, capped departmental expenditures, and sold thousands of state cars. Later in the year, he ended the practice he had long criticized of providing rent-free housing and other perquisites to state officials. He also invited business leaders to advise him how to cut expenses and improve services in all state departments and state agencies.[12]

In his first address to the legislature, Kean proposed a $6.3-billion budget. His budget increased spending over the previous year by $630 million. Of the $202 million he requested for new programs, Kean included $100 million for immediate transportation projects and repairs, $7 million for prisons (later increased to $20 million), $8 million for new job-training programs, $4 million for tourism promotion, and modest jumps in the funds for the arts. He provided $45 million in "stimulatory" tax relief to businesses. He wanted to reduce the corporate tax from 9.0 to 8.5 percent and exempt businesses from having to pay net-worth taxes on the first $100,000 of assests as the initial step in a complete phase-out of the net-worth tax over four years. At the same time as he was cutting taxes for businesses, Kean recommended taking away one benefit they were receiving when he called for decoupling state depreciation schedules from the federal code so that New Jersey businesses would not enjoy the full benefits of accelerated depreciation under the Economic Recovery Tax Act of 1981.[13]

To close the deficit, pay for new programs, and offset the tax cuts, Kean proposed raising the gasoline tax from 8 to 10 percent.[14] Kean sought to raise an additional $35 million by raising cigarette taxes by three cents per pack. He proposed raising college tuition between seventy-five and one hundred dollars per student, transit fares 25 percent, and suggested raising at least an additional $10 million through the sale of state-owned land. Kean's advisers expected the gas tax to generate an extra $200 million and recommended a constitutional amendment that would ensure that funds raised through this source would be dedicated to road and infrastructure repairs.

Kean proclaimed transportation among his highest priorities, arguing that improvements in the state's transportation system were a precursor to economic recovery.[15] The state senate's minority leader estimated that nearly a third of the state's 10,500 miles of roads and its 2,271 bridges needed repair and at a cost of $15 billion over the next decade.[16] Kean said that the increase in the gasoline tax would cost the average motorist an additional thirty to forty dollars each year. He predicted they would find this preferable to paying more money on automotive repairs if the state continued to put off necessary repairs to its roads.[17]

To obtain additional revenues, Kean had the state retain money it raised through the gross-receipts taxes—money that it had traditionally passed along to municipalities. Utility companies paid these taxes in lieu of property taxes to locales in which they operated generating stations or ran power lines. Rising energy costs had caused gross-receipts revenues to swell at a time when revenues raised through other means fell during the two recessions. With gross-receipts taxes totaling $650 million in 1981 and rising on average $150 million a year, and the state increasing other aid it gave municipalities, they proved a tempting place for any governor to look when trying to balance a budget.

Democrats wasted no time denouncing Kean's budget. Senator Lawrence Weiss (D-Middlesex), chairman of the Joint Appropriations Committee, declared it out of balance because it presupposed passage of the gas and cigarette tax increases. Other Democrats proclaimed that the corporate tax reductions were giveaways to the rich and argued that the hike in the gas tax was a regressive tax increase on the middle class and the poor. "Robin Hood in reverse" became a refrain they took to using while condemning Kean's tax cuts and gas tax hike. In what would be the first of several self-revelatory outbursts, Karcher suggested that his reservations were rooted not so much in his recently acquired populist ideology as in personal pique. "What really upsets me," he said, "is that two years ago, I proposed a 10 percent tax on gasoline instead of the 8 percent tax, and the Republicans denounced it as 'repugnant' and now their Governor [Kean] is asking them to vote for it . . . that's what I find hypocritical."[18] The Speaker declared that before any Democrat voted to increase the gas tax, every Republican in both legislative chambers would have to go on record as favoring the measure. That proved a tall order.

Some Republicans opposed raising the gas tax on principle. Others wanted deeper spending cuts. Many, including some of Kean's leading allies in both chambers, complained that they had not been consulted beforehand about Kean's proposals and first learned about them in the press.[19] Days before Kean's budgetary address, Edwards and Biederman briefed several editorial boards on their budget proposals on an "embargoed" basis. "That," Kean recalled, was when "all hell broke loose." The *Bergen Record* printed many of the details on its front page. The *Star-Ledger* followed with pie charts, replete with spending figures and percentages.[20]

As Karcher and other critics of Kean's budget concentrated their fire on the gas tax, Kean became more aggressive about withholding funds raised through the gross-receipts tax. He said he would veto any bill that allowed municipalities to keep 100 percent of funds they were receiving through this levy. Karcher charged that Kean was trying to steal money from taxpayers and called Kean's maneuver a subtle attempt to establish a statewide property tax. As Kean's gas tax proposal neared a vote in the assembly, it was Karcher who went on the offensive. In the absence of 100 percent Republican support for Kean's measure, Karcher submitted a budget that underspent Kean's by $266. It included two items Kean had deliberately left out of his budget submission: a return of $35 million in gross-receipts tax revenues to municipalities and $43 million in additional school aid. Karcher also removed from his budget items that Kean especially wanted, such as his requests for additional funds for roads, prisons, and job training.

Karcher suggested that in the event Kean could get the gas tax increase through the legislature, Democrats might rescind the cuts they had made to his proposals. He stated that the price for this accommodation would be retention of the gross-receipts tax refunds and the school aid. Kean suggested he might be amenable to this deal if the legislature found a way to fund Karcher's priorities. Kean then threatened additional cuts in spending to meet any existing and mounting shortfalls. When Kean mailed layoff notices to five thousand state workers, Karcher branded his action an exercise in terror.

As the fiscal year drew to a close, Kean, Karcher, and Orechio came together temporarily in order to meet the constitutional requirement that the budget be balanced by the end of the fiscal year. Democrats cut Kean's $45 million in tax cuts for business to $14 million, but agreed to his proposal to reduce the corporate net-worth tax by 25 percent each year until it had been phased out. They also ap-

'Stick 'em up, I'm desperate!'

Fig 10.2. Kean's plans to close a mounting budgetary deficit by raising the gas tax aroused much opposition, much of it within his own party. (© 1982 *The Star-Ledger.* All rights reserved. Reprinted with permission.)

proved his recommended increase in the cigarette tax. As a result of intensive administration lobbying, eleven assembly Democrats, breaking away from Karcher, joined thirty-one assembly Republicans to approve Kean's gas tax increase. The measure fell one vote short in the senate, where fourteen Republicans and six Democrats voted in its favor. A yes vote from any of three Republicans who abstained from voting would have secured its passage.

When the senate returned from a brief recess, four Republicans who had voted yes, citing pressure from their constituents, switched their votes to no.[21] Afterward, legislators of both parties complained that Kean might have picked up the necessary number of votes had he been willing to engage in conventional arm-twisting and horse-trading, to which legislators had grown accustomed. Kean eschewed such tactics. He also believed that they would prove ineffective, because legislators, learning of what had been promised their counterparts, would begin upping the ante. "My idea is to reason with them, to explain that a program is right and that it meets the needs of the state," he said upon learning that his gas tax proposal had been defeated.[22] Kean volunteered that one legislator offered to vote the administration's way if Kean made a certain person a judge and that he had refused.[23] Some of Kean's critics charged that he might have been able to attract the additional vote he needed had he called the legislature into special session rather than allowing it to recess.

When Kean complained that the defeat of his budget proposals, which included not only the gas tax increase but also his proposal to cut corporate taxes, dealt a serious blow to the state's economic revival, Karcher countered that the primary impediment to the state's recovery was Kean's leadership. He suggested that Kean had become "literally paralyzed by his own party."[24] Kean refused to take defeat personally or to respond in kind, saying only that there was plenty of blame on all sides. He vowed to press on with alternative proposals to improve the state's business climate.[25]

In the aftermath of the defeat of Kean's gasoline tax increase, Democrats seized the initiative. They slashed from the budget Kean's recommended $100-million increase for roads, the $4 million in additional funds he wanted to promote tourism, and $13 million of the $20-million increase he requested for prisons. They also removed $15 million in minimum school aid, intended for suburban districts, reopening an argument that the two parties had waged since the state began providing aid to municipalities at the end of the Hughes administration. Gloating at Kean's predicament, Karcher offered to bail him out. He suggested that Democrats might help Kean raise the gas tax, in order to avert a "collapse of the state's transportation system," in exchange for Kean giving them a greater say over appointments and the setting of state priorities. "In effect," the speaker said, "we are looking to form a coalition government."[26] In what he considered a moment of triumph, the Speaker overreached.

Karcher had admitted that he shared Kean's assessment of the condition of the state's infrastructure and that he had refused Kean's requests solely on partisan grounds. In suggesting that he might be open to Kean's ideas, in exchange for a sharing of power, Karcher had also revealed that he thought they would work. Kean ignored Karcher's power-sharing offer. Instead, he sought to bring the budget into greater balance through his ability to "line-item veto" spending measures. When Kean made good on his promise to veto municipal and school aid, Karcher charged him with perfidy and treachery.[27]

A Glowing Success amid Mounting Frustrations

Days later, after touring the Mid-State Correction Facility at Fort Dix, Kean, most uncharacteristically, lashed out against his Democratic adversaries. He called the reductions in his prison aid both stupid and insensitive.[28] Weiss pronounced Kean's remarks "not worthy of a governor," but of a "petulant child."[29] Kean insisted that the cuts in his recommended increases would undermine his efforts to relieve prison overcrowding.

In the years preceding his election, rising crime rates, coupled with legislatively imposed mandatory minimum sentences and restrictions on parole, had produced a dramatic increase in the prison population. Simply put, more prisoners were entering correctional institutions each year than were leaving them. By the time of Kean's inauguration, incoming prisoners were exceeding parolees by several hundred a month.[30] County jails, ill-equipped to house violent criminals, overflowed with prisoners bound for state penitentiaries that lacked space to house them. Following up on a request Kean had made during his campaign, the Reagan administration allowed the state to construct a prefabricated five-hundred-bed unit at Fort Dix on land leased from the military. The site would house less violent criminals, freeing up room in the prison system for those who had committed more serious crimes. In his budget, Kean had allocated funds to construct additional prefabricated units elsewhere. Creative though it was, the Kean-Reagan plan was, at best, a short-term solution. During his time as governor, Kean doubled the size of the state's prison capacity through construction of new prisons, financed through two bond issues.

In addition to seeking temporary shelter for prisoners not needing to be housed in maximum-security facilities, Kean's administration sought out ways to prevent less violent offenders from turning into hardened criminals. Stein had worked out an arrangement through which four hundred of these offenders would, under strict supervision, be able to avoid incarceration and hold paying jobs. They would pay the costs of their rehabilitation and counseling, perform community service, participate in drug and alcohol rehabilitation, and make restitution to their victims. Costs to the state per parolee were five thousand dollars annually, as compared to the fifteen thousand dollars per year it cost to incarcerate them.[31] Kean became the plan's strongest advocate. When the legislature cut the $2 million he had included in his budget to launch the pilot program, he grew incensed. His uncharacteristic outburst was anything but the temper tantrum Weiss had called it, but a calculated endeavor to draw public attention to the issue and to put the legislature on the defensive. Soon he was applying pressure to it in other ways.

Aware that public support for new prisons had not kept pace with increasing clamor for tougher sentences, longer incarcerations, and the death penalty, Kean warned that unless overcrowding were relieved, judges would turn violent criminals loose on the streets. He made prison construction a part of his overall anticrime package, which included reimplementation of the death penalty, thirty-year minimum prison terms for those who had committed capital crimes, consecutive sentencing, and trying juvenile offenders as adults. In April of 1982, he proposed placing on the November ballot a referendum that would allow the state to borrow $170 million to build new prisons and renovate existing ones.

Rather than oppose the measure, Democrats, seeking to benefit from the anticipated regional competition for the new facilities, demanded that the referendum state precisely where new prisons would be built. This was the first of several occasions when Democrats sought to set spending and other priorities for Kean initiatives they considered inevitable. While Kean's team cautioned that bond houses took a dim view of referenda that specified in detail how proceeds would be allocated, they were quick to inform big-city mayors that their locales would receive consideration.[32] To serve as one of the honorary chairmen of a citizens committee to campaign for the bond issue's passage, Kean named former governor and chief justice Richard Hughes, perhaps the most popular Democrat in the state.

With his proposal coming on the heels of New York State voters' rejection of a prison construction program two years earlier, Kean left little to chance. His efforts on behalf of the prison bond issue became the first of many public education campaigns Kean launched in which he would take his case directly to the public, going over the heads of entrenched politicians. In reaching out to political leaders of the Democratic strongholds of Newark, Paterson, and Camden, and in drawing to his side an esteemed Democratic predecessor, Kean had found a way to get his priorities out from under Karcher's grasp. He would revert to this practice repeatedly during his first term. That fall, the prison referendum passed. Another one, requesting $198 million, would be approved by voters five years later. By the time Kean left office in 1989, no one spoke of a prison crisis.

One thing Kean did not envision when he put this strategy into place was that he would sign the measure that put the prison bond issue on the ballot from a hospital bed. As part of the visible cost-cutting measures he had taken to demonstrate his commitment to holding down the costs of government, Kean flew to his first meeting of the National Governors Association in a National Guard plane. After sitting for several hours on a wooden bench affixed to the floor on a flight to Oklahoma, he complained of pain in his legs and lower back. Upon his return, he was diagnosed with a disc ailment and spent nearly a month in St. Barnabas Hospital. His hospitalization attracted more attention and expressions of sympathy and support than had his budgetary recommendations. People with back ailments all across the country flooded the hospital with letters and telephone calls suggesting remedies and names of specialists. Though unintended, the episode established for Kean a celebrity status rarely bestowed on state political figures.

The Battle of the Budget: Round Two

With the governor and the legislature at a stalemate, Karcher made his long expected attempt to force Kean to accept an increase in the income tax. To blunt charges that partisanship was his primary motivation, Karcher cast about for Republican allies. He did not have to search far. Senator Wayne Dumont of Warren County not only opposed Kean's gas tax increase but had introduced a bill to raise the income tax while Kean's proposal was still being debated. Dumont proposed raising income tax rates on incomes in excess of $40,000 per year. He also favored increasing the rates from the then 2 percent assessment to between 2 percent and 6.5 percent. With Dumont's plan already in circulation, Karcher proposed a plan that raised the tax on incomes that exceeded $25,000 per year.[33] In presenting his plan, Karcher sanctimoniously suggested that he and Dumont had done what Kean had asked. They had, he said, found a way to fund Democratic and Republican budgetary recommendations through an alternative to the gas tax. Kean responded that raising the income tax would be the worst thing the state could do during a recession.[34]

As the governor and the Speaker argued over the merits of various tax proposals, nine Middlesex County municipalities, all under Democratic control—presumably at Karcher's urging—took Kean to court. They argued that he had exceeded his authority by withholding gross-receipts revenues from them without legislative authorization.[35] The courts subsequently declared Kean's actions constitutional on the grounds that the governor, through his capacity to line-item veto, was part of the legislative process and that the legislature, through its power to override the executive, had the opportunity to exercise an appropriate check on his action.

As summer gave way to fall, Karcher overplayed his hand a second time when he charged that Kean's failure to find a revenue source to fund the anticipated deficit had left the state technically insolvent. Fearful of the impact such a statement might have on the state's bond ratings, Orechio suggested that his colleague had engaged in sensationalism.[36] After the congressional elections in the fall of 1982, Kean said that he would cut the budget 3 percent across the board as a cost-cutting move. To the surprise of his listeners, he also announced that he would reintroduce the gas tax increase and call the legislature into special session to consider it. Given his previously stated view that he expected Reagan to succeed in raising the federal gas tax an additional five cents per gallon and that such an action would render a subsequent hike in state gas taxes unlikely, Kean's reasons for declaring the special session were unclear.

Having convened the special session, Kean further confounded observers when he failed to request that it meet in "continuous session." Instead, Kean said he hoped that the legislature would "meet every day and on Saturday, if need be, to solve the problem." Editorial writers and even some longtime Kean allies complained the governor was not being tough enough. Dean Gallo, the assembly minority leader, suggested that he appeared "unwilling to go to the mat."[37] In the opinion of some, Kean and his team had not been hard enough on Republican senators in the spring and too soft on assembly and senate Democrats in the fall.

Denouement

As 1982 drew to a close, Kean had only two options, both of them unpleasant. He could either go along with Karcher's demands to raise the income tax or follow through with his threats to cut the budget. Legislators claimed not to know his preferences. Some suggested that in his meetings with legislators, he came across more as a sounding board than as an initiator. In his defense, Kean maintained that he had reached a point with the assembly leadership where once he indicated what he found unacceptable, that would be what they would try to give him.[38]

Kean's stance was as much the product of calculation as of circumstance. If he were to abandon his pledge not to raise the income tax during his first term, he would first demonstrate that he had exhausted all the other alternatives. The approach he settled on was one of passive aggression. Although he knew he would be criticized for going back on a promise, Kean would not have to face the electorate for another three years. Legislators, especially Democrats in "swing districts," would have to justify their votes in the 1983 off-year elections. Kean also recognized that, once he had found a way to get the budget crisis behind him, he would have time to move the rest of his program after the recession had lifted.

In December, Kean made a move which set in motion the process that produced an eventual compromise. He suggested he would be open to a one-cent increase in the sales tax in order to balance the budget without further spending cuts. He asked Jackman to ascertain what support there was in the lower house for such a proposal. At the same time, Kean said he would veto any increase in the income tax that began with people with incomes of under $50,000 per year. He said such an action would drive taxpayers and jobs out of the state. He also released a list of spending cuts he was prepared to make if he and the legislature failed to reach an agreement. On December 20, Karcher, upping the stakes, brought his income tax proposal to a vote. In a straight party vote, it passed the assembly 42 to 33. It cleared the senate in a vote of 21 to 15, with Dumont the only Republican voting for it. Moments later, Kean vetoed it. Yet he held off on the promised spending cuts.

In an all-night session on New Year's Eve, the legislature passed and Kean signed bills that raised the sales tax one cent (to 6 percent) and raised the income tax by 1 percent beginning with persons making $50,000 per year, increasing the top rate from 2.5 to 3.5 percent. "It's not what I wanted or what anybody else wanted," Kean said as he signed it into law.[39] Some speculated, many out loud, that Karcher had bested Kean, who had repeatedly vowed he would not raise the income tax. As had his father before him with price controls, Kean accepted the tax increases with resignation. After first trying to pass several other alternatives, he presented the matter as a lesser evil than either draconian spending cuts or even higher taxes. In the short term, Kean lost some face. Having run for governor promising to cut the sales tax by one cent, and not to raise the income tax, he ended his first year having raised both broad-based taxes.

Some believed he had weakened his own bargaining position when he failed to follow through with the cuts and layoffs he had repeatedly promised. Others questioned whether he had the stomach to actually do what he had threatened. Years later, Kean admitted there had been some substance to these charges. "They knew me," he said of Democratic legislators, "and they knew I just would not cut back on programs that I thought were good for the state and for which I had voted when I was in the legislature."[40]

The Third Way Redux

If there was one short-term saving grace to Kean's perceived capitulation on the tax increases, it was that he had denied his adversaries the opportunity to characterize him, as congressional Democrats had Reagan, as harsh. Kean's refusal to go along with the previous administration's recommended closing of nine state-operated day-care centers won him praise from the national president of the American Federation of State, County, and Municipal Employees union, known for its customary backing of Democrats.[41] Nor would they be able to blame him for "shutting down" the government, as Clinton would the Republican Congress, after he vetoed a budget that contained more cuts than he had been willing to accept. "He had to do something," one Kean loyalist said. "You cut services and people would be hurt."[42]

If some conservatives never forgave Kean for allowing taxes to rise and not cutting deeper into state operations, Democrats found it impossible to demonize him. Whatever else they would say or think about him, not even Karcher would attempt to "morph" Kean to national Republican leaders thought to be cold-hearted toward the poor. Twenty years after he lost the 1981 election to Kean, Jim Florio paid his former opponent a backhanded compliment when he stated that Kean's greatest achievement lay in what he refused to do. "Tom did not do bad things," Florio said, at a time when Republicans in Washington were attempting to reduce federal spending on domestic programs and shifting the burden for funding and running them to the states.[43]

Kean, however, saw no contradiction in his outward support for Reagan's agenda and the attitude he took toward social programs in New Jersey. He had insisted all along, and especially in the campaign, that the states could run such programs better than the federal government and at less cost. Just as Kean as a young legislator had cut a path between the liberal, urban-oriented governor and conservative, rurally focused Republican legislators, as governor, he steered a "third way" between Reagan Republicans in Washington and Karcher Democrats in Trenton.

In his subsequent budgets, Kean would allocate state funds to compensate for reductions in federal spending on social services, Medicaid, and mass transit. Sometimes he used the availability of matching state funds as incentives to the private sector or other levels of government to keep certain programs functioning. He would also find alternative sources of funding, such as revolving funds, to finance capital projects, in addition to increased state expenditures, public borrowing, and federal grants. Kean described increases he proposed in spending as investments that would bring the state immeasurable long-term returns. Though he would not completely satisfy either liberal or conservative ideologues, he became anathema to neither. If there were such a thing as an ideology of moderation, Kean proved its principal practitioner.

Kean broke with social conservatives when he vetoed a bill requiring a "moment of silence in New Jersey schools." However, he justified his position not only on constitutional grounds but on conservative principles, decrying the measure as one more unnecessary state intrusion into the affairs of local schools. He predicted, accurately, after the legislature overrode his veto—the only such occurrence during his eight years in office—that the courts would cite language used in legislative debates as evidence that the bill's sponsors intended to impose prayer rather than reflection. Yet in justifying his crime prevention agenda, which the American Civil Liberties Union, the American Council of Churches, and legal aid societies criticized, Kean sounded more like a liberal than a conservative. Since minority and inner-city residents were more likely than other Americans to suffer the effects of violent crime, they stood the most to gain, he said, by increased law enforcement, tougher sentencing, and a reimposed death penalty, all of which served as deterrents to crime. He proclaimed personal security a civil right.

Kean's tactical retreat on taxes in 1982 helped plant the seeds of victories that came his way the rest of his time in office. Having balanced the budget, he bought himself breathing room with which to develop strategies to break future legislative stalemates and enact the remainder of his agenda. The day Kean signed the tax increases into law, few anticipated that the taxes he agreed to raise in order to close a budget gap would fuel future surpluses through which he would both fund new initiatives and return money to taxpayers. As he charted his course for the remainder of his time in office, Kean demonstrated three characteristics that would define his overall style as governor: patience, persistence, and the capacity to cast his opponents as narrow partisans, pursuing selfish pursuits, and himself as the embodiment of the hopes and aspirations of the people of the state. He would learn to outmaneuver his opponents. As he pursued his goals, Kean received a healthy assist from his primary antagonist.

After the 1983 legislative elections, the Democratic Speaker over-reached for the third and final time. In spite of a spirited and heavily funded campaign mounted by Republicans in which Kean played a prominent role, appearing in generic television and radio ads, Democrats retained their majorities in both houses, picking up three seats in the assembly. Karcher responded to the news by launching a blistering personal attack upon Kean. Asked the day after the election to account for the Speaker's behavior, Kean feigned bemusement. After repeated entreaties that he clarify what he meant when he said that he thought the Speaker was strange, Kean replied that Karcher "could not help himself." "It's just his nature," he said. Pressed to expand on that thought, the former teacher in the governor's office recited a favorite tale from *Aesop's Fables* that he had obviously intended to deliver all along.

> One day a scorpion walked up to a frog and asked if he could ride on the frog's back as the frog swam across a stream. The frog refused at first. "You will sting me," he said.
> "If I did that," the scorpion replied, "we'd both drown." Reassured, the frog allowed the scorpion onto his back and jumped into the stream. Midway across, the scorpion stung the frog. "But you said if you stung me we would both drown," cried out the frog. "I know," the scorpion replied, "but it's my nature, I can't help myself."
> So that's his nature. He just cannot help himself.

The press roared.[44]

A Senate Appointment

While still settling into his new role as governor, Kean was presented with an opportunity to appoint an interim U.S. senator to complete the term of Harrison A. Williams. Reelected by a wide margin in 1976, Williams resigned on March 11, 1982, after being convicted for taking bribes in Abscam, an FBI sting operation. As was his practice in making other critical decisions, Kean was slow to declare his intentions and kept his own counsel. Twenty-seven days after Williams stepped down, Kean appointed Nicholas Brady to the U.S. Senate. In accepting the appointment, Brady stated that he would not campaign for Williams's seat, which fell open that very year. In naming a "caretaker" to replace Williams, Kean spared himself having to choose between two New Jersey Republicans known to be interested in running for the U.S. Senate in 1982.

Much of the party establishment urged him to appoint Millicent Fenwick. In the eight years since she defeated Kean in the 1974 congressional primary, Fenwick, through her aristocratic style, eclectic set of interests, and capacity to capture headlines, enjoyed a following that extended beyond her congressional district.[45] Most pundits considered her the front-runner in the upcoming primary and general elections. Conservative political activist Jeff Bell, who had defeated incumbent U.S. senator Clifford P. Case in the 1978 senatorial primary before losing the general election to Bill Bradley, also declared his intention to run. In the intervening years, Bell had crafted presidential candidate Ronald Reagan's tax cut proposals in 1980 and helped shape Kean's in New Jersey a year later.

Naming a former opponent over a key adviser might have made Kean appear ungrateful—especially to party conservatives. Yet naming Bell, whose electoral prospects in 1982 appeared no better than in 1978, appeared risky. A third possibility might have been Kean's 1981 campaign chairman, Representative Jim Courter, a conservative who had been helpful to him and who stood a better chance than Bell of retaining the Senate seat for the Republicans. With Courter and his backers not pressing his case as vigorously as had Fenwick's and Bell's, Kean turned to Brady. A former chairman of the investment firm Dillon Read, Brady had been active in New Jersey politics for decades and was a close friend of Vice President George H. W. Bush.

By opting to fill Williams's seat in the method he had, Kean left himself open to criticism that he had not done all he might have to keep the Senate seat in Republican hands. The victor of an ideologically divisive primary, Fenwick proved a weaker candidate than anticipated in the general election. Fated to run at the height of a national recession, when Reagan's standing in the polls was low, and unwilling either to invest her personal resources into her campaign or to accept money from political action committees, she lost to businessman Frank Lautenberg.

In his short time in the Senate, Brady, through his ties to the vice president and his knowledge of the financial industry, quickly established himself as a Senate insider. On several occasions, he used the access he enjoyed to the Senate's leadership and committee chairmen to give Kean the opportunity to make a case for policies he considered beneficial to New Jersey. Brady also helped end a stalemate between Kean and U.S. secretary of labor Ray Donovan over the dispensation of federal patronage to New Jersey. Prior to Kean's election, the Reagan administration had relied on the recommendations of Donovan, who had chaired Reagan's New Jersey campaign. With the senator of the president's party, by tradition, extending the courtesy of recommending nominees for federal posts requiring confirmation, Brady took to recommending candidates agreeable to Kean.[46]

The Transportation Trust

While he was still working to salvage his gas tax proposal in the legislature, Kean began to explore alternative ways to find "an adequate and stable source of funds" to finance transportation and infrastructure improvements. In consultation with the financial community, he and his team conceived of the "New Jersey Infrastructure Bank." The plan called for the state to pool together into a common fund unspent monies from previously passed public bond issues, previously authorized federal grants, additional state expenditures, and surpluses from three toll roads, all operated by independent authorities.[47] The infrastructure bank would then lend funds, on a revolving basis, at low or no interest, for up to fifteen years to municipalities seeking to repair or rebuild roads, bridges, sewer systems, or to meet other needs. As municipalities repaid the loans, the state would lend the funds out to others. Though the concept by which the bank would operate was simple, putting it into practice was cumbersome. Kean's administration would have to seek approval from voters to make changes in how proceeds raised through previously passed bond issues were allocated and approval from both the state legislature and Congress to place into the revolving fund state and federal monies they had appropriated for other purposes.

The plan promised to meet several delayed and competing demands over a short period of time. Environmental protection commissioner Robert Hughey, one of its initial proponents, projected that the state's need for sewer repairs totaled $2.8 billion. Federal cutbacks meant that over two hundred projects that had made federal priority lists would not receive funding anytime soon. To fund infrastructure repairs on facilities it operated, the Port Authority of New York and New Jersey had sought to establish an infrastructure bank of its own, financed through rents collected from the World Trade Center.[48] As soon as Kean advanced the idea, it became immersed in the same partisan political squabbling that had already beset both his budget and prison proposals. Proclaiming the concept a shell game, Florio questioned why federal money already set aside as grants should be converted into loans. He criticized Kean for recommending ways to accommodate Reagan's spending cuts, when, in the Democrat's view, the governor should be resisting them. The congressman predicted that the only beneficiaries of Kean's plan would be bondholders, bonding attorneys, and bonding brokers.[49]

Back in Trenton, Karcher, assuming a posture similar to that which he had taken when he opposed Kean's gas tax proposal, declared that the legislature would appropriate no funds to the infrastructure bank until after Congress consented to the state reallocating funds it had already made available to New Jersey for other purposes. When Congress showed signs of going along, the assembly Speaker changed tactics. For example, when Kean requested permission from the state legislature to reallocate $385 million in federal clean-water projects, Karcher had the assembly deny it on the grounds that the money had been earmarked as grants to eleven municipalities for sewer projects. He failed to mention that the same eleven local jurisdictions could expect no additional federal funds for transportation or that an additional 227 municipalities would receive no future federal funds for sewers.[50] All these projects would be eligible for funding over time under Kean's plan. As he had attempted with the prison bond issue, Karcher demanded legislative concurrence as to what projects Kean's plan would fund and in which localities.[51]

As the months dragged on, the battle to enact what became the Transportation Trust Fund moved to center stage in Trenton. In June of 1984, Kean proposed establishing the trust with $235 million in state funds, leveraging $600 million in federal funds. He proposed that the state's portion be raised through increased truck registration fees, surpluses from the state's three toll roads, and public borrowing over a ten-year period. Karcher suggested funding the projects through what was becoming a growing surplus, courtesy of the national economic recovery and the increases in state revenues, fueled in part by the tax increases Kean had approved. Kean countered that such an approach would ensure funding for infrastructure repairs for only one year, while under his plan, repairs would continue for at least four. For years, the state's AFL-CIO had complained that shifting state priorities and fluctuations in the national economy had cost their members jobs. With Kean's proposal providing what labor leaders regarded as assurances of regular and predictable work, union officials and rank-and-file workers weighed in on its behalf.

One evening after Kean had gone home, a group of union members descended upon the statehouse. One waved his finger in Karcher's face, repeating the words, "Accountability, Alan."[52] Days earlier, Senator Walter Rand (D-Camden) had introduced a plan similar to Kean's but with milder increases in trucker fees. In a deal essentially brokered during a late-night session in the governor's office, supporters of Rand's and Kean's proposals came together. The final version established the fund with an increase of $30 million in trucking fees, a dedication of two and one-half cents from the existing gas tax, and $25 million in revenues from the toll roads. The transportation trust fund would then be empowered to sell up to $600 million in short-term bonds. The new authority, which would have a life span of seventeen years, was expected to "invest" $3.3 million in construction projects over the next four years, creating between 120,000 and 150,000 new jobs.

In a last-ditch effort to deny Kean his plan, Karcher proposed the creation of a new independent authority through a $450-million bond issue package. Aware that transportation bond issues were faring poorly at the polls elsewhere in the country, Kean agreed to a bond issue for the much smaller amount of $88 million. If voters disapproved the package, the transportation trust fund would still be able to go forward. With the bond issue dispute resolved, legislative demands for control over which projects were funded remained the final stumbling block. "We wanted to get our footprints on this thing," one Democrat said.[53] The two sides agreed that the authority would submit its proposals to the legislature by April 1 of each year. It would have until the end of the fiscal year (June 30) to approve it or offer a substitute version. Kean signed the measure into law at the War Memorial on July 10, 1984, before a crowd of 450, mostly construction workers. By the year's end, the State Building Trades Council was publicly urging Kean to seek reelection.[54]

High Technology and Higher Education

Higher education, like roads, prisons, sewer lines, and bridges, had not been an area in which New Jersey state government had invested heavily in the decade prior to Kean's election as governor. Aware that Kean had campaigned on a platform to attract jobs to the state, the New Jersey Board of Higher Education, acting through its chairman, Ed Barr, president of the Sun Chemical Company, and Chancellor T. Edward Hollander, presented a proposal to the new administration to attract high-technology companies to the state by upgrading university laboratories and research facilities and investing public funds in start-up companies.

The two men informed Kean that, although 2,500 patents were issued annually to firms working at the 700 corporate research laboratories in New Jersey, most of the products that developed from this research were manufactured elsewhere. That meant that ideas generated in the state were being used to grow the economies of other regions. A major reason New Jersey had lost its competitive edge, they cited, was the absence of significant transfers of technology between research-based and applied technology. Other states, they pointed out, offered tax incentives and investments in public-private partnerships in order to promote such activities.[55] A prime example of where this was working well was at the research triangle that had developed with state assistance around the cities of Raleigh, Durham, and Chapel Hill in North Carolina. Another reason New Jersey lagged behind, they argued, was that it had permitted a decline in the quality of its university laboratories.

The issue that Barr and Hollander brought to Kean's attention dovetailed with his overall objective of making the state more attractive to business, so that rather than being known for its polluting smokestacks, it would be seen as incubator of ideas, fueled by a highly skilled and well-trained workforce. Along with prison overcrowding and infrastructure repairs, the high-tech initiative soon became part of Gary Stein's portfolio. During his first year in office, Kean named a twenty-one-member commission on science and technology, with Barr as chairman. He charged it with finding ways to make the state more attractive to high-tech companies. "What would it take to get them to want to locate here?" Kean would inquire of its members. The commission included the chairman of Exxon, the heads of New Jersey–based pharmaceutical firms, entrepreneurs affiliated with smaller high-tech companies, and university presidents.

Barr's group divided into task forces that also drew upon middle-level managers of companies. To attract and retain public attention, the commission issued periodic progress reports.[56] In its report, issued in early 1984, the commission made thirty-eight recommendations. Its primary proposal was that four advanced technology centers be established at northern New Jersey universities.[57] The commission called for the state to create a venture-capital partnership, which would make equity investments to start-up companies and assist with initial financing for firms that financial institutions deemed too risky to qualify for the kind of loans they habitually made to more conventional businesses.

Kean became the report's most ardent champion. "We're going to the gold and to make New Jersey Number One," he proclaimed during the Olympic year of 1984.[58] He named a cross-section of leaders from higher education, business, labor, and government to press for passage of a $90-million bond issue. He also studied why voters in New Jersey and elsewhere had rejected past higher-education bond issue of similar sizes. To make his proposals more attractive, he emphasized their capacity to create high-paying jobs: "The bond between the strength of our economy and the quality of our education is more apparent every year. To attract the best jobs, we must attract the best minds. To attract the best minds, we must maintain the resources on which they depend. We must compete with other states to keep them here, if we want to compete to keep jobs here."[59] To dramatize the capacity of the bond issue to transform the state's economy, Kean signed the bill that put the bond issue on the ballot at Thomas Edison's laboratory in West Orange. "New Jersey is an old and distinguished state," he said. "But she is never too old to make her fresh starts, to keep making fresh starts, to turn her starts into first place finishes and then to start again."[60]

Kean's second major achievement in the area of higher education came in the form of "challenge" grants to state colleges and universities. Rather than see increases he made in institutions' budgets, over the rate of inflation, go primarily to fund overall operations, Kean asked their presidents to demonstrate how the infusion of funds earmarked for particular purposes, often matched by private-sector donations, could achieve national prominence for specific colleges and universities in certain areas. "You convince me that they [the areas the presidents designated] can be the best in the world," Kean told them, "and I will put money in the budget to make them the best in the world."[61] Through a symbolic $5 million he added to one of his early budgets to establish the Center for Information Age Technology at the New Jersey Institute of Technology, Kean signaled what lay ahead for other institutions interested in achieving world-class status.[62]

Kean admitted nearly two decades later that he saw challenge grants as a way not only to prompt university leaders to stretch their imaginations but also to demonstrate to a skeptical, and often hostile,

'Puts us in the driver's seat!'

Fig 10.3. Kean devised several strategies to make the state more attractive to business. This cartoon captured his competitive instincts with regard to what other states were doing to lure high tech-firms into their borders. (© 1984 *The Star-Ledger.* All rights reserved. Reprinted with permission.)

legislature that such investments would indeed bring results that could be both seen and measured. "The legislative leadership told me," he said, "that I had too many idiosyncrasies like higher education and the arts. They could see the return on what they had spent in other areas."[63] As part of his endeavor to achieve both goals, Kean twice featured the challenge grants in his State of the State address. On the first occasion, he singled out for praise college presidents who were willing to meet Kean's challenge. On the second, he introduced professors hired under the program and read their credentials aloud so "that legislators would see what they had gotten for the money they had appropriated."[64] Also during his administration, to allow state college presidents more freedom in the management of their institutions, Kean shepherded through legislation granting state colleges autonomy from state civil service and collective bargaining procedures.

Passage of the high-tech bond issue and the challenge grants program marked major milestones for Kean's administration. As governor, he worked hard to keep both free from politicization. Sensing that support for high technology was strong among both voters and contributors, some within the legislature sought to establish a high-technology commission through legislation. Kean preempted them by establishing his own. Rather than fund it through a separate legislative appropriation, he provided for its operations through existing monies previously allocated to the state's Department of Commerce. When the legislature tried to pass an appropriation afterward, Kean, fearful of legislative intrusion in the commission's affairs, threatened a veto. He would prove just as vigorous in protecting other of his initiatives.

chapter 11

Building New Jersey Pride

"New Jersey and You—Perfect Together"

None of Tom Kean's initiatives as governor became more identified with his persona in the public's mind—both inside New Jersey and out—than his televised appearances promoting the state. The slogan that became his trademark, "New Jersey and You—Perfect Together," encapsulated much more than the tourist sites it was designed to promote. It became synonymous with all Kean attempted to do while in office as well as with the man himself. At a statehouse ceremony at which Kean's portrait was presented for permanent display, his successor as governor, James J. Florio, captured the spirit of Kean's administration when he said, "Tom gave us back a very important thing, our pride."[1]

Kean came into office believing New Jersey had for too long been the butt of too many national jokes and fodder for too many late-night comedians. Most of the put-downs revolved around the state's reputation for having a high tolerance for political corruption, organized crime, and pollution. Kean resolved that if he ever got the chance, he would use the powers and visibility of the governorship to erase this stereotype and establish a new image for the state in which its residents could take pride. He was convinced that the long-term economic health of the state rested on its ability to attract information and service industries to replace the heavy manufacturing industries that had departed to the Sunbelt or gone offshore. Success in attracting these industries, he would say, hinged on the state's ability to train a workforce capable of performing the tasks that an increasingly global and

technological economy demanded and to establish a tax and regulatory climate favorable to business. Kean would justify not only his
education proposals but his transportation initiatives, his environmental policies, and his support for the arts on the grounds that corporations could be choosy in deciding where to locate and that the
state needed to do more to attract them. He pitched his promotional
enterprises to two audiences: (1) tourists and employers located outside of New Jersey's borders and (2) consumers of state services
within them.

In his first budget, Kean sought to make good on his promise to
make more funds available to promote tourism. Karcher and his
Democratic allies cut Kean's request from $4 million to $1.2 million
at the same time they cut his prison funding recommendation. That
limited amount proved sufficient for Kean to launch a pilot advertising program in the hope that once the public and the legislature
saw the results, he might be able to expand it. Kean and his team
were determined to replace the then existing slogan the state had
used to promote tourism: "New Jersey's Got It." The phrase had given
cynics, comedians, and would-be New Jersey detractors fodder for
further New Jersey jokes. Kean asked the state's Department of Commerce to launch a public competition to find a replacement slogan
and to propose a suitable advertising campaign to go with it.

By September 1982, they had narrowed the field of contenders to
four finalists.[2] Among them was Bozell and Jacobs, which submitted
the slogan that would make the state's forty-eighth governor one of
its most famous. In April 1983, Kean held two press conferences, one
at the Meadowlands, the other at the statehouse, to announce the
launching of a seven-week advertising campaign. He brought to the
tourism campaign the same energy and enthusiasm he had invested
in his campaign for governor two years earlier. After briefly reciting
the reasons many nonresidents had been quick to sell the state short,
Kean pointed to its greatest assets. "We are the cockpit of the [Amer-
ican] Revolution with many historic sites," he boasted. "New Jersey
residents enjoy a tradition steeped in history, inventiveness, and in-
dustriousness. These traditions, coupled with our natural beauty, our
economic vitality and our geographic location, give us a definite edge.
When you add our greatest asset—our people—you have a winner."[3]
He explained that he had timed the advertising campaign to coincide
with the period when most people were planning their summer vacations. Bozell and Jacobs's plan meshed perfectly with Kean's vision
of how best to attract both visitors and businesses, while building a
sense of pride among New Jerseyans. The television spots featured
New Jersey beaches, mountains, and historical sites replete with a

catchy jingle and a readily identifiable catch phrase: "New Jersey and You—Perfect Together." The advertising executive Ron Vrba patterned the campaign after two other publicly supported tourism campaigns: "Virginia Is for Lovers," introduced in 1969, and "I Love New York," which debuted in 1977, in the aftermath of New York's City's fiscal crisis.

Kean was impressed by how effectively and aggressively New York City promoted its theaters and other cultural attractions in its tourism advertising. He would point to the success of the city's tourism campaign as an example of what New Jersey might be able to achieve, provided its cultural attractions proved of similar caliber and the state legislature and the private sector recognized that by "investing" not only in them but also in the state's beaches and historic sites, they would reap multiple rewards in increased tourism and business investment.

The first "I Love New York" television advertisement had featured *Dracula* lead actor Frank Langella, attired in full costume, proclaiming his love for New York, "especially in the evenings." Elizabeth Taylor, then starring in a revival of Lillian Hellman's *The Little Foxes*, followed. Name performers affiliated with the Metropolitan Opera, New York City Ballet, and New York Philharmonic made future appearances. Subsequent ads highlighted the city's museums, zoos, and other tourist destinations. The New York State Chamber of Commerce credited the "I Love New York" campaign with a $3.8-billion jump in tourist activity and ten thousand of the new jobs the city and state reported during its first year in operation.[4] Soon, the campaign that had been intended to promote the city was expanded to include the entire state.

New York City's use of celebrities aroused Kean's competitive instincts. He enticed multifaceted entertainer Bill Cosby to kick off the New Jersey commercials. Kean had first met Cosby at the Garden State Arts Center. Cosby performed there while Kean was serving on the highway authority, which administered the facility. Then starring in a highly popular situation-comedy television show, Cosby appealed to audiences of all social, economic, and racial backgrounds. He not only agreed to star in the commercials, but also refused any payment over the required prevailing union rate of nine hundred dollars.[5] In the pilot advertisement, Cosby and his wife were depicted loading up their car, preparing to go on vacation in New Jersey. Looking into the camera, Cosby recited all the things the couple hoped to see and do while in the state. Actress and Bergen County native Brooke Shields, then a Princeton undergraduate, followed Cosby in a subsequent wave of ads.

Vrba's third selection to appear in the commercials proved both more controversial and more memorable than his first two. He reported that he had conducted a survey to ascertain which persons New Jerseyans found the most "credible." Longtime CBS news anchor Walter Cronkite placed first, followed by Cosby. Kean, Vrba said, polled third. With Cronkite unavailable and Cosby already lending his services, Vrba decided to ask Kean to appear in the campaign's television commercials. Democratic legislators, concerned that Kean's commercial appearances would boost his political standing in the run-up to his 1985 reelection campaign, capped the amount of funds the state could expend airing the commercials that featured Kean in media markets that included New Jersey residents.[6]

While photographs of past governors had graced state highway maps and other publications, the New Jersey commercials marked the first time an incumbent governor was featured in state-financed television spots promoting tourism. To viewers, both in-state and out, Kean belied the caricature of the conventional New Jersey politician. Instead of the potbellied, cigar-chomping, balding man of late middle age, about to be hauled off to jail, an image of New Jersey officials so familiar to national audiences, Kean, vigorous, genial, fit, and amicable, with a full head of light brown hair, appeared in people's living rooms walking along a quiet beach, proclaiming his state's most attractive places.

Vrba later volunteered that he had considered retaining a Hollywood actor to perform in this role but had decided that Kean would prove a more effective salesman. That the commercial's spokesman was actually the state's governor underscored the image of the state Kean intended to project through the commercials. Evidence of the success of Vrba's strategy appeared in a *New Yorker* cartoon four years into the advertising campaign. In it, a wife, viewing the commercial, says to her husband, "Tom Kean seems awfully nice. We should hop over to New Jersey sometime."[7] The commercials helped Kean achieve a celebrity status none of his recent predecessors had attained. "Gee, he's nice," remarked a woman who met Kean as he toured Trenton's predominantly Italian American Chambersburg neighborhood, "he's so much better-looking in person than in his pictures."[8] Everyplace he went residents would greet him by repeating the words in the slogan, some good-naturedly imitating his accent.

The immense popularity of the ads fueled reporters' interest in where Kean spent his own vacations. For several years, the Keans had been renting summer quarters on Fishers Island, New York. After they purchased a vacation home there, the *New York Daily News* ran a headline proclaiming that New Jersey's chief executive had not found his state as perfect a setting for his vacation as he was recommending to others. Years later, Kean told of how far his Fishers neighbors had gone to protect his family's privacy: "A reporter walked up to the check-out counter of a grocery store and asked the cashier whether she had seen the Keans. 'No' she said, 'haven't seen 'em; don't know 'em.' Debby was standing right behind the reporter on line, waiting to pay. Everyone in the store knew who she was. Yet no one let on. Nice people."[9]

Like the two models on which it had been patterned (those in Virginia and New York), Kean's tourism promotion exceeded expectations. In three years, New Jersey moved from seventh in annual visitors to fifth, attracting 54 million visitors and generating $12 million in economic activity. The ads also helped further another of Kean's goals: raising state pride. The year Kean ran for reelection, polls showed that 80 percent of state residents thought the state a good or an excellent place to live. This was a jump of 12 percent from previous surveys, conducted in 1977 and 1980.[10] Some of the shift, no doubt, resulted from the improved state economy. Yet much of it flowed from the intensive effort Kean had made to alert his constituents to

"Tom Kean seems awfully nice. We should hop over to New Jersey sometime."

Fig 11.1. Kean's heavy promotion of New Jersey as a tourist designation elicited this response from a *New Yorker* cartoonist. During his eight years as governor, his face and voice on television came to personify much of what was good in New Jersey. (© *The New Yorker* Collection 1986 Edward Frascino from cartoonbank.com. All rights reserved.)

the good things that were transpiring within its borders. "Hardly a day goes by," he wrote, "when I am not approached by a constituent who asks me to say, 'New Jersey and You—Perfect Together.'" The slogan, he suggested, became residents' "shorthand way of saying the jokesters are wrong: New Jersey is a good place to live."[11]

As tourism rose and state pride increased, Kean pursued another of his promotional goals: business development. In addition to the television commercials, Bozell and Jacobs prepared promotional materials and advertising supplements to business journals, stressing the state's low tax structure and favorable business climate. Kean's commerce commissioner, Borden Putnam, as had Vrba before him, enlisted Kean personally in these efforts. Kean began paying visits to the heads of companies that he learned were contemplating expanding their operations in the hope that he might entice them to consider New Jersey. "We will do everything we possibly can to avoid second place," Kean said after he had asked General Motors to locate a Saturn manufacturing plant in New Jersey.[12] After GM settled on Tennessee, citing lower operating costs as well as a state package of land, tax abatements, and subsidies, totaling $250 million, Kean continued his efforts with other companies. Many of his most likely targets were situated closer to home.

When not promoting New Jersey's assets, Kean would stand guard over the new image he had helped forge for his state. He would telephone television and radio producers to demand equal time whenever someone disparaged his state on their stations. Presidential aspirant Gary Hart experienced the full extent of Kean's ire in 1984. With the New Jersey and California primaries held on the same day, Hart and his wife campaigned on opposite coasts. Hart proclaimed that the "good news" in that situation was that his wife had held a koala bear in California. "I won't tell you what I got to hold in New Jersey," Hart went on, "samples from a toxic waste dump."[13]

"We don't like New Jersey jokes anymore," Kean, who just happened to head Ronald Reagan's reelection effort in New Jersey, told the press. He suggested that Hart apologize the next time he was in New Jersey.[14] When he returned to the state, Hart found that his New Jersey remark was all New Jersey reporters wanted to discuss with him. Essex County executive Peter Shapiro, a booster of Hart's opponent, former vice president Walter F. Mondale, said that Hart had hit a "very tender spot."[15] Years later, Kean confessed that his former television sparring partner, Richard Leone, a Mondale adviser, had directed his attention to Hart's remark as a means of revving him up. "I didn't need revving up," Kean confessed.[16] That Kean had been able to inject himself into the Democratic primary, possibly influencing the results, added to his enjoyment.

If Kean was prepared to take on those who besmirched his state, he was just as ready to poke fun at his own propensity, as journalist Michael Barone observed, to promote the state shamelessly.[17] On the *ABC Comedy Special,* in a spoof on the television show *Miami Vice,* comedians Joe Piscopo and Eddie Murphy, cast as detectives, stopped Kean's limousine on the mistaken assumption that it had been stolen. Upon discovering that its occupant actually was the governor, they excused themselves and sped off. "Drive safely," Kean shouted after them, "we have the best highway system in the East. We have seventy-two airports, two hundred and sixty-two farms; we are fourth in the nation in wine production."[18]

The War with New York

The press called it the second "war between the states."[19] Headline writers, unaccustomed to New Jersey's new aggressiveness, used the phrase to describe Kean's attempt to bring into Hudson and Bergen counties back-office operations that New York City–based financial firms wished to locate outside of Manhattan. New York City mayor Ed Koch was equally determined to frustrate him. The so-called war between the states produced some of the most dramatic episodes of Kean's years in office. Representatives of the two localities clashed over jobs, revenues, the homeless, sports teams, shore protection— and even the Statue of Liberty.

The "war's" opening salvo came on September 22, 1982, when Kean announced he would seek legislation to allow the Port Authority of New York and New Jersey to assemble acreage in Hoboken for a $500-million redevelopment project. The bi-state agency would invest $100 million in the enterprise, with the private sector providing the rest. The project would consist of 670 residences, multiple retail operations, office buildings, a four-hundred-room hotel, restaurants, recreational facilities, and a marina along the Hudson River. For this to happen, the New York and New Jersey legislatures and the U.S. Congress would have to amend the Port Authority's charter, allowing it to broaden its mission to include waterfront redevelopment. Kean predicted that the project would "breathe new life into one of New Jersey's most valuable and underutilized resources." He suggested that the proposal would be balanced with a similar Port Authority–initiated project on New York's side of the Hudson.[20]

The following spring, Kean announced a $200-million renovation of the Harborside Terminal in Jersey City. Bankers Trust, eager to relocate its computer operations from lower Manhattan, would be a major tenant. To lure the financial institution, Jersey City offered a fifteen-year tax abatement. It planned to develop the site with $9 million of an Urban Development Action Grant (UDAG) it expected to receive from the U.S. Department of Housing and Urban Development (HUD). The site was a mile from Harbour City, a mixed-use development for which the city had already received $40 million in UDAG funding. In announcing the news, Kean called the New Jersey waterfront the "most valuable real estate in the world."[21]

New York mayor Edward I. Koch did not take kindly to the two New Jersey projects, subsidized in part by a bi-state agency and the federal government. He used his influence to block the change in the Port Authority's charter in the New York State Senate. As his price for dropping his opposition, Koch demanded that the amount of office space development in Hoboken be scaled back. Kean immediately informed New York governor Mario Cuomo that he would find it "very difficult" approving a Port Authority plan to spend $15 million to build a home port for the U.S. Navy on Staten Island when John Marchi, the state senator from Staten Island, was holding up the Hoboken project.[22] Governor Cuomo, not on the best of terms with Koch, voiced sympathy for Kean's position. "The truth is we made a gentleman's agreement with Kean, which included the mayor, and then we turned around and said 'sorry we can't deliver,'" Cuomo said.[23] Once again, Kean was benefiting from divisions within Democratic ranks. (Cuomo and Koch had been rivals in the 1977 mayoral and 1982 gubernatorial primaries.)

Koch next turned his attention to the federal government's role in funding the Jersey City projects. Arguing that the UDAG program had not been intended to benefit one depressed area at the expense of a neighboring locale, he sought to persuade HUD secretary Sam Pierce, a fellow New Yorker, to write provisions into grants that would prohibit localities from using the funds to lure firms from other jurisdictions within the same region. Koch also threatened a lawsuit to prevent the already-approved $40-million UDAG funds from going to Jersey City.

Kean offered both a counteroffensive and a truce in a talk before the Association for a Better New York, a group of business leaders dedicated to New York boosterism. He told his audience—which included former New York City mayors Robert F. Wagner and John V. Lindsay, leading real estate developers (Donald Trump among them), and the Port Authority leadership—that he had been informed that the city was considering a suit to block grants to New Jersey. To the bemusement of his listeners, he suggested that New Jersey was contemplating a suit of its own to block construction of what would become the Jacob K. Javits Convention Center. He proposed that both entities drop their plans to go to court for the good of the region, arguing that the only victors of the lawsuits would be law firms and other parts of the country.[24]

"New Jersey is no pirate," Kean declared, insisting that there was a difference between enticing Manhattan-based firms to leave New York and competing with the outer boroughs for new operations that firms intended to be built outside of Manhattan. He suggested that if such companies were prevented from locating part of their operations in New Jersey, they would abandon the tri-state area completely and relocate to the Sunbelt. Many of his listeners found his arguments persuasive. Lindsay stated that Kean had been "right on target" and called upon the city to drop its opposition to the Jersey City project.[25] Koch proclaimed that Kean's threat of a countersuit was "not nice."[26] Full-page advertisements began appearing in the *New York Times*, listing New York's competitive advantages over New Jersey. Accompanying them were photographs of Koch nailing shut the New York entrance to the Holland Tunnel.[27]

As the UDAG dispute raged, members of New Jersey's congressional delegation, picking up on an argument Kean had been making, complained that New York City's continued discharging of raw sewage into the Hudson River and the Atlantic Ocean posed an environmental hazard to New Jersey's beaches. Koch countered that the city discharged residential waste, while New Jersey discharged chemical ones. "If you come into contact with one or the other," he said, "one is unpleasant, the other kills. New Jersey kills," he said.[28] As charges and countercharges continued, Pierce revoked the $9-million grant to the Harborside Financial Center. The interregional squabbling provided the Reagan administration with an excuse to terminate the UDAG program, of which it had never been fond.[29]

While these disputes raged, the two localities also engaged in a tug-of-war over the use of federal funds for the homeless. In March 1983, New York City began placing one thousand homeless persons in hotels in Essex and Hudson counties. Calling its action the "height of irresponsibility," Kean said that New York had put a strain on New Jersey's already overburdened service providers and harmed the homeless by removing them from support systems to which they had become accustomed.[30] His annoyance grew when he discovered that the city relocated these residents so that it could renovate buildings where they had been sheltered in order to accommodate the growing demand for middle- and upper-income housing. Kean and his administration embarked on a strategy to persuade the city to change its mind through repeated criticisms in the press. The city backed off.

In yet another area, Kean's administration provided the New York Jets football team with the opportunity it had been seeking to play in a state-of-the-art facility. Team owner Leon Hess frequently complained about the city's slowness in renovating Shea Stadium, then the team's home. Hess had been in negotiations with the sports authority chairman, Kean appointee Jon Hanson, about a possible move to the New Jersey Meadowlands. Discussions bogged down over Hess's desire for an escape clause in his contract that would allow him to move the team back to New York City in the event that the city made good on its past promises to the team. Amid one such discussion, Hanson telephoned Kean and handed Hess the telephone. The two agreed that in exchange for the escape clause, Hess would promise to pay the New Jersey sports authority $10 million in the event that he exercised that option.[31] As both parties walked away with the guarantees they sought, Koch broke the news that the Jets were leaving New York. In a burst of New York chauvinism, after the football team that was already playing in the Meadowlands, the Giants, won the Super Bowl, Koch denied the team permission to march in a victory parade down Fifth Avenue. Kean and Hanson staged one instead in Giants Stadium in the middle of a snowstorm.

As the "war between the states" progressed, its principal generals called periodic truces. Kean and Koch paid each other occasional visits, becoming good friends in the process. Each found much to admire in the other. To Kean, Koch epitomized New York City in all its brashness. He enjoyed watching the mayor march in parades, exchange insults with hecklers, and ask residents to evaluate his performance.[32] Koch came to admire Kean for his gentlemanly qualities. He voiced surprise when Kean telephoned him in 1985 to ask whether the mayor had objections to Stephen Berger succeeding Peter Goldmark as the Port Authority's executive director. Koch and Berger had been feuding at the time. As Koch recalled, no governor of New York had ever thought to sound him out about prospective Port Authority appointments. Kean, Koch said, had been willing to go so far as to veto the bi-state agency's minutes if Koch expressed objections to Berger. Koch told Kean he would not ask him to do so.[33]

On his frequent visits to the city, Kean occasionally accompanied Koch on his excursions to favorite restaurants, where the mayor would hold court. When not in the mayor's company, Kean would look for Koch's picture in windows of restaurants before going inside. A smile on the mayor's face indicated that Koch thought well of the establishment. Through their different styles—Koch through bluff and bluster, Kean through boosterism, tempered by gentility—both worked to restore pride within their respective jurisdictions. Koch had been elected mayor in the aftermath of the worst fiscal crisis in the city's history. Kean had become governor during the worst economic downturn since the Great Depression and in the aftermath of a decade-long battle over whether to impose an income tax and how activist a government New Jersey should have. Both had promised to lead their respective locales to prosperity through economic development. Asked Kean's greatest achievement as governor, Koch said that his counterpart "established that you could be courteous in public as well as in private and not scream to get it [the job] done."[34]

As the second "war between the states" waged, New York governor Mario Cuomo proved as willing to compromise with Kean as Koch had been to confront him. Away from the cameras, the two governors would have breakfast every six to eight weeks to discuss mutual concerns.[35] Each came with a list of items he most wanted to see implemented. Cuomo supported not only the Hudson redevelopment projects but also the Port Authority's plans to enter into a joint venture to finance construction of a legal center along the Passaic riverfront in Newark. He also helped Kean make good on his long-standing dream of restoring ferry service between New Jersey and New York City. The two governors used the centennial of the Statue of Liberty to resolve an ongoing dispute as to which location maintained jurisdiction over the monument. To make their peace, they boarded a New York City police barge to Liberty Island, where they signed an agreement to divide sales tax revenues raised at the facility to fund programs for the homeless. True to form, Kean persuaded the New Jersey legislature to enact the measure, while its counterpart in Albany balked at Cuomo's request.

Kean Goes International

Kean's efforts to improve the health of the state's economy took on more of an international flair as he strove to attract foreign investment and to market New Jersey products abroad. During the 1980s, state governments became more involved in both of these endeavors, opening offices abroad, sponsoring trade missions, offering tax and other incentives to entice foreign companies to locate within their borders, and signing "sister state" agreements with subnational political entities in other countries.[36] Kean engaged in all of these practices. Because of its close proximity to New York and Pennsylvania, its good transportation network, skilled workforce, competitive tax rate, and good research universities and research laboratories, Kean maintained that New Jersey could be as attractive to foreign companies expanding their operations as it was to domestic ones. To help him make that case to them, Kean designated as his special trade representative Ming Hsu.

Born in China, the daughter of a member of Chiang Kai-shek's cabinet, Hsu came to the United States to escape the depredations that

Japan's invasion of China and the Chinese civil war inflicted upon her country. Fluent in English, Hsu found work at NBC and, eventually, at RCA. Interested in learning more about the politics of her adopted country, she attended the 1972 Republican National Convention in Miami, where she first encountered Kean, then Speaker of the assembly. "Tom just came over and said 'hello,'" Hsu recalled.[37] Kean impressed her with his curiosity both about her and her thoughts about how President Richard Nixon's 1972 visit to the Chinese mainland would affect U.S.–China relations.

Under Hsu's direction, the state began participating in trade shows abroad. At booths the state rented, partly with funds New Jersey businesses provided, business personnel promoted their products, while state officials stressed New Jersey's suitability for foreign investment. Hsu put her primary focus on small and medium-sized firms, which did not maintain offices overseas. Larger New Jersey corporations that had offshore offices often allowed her to use their facilities for meetings. Hsu shepherded the founding of export trading companies, maintained a directory of state firms interested in establishing joint ventures with foreign counterparts, and enticed foreign companies to open facilities in New Jersey. In 1984, Samsung became the first Korean concern to open an operation in New Jersey. Daewoo, Hyundai, and Lucky Star followed.

In 1986, Kean embarked on his first official trade mission. He spent seventeen days in China, Hong Kong, and Korea, addressing American chambers of commerce, calling on government officials, visiting schools and universities, and courting potential investors. He stopped in Hangzhou, an ancient Chinese capital, in Zhejiang Province, to renew a "sister state" relationship Brendan Byrne had signed late in his administration. The following year, Kean embarked on a three-week journey to China and Japan. As Kean prepared for his first trip to China, he asked Richard Nixon to supply him with information about people he would be seeing and places he would visit. Aware that Kean planned to visit Hangzhou, where he and his national security adviser, Henry Kissinger, had drafted the Shanghai Communiqué, Nixon asked Kean to find out whether a California sequoia he had planted in the city in the presence of Zhou Enlai had survived. Experts in the U.S. Department of Agriculture had doubted that it would take root. Kean found that the tree had prospered and that it stood surrounded by its children and grandchildren. In a toast he offered to his Chinese hosts, Kean offered the hope that the friendship between the United States and China would become as strong as the tree, which, he later reported to Nixon, "looked like it was good for a thousand years."[38]

On his travels, Kean grew acutely aware of growing competition among the states for foreign investment. "Everywhere I went, there was a governor coming in behind me and one in front who was just leaving," he said upon his return from one trip.[39] He opened a small office for the state in Tokyo, from which state officials could travel to the rest of Asia. Late in his governorship, he led a trade mission to the United Kingdom. He returned to China as the only elected official on a corporate visit Henry Kissinger had organized. He also visited Singapore, Malaysia, and Indonesia. Kean capped his international ventures by sponsoring "China Expo '88," a weeklong exposition of Chinese products held at the County College of Morris in Randolph. To preside over its opening, Kean invited Henry Kissinger, who regaled the national press with stories of his early experiences trying and failing to outfox Chinese diplomats. In typical Kean fashion, the expo contained an educational component, bringing Chinese artists and performers to high schools across the state.

Kean's international endeavors sparked some controversy when the *Bergen Record* ran a story questioning whether his travels actually helped influence where foreign companies decided to locate and whether his trips justified their costs. "I don't often write letters to newspapers, in fact this is my second in 20 years in public life," he began his written rebuttal. Then he let fly: "I have participated in three trade missions in my 6½ years as governor. That ranks in the bottom five percent of all governors in the country. I'm not proud of that. I should have done more."[40]

By the end of Kean's tenure, New Jersey ranked fourth among the states in foreign investment in an American state.[41]

chapter 12

The Education Governor

Setting Educational Goals

Of all Kean attempted to do as governor, improving the quality of public education remained his highest priority. It was in this area that he achieved his most significant accomplishments. As a former teacher and onetime chairman of the assembly's Education Committee, Kean came into office knowing more about education and with more experience in the politics of education than any New Jersey governor since Woodrow Wilson. Because much of what he wanted to do did not require legislative approval, education was also the area that offered Kean the widest latitude in which to act after winning his election by the narrowest of margins and having to face two legislative chambers in which the opposition party commanded substantial majorities. Kean had made education a major issue in his campaign for governor. Whenever he would speak on the subject, he seemed less the politician and more the teacher he once was. "Nothing can compare with the excitement you feel when you see the first glimmer of understanding in a student's eyes or when you find out that after the bell rings kids want to stay and finish the discussion," he would say.[1] He took office determined to improve the entire educational enterprise in New Jersey.[2]

First and foremost, Kean wanted to better the quality of education by improving the quality of teacher training. He argued during the campaign that the teacher certification requirements then in existence worked to keep out of classrooms the very people the state should be enticing to enter them: highly motivated and high-achieving liberal arts majors from the best colleges and universities and people who had distinguished themselves in other fields. Opinions he voiced came directly from his own experience. Kean witnessed at close range the impact well-trained and dedicated teachers at St. Mark's could have on students. He saw no reason why every school should not strive to provide the kind of education he had received as a student and tried to impart as a teacher.[3]

Kean's experience prior to his election as governor persuaded him that neither school systems nor prospective teachers placed students' needs at the head of their concerns. While at Columbia's Teachers College, he encountered people who had enrolled in graduate school not to increase their knowledge in their subject areas in order to become better teachers, but primarily to earn higher pay or to become administrators.[4] All the incentives for advancement, he concluded, "ran the wrong way" and to the benefit not of children but of professional educators and their allies. By the time Kean entered the assembly, he grew concerned at the number of people who told him they had decided to teach either because they did not know what else to do or because they wanted a profession that they could fall back on after pursuing other options. Kean was also troubled that education, as a major, was attracting students with the lowest grade point averages and who had compiled the lowest scores on the Scholastic Aptitude Test.[5]

To illustrate his point that licensing practices then in existence served as barriers keeping the most qualified potential teachers out of classrooms, Kean noted that Albert Einstein had been allowed to teach at Princeton University but would not have been considered qualified to teach in the public schools because he had not taken the eighteen credits in education courses the state required prospective teachers to complete. "If an Einstein could not set foot in a New Jersey public school," he would ask, "what chance did scientists at any university or corporate laboratory have at a time when the nation was experiencing a shortage of science teachers?"[6] At Columbia, Kean had taken his share of methodology courses the state still required of aspiring teachers. He considered them worthless. None of the syllabi he had perused in the intervening years had persuaded him otherwise.

Kean wanted prospective teachers to spend more time familiarizing themselves with the substance of what they would teach and less time learning how to teach it. Rather than attract the "best and the brightest" college students into New Jersey classrooms, Kean argued, the then-prevailing practices catered primarily to those who were available. Such practices, he said, led to the acceptance of minimal student performance, when schools should be striving for excellence. Having made the case, while a legislator, for mandatory basic-skills testing and higher standards, he grew disturbed when the Education Department failed to impose universal standards against which student performance across the state could be measured.

At the outset of his term, Kean made clear that he would travel in a different direction in forming education policy than had his predecessor. Brendan Byrne had invested considerable effort enacting a state income tax as a mean of complying with the state supreme court's ruling in *Robinson v. Cahill* that reliance exclusively on the property tax as a means of funding education violated the constitutional mandate on the state to provide a "thorough and efficient" education to every child. After it enacted the tax, the state began to channel revenues raised in this manner to school districts less able to raise funds through the property tax than their ratable rich counterparts. Having succeeded in that objective, Byrne allowed the state education bureaucracy to set policy. Its critics maintained that its policies worked to further not so much the interests of children as those of professional educators, primarily the New Jersey Education Association, which had favored Byrne's reelection. (With the advent of collective bargaining, the NJEA, like its counterparts across the country, began to function increasingly less like a professional association and more like a trade union, concerned primarily with protecting the economic and other interests of the majority of its members.)

Kean defined education policy more broadly. He believed that all who held a stake in the educational enterprise (parents, teachers, school boards, and employers) should have a say over what went on in the public schools. He knew that if he was to raise standards for both students and teachers, he would have to take his case beyond the small world of education politics to wider audiences. As he pursued those goals, Kean relied more heavily upon the "bully pulpit" powers of his office. Repeatedly, he used public support he had obtained as leverage against an entrenched educational bureaucracy and a legislature beholden to interests resistant to reform.

In his educational philosophy, Kean placed among conservatives, in that he believed there was a certain body of knowledge that both students and teachers needed to master in order to perform at their maximum capacity. He decried what he saw as the dumbing down of curricula and the introduction of fads, such as the "new math" and the "socially relevant," for tried-and-true methods such as phonics, multiplication tables, history, and geography. While his critics may have condemned his overall approach as elitist, Kean considered a quality education, in the manner in which he defined it, a universal right that no child should be denied because of the economic circumstances of his or her parents or where he or she happened to live. He continually made the argument that a quality education was the path toward a high-paying job. If the state did not fulfill its obligations to produce a well-educated and well-trained workforce, he argued, businesses in need of such employees would locate elsewhere, and the economic health of the state would deteriorate.

Finding the Right Education Commissioner

As governor-elect, Kean announced that he intended to make good on his campaign promise to replace Education Commissioner Fred Burke. In addition to the controversies surrounding declining SAT scores and the alleged watering down of basic-skills tests, Burke was dogged by allegations of mismanagement and conflicts of interest.[7] Claiming that two years remained of his five-year term, Burke at first refused Kean's demand that he resign. He gave way after Kean's staff discovered that, technically, the commissioner's term had expired, and after Kean let it be known that he was prepared to press the matter in court.

Kean thought he had found Burke's ideal replacement in Ronald Lewis, deputy to the Pennsylvania secretary of education and former superintendent of schools in Plainfield. Given the emphasis he placed on urban education, Kean found the prospect of naming the first African American education commissioner in the state's history, who also had experience working with inner-city schools, appealing. Five days after Kean announced Lewis as his choice, the *Star-Ledger* disclosed that the prospective appointee had copied more than half of his doctoral dissertation from several sources.[8] Within days after Lewis stepped aside, Kean announced his intention to appoint Saul Cooperman, school superintendent of Madison, New Jersey, and former head of the Montgomery Township school system, as Burke's successor. Cooperman shared Kean's concept of the schools as providers of a service and of students and parents as consumers. "You are the means," the commissioner-designate told his staff. "The kids are the ends."[9]

The path that Cooperman had followed into the classroom was not much different from the one Kean had traveled. After graduating from Lafayette College, Cooperman set out to pursue an M.A. in political science at Rutgers. Realizing that such a degree would not qualify him for an administrative post in most school districts, he shifted the focus of his academic interest to education and obtained an M.A. in that field. Aspiring to work on curriculum matters for a school district, he resigned his post as principal of Belvedere High School to pursue a doctorate in education, also at Rutgers.

Cooperman came to his post as commissioner with decided ideas on how to improve the quality of instruction based on his personal experiences. In the school district he had most recently left, 90 percent of teachers had tenure. Unable to replace poorly performing teachers at will, he had tried to rejuvenate those he called "burned-out cases" through training sessions and motivational seminars. Part of his approach had been to have teachers who had been exposed to such training impart what they had learned to their colleagues. Cooperman was eager to see whether he could replicate what he had achieved at the state level.

In his first meeting with Kean after his appointment, Cooperman asked the governor what he had in mind when he spoke about excellence in education. "That's why you're here," Kean replied with a chuckle.[10] That remark, Cooperman said years later, defined their relationship. Kean would set broad goals and leave it to Cooperman to devise the means to attain them. Kean, the politician who had spent part of his professional life in the classroom, and Cooperman, the political neophyte who, by his own admission, could not find his way to a political clubhouse in a taxicab, forged a partnership between a governor and an education commissioner unique in New Jersey history. The more Kean saw of Cooperman's earnestness, idealism, and passion, the more he backed his commissioner up. Cooperman attributed the governor's willingness to support him to Kean's self-confidence, which allowed him to take a chance on someone he did not know. "He could sense I would never do anything but support him," Cooperman said.[11]

Early Efforts at Educational Reform

In the months that elapsed before Kean had in place a commissioner of his own choosing, he cast his lot behind whatever efforts others were making to improve teacher training. The Board of Higher Education (BHE), at the initiative of Chancellor T. Edward Hollander, bolstered by recommendations of a legislative commission chaired by Assemblyman Daniel Newman, encouraged students in teacher-training programs to take additional courses in the liberal arts, spend additional hours practice-teaching, and demonstrate mastery of an assigned body of knowledge. The BHE enacted these requirements in summer 1981. Then the recently selected Republican nominee for governor, Kean praised its actions. In his first weeks in office, Kean demonstrated his continued support for the board's approach.

Although the BHE could influence what prospective teachers studied through its ability to approve curricula for teacher-training programs at state colleges, the ultimate authority over certification rested with the Education Department. Hollander wanted this power transferred to the BHE. He also wanted to require new teachers to hold master's degrees. With the change in departmental jurisdiction over licensing requiring legislative approval, Hollander sought to obtain it before Burke's successor took office. With the cooperation of Kean's counsel, Cary Edwards, the chancellor had the appropriate legislation introduced.

Once in the assembly, teacher licensing, like prison overcrowding and infrastructure repairs, joined the list of measures Speaker Karcher tried to hold up in order to extract concessions from Kean on other matters, especially on taxes. Karcher was not the only legislator who voiced objections to the bill. Members of the assembly's Education Committee who worked in the very teacher-training programs also objected to the measure. In order to entice at least one, Assemblyman John Rocco (R-Camden), dean of education at Rider College, to be more receptive to Kean's proposal to raise the gas tax, Edwards acquiesced to legislative demands that the bill be put on hold. Edwards's action proved fortunate for Kean in that it allowed Cooperman the time he needed to devise an even more radical transformation of the certification process than what Hollander envisioned.

Before he could advance an agenda, Cooperman had to take control of his department. He replaced staff, reduced layers of management, and created internal "swat teams" to guard against improprieties. Turning his attention to basic skills, Cooperman replaced the test that Burke had in place with a more difficult version and added a writing requirement. The new test became part of state-imposed requirements for graduation. Along with Kean, Cooperman demanded that student performance be measured against state-established standards, rather than against past student performance in particular districts or regions. Cooperman signaled his willingness to break with both tradition and the state's premier education lobby when he opted not to appoint NJEA designees automatically to each of four slots reserved for teachers on the state certification panel. (He named only one.) He also resisted expanding the scope of collective bargaining.

As Cooperman went about his tasks, Kean announced initiatives of his own. Through funds raised from private donations and foundation grants, Kean initiated a series of Governor's Schools in several disciplines and located them at colleges across the state. The first, devoted to global studies, began operations in 1983 at Monmouth College. Others, taking as their themes science, social studies, environmental studies, and the arts, would follow in subsequent years. Kean proclaimed the purpose of the Governor's Schools the "recognition of excellence."[12] Each summer, he would visit each of the

Governor's Schools he had established. Their very existence, he argued, would result in the raising of standards in most schools as students competed to gain entry into this selective program. To advance science education in New Jersey, Kean breathed life into a long-percolating, but previously unfunded plan to build a science center in Jersey City. The facility, heavily geared to children's and educational programs, would become the only one of its kind between Boston and Philadelphia.

A Nation at Risk

During their second year in office, Kean and Cooperman received a powerful boost in their attempt to rally public opinion behind reform of teacher training and higher educational standards. In April 1983, the National Commission on Excellence in Education, a group U.S. secretary of education Terence Bell had convened to assess the quality of public education, released a report titled *A Nation at Risk.* It warned that the United States was on the verge of losing its competitive edge over much of the world because of a decline in the quality of the education it imparted to its students. "If an unfriendly foreign power had attempted to impose on Americans the mediocre educational performance that exists today, we might have viewed it as an act of war," it said. The report documented case after case of students in other countries outperforming their American counterparts in tests in various academic disciplines.[13] Its release set off a firestorm of calls for reform. In linking educational improvement to students' ability to obtain high-paying jobs, Bell's report dovetailed with what Kean had been saying for nearly two years.

Michael Deaver, then deputy chief of staff to President Ronald Reagan, attributed Reagan's rising popularity in the fall of 1983 to his success in identifying himself with this increasingly salient political issue. Deaver explained how Reagan, through his use of the bully pulpit and his delivery of a consistent message at different venues, reaped numerous political and policy rewards.

> I remember . . . the President throwing his speech cards across the table . . . and saying to me, "I'm not going to give the speech any more. . . . I've been doing it for a week and a half now, and those guys [the media, seated in the back of the plane] aren't paying any attention." . . . I said, "Well, Mr. President, . . . four days before you were in Atlanta, the local news there was covering the arrangements, talking to local education people, talking to the mayor, the superintendent of education, watching and

following the Secret Service and the advance people making the details. From the time the airplane set down in Atlanta until the wheels were up four hours later, you were live in one of the five major media markets in the country, and tomorrow the Secretary of Education and your education adviser from the White House are going to be on all the talk radio and television shows in town, being interviewed in the newspapers."[14]

Reagan, Deaver said, gathered up his cards. Several governors, Kean first among them, threw themselves into this effort with an even greater enthusiasm than had Reagan.

To mark the beginning of the first school year since the release of *A Nation at Risk,* Kean convened a special session of the state legislature. He termed his proposals a "blueprint" for educational reform. His was a most ambitious agenda: increasing beginning teachers' annual salaries, then averaging between $11,000 and $14,000, to $18,500; implementing new licensing requirements, allowing prospective teachers to obtain certification through avenues other than existing teacher-training programs; rewarding outstanding teachers with merit pay, carrying a cash component of $5,000; establishing an academy for the advancement of teaching and management; adopting new approaches to urban education; accrediting well-performing local schools for five-year periods; instituting new statewide high school graduation tests; making proficiency in English a precondition for high school graduation; monitoring school districts; and, where necessary, removing disruptive students from classrooms.

Kean initially proposed offering the $18,500 salary only to teachers who passed tests required of all new teachers. "People have got to be assured they are getting better teachers, as well as better paid teachers," he said.[15] He would eventually agree to make the higher starting pay universal. When Cooperman first proposed higher starting salaries to Kean, most gubernatorial aides objected on the grounds that it would cost too much money. Pretending to be noncommittal, Kean, Cooperman said, smiled broadly as "it was all being fought out before him."[16] The commissioner had gotten his first glimpse of "that grin."

While the NJEA had not resisted Kean's efforts to raise teachers' starting salaries, neither had it reacted to the proposal enthusiastically. Known for its skills in successfully negotiating higher benefits for its members, the union's leadership had been cast in the role of acquiescing to an idea the governor advanced. Its pattern had been to press for overall increases in education spending and allowing districts to set spending priorities. Starting salaries for new hires had not traditionally ranked high among their concerns. As it prepared to make the case for alternative uses for the funds Kean was making available to cover the costs of increasing starting teachers' pay, the governor undercut their argument by funding fully, for the first time ever, the state school-aid formula. Bolstered by an $800-million state surplus, fueled in part by a recovering national economy and the tax increase to which he had reluctantly agreed two years earlier, Kean was able to fund both his initiatives and the union's preferences. With the matter of starting salaries settled, the NJEA concentrated its fire on two of his other proposals: alternate teacher certification and merit pay, which it regarded as a direct threat to the principle of trade unionism.

Alternate Teacher Certification

The day after he delivered his special message, Kean appeared before the New Jersey Board of Education to obtain its support for his educational initiatives. "You've got to be prepared to defend your position in the face of a crisis," he said, in what was taken to be a reference to *A Nation at Risk*.[17] Cooperman succinctly defined what the administration intended its alternative teacher certification plan to achieve: "We will move from a system that will certify people of limited ability to a system that will deny these people admittance to the profession. We will move from a system that systematically discourages talented people to a system that will make it possible for them to teach."[18]

Under the new plan's provisions, all new teachers would have to pass nationally devised tests in their respective fields. High school teachers would be examined in an academic discipline, elementary teachers in general knowledge. The power to certify would be transferred from the New Jersey Department of Education to local districts that did the hiring. All graduates of existing teaching programs would have to major in the liberal arts or the hard sciences, as opposed to education, and take up to sixty credits in general studies. Teachers pursuing the nontraditional route would, after passing the test, receive provisional certificates for a period of one year. During that time, they would undergo additional training by teams of educators from districts in which they worked. To avoid going to the legislature for funding, thereby risking "poison pill" amendments to the program, Cooperman financed the additional training in multiple ways: subsidies by hiring districts, scholarships to students, foundation grants, and the withholding of part of starting teachers' salaries.

In order to build public support for his ideas, in the course of two days, Kean delivered two speeches and held three press conferences in three separate locations. He made alternate teachers the major topic of each. The NJEA ridiculed Kean's efforts as a carefully rehearsed media event. It accused him of seeking to implement his plan through a "naked show of force."[19] Predicting that Kean's proposals would make guinea pigs of New Jersey students, Assemblyman John Rocco threatened to introduce legislation to block the implementation of the alternate teacher certification plan.[20] Kean pledged a veto. Through his relentless public advocacy of the proposal, he created an aura of its inevitability. Cooperman appointed a panel of nationally recognized educators, headed by former U.S. education commissioner and then-current president of the Carnegie Foundation for the Advancement of Teaching, Ernest Boyer, to establish guidelines for the test that new teachers would have to take and for the course of study noneducation majors would receive during their first year as teachers. Kean personally presented Boyer to the state board and threw his weight behind the panel's recommendations.

During its first year in operation, under the alternate teacher certification program, nearly two hundred provisional teachers entered New Jersey classrooms. Most came from other professions or private schools; 34 percent had graduated from college with honors; 14 percent held graduate degrees; 71 percent had prior teaching experience.[21] Three years later, nearly one-third of newly licensed teachers had come to the positions through the alternative certification route.[22] A decade after Kean left office, the number approached 40 percent. Contrary to critics' predictions, the requirement that new teachers pass the National Teacher Examination did not result in the diminution of minorities among the ranks of new teachers. Their number had actually increased as minority graduates of better colleges found this route into the classroom more attractive than traditional teacher-training programs, just as Kean had predicted.[23] New Jersey's alternate teacher program was the first of its kind in the nation. Several states followed its lead. Kean expressed particular pride when British prime minister Margaret Thatcher's government, eager to ease a teacher shortage in the United Kingdom, sent a delegation to observe how New Jersey's plan was being implemented.[24]

Other Educational Initiatives

Kean and Cooperman undertook several initiatives designed to motivate existing teachers to excel. One of their favored methods was teaching academies. The concept expanded on programs Cooperman had already implemented in Madison. Kean, the once and future teacher, found appealing the idea of professionals, having bettered themselves, imparting what they had learned to their colleagues. As he had in the case of the Governor's Schools, Kean proposed funding them through partnerships with the private sector. "Nobody's got a greater stake in teaching effectiveness than the many companies that will be hiring many of our children."[25]

As a means of advancing their proposal to reward "master teachers" with cash awards, Kean and Cooperman established a pilot program through which locally appointed committees in a handful of districts would select honorees. The NJEA denounced the initiative. It claimed that would lead to "undesirable competition that could destroy morale and collegiality."[26] Speaker Alan Karcher predicted that school boards would use the money to reward "those with political advantages."[27] Kean insisted that competition for this designation would improve the quality of teaching throughout the system. Upon learning that the NJEA had discouraged all but ten districts from participating, he tried going over its head by appealing to teachers directly. "No one controls good teachers, not even their unions," he stated.[28] Kean was particularly frustrated that the union took this stand after he had taken steps to involve its members in the program's implementation. "To turn it down was totally wrong," he said. "Teachers would have seen that they had the opportunity to be paid for excellence and competence."[29]

Rather than fold the funds he had set aside into those allocated to districts, as the union wanted, Kean earmarked them for other education initiatives, including a scholarship program for high school graduates desiring to become teachers and a program to forgive student loans to undergraduates who agreed to teach in urban schools. He also began a program through which he would annually present a modest award to the "best teacher" at each New Jersey school, nominated by students and staff. Each year, Kean would host convocations at which he presented one-thousand-dollar checks to the honorees at Princeton University's Jadwin Gymnasium. The event became so popular among teachers that the NJEA pressed Kean to allow its leaders to appear with him on stage as he recognized each winner.[30] Kean and his commissioner also established the Governor's Teaching Grants, thirty awards of up to fifteen thousand dollars annually bestowed upon a teacher or group of teachers who developed effective teaching techniques that could be replicated elsewhere.

Along with improving teacher training and raising the morale of teachers, Kean and Cooperman made urban education a high priority. They eschewed advice from specialists who urged educators to place emphasis on student self-esteem rather than on improved academic standards. Self-esteem, they maintained, would rise with academic achievement, accurately measured.[31] Kean refused to accept prevailing notions that the problems of urban schools were insoluble. His approach, as well as his words, anticipated President George W. Bush's subsequent description of such attitudes as the "soft bigotry of low expectations." In a speech before the College Board, Kean urged his audience not to lower standards in order to increase the number of minority graduates, but to "raise the students." "We kept the test," he said," and put more money into ensuring that the kids got the skills to pass it."[32] He proclaimed the lowering of standards "racist," because it presumed that students from certain backgrounds could not excel.

Kean introduced a pilot program, Operation School Renewal, through which three urban school districts signed three-year contracts with the state in which they promised to improve students' performance on state-administered tests, increase attendance, reduce disruptive behavior, improve the principal's performance, and enhance efforts to place graduating seniors in jobs. In exchange, the state provided additional aid and technical support. Kean found the idea of having recipients of assistance contract with its provider particularly attractive. "Even if we try, even if we try our best, there's always the chance we may not succeed," he said. "But if we don't try, then we will certainly fail."[33]

Taking His Case Nationally

Kean's achievements in education put him in the forefront of a national reform movement that spread across the country in the aftermath of the publication of *A Nation at Risk*. As his involvement in national educational affairs increased, he found that he needed a full-time aide just to keep him abreast of what was happening on the national scene and to identify areas in which he might assert his influence. Cooperman recommended Richard Mills of his staff. Mills's appointment proved anything but popular within Kean's official family.

First, the young educator had been in the employ of the much-maligned Fred Burke. He had also recently been elected to the Rocky Hill Borough Council, gubernatorial aides maintained, as a Democrat. Cooperman stood his ground. He related to any Kean adviser within hearing distance that he thought it outrageous to deny the governor the services of a highly qualified man. As nonpartisan as he was nonpolitical, Cooperman reminded Kean's aides that Mills had run as a *Republican*. The dustup between Cooperman and Kean's staff did not abate until after Mills had been hired. Mills first discovered that Kean had retained him when the governor telephoned him to give him his first assignment.

Having ridden the crest of a wave of national education reform to implement changes in New Jersey, Kean used the successes he had attained at the state level as his vehicle to press for change in education policies nationwide. He explained his manner of operation.

> I deliberately set out to influence national policy. . . . As word of New Jersey's reforms spread other governors called me up and asked for advice. I also lobbied for and won the chairmanship of the Education Commission of the States [ECS]. I used that position to become the only governor on the Carnegie Forum Task Force on Teaching. There I tried to give some intellectual consistency to the spate of reports that were coming out on education . . . I made sure that it [the alternate teachers certification program] was both in the Carnegie report and the report I helped write for the National Governors Association.[34]

Founded in the early 1960s by North Carolina governor Terry Sanford and underwritten by foundation grants, the ECS is a forum where governors, legislators, education commissioners, and members of state school boards come together to learn about education programs in other jurisdictions. Kean transformed it into one of the most active educational advocacy groups in the nation, through which policy makers from one part of the country learned about innovations that had been made in another.[35] Arkansas governor Bill Clinton served as the ECS's vice chairman under Kean and succeeded him as chairman.

Kean and Clinton first came into contact at a meeting of the National Governors Association in 1983. The two governors found that they had similar ideas about education. The very month Kean convened a special session of the New Jersey legislature to deliver his blueprint on education in New Jersey, Clinton did likewise in Arkansas. Like Kean, Clinton had also proposed higher teacher salaries, competency tests for teachers, and elevated standards for students. He earned the enmity of his state's teacher's union when he linked raises in teachers' pay to improved student performance and initiated tests to measure both.[36] In working toward common ends, Kean and Clinton enjoyed each other's company.

"He would quiz me about things we were doing back home," Kean said of Clinton. "He would come up to me and say, 'I've got this question.' His inquiries got right to the substance of things."[37] Clinton recalled being impressed with Kean's capacity to get other people to want to work with him. "He wears well," Clinton said of Kean. "He sort of grew on you."[38] Hillary Rodham Clinton, then heading a task force charged with formulating Arkansas's response to *A Nation at*

Risk to improve its own educational enterprise, shared her husband's assessment of Kean. Her first encounter with the New Jersey governor occurred at an ECS conference, where she served on a panel with Kean. As a third panelist recounted how children's formative experiences impacted upon their ability to learn, Mrs. Clinton glanced in Kean's direction. She noticed how intently he was following what was being said. "You could tell he really got it," she recalled.[39]

The Carnegie report, *A Nation Prepared,* called for national standards of certification, increased pay for teachers, differentiated staffing and pay scales, delineation of a core body of knowledge every teacher should know, more time in the classroom for teachers, and greater participation of teachers in school governance. All were measures that Kean had advocated at home. The underlying goal of the Carnegie report was to effect a change in school governance from one that pitted management (school boards) against labor (teachers unions) to a more collaborative enterprise in which teachers, principals, school boards, and parents (all stakeholders in the educational undertaking) participated in the running of schools.[40] Such a transition, its authors hoped, would cause both teachers and their supervisors to put a premium on excellence, acquired through the acquisition of skills, rather than on collective bargaining. Kean's hand could be seen in the creation of the National Board for Professional Standards, established one year after the Carnegie study was released. Its goal was to enhance the prestige of the teaching profession.

Kean's goal was to have schools compete for teachers who fulfilled the board's requirements, hopefully through the ability to provide higher compensation. He boasted that the Carnegie documents contained many "New Jersey ideas," including a state monitoring system that measured adherence to state goals, abolition of "emergency certificates," and preference for liberal arts over education majors in teacher recruitment. Kean made that report, and the previous work he had done with the ECS, the foundation for the National Governors Association report *Time for Results,* released in 1987. By the decade's end, a consensus had formed among governors and educational reformers around the recommendations contained in the Carnegie study.

As his participation in the national education reform movement broadened, Kean sometimes found himself having to walk a delicate line between policies recommended by the national bodies on which he sat and those he was administrating back home. Taking issue with his own chancellor of higher education, in one instance, Kean proclaimed himself "dead against" requiring graduate degrees as a precondition for teacher certification.[41] Acting through the National Governors Association and not always in sync with the national

Republican Party, Kean asked Congress and the Reagan administration to commit to certain principles, such as the right of children to good schools and of qualified applicants to attend college, and to set national standards against which states could monitor students' progress. Through the ECS he initiated "talking with teachers," an undertaking through which teachers, selected by their peers, shared with governors their views on how they regarded their profession. Kean and his peers found such an approach preferable to relying solely on results of surveys educational organizations commissioned. Their hope was that those who participated in these sessions would take a more active role in the governance of their respective schools. In New Jersey, Kean made it his practice to visit one school every five or six weeks on average. He visited seventy in the course of his eight years in office.

Widening the State's Role in Education

As Kean began his second term, observers and pundits expected him to use the size of his mandate to press for even more comprehensive changes in how the state conducted its affairs than he had in his first term. In his fifth State of the State address, Kean took government reform as his theme. He came out in favor of expanded initiative and referendum for voters, advancing the date of the state's presidential primary (from June to early spring), removing judicial discretion over housing policy, denying bail to violent offenders, setting legal thresholds on "pain and suffering" in lawsuits resulting from car accidents, and revamping the state's civil service. His suggestion to establish the post of lieutenant governor attracted the most attention. He saw this change as a means of improving the state's archaic gubernatorial succession practice of having the senate president serve simultaneously as acting governor and as senate president in the event the governorship fell vacant.[42]

As they dissected Kean's "good government" package, his allies and adversaries alike overlooked what he said about education reform. Kean called for amending the school funding formula to make more money available to schools that showed improvement in student performance over previous years. His suggestion ran counter to the then-prevailing practice of routinely (and automatically) increasing aid to underperforming districts. Kean considered such practices rewards for failure. When schools continually fell short of meeting state-imposed measurements of competency, he favored a more drastic remedy: replacing those who ran the school districts with administrators named by the state. Kean's advocacy of the state taking over failing school districts was so unprecedented that few in his audience managed to grasp the significance of what he had said. In its published excerpts of remarks from his speech, the *New York Times* omitted its most critical passage: "A handful of districts in the future may continue to fall short. . . . If the situation cannot be resolved any other way, then the state will have to intervene in a most assertive way in the operation of these school districts."[43] In his oral delivery, Kean substituted the word *directly* for *in a most assertive way.* He reported that he had asked Cooperman to draw up an appropriate plan and suggested he would be asking the legislature to act upon it.

Cooperman was already at work. Shortly after Kean won reelection, the commissioner mentioned that he had been reviewing Chapter 11, the federal bankruptcy statute, which allowed courts to name receivers to manage and reorganize failed companies. He wondered whether such a practice could be applied to failing school districts. Kean's eyes, Cooperman recalled, "lit up." The governor jumped out of his seat, shook his commissioner's hand, and exclaimed, "We are going to do it!"[44] Kean told Cooperman that he wanted to include the idea in his State of the State speech a month later.

Kean and Cooperman's decision to go the takeover route was as much an admission of failure as it was a hope for future success. During his first term, Kean increased education spending in all districts, devised special programs to assist urban schools, directed federal block grants to failing districts, funded the "thorough and efficient" formula fully, devised improved measurements of student performance, and took steps to bring better-trained teachers into classrooms. Few of these measures had much of an impact on districts Kean would later call "faulty, flawed, and failed." His advocacy of direct intervention in such districts was a bolder assertion of state power than any his predecessors or the courts ever proposed. Prior to his administration, the state had limited the extent of its participation in schools to the manner in which they were financed.

For a quarter century, legislative debates and court decisions centered on how to reduce disparities in funding between districts so that spending levels would meet what courts considered sufficient to satisfy the constitutional mandate on the state to provide a "thorough and efficient" education to every child. Kean sought a role for the state in improving upon the way in which children learned and what they learned. At the time he advanced them, Kean's views were gaining currency nationwide. Partly through his urging, the National Governors Association urged governors to use their power to seize control over districts that had been proven "academically bankrupt."[45]

The same year Kean offered his proposal, Kenneth Clark, whose research on the adverse effect segregated schools had on the self-esteem of African American children was cited in the Supreme Court's *Brown v. Board of Education* desegregation decision, called upon the New York State Board of Regents to supersede the authority of local school boards if they continually reported low test scores.[46]

Although several districts qualified for the designation "academically bankrupt" according to state criteria, Jersey City's, having failed thirty-two of fifty-one state requirements for certification and rumored to be rife with political corruption, patronage, and nepotism, appeared the ideal place to test Kean's ideas. His bold assertion of the powers of the state government over those of a local and rumored corrupt administration beholden to special interests won him praise across the country, from conservatives as well as from moderates and liberals. Future Speaker of the House of Representatives Newt Gingrich attributed his own radicalization on school governance to what he learned from Kean about how one city had used taxpayer funds the state had poured into it. "He showed me a thousand-page study of the Jersey City Schools. . . . Governor Kean's study group discovered the schools had been looted by the local political machine for patronage purposes. There was a $54,000-a-year fire extinguisher inspector who failed to show up for three years. Not only was he freeloading, but the schools were left with faulty fire extinguishers. . . . The study led to a state takeover of the city school system."[47] Kean described that city's school system as one that had "everybody's brother-in law and campaign manager" on its payroll.[48]

Kean consciously took up the role of the public's guardian, exercising his powers as chief executive to enforce the rights of students, parents, and taxpayers against the special interests, the incompetent, and the corrupt. The public image he created for himself was that of a George Wallace in reverse. Whereas the Alabama governor, in 1963, stood in the doorway of the University of Alabama to prevent African American students from entering, New Jersey's two decades later would send state-appointed administrators to supersede or remove officials who failed to educate children. Kean's use of his office to hold schools accountable and his belief that schools existed to benefit children rather than educational bureaucrats set a precedent for other education reforms that came to the fore after he left office, such as charter schools, school choice, and vouchers. All took as their underlying premise Kean and Cooperman's concept of students and parents as consumers of education and school boards and teachers as providers of a service.

Kean's Battle to Establish State Control of Failing School Districts

In June 1986, Kean unveiled a plan through which the state would intervene in the operations of school districts that consistently failed to meet state competency levels. Under its provisions, the state would send two sets of monitors into districts, one to investigate why they consistently failed to improve and another to assess their governance, management, and finances. Based on their findings, the education commissioner would be empowered to establish a state-operated district, replacing the local school board with persons sent by the state.[49] Kean proclaimed that the quality of the education children received in certain schools was neither "thorough" nor "efficient." He insisted that he could not philosophically or legally allow that situation to continue.[50]

On June 30, at his initiation, legislation was introduced to allow the state to establish state-operated districts and the commissioner to

Fig 12.1. Having made education his major priority as governor, Kean enacted more than three dozen reforms. Many, such as his efforts to hold schools accountable and reform teacher training, drew national attention. Kean and his education commissioner, Saul Cooperman, saw their roles as advocates for students and parents rather than for professional educators and bureaucrats. (© 1986 *The Star-Ledger.* All rights reserved. Reprinted with permission.)

replace local boards. State takeovers would last for a minimum of five years. Districts found to be in compliance at any time after that initial period would be free to decide their future form of governance. To make the measure more palatable to its opponents, the bill allowed teachers to retain tenure. The state's three major education associations were initially temperate in their reactions to Kean's proposal. The NJEA concentrated its efforts on retaining principals' tenure. All the state school boards association said was that it had not been consulted when the plan was assembled. The New Jersey Association of School Administrators announced that it would "weigh the potential benefits to the children against the rights of affected administrators."[51]

As the bill's opponents, primarily city governments and teachers unions, worked behind the scenes to weaken, if not bury, the legislation, Kean worked to build public support for his proposals. He especially cultivated organizations that saw their mission as improving conditions for minorities. In a speech before the National Urban League, Kean, the *New York Times* reported, brought his audience to its feet when he said: "We are telling our urban school districts that no longer will we turn our backs and tolerate mediocrity. We are no longer going to blame our children. We are going to fix the schools."[52] He suggested that some urban schools had become "warehouses filled with unfulfilled human potential." Calling the right to a decent education the new civil right, he suggested that those who administered systems that failed to educate were harming minority children just as severely as had segregationists of years past.[53]

A year later, Kean, speaking before the seventy-sixth annual gathering of the National Association for the Advancement of Colored People (NAACP), proclaimed that the failure of urban schools to teach was a form of "educational child abuse." After citing statistics that suggested that urban youngsters were more likely to suffer the effects of drug and alcohol abuse, unemployment, teen pregnancy, and other maladies, he said that schools were among the few institutions able to provide such youngsters with a means to a better life. That was why, he insisted, it was important that they not fail. Keith Jones, president of the Newark branch of the organization, summarized the dilemma Kean made its members confront: "If something is not working, then we need a change. We don't want to see black administrators replaced. We don't want to see local control lost. But we must make some decision about how to make improvements."[54]

To ease the takeover bill's passage in the assembly, Kean made a series of compromises that may have impeded the statute's subsequent effectiveness. He accepted amendments that shifted the burden of proof from localities to the state in establishing the justification for takeovers. He allowed removed school board members to serve out their terms, but only in an advisory capacity. Although he had repeatedly held firm against allowing principals to retain their tenure and on not increasing state aid to districts to prevent turnover, he yielded considerable ground on both points before the bill passed, just as he had consented at the outset to allow teachers in failing district to retain their tenure. Even with these compromises, the city's decision to sue the state delayed the statute's implementation by a year.

When the senate initially considered Kean's takeover legislation, it rejected it in a vote of 21 to 18. Most troubling to Kean was the defection of seven Republicans. The takeover battle produced some unconventional alliances and frayed some long-established coalitions. Big-city mayors, fearful of losing control of local schools and the patronage that came with it, opposed the bill. So did conservative Republicans, not eager to set a precedent for future state incursions upon home rule. Eight Democrats, convinced that Kean's plan might actually work, supported it.

For the first time during his administration, Kean threatened reprisals. He suggested that he would find it "very difficult" to campaign in 1987 with Republican senators who voted against the takeover bill. He vowed to stop funding schools that "will not educate children." He declared that he would not be bound by an agreement he had made with the NJEA to expand the scope of collective bargaining. "I'm willing to talk with anyone about any issue," he said, "but that one's dead." "The problem is that poor black children don't vote," he declared[55] Editorial support was all but universally with him. Representative of press opinion was a *Trenton Times* editorial declaring the senate's vote a "victory only for incompetent school officials, including principals who can continue sabotaging education behind a shield of tenure."[56]

Three days after the senate vote, Kean stunned the New Jersey political community when he suggested that funds raised at the GOP's annual Governor's Ball might not be made available to the campaigns of Republicans who had opposed the takeover bill.[57] Guests arrived to hushed tones as Kean and GOP state chairman Frank Holman, in formal attire, huddled to discuss how to allocate the dinner's proceeds. "If all these guys want to run on their own then let them run on their own," Holman said later.[58] Barely eighteen months after winning his record-setting reelection, Kean had seen legislators from his own party sabotage not only the major policy initiative of his second term but also one he had been advancing all over the country.[59]

At first glance, Kean's threats against his fellow Republicans appeared shortsighted and self-defeating. How, some inquired, could chances for the passage of the rest of his program improve in a senate chamber in which Democrats controlled twenty-three seats and the Republicans seventeen, with reduced GOP margins brought about, in part, by his actions? Kean let them speculate. After issuing his threat, he departed for a trade mission to the Far East. When he returned, the governor announced that he would campaign, after all, for Republicans who had voted against the takeover legislation. He added that he would find the chore easier if he received an indication that some who opposed the measure "may be able to vote for it in the future." Seeing an opening, Louis Bassano (R-Union) let it be known that he might be supportive, providing that the legislation were accompanied by language extending legislative oversight of the commissioner, once a takeover was under way. Kean was amenable.[60]

While he had voiced uncertainty as to whether he would appear in public with Republicans who had opposed him, Kean left no doubt that he would support those in difficult races who had supported him. Frank Gargiulo, a Jersey City resident and one of four Hudson Republicans to win election to the assembly on Kean's coattails in 1985, was a case in point. Late in October, Kean, with U.S. Secretary of Education William Bennett at his side, staged a rally on behalf of the beleaguered Republican. "If you own a hamburger stand and you serve one rotten hamburger," Bennett said, "the state and federal government will shut you down. If you serve up a rotten education, nothing happens."[61] Bennett would return to Washington fired up about what he had heard and seen of Kean's reform efforts. Years later, Bennett still spoke admiringly of Kean's "willingness to put in the work, make the argument, and do the gritty things that assure [educational] progress." He also recalled the pleasure Kean derived in relating how he had defied the NJEA on several occasions. "I just go at 'em," Kean gleefully told Bennett.[62] "That grin" was beginning to get national exposure.

In the New Jersey election, Republicans lost four seats in the assembly and one in the senate. In a lame-duck session, the lower house passed a version of the takeover bill Kean had conditionally vetoed. The new version restored tenure rights to principals. After the measure passed, the NJEA, having achieved its major objective and still hopeful of extracting concessions from Kean on other issues, reversed its position and supported the takeover bill. To assuage him, the assembly added a provision expediting the hearing process for principals whom state-appointed administrators wished to remove.[63] After an amendment was added in the senate that required the state to pay the costs of actions taken by districts to avoid a takeover, Kean, disappointed, proclaimed that "politics came above children." He suggested that the senate had sent a message to schoolchildren that if they got an F, they would be rewarded, but not if they received an A.[64] Reworking Kean's phraseology, Senator Bill Gormley (R-Atlantic), a

Kean loyalist, termed the amendment an "incompetence grant," reserved only for "incompetent districts."[65]

In subsequent weeks, a tug-of-war ensued between Kean and Democratic senate president John Russo over whether the takeover bill, even in its weakened form, would become law. Observers attributed Russo's insertion of the provision Kean found so offensive to the Democrat's cultivation of Jersey City mayor Anthony Cucci's support in the 1989 Democratic gubernatorial primary. A Democrat elected from a heavily Republican county, Russo was basing his claim to be the Democratic standard-bearer on his professed and demonstrated political independence. It would not be good for his image for him to be identified in the public mind with the Jersey City clubhouse. Russo denied Kean's suggestion that the senate president had entered into a secret deal with Jersey City's mayor. He suggested that Kean had lost his cool.[66] As the public rift between the two widened, Russo began substituting the word *marbles* for *cool.*[67]

As Kean and Russo traded accusations, their staffs began working out their differences. One Kean aide said that the bill had been amended so many times that its entire text was in italics.[68] Having already made concessions on principals' tenure, Kean eventually agreed that the state would assume the costs of actions districts took in advance of a takeover, but in the same proportion as it supplied aid under existing school-aid formulas. They also agreed to speed up the timetables through which municipalities received state funding. In signing the legislation, which each chamber had voted upon no less than four times, Kean declared that the state was making a moral statement that "when schools fail, adults are the ones who have failed and . . . who must pay the price."[69]

He laughed when Russo presented him with a bag of marbles and referred to the senate president as a "class guy." "When the history of Tom Kean is written," Russo predicted "no one will be able to challenge his belief in the children of the state." One observer described the tenacity Kean had exhibited in pursuit of a cause in which he deeply believed: "More than once . . . Governor Thomas H. Kean faltered and almost lost the fight for the plan. But each time, the governor . . . was able to rally, go to the people through the press and build a base of support for the plan that he believes will determine his place in New Jersey history."[70]

Winning the Takeover Battle

Kean's signature on the takeover bill in no way ended the battle over who would control Jersey City's schools. Cucci, spending one million dollars in public funds, much of it from the state, filed suit to prevent Cooperman from asserting his powers under the newly passed legislation. Kean, arguing that such funds might have been better spent educating children, tried to impound them.[71] The legal dispute dragged on for more than a year. Ruling in the state's favor, an administrative law judge declared: "Ample proofs establish that the children attending public school in the Jersey City school district are not receiving the thorough and efficient education to which they are entitled, that political interference originating in earlier school administrations has continued, that public money allocated to education in the district is being misspent and that district problems chronicled in so many state reports are deep rooted and serious."[72]

On October 4, 1989, with three months remaining in Kean's administration, New Jersey became the first state in the country to assume both educational and administrative control of a school district. By unanimous vote, the New Jersey Board of Education abolished the city's school board, fired its superintendent and six administrators, and named to key positions individuals of Cooperman's choosing. Across the political spectrum, analysts and policy makers recognized the historical significance of these actions and applauded Kean for initiating them. Liberal columnist Carl Rowan called upon other states to follow New Jersey's lead in rising above the "local control trap."[73] Conservative William F. Buckley Jr. saw Kean's *blitzkrieg* against Jersey City" as the first in a series of steps that would lead parents, energized by Kean's assertion of the accountability principle, to withdraw from failing schools both their children and their tax dollars.[74]

In future years, other cities besides Jersey City would have state-operated school districts. Looking back, Cooperman reported that by all measurements, the takeover bill achieved several of its objectives: corruption and nepotism had been significantly reduced or eliminated; facilities had been repaired; new textbooks and equipment had been provided; parents and communities had become more interested in what transpired within the schools. While student average performance still did not meet state-imposed minimum standards, it had, Cooperman said, increased dramatically and more substantially than in other poorly performing districts the state had not taken over.[75]

Analysts assessing the takeover's progress believed that even more progress would have been made had officials spent less time supervising the shuffling of personnel from position to position as dismissed principals asserted their tenure rights to teaching positions. This had been an unintended consequence of concessions Kean and his advisers made to smooth passage of the legislation. The question of how much in the way of additional state funds should be spent in poorly performing districts remained a topic of debate. The year after Kean left office, the state supreme court ruled in *Abbott v. Burke,* which was first filed the year before his election, that, after passage of the state income tax, disparities in spending between rich and poor districts had widened. It ordered additional funds allocated to poorer districts in order for the state to comply with the "thorough and efficient" mandate.

For the Jersey City school takeover to have been more effective, Cooperman said, the state would have had to find ways to compensate for the negative aspects of students' lives outside the classroom and the impact those have on their ability to concentrate, let alone learn. One insurmountable barrier he cited was the high turnover each year in poorly performing schools. "Being first is difficult," he noted. "There were no existing models."[76] Kean predicted that those who followed the road he had traveled would have the benefit of discoveries made after he left office, especially the impact early childhood education can have on children's ability to learn.

As he waged battle on behalf of the legislation, Kean had taken a long view. "If we fail," he said at the time, "those kids are no worse off than before. If I'm right," he continued, "those kids have a chance for a future that they would have no other way."[77] He voiced the disappointment that the administration that succeeded his did not vigorously pursue reform and regret that he had not pushed even harder than he had to link increased school aid to administrative, curriculum, and other reforms. Still, Kean's pursuit of the first state takeover of failing schools in the nation ranked among his most courageous as governor. "If anything is said of Tom Kean as governor, I hope it is that I did not sit by and watch another generation of city children treated like pawns in a political game, the resulting ignorance enslaving them just like the chains that once bound their great-grandparents," Kean wrote.[78]

Years later, Kean cited among his major regrets his failure to act unilaterally, whether in advance of or in lieu of legislation, to take over failing school districts. Had he gone this route, Kean would have argued that, as the state's chief executive, he had an obligation to enforce the constitutional mandate to provide a "thorough and efficient" education to every child. "The lawyers advised me that we would be better served to get the legislation," he said.[79] Several of his advisers believed the courts would look more favorably on Kean's actions if they could point to a statute that explicitly granted him authority to do what he intended. Had Kean relied on his initial instincts, the courts might well have sustained him.[80] After he left office, a retired state supreme court justice told him that had he as governor acted on his own, the court "would have been delighted."[81]

President Reagan Gives Kean High Marks for Education

Ten days after Kean signed the takeover bill into law, he received a call from a White House aide. The staffer urged Kean to tune in to President Reagan's State of the Union address scheduled for the following evening. He suggested Kean might find it of interest.[82] Before a national television audience, President Reagan lauded Kean's alternate teacher certification program, passed in his first term, as a model for the nation. Reagan's comments suggested support for Kean's other initiatives in education: "As a nation, we do, of course, spend heavily on education—more than we spend on defense—yet across our country, governors like New Jersey's Tom Kean are giving classroom demonstrations that how we spend is as important as how much we spend. Opening up the teaching profession to all qualified candidates; merit pay, so that good teachers get A's as well as apples; and stronger curriculum, as Secretary [William] Bennett has proposed for high schools—these imaginative reforms are making common sense the most popular new kid in America's schools."[83]

Preparations for Reagan's address were already under way when Bennett had visited New Jersey during the 1987 election. William Kristol, then Bennett's chief of staff, referred to Kean's alternate teacher certification initiatives in talking points he had prepared for Reagan's speechwriters.[84] In addition to recommending that the president commend Kean for implementing the idea, Kristol had suggested that Reagan, in order to encourage other states to follow New Jersey's lead, announce that the federal government would offer to pay some of the costs of administrating the alternative teacher certification program. Mindful of criticism the president was receiving over the growing size of the federal deficit, Reagan's advisers balked at the suggestion. Reagan's successor, George H. W. Bush, embraced the idea on a visit to a New Jersey school with Kean accompanying him.[85]

After the president delivered his remarks, Kean wrote to Reagan informing him of how "deeply honored he was" to have been mentioned in a "great speech by a great president."[86] In his own hand, Reagan wrote a response, which he passed on to his secretary to type. "Dear Tom," it began. "Thank you for your kind words about my speech. I meant what I said about you because you have done and are doing a great job. You have turned your state around and made it a shining example of fine government. Best regards, Ron." By the time the letter had been readied for his signature, word reached Reagan that Elsa Kean had died. Before affixing his signature, Reagan dictated a postscript: "P.S. Just as I was preparing to sign this note, I learned of your mother's passing. Nancy joins me in sending you deepest sympathy on your loss."[87]

Reagan's State of the Union address marked the third occasion during his presidency when he singled out Kean by name while talking about education. In Indiana in 1983, while attending a conference as part of his response to Bell's *A Nation at Risk* study, Reagan had referred to the alternate teaching certification plan that Kean had introduced: "In New Jersey, Governor Tom Kean has a proposal that deserves wide support. Under his plan, the New Jersey board of education would allow successful mathematicians, scientists, linguists, and journalists to pass a competency test in their subjects and then go into classrooms as paid teaching interns. If they performed well, they would be given permanent teaching certificates at the end of the year."[88] Reagan returned to this theme in his radio address five months later: "In New Jersey Governor Tom Kean had another creative idea—give scientists and mathematicians in private industry a form of teaching accreditation so they can go into the schools and teach what they know."[89]

On a stopover in New Jersey during the 1981 recount, Reagan, trying to lift Kean's spirits, urged his youthful protégé to "hang in there." The president reportedly told Kean that being governor was worth all the effort and occasional inconveniences. "There would be days," he said, when because of something he had achieved, Kean, as governor, would feel "ten feet tall." January 13, 1988, the day Kean signed the takeover bill, and January 26, 1988, the day Reagan praised Kean before the nation, were two such days.

chapter 13

Kean and the Arts

The Governor as Arts Advocate

Anyone paying attention to what Kean said during his 1981 campaign about the role the arts might play in rekindling state pride would have expected his administration to pay increased attention to cultural affairs. Just how high a priority Kean accorded them, in the investment of both time and funds, surprised even his closest advisers. He had certainly given hints. When declaring his candidacy for governor, he had praised the quality of New Jersey cultural organizations and had made note of the number of internationally acclaimed performers who routinely graced New Jersey stages. Once elected, he asked the state's leading performing and visual arts organizations to participate in his inaugural festivities and allocated to them a major share of the proceeds.

Much as Kean may have believed in what he was saying about the quality of New Jersey arts organizations, he was well aware that many, both within and without New Jersey, influenced by late-night comics and New York arbiters of taste, accepted the caricature of the state as a cultural wasteland. Thomas Michalak, the recently departed conductor of the New Jersey Symphony Orchestra, complained that the state suffered from an inferiority complex. "You know, if the product is named New Jersey, it can't be any good," he observed; "people simply do not seem to have enough pride."[1] Kean had come into office determined to change that.

Taking office amid a deepening recession, he could do little at first about the situation other than use the visibility of his office to showcase groups and individuals he believed merited support. Allies, who might have been able to assist him under other circumstances, were in short supply. The state's premier performing arts organization, the New Jersey Symphony, teetered on the brink of bankruptcy, while the New Jersey State Council on the Arts, the agency through which the state provided partial funding to the arts, was beset with petty scandals and had fallen victim to a political feud not of its own making.

The symphony's executive director, John L. Hyer, attributed the orchestra's plight to its inability to attract support from corporate and individual donors in the same proportion as its counterparts in other states.[2] He also cited as a contributing factor to its financial difficulties the absence of a world-class performing arts center to which audiences would want to come and where the orchestra could record, broadcast, and telecast. One of the few performing arts organizations with a statewide audience, the symphony spent much time playing in high schools, gymnasiums, and renovated theaters, many of them substandard venues for the presentation of great music and, often, in need of repairs. Hyer's knowledge of the music industry, media savvy, perseverance, and biting sense of humor made him a natural leader for the still nascent arts advocacy movement in New Jersey. He knew how to mobilize audiences and patrons, argue his case to politicians and potential donors, and make common cause with groups that stood to benefit from a thriving arts community, such as building-trades unions, restaurateurs, and the recording and publishing industries.

Aware that he would have few additional funds to invest in the arts during his first year in office, Kean made symbolic increases to the arts council's budget as he cut back in other areas. He also encouraged nongovernment sources to invest in cultural institutions. He often cited a study by the Port Authority of New York and New Jersey that suggested the arts contributed four dollars in economic activity to their host communities for every dollar of public funds spent on them.[3] Kean appeared regularly at performances and openings. During intermissions, he would recite the performing or exhibiting organization's strengths to reviewers and donors. CEOs, hopeful of catching the governor's ear, started attending such events in person, rather than sending lower-level officials to represent their companies. Reporters (whose beats did not include the arts) took to standing outside theaters and museums in the hope of catching exclusives from Kean. Before long, news from the state's cultural scene began appearing in the front sections of newspapers, as well as on the arts pages in the back.

"The emphasis we place on the arts," Kean liked to say, "says a lot about the values we hold as a people and the quality of life we hope to build in our state."[4] Each spring, Kean hosted an invitational tennis tournament and donated the proceeds to a half-dozen cultural organizations. Although his predecessor had also held such tournaments to raise funds for non-profit organizations, Kean changed their focus. During Byrne's time, proceeds went to the Robert F. Kennedy Memorial Foundation, which used them to fund projects across the country. Kean decreed that funds be used for the benefit of New Jersey arts organizations. On average, the tournaments netted between $130,000 and $200,000 annually.

The Return of the Prodigal Agency

In order for Kean to establish for the state a reputation for excellence in the arts, he needed a partner that could with credibility attest that organizations the state supported were of a quality worthy of audience and private-sector support. A state arts agency, respected throughout the cultural community and known to disburse limited funds through a fair, competitive process, might have played such a role. At the time Kean took office, the New Jersey State Council on the Arts was hardly in a position to do so. The legislation that had established the arts council in 1966 placed it under the auspices of the secretary of state. During Byrne's last year in office, the agency was moved to the Department of Education at Byrne's request. The transfer was part of Byrne's attempt to curb the secretary of state's powers after incumbent Donald Lan refused Byrne's ultimatum to either abandon plans to run for governor or resign his office.

Lan called the transfer of the arts council a "monument to political retribution."[5] As one observer put it, "The normally placid world of the arts" had "become a political pawn in the war between Brendan Byrne and Secretary of State Donald Lan over who would control it."[6] Byrne loyalists charged that Lan had impeded the council's ability to function by not signing off on grants and travel vouchers. Lan cited irregularities in how the council awarded and handled its funds as his justification. Adding to the agency's woes, the National Endowment for the Arts held up payment of its annual basic state grant to New Jersey, calling the council's application "inarticulate" and its procedures for awarding grants "questionable."

Not long after Kean took office, the state's commission on ethical standards, after investigating allegations Lan had made against the council's executive director, Eileen Lawton, recommended that she be dismissed for ethical improprieties. An administrative law judge subsequently ordered she be removed from her post.[7] She resigned three days later. Even before her case was resolved, Kean was taking steps to build the kind of arts council in which he could have confidence. During the transition, secretary of state–designate Jane Burgio told Kean that she would like to see the arts council returned to its traditional home. Kean was supportive.

Days after Cooperman began his duties as education commissioner, Burgio approached him to ascertain whether he wished to see the agency remain part of his department. He replied that although he would fulfill his statutory obligations to it, he would not be able to give it a high priority. He also said that he would not oppose the transfer. This part of her homework completed, Burgio asked her successor in the assembly and sister arts supporter, Maureen Ogden (R-Essex), to submit the necessary legislation. When he signed Ogden's bill into law, Kean announced that he and Burgio would place "greater emphasis on a vigorous promotional effort for the arts in New Jersey." He also promised that the council would be "free of the kind of political controversy which surrounded it in recent years."[8]

Even before Ogden introduced her measure, Burgio had taken steps to prepare her department to function as a cultural advocate within the cabinet. This prospect was much on her mind when, shortly after taking office, she asked me to serve as her principal deputy in the post of assistant secretary of state. I had known Burgio from the time she served as vice chairwoman of the Essex County Republican organization and had campaigned for her when she first ran for the assembly. Although I was not familiar with the workings of the arts council, I had worked with two organizations it helped fund: the Newark Museum and the New Jersey Symphony. I was aware of the controversies that had swirled around the arts council, the ethical infractions that had resulted in indictments of three of Burgio's predecessors, with one going to prison, and the conviction of the immediate past assistant secretary of state for laundering funds to Byrne's 1977 reelection campaign.

Prior to my appointment, some Kean aides had been pressing Burgio to fill the assistant secretary's post with a county political leader. In naming me to the position, Burgio had reinforced her personal ties to Kean, while distancing her department from his political operation. A less self-assured cabinet officer might have regarded my prior association with Kean as a threat to her authority. Burgio considered them an asset.

Until the day I was sworn in, June 17, 1982, some on Kean's staff, still hopeful that the post would go to a political operative, tried to convince me to take another appointment. Hearing the rumors, Burgio informed Kean that in the event that I declined her offer, she had others in mind for the post and would like to discuss these possibilities with him. Raising his eyebrows, Kean declared sternly, "Well, that young man is going to have to make up his mind." I telephoned both Kean and Burgio to accept the appointment. Six months later, the arts council had "come home."

A New Focus for the State Department

The removal of the arts council back to the Department of State was one of many steps Kean took early in his term to transition Burgio's department away from political and patronage matters and toward the formation of policies consistent with the rest of his agenda. Upon his release from the hospital on September 9, 1982, Kean signed an executive order placing the Governor's Advisory Commission on Ethnic Affairs in the State Department.[9] In the spring of 1983, Kean, also by executive order and with Cooperman's concurrence, placed the New Jersey Historical Commission and the New Jersey State Museum under Burgio's aegis.[10] A year later, Kean did the same with the state archives. He subsequently assigned the State Department responsibility for New Jersey's participation in such celebratory activities as the centennial of the Statue of Liberty (1986) and the bicentennial of the U.S. Constitution (1987). By the end of Kean's second term, the State Department was functioning in all but name as the Department of Cultural Affairs. Repositioning it so that it could do so effectively became part of my portfolio.

The State Department received its first opportunity to act in its new capacity in the summer of 1983. As a means of promoting state tourism, Kean accepted the Smithsonian Institution's invitation to make New Jersey its featured state at its annual folk life festival, held on the National Mall. Initially, he had rejected the offer on the grounds that, in time of recession, the state had better use for the $250,000 the Smithsonian required its invitees to expend. Seeing an opportunity to promote the state at the height of the tourist season in a sluggish economy, he decided that New Jersey would participate, but that it would pay for the exhibition with private funds.

Kean turned what had been billed as a two-week festival outside the state into a yearlong celebration of New Jersey's treasures within it. Under the leadership of John Horan, chairman of the Merck Chemical Company, Festival New Jersey '83, the nonprofit organization charged with fund-raising, generated $1 million, nearly five times the figure the museum cited, enabling the exhibition to tour the state. Under the direction of Paterson mayor Pat Kramer, Festival New Jersey '83 held events in every county, culminating with an opening-night gala concert at the Smithsonian's Castle featuring the New Jersey Symphony.[11] "This is what you get to do when you come in second in a state primary," Kramer deadpanned. The most prominent feature at the exhibit was the 150-foot replica of the Atlantic City Boardwalk the state carpenters' union erected between the Washington Monument and the Capitol. After a hurricane devastated boardwalks along the shore later that year, Kean donated the Smithsonian boards to Bradley Beach as a symbol of the shore community's renewal.

On the heels of the Smithsonian celebration, New Jersey's cultural organizations, again at the State Department's impetus, sprang back into action. To commemorate the bicentennial of the signing of the Treaty of Paris, which recognized the independence of the United States, it brought to Princeton, which served briefly as the nation's capital in 1783, representatives of the signatory countries as well as reenactors, musicians, amateur historians, and scholars. Featured speakers in addition to Kean and Princeton University president William G. Bowen included Richard B. Morris, author of the definitive account of the treaty and one of Kean's former professors at Columbia. "I'm so proud to be governor of a state with that kind of history," Kean bellowed after recounting the role that New Jersey had played in the American Revolution to a hall packed with television cameras from around the world.[12] When the state's archivist presented him with an original copy of the document that had been returned to the state's possession, Kean, his competitive instincts aroused, boasted that his was the only state to have such a document in its possession.

When a reporter interrogated Morris about Kean's record as a student, the professor remembered Kean as "outstandingly good." Unwittingly, Morris let go a line Kean had been using for well over a year to the delight of listeners. Noting that Kean was not a lawyer, Morris said that he would like to see more nonlawyers in politics.[13] When Kean ran for governor in 1981, he mentioned in a speech that, if elected, he would be the first governor to serve under the 1947 constitution who would not be a lawyer. To his surprise, his audience burst into thunderous applause.

The Arts Council Gets the Message

After the top position at the arts council became vacant, Kean instructed its leadership to conduct an open search to fill it. He said that after it had decided upon a new executive director, he might like to meet with its designee. He asked that it not make its choice public until after it had notified him. Its failure to follow Kean's directives produced some comical and suspenseful episodes. After months of deliberation, the council settled on Jeffrey A. Kesper, director of the Middlesex County Cultural and Heritage Commission. After Margaret Hager, one of Kean's first appointments to the arts council, reminded her colleagues of Kean's instructions, its acting assistant director telephoned Kean's office and left a message informing him of the council's decision. She then issued a press release announcing Kesper's appointment.

The following day, Greg Stevens, who had replaced Lew Thurston as Kean's chief of staff, informed Burgio that the forms necessary to add Kesper to the state payroll would not be signed. He added that Kean was upset that the council had not extended him the courtesy he had requested of meeting with the council's choice before it made its decision public. For the next six months, Burgio worked to break the impasse. Repeatedly, she invited Kesper to join her at events she knew Kean would be attending. Each time, she introduced Kesper to Kean. Each time, Kean was cordial. Yet Kesper's papers failed to move. One day at an event Kesper did not attend, Burgio walked up to Kean and said, "Governor, I want to talk to you about the situation at the arts council." "Oh, is that thing still going on?" Kean inquired, flashing "that grin." He suggested that she bring Kesper in to see him. Kesper was hired the day after he met Kean.

Kean had made his point and in a way that avoided what could have been a costly political battle. When he called on the council to dismiss Lawton after the administrative law judge recommended she be removed, Kean said that personnel actions rested not with the governor but with the council, which, he said, "was set up independently."[14] Although Kesper had not participated in partisan politics, he had been in the employ of a county government that was overwhelmingly Democratic in its composition. He was on good terms with New Brunswick's Democratic mayor John Lynch, who also served concurrently in the majority leadership in the state senate. Also representing Middlesex in the legislature was assembly Speaker Alan Karcher. Either Middlesex Democrat might have welcomed the opportunity to contest with Kean, possibly in court, over how far the governor's powers extended into the internal workings of the arts council. By basing his reluctance to add Kesper to the state payroll in terms of a "courtesy," Kean had avoided a potential showdown with the legislative leadership. By the time he signed off on the council's appointment, he had ensured that the agency would march in step with his administration. From that moment on, Kean became the first rather than the last to learn of the council's decisions.

Figure 1. John Kean 1756–1795. The first of Tom Kean's forebears born in North America and the first to hold public office, John Kean was serving in the Continental Congress when George Washington appointed him Cashier of the United States. Kean wed Susan Livingston, niece of New Jersey's revolutionary governor William Livingston, a signer of the Declaration of Independence and of the U.S. Constitution. (Courtesy of Thomas H. Kean.)

Figure 2. Senator John Kean, 1852–1914. Party stalwart and businessman John Kean, Tom Kean's great-uncle, served in the U.S. Senate from 1899 to 1911. In an era when state legislatures, rather than voters, selected U.S. senators, Kean's political career was cut short when Woodrow Wilson was elected governor of New Jersey in 1910, along with a Democratic legislature. (Courtesy of Thomas H. Kean.)

KEAN ACTION NEWS

SENATOR KEAN'S FIGHT AGAINST CHEAP FOREIGN LABOR WINS SUPPORT OF JERSEY WORKERS

U.S. SENATOR H. F. KEAN

At every opportunity Senator Kean has fought to protect American labor against the disastrous effects of the importation of foreign goods produced by peasant, peon or coolie labor. Every time the Democrats tried to enact vicious Free Trade Legislation that would lower the bars to cheap foreign goods, Senator Kean fought tooth and nail to protect American workingmen's jobs.

❖ Senator Kean voted to raise or maintain at high levels import taxes on nearly 100 items. Fifty-three times he was on his feet in the Senate addressing that body on behalf of American labor, a record of which Jersey labor should be proud.

VETERANS O. K. SEN. KEAN'S RECORD

Senator Kean has always been a staunch friend of the veteran. At a meeting not long ago the Senator spoke of his efforts to help the veterans receive proper medical attention and recognition from the government. The sincerity of his statement is proven by his voting record of 800% for veterans' legislation. After the meeting while vets crowded around the Senator and voted him a "buddy," one of the vets said: "Gee Senator you talk as tho you really knew something about what us fellows went thru over there." The Senator did know

(Continued on Page 2 - Col. 2)

GOV. MOORE BREAKS FAITH WITH LABOR

Calling on New Jersey organized labor and workingmen to re-elect Senator Kean as a proved friend of labor, Harry Wendrich, A. F. of L. organizer, in a Labor Day Radio address scathingly denounced Gov. Moore for breaking his promise to appoint a labor man as New Jersey Secretary of Labor. After promising to appoint a labor man to this important post, Wendrich declared

(Continued on Page 3 - Col. 1)

Central European Textile Workers
68c a Week is BIG PAY

PAGE 3 TELLS HOW YOU CAN HELP RE-ELECT SEN. KEAN

Figure 3. Hamilton Fish Kean, 1862–1941. Named for his uncle-in-law and U. S. Grant's secretary of state Hamilton Fish, Hamilton Fish Kean was elected to the U.S. Senate in 1928 and served for one term. The brother of Senator John Kean and grandfather of Tom Kean, Hamilton Fish Kean worked to protect domestic industries, curb ocean pollution, and extend civil rights to African Americans. (Courtesy of Hamilton Fish Kean II.)

Figure 4. Tom Kean, as an infant, makes an early appearance in a family photograph. (L to R: Hamilton, Rose, Robert W. Sr., Elsa, Tommy, Beth, and Robert W. Jr.) Tom's father's dog, Adolf, grew especially fond of Tommy, first standing guard over his crib and later following the toddler around the Kean house and grounds in Livingston. (Courtesy of Hamilton Fish Kean II.)

Figure 5. Five-year-old Tommy Kean (center) holds a baseball bat with his family gathered around him. This picture appeared on the cover of the Christmas card that freshman representative Robert W. Kean (R-NJ) mailed to supporters and constituents in 1940. (L to R: Hamilton, Elsa, Katharine, Rose, Tommy, Robert W. Sr., Beth, and Robert W. Jr.) (Courtesy of Hamilton Fish Kean II.)

Figure 6. Tommy Kean poses with his sister's dog, Rusty. He received his first dog, a cocker spaniel, when he was twelve. He named it Pepsi after a favorite beverage and proved a conscientious master. Dogs would always fill an important place in Tom Kean's life. (Courtesy of Thomas H. Kean.)

Figure 7. Seven-year-old Tommy at his sister Beth's wedding. As the photographer struggled to take a picture of the bride and groom with the bridesmaids, Beth's "bratty little brother" raced across the room to be included. Tom had been planning his move carefully for several minutes. (Courtesy of Elizabeth Kean Hicks.)

Figure 8. Tom (standing, far right) at St. Mark's School. Like his father and brothers before him, Tom Kean was selected by his peers to be a monitor during his final year at the school. Tom Kean's self-esteem and self-confidence rose substantially during the years he spent there, largely, he recalled, through the efforts of an exceptionally diligent and dedicated teacher, William Gaccon. The impact such a teacher might have on students was one of the lessons Tom drew from his experiences at St. Mark's that he would apply later in life. (Courtesy of Thomas H. Kean.)

Figure 9. Tom Kean presides over a meeting with his fellow counselors at the Brantwood Camp. During the six summers he spent at this camp for underprivileged children, Tom exhibited leadership skills he would later bring to bear in various positions he would occupy in public service. He also developed a sense of humor and empathy for which he became equally well known. (Collections of the Peterborough [N.H.] Historical Society.)

Figure 10. Freshly graduated from Princeton (class of 1957), Tom (standing, third from right) poses with his family as his father prepares to run for the U.S. Senate in 1958. Although Robert W. Kean lost that election to Harrison A. (Pete) Williams, Tom, having served as one of his fathers main surrogates on the stump, found that he liked the political process. (Courtesy of Hamilton Fish Kean II.)

"Let them continue....."

Tom Kean and **Phil Kaltenbacher** have sponsored and supported measures to:
...**Reform Welfare Systems**
...**Create a Successful Lottery**
...**Fight Organized Crime**
...**Create a Major League Sports Complex**
...**Improve our Environment**
...**Fight Drugs**
...**Provide Meaningful Consumer Protection**
...**Bring about Tax Reform**
...**Expand New Jersey's Colleges**

Re-elect Tom
KEAN &
Phil
KALTENBACHER

Vote Republican

Governor Cahill's Leadership Team, Let them continue...

Paid for by Charles I. Nadel, M.D. / 986 Sanford Ave. / Irvington, N. J.

Figure 11. "The Leadership Team" of Tom Kean and Phil Kaltenbacher seeks reelection to its second term. Elected to the assembly in 1967, Tom Kean compiled a prodigious record during his freshman term. Five years after he entered the assembly, his colleagues elected him Speaker at the age of thirty-six. (Author's collection.)

Figure 12. Assistant assembly minority leader Tom Kean and President Richard Nixon in 1969. As vice president during the 1950s, Nixon knew Tom as "Bob Kean's son." After retiring to New Jersey, the former president took an avid interest in Tom Kean's career, offering political advice and information in advance of Kean's trips abroad, especially to China. (New Jersey Department of Community Affairs, Ace Alagna Photos.)

Figure 13. As a young assemblyman, Kean made the environment a major priority. Here he participates, along with folksinger Pete Seeger, in one of the earliest celebrations of Earth Day in New Jersey at Drew University. (Kean is far right; Seeger is far left.) He would return to the campus two decades later as its president. (Courtesy of Drew University.)

Figure 14. President Gerald R. Ford flanked by Kean the elder (Robert on the right) and Kean the younger (Tom on the left). Standing behind Ford and Robert W. Kean is Kean family friend and adviser Tony Cicatiello. While a junior member of the House, Ford "stood in awe" of Robert W. Kean because of the more senior congressman's expertise on Social Security. In 1976, Ford, the incumbent president, passed over several more seasoned Republicans when he designated Tom Kean, then assembly minority leader, as chairman of his reelection effort in New Jersey. (Courtesy of Thomas H. Kean.)

Figure 15. President Ronald Reagan takes measure of Tom Kean in 1981. Reagan campaigned for Kean during his two successful campaigns for governor. He singled out Kean for praise in his 1988 State of the Union address and on multiple other occasions. Former aides say Reagan especially looked forward to his visits to New Jersey so that he could discuss public policy with Kean. As the two were driven to presidential venues, Kean used his time with Reagan to discuss state programs and to seek assistance on various matters. (Courtesy of Thomas H. Kean, Harold Brown, photographer.)

Figure 16. Tom Kean looks on as his 1981 Democratic opponent for governor, Representative James J. Florio, makes a point during one of their debates. Both would later describe their square-off as the last "high-minded" campaign in recent New Jersey history. Kean defeated Florio by the narrowest of margins in modern times and the second narrowest in a New Jersey election. (AP/Wide World Photos.)

Figure 17. The Kean family on the eve of Tom's election as governor in 1981. (L to R: Reed, Debby, Alexandra, Tom Sr., and Tom Jr.) (Author's collection.)

Figure 18. Governor Tom Kean heads a communitywide demonstration of solidarity in Manalapan after teen vandals smeared graffiti on the walls of a synagogue. As governor, Kean repeatedly lent his voice and the powers of his office to promote greater understanding among people of different backgrounds. He advocated efforts to right wrongs against Jews, African Americans, Italian Americans, Asian Americans, Hispanics, and others. (Photo © *The Star-Ledger.* All rights reserved.)

Figure 19. Governor Tom Kean takes a refreshment break at an ethnic festival at Liberty State Park with Secretary of State Jane Burgio and Assistant Secretary of State Alvin S. Felzenberg. (Lucinda Dowell Photographs.)

Figure 20. Metropolitan Opera singer Jerome Hines flanks Kean and his 1985 Democratic opponent, Peter Shapiro, in a display of bipartisan support for the arts. Kean defeated Shapiro in the fall by the widest margin in the history of the state up to that time. (Photo © *The Star-Ledger*. All rights reserved.)

Figure 21. Tom and Barbara; Debby and George H. W. The friendship between the Kean and Bush families extended through several generations. Kean's and President George H. W. Bush's fathers served together in Congress. Their grandfathers were classmates at the Stevens Institute of Technology. Kean jokingly referred to the forty-first president as his only rival for Debby Kean's attentions. (Photo © *The Star-Ledger*. All rights reserved.)

Figure 22. Tom Kean enjoys a light moment in the Oval Office with his friend Bill Clinton. When the two served concurrently as governors of their respective states, they often collaborated to reform education and welfare. Clinton considered Kean one of the nation's most successful governors. As president, he named his former colleague to advisory panels on entitlement reforms and race relations. (Courtesy of the William J. Clinton Presidential Library.)

Figure 23. After stepping down as governor in 1990, Tom Kean became president of Drew University. The post afforded him ample opportunities to apply the administrative skills he had acquired as governor and to return to his first calling—teaching. Here he shares a laugh with students enrolled in his course Governing a State, one of the most popular at the university. While at Drew, Kean was summoned back to public service by three successive president of the United States. (Photo © Bob Handelman.)

Figure 24. The chairman of the 9–11 Commission, Thomas H. Kean, and its vice chairman, Lee H. Hamilton, brief the nation on the progress of their investigation on NBC's *Meet the Press*. The two made it their practice to appear together in such forums, underscoring the bipartisan nature of their common mission. (Alex Wong/Getty Images.)

Figure 25. The author as spokesman for the 9–11 Commission confers with its leaders, Tom Kean and Lee Hamilton. None of the three knew that they were being photographed or that this picture would appear on the front page of the *Washington Post* the next day. (Photo © 2004 *The Washington Post*. Photo by Gerald Martineau. Reprinted with permission.)

Figure 26. Thomas H. Kean, chairman of the 9–11 Commission, presents its final report to President George W. Bush. (AP/Wide World Photos.)

Figure 27. Thomas H. Kean with the next generation of Keans to take an interest in the family business of public service Thomas H. Kean Jr. Tom Jr. is the Republican candidate for New Jersey's U.S. Senate race in 2006. (Author's collection.)

Organizations of National Prominence

With the arts council back in the State Department and with its new director in place, Kean turned his attention to its funding. Launched with an annual budget of $75,000 during Richard J. Hughes's administration, the council's budget remained flat during its first four years of existence. Cahill increased it to $271,577. By the end of Brendan Byrne's second administration, its budget stood at $3 million. Kean, during his first three years, raised the council's budget by $250,000, $65,000, and $77,000, respectively. With the economy improving, Kean recommended an additional $2 million to the council for fiscal year 1984. With that action began a series of steady annual increases under Kean that culminated in an all-time high appropriation of $23 million in operating funds by the time he left office. Kean's cultural legacy would also include substantial additional funding, raised through bond issues, for improvements to capital facilities.

Prior to announcing his first major increase to the arts council's funding, Kean cautioned Burgio to keep a watchful eye over how the council spent the additional money. "Don't let them squander it," he told her. His comment reflected the council's past practice of providing small grants to many groups. When I asked him whether he had any preferences in how the council made use of its additional funds, Kean said he wanted it to invest much of them in organizations capable of achieving national prominence. The council set up a special program to identify such organizations and provide them with funds beyond their basic operating grants to help them attain such standing. Over the next six years, it bestowed $11 million in this way to eight groups.[15]

To ensure that groups it assisted would not slide back down the ladder of achievement, the council set a policy that no organization would receive more than 20 percent of its funding from the state. It also required that organizations on which it bestowed significant increases in funding match the state's contribution several times over with private donations. During Kean's time in office, the arts council began to function less like a state agency and more like a foundation, toughening eligibility requirements, disseminating clear and consistent guidelines for prospective applicants. Eventually corporations, foundations, and individual donors began to regard an organization's receipt of council funding as less a sign of its political influence and more as a demonstration of quality, as assessed by a panel of neutral, qualified judges.

Jerome Hines and the "Seven Majors"

In the years in which the arts council's budget had remained flat, cultural organizations with the largest budgets and audiences lobbied the legislature for direct funding. Sometimes, with the help of friendly legislators such as Kean, they succeeded in obtaining it. Most considered having to depend on legislative whims too precarious a method of planning their budgets. When they learned that Kean planned to increase the arts council's budget by 40 percent, a delegation of arts administrators paid him a visit to make their case for what they considered to be their "fair share" of the new funds. South Orange resident Jerome Hines, then a principal bass with the Metropolitan Opera Company, acted as their spokesman.

Hines maintained that the organizations he represented (the New Jersey Symphony, New Jersey State Opera, New Jersey Ballet Company, McCarter Theatre, Waterloo Village, Newark Symphony Hall, and the Paper Mill Playhouse) should receive all or most of the $2-million increase Kean recommended for the arts council. He asked that Kean set a goal of providing $1 million in state aid to each of what he considered the seven major arts organizations. "Seven Million for Seven Majors" Hines took as his slogan.[16] While Kean found Hines's idea laudable, he did not explicitly commit to meeting it. Kean found it useful to have a state agency—accountable to a board whose members served staggered terms—decide among competing claimants. While he would, on occasion, express surprise or disappointment at certain council funding decisions, he never instructed it to raise or lower the size of an award.

At its core, the disagreement between Hines and the council was not over whether to provide more funds to major organizations, but which among them had the capacity to attain Kean's objective of national prominence. For months, the council and the opera singer and his cohorts engaged in a protracted struggle, each claiming, with some justification, to have Kean's support. Yes, Kean wanted to see more of the funds he made available to the arts go to major organizations. And yes, mindful though he was of past allegations that the council had awarded grants based on favoritism, Kean wanted the council to render objective assessments as to which groups best merited funding. Eventually, Kean appointed Hines to the arts council, hoping both that the singer's presence would enhance its prestige and that battles over funding decisions would be waged someplace other than in the governor's office. Before Kean's hopes could be realized, an external threat to Kean's budgetary recommendations did more to unite the squabbling arts community than had any amount of gubernatorial coaxing.

Senator Stockman Sparks an Advocacy Movement

Professing anger that Kean declined to reappoint one of his constituents to the arts council, state senator Gerald Stockman (D-Mercer), in his capacity as member of the Joint Legislative Appropriations Committee, slashed $1 million from Kean's requested $2-million increase to the arts council's budget. Asserting that Kean sought to load the council with "elitist wealthy suburbanites," Stockman also persuaded his fellow senators to hold up three of the governor's appointments to the council. Observers found Stockman's charge fallacious. Although Mollie Merlino, the council member Kean had not reappointed, lived in Trenton, she was hardly the kind of inner-city resident Stockman asserted should be on the arts council. She was the wife of a former president of the New Jersey State Senate.

Stockman's willingness to take retribution on Kean by reducing funds available to arts organizations, including those in his own district, struck some legislators, even within his own party, as petty, excessive, and self-defeating.[17] While most Democrats professed support for Stockman, public and editorial opinion ran in the opposite direction. Under the heading "Rembrandt He Ain't," the *Star-Ledger* ran a cartoon depicting three portraits, including one of Kean, on which a vandal had painted beards and mustaches. On a nearby table was a bucket of paint and a brush, labeled "Senator Stockman's budget cuts."[18] Kean called the cuts outrageous, asked the legislature to restore the funds, and urged his three nominees to "hang tough." "How is my 'elitist' friend today?" Kean asked one of them, Celeste Penney, an assistant curator of painting and sculpture at the Newark Museum, as he encountered her one Saturday on his way to play tennis. To scores of artists angry that they were being denied the additional funds Kean had recommended, he had some advice: "Make yourselves heard. Let your local legislators know how you feel."[19]

Hyer did not need much prodding. As the legislature prepared to complete the budget in the spring of 1984, he and Hines organized the first rally in support of the arts in New Jersey history. Wearing buttons proclaiming, "New Jersey and the Arts: Perfect Together," a takeoff on the state slogan Kean had made famous, Hyer and Hines led a crowd of hundreds on a march to the statehouse. "Man does not live by bread alone," Hines told the gathering. To the delight of the crowd, Kean made an unscheduled appearance. Overjoyed at the turnout, he exclaimed: "If it weren't for the pleasures you have given so many in New Jersey, none of us would be here. And I wouldn't have had the confidence to put that money in the budget and you would not have the confidence to come here and get it back."[20]

Within days, the legislature had restored to the council its "missing million." Soon, Kean and the legislature reached an accord that resulted in the confirmation of 210 of Kean's nominees, his three to the arts council among them. Kean's counsel, Cary Edwards, attributed the resolution of what had been a stalemate to the publicity the arts council controversy generated. "If there was any benefit from the arts fiasco, this was probably it," he said.[21]

Second to None

In the fall of 1984, anticipating a budget surplus approaching $413 million, Kean suggested separately to Burgio, to Ogden, and to me that many constituencies had been agitating for some of the anticipated additional funds. "If the arts want to be included, they had better speak up," he said. It did not take them long to take the hint. "Think big," Hyer told his compatriots.[22] He urged them to press for funds to renovate antiquated theaters, concert halls, and museums and described their poor condition as the last obstacle to their ability to achieve Kean's goal of national prominence for New Jersey cultural institutions. Estimating the costs of repairing twenty-five facilities to be $50 million, they called for the creation of a capital investment of that amount. So that the issue would attract both legislative and press attention, Ogden introduced a bill in the assembly allocating $50 million from the general fund to the arts council for this purpose. Stockman, anxious to reestablish his bona fides as an arts advocate, offered a companion version in the senate.[23]

As the arts groups pressed their requests for capital funding, Kean announced he was requesting a $3.1-million increase to the council's budget. This time, no one moved to cut back on his request. "Raising the amount of funds the arts received was one of the things I ran on," he said. "Each year, I put in every penny I thought I could get by the Democrats in the legislature."[24] Each year, Kean would decide by himself exactly by what amount he would increase the size of the arts budget. Ed McGlynn, Kean's last chief of staff, described what ensued when a Trenton bureaucrat inadvertently questioned the wisdom of Kean's actions: "A budget official, obviously new to the process, began the meeting by saying, 'You asked me to hold most of the departments to their last year's appropriation and to cut others back. I did what you requested. So, could someone please tell me, who was the jerk who inserted $21 million into the budget for the arts council?'After a lengthy silence, Kean began to speak. Sheepishly, he said, 'Well, I was taking a look at the numbers, and I decided . . . '"

"You never saw a redder face in your life," McGlynn said of the bureaucrat.[25]

Taking as their slogan "Second to None," a phrase Kean had used when he challenged state arts organizations to strive to be the best they possibly could in their respective disciplines, Hines and Hyer led a second march to Trenton on June 6, 1985. This time, the press estimated the crowd at two thousand. In his references to the legislature, Hines was as confrontational as Kean was conciliatory. "When you walk into New Jersey's symphony halls and its theaters," the singer said, "you see that they're falling down, they're junk. It's a message from the legislature that you're not welcome in the arts in this state."[26]

Kean began by recognizing the presence of Charles Marciante, president of the state's AFL-CIO, at the rally. The governor then said that he hoped the legislature would prove receptive to the needs of the theaters and recognize that their repair would create jobs all across the state.[27] To demonstrate the bipartiship of their cause, Hyer and Hines had invited Kean's Democratic opponent Peter Shapiro also to address the rally. Playing to the cameras, the opera singer threw his arms around both candidates, and the three led the crowd in a new rendition of a well-known song. To the tune of "Row, Row, Row Your Boat," the candidates, the opera singer, and the marchers chanted, "Vote, vote, vote the bill. Fifty mill today. Merrily, merrily, merrily, merrily, the arts are here to stay." Prior to Kean's arrival, Shapiro, who had won his party's nomination for governor only days earlier, offered himself as a mediator between the governor and the legislature to release the necessary funding. With the Democrats in control of both houses, Kean voiced no objections.

Carl Shaver's Report and the "Quality of Life" Bond Issue

When he approved the budget for fiscal year 1986, Kean cited as his sole disappointment the legislature's failure to include the $50 million Odgen had recommended for capital repairs of cultural facilities. Kean said that if he could not get the entire amount approved, he would press "to get part of it to get it [a capital cultural construction fund] started."[28] He would succeed, but in another year and through other means.

The process started weeks after Kean's triumphal reelection to a second term with a call I received from Margaret Hager, recently elected chairwoman of the arts council. Hager became convinced that if the symphony was to attain the kind of national prominence both Kean and Hyer sought, it had to have a new world-class facility in which to perform. All the state's existing facilities were inadequate for such purposes, she said, and the costs of renovating any of them to the point where it could function in this capacity would approximate what it would cost to start from scratch.

She and I agreed that, if the governor were to select a site for any new facility, community leaders from locales passed over would lobby their legislators to block funding for his proposal. We also agreed that even after the new hall was built, existing facilities would continue to operate as regional cultural centers. Most were in need of repair. We talked about raising part of the money necessary to assist their renovation through a bond issue. We concluded that as we pressed for such a bond issue, we should consider retaining an internationally respected arts consultant, with no ties to any existing New Jersey facility, to assess whether New Jersey businesses, donors, and audiences would support a world-class facility and, if so, where to locate it.

Kean did not need to be convinced that something was sorely lacking in the state's cultural fabric. In his travels to governors' conferences across the country, he had attended meetings held in brand-new facilities that housed the hosting area's leading performing arts organizations. He had also been subjected to intense lobbying from operators and patrons—eager for their facilities to serve as the "official home" to the state symphony and other organizations—for funding to upgrade their structures. Kean said that he would finance an independent consultant's study through discretionary funds at his disposal. A five-person committee (Burgio, Hager, Kesper, a representative of the state treasurer, and I) decided, after weighing competing proposals, to retain C. W. Shaver, based in New York City, for this purpose. Its principal, Carl W. Shaver, had participated in the planning of Lincoln Center. More recently, he had helped create the Pioneer Square Cultural District in Cleveland, Ohio. We gave Shaver six months to make a recommendation.

"New Jersey citizens should have the alternative of seeing good performances in our own state rather than having to go to New York or Philadelphia," Kean said in announcing the awarding of $208,000 to Shaver's firm toward the end of 1986. He suggested that Shaver's study could be the beginning of a "big plan," which might lead to the creation of a complex, perhaps on the scale of Lincoln Center.[29]

When Shaver was two months into his work, Assemblywoman Odgen and Senate majority leader John Lynch introduced a bond issue that would appropriate $50 million, on a matching-fund basis, for repairs of cultural facilities and $40 million for renovation of historic sites. What they called the "qualify of life" bond issue would become the first in the nation that allocated funds to cultural centers.[30] To enhance its chance of passage, Kean brokered a compromise through which the state would borrow $100 million, with $40 million going to cultural facilities, $25 million to historic sites, and $35 million to the state's Green Acres program.

In signing legislation to put the proposal on the ballot, Kean lifted verbatim Hyer's description of the state of New Jersey's cultural facilities: "The stages, auditoriums and lobbies . . . are falling apart. Piano legs have crashed through stage floors, the bottoms of audience seats have collapsed and leaky roofs have cut short too many performances. In fact, we are the only state in this country that can say its orchestra has been rained out in an indoor performance."[31]

On Election Day, 1987, the Ogden-Lynch bond issue passed by a two-to-one margin. Before any funds could be awarded, Kean removed from the list of potential applicants the War Memorial in Trenton, which he was prepared to have the state take over from the governments of Mercer County and the city of Trenton.[32]

On July 22, 1987, Shaver released his recommendation at a press conference in Kean's outer office. He proposed a $200-million performing arts complex in the city of Newark and an additional $100 million in improvements to regional facilities across the state. Shaver's proposal for Newark called for a 3,000-seat theater for opera, drama, and dance; a 2,500-seat world-class concert hall for the symphony; an 1,800-seat music theater; a 750-seat theater for drama and smaller productions; and a 250-seat children's theater. Shaver said he had selected Newark because it was within a twenty-five-mile commute for 4.5 of the state's 7.5 million residents. He cited its proximity to all the state's major roads and highways, Amtrak and New Jersey Transit, and Newark airport as major assets.[33]

Kean's consultant suggested erecting the complex on the site of the abandoned Hahne's department store on Broad Street. He also proposed creating a cultural district running a quarter mile from the arts complex, encompassing the Newark Museum and several colleges and universities. He recommended that the city be allowed to retain sales tax revenues that poured in from parking facilities, restaurants, shops, and boutiques that he expected would spring up around the arts centers to reinvest in the cultural district.

Kean dscribed the proposal as "bold, imaginative and extremely ambitious." "You've got to have faith in the city of Newark," he proclaimed. Anticipating that the project's opponents would argue that people would be afraid to venture into the city at night, Kean declared, "What drives away the criminal element is people"[34] As he spoke, his thoughts carried him back to the days when, as a graduate student at Columbia, he had seen Lincoln Center transform a crime-ridden part of New York City into a tourist destination. He suggested the same phenomenon could take place in Newark.

The *Bergen Record* called the proposal "a star for the state's crown."[35] The *Star-Ledger* made it the latest of New Jersey booster-ism projects it supported, running an extensive series along with pe-riodic editorials and cartoons in support. Breaking with the pack, a writer with the *New York Daily News* deemed the plan "the dumbest idea since Napoleon Bonaparte decided to invade Russia." He sug-gested the center be located not in a city that was all but abandoned at night but in a suburban location near the intersection of Routes 206, 22, 78, and 287 in Somerset County.[36] Opinion leaders of re-gions Shaver had not recommended for the arts center's location voiced their dissent.[37] A *New Brunswick Home News* headline asked what was on many people's minds, including Kean's: "Million-Dollar Question: Will Business Back Arts Complex?"[38]

Rather than press for the immediate adoption of Shaver's plan, Kean said he wanted to ascertain from the legislature and business community whether they were prepared to establish for New Jersey a "reputation for excellence" in the arts, as they had already done in sports and other fields. His comments suggested he expected the re-action to be mixed. Within the city of Newark, praise for the proposal was far from universal. Small businesses along the block where Shaver proposed building the arts center asked where they were to go. A media-savvy monsignor of Newark's 137-year-old St. Patrick's Pro-Cathedral, located on the corner of Washington Street and Cen-tral Avenue, complained that Shaver's etchings had shown a parking lot on the site the house of worship occupied. "You wouldn't believe how our old Irish parishioners can get their tempers up about their old church," Monsignor John Maloney exclaimed. "We have no de-sign to take away an asset that has meant so much to the spiritual and physical life of the city," I nervously told the *Star-Ledger*, after in-structing Shaver to change his drawings.[39]

Robert Van Fossan, the chief executive officer of Mutual Bene-ficial Life and the unofficial chairman of the Broad Street Gang, a collection of corporate leaders who functioned as the backbone of philanthropic activities in Newark, posed more serious opposition. Van Fossan had taken on the responsibility of renovating Newark's Symphony Hall, one of the few structures where the symphony, opera, and other groups could perform before large audiences.[40] Symphony Hall was located a mile away from the site Shaver proposed. It also stood in a part of town that boasted few amenities. Van Fossan tried to persuade Shaver to recommend Symphony Hall as the site of the performing arts center. After Shaver proposed that a new structure be built in another part of town, Van Fossan said that he was ecstatic that the consultant had recommended Newark over other municipalities, but that he was uncertain that the business community would commit the $150 million Shaver cited as the cost of implementing his plan.[41]

Owners of the land on which Shaver wanted to build the performing arts center had other designs for its use. Lowell Harwood, chairman of Square Industries, planned to erect two office buildings on the site of the long-defunct Klein's department store and the long-evacuated Loew's theater. Shaver's envisioned complex would have engulfed part of Harwood's property. Taking his case to Trenton, Harwood, through lobbyist Alan Marcus, argued that his office structures would bring more immediate economic benefits to the city than the arts center would. They found a receptive ear in senate appropriations chairman Larry Weiss. The sale of the Hahne's site to a New York developer for $5 million appeared to present yet another obstacle to achieving Shaver's objective. "The sale of a building does not an arts center stop," I told the press, suppressing my private doubts.[42]

Within the city of Newark, the arts center had no firmer advocate than Mayor Sharpe James. Over and over again, the mayor proclaimed that when the state sought a site to locate a prison, a halfway house, a place to treat people with AIDS, or a trauma center, it had selected Newark. Now that the state was offering its largest city some succor, James resolved to fight hard to get it. Before long, Harwood was complaining that the city was dragging its feet on his proposal to develop the property he owned.[43]

Making Way for the Greats

Kean's support for the construction of a Lincoln Center–type arts complex in downtown Newark caught the attention of arts producers all across the country. One spring day, Kean's cabinet secretary, Jane Kenny, informed me that Joseph Papp had telephoned, requesting an appointment with the governor. She asked if I could ascertain what he wished to discuss with Kean. Papp, founder and chairman of the New York Shakespeare Festival, had burst on the cultural scene in the 1950s when he stood down New York City parks commissioner Robert Moses to present free performances of Shakespeare plays in Central Park.[44] Beginning with Shakespeare's *Two Gentlemen of Verona*, which he had turned into a musical, Papp produced a string of hits on Broadway. At the time he telephoned Kean's office, his *A Chorus Line* had set a record as the longest-running production in history.

Having read in the *New York Times* about Shaver's proposal, Papp wondered whether the state would be interested in having the Festival Latino—a new theater company he had founded—perform in the new structure. After meeting with Papp, Kean invited the producer to join him at the annual presentation of the governor's arts awards to junior and senior high school students. As the two came out on stage, the audience, recognizing Papp, burst into delayed but sustained applause. Papp regaled his youthful fans with tales of Broadway and of his lifelong affinity for the works of Shakespeare. Of Kean, Papp observed, "He actually loves the arts. His face takes on that funny expression when he talks about them."[45] The Shakespeare enthusiast had become the latest to discover "that grin."

Before departing, Papp participated in a ritual Kean performed each year during his tenure as governor. One reporter described the scene from a prior year: "He [Kean] stood on the stage for more than an hour, posing for individual photographs with nearly 120 children and 16 educators. For each of the kids, [and] for the adults, Gov. Thomas Kean had a word of congratulations, delivered as if he were personally familiar with their work."[46]

The following summer, Papp's company became one of several to perform free presentations of plays that the arts council and the New Jersey Theater Group presented in New Jersey parks.[47]

The Metropolitan Opera was next to phone. The company had, in prior years, presented free concerts in New Jersey parks. It wondered whether Kean's administration was interested in reviving that tradition. Some state legislators did not share the governor's enthusiasm for the idea. When I appeared with Burgio before the Joint Appropriations Committee to defend the arts council's budget, one legislator asked how local groups would respond to the news that the state had used public funds to bring in an out-of-state organization to perform. I offered the opinion that, given the Met's capacity to build audiences for opera, local groups would be delighted. When I told Kean afterward that I had misjudged their reaction, the governor, flashing "that snarl," replied, "Well, they *ought* to be delighted." Appropriations chairman Larry Weiss ordered an investigation of whether the council, in awarding funds not only to the Met but also to the Alvin Ailey Repertory Ensemble, which it brought to perform in New Jersey schools, and the Kirov Ballet, which it helped bring to a southern New Jersey college, had violated state law.[48]

When not celebrating the achievements of cultural organizations, Kean went out of his way to salute state residents who won acclaim for their talent. After Olympia Dukakis, of Montclair, was nominated for best supporting actress in the film *Moonstruck* in 1988, Kean presided over a rally at Newark airport to cheer her on as she departed for Los Angeles to attend the Academy Awards celebration. "The last time I came here on an occasion like this was to welcome the Super Bowl Giants," Kean said as he proclaimed Dukakis "one of the good reasons" New Jersey was "second to none" in the arts.[49] The state legislature waited until after Dukakis had won her Oscar to honor her. Just as she had turned her acceptance speech into a cheer for her cousin Michael Dukakis's presidential campaign ("Come on Michael!"), Dukakis used her time in Trenton to thank legislators for funding Kean's arts budgets.[50]

While all this other activity was taking place, the New Jersey Symphony continued to gain Kean's confidence. Between Kean's second and fifth years in office, the symphony's annual budget grew from $530,000 to $1.9 million, 20 percent of it coming from the state. It expanded the number of its performances, attracted favorable critical attention, and became the talk of the music world when it retained Hugh Wolff as its conductor.[51] A young rising star in the musical world, Wolff, then thirty-two, had been serving as associate conductor of the National Symphony Orchestra under Mstislav Rostropovich when Hyer had tapped him. When Hyer brought Wolff to see Kean, the governor turned what had been billed as a courtesy call into a recruiting session. Wolff and Hyer came away impressed with the depth of Kean's knowledge about classical music and with his willingness to give them as much time as he had.

Three months before Shaver presented his report, Wolff took the orchestra to Carnegie Hall. With Kean in the audience, beaming at the prospect of another "New Jersey first," Wolff led the orchestra through a powerful performance. *New York Times* critic Donal Henahan observed that "high level results were accomplished with what until Mr. Wolff's arrival had been considered a good community orchestra."[52] Three months after Kean threw his weight behind Shaver's recommendations, Wolff and the orchestra returned to Carnegie Hall, where they performed an entire program of Leonard Bernstein's compositions on the occasion of the composer's seventieth birthday. The *Star-Ledger* plastered on its front page the next day Bernstein's praise of the "terrific" symphony and of Wolff, who Bernstein had said made him forget that he was a conductor.[53] One of Wolff's players likened the experience of performing in Carnegie Hall after playing in New Jersey facilities to "going from the ridiculous to the sublime."[54] Shaver and Hyer sent copies of these quotes and accompanying reviews to people they believed might be interested in helping to finance construction of a performing arts center in New Jersey.

The Project Gets a New Recruit

With the legislature showing no interest in Shaver's proposal in spite of Kean's prodding, the governor, in an attempt to regain the initiative, asked Shaver to identify individuals who might assume responsibility for raising the private funds necessary to build the center. The two assumed that major corporations would contribute to the costs of constructing such a center, but only after they had been approached by a known philanthropist who believed deeply in the project. Although he had identified five such individuals, Shaver focused primarily on one: Raymond G. Chambers. Shaver approached Chambers at a time when he was particularly anxious to do more for the children of the city of Newark.

A graduate of Newark's West Side High School and Rutgers University, Chambers had made his fortune in leveraged buyouts in the late 1970s and early 1980s. In recent years, he had been focusing on efforts to assist poor children in the city of Newark. After assuming the reins of the city's Boys Club, which he soon merged with the Girls Club, Chambers devised a program he called Rigorous Educational Assistance Program for Deserving Youth (READY). Participating youngsters pledged to remain in school, stay off drugs, receive decent grades, and abide by certain rules. In exchange, Chambers and his organization promised to pay the complete costs of their college education.

In February 1987, five months before Shaver released his report, Chambers grew concerned when an associate of his, working in Newark's South Ward, reported to him that the majority of the younger people she encountered were so hopeless, they did not care if they lived or they died. "Then the arts center came along," Chambers said. He began to envision what it would mean to the city's children.

As I had with Papp, I visited Chambers and subsequently arranged for him to meet with Kean. Chambers remembered being taken by Kean's "grace, interest in reviving the city, and . . . his persuasiveness." He was also intrigued that a Republican patrician, who had graduated from both St. Mark's and Princeton, and whose political base had been the wealthy suburbs, would take such a keen interest in what was transpiring in Newark. He promised Kean he would see what he could do to advance Shaver's proposals.[55]

Chambers asked his staff to investigate what it would cost to construct a hall that conformed to Hyer's specifications. They returned with an estimate of $66 million. He pledged to commit to raise half the amount if the state agreed to match it. By the end of the year, he had at his command, whether in hand or in pledges, $17 million.[56]

Breaking the Impasse

Kean made the arts center a major theme of his 1988 State of the State address. After hearing his speech, Assemblyman Willie Brown (D-Essex), with Republican assembly Speaker Chuck Hardwick as cosponsor, introduced a resolution awarding $33 million from the general fund toward the construction of the arts center. Not only was that figure approximately half the amount of Chambers's initial estimate of the center's total costs, but, perhaps by coincidence, it was just $1 million higher than the amount the legislature had authorized to construct an aquarium along the Camden waterfront. With Camden getting an aquarium and Jersey City a science center, Kean could argue with credibility that the time to build a world-class amenity in the state's largest city had come.

Though Brown had introduced his resolution with considerable fanfare, Weiss, in his capacity as chairman of the senate's Appropriations Committee, maintained that Brown's action had taken him by complete surprise. For the remainder of the year, Weiss presented one

Fig 13.1. Obtaining legislative approval for the state to match the private sector's commitment to build a performing arts center in Newark proved to be Kean's last battle as governor. With key legislators reluctant to go along with Kean's plans, he kept up the pressure, enlisting allies in the business and cultural communities. (© 1989 *The Star-Ledger.* All rights reserved. Reprinted with permission.)

procedural hurdle after another to block any state appropriation for the proposed arts center. The senator had been pressing to allocate part of the surplus into a rainy-day fund the state could tap during future economic downturns. He was suspicious of any large authorizations that threatened to cut into the size of the fund he wished to create. Weiss also voiced suspicions that, in addition to the initial $33 million, the state would be asked to contribute to the center's subsequent operating budgets. He pointed out that Lincoln Center required $67 million in subsidies each year to balance its books. "This could be the best thing in the world. But the question is can we afford the best thing in the world?" Weiss took to saying.[57] As the talks dragged on, Weiss, as had Van Fossan before him, asked why the orchestra did not just settle for a renovated Symphony Hall. He also echoed Harwood in suggesting that Shaver had been overly optimistic in his projections of the economic benefits the center would bring to the city.

Weiss's refusal to budge on the $33 million meant that Kean's proposal received no funding from the state for the remainder of 1988. Many assumed the project was dead. During this hiatus, Chambers quietly assembled parcels of land on a site not far from the one Shaver had proposed. In his final budget, Kean set aside $33 million for the construction of a concert hall. The accompanying language suggested that funds could only be expended if matched on a dollar-for-dollar basis. "The state of New Jersey and the city of Newark deserve a world-class performing arts center," Kean said, not for the first time. Shortly thereafter, Chambers told a packed press conference in Newark that his company, Wesray, and Van Fossan's, Mutual Benefit, would guarantee the remainder of the necessary funds to match the state's appropriation.[58] His announcement put new pressure on the legislature.

Van Fossan's change of heart was the product of several factors: his high personal regard for Chambers, assurances he received that Symphony Hall would qualify for funding through the recently passed bond issue, and the unabated pressure that Kean and James had put on him. Chambers announced that he had reached an agreement with the Archdiocese of Newark to purchase 6.8 acres east of Military Park and was negotiating for the purchase of other properties.

With the private-sector "match" now in hand, Kean turned up the heat on Weiss. "The question is not whether we can afford it but whether we can afford not to do it," he said.[59] With Van Fossan now backing the project and Harwood neutralized, the number of the arts center's opponents was dwindling. Eager for James's support in the upcoming 1989 Democratic gubernatorial primary, Democrats seeking to succeed Kean as governor went on record as favoring construction of the performing arts center in Newark. This combination of factors proved too powerful for Weiss to overcome. Asked what turned the powerful legislator around, Kean supplied a three-word answer that Weiss himself used to explain his change of heart: "It was time."[60]

As an alternative to a $33-million appropriation, Weiss proposed the state contribution consist of a $20-million Economic Development Loan, which the state would repay and eventually assume title to the property. The money would be used for the purchase of a twelve-acre tract bordered by Route 21, Military Park, and the Passaic River. What Weiss found most appealing about this approach was that the state had secured its investment.[61] Kean immediately accepted Weiss's offer. Days later, Chambers announced the appointment of Lawrence P. Goldman, who had overseen a recently completed renovation of Carnegie Hall, as president of the New Jersey Center for the Performing Arts Corporation. With additional infusions of funds from both the state and federal governments and the private sector, necessitated by unanticipated environmental and other difficulties, the New Jersey Center for the Performing Arts opened its doors in 1996. The $190-million facility, designed by architect Barton Myers, instantly established its place among the great concert halls in the nation.

"One thing about being governor is that you have staying power," Kean said decades later. "If you persist—if you keep coming back at it—you can eventually prevail."[62]

chapter 14

Kean the Environmentalist

After education, environmental policy was the issue with which Kean had the most experience at the time he assumed the governorship. Although he had plenty of time to develop plans and strategies to achieve educational reforms, in the environmental area he found himself reacting to a series of uninterrupted crises that threatened the public health. During his eight years in office, he responded rapidly and forcefully to discoveries of dioxin in the cities, radon in suburban basements, asbestos in schools, acid rain in the skies, medical wastes washing up on New Jersey shores, PCBs in fish caught in New Jersey waters, and such natural disasters as hurricanes and floods—to name just a few. How Kean responded to these scares and others contributed in no small way to the high regard in which so many New Jersey residents came to hold him.

Tackling Hazardous Wastes

The first environmental issue to confront him was one Kean had made a leading issue during his 1981 campaign: toxic wastes. He and his first environmental commissioner, Bob Hughey, moved swiftly to ensure that all such facilities were properly inventoried so that New Jersey would be among the first states to qualify for clean-up funds under the newly established Superfund program. When the Environmental Protection Agency published its list of the 418 most dangerous hazardous waste sites in the nation, 65 in New Jersey appeared on it.[1] Reagan's critics saw the speed with which the national administration responded to Kean's request as evidence that the president's aides had politicized Superfund. They argued that the federal administration, not known for its activism in environmental matters, expedited grants from the program in order to assist friendly state administrations.[2] Kean attributed New Jersey's receipt of 80 percent of the grants Superfund awarded in its first year in operation to the diligence Hughey had shown in complying with federally imposed requirements and deadlines. If money flowed his way for other reasons, he was just as happy to take it.

When the federal government attempted to delay distribution of Superfund grants until after scientists determined what constituted a "cleaned-up" site, Kean pushed to continue work that had begun, offering to advance state funds with the federal government reimbursing it later. He took a similar approach when the program ran out of money. Together with U.S. senator Bill Bradley (D-NJ), Kean lobbied the federal government to reduce the amount of money a state had to invest in clean-up efforts in order to qualify for assistance.[3]

To curb what was becoming an avalanche of new toxic discoveries, Kean pressed for and obtained legislation that required sellers of property to certify that their sites were free of hazardous materials.[4] He also signed into law bills that imposed jail sentences on those who allowed toxic substances to be disposed of anywhere other than a licensed facility and granted the New Jersey Department of Environmental Protection (DEP) permission to close down sites until they had been cleaned up.[5] He pushed for rapid appropriation of monies raised for toxic cleanups through a recently passed bond issue, which he had supported, and through the New Jersey Spill Compensation Fund, both initiatives of the Byrne administration.

Offshore Drilling

After he became governor, Kean's relations with U.S. Interior secretary James Watt, whom he had criticized during his campaign, continued to deteriorate. Kean and Watt had already been at odds over the necessity of preserving the Pinelands. Their relations worsened after Kean filed suit in federal court to block the Interior Department from allowing oil and gas companies to drill on twenty-three tracts off the New Jersey coastline.[6] He charged that drilling would irreparably damage the commercial and recreational fishing industries, which, he maintained, contributed $1 billion annually to the state's economy.[7] Kean noted that the federal Continental Shelf Land Act and Coastal Zone Management Act required the interior secretary to accept a governor's recommendations if they reflected a balance between federal and state concerns and were consistent with the state's federally approved coastal plan.

With the suit pending, Watt proposed selling drilling rights on tracts at the edge of the continental shelf. Watt and Kean declared a temporary truce after the federal government signed a memorandum of understanding in which it pledged to protect species deemed important to the fishing industry. Kean and Watt remained at odds over the extent to which the federal government could overrule the environmental concerns of governors of the coastal states.[8] After the U.S. Supreme Court, in a 5-to-4 decision, ruled that states lacked authority over economic activities that occurred more than three miles beyond their coastline, Kean took his case to the National Governors Association. He hoped that he and his colleagues from coastal states could persuade congressional representatives from their respective states to get Congress to write outer-continental-shelf protection into coastal management plans. This would, in effect, have negated the Supreme Court's ruling. What Kean most feared was that the federal government would allow the very incursions into the coastline by private industry that he had succeeded in having the state ban a decade earlier with the passage of the Coastal Area Facility Review Act (CAFRA).[9] He found it ironic that a national administration elected on a promise to return more powers to the states sought, in this instance, to undercut their powers.

Dioxin

In the spring and summer of 1983, Kean turned his attention to more immediate concerns. In April, discoveries of high concentrations of dioxin in Times Beach, Missouri, resulted in the federal Environmental Protection Agency evacuating the entire town and buying up residents' homes at a cost of $33 million. In the aftermath of the Missouri episode, most states began testing for the presence of toxic chemicals. In New Jersey, Hughey incorporated testing for dioxin into his ongoing efforts to identify toxic substances in the soil. On May 31, Kean rushed to Belleville after a toxic chemical leak had occurred at a chemical plant.

Donning a gas mask, a white Teflon suit, and boots, he and several officials toured the plant. When he emerged, Kean announced that although nothing damaging to the public health had been found, the state would provide free medical screenings for all who wished them. He also promised to make public as soon as they became available results of the tests that DEP had conducted at the plant. "We don't want to be 99 percent sure. We want to be 100 percent sure," Kean told local residents.[10] Maryann McCrea, head of the local PTA, gave voice to sentiments shared by other residents when she said, "I'm still not at ease. But it's good to know that someone higher up is on your side."[11]

On June 2, DEP reported high dioxin levels at a shuttered factory in Newark's Ironbound section. Kean visited the site. In what he termed a "precautionary measure," he offered to relocate about one hundred residents living within three hundred yards of the plant to a nearby YMCA and made $500,000 available for this purpose. He also set up two hotlines that residents could telephone for information about dioxin. Kean's moves won him praise from local Democrats, including two known to be considering running for governor in 1985. One, Newark's mayor Kenneth Gibson, reported that the state had advised him six months earlier that it was looking for contaminants on the site.[12] The other, county executive Peter Shapiro, said, "The state's efforts can't be faulted. They've gone about it in a very hard-hitting, expeditious manner."[13] Early sample tests suggested that levels of dioxin exceeded the danger point.

On June 4, Kean toured the Ironbound neighborhood to offer further reassurance to residents. The front page of the Sunday *New York Times* the next day carried stories and photographs of him standing outside peoples' homes, explaining state testing procedures to groups.[14] Not everyone he encountered voiced satisfaction with the way the state was handling things. Operators of a farmer's market that served as a major distribution center to residents and stores in the tristate region protested having to relocate miles away from their customers. "You're ruining us," one shouted at Kean. "Hey listen" was all Kean could say before being interrupted.[15] Kean convened a meeting of merchants, health officials, and representatives of his office the next day, a Sunday. He promised to get the local telephone company to transfer lines to the alternative site immediately. "We will get you taken care of," he told them. "You are businessmen and we want you to stay businessmen."[16]

Once he learned that the contamination had been confined to the factory site, Kean returned to update the community. Not finding many people at home, he made his way into one of the few business establishments open, the Lisbon at Night tavern. Word spread that he was there, and an impromptu town meeting ensued, with people pouring in by the dozens. Kean recounted the scene: "I explained that the threat was not as great as first feared, and they would be able to stay in their homes. We believed there was a good chance that no health threat existed. As I answered questions, I could feel people grow a little more confident, a little less worried. By the end of the two hours, my shirt was soaked with sweat, but the tension was gone.

Before I left, I bought the house a round of beer and we toasted each other."[17]

Carl Golden, who accompanied Kean on that visit, cited the incident, coming on the heels of Kean's previous visits and intervening actions, as evidence that Kean truly "understood what the presence of a governor on the scene meant" to a community, or for that matter, the people of the state.[18] Kean's response to the dioxin crisis set the pattern for how he and his administration responded to other environmental crises that erupted during his tenure as governor. One reporter, who frequently faulted Kean's approach to other issues, commented on his apt handling of environmental emergencies: "Kean personally took charge and rallied the various agencies of government like a seasoned field general."[19]

In the aftermath of the dioxin scare, the New Jersey legislature passed a statute requiring all manufacturers to list at workplaces substances with which workers would come into contact, both hazardous and nonhazardous, by their chemical name. Business interests objected to having to itemize the chemical names of nontoxic substances. The New Jersey Chemical Industry Council estimated that the bill would cost the industry between $40 and $60 million. Throughout the legislative debates, Kean remained noncommittal on the legislation. He said he favored the "right to know" concept in principle, but expressed sympathy to business's concerns. After the measure passed, labor and environmental groups mounted an intensive campaign to pressure Kean to sign the bill. On the last possible day he could act before the bill became law without his signature, Kean complied. In affixing his signature, he repeated his often-stated belief that "the goal of a strong economy and that of a clean environment were complementary [rather than contradictory] goals."[20] Environmentalists called the bill the strongest of its kind in the nation. Bruce Coe, president of the New Jersey Business and Industry Association, characterized it as the "single most anti-business bill to become law" in years.[21]

Acid Rain

As he had in his efforts to protect the coastline, Kean worked through national associations to tackle other environmental hazards that extended beyond the borders of any one state. Acid rain was a case in point. A combination of sulfur and nitrogen oxides produced at coal-powered electrical generating stations, acid rain, when carried to earth through precipitation, rendered harmful effects to air, soil, and water and defaced building and monuments. Upon assuming the chairmanship of the Coalition of Northeastern Governors, Kean rallied his peers behind measures to contain an environmental malady emanating from the Midwest.[22] His proposal that Congress establish a "national acid rain trust" had a New Jersey ring. Patterned after the still-to-be-enacted transportation trust fund, it had the federal government make loans on a revolving basis to localities. Repayment schedules would span twenty years.

Kean proposed funding the trust through a fee imposed on industries that burned fossil fuel and a nine-dollar annual assessment on homeowners who consumed 500 kilowatt-hours of electricity per month. He envisioned his plan raising $35 billion over a decade and in that time reducing sulfur emissions dramatically.[23] Kean led a bipartisan delegation of five governors to persuade President Reagan to support the idea. When a skeptical Reagan asked whether the matter was truly an emergency or whether the entire acid rain matter could await further study, Kean, mindful that the president would be seeking reelection later that year, replied that 70 percent of the public recognized the extent of the problem and were willing to "spend a small amount of money" to address it.[24] In his 1984 State of the Union address, Reagan referred to the problems acid rain posed but did not endorse Kean's remedy.

Reagan's successor, George H. W. Bush, proved more receptive, after his advisers and Kean's found a way to address the problem through market-based solutions, rather than through tax increases and fines. Bush's team, with Kean's coaching from the sidelines, inserted into the reauthorization of the Clean Air Act provisions establishing a national cap on acid rain emissions. The legislation allowed high-polluting utilities to transfer to lower-polluting ones the right to burn sulfur emissions up to a certain level.[25] In this manner, the federal government encouraged polluters to cleanse their plants at a lower cost than they would have paid in fines. By the time both Bush and Kean had left their respective offices, few considered acid rain as serious a problem as it had been a decade earlier.

Freshwater Wetlands

"Well, I'm practically speechless," Maureen Ogden, the assembly's most ardent environmentalist, declared in March of 1987 upon learning that Governor Thomas H. Kean had announced that he would veto, conditionally, a wetlands protection bill she had guided through the assembly and which was working its way through the state senate.[26] Kean contended the measure did not go far enough, describing it as a recipe for the plundering of wetlands. Ogden had not been entirely happy with her bill either. After a four-year stalemate, in which she had negotiated her way through as many as fifty-six drafts of the bill, she concluded that the bill at hand represented the best she could obtain. Kean's unexpected weighing-in at the eleventh hour changed the entire dynamic of the debate.

Kean had hardly been silent about freshwater wetlands. In three successive State of the State addresses, he had spoken in support of the original legislation Ogden had introduced. Yet he had not commented publicly, or, some said, even privately, on the substance of the negotiations between and within the two legislative chambers. Save for those that pertained to education, Kean made it his practice, especially after the difficulties he experienced in his first year, not to say whether he would sign controversial legislation until after it had reached his desk. He had followed such a course with regard to bills requiring a moment of silence in the schools, the "right to know" measure, and the South African divesture statute (see chapter 15). He did not change his approach after Republicans took control of the assembly in 1986. He would allow advocates for and against controversial legislation to argue their case before him. By keeping his own counsel up to the last minute, he sometimes antagonized members of his party who voted against certain bills they expected him to veto.

In the wetlands episode, Kean intervened earlier in the process, but not in the form of a thumbs-up or -down decision. At the heart of the dispute was not whether the state would protect wetlands per se. (Section 404 of the federal Clean Water Act of 1970 already ensured their protection to some extent. State law defined *freshwater wetlands* more broadly.) The compromise Ogden had negotiated established a sphere of buffer zones, near the protected areas, in which the state could regulate development. Industry and environmentalists had been at odds over how large an area these buffers would encompass. During Kean's first term, Democratic senate majority leader John Lynch had guided through the senate a version of a strong bill Ogden had introduced in the assembly that had buffers extending over the widest possible area. In the assembly, Karcher refused to post it and was later honored by the builders' association for his efforts. After partisan control of the assembly shifted, the Republican leadership agreed to bring the measure to a vote, but only after Ogden, who sided with the environmentalists, and her colleague Jack Penn, who took business's position, came to an agreement.

At the time he issued his veto threat, tilting his hand strongly in favor of the environmentalists' position, Kean was attempting to draw national attention to the wetlands issue. He termed his own state's failure to act on the measure a national embarrassment. He announced that he would delay his acceptance of the chairmanship of the National Wetlands Policy Forum until after he had seen signs that the legislature was prepared to enact a strong bill.[27] His public pronouncement, coming after his veto threat, attracted considerable media attention and favorable editorial support and kept public pressure on the legislature.

While the legislature was contemplating how to react to his veto threat, Kean struck again. On June 8, 1987, he issued an executive order in which he placed an eighteen-month moratorium on development around more than three hundred thousand acres of freshwater wetlands.[28] As precedent for his action, Kean cited Brendan Byrne's 1979 executive order that had barred more than one million acres in the Pinelands from development. Byrne's executive order hastened legislative passage of a bill establishing the Pinelands Control Commission to regulate future development. Kean hoped that his action would also result in legislation to his liking. Calling Kean's actions the "arrogance of power," senate president John Russo (D-Ocean) suggested that Kean had acted as he had in order to "get

Fig 14.1. Kean regarded the preservation of the state's beaches, open space, and wetlands and reversal of damage done by toxic substances and natural disasters as major parts of his legacy. As a state legislator, he authored every environmental bill of significance, including that which established the Department of Environmental Protection. (© 1988 *The Star-Ledger*. All rights reserved. Reprinted with permission.)

radon off the front pages."[29] Kean would resolve both environmental
problems within a similar time frame.

Radon

In 1983, after state testing revealed the presence of high levels of
radon in sixty homes in suburban Essex County (all in Montclair,
Glen Ridge, and West Orange), Kean signed an executive order requiring its removal. His action set off a four-year dispute over where
to locate the contaminated soil. Radon is a colorless gas emitted during the decay of radium. When allowed to escape into the atmosphere, experts maintain, the gas produces no harmful effects. When
trapped in a given area, such as under a roof or ceiling, it becomes a
primary producer of lung cancer. The sixty homes had been built on
a site once occupied by a factory where luminescent clock faces were
manufactured.

Initially, a firm in Nevada offered to receive and bury the contaminated soil, but changed its mind. Several New Jersey locales
refused state entreaties to store the drums of soil temporarily at licensed facilities for a fee. Kean's administration abandoned a plan to
blend the "bad" soil with noncontaminated soil in a quarry in the
town of Vernon in Sussex County, where the radon could escape into
the atmosphere, after local residents protested strenuously. One legislator told Kean that he was prepared to lie down in front of state
trucks to prevent the soil from entering his county.[30] Noting an increase in gun sales in western New Jersey, state police feared that
the protests would erupt into violence. Around the time Kean issued
the executive order barring development around the wetlands, his
staff was investigating whether the radon-contaminated soil could be
stored at the Colliers Mills Wildlife Refuge in Jackson Township (in
Russo's district). Again protests erupted. Congressmen from the region voiced their opposition to the state's plan to the federal government. Whether at their behest or perhaps to settle a score with Kean,
the Interior Department objected to the state's proposal.

Kean charged Richard J. Sullivan, the state's first environmental
protection commissioner, with finding a solution to what was becoming a major public relations problem as well as an environmental
one. After weighing twenty-two alternatives, Sullivan recommended
shipping the soil to a Tennessee facility, where it would be mixed
with materials with an even greater level of radioactivity and buried
in a licensed low-level facility.[31] Kean mused over the irony in the
state's having to make the soil more hazardous in order for it to be
disposed of.

Ogden's Bill Passes

Upon learning that the state supreme court had denied developers' motion to stay his executive order on wetlands, Kean used his appearance at a ceremonial function both to up the ante and to savor his victory. At a traveling exhibit devoted to the Magna Carta, Kean stopped at a display case bearing a replica of one of King John's swords. "I have a sword too," Kean snapped, "it's called an executive order."[32]

On July 25, days after he had put the radon controversy behind him, Kean announced that he could accept the latest in a series of bills the legislature had been considering since he issued his veto threat in March. Russo advised builders that they had so many hours in which to submit amendments to Kean's liking or be prepared to see his executive order remain in place throughout the legislature's summer recess.[33]

At a dramatic public ceremony at which he signed Ogden's bill and tore up his executive order, Kean proclaimed the new statute one of the most important ever enacted in the state. He said that it would protect 6 percent of the state's landmass from haphazard development, set aside buffer zones from 75 to 150 feet to protect trout production and endangered and threatened species, and set aside 25 to 50 feet of additional buffers for wetlands of lesser value.[34] Asked what impact Kean's action had had on shaping the legislation, Ogden wryly observed that "it obviously speeded up the process."[35]

Beach Protection

During his first term, Kean acted often and decisively to protect New Jersey beaches from erosion and to safeguard residents living along the coastline from the ravages of nature. When storms, hurricanes, and floods devastated parts of the New Jersey shore and forced residents out of their homes, Kean joined the staff at the New Jersey State Police bunker in West Trenton, where its emergency management unit maintained operations. Under a statute enacted during World War II, the state police assumed responsibility for civil defense. Under that authority, it came to exercise command and control over state, county, and local emergency responders and agencies during natural disasters. Kean participated in the unit's emergency service planning operations and became its public spokesman during emergencies. Colonel Clinton Pagano, superintendent of the state police, attributed the high level of cooperation the public gave the unit in times of stress to Kean's credibility.[36]

The governor pushed a $50-million bond issue to rebuild areas of the coastline that had been damaged during the worst storm to hit the region since 1962. Kean, acting through the National Governors Association, also pressed Congress to earmark $200 million to protect the coastline from the dual threats of flooding and beach erosion. During his second term, his priorities shifted from how to shield the shore from disasters nature inflicted to how to protect it from actions humans committed.

On August 14, 1987, a day Kean would later term "New Jersey's own day of infamy," a fifty-mile-long slick of hospital wastes appeared along the New Jersey shore and washed up on its beaches.[37] The debris included syringes, hypodermic needles, pill bottles, and an assortment of other hospital instruments. Their discovery forced closings of Monmouth and Ocean county beaches at the height of the tourist season. After flying over the area with a host of federal and state officials, Kean held a press conference at Island Beach State Park. He was clearly in a fighting mood. "I'm angry, frankly. Very angry," he said. "The ocean is not a cesspool," he added. He vowed to sue in federal court "to have the guilty party pay every penny of damage" the wash-up caused.[38]

Kean's comments reflected his and his constituents' growing impatience with New York City's dumping practices at the time. What distinguished the latest incident from those that preceded it were its massive scale and the nature of the debris involved. In one day, the $11-billion tourism industry, the state's second largest after petrochemicals, stood on the verge of collapse for the remainder of the 1987 season and beyond. Immediately, Kean embarked on a two-part strategy to confront the situation and prevent its reoccurrence.

First, he assured the public that the state was doing all within its power to reverse the damage. As he had during previous environmental alerts, Kean had the state conduct tests, this time of the water, and apprise the public what they revealed. While most beaches reopened within a day, the discovery of fecal coliform bacteria off Atlantic City resulted in the first closing of this beach in the city's history, reigniting fears along the rest of the coast. Kean responded to all that ensued in what he called "one dreadful week" with a new series of televised ads. In a manner reminiscent of how he had approached the toxic waste issue, Kean said in the commercials that New Jersey was doing more than any other state to ensure the safety and cleanliness of its beaches.

Second, he announced too that the state would offer a five-thousand-dollar reward to anyone who supplied "hard evidence to convict and jail" the perpetrators, and set up a hotline citizens could use to provide or receive information.[39] After the initial beach closings, Kean had commissioned a poll to ascertain what measures the state needed to take to convince the public that it was taking ocean pollution seriously. "Jail sentences for offenders" topped the list of suggestions. He incorporated this and similar phrases into most of his public statements. "If they are dumping illegally in the ocean," Kean took to saying, "we can find them and bring them to justice; we can even put people in jail."[40]

As he lambasted the still-to-be-identified polluters, Kean was surprisingly conciliatory in comments he made about New York City's possible culpability. In a joint appearance with the city's mayor, Ed Koch, Kean said, "We can't just look at our neighbor. We have to look at ourselves," pointing out that New Jersey locales and residents had also engaged in the very activities they had been deploring.[41] Preliminary evidence suggested that the much-maligned Big Apple, long the source of untreated sewage that washed up along New Jersey shores, was not responsible for the most recent incident. Both New York and New Jersey had passed laws specifying how medical wastes were to be handled. Officials on both sides of the Hudson suspected that a private contractor illegally discharged debris en route to a municipal incinerator, treatment site, or landfill.

Kean and his administration used the publicity the beach closings received as an opportunity to resolve its remaining disputes with New York City over the dumping issues. In November, Kean and Edwards, now the state's attorney general, announced that New Jersey would not join a federal suit the township of Woodbridge had filed against New York City for polluting its beaches. In return, the city agreed to install floating "sweepers" in waters around the Southwest Brooklyn Transfer Station and below the surface at the Fresh Kills Landfill in Staten Island to prevent wastes from seeping into New Jersey waters. The city also offered restitutions to Woodbridge for its past actions. Beaming with optimism, Kean hailed the agreement as "a major step to make sure that New Jersey shore vacationers only have to worry about surf and sunburn, and not soda cans, syringes or whatever else washed up in that particular tide."[42]

A year after the garbage slick made its appearance off the New Jersey coast, Kean and New York governor Mario Cuomo boarded a New York City fireboat to announce, with the Statue of Liberty and the World Trade Center visible behind them, that the two states were adopting "cradle to grave" regulations that would require producers of medical waste, from its creation to its disposal, to keep continuous logs of how the materials were handled.[43] Both governors pointed out that their actions would only control medical wastes.

Having called a truce with New York, Kean took aim at more local causes of beach and ocean pollution. His administration turned its attention to trash and sludge that had made its way into the ocean during heavy rains, bypassing local treatment plants. The day after he announced the court settlement with New York, Kean unveiled a fourteen-point, $200-million program to safeguard ocean waters off New Jersey shores. He revealed that he would include the first $50 million in his next budget and the remaining amounts in ensuing years. His plan would ban sludge dumping into the ocean in five years, mandate removal of lead and cyanide from material discharged into sewage systems, prevent municipal trash from washing out to sea during storms, and require marine policing to enforce the new rules.[44]

After putting his own house in order, Kean set out to press the federal government—again by working through the National Governors Association, together with Mario Cuomo— to outlaw the dumping of sludge into oceans. With the memory of the "infamous" summer of 1987 fresh in its memory, Congress passed a measure sponsored by representatives and senators from the coastal states that banned the practice by a certain date. President Reagan signed the measure into law in October 1988. Not for the first time, Kean had used his increasing national clout to bring about change at home.

Kean's Environmental Legacy

Kean's actions to speed cleanups of toxic wastes, resolve the radon controversy, establish buffer zones around wetlands, and provide for sewer and infrastructure repairs were but some of his major environmental achievements as governor. He also furthered the planning process in the state's Green Acres program, allowing for the state and municipalities to plan for acquisition of properties that came on the market in the future, ending what had been a haphazard approach to the acquisition of open space.[45] In addition, he brokered a stalemate that had prevented the creation of a nuclear power plant in southern New Jersey. Interestingly, given the controversies that surrounded radon and dioxin, this dispute revolved not around safety considerations (all sides were satisfied that industry would meet the most stringent requirements at the Hope Creek site) but costs overruns. In his office, Kean brokered a deal with his energy commissioner (Leonard Coleman) and public advocate (Joseph Rodriquez) that industry, rather than ratepayers, would assume these additional costs.[46]

Kean tried but failed to establish another revolving fund, this one financed through a minimal tax on home sales, to control floods, dredge lakes, and maintain parks. He also proved unsuccessful in efforts to create a coastal commission to regulate, if not restrict, runaway development along the shore. The latter would have closed a loophole in CAFRA, a measure Kean had sponsored as assembly Speaker, that had exempted projects of up to twenty-four units from state regulation.[47] Nearing the end of his term, however determined he remained to use the fullest powers of his bully pulpit to press for change, Kean had simply run out of time.

Speaking at the Governor's School on the Environment, established in his final year in office, Kean repeated before one hundred students in attendance a message he had delivered before citizen activists in what was then a nascent environmental movement. "Where the public is not involved," he told them, "the special interests have their way; when the public is involved, it doesn't matter how much money the special interests give to legislators."[48]

chapter 15

The Politics of Inclusion

Reaching Out to Diverse Communities

Throughout his political career, Kean displayed an ability, rare among national Republicans and many Democrats, to relate to ethnic constituencies. He encapsulated his attempts to reach out to African American, Italian American, Asian American, Ukrainian American, Polish American, Jewish, and other voters who had not habitually voted Republican in the phrase "the politics of inclusion."[1] In the manner in which he approached diverse communities, Kean came across less as a politician than as someone genuinely interested in learning about people with backgrounds different from his own.

Undoubtedly, Kean acquired some of the dexterity he exhibited in reaching beyond traditional Republican constituencies by observing his father. Robert W. Kean ran strong in ethnic wards and remained in contact with the disparate groups he represented. He kept the diverse elements of his district informed of what he was doing on their behalf through his newsletter, *Kean Comments,* the press, and through word of mouth, spread by friends and advisers who had deep roots in various ethnic enclaves. He diligently performed the "casework" that congressmen habitually undertake on behalf of constituents: locating missing Social Security checks, following up with the Veterans Administration, inquiring about constituents' relatives caught up in the flames of war-torn Europe.

In Robert W. Kean's day, people of similar ethnic extractions lived largely among themselves. His descriptions of Essex County's Italian, Jewish, Polish, and Irish wards in the 1930s read like a textbook on immigrant settlement patterns, urban politics, and boss rule, all areas with which he was familiar. By the time Tom Kean ran for office in the late 1960s, geographic barriers, at least among whites, had broken down. Children ceased speaking the native tongues of their parents at home or on the street. Many of them as adults married someone of a different ethnic background and moved to one of the newly developed suburbs, returning to the old neighborhood for Sunday and holiday meals at "Grandma's." Older generations passed from the scene and newer immigrants, many not from Europe, moved into their former dwellings.

The civil rights movement and its accompanying assertions of black power and black pride prompted many assimilated white ethnics to reconnect with their roots. Outlets for them to do so appeared in the form of language schools, ethnic festivals, radio broadcasts, and museum exhibitions. Tom Kean came to know this part of New Jersey well. As a highway commissioner, he attended ethnic festivals at the Garden State Arts Center. The office of ethnic affairs Governor Kean established in his secretary of state's office provided him with opportunities to interact with representatives of more than one community simultaneously at annual events at Liberty State Park. It also kept him abreast of issues of concern to various communities, serving as the statewide equivalent of listening posts his father had maintained throughout his congressional district.

When he issued proclamations commemorating events of concern to one particular group, such as Greek Independence Day, Soviet suppression of the 1957 Hungarian uprising, or Stalinist-imposed famine in Ukraine, Kean turned his outer office into a classroom, regaling onlookers with tales of heroic deeds performed by people with unpronounceable names in centuries past. On the stump, Kean established common bonds with constituents of different ethnic backgrounds. He, like his father before him, delighted Polish Americans when he told them that one of his ancestors had married a Polish noble. "On my mother's side, we are Dutch, you know," Kean informed acquaintances as he departed for a ceremony honoring the queen of the Netherlands.

The year Ronald Reagan became president, Kean related to Irish Americans that both he and Reagan might both be descended from Brian Boru (940–1014), the last king of a united Ireland, whose biography he kept in the trunk of his car for ready reference. Asked how far back his Irish lineage extended, Kean, grinning, said that the official at the Irish tourist board who had researched the origins of the Kean name told him that "much of it had vanished in the mists of Irish history."[2] Yet, Kean maintained a deep interest in Irish history and culture. Years after he had left office, he was still sporting a patched tweed hat he received as a gift from a woman selling Irish crafts at a festival.

Bonding with Italian Americans

Sometimes, Kean used his familiarity with history to win the affection of audiences others had tried to turn against him. Such proved the case during his first year in office when he was asked to speak at an Italian American event on Columbus Day. Typically, he was running late. Marie Garibaldi, whom Kean had recently nominated to the state supreme court, making her the first woman to serve in this capacity, delivered the keynote address. After she had finished, the program chairman recited the names of Italian Americans who had distinguished themselves in various fields. When he turned his attention to public service, the speaker admonished his listeners that, had they worked harder the previous year, he would be introducing New Jersey's first Italian American governor instead of Tom Kean. At that juncture, Kean walked into the room to hushed tones.

Seeking to break the tension, he offered biographical information about himself. "Some of you may know," he said, "that before I got into this government and politics business, I had been a teacher." Lamenting how little students knew about history "these days," Kean said that he doubted that many knew that Churchill had lifted his "blood, sweat, and tears" speech directly from the writings of nineteenth-century Italian patriot Giuseppe Garibaldi.[3] Offering further information about himself, Kean noted his fondness for opera. In a reference to what he termed the "mysteries of the Italian language," he described a scene from Puccini's *La Bohème* in which Rodolfo touches Mimi's hand and sings the aria "Che gelida manina." "How do you translate that?" Kean asked. "Sorry," he volunteered, "the literal translation, 'your little hand is cold,' just doesn't do it." His listeners responded with sustained applause. After Kean had departed, Arthur Imperatore, president of APA Transport, proclaimed in a loud voice that he was "proud to have a governor like Tom Kean." Twice embarrassed, the program chairman who had publicly lamented Kean's election slumped into his seat.[4]

Kean knew the Italian American community in New Jersey well. His familiarity with many of its members came less from opera than from politics. For generations, this community supplied both parties in Essex County with workers, votes, and candidates. In the eras in which both Robert W. Kean and Tom Kean were politically active, Italian Americans participated heavily in the affairs of the Essex County Republican Party, while their Irish American counterparts sought political advancement through the Democratic Party. Kean described one particular Republican leader, Joseph Intile, as someone who had risen through the party's ranks by working harder than everyone else. "He knew the names of all the voters, those of their families, and even where in Italy they or their forebears came from."[5] Kean would joke that many of the rivalries and alliances that manifested themselves in then current election cycles carried over from Italy.

As the son of a politician who had run well in Italian American communities, Kean grew up aware of the prejudice that existed against Italian immigrants. After Senator Bill Bradley introduced legislation to return land in South Dakota's Black Hills to the Sioux, that state's attorney general suggested that New Jersey be given to Sicily, on the grounds that "Sicilians run and own New Jersey anyway." Kean demanded an apology.[6] He told a group of Italian American war veterans that the South Dakotan's crudeness may have served a useful purpose by reminding people that the "specter of bigotry" was not dead. A decade after he had left office, a popular cable television show *The Sopranos* would present millions with the very same stereotypical view of Italian Americans in New Jersey that Kean had found so offensive.

The Liberation Monument

Four months after taking office, Kean, along with David Kotok, 1980 presidential contender John Anderson's former New Jersey campaign manager whom he had befriended when he commented on politics for New Jersey Network, visited Temple Shalom Synagogue in Plainfield to partake in a "Days of Remembrance" ceremony, honoring victims of the Holocaust. The program called for Kean to say a few words and receive a curriculum on Holocaust education that the Anti-Defamation League of the B'nai Brith had prepared. As he introduced Kean, Kotok read from the *Congressional Record* Robert W. Kean's remarks of March 23, 1943, urging the U.S. government to speed up efforts to rescue Jews in Europe. Kotok said afterward that he could tell from the expression on Kean's face that the governor was hearing his father's words for the first time.[7] (Kean was about to turn eight years old when his father uttered them.)

Later that evening, Kean presided over the unveiling of a nine-foot bronze relief by sculptor Nathan Rapoport, depicting a mother and child about to be consumed by flames and soldiers attempting to rescue them. The synagogue's president, Luna Kaufman, and her husband had commissioned the work as a gift to the temple. When Kean indicated that he wanted to know more about the artist, Kaufman told him that she became acquainted with Rapoport's work in 1948 when she attended the dedication of the monument he had created to commemorate the heroes of the Warsaw Ghetto uprising. Kaufman had spent much of the war in a forced labor camp near Leipzig, Germany, an area she described as a no-man's-land. "After those horrible years, you didn't know what to do about your Jewishness," she explained. "We didn't know whether we should give up being Jews, forget about being Jews, or be ashamed of being Jews," she said. "There was pride and dignity to the monument, which gave us courage to go on," she remembered.[8]

Kaufman told Kean that Rapoport wanted to build a monument to American soldiers who had rescued a half million Jews during World War II. She volunteered that the artist had a model of such a work in his New York studio. Kean paid Rapoport a visit. The model depicted an American soldier, arms outstretched, carrying a survivor in his arms. As he gazed at the pietà-like work, Kean said that he wanted to see the monument built. Rapoport told him that Westchester County, New York, had expressed interest in erecting it but had changed its mind. The two discussed Arlington National Cemetery as a possible site. Rapoport told Kean that children don't frequent cemeteries and that he wanted his work to teach them compassion. Kean later telephoned Kaufman to inform her that the monument could be built at Liberty State Park in Jersey City, across from Ellis Island and the Statue of Liberty. He also said that he wanted the artist and his backers to meet two conditions.

"Build it as big as you can," Kean instructed Rapoport, who changed the statue's dimensions from nine to fifteen feet.[9] It would eventually stand on a two-and-one-half-foot pedestal of Vermont granite. Kean also insisted that it be financed exclusively with private funds. At an exhibition of Rapoport's work at the New Jersey State Museum, the first to honor the sculptor in this way, Kean kicked off what would be a yearlong campaign to raise $1 million in private donations. Kotok and Kaufman served as cochairmen, with Kean and U.S. senators Bradley and Frank Lautenberg as honorary chairmen.[10] "It's not just a Holocaust memorial," Kean said of the proposed monument, but a "memorial to the idea that America fights wars to liberate."[11] Kean said that when he beheld Rapoport's model, he thought of his two brothers and of other relatives who had fought in World War II. Following Kean's instructions, Kaufman, through a series of public programs and concerts, found ways for schoolchildren, corporations, unions, farmers, veterans' groups, and cultural organizations to participate in what had become a statewide effort.

As construction of Rapoport's monument proceeded in Jersey City, events ensued in Manalapan that underscored the need for it. On

October 17, 1984, three teens hot-wired the ignition of a bulldozer and drove it through the walls of Temple Beth Shalom. So that all would know why they had committed this vandalism, they sprayed swastikas and anti-Semitic slogans on the walls of the building. Several youths were later charged with throwing a Molotov cocktail in front of another synagogue in town. Weeks later, Kean spoke to a gathering of more than three thousand residents who assembled in a show of solidarity at the local high school. Giving voice to its collective outrage, he praised the audience for demonstrating "what it truly means to live in an American community."[12] Afterward, he participated in a ceremonial cleanup of the building, personally scrubbing graffiti from the synagogue's walls. Observing local children compete to see who could wash off the most letters in the shortest amount of time, Kean prodded them to speed things up. Within an hour it was all gone.[13]

On May 30, 1985, in the run-up to the fortieth anniversary of the end of World War II, Kean dedicated Rapoport's Liberation Monument. Later that year, he told students at the Governor's School for the Arts he had established at Trenton State College that as long as Rapoport's works continued to stand, "we will not let the Holocaust happen again."[14] Looking back on the event nearly two decades later, Kaufman said her experiences working with Kean marked the first time she actually felt at home in a country to which she had immigrated thirty years earlier, coming out of "nowhere," knowing nobody, and having nothing. "Tom Kean," she said, "was the first Christian I encountered who I thought really cared about the Holocaust and the Jews."[15]

Standing Up for a Refusenik

On March 16, 1983, Kean, Kotok, and a gubernatorial aide departed for a ten-day private trip to Israel.[16] At Yad Vashem, Israel's national memorial to the six million Jews who perished in Hitler's death camps, Kean inspected another of Rapoport's works, *Scroll of Fire*. His Israeli hosts held a memorial service in honor of Robert W. Kean on the fortieth anniversary of his now celebrated speech on the floor of the House of Representatives. By coincidence, the World Conference of Soviet Jewry had been meeting in Jerusalem at the time of Kean's visit. After Kean retired for the evening, he was awakened by a telephone call. Several dignitaries had addressed the conference. The caller wanted to know if Kean would like to as well.[17] He did.

Among the items on the agenda at the WCSJ conference was the protection of Soviet Jewish "refuseniks" (persons declared "enemies of the state" after requesting permission to depart the USSR to settle in Israel) by having prominent persons in the West "adopt" them. By the time he had returned to New Jersey, Kean had "adopted" thirty-seven-year-old mathematician Boris Klotz, a resident of Moscow.

Kean began writing Soviet leaders to request that Klotz and his family be allowed to emigrate. His files show the extent to which he exerted himself on Klotz's behalf. In his own hand, Kean reworked a staffer's draft of a letter to Yuri Andropov, Brezhnev's short-lived successor. Forgoing the traditional niceties the aide had inserted, Kean said that Klotz and his wife were "close personal friends of some good friends." He asserted that they had "no involvement whatsoever in politics" and that they wanted to "immigrate to Israel for personal reasons." Kean concluded that he would consider it an act of personal friendship for Andropov to grant his request.[18] Receiving no reply, he wrote again and again. Upon learning that Soviet authorities had interrogated Klotz, his western contacts began to fear the worst.

Through mutual friends, Klotz got word to Kean that he wanted to talk with him by telephone. Kean tried to reach the refusenik for several months. After he succeeded in getting Klotz on the line, Kean kept a crowd waiting outside his office for nearly an hour as the two men exchanged pleasantries, mostly about their twin sons. Kean let on afterward that he did not want the conversation to end out of concern for what might become of Klotz.[19] Kean then renewed his efforts on the refusenik's behalf. News of the extent to which Kean had gone on Klotz's request reached Moscow.

On October 6, 1986, in a letter he sent to Kean through an intermediary, Klotz wrote: "Lately we were told about President Reagan's visit to New Jersey. We were told that during your discussions with the President you mentioned our case and as a result we were included in a list of about ten or a dozen families, which are of special concern for the President." In the same letter, Klotz asked whether the information he had received was accurate.[20]

It was. In the eight years Kean served as governor, Reagan visited New Jersey on twelve occasions With Newark the only airport in the state able to accommodate Air Force One, presidential visits to New Jersey entailed thirty- to forty-minute car rides to various engagements. Accompanying Reagan as his official host, Kean would use his time with the president to discuss policy concerns or seek the president's assistance in certain matters. Files in the Ronald Reagan Library reveal that Kean was not the only American to show his concern for Klotz.[21] He may well have been the first, however, to bring this refusenik's plight directly to Reagan's attention.

As enclosures with his October 6 communication to Kean, Klotz included letters he had written to both Reagan and Gorbachev, who were scheduled to hold a summit in Iceland. After explaining that he could only petition his own government through the intervention of foreigners, Klotz asked Kean to forward the letter he had written Gorbachev to the Soviet embassy in Washington.[22] On February 27, 1987, Kean wrote to Gorbachev expressing his concern that Klotz had been interrogated. Again, he asked that Klotz and his family be allowed to emigrate. To entice Gorbachev to do his bidding, Kean tried several approaches. He mentioned his past advocacy of a nuclear freeze, hinted at increased trade and cultural exchanges between the two countries, and praised Gorbachev's reforms.[23] Seven months later, Kean received a one-sentence letter from the Soviet embassy in Washington. "In response to your letter this is to inform you that the Klotz family is allowed to go to Israel," it said.[24]

Outreach to African Americans

Of all the bridges Kean built to "nontraditional" constituencies, he worked the hardest at forging ties with African Americans. His winning of more than 62 percent of the votes New Jersey African Americans cast when he sought reelection in 1985 attests to his success. Although Kean's legislative district had included few African Americans and he had paid attention to their concerns, he fared no better in predominantly African American precincts than had other Republicans. After he became governor, Kean continued the outreach efforts to African Americans he had already been making, but over a wider terrain. What had changed after he became governor was not Kean's operating style but his visibility. Because of the post he occupied, the media paid greater attention to his activities and more people learned about them.

That Kean would take an active interest in the problems of African Americans was not surprising, given his and his family's longstanding commitment to civil rights and his own record as a state legislator. After he was declared the winner of the 1981 election, Kean made it one of his highest priorities to earn the trust and support of his African American constituents. He had done it so effectively that by the time he sought reelection in 1985, not even his staunchest critics, including Alan Karcher, saw any advantage to be gained by bringing up the ballot security controversy that arose in the aftermath of the previous gubernatorial election.

As governor, Kean increased his efforts on behalf of Babyland. "I could not always pick up the phone and get city officials on the line, but I could always get the governor," its director, Mary Smith, later said. Smith recalled that word soon spread among the neighborhoods and throughout the community that Kean was a different kind of Republican. She cited the following example to show the lengths to which he was willing to go to assist Babyland. Kean overruled his own attorney general after the state had determined that it lacked the power to condemn a tract of land on which a nonprofit organization sought to build a supermarket in Newark's Central Ward. "These people [including those served by Babyland] need a supermarket," he declared, "and we should be helping them attract it." The market was built.[25]

Upon discovering that the Port Authority of New York and New Jersey had rejected a $5-million maintenance contract to a New Jersey minority businessman named Malcolm Dunn, even though Dunn had submitted the lowest bid, Kean vetoed the authority's minutes in protest.[26] He remained undeterred when the bi-state agency informed him that if it awarded a contract to Dunn, who ran a nonunion shop, it risked provoking labor unrest in New York. Turning his attention toward transportation projects within his state, Kean listened to complaints that the state was not taking seriously its obligation to award 10 percent of roadwork contracts to minority-owned businesses. He soon discovered that personal intervention would not be enough to change the bureaucratic culture he had inherited. "The things Tom Kean can do himself get done," said a black community leader. "Those things he has to have the cabinet do don't get done."[27] Taking such comments to heart, Kean asked his energy commissioner, Leonard Coleman, to take on two additional roles: external liaison to the African American community and internal ombudsman for minority concerns.

At the time of Kean's election, Coleman was serving as head of the Newark Urban Coalition. Like the Newark business executives who funded his operation, Coleman backed Pat Kramer in the 1981 Republican primary. Through his work in Newark and with the Episcopal Church, Coleman came Kean's way with an expansive network of contacts. After joining Kean's cabinet, first as energy commissioner and later as head of the Department of Community Affairs, Coleman met regularly with black executives, educators, and professionals, offering his assistance with problems they encountered with state government. It was through one such group, the Brain Trust, that he learned of Dunn's difficulties with the Port Authority.

Having taken on the Port Authority bureaucracy, Kean set out to change its management structure. He appointed Henry Henderson, owner of one of the one hundred largest minority-owned businesses with experience in international trade, to its board, making him the first African American commissioner in the bi-state agency's sixty-two-year history.[28] Unhappy that minorities were underrepresented on boards of utilities, over which the state exercised regulatory authority, Kean had Coleman spread the word that his administration would be reluctant to grant rate increases to concerns that excluded representatives of their minority customers from positions where they could influence company policies.

Kean worked to increase the number of minorities serving as judges and in law enforcement. He was particularly concerned that minority citizens who came into contact with the judicial system did not regard it as a whites-only preserve. Kean appointed to the superior court Elliot Heard, making him the first African American ever to serve as a judge in southern Jersey. He also named to the superior court Shirley Tollentino, the first African American woman to serve at this level. As Essex County prosecutor, Kean tapped Herb Tate Jr., whose father Robert W. Kean had added to the county GOP legislative ticket a generation earlier.

Kean and Coleman worked to improve communications between the state administration in Trenton and the broader African American community. Often, they acted through minority ministers. Two they consulted often were the Reverend Benjamin F. Johnson Sr. and Edward Verner, president of the Newark–North Jersey Committee of Black Churchmen. Johnson, then in his eighties, had been a friend of Robert W. Kean. In 1981, he had been among the few black leaders who supported Tom Kean for governor over James Florio.[29] Coleman arranged to be invited to meetings Johnson and Verner held every Wednesday with all black ministers in the city of Newark. Kean occasionally went along. The ministers kept their parishioners informed of what Kean was doing and in turn brought their congregants' concerns to Kean's and Coleman's attention. Kean made it a practice to visit black churches frequently and not only when he was a candidate seeking votes.

When he appeared before minority audiences, Kean would first recite his bona fides in civil rights. He then related how policies he was pursuing would impact positively on minority communities, placing special emphasis on reducing crime, improving education, and attracting jobs. As a means of relieving minority unemployment and attracting capital into the inner cities, Kean, following up on a campaign promise, guided to passage legislation establishing urban enterprise zones. An idea of Representative Jack Kemp (R-NY), the concept entailed using tax and regulatory incentives to entice companies to locate in areas of high unemployment and employ local residents. Kean became the first public official in the United States to implement it.[30] With Kemp's measure to establish the program at the federal level stalled in the House Ways and Means Committee, its supporters began pressing for its implementation at the state level.

Newark and Camden were the first of several cities to have enterprise zones established within their borders. Recreating one of the most memorable episodes from his campaign, Kean signed the bill into law in Camden with Kemp at his side.[31]

Kean and Coleman also worked through conventional black organizations such as the National Association for the Advancement of Colored People and the Urban League to spread Kean's message. Each year he served as governor, Kean addressed the Black Issues Convention. Though his choice of topics varied, his political pitch remained the same: that the best way for minority voters to benefit from the political system was by participating in both political parties. Otherwise, he suggested, one party would continually take African Americans and their votes for granted, while the other wrote them off. Kean, ever the historian, reminded his listeners that this is what had occurred toward the end of Reconstruction.

Bringing African Americans
Back to the Party of Lincoln

As a means of building an African American presence within the New Jersey Republican Party, Coleman founded the Republican Progressive Association (RPA). Most African Americans who served in Kean's administration joined, as did several of their Caucasian colleagues. The RPA's membership consisted primarily of African American businesspeople and professionals. Its leadership included aging GOP African American stalwarts, such as Essex County College president J. Harry Smith and former congressional hopeful Bill Stubbs, and promising newcomers like Pat Stewart, the deputy chairwoman of the Bergen County GOP organization, who had presided over the tally at the 1980 Republican National Convention. The organization staged weekend retreats at which Kean, Coleman, and top officials in Kean's administration appeared. Kean, Coleman, and state party Republican chairman Frank Holman looked upon the RPA as a source of possible African American appointees to state boards and commissions.

With the state and county Republican parties lacking an institutional structure within the African American community from which to build electoral support for Kean and other Republican candidates, Coleman reached out to disaffected African American politicians in the Democratic Party. Several had at their command civic associations and booster organizations that could bring support Kean's way, often in exchange for access, appointments, and favors. Among those who helped him in this fashion were former Newark councilmen Calvin West and Earl Harris and incumbent Trenton councilman Bo

Robinson. Though it proved beneficial to Kean when he sought re-election in 1985, this approach did little to plant roots for future GOP successes in minority communities after Kean left office. Several minority officeholders who supported Kean's reelection either returned to the Democratic fold or departed from civic life.

After Kean's reelection, the New Jersey Republican State Committee and the county party organizations did little to cultivate, on the party's behalf, African Americans who benefited from Kean's education, welfare, and other policies. One reason may have been that the party was less likely to plant roots among such voters than among middle-class African American voters, many of whom resided outside the inner cities. With Kean and Coleman continually cultivating big-city (Democratic) mayors for support for administration initiatives in the legislature, their would-be allies would not have taken kindly to Trenton's instigating insurgencies in their home bastions. Surprisingly, given Kean's pro-business policies and his close association with national conservatives such as Kemp, his administration contained among its ranks few identifiable black conservatives. Coleman downplayed the significance of ideological diversity within the African American community. As Kean prepared to leave office, Coleman observed: "There is a strong rapport and collegiality between the black Republicans and black Democratic political leaderships. The interests of the ethnic group outweigh partisan differences."[32]

Nor had Kean and Coleman managed to increase significantly the numbers of African American Republican elected officials. Throughout Kean's eight years as governor, all African Americans serving in the state legislature were Democrats. All won election in districts with predominantly minority populations, areas where Republican organizations were at their weakest. In areas where the party was stronger, Republican county organizations showed little of Robert W. Kean's enthusiasm for running African American candidates. These setbacks notwithstanding, Kean and Coleman made the most of the one opportunity that came their way to develop at the local level a pool of talented African American Republican officeholders and appointees.

After Atlantic City mayor Michael Matthews, under indictment, was forced into a recall election in 1983, Kean, Coleman, and Republican state chairman Frank Holman worked to elect James Usry as the city's first African American mayor. Born in Athens, Georgia, in 1922, Usry was six months old when his parents moved to Atlantic City. During World War II, Usry fought in Africa and Italy with an African American unit called the "Black Buffaloes." After graduating from Lincoln University, he played professional basketball with the Harlem Globetrotters before returning to Atlantic City. He taught in its public schools, rising through its bureaucracy to become a principal and assistant school superintendent. Usry became known for the personal interest he showed in the city's students. "You will never do anything more important than what you are about to do," he once told a new teacher.[33] Comments such as this explain why Kean was so taken with him.

Kean had the state Republican Party get behind Usry again when he ran for a four-year term in 1986, even though his opponent in the nonpartisan election was incumbent Republican assemblywoman Dolores Cooper. The state party provided Usry with money, workers, and advice. Before state and national audiences, Kean cited Usry as an example of the politics of inclusion.[34] Usry won national recognition with his election as president of the National Conference of Black Mayors. Kean's hopes of building upon Usry's example evaporated when the mayor, along with other Atlantic City officials including its city council president, also a Republican, were arrested in a sting operation. In a plea bargain, Usry pleaded guilty to minor campaign violations, rather than to taking six thousand dollars in bribes as the state alleged.[35] He was defeated for reelection in 1990.

Kean missed a chance to embarrass Democrats nationally when he failed to commandeer party leaders to support Coleman when he expressed interest in running against incumbent U.S. senator Frank Lautenberg in 1988. Had he been elected, Coleman would have been the second African American elected to the U.S. Senate since Reconstruction.[36] Had he been defeated, Coleman's candidacy would have demonstrated that Kean's concept of inclusion extended to running minority candidates for statewide office. Years later, Kean listed among his few regrets his failure to press Coleman's case upon the party establishment.[37] Several factors led to his reticence.

Coleman expressed interest in the seat after party fund-raisers had settled on Vietnam war hero, Rhodes scholar, and West Point Heisman Trophy winner retired brigadier general Pete Dawkins. They based their decision on the assumption that, through his personal wealth, Wall Street connections, and commanding biography, Dawkins could raise the funds necessary to mount an effective campaign against the wealthy Lautenberg. Never the favorite of party leaders when he had sought party nominations, Kean proved unwilling, after he had become governor, to play the role of the supreme political boss, able to foist his choice upon the party. How Kean might have reacted had Coleman, who had some organizational support, been as willing to oppose Dawkins in a primary as Kean had been to challenge Fenwick, Bateman, and Kramer, all choices of the party establishment, is anyone's guess.[38]

Celebrating African American History

Kean made the first observance of Martin Luther King's birthday as a federal holiday the occasion for multiple celebrations and educational programs all across the state. As cochairmen of a forty-member commemorative commission, Kean designated one of his Democratic predecessors, Richard J. Hughes, and civil rights leader, labor activist, and former member of the Democratic National Committee Connie Woodruff. Hughes had been governor at the height of the civil rights struggles and had personally known King. His recollections of his conversations with the civil rights leader in the aftermath of the Newark riots captured the imagination of a generation that came into political consciousness after King's death. As he reminisced about his time in office, Hughes recounted to his audiences the work he and Kean had done together in the late 1960s to broaden opportunities for African Americans and to alleviate urban ills.

Kean made it his practice to attend conferences the New Jersey Historical Commission sponsored each year as part of Black History Month. Rather than read a proclamation and depart, he would often remain through the proceedings. He also tailored his remarks to fit with the theme of the gathering he addressed. At one conference, "Books in Chains," at which participants considered the failure of mainstream publishers and academicians to take seriously works by African American historians, Kean related his own experiences as a graduate student as evidence in support of its underlying premise. Kean challenged his audience to fill the gap with writings of their own and to press to get their works published and assigned.[39] At a similar gathering another year, which took as its theme the role humor played in black culture, Kean expounded extemporaneously on the importance of folktales. To the delight of his audience, he recounted the old Brer Rabbit tales he had learned as a youth. WBGO, a Newark-based radio station, subsequently aired a tape of Kean's remarks.[40]

If Coleman served as Kean's liaison to the state's African American political leadership, Rutgers-Newark history professor Clement A. Price, who organized the annual African America history conferences, became his emissary to African American artists and intellectuals. Price was serving as chairman of the state arts council when Kean took office. As Price's term was about to expire, he received a phone call from Kean, who said that he intended to reappoint him.[41] An easy rapport soon developed between the historian and the governor determined to make history.

South African Divestiture

On August 21, 1985, Kean, in his boldest action as governor, announced that he would approve a bill requiring the state to divest $2 billion in state pension funds from firms doing business with South Africa. "There are instances in human history," he said, "when the gravity of an evil is so clear, and the cost of its continuance so great, that the governments at every level must use every tool at their disposal to combat it." "Apartheid," he maintained, was "such an evil."[42] Kean's words caught the attention of African Americans all across the country and opponents of apartheid all across the world.

Although seven other state legislatures had passed measures similar to the one that reached Kean's desk, financial analysts expected New Jersey's divestment to exert a more immediate impact on financial markets because its $10-billion public pension portfolio was the forty-second largest in the country and one of the largest among the states. Analysts anticipated a loss to the state's economy of between $60 and $100 million in investments.[43] Kean took this action after keeping the state's political and business communities in suspense for months. When the legislature passed the divestment measure in June, pundits attributed the timing of its action to Democratic desires to present Kean with a political dilemma the year he sought reelection.

If the governor signed the measure, he would be stripping from the state's portfolio investments in some of the state's largest employers. Promoting a healthy business climate had been one of Kean's highest priorities, and business was one of his party's rock constituencies. If Kean vetoed the bill, Democrats would be certain to castigate him, not only to African Americans, but to moderates and liberals in both parties, as insensitive to the plight of black South Africans.

Kean spent much of the summer soliciting opinions from people on both sides of the divestiture question. Hodding Carter, Kean's Princeton classmate and fellow Princeton University trustee, remembered observing a decided change in Kean's views on the issue over a period of months. Like the state legislature, Princeton officials had come under pressure to drop from the university's portfolio investments in companies that did business in South Africa. "At first, he sided with the university administration, which opposed divestment and supported the Sullivan principles," Carter remembered. "But as time wore on, I could tell that he seemed to believe less and less in that approach. I was not at all surprised when he signed the bill."[44]

Kean said that he had decided to sign the bill because of actions the South African government had taken in the time that had elapsed since the legislation had passed. These included violent crackdowns against student demonstrators and Prime Minister P. W. Botha's denunciation of people outside his country who urged his government to abandon apartheid. Kean's actions earned him praise from some old adversaries and criticism from once and future allies. Karcher called Kean's action his "finest hour."[45] The American Federation of State, County, and Municipal Workers and the Communications Workers of America agreed.

The New Jersey Business and Industry Association, worried about the precedent-setting nature of the legislation, said that South Africa was not the only country violating human rights. Republican legislators, who had voted against the measure on the assumption that Kean would veto it, criticized Edwards's staff for having misled them. Sheepishly, but truthfully, many an assistant counsel replied that they had not known that Kean would sign it.

The same day Kean signed the divestiture bill into law, he conditionally vetoed another bill the Democratic legislature had also passed in June. That measure would have required companies planning to cease operations in New Jersey to give 180 days' notice. By taking both actions at once, Kean had found a way to play the idealist and the pragmatist at the same time. He could truthfully remind his critics in industry that his Democratic opponent would have signed both measures, whereas he had only approved one. Kean's signing of the South Africa divestiture bill earned him respect and standing within the African American community that no other Republican in his lifetime—and few Democrats—would ever match.

Japanese American Redress

During his second term as governor, Kean had an opportunity to help rectify another injustice. While he was working on his autobiography, *The Politics of Inclusion*, his editor at Free Press, Grant Ujifusa, informed him that legislation was working its way through Congress that would have the United States issue a formal apology to Japanese Americans who had been sent to internment camps during World War II as part of the nation's civil defense program. The bill also called for the awarding of twenty thousand dollars to each of the approximately 120,000 American citizens and registered aliens who had spent part of the war years in internment camps—or their descendants.

Ujifusa was concerned that President Reagan might veto the bill. The legislation appropriated $1.25 billion over several years to fund the payments. Although this was a relatively small amount by federal standards, congressional Democrats had been criticizing Reagan for adding to the size of the federal deficit. Here was an expenditure he could easily avoid making. Moreover, Justice Department officials were resisting efforts to have the Supreme Court reconsider its decision in the *Korematsu* case, where it ruled that internments of the kind of which Ujifusa complained were constitutional during wartime. The president's signing of the redress bill, they maintained, would undermine their argument. In addition, U.S. senator S. I. Hayakawa, Reagan's fellow California conservative, insisted that those who were pressing the redress bill were troublemakers, left-wingers, and radicals. Some within Reagan's camp agreed.[46]

Kean promised his editor that he would talk to Reagan about the redress bill at his earliest opportunity. As he had in the case of Boris Klotz, Kean raised Ujifusa's concerns to Reagan while riding in an automobile. Kean made his case in the fall of 1987, when Reagan visited New Jersey to campaign for Republican legislative candidates. The president voiced skepticism about the legislation. He volunteered that he had heard that Japanese Americans had gone to the internment camps of their own volition seeking "protective custody." After Kean told the president that the bill presented him with an opportunity to erase "one of the few black marks in American history," Reagan turned to his deputy chief of staff, Ken Duberstein, and said, "Maybe we should take a re-look at this one."[47]

Kean followed up with a letter to Reagan, reminding him of their conversation. He inserted two enclosures. One was a letter from Ujifusa to Kean explaining that the "protective custody" argument had been raised "after the fact." The editor supplied photographs showing armed personnel pointing guns at those about to be interned.[48] Kean's second enclosure was a letter to Reagan from June Masuda Goto, whose brother, Sergeant Kazuo Masuda, had been killed late in the war while leading a night patrol across the Arno River in Italy. Goto reminded Reagan that as a recently retired captain in the U.S. Army, he had participated in a ceremony honoring her brother in Santa Ana, California. A local cemetery had refused to bury her brother's remains, igniting a public controversy. When General Joseph ("Vinegar Joe") Stilwell had paid a visit to Goto's parents to present them with the Distinguished Service Cross their son had been awarded, the fallen soldier's mother refused the medal. After Masuda's sister Mary accepted it, the general and his party then withdrew to the Santa Ana Bowl to participate in an "Americans United" gathering.

Joining a debate in which Robert W. Kean had engaged years earlier, Stilwell asked his audience what constituted a *real American.* The general defined the term as someone "who calls it a fair exchange to lay down his life in order that American ideals go on living." By those standards, he proclaimed Sergeant Masuda "a better American than any of us here today."[49]

Captain Reagan spoke next. His remarks anticipated the eloquence he would later exhibit as president: "The blood that has soaked into the sand is all one color. America stands unique in the world, the only country not founded on race, but on a way—an ideal. Not in spite of, but because of our polyglot background, we have had all the strength in the world. That is the American way. Mr. and Mrs. Masuda, just as one member of the family of Americans, speaking to another member, I want to say for what your son Kazuo did— Thanks."[50] ("You can imagine," Ujifusa later said, "what it felt like to a group that had been derided as 'sneaky' and 'treacherous' to have a white movie star affirm their worth as Americans.")[51]

Along with her letter, Goto included a clipping from the *Pacific Citizen* that made mention of a letter to the editor of a North Dakota newspaper that Reagan had cited at the beginning of his remarks. "I know where some good Japanese are buried," it began. Reagan had intended his speech as a rejoinder to such sentiments. The article noted that Reagan had addressed the Santa Ana gathering as a representative of the American Veterans Committee, a group that "had much to do with the Navy's decision to drop its ban on Japanese Americans."[52]

After Kean had sent his letter and Ujifusa's enclosures to Reagan, Ujifusa heard that the Office of Management and the Budget recommended that Reagan veto the bill. When Ujifusa voiced concern to Duberstein, the president's aide replied, "Grant, look, this has been talked about at a much higher level." On August 10, 1988, in language reminiscent of Kean's, Reagan cited the legislation as an effort to "right a great wrong" and signed the bill into law.[53] In his prepared remarks, the president referred to a prior speech delivered four decades ago by a young actor who had gone by the name Ronald Reagan. Making his way through the assemblage, Reagan stopped before Mrs. Goto. "Mary?" he inquired as he gazed. "No, Mr. President," she replied. "My sister Mary passed away. I am here representing my family."[54] Reagan nodded. "Were it not for Tom Kean, none of this would ever have happened," Ujifusa said.[55]

chapter 16

The Administrator

Personnel Changes

Just as Kean and the Democrats were putting the final touches on the budgetary agreements of late 1982 and early 1983, another story began making the rounds. Kean was about to name his 1977 campaign press secretary, Greg Stevens, to a newly created post in his office: director of public information. Speculation arose that Stevens would ultimately replace Kean's press secretary and principal spokesman, Carl Golden.[1] Under the headline "There's Always Room for an Old Pal," one newspaper criticized the governor for awarding a patronage post to an old friend when he was still talking of budget cuts and layoffs.[2] Less widely reported was Kean's growing frustration with how his office was being managed. If Kean was indeed contemplating replacing someone, it was not his press secretary, but his chief of staff. In effect, Stevens assumed two roles when he joined Kean's operation: conveying Kean's message to state residents through avenues beyond the statehouse press, such as cable television, radio, and network television, and advising Kean as to how his internal operation might be improved.

Lacking Cary Edwards's political base and coterie of personally loyal aides and Gary Stein's sheer intellect, self-confidence, and personal friendship with Kean, Lewis Thurston, from the start of Kean's administration, appeared the weakest member of his troika. During Kean's first months in office, state officials, legislators, and party leaders complained about Thurston's failure to return telephone calls. Some suggested they had an easier time getting through to Kean than to his chief of staff. When they did, some would jokingly ask Kean to pass along their concerns to Thurston. The chief of staff's failure to make decisions in a timely manner made for some short-term embarrassments to the administration. A case in point was when, after receiving no response for six months to requests that the salary of the executive director of the New Jersey Motion Picture Council be increased, Emmy-winning playwright J. P. Miller resigned from the panel in protest. After reading about the problem, Kean ordered that the paperwork required to approve the pay raise be processed.[3] Problems ensued in the vetting of nominees. Several appointees withdrew from consideration after the press reported that they had inflated professional credentials on their résumés.[4]

There was the peculiar manner in which the administration tried to appoint Anthony Imperiale to a position where he would work with local police in high-crime neighborhoods. News of the appointment was made public through a press release issued by the Department of Community Affairs. Because the announcement had not come from the governor's office, as had those of other appointments, reporters assumed both that Kean sought to distance himself from the appointment and that its primary purpose was to reward Imperiale for his work on ballot security on the previous Election Day. In both an editorial and a political cartoon, the *Star-Ledger* declared the naming of Imperiale a case of "creative patronage."[5] The *New York Times* called it inflammatory to minorities.[6] At a news conference, Kean defended the need for the new post but, in uncharacteristic fashion, allowed Golden to end the session abruptly when reporters inquired why Imperiale would be filling it.[7] Although Imperiale never served in the position, the controversy took a toll on the young administration's credibility.

Another public relations flap concerned Paul Sherwin, a former secretary of state. Recently released from prison, Sherwin showed up in Kean's outer office and demanded a meeting with the governor. The former official was concerned that, because of his conviction, he might be removed from the list of approved insurance agents for the South Jersey Port Corporation. When Sherwin refused to leave, Thurston brought him in to see Kean. This created the impression afterward that Sherwin's continuation on the list of approved contractors resulted from gubernatorial intervention.[8]

Insufficient vetting, botched appointments, and publicized visits from controversial office seekers and favor seekers were not the only personnel problems that plagued Kean's administration in its early months. Republican activists complained that too few of their number were being appointed to positions. County chairmen insisted their patronage requests had been ignored. At first, Kean was unconcerned.

For a time, he and his aides attributed their slowness in making appointments to the recount, which shortened the time they had had to sort out résumés and interview job candidates. Kean was also averse to removing competent people from posts solely because of their political affiliation. After Brendan Byrne joked at a legislative correspondents' dinner that with so many of his appointees still in their jobs fifteen months into Kean's administration, the former governor would not need a transition should he return to his old job, Kean's team realized it had a problem. The paperwork necessary to place appointees in positions had been allowed to pile up, along with unanswered mail.

Overenthusiastic political fund-raisers posed further difficulties for Kean. Early in his administration, a letter went out to potential donors, promising special access to Kean and state officials if they joined the Governor's Club, a group of Republican contributors.[9] Kean nixed the idea after he read the text of the letter in the press. Were this not enough, Kean watchers of long standing wondered why Kean, who had in the past been able to dramatize issues in ways that captured the attention of the media, so often found himself playing the defensive to Alan Karcher. One reason was that Kean spent time cleaning up for others he might have used building public and legislative support.

On April 11, 1983, before a crowded press conference, Kean announced that Thurston had accepted a post at the sports authority, where he would oversee maintenance, security, and traffic control, and that Stevens would replace him as chief of staff. Barely bothering to conceal their sense of relief, Kean intimates transformed what had been billed as a routine reception, honoring Cape May Republican chairman Philip Matalucci upon his appointment to the Civil Service Commission, into a major celebration. "It was kind of tacky of everybody to be dancing in the streets 10 minutes after the press conference," one told a reporter.[10]

A New Chief of Staff

Thurston's departure marked the end of the troika system around which Kean had organized his office. While Edwards and Stein would continue to run their respective bailiwicks, Stevens would be first among equals. Upon assuming the chief of staff's post, he made personnel changes, took control of scheduling, honed the administration's message, and ensured that departmental decisions and announcements synchronized with Kean's policies and priorities. In the course of a few weeks, mail was being answered in three days. If the writer's concerns could not be resolved in that time, Kean staffers provided status reports. Vacancies were filled more quickly. Events and meetings were placed on Kean's calendar in order of their importance to his overall objectives, rather than as favors to those requesting his presence.

Confident that things were functioning better at home, Kean felt free to take to the road. With an eye sensitive to the demands of television, Stevens sought out events and visuals that showed Kean at his most photogenic and in ways that captured his upbeat and jovial personality. Rather than sign a high-tech bond issue or an urban aid bill in the statehouse, Stevens sent Kean to Thomas Edison's laboratory in West Orange and Paterson's city hall. At Stevens's prodding, Kean began holding town meetings. For the rest of his time in office, he would hold one in a different county every six to eight weeks. In preparation for these appearances, cabinet departments would supply Kean with an inventory of programs they maintained in particular locales, as well as with a list of anticipated questions and suggested answers. As questioners left the microphone, gubernatorial aides took their names and addresses so that Kean's staff could follow up on people's questions.

Stevens tended to the smallest detail. One newspaper, noting that Kean, not known as a fastidious dresser, appeared at a town meeting dressed in "Kennedyesque garb of gray slacks, a loosened red tie and a blue shirt with the sleeves rolled up and top button undone," called it the "perfect uniform for television."[11] In addition to the town meetings, Kean hosted a cable television and call-in radio shows. Stevens's administrative strengths were also on display in Kean's manner of handling emergency situations, ranging from dioxin in Newark to evacuation of shore residents during hurricanes. Kean came to know that whenever he committed to a course of action, competent hands in Trenton would follow up.

Unlike Thurston, Stevens took an active interest in partisan politics and paid attention to developments within the state GOP and the county organizations. Seeing as his primary function securing Kean's reelection in 1985, he imposed discipline on Kean's operation, relieving Kean of having to tend to minor administrative details. Stevens used the 1983 legislative elections as an opportunity to try out techniques he would use to Kean's benefit two years later. His decision to feature Kean in generic party radio advertisements in the off-year election, while failing to increase the number of Republicans in the legislature, increased both Kean's visibility and his popularity.

Early in his tenure, Stevens helped extricate his boss from a situation which, while it had begun as a minor irritant, showed signs of becoming a major public relations problem. It went by the name Drumthwacket.

Hairy Legs and Claw Feet

Until 1956, New Jersey maintained no official residence for its governor. That changed when former governor Walter E. Edge, who served in the post during World Wars I and II, deeded his Princeton home, Morven, to the state with the proviso that it be used either as an official residence for the governor or as a museum. Governor Robert B. Meyner and his wife, Helen, were the first "first couple" to take up residence at the historic house, which once belonged to Richard Stockton, a signer of the Declaration of Independence. Following the childless Meyners, the Hugheses, Cahills, and Byrnes, all large families, moved into Morven. Finding its quarters cramped and complaining about the lack of privacy, Cahill cast his eye on another facility the state owned a mile down the road: Drumthwacket. Its name was Scottish Gaelic for "wooded hill." Some expected him, should he be reelected, to move to the larger house, once the home of Charles Olden, New Jersey's Civil War governor. He never had the chance. During Byrne's last year in office, the New Jersey Historical Society offered to raise $2 million in private donations to transform Drumthwacket into a suitable residence for Byrne's successor. In exchange, the society would operate Morven as a museum.

During the 1981 gubernatorial campaign, neither Kean nor Florio, not wanting to appear presumptuous, commented on the arrangement. After his election, Kean announced that he and his family would remain in Livingston for the time being. He cited as his reason his disinclination to move his children in the middle of a school year. Six months later, Kean again said that he had no plans to relocate. This time, he said he based his decision on the need to save the state money during a recession. "I think the Governor has to set the example," he declared.[12] So as not to hamper ongoing fund-raising activities, neither the society nor the Keans made public that New Jersey's first family had already decided they would not occupy the mansion.[13]

His own childhood having been disrupted by his father's change of careers, Kean resolved not to allow his election as governor to alter his family's routine. When Kean's twin sons, Tom and Reed, became old enough to attend boarding school, he left it to them to decide whether to follow in his footsteps to St. Mark's. He was delighted when they chose to attend the Pingry School nearby. Once they had decided to remain at home, Kean saw no reason to separate them or their sister, Alexandra, from their friends. Years later, Kean said that not moving his family to Drumthwacket was the best decision he ever made: "The children were very small. Growing up in a goldfish bowl would not have been good for them."[14]

Other factors contributed to his decision. Although Debby Kean had proved a loyal and steadfast campaigner for her husband, her highest priority was her family. She saw little reason to modify her routine after her husband became governor. Nor did she sense a need to become a public person. "You don't see the mailman, the plumber and the UPS driver bring their wives to work," she once observed. "They are out doing their jobs leaving their wives at home and I will stay at home doing mine."[15] The high point of her day, and of her children's, she observed, was when her husband returned home each evening. "He goes to all these dinners and always comes home not having eaten dinner," she joked.[16] Kean's choice of where he would dine was deliberate.

Debby resisted pressure, especially from the press, to change her ways in order to accommodate the demands of being first lady. "I could never play Mrs. Reagan's role as hostess and companion to her husband everywhere, with three kids so young," she explained.[17] Nor did she see any need to comment on public issues. One of her admirers, New York City mayor Ed Koch, found out for himself just how difficult it could be to get Debby Kean to comment on political subjects. At dinners he hosted at Gracie Mansion, the mayor's official residence, Koch customarily brought up issues currently in the news and asked his guests to comment on them. When it became Debby Kean's turn to speak at one of these dinners, he recalled, she smiled and said, "I don't comment about things like that in New Jersey. Why should I do it here?"[18] Some attributed Debby's reticence to shyness. One shrewd observer saw behind her reluctance to partake in political discussions a desire not to embarrass her husband.[19]

With his children settled into a steady routine and his wife disinclined to the public limelight, Kean saw advantages to establishing physical as well as psychological boundaries between his life at work and at home. Commuting to one's place of business was the norm in the community in which the Keans lived, and, as governor, Tom Kean was no exception. With a state trooper driving, Kean would catch up on his work and keep in touch with his staff by telephone from his makeshift office in the backseat. As the Keans anticipated, with so much else on the state's agenda at the time Kean took office, where they would live was not a topic of much public interest during his first year as governor.

That changed with a front-page story in the *New York Times* on January 24, 1983. Under the headline "Mansion Antiques Are Rejected by Mrs. Kean," it informed readers that Debby Kean had ordered furnishings of the French Empire style, estimated to be worth in excess of two hundred thousand dollars, "carted away for sale."[20] "She did not think it had been tastefully done," Golden was quoted as saying.

Antique dealers across the country weighed in with comments about the first lady's actions, her taste in furnishings, her qualifications as an interior decorator, and whether a temporary "tenant" should quibble about how a nonprofit organization adorned a mansion she did not occupy.

The story appeared while Kean was attending a meeting of the Coalition of Northeastern Governors in Providence, Rhode Island. This was an important meeting for him. A year earlier, Kean had voiced displeasure that the group was not fulfilling its potential and had suggested that New Jersey might sever its association with it.[21] The group reorganized itself, focused its attention on issues of concern to the region, and elected Kean as its chairman. At a press conference at which he was to outline the coalition's objectives for the next year, Kean found that reporters only wanted to discuss Drumthwacket. By the time he returned to New Jersey, he had grown particularly angry at how his wife was being portrayed in the press. "Families of people in public life put up with a lot," he recalled years later. "And when someone attacks somebody you really care about, the arrows pierce right through your armor."[22]

Back in the statehouse, he said that the decision to reject the furnishings had been his. He ridiculed the French Empire style that was characterized by "furniture with claws and hairy legs." Were that not enough, he noted that "the chairs weren't very comfortable to sit on." He even derided the name of the mansion, inquiring rhetorically why anyone would want to reside in a place with such a funny name as Drumthwacket. He went on to say that neither he nor his wife had ordered the furniture sold and that he understood the New Jersey Historical Society would be holding on to some of the pieces for its own use. He explained that his wife had been working with Finn Caspersen, chairman of the Beneficial Management Corporation, and art historians and decorators to make the house suitable as a governor's residence. "These things cannot be done quickly and shoddily," Kean added, in a not too oblique reference to how the society had placed borrowed institutional office furniture next to the antiques it had assembled.[23] The *New York Times* followed with an editorial ridiculing Kean's "claws and hairy legs" comment, reminding him that the French Empire style was also noted for "hairy knees, cloven hoofs, bird feet, lion hocks, acanthus leaves, plumes and cornucopias."[24]

Sensing the unfurling of a public relations disaster comparable to that which circled around Nancy Reagan when she solicited private donations to acquire new china for the White House in the midst of a recession, Stevens moved to bring the Drumthwacket saga to a close. Stevens had Kean announce that he would not be moving to the mansion. Next, the state documented proposed expenditures on the mansion Kean had vetoed such as the purchase of a thirty-thousand-dollar Jacuzzi, and unanticipated expenditures the state had to make on the building and the grounds.[25] Caspersen's group swung into full gear. The Newark, Princeton, and New Jersey State museums loaned the mansion paintings and sculptures from its collections. I contacted authors and publishers requesting that they donate copies of books either about New Jersey or by New Jersey authors. Princeton professor and Hemingway biographer Carlos Baker was first to respond, sending by messenger signed copies of his complete works. By the time Kean sought reelection, Drumthwacket had been restored to the point where Kean could receive visiting dignitaries in a manner which their positions commanded.

Stevens Plays the Heavy

In the course of his tenure as chief of staff, Stevens's propensity to act quickly and decisively proved as embarrassing to Kean as had Thurston's indecisiveness and sluggishness.

In March 1985, the Department of Motor Vehicles announced in a joint press release with the attorney general's office that the state had entered into partnership with Sears Roebuck to issue photo drivers' licenses. The program was to have been the largest privatization effort of its kind in the nation. As they had in the case of the Imperiale announcement, reporters wondered why the news of a program bound to attract attention had not been released by the governor's office. A month later, the *Asbury Park Press* reported that the contract would be awarded not directly to Sears but to one of its concessionaires, William Taggart, owner of several profitable driving schools, a friend of Kean's, and a major GOP donor.[26]

Kean called the omission of Taggart's name from the release "ill-conceived," "stupid," "inexcusable," and contrary to his administration's policies of "candor, honesty, and forthrightness in matters dealing with public issues and public money."[27] Kean said he had known of Taggart's involvement but was shocked to learn that his friend's name had been omitted from the release. He also said, quite correctly, that under the rules then in existence, there had been nothing untoward or irregular in the issuance of the contract to Taggart, who operated a highly respected network of driving schools.[28]

Kean announced that he had asked Stevens to investigate the genesis of both the release and the contract. With Democratic gubernatorial hopefuls alleging that the administration had entered into a secret deal with the GOP donor, Clifford Snedeker, director of the Department of Motor Vehicles, announced that he had violated the ethics code in abnegating powers that remained with the state to a private vendor. He voided the contract with Taggart and resigned.[29] Legislative hearings revealed that Snedeker had written Stevens's office for guidance in how the release should be worded and had met with Kean's chief of staff and other officials to discuss the matter.[30] The bipartisan State Commission of Investigations concluded weeks later that Snedeker had not violated the ethics code but had been forced from office on a pretext. The SCI findings invited the conclusion that administration officials, primarily Stevens, regarded Snedeker's forced resignation as a means of cutting the controversy short.[31] In trying to avoid the appearance of cronyism, where none may have existed, Kean's advisers turned what ordinarily would have been a two-day story into months of controversy. For the only time in Kean's administration, the press appeared suspicious of the administration's motives. "Forthrightness was replaced with uptightness," observed one reporter. "Instead of candor administration officials showed dander."[32]

Months after the DMV story broke reporters spotted the strong arm of Kean's chief of staff on the shoulders of a longtime Kean supporter. Upon her confirmation as director of the Essex County Board of Elections, Karla Squier received a letter from Stevens instructing her to retain a certain attorney, who happened to be a friend of Essex County Republican chairman Michael Francis, as her legal counsel. He said that such action on her part had been a "condition" of her appointment. Not only had Squier not agreed to these terms, she had protested to Stevens that state law required that boards of election be represented by the state attorney general. When news of this dispute within Kean's official family broke into the open, it exuded an odor of the kind of backroom deals and "no-show" political jobs that had characterized so much of New Jersey government in the past, sullying its reputation. This time, Kean kept his silence. He neither rebuked his chief of staff nor ordered Stevens's instructions carried out. Weeks later, the reporter who broke the story observed that Stevens was still "running the show in Trenton," while Squier remained boss of her office in Essex.[33]

If it was not Snedeker's idea to drop Taggart's name from a press release or Squier's to retain a counsel for her office, it is equally inconceivable that Borden Putnam, Kean's commerce commissioner, a meticulous businessman, would on his own have exceeded limits the legislature placed on the airing of tourism commercials featuring Kean in media markets that encompassed New Jersey the year Kean sought reelection. When a legislative audit revealed that the Department of Commerce had spent twice its allotment in the Philadelphia and New York media markets, Putnam accepted the responsibility but noted that he had cleared his action with gubernatorial aides.[34]

Creative Tension within Kean's Inner Circle

Sometimes in his eagerness to advance what he perceived to be Kean's best interests, Stevens found himself at cross purposes with other Kean appointees, who believed that they too were attempting to do what was best for Kean, often with his concurrence. Stevens's deputy and successor Ed McGlynn recalled that, within Kean's office, the arts had become a running joke.[35] "I had a wonderful group of people around me," Kean said, "but they would be appalled if I told them to go to a museum with me."[36] Stevens and the team he assembled could not understand why Kean spent so much time talking with opera singers and orchestra directors and attending cultural events. Some thought Kean's association with the arts worked to his disadvantage by giving him the air of an elitist, when they were trying to present him as an "all-around guy" to "Reagan Democrats" and other constituencies they were pursuing.

After Stevens cast cold water on a proposal to organize a Roemmele-styled "Artists for Kean" committee to advocate the governor's reelection, Burgio and I arranged for opera singer Jerome Hines, actor Paul Sorvino, actress Celeste Holmes, and other celebrities to walk up to Kean, after he signed a proclamation saluting the National Endowment for the Arts on its twentieth year in operation, and endorse him for reelection. We received grudging praise from Stevens the next day after several newspapers, not all of them New Jersey–based, awarded prominence to photographs of Kean and the stars. Before long, artists and arts patrons became yet another constituency, known for its Democratic leanings, to become part of Kean's expanding base of support.

Within Kean's inner circle, the equally energetic, high-powered, and competitive Stevens and Edwards locked horns over everything from office procedures and travel allotments to legislative negotiations and strategy, once Edwards's exclusive preserve. Their vociferous disagreements, sometimes in Kean's presence, ensured that options would be weighed, alternatives considered, and decisions reached. Both Stevens and Edwards characterized the ambience of the governor's office in which they collaborated and competed as a highly charged atmosphere in which each pressed vigorously for their point of view. Having no agenda other than to reelect Kean and move on, Stevens found Edwards, known to harbor political aspirations of his own, too willing to give away too much to legislators in exchange for too little. Edwards, meanwhile, found Stevens impatient with legislative nuance and too willing to "go nuclear." While Kean rarely, if ever, intervened when the two came to verbal blows, he came away from these sessions satisfied that he was being well served. Sometimes, as Edwards recalled, Kean would "stir the pot," throwing out an argument just to provoke reaction.[37]

Stevens and Edwards, aped by their junior aides, competed for Kean's attention and approval. "Someone was always in the doghouse," McGlynn recalled. "You never knew actually why, but suddenly you found yourself let back in."[38] To relieve tensions, Kean would play the tease, often reminding them of the very things to which they had taken an aversion. Kean would delay a meeting in order to tell a grimacing Stevens about an arts event he had attended the previous evening. "Well, I spoke to that state senator friend of yours," Kean would tell an assistant, who had badgered him to return a telephone call to a particularly testy legislator Kean knew the assistant disliked. Never would Kean speak disparagingly about one adviser to another. If others did, he would instinctively jump to the defense of the absentee. Sometimes, to the frustration of those closest to him, Kean would go out of his way to say good things about people he knew that his colleagues found insufferable. Once, an exasperated Burgio came in to my office and, shaking her head, blurted out, "The people your friend Tom Kean likes!"

The Governor and the Gipper

Among the many challenges Kean faced during his first term as governor was how best to advance the interests of New Jersey while retaining the Reagan administration as an ally in his efforts. Kean struck a delicate balance between supporting an administration whose help he needed to direct federal funds and attention to New Jersey problems and opposing it when it pursued policies he believed would hurt the state. In striking a balance between the agenda he was pursuing at home, which was decidedly centrist, and, on occasion, even liberal, while retaining his bona fides with a conservative administration, Kean sometimes went through a series of strained contortions.

In his stance toward the Reagan administration, Kean reverted to the "third way" posture he had adopted in the assembly. This time, he would occupy ground, not between a rurally focused conservative Republican caucus and a liberal Democratic governor, but between a conservative national Republican administration, trying to cut back on Great Society programs, and liberal Democratic majorities in both houses of the state legislature that had come to expect a steadily increasing federal role in funding state programs. Kean's success in bridging this gap resulted in no small part from the rapport he established with the former actor-turned-politician-turned-president, whom Republicans affectionately nicknamed the "Gipper."[39]

At first glance Kean and Reagan seemed an unlikely pair. They were on opposite sides of the same political fence for most of the time Kean was in public life. They were also of different generations. In 1938, when Tom Kean was the three-year-old son of a recently elected member of the House of Representatives, Reagan was beginning to make his mark in Hollywood. Reagan played the role of George Gipp, whence his nickname the "Gipper," in *Knute Rockne—All-American*, in 1940, when Kean was five. In 1964, the year Reagan burst on the national political scene with his "Time for Choosing" speech in support of Barry Goldwater, Kean, as Bill Scranton's national youth coordinator, had worked to stop Goldwater's nomination. Four years later, when Reagan made a last-minute try for the Republican presidential nomination, Kean backed Clifford P. Case's favorite-son candidacy as a means of enhancing Nelson Rockefeller's chances. Eight years later, Kean, as Gerald R. Ford's New Jersey campaign manager, worked feverishly to fend off Reagan's attempts to capture some of New Jersey's "uncommitted" delegates. Although Kean professed neutrality during the 1980 primary season, his neutrality bespoke a decided tilt toward Reagan's principal opponent and eventual running mate, George H. W. Bush.

Although he had opposed Reagan in Republican Party contests, Kean, who closely observed the political styles of other politicians, carefully studied Reagan's. He admired the former California governor's respect for ideas and his strengths as a communicator. He also admired Reagan's capacity to instill intense loyalty among his supporters. As he geared up for the 1981 gubernatorial primary, Kean incorporated elements of Reagan's style into his own. On the stump, Kean all but proved Reagan's equal in his demonstrations of buoyant optimism. At a time when conservatives exerted a strong influence in primaries, even in New Jersey, where they had ended the careers of liberal Republicans William T. Cahill and Clifford P. Case, Kean's positions on crime, taxes, and regulation, all similar to Reagan's, put him in good standing with them.

While Kean would never become New Jersey's equivalent to Reagan—as conservatives in New Jersey or elsewhere might have hoped—he came closer to filling that role than any other viable public figure of his era, given where the political center of gravity was in New Jersey at the time he was elected. By those lights, Kean was the most conservative governor the state had seen since the 1950s. As the state's first governor to link increased spending on education to improved student performance, to regard parents as "consumers" of education, and to advocate state takeovers of failing school districts,

Kean was clearly in the camp of accountability advocates, most of whom were conservatives. It was for these stands and actions that Reagan most praised Kean.

While Kean opposed school prayer (which Reagan favored), came down on the pro-choice side of the abortion debate (Reagan was pro-life), and was prone to favor more environmental regulation and gun-control legislation than the president—Kean managed to keep most New Jersey conservatives at his side. His pro-business, low-tax, and regulatory policies, together with his advocacy of the death penalty, appealed to them. So did his willingness to appoint conservatives to policy positions, his readiness to listen to their ideas, and his willingness to adopt some of their ideas. Plaudits not only Reagan but also Kemp, Bill Bennett, and Newt Gingrich threw his way bolstered his credentials with them.

As governor, Kean continued to incorporate Reagan's techniques into his own style. Reagan cadences found their way into Kean's speeches. Kean followed Reagan's practice of inviting to his annual State of the State speech individuals who performed extraordinary deeds and, as he spoke, asking them to stand to receive the thanks of their elected representatives. Like Reagan, Kean seemed at his best when he voiced the collective sentiments of those on whose behalf he governed. In the public mind, Reagan did that best during the observation of the fortieth anniversary of the D-Day invasion, the opening of the Olympics in Los Angeles, in the aftermath of the *Challenger* tragedy, and at the Brandenburg Gate. Kean struck an indelible image of the governor as the state's leading cheerleader and defender, walking its beaches to entice tourists or warn would-be polluters, tirelessly reciting the state's assets, and enthusiastically hailing achievements of residents who distinguished themselves. Whereas some within Reagan's camp voiced displeasure when he opted to run his Morning in America–style re-election campaign devoid of ideology, Kean looked to it as a template upon which to model his own reelection effort in which he would attract support from voters who identified with the opposition party.

On foreign and defense policies, Kean usually, but not always, sided with the president. When the National Governors Association attempted to pass a resolution critical of Reagan's defense buildup, Kean said that he found it very strange to see governors "standing around the halls debating defense expenditures."[40] He maintained that when they ventured beyond their respective competencies, governors weakened their credibility. Yet he never attempted to reconcile that stand with his own advocacy of a nuclear freeze. Years later, Kean cited his support for the freeze as one of his major regrets. Reagan, he said, "understood better than I that the chances for peace were greater when we projected strength."[41]

When the Soviet Union shot down Korean Airlines Flight 007 in September 1983, Kean cancelled a trade mission to the Soviet Union. Together with New York governor Mario Cuomo, he ordered the Port Authority of New York and New Jersey to deny permission to a plane carrying Soviet foreign minister Andre Gromyko and other Soviet diplomats to land at airports in the New York City region. "The Soviet Union acted in an uncivilized manner," Kean declared. "We said '*nyet.*'"[42] Gromyko canceled the speech he was to deliver before the United Nations. If he were paying attention, Reagan might well have wondered whether a younger version of himself had taken hold of the reins of New Jersey state government. Kean proved a staunch defender of Reagan's tough negotiating stance toward the Soviet Union, of his efforts to eliminate nuclear weapons, and of his support for the contras in Central America.

If Kean occasionally tempered his support for the national administration, especially on domestic policy, Reagan consistently supported his junior partner in Trenton. His administration allowed the state to erect prefabricated housing units at Fort Dix to relieve prison overcrowding. It responded speedily to Kean's efforts to place New Jersey's toxic sites among the first to receive federal funds from the Superfund for cleanups. Reagan incorporated Kean's concerns about acid rain in his 1984 State of the Union address and endorsed the Kean-Cuomo proposals to ban ocean dumping. On three different occasions Reagan singled out Kean for praise for his record in education reform. Reagan's administration granted Kean's administration waivers allowing it to depart from federal procedures to facilitate welfare reform.

While much of the cooperation between the state and national administrations resulted from negotiations conducted at the staff level, Kean proved especially persuasive in personal meetings with Reagan. His conversations with the president undoubtedly sped up Soviet refusenik Boris Klotz's departure from the Soviet Union and helped shape Reagan's position on redress for Japanese Americans. The two found that although they did not agree on every subject, the chemistry between them was good. "Ronald Reagan genuinely liked Tom Kean," Reagan's last chief of staff, Ken Duberstein, remembered. "He would love going to New Jersey just so he could discuss policy with Tom Kean, just like he liked going to Wisconsin so he could discuss policy with Tommy Thompson."[43]

The ultimate test of how durable the Reagan-Kean partnership would remain came in 1985 as Kean prepared to seek reelection. Kean began the year by denouncing Reagan's budgetary recommendations for fiscal year 1986 as "unacceptable, harsh, not fair, and not right." Reagan's requests, he said, would deny the state $800 million in aid to education, mass transit, revenue sharing, housing, and student loans. Departing from his past position that governors lacked the necessary expert knowledge with which to comment on defense policy, Kean suggested that cuts could be made in the defense budget without undermining Reagan's strong defense posture, which Kean said he continued to favor.[44] By attacking the federal budget before his would-be Democratic opponent had a chance to do so, Kean strengthened his position within the state. Again, he had demonstrated independence from his national party when it came to advancing New Jersey's interests.

Reagan played along. He uttered not a word of criticism about Kean. Nor did the money stop flowing. As a former governor himself, Reagan understood Kean's predicament. Like Kean, Reagan had to face hostile Democratic majorities in both houses of his state legislature during most of his two terms. He, like Kean, learned how to bargain with legislators and their leaders and when to maneuver around them. Had the two compared notes, they might have found the difficulties Kean encountered working with Alan Karcher to be mere inconveniences in comparison to those Reagan endured squaring off against Jesse Unruh, Speaker of the California assembly, and "Tip" O'Neill, Speaker of the U.S. House of Representatives.

While in Sacramento, Reagan compiled an environmental record that paralleled Kean's as a legislator and governor. Governor Reagan declared the Minareto—the crest of the Sierra Nevada, south of Yosemite National Park—off limits to highway builders. Together with Nevada governor Paul Laxalt, Reagan prevailed upon Congress to create a bi-state agency to oversee preservation and development in the Lake Tahoe basin. Around the same time Kean was attempting to prevent the construction of the Tocks Island Dam, Reagan blocked a federal dam on the Eel River, preventing the flooding of a valley of Indian ranches and burial grounds. Although as president, Reagan took a less interventionist approach to the environment, as governor, he, like Kean, argued the case for an activist state government, as he urged the federal government to play less of an intrusive role in state affairs.[45]

As Kean geared up for his reelection, he looked to Ronald Reagan's 1984 landslide, particularly in New Jersey, as a foundation upon which to build. Reagan had carried the state over former vice president Walter Mondale by 658,000 votes, double the size of his victory over Jimmy Carter in the state four years earlier. Reagan's enormous popularity made Democrats less eager to turn the 1985 gubernatorial election into a referendum on the national administration, as Florio had done in 1981.

As Reagan's New Jersey campaign chairman, as he had with Ford eight years earlier, Kean traveled with the president whenever he visited the state, staffed Reagan's New Jersey campaign operation, and suggested places for the president to speak. On each of his stops, Reagan found something in Kean's record to praise before their mutual constituents.

In a June 1984 "nonpolitical" appearance at River Dell High School in Oradell, Reagan threw his weight behind state efforts to reduce teen driving fatalities by raising the drinking age to twenty-one. Reagan noted that New Jersey, with the support of his "good friend" Tom Kean, had reduced nighttime, single-vehicle fatalities among nineteen- and twenty-year-olds in one year. To his youthful audience, the oldest man ever to serve as president made a heartfelt appeal to stay off alcohol and drugs.[46] A month later, at a White House ceremony at which he signed a bill that set a national minimum drinking age, Reagan twice recognized Kean.[47]

As in 1980, Reagan kicked off his campaign in New Jersey. In 1981, his managers chose Liberty State Park in Jersey City as the venue. At a rally at Elizabeth's city hall in 1984, after repeating the city's motto, "Elizabeth Is a Proud Lady," Reagan defined what it meant to be a "Reagan Democrat" in the Northeast: "You know, so often when people talk of America's heartland, they speak of the Middle West or the Great Plains. . . . But there's another heartland in America—a heartland of the streets; a kind of place that welcomes tremendous numbers of people—Italians, Cubans, Puerto Ricans, Portuguese, Blacks, Irish, Polish-Americans."[48] Reagan's next stop was the St. Ann's Festival in Hoboken. Flanked by both Kean and Hoboken's native son Frank Sinatra (making a rare visit to New Jersey), Reagan worked his way through the crowd gathered on the church grounds, stopping to play games of chance on his way to having a meatball-and-spaghetti dinner in the gymnasium in Sinatra's former church. Parishioners paid fifteen dollars a head for the privilege of dining with the president. To the assemblage of more than four hundred of the kind of people Kean and Stevens hoped to bring to Kean's side the following year, Reagan turned on his celebrated charm. He began by reciting the two reasons he had wanted visit Hoboken: the colorful, handmade invitation that local resident Santo A. Milici had sent him and the reputation of the area's *zeppoles*.[49]

After paying tribute to the importance of neighborhood, tradition, faith, and family, Reagan challenged the Democratic Party's claim to be the party of compassion. He then asked his listeners why the national Democrats showed no compassion for the unborn, for middle-class parents seeking tuition tax credits to ease the burden of sending children to parochial or independent schools, for children desiring to pray in public schools, and for all who suffered under the repressive Sandinista regime in Nicaragua.[50] Intended for a national audience, this was not the kind of speech Tom Kean, who agreed with the president only on the last point, would have delivered to the same audience. Reagan's talk had been intended as a rebuttal to the Democratic vice presidential nominee, Congresswoman Geraldine Ferraro, who days earlier at the Democratic National convention had declared that Reagan was not a good Christian because his budget-cutting policies were so "terribly unfair."[51]

More important to Kean's 1985 reelection strategy than the specifics of what Reagan had said was how the crowd reacted to the president. Asked what he thought of the president, an electrician declared that he supported Reagan because he had pledged to create more jobs and had delivered on his promise.[52] Kean, who compiled a similar record, hoped to appeal to precisely such voters. He and Stevens made certain that people knew what Kean had achieved in infrastructure repairs, prison construction, laboratory upgrades, recruitment of businesses, and waterfront redevelopment.

The St. Ann's spaghetti dinner for the president was so successful that New Jersey Republicans decided to repeat the event five years later in West Orange, where 1,400 diners, each paying twenty dollars, heard Reagan boost the campaigns of George H. W. Bush for president and General Pete Dawkins for U.S. senator. In introducing his celebrated guest, Kean said that Reagan had made it respectable again to say three simple words: "God Bless America." He then quoted John Adams's tribute to George Washington, noting that it applied to the fortieth president as much as to the first: "I glory in that man's character because I know him to be only an exemplification of the American character."[53]

Eight weeks after sampling the food at St. Ann's, Reagan was back in New Jersey. Before a rally in Hammonton (the "Blueberry capital of the world"), standing on a green at which John F. Kennedy had spoken in 1960, Reagan recited what would become the theme of Kean's own reelection campaign: "And I'm glad to be back with a leader that I know you respect as much as I do, your fine governor, Tom Kean. Tom understands that we build a better future with economic growth and that we build economic growth from opportunity and that we create opportunities by ensuring excellence in education. Well. Your governor has helped you create economic growth. He's helped you bring unemployment down and is helping you create one of the best educational systems in the country. And in my book, that makes Tom Kean one of America's best."[54]

None of Kean's staff would be able to improve on that passage a year later. On October 26, Reagan made his final foray into the state as part of his reelection effort. He used his stop in Hackensack to reiterate his reasons for his prior visit to Hoboken to laud the economic growth of Bergen and Hudson counties: "And now, my friend and your great governor, Tom Kean, has told us about the good news about Hackensack—that you're not only growing up, you're growing out. You're rebuilding the inner city. You're attracting new businesses and new homeowners. So, you're very much a part of the great renewal that we've been trying to lead in Washington, but which has really been made possible by you, the people of this community, and you the people of this state and this country."[55]

Tom Kean had not lost his knack for briefing presidents.

chapter 17

The Reelection
of the Governor, 1985

From Deficits to Surpluses

Planning for what became Kean's record landslide reelection in 1985 began the instant that Greg Stevens replaced Lew Thurston as Kean's chief of staff. Early in Stevens's tenure, he put in place a strategy through which Kean's genial personality and "third way" approach to issues would appeal to voters across all segments of the population and in both political parties. By the time the 1985 political season was upon them, Kean and Stevens had established in the public mind a bond between Kean and New Jersey state residents. This image they had of him was based on reality. A newspaper not known for its support of Kean or his policies recognized the political appeal of Kean's personality at the time he sought reelection: "There is no question that Mr. Kean is an engaging and extremely likable individual. Even his political detractors will admit that is he a very charming fellow, possessed of a good nature and almost impossible to dislike. Though he comes from an elitist heritage, and has a 'Hahvad' accent that separates him somewhat from other New Jerseyans, he fits in well with people of all classes and backgrounds."[1]

After Stevens had come on board, Kean's team recognized the value of using the governor's popularity as leverage to prod the Democratic legislature to do his bidding. When this proved insufficient by itself to pass legislation, they enlisted help from outside interest groups that his adversaries dared antagonize only at their peril. Kean brought in labor leaders to press for his transportation trust fund, employers to campaign for his high-technology proposals, a popular

former governor to assist with the prison bond issue, parents on behalf of school reform, and big-city mayors in support of his budget and
bonding requests. On other occasions, Kean took his case directly to
the public through the media and waited for public opinion to turn
legislative opposition around. Sometimes, he was able to maneuver
his way around the legislature entirely, enlisting private-sector support in the case of the Governor's Schools, or federal assistance with
prison overcrowding and the Superfund program, to achieve his goals.

Signs of a turnaround both for the state's economic well-being
and Kean's political fortunes were much in evidence by early 1984. In
his first State of the State message, Kean spoke of the worst economic
downturn since the Great Depression; in his second, he detected a
"fresh new breeze in the state's sails"; by his third, he sounded confident enough to advocate major financial investments in the state's
future, with the transportation trust fund, high technology, higher education, and the arts as the perfect vehicles. In his budget proposals
for fiscal year 1986, Kean proposed increasing state spending to $7.6
billion without raising taxes. He would be the first New Jersey governor in a decade to announce a budget in surplus rather than in deficit.
He proposed spending additional funds on education, senior citizens,
welfare, and computer literacy, prompting Assemblywoman Mildred
Barry Garven (D-Essex) to say that Kean sounded "like a Democrat."[2]

Months later, as Democrats and Republicans debated how large
they believed the surplus would be, Kean donned the clothing of the
tax cutter he had campaigned as in 1981. He called for a one-shot tax
rebate to low- and middle-income homeowners and credits to tenants.
"I strongly believe that the legislature and I, as governor, have a
tremendous obligation to return a major portion of this surplus to the
taxpayers, from whence it came," he announced.[3] Refunds would be
added on to the rebate checks residents were already receiving to offset some of their property taxes. (Taxpayers began receiving rebates
in 1976 with the passage of the state income tax.) Recipients would
receive, on average, an additional fifty-four dollars. Senior citizens,
the disabled, and renters would receive higher amounts.

Kean said that he preferred the onetime tax reduction to a permanent cut in the broad-based taxes because he was not convinced
the surplus would be permanent. In addition to $90 million in rebates,
he proposed using the balance of the projected $200- to $400-million
surplus for flood relief, road repairs, toxic cleanups, and other immediate needs. His caution about the likelihood of future surpluses and
his short-term proposals to return part of the current surplus, while
spending the rest on immediate needs, partially met conservative demands that he work to rescind the tax increases he had signed into
law the previous year. Given that Kean had singled out the sales tax as

the revenue source that had contributed the most heavily to the surplus, demands that it be lowered were hardly unreasonable. Whatever the merits of Kean's cautious approach to cuts in broad-based taxes in 1985, Karcher's refusal to allow even Kean's modest measure to advance in the assembly, where all money bills originate, helped keep conservatives of all stripes and many moderates in Kean's corner.

Karcher said that he agreed with Kean that property taxes were too high. He proposed reforming the state's tax structure by making the income tax more progressive. His efforts to impose on Kean the same steeply graduated income tax rates the governor had previously vetoed left the Democrat open to charges that, whether budgets were in the red or in the black, the Speaker's position remained the same: raise the income tax on some citizens. Just as they had resisted Kean's effort to pass a gas tax in 1982, Democrats now opposed Kean's every attempt to return part of the surplus.

Whatever its limitations, Kean's tax proposal remained the only tax reduction either party had put on the table in 1984, a fact Stevens made certain the Republican State Committee conveyed to voters in paid media advertisements. Once again Kean found a "third way" position between Republicans and Democrats, this time with all but the most left-leaning Democrats behind him. Kean's decision to steer the majority of the rebates to households with annual incomes of less than sixty thousand dollars shielded him from charges that the Republican plan "favored the rich," arguments Democrats had used against Ronald Reagan and would again against George W. Bush. Stevens had intended the radio ads to be aired in support of Kean's plan to entice middle-income voters to question why the Democrats opposed cutting their taxes. In the end, both the executive and legislative branches found ways to spend the entire surplus on matters other than tax rebates.

Having broached the subject, Kean was only too happy to return to it the following year, when he sought reelection and when the surplus would be even higher, in the range of $800 million. In his budget for fiscal year 1986, he proposed increasing the homestead rebates for residents earning less than sixty thousand dollars per year. Karcher blocked it a second time. Now Karcher and several Democratic contenders for governor argued that Kean's proposed refunds were "too low." They did not repeat their demands that the income tax be raised.

Stymied again, Kean proposed a onetime 10 percent reduction in the income tax. He also recommended capping the amount at seventy-five dollars, so that high wage earners not receive a disproportional amount of the benefit. The assembly instead passed a measure freshman Marlene Lynch Ford (D-Ocean) introduced (at the initiative of assembly leader John Paul Doyle), allowing homeowners to deduct their property tax payments from their state income taxes.[4] Kean objected to it, citing its regressive nature—inflation in the past decade had bumped up the value of property assessments upon which property tax rates were based. In allowing the bill to pass, Karcher had clearly positioned himself to Kean's right. Given his previous advocacy of raising the income tax, his shift in position further fueled speculation that the Speaker would oppose almost anything Kean advocated and advocate almost anything Kean opposed.

If Karcher intended to bait a trap for Kean, it was one the governor was only too happy to fall into. While opposed to the Ford bill in principle but convinced that the measure would be the only direct tax cut to pass the legislature that year, Kean signed it. Thus his approach to tax cuts in his fourth year in office resembled that which he had taken toward tax increases in his first. Both times, he accepted certain provisions that had not been to his liking after his recommended alternatives had been rejected. He reaped considerable benefits through both actions. The election-year tax cut came on the heels of passage of proposals in Kean's budget to stimulate the state economy and improve its business climate. Those included phasing out the corporate net-worth tax over four years and the inheritance-transfer tax over ten. In addition, labor secretary Roger Bodman conducted negotiations with the federal government and state labor unions that produced an agreement through which the state was able to pay down its debt to the federal unemployment compensation fund. The immediate result was a reduction in payroll taxes.

On the spending side, Kean, in his $8.8-billion budget, included several popular provisions, such as full funding of the school-aid formula, additional money for transportation projects, infrastructure repairs, municipal aid, and the arts. Foreshadowing Bill Clinton's future anticrime package (which included funding for one hundred thousand police personnel), Kean called for placing an additional one thousand police officers on New Jersey streets. "If you didn't know the internal politics of the state, you would swear that Tom Kean is a liberal Democrat," Karcher said of Kean's budget.[5] Kean, thanks in part to the national recovery and the tax increases Karcher had forced on him, was now in a position to cut enough taxes and enact enough measures favorable to business to be able to present himself at the same time as a conservative in the Reagan mold.

Opening Moves in the Governor's Race

As the 1985 political season was about to begin, Stevens hinted that Kean might forgo state matching funds. He suggested that Kean might spend $5 to $7 million on his campaign. Pundits saw in Stevens's remarks an attempt to dissuade Florio, still believed to be Kean's strongest possible challenger, from entering the race.[6] Though he had deftly managed to keep himself in the news throughout Kean's term, the Democrat had not yet said whether he would seek a rematch with Kean. A loss to the increasingly popular incumbent would be his third failed attempt to become governor. Stevens saw little harm in forcing the Democrat to show his hand early. Running against such a well-known Democrat in a Democratic-leaning state, Kean's chief of staff pointed out, would require Kean to spend more money than he intended in order to remain competitive. Ultimately, Florio opted to delay another statewide run until such time when Kean would not be on the ballot.

Toward the end of 1984, Kean conditionally vetoed a bill revising the state's campaign finance law, claiming that it did not go as far as he wanted. He called for an increase in the amount of funds candidates needed to raise in order to receive state matching funds from $50,000 to $200,000, a state match on a dollar-for-dollar basis rather than two dollars for every dollar raised, a maximum contribution of $1,000, and an overall spending limit of $2 million per candidate in the primary and $4 million in the general election. By acting as he did, Kean had once again found a way to play the reformer and the partisan at the same time. The changes he wanted to see in the rules that governed the 1985 general election were identical to those that reformers had been pressing for years. But by making his feelings known at the last possible minute, when the legislature was not in session, and six days beyond the forty-five days in which he had to offer his conditional veto, he had ensured that the old rule stayed in effect, at least through the primary. Together, the low threshold and the two-to-one match would, as they had in 1981, encourage a proliferation of candidates, at least on the Democratic side. Unopposed in the Republican primary, Kean nevertheless was able to accept matching funds under the law. Like incumbents Ronald Reagan before him and Bill Clinton and George W. Bush after him, Kean accepted the funds, arguing that he had little choice but to get his message out at a time when several gubernatorial hopefuls were attacking him.[7] "It's always amusing to hear a group of politicians denounce another politician for 'playing politics,'" one wag observed.[8]

Kean announced for reelection on April 2, 1985, ten days before the deadline for filing petitions. He later said he delayed his declaration because his ten-year-old daughter, Alexandra, had misgivings about his seeking a second term. Weeks earlier, Kean convened a family summit at which he announced that any decision he made about running again would have to be unanimous. According to Debby

Kean, their two sons kept quiet at first but eventually said they wanted their father to run, while their daughter asked him not to.[9] Alexandra disliked the amount of time her father's job required him to spend out of the house. She relented, Kean said, when she realized that he would be "unhappy most of the time" if he followed her wishes.[10]

In 1981, Kean had made three stops to announce his candidacy; this time, he did it in twelve. Said one observer who found his action totally consistent with Kean's nature: "Kean took two days to make his announcement, building enough time into his schedule for him to loiter and talk to people, rather than at his audiences—the hallmark of his successful 1981 campaign, and the way he has spent a good part of his first term in office."[11]

Kean put forth two themes for his campaign. One, reminiscent of Ronald Reagan's 1984 campaign, was based on a combination of renewed state pride and the sense that the state under Kean was indeed better off than it had been four years earlier. "We must never turn back the clock," Kean said. "We must never return to the old days of more government, of tired schools, of missed opportunities, of failed promises and of self-doubt."[12] His second message was slightly different from what other Republicans were saying outside New Jersey's borders: "Our Republican Party must be inclusive, not exclusive, the party of the worker in the factory, of the student starting college, of the small businessman seeking to expand, of black as well as white."[13]

The "Phenomenon"

As the June primary approached, the fate of the Ford "tax cut" bill attracted more attention than any of the six Democratic gubernatorial candidates competing for the right to oppose Kean in the general election. When the ballots were counted, Essex County executive Peter Shapiro, age thirty-three, won the Democratic nomination with 31 percent of the vote in a primary that had attracted a 12.8 percent turnout, the lowest in sixty years. He received 100,798 votes. Senate majority leader John Russo finished second with 86,086, Newark mayor Kenneth Gibson third with 85,237, Morris County state senator Stephen Wiley fourth with 27,913, former U.S. attorney Robert Del Tufo fifth with 19,982, and a minor candidate, Elliott Greenspan, further back. Running unopposed, Kean received 148,750 votes in the Republican primary. He joked that he wanted to say yes when asked if his high popularity kept Democrats who intended to vote for him in the fall away from the polls in the spring.[14]

In spite of his narrow win, pundits and professionals considered

Shapiro's victory an upset. Running as a maverick, he had twice before in primaries defeated party regulars, years his senior in both age and experience. In placing ahead of both the senate majority leader and the mayor of the state's largest city, he appeared to have bested the party establishment once again and across a wider terrain. With Florio absent from the field, Russo, because of his following in normally Republican Ocean County and much of southern New Jersey, his Italian American ancestry, and strong backing in Hudson County, had entered the race the presumed favorite. His fortunes changed after Jersey City mayor Gerald McCann lost a runoff election for mayor to Anthony Cucci, an ally of Shapiro, a month before the primary.[15] One bit of foreboding for the Essex County executive was that, although he had carried ten of the state's twenty-one counties, he had lost his own to Gibson. In the fall election, many of the mayor's African American supporters would flock to Kean.

When Shapiro declared his intention to run for governor, conventional wisdom held that he neither intended nor expected to be his party's nominee in 1985. Both Kean and Florio had run and lost a statewide primary before capturing their party's gubernatorial nomination, increasing their name recognition and base of support in the process. Many believed Shapiro was running in order to enhance his chances of becoming governor in 1989. Though this scenario was plausible, Shapiro had hardly comported himself as a conventional politician before. By his account, he had decided to run during Kean's first year in office with the expectation that he could win.[16]

Once in the race, Shapiro placed a premium on younger and reform-oriented voters. Though he had supported Walter Mondale in the 1984 Democratic presidential primaries, Shapiro borrowed heavily from the former vice president's rival Gary Hart's "new ideas" rhetoric. Whether by intention or by accident, his slogan, "There Is a Way," bore a striking similarity to that used by a character Robert Redford had played in the movie *The Candidate.* Uncertain as to whether this resemblance was an asset or a liability, Shapiro's manager, Paul Bograd, reminded skeptics that in the film the Redford character won.[17] Tailoring his message to younger voters, Shapiro cut a video featuring images and sounds of President John F. Kennedy and Bruce Springsteen. It was aired on cable television stations and copies were mailed to a select number of households. The technique, considered a novelty at the time, given the newness of both VCRs and cable television, brought Shapiro's campaign ample media attention. Reporters joked after the primary that more voters read or heard about Shapiro's video than had actually seen it. The night Shapiro won the nomination, Alan Karcher, during an interview on television, proclaimed the Democrats' new standard-bearer a "phenomenon."

The son of an ear, nose, and throat specialist, Shapiro grew up in South Orange, where his mother managed a bookstore. He maintained that he acquired his liberal Democratic politics from his parents. "They always said, 'vote for the man,'" he said, "but the man was always a Democrat, except for Clifford Case." In 1969, when Kean was completing his first term in the assembly, the precocious Shapiro was suspended from Columbia High School for two days after he distributed leaflets inviting students to an antiwar rally in Manhattan. The American Civil Liberties Union took his case, and Education Commissioner Carl T. Marburger ordered the school to reinstate the teenager.

Shapiro initially intended to make journalism his career. After serving as managing editor of the *Harvard Crimson,* he began a brief internship with the *Wall Street Journal* covering Congress. The very month Kean lost his congressional primary (June 1974) to Millicent Fenwick, Shapiro graduated from Harvard and began a one-year stint in the merchant marine. A year later, he took a job as assistant to Brendan Byrne's transportation commissioner, Alan Sagner, a family friend. While in Trenton, Shapiro had ample occasion to observe the workings of the legislature. When his eyes focused on one of the two Democrats who represented his home area, the twenty-three-year-old Shapiro thought to himself that he could "take" the regular Democrat in a primary.[18]

The district in which Shapiro competed included, in addition to South Orange, Newark's West Ward and Irvington. Through a well-financed media campaign, Shapiro won one of the two assembly nominations, finishing second in a field of three. He took out billboards proclaiming, "The Bosses Picked Their Candidate. Now, Pick Yours." The day before the primary, the New Jersey edition of the *New York Daily News* ran on its cover a picture of the tousled-haired Shapiro walking the streets of the district accompanied by Robert F. Kennedy Jr., whose acquaintance he had made at Harvard. His nomination in the heavily Democratic district ensured his election. In the interval between his nomination and election, Shapiro encountered Kean for the first time. Then assembly minority leader, Kean was on his way into a movie theater in Maplewood when Shapiro walked up to him and introduced himself. They developed a cordial but cautious relationship.

Once elected, Shapiro did little to endear himself to the Democratic organization he had taken on. He began his legislative career by informing Essex County Democratic chairman Harry Lerner that he would, contrary to party custom, select his own legislative aides. At the time, such "employees" were considered patronage appointments to be disbursed at the pleasure of the county chairman. He also balked at allocating two-thirds of his legislative budget to the Essex party organization, another long-standing practice. When Lerner tried to retaliate by denying the young upstart a seat he coveted on the Joint Appropriations Committee, Shapiro maneuvered around him. While Lerner was pressing a case on his fellow county chairman, Richard Coffee of Mercer, then executive secretary to the assembly majority, Shapiro appealed directly to the Speaker, Joe LeFante. A fellow reformer, who had helped Jersey City mayor Dr. Paul Jordan wrest the last vestiges of control away from John V. Kenny's dying organization in Hudson County, LeFante regarded Shapiro as a kindred spirit and appointed him to the committee. Always one to pick up on divisions within Democratic ranks, Kean could not have helped but notice.

In the time they spent together in the legislature, Kean and Shapiro found themselves on the same side of several "good government" issues. One on which they worked together was legislation enabling counties to reorganize their systems of government. In their home county of Essex, Republicans endorsed electing freeholders (county legislators) along district lines, rather than countywide, in order to improve their chances of representation on the nine-member body. They, along with Reform Democrats and "Good Government" groups, favored an elected county executive as a means of improving the way in which the county was managed. This coalition proved strong enough to make "charter change" a reality in Essex.

In 1978, the year after Kean left the assembly, Shapiro declared for county executive. Profiting from a split in the Democratic organization between rival candidates Newark councilman and future congressman Donald Payne and Sheriff John Cryan, Shapiro won the nomination by a mere 2,100 votes.[19] He received a subtle assist from Governor Brendan Byrne, a Princeton resident and West Orange native, who had said that if he could still vote in Essex County he would vote for Shapiro. Kean, out of office but still the most respected Essex Republican, cast aside suggestions that he seek the county executive post. As the honorary chair of Shapiro's opponent's campaign, Kean found himself having to explain why his candidate, Robert Notte, had not registered to vote until he decided to run for office.

Shapiro defeated Notte by over 20,000 votes. In 1982, having survived attempts to recall him, Shapiro won reelection on a slate that included Democrats from each of several warring factions. So that he would not have to ask the Essex County clerk, Nicholas Caputo, a Lerner partisan, to swear him in when he first became county executive, Shapiro asked Governor Brendan Byrne to officiate. Four years later, he extended the same request to Kean. Before performing this ceremonial function, Kean paid a tribute to his former assembly colleague that caused Republicans in the audience to cringe. Praising

Shapiro's successful reorganization of the county, Kean turned to the county executive and said, "Peter, what you did for Essex County is precisely what I am attempting at the state level."[20] In his term, Shapiro had cut the county's payroll by 20 percent and replaced political operatives holding county posts with professionals. In a county known for widespread corruption, such a record, as Kean suggested, was indeed impressive.[21]

Local Republicans, aware of Shapiro's ambitions, worried whether Kean set a tough challenge for himself, given that much of what he intended to achieve, Karcher was still holding hostage in Trenton. They feared that the day might come when Shapiro would use Kean's words against him. Whether delivered as a slip of the tongue, as a burst of unguarded exuberance, or as a sincere appraisal of a colleague's performance, at the time Kean uttered those remarks, Peter Shapiro was not the Democrat giving him cause for concern. In 1982, the shadows of both Karcher and Florio loomed larger.

The Candidates Square Off

Once the Democrats designated their candidate for governor, Kean immediately went on the offensive. He aggressively defended his record and, wherever he could, took the battle to his opponent. Days after the primary, Kean, lifting a page from the book of Harry Truman, tried drawing his opponent into disputes he was having with the Democratic legislature. He publicly invited Shapiro's assistance in persuading Karcher to release legislation both gubernatorial candidates favored: an environmental trust fund, reform of the state's civil service system, a monetary threshold for lawsuits resulting from automobile accidents, and autonomy for state colleges.

Through his challenge, Kean presented Shapiro with a dilemma. If Shapiro intervened and the stalemate continued, Kean could rightly claim that his rival would fare no better with a Democratic legislature than had the Republican governor. If Shapiro jumped into the fray and the legislature passed these initiatives, Kean would receive much of the credit and would be certain to stage an elaborate bill signing. With Shapiro dodging his challenge, Kean continued pressing the legislature for results. When it eventually passed Kean's environmental trust fund, a program allowing municipalities to borrow from a revolving fund to build sewage treatment plants and upgrade recycling systems, many of Shapiro's fellow Essex County officials showered Kean with accolades.

When not daring his opponent to participate in the legislative jostling, Kean did his best to ignore Shapiro. Often, he tried to create the impression in voters' minds that he was actually running against someone else. "Alan Karcher blocks everything we try to do," Kean told the Monmouth County Federation of Republican Women. "If you elect a Republican Assembly with me, we will be able to throw him out of office," he continued.[22] Kean made this argument several times throughout the rest of the campaign, even asking national Republicans who came into the state on his behalf, including President Reagan and Vice President Bush, to concentrate their attacks not on the Democratic nominee but on assembly Democrats. He reminded party workers and supporters that if he was to be even more successful in a second term than he had been in his first, he needed help in Trenton.

A week after the primary, Kean took time away from both his governmental and campaign obligations to hear an admiring visitor praise his achievements. On an ostensibly "nonpolitical" visit designed to stir up support for proposed changes in the tax code, President Ronald Reagan journeyed to Bloomfield. Proclaiming the state lucky to have Kean as its governor, the Gipper called Kean "one of the ablest state executives in the country" and one of his favorites: "He [Kean] calls me now and then, and I'll ask him, 'Well, Tom, what should I do about the budget?' And he says, 'Come to New Jersey.' And then I say, 'Tom, what should I do about taxes?' And he says, 'Come to New Jersey.' He's a great booster of your state, and I've been here four times in the past year alone, so you can see I take his advice seriously."[23]

For weeks, Shapiro struggled to develop an argument to give voters a reason for turning out an incumbent governor the president had described in such glowing terms. He tried peddling the argument that Kean's administration had been "soft on corruption," citing the motor vehicle photo-licensing comedy of errors and a $7-million noncompetitive contract the Department of Motor Vehicles awarded Price Waterhouse days after the company had contributed to the state Republican Party. When he found few takers, Shapiro fell back on an even less glamorous issue, but one on which Kean had already been working, reorganization of state government. Two "new ideas" Shapiro said he would implement were using sales tax revenues to decrease property taxes by 15 percent and lowering automobile insurance premiums. As the campaign advanced, Shapiro directed most of his fire on one issue where polls suggested that Kean might be vulnerable: the slowness with which the state had cleaned up toxic waste sites.

By summer's end, the *Star-Ledger*–Eagleton Poll reported that Kean was leading Shapiro by forty-nine points (68 percent to 19 percent, with 13 percent undecided).[24] It showed Kean running equally well across occupational groups, ethnic and racial groups, and equally well among men and women. It also showed him pulling 41 percent of self-identified Democrats. While 40 percent of responders cited pollution and toxic cleanups as the major issues, 57 percent thought Kean would do a better job of addressing them than his opponent. Kean set out to deny Shapiro the slightest opening by reciting his own environmental record before his opponent had the chance. Wherever he went he spouted statistics: sites identified as toxic, 200; sites placed on Superfund priority list, 98; sites undergoing Superfund feasibility studies, 54; sites undergoing engineering studies, 12; number of projects under way, 14.

On this issue, Kean spoke with such authority that few wondered whether Shapiro's proposal to finance a $2-billion cleanup over ten years would get the job done any faster than what Kean was already doing. For those who did, Kean's surrogates, all with credible credentials within the environmental movement, pointed out that Shapiro's plan to clean up toxic sites would take even longer than Kean's because it relied more heavily on funds from penalties established after prolonged litigation. Given Kean's success in handling other issues such as crime, prisons, education, and transportation, pundits and voters seemed prepared to give the incumbent the edge on what increasingly appeared to be an argument between two "policy wonks."

In mid-September, the AFL-CIO officially made Kean the first Republican candidate for governor to receive its endorsement. Lest

Fig 17.1. The *Newark Star-Ledger* ran this cartoon alongside its endorsement of Kean for reelection in 1985. Depicted beside him is the logo of the campaign Kean initiated to promote the state. (© 1985 *The Star-Ledger*. All rights reserved. Reprinted with permission.)

any of its members fail to recall the reasons, Kean was only too happy to remind them, pointing out the number of construction projects his transportation and environmental trust funds had rendered possible.[25] Unable either to derail Kean's education reforms or to defeat him politically, the New Jersey Education Association followed suit. Shapiro attributed these union defections as much to anti-Shapiro sentiments as to pro-Kean ones. As Essex County's county executive, he had tried to strip government workers of some of their union protections and attempted to make wage increases contingent on merit rather than time served. He angered unions further when he contracted out services in county parks and recreational facilities to community-based organizations. Nor did he endear himself to the NJEA when he came out against granting tenure to school principals. Shapiro predicted that voters would see a secret deal behind the "power brokers'" endorsement of Kean.[26]

Guarding his lead, Kean tried to minimize the number of times he shared a stage with his opponent. When he learned that Shapiro was to speak at the inauguration of Jersey City mayor Anthony Cucci, Kean waited in his car as an aide telephoned ahead, threatening that the governor would leave unless the format was changed. Some saw the heavy hand of Stevens again at work in Kean's uncharacteristic testiness. Faced with a choice of carrying out his threat or disappointing an assembly of three thousand potential Democratic defectors, Kean relented.[27]

In the run-up to the first debate, Kean's camp demanded that Shapiro sign a written pledge not to use any video excerpts of his exchange with Kean in future television commercials. When the Democrat refused, Kean threatened not to go ahead with the debate. With fifteen minutes to spare, the governor arrived, ready to participate, saying he did not want to disappoint the hosts, the New Jersey State Chamber of Commerce. Shapiro boasted that he had gotten Kean to back down. Commentators gave the challenger the edge on the "debate about the debate" exchange.[28] In the main event, Shapiro came across as scrappy, Kean, statesmanlike, but uncharacteristically defensive. Trying to capitalize on what he saw as a potential weakness in Kean's record, Shapiro termed the governor's environmental record shameful and appalling. Kean, obviously irritated, responded, "Pardon my expression, but that's bull."[29] He repeated what to his listeners appeared a familiar refrain of statistics on how many sites were on the list to be cleaned up and timetables as to when work on each of them would begin.

In a move to undermine Shapiro's credibility, Kean disputed Shapiro's claim to have lowered his county's tax rate by 25 percent in six years. His Democratic challenger had cited his record of holding down taxes as evidence of his ability to reduce property taxes statewide by 15 percent. Taking from his pocket sheets of paper he identified as his tax bill and Shapiro's, Kean noted that in the time that Shapiro had been county executive, the Keans' tax bill jumped 50 percent and his opponent's had gone up 30 percent.[30] "If you're watching television in Essex County," Kean said to the viewing audience, "get out your tax bill. Did it go up or down?" Shapiro countered that he had been talking about tax *rates* rather than the amount of taxes collected. Proving that residents would have paid even more in taxes had he not been able to keep the rate of taxation down proved too steep a climb for Kean's challenger, however valid his assertion may have been.

After the debate, Kean, obviously still annoyed at the tenor of Shapiro's assaults, volunteered to reporters that "the only time" his taxes didn't go up was "when Peter [ran] for election."[31] When Shapiro tried to interrupt, challenging Kean to join him on a tour of a toxic dump in Sayreville, Kean pretended not to hear. When Shapiro persisted, Kean, continuing his chat with reporters, almost in an aside said, "I'll join you in Sayreville some other time." When Shapiro suggested Kean was ducking further debates, Kean feigned surprise. Softly, he said, as if talking about a social event, "We'll do some things together."[32]

"Keen on Kean"

In order to blunt any unexpected attention Shapiro received from his first square-off with Kean, the Republican's campaign scheduled events the day before and the day after the debate that were certain to attract headlines. The day preceding the debate, Kean appeared with Jack Kemp at a fund-raiser in West Orange. The day after it, Kean shared a podium with Ronald Reagan in Parsippany. Proclaiming himself "keen on Kean," Reagan called New Jersey's good economy a bellwether for the nation. The president referred to Kean as "the single most popular governor in the history of the state." Noting that for seven out of the eight years he had been governor of California, he had to face a legislature dominated by the other party, Reagan called on his audience to get Kean "the help he needs" by electing a Republican assembly.[33] Picking up on Reagan's theme, Kean stated that during his first term, New Jersey had witnessed the creation of 350,000 new jobs and the lowest unemployment rate in fifteen years.[34] By the end of his second term, he would claim to have created more than double that amount of jobs through his tax, regulatory, and pro-growth policies.

As the campaign progressed, Kean demonstrated his flair for finding common ground with ethnic and non-Republican audiences. He ended one day of campaigning with a stop at an event intended to raise funds for a young musician battling cancer. Aware that the teen-ager belonged to a band that performed Irish tunes across the state, Kean talked about the special place that music had in Irish culture. The chairman of the event happened to be none other than Essex County sheriff John Cryan, one of Shapiro's local Democratic rivals. After Kean's words of greeting, musical performers, echoing the sentiments of the donors, began to play, keeping time with the refrain "Shapiro don't stand a chance."[35] Elsewhere, Kean told a Columbus Day gathering that the "spirit of discovery" should spur all Americans, not only Italian Americans.[36] At a breakfast at Temple Beth Sholom in Fair Lawn, Kean compared the obligation to vote with the contract God made with Noah.[37]

On October 13, the *Star-Ledger*–Eagleton Poll showed Kean leading Shapiro 67 percent to 16, with 17 percent undecided. The major change since its previous survey was the reduced number of Kean voters who said they were likely to change their minds.[38] In interviews, Shapiro and his manager, Paul Bograd, conceded the difficulty in asserting a "change" theme when voters appeared to be satisfied with existing conditions. Some Democrats publicly worried that in focusing exclusively on toxic waste, Shapiro had cast himself as a Johnny one-note.[39]

As he had in his previous campaign, Kean sandwiched his second joint appearance with Shapiro between visits by national celebrities. Prior to their exchange, Vice President George H. W. Bush, at a partisan luncheon at the Kean ancestral home, Liberty Hall, castigated Democrats as the party of "whining, weakness, and despair."[40] The next day, Kean's campaign dropped an earthshaking political bombshell. Ostensibly in the state to present Kean with an award for New Jersey's support of the Martin Luther King Jr. Center for Nonviolent Social Change, Coretta Scott King called Kean a "contemporary Republican in the tradition of Abraham Lincoln and Frederick Douglass." Though she stressed that her comments did not constitute a political endorsement, King noted that "to the extent decent and concerned New Jerseyans—especially blacks and Hispanics—say 'thank you' at the polls, they will set in motion a revolution in party attention and respect."[41] King's "nonendorsement" helped galvanize the GOP's ongoing efforts to persuade African American voters to move into Kean's column. Many pundits interpreted her words as a clear sign that the top ranks of the civil rights leadership approved of Kean's reelection.

Frustrated, if not stunned, at the potential defection of thousands of his party's most steadfast adherents, Shapiro accused Kean of trying to buy support from influential New Jersey black officials. He charged that Kean had named Julian Robinson, a former Jersey City Democratic chairman, to the New Jersey Highway Authority in exchange for political support and that Jersey City councilman Robert Jackson, head of Democrats for Kean, received five thousand dollars in consultant fees from the state GOP. Kean replied that he had appointed Robinson because he had worked well with him in the past. Of Jackson, Kean said, flashing "that grin," he was not certain that the councilman was working with the Republicans, but certainly hoped that he was.[42]

In the candidates' final debate, Shapiro sharpened his criticisms of Kean. Citing Kean's promise not to sign an increase in the income tax and to cut the sales tax, Shapiro said that if his opponent had been a "TV set or a toaster, he'd be under investigation by the Division of Consumer Affairs."[43] Kean again questioned Shapiro's credentials as a tax cutter. Had Shapiro's challenge been issued by a conservative Republican in the primary, it might have had credence. Coming as it did from a liberal Democrat not known as a fiscal conservative, Shapiro's remark came across as that of a "smart aleck," an impression he reenforced on his way out of the hall. Spotting two women with signs that read "Arts for Kean," the Democrat suggested they paint an *F* before the word *Arts*. Their groans could be heard out into the parking lot.

Two-Term Tom

The weekend before the election, the final *Star-Ledger*–Eagleton poll put Kean ahead of Shapiro 61 percent to 21 percent. Approval of Kean's job performance stood at 80 percent. Among Democrats, Shapiro led by only four points, 41 percent to 37 percent.[44] When the ballots were counted, Kean won by the largest margin in the state's history. He won with 68 percent of the vote, carrying all twenty-one counties and all but three of the state's 567 municipalities.[45] Kean received 60 percent of votes cast by African Americans. He won Democratic Essex County by 64,000 votes, Newark by 6,000, and East Orange by 1,200. He credited his large win to the strength of his message, his record of achievement, and the manner in which he communicated it: "We proved tonight people of all backgrounds and political persuasions will support you if the cause is worthy enough and the evidence solid. Our cause is building pride in New Jersey and our record speaks for itself. This election proves that New Jersey can't be stopped."[46]

Elected with Kean were fourteen new Republican members of the assembly. Partisan control of the chamber shifted from forty-four

Democrats and thirty-five Republicans to forty-nine Republicans and thirty Democrats. Charles Hardwick would be the first Republican to serve as Speaker since Tom Kean.

Kean's consultant Roger Stone noted that to the coalition of blue-collar ethnic Catholics that fueled Reagan's landslide in the Northeast, Kean added blacks, Hispanics, union members, Jews, and other traditional Democratic voters. He predicted a boomlet of publicity and a wider role for Kean in national politics as the 1988 presidential season got under way.[47] Typical of the kind of voter who fueled the size of Kean's landslide was Irma Abrams, a geriatric social worker who had supported Florio in 1981: "I think because the last election was so close he [Kean] has made a special effort not to toe any party line. He's tried to be fair to the majority of people, more so than a lot of governors we've had previously."[48]

chapter 18

The Storm over the Wilentz Case

An Unlikely Fight

With Kean freshly reelected, many observers expected that with the assembly now in Republican hands, the first major controversy of his second term would pit Kean against the Democratic state senate. Kean did, indeed, face down a determined group of senators early in his second term. All of them, however, were Republicans. In some respects, the standoff with them was reminiscent of his earlier ill-fated battle to raise the gas tax in 1982 (see chapter 10) and a precursor of his efforts in 1987 on behalf of school-takeover legislation (see chapter 12). The major difference in this instance was that Kean was not trying to enact his own agenda but to uphold a principle. Kean precipitated the battle when he announced his attention to reappoint a Democratic chief justice.

Under the New Jersey Constitution, state judges receive initial confirmation of seven years. Upon their reappointment and reconfirmation, they are allowed to serve until they reach the age of seventy. Governor Brendan Byrne appointed Robert N. Wilentz chief justice in 1979. The chief justice's initial term of appointment was to expire in August of 1986. Under ordinary circumstances, Kean's decision to reappoint Wilentz would hardly have caused a stir. Wilentz's intellectual and judicial capacities and his personal integrity were beyond reproach. Moreover, no member of the state supreme court had been denied reconfirmation since the adoption of the 1947 constitution, which had streamlined and unified the state judiciary. Were this not enough, Kean respected Wilentz and had much in common with him. Both hailed from politically prominent families and had served together in the assembly.

Wilentz was the younger son of David Wilentz, a former state attorney general, who in 1935 successfully prosecuted Bruno Hauptmann, the defendant in the Lindbergh kidnapping case. For decades after he had stepped down from state government, the elder Wilentz remained a major force within the state's business, legal, and political circles. In addition to his business interests, he simultaneously served as Middlesex County Democratic chairman, member of the Democratic National Committee, and founder and partner of the law firm that bore his name. As a result of his fortuitous break with Jersey City mayor Frank Hague, just as the Hudson County boss was about to fall from power, Wilentz played a leading role in the recruitment and election of Governors Robert B. Meyner and Richard Hughes. He worked behind the scenes in the staffing and running of both administrations. The senior Wilentz became acquainted with Robert W. Kean through their mutual service on the board of the Perth Amboy Bank.

Wilentz's older son, Warren, running under the slogan "Wilentz Makes Sense," took on the thankless task of opposing U.S. senator Clifford P. Case in 1966. Afterward, he returned to the family law firm, eventually taking his father's place at its helm. Wilentz's daughter, Norma, married Leon Hess, owner of the New York Jets and chairman of energy concerns that bore his name (Amerada Hess). The interaction between the Kean, Wilentz, and Hess families grew stronger as Kean's friendship with Leon Hess developed after Kean enticed him to relocate the Jets to New Jersey. Hess became an enthusiastic contributor to many of Kean's special causes, including the construction of the New Jersey Performing Arts Center in Newark. Kean would eventually serve on the board of Amerada Hess.

Robert N. Wilentz was in his second term in the assembly when Kean was elected to his first in 1967. Although of opposite parties, the two worked well together. After Kean succeeded Wilentz as chairman of the Education Committee, he often called upon the Democrat for advice. In 1969, Wilentz left the assembly in order to comply with a "conflict of interest" law he sponsored. The legislation barred law firms that retained state legislators in their employ from appearing before state agencies. For the rest of their careers in public service, Kean continued to oppose the law that drove his friend from elective office, while Wilentz continued to favor it.

His reputation for brilliance and hard work notwithstanding, Wilentz's reconfirmation turned out to be anything but routine. As chief justice, Wilentz antagonized much of the political establishment and the legal community of which his family had for so long been a part. To many, he and the court he led, if not dominated through his strong personality, became symbols of increased judicial activism and arrogance.

Two Chief Justices

In one sense, Wilentz was merely following in the activist tradition of three of his predecessors: Arthur T. Vanderbilt, Joseph A. Weintraub, and Richard J. Hughes. Under Hughes, the court ventured upon new legal ground when it ruled, in the Karen Ann Quinlan case, that life-supporting instruments could be turned off if certain conditions were met; declared exclusionary zoning unconstitutional; and closed the state's schools to prod the legislature to enact a state income tax as a means of conforming with the court's decree to find alternatives to exclusive reliance upon the property tax in the funding of public education.[1]

As he rendered his decisions, Hughes remained sensitive to public opinion, the demands of the political system, and professional courtesies to which lawyers and judges were accustomed. Hughes had served as Mercer County Democratic chairman, superior court judge, and governor before he became chief justice. In 1938, the year Robert W. Kean won his first election, Hughes had also sought a seat in Congress. Running as a 150 percent Roosevelt Democrat in a Republican district the year FDR had tried to "pack" the U.S. Supreme Court, he lost. He came away from the experience a firm believer in both judicial independence and the importance of judges not veering too far ahead or behind prevailing public opinion.[2]

The manner in which Hughes approached the school-closing decision reflected his style of leadership perfectly. Rather than press for a unanimous decision, he was content to speak for four out of seven justices, once he had craftily carved out a majority, centrist position. Two colleagues to his right believed the court had exceeded its authority. One, to his left, was of the mind that it had not gone far enough in not mandating an income tax. Hughes let all three have their say. He issued the long-awaited decree in the summer, when the fewest number of teachers, students, and administrators would be inconvenienced, thereby minimizing the potential backlash against the court. Those who opposed his ruling directed most of their animus at the sitting governor, Brendan Byrne, who had tried and failed several times to enact an income tax prior to the court's ruling. It had not been for naught that Hughes's associates, extending as far back as his days in the Young Democrats, had referred to him as "old two buckets." The reference captured his capacity to balance two pails of water on his shoulders without spilling a drop.[3]

Though Hughes's equal in his liberalism and his activism, Wilentz proved to be a justice of a different sort. He also came to his post through a different path. Hughes was a graduate of St. Joseph's College in Philadelphia and Rutgers Law School in Camden. Wilentz was a product of Harvard and Columbia Law School. Though both came from political families, Hughes's father was a political functionary, whose livelihood depended on how well the party fared at the polls, how much he had done to produce Democratic victories, and how well he got along with the party's leadership. Wilentz's father was a major power broker within the state Democratic Party. Considered a political dark horse and a decided underdog when the county party chairmen declared him their choice for governor in 1961, Hughes, through his constant campaigning and his "happy warrior" temperament, defeated the better-known James Mitchell, Eisenhower's former secretary of labor. Hughes's wife joked that if her husband learned that the Public Service Electric and Gas Company was replacing a manhole cover, he would rush to the site to say a few words about how the company was contributing to the well-being of the economy.[4] Having contended with a legislature under control of the opposition party for six of his eight years in office, Hughes had mastered the art of compromise by the time he ascended to the bench.

Twice elected to an assembly seat specifically drawn to favor his party and having won on a ticket his father had selected, Wilentz seldom had to justify his positions to sizable portions of the electorate. Nor had he faced the prospect of defeat, as had Hughes in 1938, 1961, and 1965. Having to convince people of the rightness of his cause was not part of Wilentz's experience. Nor did he demonstrate Hughes's capacity to "suffer fools," his flexibility, his likeability, or his temperament, judicial or otherwise. Once on the court, Wilentz sought to impose his will through the force of intellect, argument, and personality. Under his aegis, unanimous, rather than split decisions were the order of the day. On more than one occasion, he appeared to inject himself, if not his court, into the legislative process, through his person as well as through his decrees. In addition to his willingness to break new judicial ground, Wilentz was prone to impose regulatory and administrative methods to implement them.

In his capacity as administrator of the court system, he reorganized the court system, created new superior court districts, reduced backlogs, appointed nonlawyers to court-appointed commissions and committees, computerized the judiciary, and worked to eliminate discrimination against women and minorities. More than a few attorneys balked when he required members of the legal profession to contribute to a fund to compensate victims of unethical conduct by lawyers. Some lower court judges objected when he issued standards to assess their performance. Wilentz's detractors within his profession, unwilling to oppose him openly for fear of reprisals, began whispering their displeasure to their state senators.[5]

A Controversial Nominee

Those who were willing to confront Wilentz publicly found much in his public record to criticize. Pursuant to state law, the chief justice appointed the tie-breaking vote to a legislative redistricting commission. After Wilentz's choice, Donald E. Stokes, dean of Princeton University's Woodrow Wilson School of Public and International Affairs, cast the deciding vote for a plan Democrats favored, Republicans accused the chief justice of misusing his powers of appointment. Stokes, a registered Democrat, denied that he had played the role of the partisan, arguing that the Republicans' success in capturing control of the lower house in 1985 demonstrated that the revised legislative map had not worked to the Democrats' favor.

Wilentz issued two decisions that provided his detractors with additional ammunition. The one that nearly derailed his judicial career, "Mount Laurel II," mandated that specific numbers of low-cost housing units be built in developing communities as a corrective to exclusionary zoning. In a ruling characteristic of the Hughes court, the state supreme court in its "Mount Laurel I" ruling had outlawed exclusionary zoning. Having made its point and won plaudits from civil rights organizations and most of the political establishment, including Kean, Hughes left it to local and state governments and his successors to implement his decision.

Speaking for a unanimous court in 1983, Wilentz ruled that towns desiring new development revise their zoning ordinances to provide sufficient housing for low-income residents. He divided the state into three units and named a superior court judge to implement his ruling in each. If any of the judges found that a town did not go as far as they believed it should under the ruling, they could, under Wilentz's order, impose a "builder's remedy." Under its provisions, developers could construct more housing than local ordinances allowed, providing a sufficient number would go to lower-income residents. In practice, the decision meant that four market-priced units would be built for every low-cost one erected. Buyers of higher-priced units would subsidize the lower-selling ones. The decision sparked litigation throughout the state, with builders often the plaintiffs, using the court's ruling as a way of forcing towns to build more units than its residents and elected governments deemed desirable. Fearful of costly lawsuits, towns often settled out of court.

The Mount Laurel II decision sparked considerable opposition. Kean was among its harshest critics. He called the decision "communistic" and went so far as to request a constitutional amendment to restrict the power of the state supreme court to rule on zoning cases.[6] Eventually, he named a seventeen-member state council to propose a statewide "master plan" to regulate state development.[7] Years later, the flood of litigation sparked passage of legislation, which Kean supported, allowing builders to transfer "rights" they had acquired through the "builder's remedy" from growing suburbs to other areas, including the cities.

Wilentz added to his opponents' "bill of particulars" a year after he had issued the Mount Laurel II decision when his court ruled that owners of private residences at which alcohol was consumed were responsible for acts their guests committed after they had departed. Critics of the "host liability" decision asserted that such a means of cutting down on drunk driving, even if it proved effective, "stretched" the constitution by creating a new class of defendants, who themselves had violated no law. Kean seemed to share in that opinion. His outspoken opposition to these two rulings led some to speculate that he might not reappoint the chief justice. They did not know their man.

Kean Makes His Move

Kean learned that Wilentz's continuity on the court would be a controversial matter early in his second term, when Republican senators turned what was supposed to have been a pro forma get-acquainted meeting with Kean's new chief of staff, Ed McGlynn, and his new counsel, Mike Cole, into a gripe session over the chief justice's tenure on the court.[8] The sole bit of good news to emerge from the get-together was the senators' purported delight over Kean's choices of his two principal senior aides. McGlynn, formerly Stevens's deputy, was well known around the statehouse and well liked. The brother of one of Kean's 1981 primary opponents, McGlynn had come into Kean's administration as an aide to Kean's first attorney general, Irwin Kimmelman. The affable McGlynn proved a better administrator than Thurston and was less intense in his dealings than Stevens. McGlynn's reputation as an honest broker stood him in good stead with legislators and other members of the administration.

Kean first encountered Michael Cole during the 1981 recount. Cole was then representing the state in the legal proceedings. Kean had found him judicious, meticulous, and fair, qualities he demonstrated again when he absolved DMV director Cliff Snedeker of having violated the state's ethics code, after higher-ups in the administration had insisted to the contrary. While Edwards, now Kean's attorney general, had concerned himself with legislative strategy and politics, Cole focused on legal craftsmanship. Because he exuded the demeanor of a disinterested staffer, rather than that of a principal, legislative leaders did not regard him as a potential political rival. That made them more likely to go along with what Cole wished to achieve on Kean's behalf.

If Kean's new lieutenants entered the meeting believing Wilentz's reconfirmation would be an easy sale, they departed shed of any illusions. "He's worse than a criminal," Bergen County senator Gerald Cardinale said of him. "Criminals steal money and goods; Wilentz steals democracy from the people."[9] Seven Republican senators who were opposed to the reappointment sent letters to between seven and ten thousand Republican activists, advising them to urge Kean not to reappoint the chief justice.[10] Some argued flat out that Kean should appoint a Republican chief justice. Had Kean taken that advice, the court's partisan composition would have shifted from four Democrats and three Republicans, to four Republicans and three Democrats.

Of the three Republicans on the court, Kean had appointed two: Marie Garibaldi, its first woman, and Gary Stein, his first director of policy and planning. The third, Stewart Pollack, whom Kean would reappoint, had served as counsel to Brendan Byrne. That the Republicans on the court voted in a similar if not identical fashion to Wilentz somehow escaped the notice of the chief justice's Republican critics. When conservative activists circulated petitions urging Wilentz's replacement, Kean grew angry at such attempts to force his hand. "That's not the way to convince Tom Kean to do something," one of his aides commented.[11]

Once he had decided that he would reappoint Wilentz, Kean resolved to act before the opposition had crystallized into an organized movement. Although Wilentz's term would not expire until August, Kean announced his decision in May. On his way back to his office from a meeting with the overseers of the Governor's Schools, Kean let slip to a reporter that he intended to renominate Wilentz.[12] Not known for his coverage of the arts or education, "Moon" Mullins of the *Passaic Herald News* went to the meeting in the hope that Kean would drop a tidbit of news. He did not go away disappointed. "But you can't tell just one reporter," Golden told Kean upon learning what he had done. "But he asked me," Kean replied, trying to conceal "that grin." He acceded to Golden's demand that he announce his decision at a hastily convened press conference. "He probably figured I was having too slow of an afternoon," Golden reflected.[13]

Kean's declaration of his intentions regarding Wilentz was no slip of the tongue. He demonstrated at his press conference that he had carefully rehearsed in his mind the arguments he would make in defense of his decision. His rationale was preserving the independence of the state's judiciary: "I feel very strongly about that because if any judge in the state is worried about how he should make a decision and that would affect his or her re-nomination, then the quality of justice is not going to be what you and I want it to be."[14]

Having taken his stand, Kean, the politician, was quick to point out that the court had become more activist than he liked in some instances.[15] His subsequent statement that Wilentz had served honorably in the post made clear that Kean considered good behavior on the bench the sole criterion in deciding whether to reappoint jurists. Kean volunteered that he had not discussed the reappointment with Wilentz, asserting that such a move would have been improper, given the separation of powers among the branches of government. That they would speak several times, often at Wilentz's initiative, before the controversy subsided became but one of the ironic turns that Wilentz's path to reconfirmation would take.

"Discourteous" Senators

Having declared his intentions, Kean's next move was to demand an up or down vote for his nominee in the senate. He reasoned that once the nomination made its way to the senate floor, the Democratic leadership, exerting party discipline, would rally the majority caucus behind one of their own. If they did, Wilentz would win reconfirmation in a vote of 23 to 17, assuming no Republican voted in his favor, an unlikely prospect, given that Wilentz was now the choice of a Republican governor. Kean's appeal for an open vote had the additional strategic benefit of rallying editorial and "good government" opinion behind the nominee.

Senator Peter Garibaldi (R-Middlesex), who represented Wilentz's hometown of Perth Amboy, suggested early in the process that he might seek to block Wilentz's reconfirmation by evoking "senatorial courtesy," an informal privilege senators granted each other, through which no vote would be taken to confirm an individual if his or her home county senator objected. In addition to serving in the senate, Garibaldi was mayor of Monroe Township. In that capacity, he once proclaimed that he would rather go to jail than comply with the Mount Laurel II ruling.[16] Garibaldi's Democratic colleagues cited a precedent from recent state history that might allow the senate to disregard Garibaldi's objection. Years earlier, after Senator James Wallwork (R-

Essex) had evoked senatorial courtesy to block conformation of one of his constituents, Joel Jacobson, to the Casino Control Commission, Jacobson changed his legal residence to Ocean County, where he maintained a vacation home. He subsequently won confirmation. Many believed that Wilentz, who also maintained a summer residence outside of Garibaldi's district, would do likewise.

The Jacobson case had not been the only instance in which the senate had disregarded the wishes of one of its own after he evoked his right to senatorial courtesy. After Kean renominated superior court judge Sylvia Pressler in 1983, her home county senator, Gerald Cardinale, charging that the judge had been "arrogant, intemperate and flippant," declared his intention to block her reappointment.[17] When it became public that Cardinale had been an unsuccessful litigant before Pressler's court, his colleagues, citing a conflict of interest, stripped him of his "courtesy" privilege. Pressler won reconfirmation.

While some of Wilentz's backers saw in the Pressler matter evidence of the senate's willingness to set aside its "courtesy" custom, Wilentz's intrusion into the Pressler controversy provided his enemies with additional information to use against him. He mounted nothing less than a full lobbying campaign on Pressler's behalf. He said that if Cardinale were allowed to succeed in his efforts to force Pressler off the bench, the independence of the judiciary would be forever undermined. The chief justice asked to address the senate on the constitutional issues he said the Pressler controversy had raised. Terming Wilentz's request unusual and unprecedented, a spokesman for senate president Carmen Orechio said that he doubted that Wilentz would be well received.[18]

His request denied, Wilentz retreated, presumably with Kean's permission, to the governor's outer office, where he staged a press conference. Before taking questions, he read from a seventeen-page handwritten statement. Some of his listeners wondered whether Wilentz, however strong his dedication to principle, through his intrusion into a matter currently before the legislature had violated the spirit of the very independence that he was defending.

Before the Democrats would figure out how to circumvent the courtesy issue, Kean, through his aides, hinted that he might instigate primary challenges against any Republican senator who evoked senatorial courtesy in order to deny Wilentz the up-or-down vote in the senate. Kean was obviously gambling that Garibaldi, who represented a swing district, would want when seeking reelection both the support of a popular governor and the financial resources of the Republican State Committee, which Kean controlled. Before the senator had a chance to back down, the Democratic senate majority passed a rule through which senatorial courtesy would not apply to renominations of sitting members of the state supreme court. With this obstacle removed, Wilentz was certain to receive the floor vote Kean sought, and to sail to a smooth and speedy confirmation—or so it appeared.

Wilentz's Controversial Residence in the Big Apple

Just as Garibaldi's colleagues removed what seemed the final road-block to Wilentz's renomination, another obstacle—of the chief justice's own making—appeared, which could not easily be put aside by a change of New Jersey domiciles or of senate rules. Before he became chief justice, Wilentz divided his time between his two New Jersey homes and an apartment he maintained in Manhattan. Customarily, he spent most of the week in New Jersey and his weekends in New York. In 1980, a year after he joined the court, he began spending more time in New York, where his wife began receiving treatments for cancer. When he testified before the senate's Judiciary Committee, Wilentz revealed that, because he resided more than half the year in New York, he paid state income taxes to that state as well as to New Jersey.[19]

Senators began questioning the chief justice's true residence. Although Wilentz maintained that he considered himself a resident of New Jersey, he refused to say whether he would reverse his commuting pattern should the health of his wife improve. He further antagonized his critics by volunteering that he doubted New Jersey statutes that required state officeholders to reside within the state applied to judges. Even senators sympathetic to Wilentz's family situation found it odd that a justice known for his liberal interpretation of the constitution would apply a literal, if not a strict constructionist, interpretation to the document on matters pertaining to his personal situation. For months, Wilentz's opponents publicly decried Wilentz's commuting in a state-supplied limousine to his Manhattan apartment. Some senators suggested that, through his living arrangements, Wilentz put himself beyond the reach of his own court.

Kean volunteered that he did not know how much time the chief justice spent in New York, but that he would be disturbed only if Wilentz's reasons were anything other than the health of his wife. He called the residency issue nothing but a smoke screen behind which senators, wanting to deny Wilentz reconfirmation, hid their true objections, which concerned the justice's rulings. Kean would hold this view for decades.[20] Adding fuel to his opponents' arguments, Wilentz refused to state whether he would abide by recently introduced legislation that required state judges to reside in the state.

When Wilentz's nomination came to a vote, five Democrats deserted him, while two Republicans voted in his favor.[21] When the senate called a recess, the vote stood at 20 to 19. During the three-hour interval that followed, senate president John Russo telephoned Kean, who was vacationing out of state, to inform him he had made no progress in persuading Wilentz to modify his living arrangements. Russo suggested that Kean give the matter a try. The governor extracted from Wilentz two pledges: (1) that the justice would return to the state on a full-time basis if his wife's health improved; and (2) that if Kean signed a residency law mandating judges to reside in the state, Wilentz would abide by it. That was enough to push the last undecided vote, Camden Republican Lee Laskin's, Wilentz's way.[22]

Some found it ludicrous that a governor had to plead with a chief justice he had renominated to the court to obey the very laws he would be sworn to uphold. Others saw the entire Wilentz episode as a closing of ranks on the part of the political power structure, of both parties. "Our constitutional provision for separation of powers has been violated in a public fashion by the chief justice, the governor and the senate president," Cardinale said.[23] Kean's actions almost certainly had saved his nominee from rejection. "I have to give the governor credit," Russo said afterward. "Until he made that call to the chief justice and relayed that message, we were hung up. If there was one thing that broke that 21st vote, it was Governor Kean's efforts."[24] Another New Jersey Democrat was even more ebullient in his praise. Richard J. Hughes had been sitting in the senate chamber as hours ticked away before Wilentz received the additional voted he needed in order to remain on the court. "They're gambling with the best court system in the country," he told reporters. "They're playing Russian roulette with the destiny of the state."[25] In a letter to Kean, Hughes called him a "profile in courage" for reappointing Wilentz, and ended with great effusion: "Your Father would be so proud! . . . I am very glad I know you!"[26]

Had Kean not intervened, New Jersey might well have obtained a different chief justice, one who issued rulings closer to Kean's liking on Mount Laurel, host liability, and other issues. It might also have led to a judicial reinterpretation of the "thorough and efficient" clause in the state constitution—a reinterpretation Kean favored—which defined a quality education in terms of more than equal spending per student. Having made his point about preserving judicial independence, when he initially reappointed Wilentz, and again when he threatened to oppose the reelection of senators of his own party, Kean could have held back after the residency issue surfaced and after five Democrats deserted Wilentz. This would have allowed him to blame the justice's demise on the Democratic senate. Given that he had extended himself on behalf of his predecessor's choice, it would not have been unreasonable for Kean to have demanded that the Democrats come to the rescue of one of their own.

Moreover, Kean had made and won his point about judicial independence when the senate reconfirmed Associate Justice Stewart Pollack, whose record was practically identical to that of Wilentz. Indeed, Kean had been in a position where he could have had it both ways, having preserved the independence of the court with Pollack, and, with Democratic help, obtained a vacancy he could have filled with a justice whose views were closer to his own. Yet Kean refused to take such ways out. He continued to insist that he might have looked upon the matter differently if Wilentz's opponents had not initially raised his judicial opinions as the basis for their objections to his reconfirmation. Moreover, Kean had taken on a fight and put the full prestige of his office behind the nominee. He was determined to see the matter through.

With Wilentz safely reconfirmed, Kean kept his silence when Wilentz again tried to intrude into the legislative process six months later. The law Kean eventually signed required judges to make New Jersey the center of their "domestic lives." Wilentz wanted to make certain the passage would not apply to spouses of judges.[27] Although he had taken up permanent residence in Deal, Wilentz feared that the law required his wife also to change her residence. He asked Kean's assistance in having the legislation reworded. Kean declined to intervene. The jurist next approached the owner of the *Bergen Record* for editorial help in arguing for the change. That produced only additional publicity and criticism. One observer rendered this verdict of the jurist whose opinions so heavily impacted on the lives of others: "When someone gets around to writing the history of Thomas Howard Kean's two terms as chief executive of the Garden State, the most interesting chapter may be on Robert N. Wilentz. As chief justice of the state Supreme Court, Wilentz tested first the will, then the integrity, then the principles, and, finally, the friendship of New Jersey's enormously popular governor."[28]

chapter 19

Kean Reforms Welfare

A Growing Crisis

As he had in the case of education, Kean applied a two-pronged approach to reforming welfare. At the same time that he was implementing bold initiatives at home, Kean used the prestigious forum the National Governors Association afforded him to prod the federal government to grant not only New Jersey but all states greater flexibility as they attempted to reduce welfare rolls and place beneficiaries into jobs. Through a combination of patience, persistence, and a bipartisan approach, Kean succeeded in an arena where so many others had failed.

When he assumed the chairmanship of the National Governors Association's Human Services Committee in 1984, Kean immediately turned his attention to child nutrition and welfare reform. He had already, through his work with Jack Kemp, come to believe in measures such as enterprise zones, which gave incentives to and appealed to the self-interest of potential employers and employees. He now wanted to try to wean people off welfare. In his two decades as an elective official, Kean had seen several programs at the state and federal levels fail to achieve their stated objectives of reducing poverty and dependence. He was willing to try other approaches. By the time he assumed the chairmanship of the NGA committee, political leaders and policy analysts of all ideological persuasions had come to agree that the welfare system then in place was a failure.

By the mid-1960s, a fundamental demographic change had occurred in the type of person receiving assistance under the Aid to Families with Dependent Children (AFDC) program, established as part of the Social Security Act of 1935. There had been a steady shift away from middle- and working-class widows to teenage mothers, who had never been married. In New Jersey, this group comprised half of the welfare recipients. In other states, they constituted an even higher percentage. Most of these women had never been in the workforce. Moreover, the preponderance of thirty-five-year-old grandparents suggested a perpetuation of the poverty cycle from generation to generation.

With the states responsible for providing the majority of funds for AFDC and with the federal government pressing states to increase payments to keep pace with the cost of living, welfare expenses, boosted by inflation, came to consume higher and higher percentages of state budgets, in addition to other costs they extracted in human terms. By the time Kean became governor, talk of a welfare crisis had become commonplace among policy makers and social scientists. Organizations such as the Council of State Governments, National Conference of State Legislatures, and the National Governors Association began putting welfare reform at the top of their respective agendas.

Another Man with a Plan

To head the Department of Human Services during his second term, Kean settled on a man who shared his sense that a way had to be found to help welfare recipients become productive citizens and taxpayers rather than consumers of public spending. He was Drew Altman, then the vice president of the Robert Wood Johnson Foundation, formerly with the Federal Health Care Finance Administration. Altman sensed at this initial interview that welfare, like education and the environment, was an area in which Kean wanted to assert his influence, both in New Jersey and beyond.[1] Just as Kean had known that he wanted to bring a better caliber of freshly minted teacher into the classroom, but had allowed Cooperman to develop the plan that led to alternate teacher certification, he knew he wanted to reform welfare, but left it to Altman to show him how. Altman had several ideas.

By the 1980s, *workfare* became a concept familiar to policy makers seeking to reduce welfare rolls. Under its draconian tenets, welfare recipients performed work such as painting buildings or raking leaves in exchange for benefits. They also had to demonstrate that they were looking for employment in the private sector. Kean and Altman liked the concept of making receipt of public assistance conditional on some corresponding actions on the part of recipients. They also wanted to establish a progression through which those on welfare moved into jobs that led to advancement and self-sufficiency so that they would not slip back onto public assistance. They decided on a plan that both treated welfare recipients with respect and appealed to their sense of self-interest.

Under its provisions, women on welfare with children over the age of two would sign a contract with the state in which they agreed to accept employment, continue their education, or obtain training in exchange for the state continuing to provide them with benefits.[2] When recipients took a job, returned to school, or enrolled in a job-training program, the state would cover for up to one year the costs of their transportation, day care, and health care under Medicaid. Employers who hired former welfare recipients were provided with tax and other inducements. Kean and Altman called their program Realizing Economic Achievement (REACH). The approach they took addressed what their research had already told them: that most people on welfare desired to work but had been discouraged from looking for jobs because most of the employers who would hire people with limited skills did not provide these benefits.

Kean made REACH the centerpiece of his 1987 State of the State address, a position he assigned the environment in 1985 and education and government reform in 1986. Kean and Altman calculated that such a program required up-front expenditures of $60 million a year. They reasoned that if only 15 percent of the state's 365,000 people on public assistance left welfare rolls, the state would recoup its costs and save $50 million annually after three years.[3] As he had done with education, the environment, transportation, and the arts, Kean justified such expenditures as investments in the state's future. And, as in the case of the transportation trust fund, he pointed out that his welfare reform program would pay for itself over a short period of time. The *New York Times* called the most appealing part of Kean's initiative an "attitude" that reflected the state's obligations toward the needy.[4]

The program was vintage Kean in its emphasis on counseling and social services, with a heavy dose of Jack Kemp in its appeal to economic self-interest. It combined elements of the safety nets, often associated with Rooseveltian liberalism, with hefty amounts of Reaganite "bootstrapping." It anticipated the 1996 agreement President Bill Clinton and congressional Republicans that ended "welfare as we know it" by abolishing the AFDC program, ending the federal perpetual guarantee of welfare benefits, placing a five-year cap on payments over a lifetime, and making benefits contingent on job training.

Rather than talk about "welfare queens" driving Cadillacs or buying liquor on food stamps, as Reagan had done, Kean warned of an anticipated labor shortage. Of people then currently on welfare, he would say, "We need these people desperately in the economy."[5] Bill Clinton, then governor of Arkansas and chair of the NGA, used practically identical language to Kean's in making the case for reform. "We really don't have a person to waste in this country," both would say on frequent occasions.[6] Unlike his education, transportation, environmental, and arts initiatives, Kean's welfare reform proposal aroused no opposition in the state. Calling the amount of in-state support "beyond his imagination," Kean said it confirmed his view that there was a "realization across the political spectrum" that the present system was a failure.[7] Whatever obstacles he encountered to enacting his plan arose not in Trenton but in Washington.

For REACH to become reality, Kean needed to persuade the federal government to waive more than a dozen regulations, clearing the way for the suspension of provisions that allowed women with children under the age of six to remain at home and receive benefits. When he submitted New Jersey's plan to the White House, Altman stated that it qualified as the very kind of "pilot" or "demonstration" project the Reagan administration had been encouraging states to undertake.[8] Although the national administration was sympathetic to New Jersey's willingness to try a new approach (Reagan had called for the freeing of the "creative genius and entrepreneurial energy" of self-help groups in localities), it took Washington a year to grant the waivers, as federal and state officials dickered over which level of government would reap the larger amount of the savings if the program worked.

At a White House meeting in the fall of 1987 that lasted until 2:00 a.m., Reagan's principal welfare adviser, Charles Hobbs, and the director of the Office of Management and Budget, Jim Miller, allowed New Jersey to keep all of the savings in federal as well as state spending.[9] Again the Reagan administration came through for its counterpart in Trenton. But obtaining its help had not been easy. One observer noted that before reaching agreement on the Medicaid waivers, Altman tried every tactic short of a sit-in.[10] At a bill signing the next day, an ebullient Kean called the program, the first of its kind in the nation, "one of the rare things that is really going to make a difference in people's lives."[11] On a visit to Whippany on October 13, 1987, President Reagan predicted the "New Jersey reforms could prove among the most far-reaching and significant ever in helping those on welfare get off and become productive citizens."[12]

Bridging the Partisan Divide

As REACH worked its way through the New Jersey legislature and the federal bureaucracy, Kean began working with the NGA to obtain for the states greater latitude in meeting eligibility requirements for other federal programs so that they could accelerate their push to reduce welfare rolls. Weeks after Kean's State of the State address, President Reagan invited the nation's governors to the White House to share with him their ideas on how to "establish a process that allows states and communities to implement their own antipoverty ideas based on their own unique circumstances."[13] The president said in his letter of invitation that he was convinced that "no single policy mandated from Washington "could solve the problem." In his 1987 State of the Union address, Reagan listed welfare reform among his high priorities and followed up on it with a week of speeches.

The plan that the NGA's Executive Committee put forward bore a striking resemblance to the proposal that Kean, in his capacity as chairman of its Human Services Committee, recently unveiled in Trenton—with child-care benefits and contractual components among its mainsprings. Kean's national proposal was in effect an attempt to allow the spirit of the REACH program to extend beyond New Jersey's borders. "Our current welfare system as we all know is repugnant," he said upon introducing the measure. As U.S. senator Daniel Patrick Moynihan (D-NY) had done years earlier, Kean blamed the welfare system then in place for the breakup of families because it cut benefits to women who were married to the fathers of their children. Kean said that the surest way to beat poverty was to get people to work and the surest way to get people to work was "to build a welfare system with work as its central component."[14]

Just as Kean had hoped, Reagan warmed to the idea of having the government enter into a contract with welfare recipients in which each of the parties would agree to fulfill certain obligations.[15] National Governors Association chairman Bill Clinton expressed delight that Reagan "agreed to support more of our [the governors' welfare] program" than Clinton thought he would.[16] Years later, Clinton acknowledged that Reagan had "good instincts" on welfare. "Though he told all those stories about 'welfare queens' and so forth," Reagan, Clinton remembered, "understood . . . the importance of flexibility for the states on welfare as well as on continuing child care."[17]

While serving as governor of California, Reagan, working with a Democratic legislature, had enacted a welfare reform agenda of his own that tightened eligibility requirements, increased benefits, provided counties with incentives to recover support from absentee fathers, and imposed work requirements.[18] Early drafts of the plan had included provisions for day care, job training, and continued heath benefits under "MediCal." Reagan also knew how difficult it was for states to obtain waivers from the federal government, having taken his case for a waiver to impose the work requirement all the way up to President Richard Nixon.

Among the reasons—perhaps *the* reason—that Reagan moved more in the NGA's direction than Clinton anticipated was the manner in which Kean handled negotiations with the Republican administration and the Democratic Congress. Aware that Reagan would not support either a costlier program or a minimal federal payment to welfare recipients, Kean offered an amendment to his NGA resolution proposing that any federal standard be financed through savings the states achieved by reducing welfare rolls. Unable to persuade Reagan to have the federal government fund start-up costs of state initiatives, Kean began pointing out how he had managed to finance them in New Jersey.

With Reagan in support of their proposals, the governors took their case to Congress. Kean found a sympathetic ear in Moynihan, now chairman of the Senate's Finance Committee's subcommittee on family-related issues. Moynihan was among the first to observe the changing demographics in the AFDC program. He was also the first to decry disincentives to work that were inherent in existing welfare practices and the ways in which current welfare practices were detrimental to families. In his own rhetoric, Kean had—perhaps deliberately—used language identical to that which the senator had used in the past. Moynihan immediately introduced legislation mandating that states provide education, training, and job placement, with the federal government paying 70 percent of the costs of child care and transportation.[19]

Moynihan and his counterpart in the House, Tennessee representative Wendell Ford, agreed to consult with a panel of governors for comment in drafting a bill they intended to introduce.[20] "I've been around Congress for a long time," Kean said, "and I've never seen things happen this fast before."[21] House Democrats took the unusual step of inviting Clinton to participate in the shaping of their bill. Some of their more liberal members came to adopt several of the "new Democrat's" ideas on mandatory training and work requirements. When the House and Senate failed to reach an agreement, Kean called upon Congress to "seize the moment." To dramatize his case and provide a sense of urgency, he brought several women who had left New Jersey's welfare rolls, courtesy of REACH, to testify before his NGA committee.[22] By the summer of 1988, both houses had passed a version of Kean's proposal. On October 12, 1988, Reagan signed into law the first substantial revisions to the AFDC program since its creation.

Commentators detecting a new consensus across all parties, regions, and ideologies on welfare policy credited the nation's governors for its emergence. Moynihan went so far as to proclaim the legislation Reagan signed as "the governors' bill."[23] The presence of Kean, Clinton, and other governors at the center of negotiations between the White House and the Capitol produced an air of bipartisanship rare in a city prone to partisanship and gridlock. "The time in history when we can do this in such a bipartisan and genial way is not often and this is the time," Representative Thomas Downey (D-NY) said, before thanking a group of governors for making Congress's "job a little easier."[24]

From start to finish, Kean had played a decisive role in the nation's endeavor to reform welfare. Working with a small group of governors of both parties and of similar political orientations, he advanced his plan employing language that appealed to both liberals and conservatives. "We believe it is time to stop arguing about whether poor people or government are [sic] responsible for the failure of welfare," he said.[25] Rarely did Kean miss a meeting. Seldom did he give up on obtaining a vote. Hardly was he bereft of arguments with which to make his case. All the while Reagan and his administration resisted Kean's entreaties to fund start-up costs of programs such as REACH, the president continued to laud Kean's educational reforms at White House meetings convened to discuss welfare. Clinton attributed Kean's success in achieving their common goals to a combination of the New Jersey governor's "stick-to-itiveness" and charm. "The more you know him, the more you like him," Clinton said.[26]

Back in New Jersey, Kean and Altman introduced several other pioneering initiatives before Kean's second term came to a close. Combining his interest in child services and education, Kean launched the largest school-based health service in the country. His hope was that, once at school, poor children could receive the health care they were not always receiving at home or in their neighborhoods. As an extension of their welfare reform initiative, Altman and Kean established, with federal approval, a state-run HMO for people on Medicaid. They called it the Garden State Health Plan.

A Good Samaritan Causes a Scandal

How Kean reacted to a highly bizarre and unprecedented scandal that plagued the Department of Human Services during his final year in office revealed just how much Kean actually knew about what was going on within the state government he headed and how much he was willing to overlook in the name of compassion. In the early months of 1989, an internal audit revealed that Eddie C. Moore, the director of the department's Division of Developmental Disabilities, had been overspending his budget without authorization from Altman, the N.J. Office of Management and Budget, or the legislature. Moore was a civil servant, whose tenure preceded both Kean's and Altman's. His division's total deficit was initially estimated to be $21 million.[27]

Moore had been spending the excess funds in increased grants to entities that provided services to his division's "clients," that is, people with physical or mental handicaps, the autistic, and those suffering from developmental disabilities such as cerebral palsy and spina bifida. In addition to Moore's overspending, Altman anticipated an additional deficit of $11 million, bringing his department's total deficit to $32 million. In late March, the commissioner briefed Kean and key legislators on the problem. Kean made Altman's report public several weeks later. Legislative committees conducted extensive hearings into Moore's conduct, and the Department of Law and Public Safety launched a criminal investigation. Moore not only showed no remorse but told his investigators that he was aware of what he had been doing, was proud of his actions, and, if he had the chance, would do it again. One columnist likened his zealotry to that of Colonel Oliver North, who also cited the justness of his cause as his reason for circumventing the law in the arms-for-hostages exchange that became known as the Iran-Contra scandal.[28]

After he had figured out the full extent of the problem, Altman, in what he considered to be a routine call, informed Kean of his intention to remove Moore from his post. Days earlier the two had agreed to fire one of Moore's subordinates, Ronald Melzer, who had helped his superior cover up his overspending. At the time of Melzer's dismissal, Kean termed the abuse that had transpired within the department "wrong," "inexcusable," and "indefensible."[29] To Altman's surprise, Kean urged him to hold off on taking action against Moore.[30] In prior conversation with Altman, Moore had volunteered that his wife was ill with cancer. (He did not say that he suffered from the disease as well.) Altman complied with Kean's request, with the attorney general's investigation of Moore still pending.

In the short run, Altman paid a steeper penalty for the scandal than had his subordinate. The George H. W. Bush administration had been considering him for the position of administrator of the Health Care Financing Administration. Conservatives both in New Jersey and in Washington, angered at Altman's lack of Republican credentials, used the overspending issue to undermine his credibility as an administrator. Altman would go on to run health and human services programs for the Pew Charitable Trusts, becoming president and chief executive officer of the Henry J. Kaiser Family Foundation in 1990.

Moore remained at his post until his death. Altman speculated that Kean had known that Moore suffered from cancer. "That would have been typical of [Kean]," he said.[31] Had Moore used the money for personal gain, Kean's attitude might have been different. He was not about to fire a dying man who, in his own mind, thought he had acted to help the less fortunate. To this son of St. Mark's, the entire episode boiled down to a case of hating the sin (overspending) while loving the sinner (Moore).

chapter 20

The Man with the Message

Testing the (Political) Waters

Kean's landslide reelection, buoyed by his impressive showing among minority voters, in a year in which only two governorships were in play and Democrat Gerald Baliles won in Virginia, caught the attention of GOP officials and political pundits across the country. Upon his reelection, Kean resolved to use his enhanced visibility within the Republican Party to press upon its national leaders the importance of broadening the party's base by reaching out to voters who had not traditionally voted Republican. A little more than a year after his reelection, Kean said to the Heritage Foundation, a conservative think tank: "The fact is that [the] key issues in the black and Hispanic community are the same as in the white community. The fact is that black and Hispanic voters care just as deeply about creating jobs, improving the schools, and fighting crime as anybody else." He challenged the notion that "black voters want to hear only about ways to redistribute the economic pie, not about ways to make it bigger." He also suggested that before they sought to win converts to their ideas, Republicans needed to demonstrate their commitment to civil rights. Once they had done that, he insisted, they would find audiences receptive to the rest of their message.[1]

Kean disavowed interest in running for national office. He insisted that the only role he sought was that of messenger for a concept he called *the politics of inclusion.* Though Kean never acknowledged that he harbored national ambitions or sought to position himself for consideration as his party's vice presidential nominee in 1988, word passed quietly among his inner circle that, as he began his second term, they were to raise Kean's profile. The idea, his chief of staff Ed McGlynn remembered, "was to let others run for president, while Kean continued his work on innovative policies he had pioneered in New Jersey, which were drawing increased national attention."[2] Kean's team conscientiously sought out opportunities to showcase his accomplishments, while Kean continued to work through national organizations to influence national policy. On those occasions when his out-of-state travels were billed as political in nature, Kean stuck to his basic theme that the party needed to expand upon its base by aggressively reaching out to minorities and other nontraditional voters. He accepted, on average, one out-of-state appearance a month, usually in states that held early presidential primaries or caucuses.

With Kean spending more time away, his advisers sought to minimize the number of controversies in which he became personally involved at home. Except on matters involving education and the environment, where victory would further establish his reputation as a leader and even setbacks could underscore his reformist credentials, he let surrogates press his agenda before the Democratic-controlled state senate. With Kean coaching from the sidelines, his transportation commissioner, Hazel Gluck, urged the legislature to raise the gasoline tax to replenish the popular, though all but depleted, Transportation Trust Fund that Kean had established during his first term.[3] This time the measure passed without controversy.

A month after his reelection, at a meeting of the Republican Governors Association, Kean heard both Republican National Committee chairman Frank Fahrenkopf and Vice President George H. W. Bush refer to his successful reelection campaign as a harbinger of what lay ahead for other Republicans who followed Kean's overall approach.[4] Kean left the gathering as the new vice chairman of the organization, a post that set him up to succeed New Hampshire's John Sununu as its chairman the following year. In March 1986, Kean ventured to New Hampshire to carry his message of inclusion to a strictly partisan audience. Seventy-five New Jersey Republicans, of all ethnic backgrounds, followed him to the Granite State on a bus the party's state committee chartered. "We're friends of Tom Kean," longtime Kean loyalist Karla Squier told reporters. "We came for him."[5] She did not reveal that she had been up all the previous night, ensuring that she would have enough saltwater taffy from Atlantic City to distribute to Kean's New Hampshire admirers.[6]

Kean told four hundred Republicans at the Rockingham County Lincoln Day Dinner in Portsmouth that the GOP was on the verge of achieving majority-party status. All that it needed to do to achieve that long-standing goal, he said, was to attract a sufficient number of minority voters. U.S. senator Warren Rudman, who preceded Kean to the podium, credited the New Jersey governor with showing the rest of the party how to open its doors to new people.[7] Members of the New Jersey press, following Kean's every move, thought it odd that Kean passed up an opportunity to repeat in Rudman's presence his well-known opposition to the "Gramm-Rudman" amendment, which would trigger automatic reductions in the federal budget. In his remarks at the dinner, before he introduced Kean, Rudman vigorously defended the legislation. Months earlier, Kean, speaking on behalf of several governors, had called Rudman's amendment a straitjacket, through which Congress avoided responsibility for setting policy.[8] *Washington Post* columnist David Broder explained Kean's reasoning: "He is investing heavily in education, human services and infrastructure improvements—the very areas where the domestic cutbacks of Gramm-Rudman are most likely to fall, and the ones the country can least afford for its future."[9] Taking issue with Rudman on the U.S. senator's home turf, in front of his own constituents, would have struck Kean as the height of rudeness.

One of his fellow New Jerseyans denied Kean the same courtesy when he placed in the dinner program an advertisement asserting

Fig 20.1. A cartoonist hints that Kean's impressive reelection margin and his advocacy of the "politics of inclusion" might enhance his influence in Republican Party circles, perhaps landing him a place on a national ticket. (© 1985 *The Star-Ledger.* All rights reserved. Reprinted with permission.)

that Kean, through his record on taxes, stand on abortion, and criticisms of the Reagan administration, had forfeited his right to call himself a conservative. The signer purported to be with the New Jersey Committee for Truth in Politics, a group not well known to Kean's traveling companions from New Jersey.[10]

Because New Hampshire traditionally holds the first presidential primary, Kean's speech attracted considerable attention. Consultant Roger Stone, said to be advising at least two presidential campaigns at the time, speculated that Kean would play well in New Hampshire because his education policies would appeal to the many newcomers to the state who made their living in high-technology industries. Peter Coombs, the local party chairman, proclaimed Kean a "fresh face on the national scene."[11] Scott Reed, northeastern coordinator for the Republican National Committee and future campaign manager for presidential contender Bob Dole, attributed the size of the turnout to the strength of Kean's message.[12] Kean, with his decided New England accent and knowledge of the state, forged during seven summers at Brantwood, related easily to his audience.

Kean next journeyed to Michigan. He brought a Bloomfield Hills gathering of Republicans to its feet when he praised Ronald Reagan for bombing Libya in retaliation for a terrorist attack its government had ordered against American military personnel in Germany. Kean commended Reagan for his willingness to "stand up against the piranhas who try to spread terror in this world." Later in his talk, Kean told his listeners that the Republican Party needed to "get out of the country clubs and into the union halls and ghettos if it was to stay in power after Reagan left office."[13] Three of five candidates for the Republican nomination for governor requested to meet with Kean privately. George Romney, Michigan's legendary former governor, once a presidential contender himself, came out to take the measure of the man from New Jersey. Upon his return, Kean announced that he had formed a political action committee and had tasked it to raise a half million dollars. He would use the money to fund his out-of-state travels and to assist candidates running for office in other states.[14] Observers saw his action as a sign that Kean sought to build political IOUs in the event he ran for national office.

After Kean addressed the Council for Financial Aid to Education in Cleveland, Cicatiello arranged for Kean's speech to be printed and mailed to college presidents and corporate executives across the country.[15] Foreshadowing the kind of talk he would deliver while president of Drew University, Kean challenged corporate executives to look for the risk takers at smaller, lesser-known institutions in making donations, rather than routinely funneling $1.6 billion to large universities.[16] Traveling with Kean in Ohio, Cicatiello admitted for the first time that Kean might be testing his national appeal. In a Harris poll of northeastern Republicans taken in February and March 1986, Kean placed third in voter preferences for president, right behind presidential front-runners George H. W. Bush and Bob Dole.[17] Many of those polled related that they had seen Kean on television, touting New Jersey as a tourist destination.

Kean enthusiasts were not the only ones to speculate that despite his denials, New Jersey's governor was seeking national office. The conservative journal *National Review* warned its readers that although Kean talked "like Jack Kemp," he governed "like Mario Cuomo." As evidence of his liberal leanings, it cited Kean's signing of the South African divestiture bill, his reappointment of Wilentz, his acceptance of abortion, and his opposition to school prayer.[18] George F. Will, in his syndicated column, offered a rebuttal to Kean's conservative critics. He cited Kean's embrace of enterprise zones, his tough anticrime initiatives, the decrease in the state's jobless rate, and Kean's cuts in five taxes.[19] As to Kean's criticisms of the national GOP, Will predicted that the party would benefit from whatever heterodoxy Kean would display on the stump, should he enter the already-crowded field of presidential contenders.

Observing Kean's forays out-of-state and the increased attention he was receiving, one of his associates believed he had figured out what lay behind Kean's cat-and-mouse approach to national politics. "If someone comes along and crowns him," he said, "he'll take it. That's the way he has always operated."[20]

A Leader among Governors

In the 1986 election, as the Republicans lost control of the U.S. Senate, they picked up eight governorships, bringing the total of state administrations under their control from sixteen to twenty-four.[21] Kean saw in the national returns further vindication of his politics-of-inclusion theory. "With just a small percentage of the black vote," Kean told charter members of GOPAC, a grassroots party organization founded by future Speaker of the House Newt Gingrich, "we would not have lost the [U.S.] Senate."[22]

Kean's exposure as a national party spokesman reached a crescendo when he assumed the chairmanship of the Republican Governors Association. On the eve of his installation, Kean and his advisers mounted a multiday public program in Parsippany at which leading national figures assessed future trends in business, education, and government. Secretary of the Treasury James A. Baker delivered the keynote address. Political consultants Charles Black, Roger Ailes, and Ed Rollins critiqued the 1986 elections, while pollsters Lance Torrance, Bob Teeter, and Louis Harris offered competing predictions about the future of the Republican Party. George Allen, former Washington Redskins Coach and head of the President's Council on Physical Fitness, spoke about how to keep young people off drugs. Martin Feldstein, former chair of the Council of Economic Advisers; Princeton political scientist Richard Nathan; and best-selling author David Halberstam offered commentary on issues the United States might face in the 1990s. U.S. education secretary William Bennett and David Kearns, chief executive officer of Xerox, opined on new developments in education. Bennett, in his talk, recommended that Kean's alternate teacher certification program spread to the rest of the country as a means of producing better teachers.[23]

In his role as host, Kean kicked off each session in a manner reminiscent of Ronald Reagan's introduction of upcoming presentations on the 1950s television show *General Electric Theater*. Also in a manner similar to Reagan's, Kean returned at the conclusion of every panel discussion, offering his interpretation or synthesis of what had been presented.

One in-state observer summarized the impact Kean was having on his guests: "Kean's style, familiar to State House reporters, was obviously a refreshing surprise to the national media. Casual, informal, and easily accessible to almost anyone, Kean came off as a politician with grace and intelligence."[24] "I don't think any Republican should consider running for President without Tom Kean as his Vice Presidential candidate," South Dakota's William Janklow declared after chatting with a customer and a waitress during a late-night visit to a local diner. "You can't buy that kind of support," Janklow said.[25]

Most of the New Jersey political establishment was on its best behavior during Kean's conclave. The private sector contributed two hundred thousand dollars for gala dinners at historic sites, including a Christmas-season dinner by candlelight at historic Waterloo Village in Stanhope. Making his entrance, an officer of the state AFL-CIO said, "We owe him [Kean] a great deal of thanks. . . . He's really delivered the work. We haven't had this kind of prosperity in twenty years."[26] State senate president John Russo, with whom Kean was sparring on several matters, declined to be critical of the governor. "I have to get things done here," Russo said.[27] Staying in character, Alan Karcher recited several items that awaited Kean's attention while the governor entertained his guests.[28]

In his welcoming remarks to his fellow governors, Kean urged them to use their collective clout within the national party to press for deficit reduction and greater state autonomy over programs.[29] In spite of their best efforts, Kean and his colleagues failed to divert media attention away from the unfolding Iran-Contra scandal. Kean joked that the most frequently asked question at the conclave had been "Who didn't know what and when didn't he know it?"[30]

In the months leading up to the RGA gathering in New Jersey, Kean had asked Richard Nixon to brief the Republican governors on foreign policy.[31] In a one-hour closed-door session, Nixon touched on political developments on each continent and what impact they might have upon the United States. Reporters picked up on the irony of Nixon, who had resigned the presidency in the face of scandal, appearing just as a new scandal was beginning to envelop another Republican president. Another irony was his agreeing to leave behind a tape of his remarks. On it, the man who had proclaimed the Watergate scandal a "third-rate burglary" referred to the Iran-Contra episode as a sideshow. Nixon urged Reagan's critics to "get off his back" and admonished his fellow Republicans to refrain from practicing their "favorite sport of cannibalism."[32]

The sense of foreboding among Kean's guests rose as they, also by prearrangement, departed with Kean for a meeting with Reagan in Washington, D.C. When the pilot announced that a thunderstorm would delay their arrival because several planes were stacked up ahead of them, a White House aide, who was accompanying the governors, jumped up from his seat and made a beeline for the cockpit. The next thing Kean knew, he and his colleagues were being driven to the White House.[33] Reagan related that he first learned about the diversion of $30 million from the Iranian arms sale to the contras when Attorney General Ed Meese, after the fact, provided him evidence of what Reagan termed a "smoking gun."[34] South Carolina governor-elect Carroll Campbell pointed his finger at Chief of Staff Donald Regan and said, "Mr. President, all of us here are supportive of you, but you cannot survive if you don't get rid of that man." "All options are on the table," the president replied.[35]

Rather than make his exit ahead of his guests at the end of the meeting, Reagan lingered. As Kean prepared to leave, Reagan, standing in the doorway, grabbed his arm and said, "Tom, you've got to understand that it was not Don Regan's fault; I cannot make him a scapegoat."[36] To waiting reporters Kean described the president as "a man who desperately wants to get out the facts and get them to the public."[37]

An Exciting Time to Be a Governor

With Washington beset with scandal, partisan bickering, and investigations, political commentators turned their attention to what was transpiring in the states. Writing one month after Kean's reelection, the *Washington Post*'s David Broder remarked on a phenomenon that would come to command considerable attention: "The biggest gap in elective politics these days is not between Republicans and Democrats. It is the gap between state-level officials who are meeting responsibilities and gaining confidence and federal officials who are falling down in their jobs and suffering a loss of self-esteem."[38]

Kean sensed among his colleagues a rising satisfaction in their jobs and a growing faith in their ability to influence events. "I don't think there has ever been a more exciting time to be a governor," he said upon his ascendancy to the chair of the RGA.[39] Governors of both parties showed themselves aware of the opportunities their roles afforded them to exercise power and demonstrate their skills as executives. "A lot of Americans feel more comfortable with activism at the state level than at the federal level and feel it works better," said Arkansas Democratic governor Bill Clinton.[40] *Newsweek* attributed much of the activity and innovation emanating from state capitals to the emergence of a new type of governor: "With Washington mired in the politics of austerity, state governments are boldly reasserting themselves. From job creation to education reform, innovative and exciting ideas are bubbling up from state capitals. Much of the credit goes to a new breed of activist governors who are blurring partisan labels and tangling with entrenched interest groups in an effort to solve problems once left to Washington."[41]

In his study of gubernatorial recruitment, political scientist Larry Sabato detected in the post-Watergate era a trend away from organization politicians and toward candidates who were better educated, more interested in problem solving, and more prone to having an idealistic bent than those in previous eras.[42] By the 1980s, that pattern had clearly taken hold. In *Laboratories of Democracy: A New Breed of Governor Creates Models for National Growth,* David Osborne argued that governors, regardless of their partisan differences, advocated policies that bore a greater resemblance to those advanced by their colleagues in other states than those advocated by the leaders of their respective national parties.[43]

Kean clearly agreed. "Bill Clinton and I have yet to find a subject that we disagree on," Kean told the *Wall Street Journal.*[44] He offered a reason for the bipartisan cooperation that existed among the nation's governors that went beyond the similarities of their respective roles and of the issues they confronted: "Because we don't compete with each other, there is not a reluctance to share things, privately and publicly."[45] The bipartisan spirit that prevailed among them allowed the governors to interject themselves into national policy debates and in ways that prodded members of both parties in Congress in their direction.

Through his increasing seniority among the nation's governors and his rising national profile, Kean occupied a place at the center of a small nucleus of activist governors who pressed their ideas on education and welfare reform on Congress and the Reagan administration and who persuaded their state legislatures to improve teacher training, beef-up service delivery, and retain a business climate attractive to new investment. Such governors justified increased spending on education, the environment, and the arts as investments in their state's future, establishing a link between these quality-of-life issues and job creation. To broaden the reach of their administrations, they forged partnerships with the private sector and with other layers of government. Most were moderate on social issues, cautious on spending, and more pragmatic than ideological in their approach to problems.

Two months after his second inauguration, *Newsweek* profiled Kean, along with Michael Dukakis (D-MA), Lamar Alexander (R-TN), Bill Clinton (D-AK), and Bruce Babbitt (D-AZ) as one among five of the nation's best governors. The magazine picked up on Kean's capacity to defy ideological labels, noting his endorsement of the death penalty, corporate tax cuts, and enterprise zones (positions considered "conservative"); and his support of choice on abortion, affirmative action, and South African divestiture (stances it deemed "liberal"). As if unable to decide whether Kean's advocacy of greater accountability in education was conservative or liberal, the magazine included it among the "Good Government" stands Kean had taken. Karcher told the publication that Kean had become "immensely successful once he adopted the Democratic agenda."[46]

Pointing to their common centrism, Clinton voiced skepticism that either he or Kean could ever be nominated for president. Kean, he said, was considered too liberal to emerge as a serious contender for the Republican presidential nomination. Clinton maintained that he was regarded as too conservative to become the Democrats' standard-bearer.[47] Osborne accurately predicted that, among the "new breed of governors," a Republican of Kean's ilk would encounter greater difficulty winning a presidential nomination than might a Democrat such as Clinton, because of the higher concentration of social conservatives among Republican primary voters, whose pro-life stand ruled out their acceptance of any nominees who were pro-choice on abortion, as were most of the pragmatic problem-solving governors in his study.

Clinton used the centrist Democratic Leadership Council as his vehicle to push the national Democratic Party closer to the center.

Through his denunciation of antiwhite lyrics associated with African American performer Sister Soljah, advocacy of the death penalty, and promise to reduce the deficit, he broadened his and his party's appeal, extending its reach to include moderates (and even some conservatives). No similar structure or organization, replete with mailing lists, publications, and the wherewithal to mount conferences and public programs, existed within the GOP. Nor did Kean create one. He did not follow Clinton's example of recasting, if not his views, parts of his record, to make himself acceptable to important segments within his national party, as he had done within the state GOP when he ran for governor in 1981. Nor did he grab hold of an emerging issue and make it his own, as Kemp and Reagan had both done with tax cuts. Kean's message of inclusion, appealing as it was, was at its core more of a practice or procedure than a program.

Kean used the bully pulpits of his office and his RGA platform to urge governors to exert their collective influence within the national Republican Party. Had Kean decided to run for president or had the party's presidential nominee in 1988 wanted as his running mate a governor with executive experience and a record of solving problems at the state level, Kean might well have made it onto a national ticket. His unwillingness to put his viability to a test and George H. W. Bush's inclination to look elsewhere for a running mate foreclosed that option.

A Belated Endorsement

A year after his trip to New Hampshire, Kean flatly declared that he would not be a candidate for president. He cited the amount of time he or any incumbent governor would have to devote to such as quest as his reason. Asked whether his comments about the governorship and the presidency applied to his friend Michael Dukakis, the governor of Massachusetts, Kean replied, "He's in his third term, has a legislature dominated by his own party, and lieutenant governor that he picked." Reminded that he had not said anything about the vice presidency in his remarks, Kean shot back, "You don't run for vice president." He added that he did not expect to be asked onto a national ticket.[48] The conventional wisdom within and without the state held that Kean's chances of becoming vice president were greatest with anyone other than the presumed front-runner, George H. W. Bush. He and Bush were just too similar in background, the argument went. Both were products of elite preparatory schools and Ivy League universities and members of political families.

As the presidential primary season heated up, Kean cut back on his out-of-state appearances. Between March 1986 and December 1987, he had been to thirty-six locales. "[Kean's] being talked about inside the Beltway, in the capital," said Greg Stevens, Kean's former chief of staff turned political consultant, suggesting that those who would be consulted about various vice presidential contenders were now aware of what Kean might bring to the national ticket.[49] In lieu of intensive travel, Kean published his autobiography, appropriately titled *The Politics of Inclusion.* In it, Kean relayed what he learned from people of different backgrounds in the course of his career and recounted his achievements in several policy areas. His staff made certain that every delegate to the 1988 Republican National Convention received a copy.

To the disappointment of those who actually ran for president in 1988, Kean made no early endorsement. Enjoying the attention the top contenders, George H. W. Bush, Robert Dole, and Jack Kemp, were showing him, Kean said that he enjoyed good relations with all three. He noted that he had known the Bush family ever since his father served in Congress with the vice president's.[50] Kean reminded interrogators that as Gerald Ford's 1976 New Jersey campaign manager, he had worked closely with Dole, Ford's running mate. He declared that he would never forget that Kemp came to New Jersey and campaigned for him in the 1981 primary for governor.[51]

While he took no position on the presidential race at that point, neither did Kean discourage members of his administration, the Republican State Committee, or other elected officials from backing the candidate of their choice.[52] An alternative course might have been for Kean to have endorsed Kemp, who, Kean acknowledged, had "violated one of the first rules of politics" when he supported Kean in the 1981 gubernatorial primary.[53] Bush and Dole, both known to have valued political loyalty, might well have understood Kean's motivations. Through his advocacy of urban enterprise zones, capital formation in minority communities, assistance to minority businesses, and affirmative action, Kemp came closer to practicing Kean's politics of inclusion than any of the other candidates. But an endorsement of Kemp would have entailed backing a decided underdog at a time when Bush was considered the heavy favorite for the nomination. Kean, as Roger Stone later remarked, "thought too much like a conventional politician" to have embarked on such a course.[54]

Having chosen to sit out the early primaries, Kean tried his hand at playing political referee. As the New Jersey primary approached, he voiced frustration to a national reporter that neither Bush nor Dole offered much in the way of ideas. "They both want to be Reagan's heir," Kean complained, "but they forget that Reagan had more than a pleasant television manner." Reagan, he said, "had a clear view of

America and a plan—whether you agreed with it or not—for where he wanted to take it."[55]

One month later, without any discernible increase in the output of ideas from the vice president's camp, Kean came out for Bush. He gave his endorsement two weeks after Bush had finished first in sixteen state primaries on "Super Tuesday," after Kemp had dropped out of the race, and at a time when Dole was said to be reassessing his candidacy. With Kean at his side, Bush said that he would "shamelessly steal" from Kean's example, promising to be both an "environmental" and an "educational president." Kean winced with embarrassment when one county chairman handed Bush a bumper sticker touting a "Bush-Kean" ticket. Kean suggested that Bush put it in his pocket. Bush did as Kean advised, but not before assuring the official that he would take to heart what people had been telling him about Kean.[56]

With his declaration of support for Bush, Kean became a welcome and quite public addition to Bush's team. He was the first to suggest that Bush hold Dukakis to account for the pollution of Boston Harbor,[57] an issue that would be a major one in Bush's campaign. In spite of his expressed enthusiasm for Bush, Kean showed signs of discomfort playing the part of the hatchet man. Increasingly, Bush's campaign relied on New Hampshire governor John Sununu to play that role. "Don't let them soften you up," Sununu told Kean, after observing him and Dukakis exchange compliments at a governors' conference.[58] The strain between Kean's natural proclivities and the demands of Bush's campaign intensified as the campaign wore on.

A Two-Headed Keynote Address

Six weeks before Bush's formal nomination, his campaign announced that Kean would deliver the keynote address at the GOP convention. Behind the scenes, Kean and his team had been quietly negotiating for the opportunity. Most observers, including Kean, took the invitation as a sign that the New Jersey governor would not be Bush's running mate.[59] Kean's selection as keynoter won wide praise. Kemp called Kean an "outstanding leader in our efforts to broaden the base" of the party. Gingrich referred to Kean as a "brilliant, creative governor who has applied conservative values and created a compassionate, fundamentally Republican record."[60]

Social conservatives were not pleased with Bush's selection of Kean. Paul Weyrich, chairman of the Free Congress Foundation, saw Bush's decision to go with a pro-choice opening speaker as an indication that the vice president had forgotten the pro-family component that had propelled the party to victory in 1980 and 1984.[61] New Hampshire senator Gorton Humphrey called it an affront to the right-to-life movement and threatened to organize a walkout during Kean's remarks.[62] Kean responded that he hoped his critics within the party would not "stuff up their ears" when they heard things with which they disagreed.[63]

By his own admission, the address Kean delivered was far from the best speech he ever gave. Circumstances conspired against that happening from the outset. First, Bush's managers moved the key-note address from the first night of the convention to the second, so that President Reagan could symbolically transfer the party's reins to his vice president at the convention's outset. Hours before Kean mounted the rostrum, Bush announced that he had selected as his running mate Indiana senator J. Danforth Quayle. Surprised at Bush's choice, the media scrambled for biographical tidbits about the relatively unknown Quayle. This continued throughout Kean's talk. At least one network cut away from Kean's remarks to ascertain delegate and other reaction to Quayle's selection.

It would not be until he was a quarter of the way through his speech that Kean and the operator of the teleprompter were literally on the same page. At the end of a trial run, Kean had left a draft with Bush's handlers. He continued rewriting portions of his remarks up until the time he spoke. Although he had sent his revised draft to Bush's headquarters earlier in the day, he refused to part with his own copy, arguing that he had difficulty with mechanical things such as teleprompters. When he began to speak, an earlier draft flashed on the screen.

In content, the speech bespoke a tension between the Kean and Bush camps. Away from public view, the two sides had tried to merge two different philosophies into one address. A major area of dis-agreement was how to reconcile Kean's message of inclusion with the strategy that Bush's campaign manager, Lee Atwater, had developed to secure Bush's election. At the center of their dispute was how hard the affable, New Jersey governor should be on Dukakis. As Bush's handlers accelerated their demands, Kean balked. Remembering the advice that New York governor Mario Cuomo, the keynote speaker at the Democratic National Convention four years earlier, had given him, Kean suggested that if Bush aides continued to press language upon him of which he disapproved, they could find someone else to deliver the speech.[64]

While Cuomo's situation with regard to his national party's leadership was not analogous to Kean's (he was both in greater sympathy with the views of his party's national standard-bearers and more willing to engage in personal attacks than was his New Jersey counterpart), the tactic worked—at least to a degree.[65] Asked how he thought Kean would be received, Cuomo said that the delegates would cheer Kean, recognize that he had something special to say, and, hopefully, pay him no heed.[66] As his talks with the Bush team continued, Kean seemed to enjoy playing the part of the mischievous student he once was.

What emerged from the negotiations was a speech that reflected what the *Asbury Park Press* termed a "split personality."[67] Kean later referred to his address as "a two-headed speech."[68] Kean retained enough "red meat" for party activists that the Bush team said the speech needed. These passages, while they resonated well with the crowd inside the hall, disappointed those watching on television who had heard Kean speak in other settings. Kean began holding up an hourglass Michael Dukakis had given him. Intended as a reminder to keep his talk short, the hourglass, Kean said, symbolized that "time had run out on the liberal vision of America."[69]

In an echo of Reagan's 1975 defense of outward displays of patriotism, Kean pointed to the American flag and proclaimed that Democratic media advisers thought its colors did not look good on television. "So they changed red to pink, blue to azure, and the white to eggshell," Kean stated. Americans had no use for "pastel patriotism," he exhorted. As he had said about Jim Florio in 1981 and urged Gerald Ford to say about Jimmy Carter in 1976, Kean suggested that those he now called "Dukakis Democrats" had a secret plan to raise taxes. "What does the name Dukakis sound like to you," he asked. "More taxes," he bellowed.[70] Kean's ridiculing of Dukakis's name proved the portion of the speech that was the most out of character, coming from a speaker who had made inclusion his trademark.

Having fulfilled his partisan obligations, Kean moved on to the body of his text. In his most memorable line, he said, "We will never turn our backs on the refusenik in the Soviet Union, the black student in South Africa, or the brave freedom fighter in Nicaragua."[71] While aid to the contras had been a favored Reagan cause and all Republicans wanted freedom for Soviet Jews, ending apartheid had not placed high among the national administration's priorities. Through his reference to the South African student protester, Kean echoed Reagan's stated opposition to apartheid without making mention specifically of divestiture, which Reagan opposed. Kean's insertion of his own priorities showed up elsewhere in his speech, where he added poor schools and polluted oceans to a list of maladies from which George Bush would rid the nation or the world. Kean hailed Bush for being tough on crime, failing schools, and international communism.

As he condemned racism in all its forms, Kean took as his inspiration the keynote address Hubert Humphrey had delivered at the 1948 Democratic National Convention in Philadelphia. Whereas Humphrey had challenged Democrats to "get out of the shadows of states' rights and walk forthrightly into the bright sunshine of human rights," Kean called upon Republicans to drag bigotry and racism "into the sunshine of understanding and make it wither and die."[72] Whereas Humphrey's remarks provoked a walkout by southern delegates, Kean's sparked applause.

For his peroration, Kean selected lyrics from the song "The House I Live In," which he had listened to as a child during World War II. It began with the question "What is America to me?" Among its answers provided in subsequent lines were the "right to speak my mind" and the "air of feeling free." "What the hell is that?" one Bush aide wanted to know.[73] Kean replied that Frank Sinatra had recorded the song in 1944 and had sung it again during the Statue of Liberty centennial celebration in 1986. He did not volunteer that the first rendition he had heard of the song was not Sinatra's but that of African American singer Paul Robeson. Like Robeson, the song's composer, Earl Robinson, had joined the American Communist Party.[74] "Anything Frank Sinatra sang is fine at this convention," Bush's handlers conceded.[75]

After Kean had concluded, party moderates declared his speech a success. Delaware's governor, Michael Castle, compared it to the "Time for Choosing" speech Reagan had delivered on behalf of Barry Goldwater nearly a quarter century earlier. He predicted that Kean's call to inclusion, like Reagan's message of limited government and resistance to Soviet expansion, provided the party with a new creed as well as with a winning formula upon which to build.[76] National party strategists were less certain that Kean's future would be in national politics. One, Eddie Mahe, said that Kean's stands on issues such as abortion and school prayer posed greater barriers to his advancement within the party than his advocacy of the politics of inclusion. He suggested that the way for Kean to exert the kind of leverage he sought to wield within the GOP would be for him to serve in the U.S. Senate.[77] Several times over the next fifteen years, countless others would offer the same suggestion. Kean repeatedly declined their entreaties.

Mahe's observations about Kean and national politics proved prophetic. Few, if any, Republicans opposed Kean's theme of inclusion. Reagan, after all, broadened the GOP's appeal to working-class voters, Catholics, moderate to conservative Democrats, southerners, and evangelical Christians, constituencies hardly associated in the public's mind with the culture of the country club. If Kean sought to do the same with minority voters, and especially African Americans, as Kemp and Gingrich were also seeking to do, most Republicans and conservatives had no objection. What they resisted was abandoning positions on social policies to which minority voters might adhere, but to which northeastern Republicans, such as Kean, did not. Years later, Kemp lamented that Kean never received the recognition he deserved within the party for his willingness to carry its banner into unfamiliar territory and for succeeding. "West of the Mississippi, they wrote him off," Kemp said. He attributed this reaction not to Kean's espousal of inclusion but to his pro-choice views on abortion, his advocacy of gun control, and his opposition to school prayer.[78]

Within the New Jersey political context, Kean's endorsement of pro-business and pro-growth policies, tough stance on crime, advocacy of accountability in education, and success in reforming welfare placed him on the moderate-to-conservative side of the ideological divide. To have replicated his success in New Jersey on the national stage, he would have had to edge out other conservatives whose positions on all these issues were similar to his own, but who were decidedly to his right on the social issues Kemp and Mahe identified. This proved too high a hurdle to scale even for a politician as dexterous as Kean. As Mario Cuomo had foreseen, the national GOP politely welcomed Kean as a guest into its home but refused to turn over to him the deed to its choicest real estate: a spot on its national ticket.

Exit from Electoral Politics

Kean's final opportunity as governor to influence the direction his party would take occurred during the campaign to elect his successor. While attending the 1988 Republican National Convention, Kean suggested that he might endorse a candidate for governor in the upcoming gubernatorial primary. He said that he owed the people of New Jersey his "opinion on who could best succeed" him as the state's chief executive.[79] Yet when the time came for him to choose among several candidates, Kean reverted to his previous pattern and remained neutral. He declared that he found it difficult to choose among several worthy candidates, several of whom ranked among his most ardent supporters.[80] Having shied away from endorsing a single candidate in the primary, Kean appeared in the commercials of several.

With Kean's 1981 Democratic opponent, James Florio, all but certain to prevail over both former assembly Speaker Alan Karcher and Princeton Borough mayor Barbara Sigmund, a contentious contest for the Republican nomination was hardly in Republicans' best interest. Yet Kean did nothing to reduce the number of candidates in the field. ("How can you tell someone not to run?" he asked.) He could have done so by grooming a successor, but such a strategy would have severed alliances, aroused jealousies, and, possibly, broken friend-ships. That was not Kean's way. One of Kean's friends attributed his reluctance to endorse either a presidential candidate early in 1988 or to indicate his choice in the 1989 gubernatorial primary to Kean's aversion to "making people mad at him."[81] Once again, the former upstart had refused to play the role of party boss.

Representative James Courter finished first among the Republi-can pack. Although Kean assisted Courter in the general election, he proved unable to influence some of the candidate's positions or to add a semblance of order to a divided and disoriented campaign.[82] In their debates, both Courter and Florio presented themselves as being closer to Kean's positions on education, the environment, and the arts than they were to each other's. In one debate, Kean's 1981 opponent castigated Courter for voting against measures in Congress that Kean had supported.[83] Florio defeated Courter by 541,384 votes. Elected with him were heavy Democratic majorities in both legisla-tive houses.

Although Kean would remain popular in New Jersey and would continue to exert influence on policy making both in Trenton and in Washington, his efforts to change his party substantially either on the state or on the national level ended the day he left office. As Kean was watching Florio's victory speech on television, his telephone rang at 11:00 p.m. It was Bill Clinton. "This might be as appropriate a time as any," he said, "to tell you that you have been the best governor in the country. All of us are very proud of you."[84]

Within New Jersey, most residents shared that opinion. Weeks before Clinton's call to Kean, the Eagleton Poll reported that 63 per-cent of likely voters rated Kean's performance as excellent or good.[85] In addition to Kean's efforts to improve the quality of education, pro-tect the environment, repair an aging infrastructure, reduce crime and relieve prison overcrowding, and improve the state's overall image, his economic policies exerted a positive and noticeable impact. Beginning in his second year in office and extending almost through his last, New Jersey's economy underwent a steady climb. On Kean's watch, it witnessed a net increase of 629,400 jobs.[86] Even more sig-nificant, the income of its residents, on average, rose even faster than the number of new jobs. This suggested that during Kean's two terms as governor, high-paying jobs replaced lower-paying ones as the state completed its transition from a manufacturing to an information- and service-based economy. During Kean's time in office, New Jer-sey's real gross domestic product (GDP) increased 55.9 percent.[87]

The nation's rose by 32.3 percent. (New York's grew by 38.6 percent and Pennsylvania's by 25.9 percent.)[88] The average annual increase in New Jersey's GDP per capita was 5.15 percent from 1982 to 1989, compared to the nation's 2.65 percent.[89] (New York's grew by 3.89 percent and Pennsylvania's by 2.95 percent.)[90]

It is debatable how much of this growth might have occurred had other hands been at the state's helm during that time. Nevertheless, policies Tom Kean deliberately enacted or discouraged certainly had an effect. While he may have altered both his strategy and tactics from his days as a candidate in 1981 to meet new circumstances, Kean certainly achieved his overall goal in reversing what he considered to be a downward spiral in the economic vitality and quality of life in his state. As New Jersey's chief executive for eight years, Kean did more than merely mark time. He made a major difference in the political and economic landscape of his state.

chapter 21

Citizen Kean

From New Jersey Governor to University President

On February 10, 1989, New Jerseyans awoke to some unusual news. Their governor, Thomas H. Kean, was about to become the tenth president of Drew University, a small liberal arts college of 2,200 students situated in Madison, New Jersey. He would assume his new duties when his term as governor ended in eleven months and he became Citizen Kean.[1] During his years in public service, Kean had had an intermittent association with the university. While in the assembly, he participated in an Earth Day rally with folksinger Pete Seeger on the steps of Drew's administration building.[2] As governor, Kean delivered the Drew commencement address in 1982. Beginning in 1984, he returned each summer he remained in office to participate in the Governor's School for the Sciences he established on the Drew campus. The rapport Kean established with students at the Governor's Schools presaged that which he would exhibit as the university's president. "It's great the way he comes down to a personal level," one student said. "I'm surprised that he would sit and eat in the cafeteria with us," said another.[3]

The announcement of Kean's appointment took much of the political community—in New Jersey and beyond—by surprise. Speculation had been rampant that Kean would be heading to Washington as part of George H. W. Bush's cabinet. Years later, Bush confirmed that Kean indeed had been under consideration.[4] At Drew, many believed that Kean's tenure as its president would be short, ending the instant an opportunity arose for him to return to elective politics.[5]

Fueling such speculation was his refusal to sign an employment contract. This he attributed to his disinclination to stay at Drew one day more than necessary in the event he proved a poor president or found himself unhappy in the post.[6]

Kean would be the first non-Methodist to serve as president of a university that had been founded in 1867 to train Methodist ministers. He would also be the first nonacademic to serve in the post. Drew officials had specific reasons for wanting him. They hoped that the university's next president would be able to raise the institution's visibility as well as its budget. In accepting their offer, Kean stated that his primary interests remained education and teaching. He added that the opportunities to mentor students would be greater for him at a small, liberal arts institution than at a large university. He cited Drew's close proximity to his home among its other attractions.[7] Kean's predecessor, Paul Hardin, called Kean's decision to lead Drew, when he could have easily made his way to a larger, better-known university, a "touch of class."[8] Kean proclaimed that the opportunity at Drew was more exciting than anything the national administration could have offered him in Washington.[9]

In a hall displaying the banner "Drew and You—Perfect Together," Kean responded to the warm welcome with which the campus received him upon the announcement of his appointment with a single word: "Wow."[10] He called the university a jewel and likened it to an acorn that had grown into an oak. He said that his job would be to work with the university community to "nourish that oak, to replenish it, to help it grow even stronger" and to enable people all over the country and the world "to understand just how good a thing you have created here at Drew."[11] He then literally "tied the knot" with his new institution by removing his necktie and replacing it with one bearing the school's colors, Lincoln green and blue. In the eleven months prior to taking up Drew's reins, Kean acquainted himself with the institution he would head, reading reports, showing up at athletic and cultural events, dining with students. He hosted two cocktail parties at the governor's official residence at which he invited members of the Drew community to discuss what he called "issues of interest."[12]

Rather than seek to impose his own views about the direction he believed Drew ought to follow, Kean asked disparate elements on campus to identify "areas in need of improvement."[13] While he agreed with many on campus that Drew was the "best-kept secret in higher education," he looked upon that phrase as more of an apology than a motto. One of his objectives would be to "let the world in" on the university's strengths.[14] Another would be to build pride and raise the confidence of those he sought to lead. "Once people are convinced of their worth," he explained years later, "they come to believe in what they can achieve and do."[15] Just as he had been the state's strongest promoter, he became Drew's most enthusiastic cheerleader. He peppered his speeches and interviews with tidbits about achievements of Drew students and faculty. Before long, "Drew firsts" replaced "New Jersey firsts" in his rhetorical repertoire.

On his last day as governor, Kean characterized his mood as one of both sadness and anticipation. Debby Kean made no attempt to hide her delight at the change in her husband's status from governor to private citizen. "I wanted to have fireworks tonight, but he wouldn't let me," she quipped.[16] He officially began his new duties at Drew February 1, 1990. Awaiting him was a campus in need of a guiding hand. A fire in Mead Hall, Drew's administration building, had destroyed much of its interior, forcing officials to operate out of trailers parked on its front lawn. Kean took up temporary quarters at the president's residence, from which he oversaw the 1836 structure's restoration to its former grandeur.

For the university, Kean set goals that paralleled those he had set for the state during his years as governor: excellence in education, outstanding teaching, global studies, minority outreach, and, of course, appreciation of the arts. A week after his arrival, Kean's new associates got a glimpse of how he intended to achieve them. Before Kean left office, the Amelior Foundation (headed by philanthropist Ray Chambers) presented him, as Drew's next president, with a challenge grant of $1 million. He committed to use the funds to establish scholarships for minority students. At a dinner he hosted February 8, 1990, Kean raised in one night more than the amount of funds necessary to meet Chambers's challenge. During his fifteen years as Drew's president, Kean raised $85 million in capital funds, increased alumni annual giving by 25 percent, and tripled the endowment from $75 million to $225 million.

Kean scheduled what would be his third "inauguration" for April 20, 1990. Former Tennessee governor and then current president of his state's university, Lamar Alexander delivered the keynote address. Former members of Kean's cabinet, state legislators, members of Congress, state supreme court justices, Kean friends from boarding school and college, and scores of relatives swelled the audience to 6,500.[17] Before the ceremony began, Kean injected some levity into the proceedings when he inadvertently put his mortarboard on backward. Noticing his mistake, Kean drew his audience's attention to what he had done and led the assemblage in laughter.[18]

Preceding Kean to the podium, Drew's poet laureate, Robert L. Chapman, professor emeritus of English and editor of *Funk and Wag-*

nall's Standard College Dictionary, The New Dictionary of American Slang, and *Roget's Thesaurus,* treated the gathering to a pun-laden ode he had composed for the occasion. It read in part:

> The question arises: Is Kean also able?
> And we of this dear and forested spot,
> Met to affix the presidential label,
> Respond with a question: Who is, if he is not?
> · · ·
> He is a hale Columbia ABD,
> And learned the graduate student's bag of tricks
> Before he found another cup of tea,
> And deviated into politics.
>
> He governed our state and left it in a state
> Of fitness and of much enhanced repute;
> · · ·
> May he be our pacifier, sugar cane,
> To harmonize all jarring quirks and biases;
> And be our stern physician, to contain
> Administrational elephantiasis.[19]

Not surprisingly to his listeners, Kean took the politics of inclusion and global interdependence as his inaugural themes. In his praise of Drew's academic quality, he issued a challenge to his listeners, reminiscent of those he once heard at St. Mark's: "We say we are selective, and we are. We say we admit only the best, and we do. And we charge an extraordinary amount of money for our services. All this gives us a special obligation to ensure that when we are through, a young man or woman is ready to make his or her contribution to the world."[20] Kean lauded the university's study abroad program. (As its president, he would broaden its reach to Asia, Africa, and Latin America. He also expanded the university's offerings in African, Asian, Islamic, and Russian studies. As if thinking back on his first job, he initiated a semester on Wall Street program.) In his first formal address as Drew's president, as in his State of the State addresses, Kean cited educational excellence and technological advances as the most effective means for the United States to remain competitive in a global economy.[21]

Upon settling into his new post, Kean let it be known that he considered the title of president too stilted. He preferred to be addressed as "Governor," he said, leaving open the possibility that students might refer to him as "Guv."[22] Eventually, they started calling him

"T.K." Whether on foot or by bicycle, he made himself a visible presence on campus, turning up at sports events, in cafeterias, and at student plays, usually unannounced. Each week he would hold an "open hour" at which students could share with him whatever was on their mind. Quickly, Kean took on the persona of someone who extended himself on behalf of students, writing letters of recommendation, passing along leads on summer jobs, sharing confidences.

Once, Kean popped up while a student he knew was defending her honors thesis and began asking questions.[23] Having arranged for a Drew student to attend the 1996 Republican National Convention, he handed his protégé his own floor pass so that the budding politico could mingle with governors, senators, celebrities, and journalists. On another occasion, he officiated at the wedding of two Drew alumni, after obtaining a dispensation from the governor of Massachusetts in order to do so.[24] Kean enjoyed his interaction with students more than any other aspect of his job.[25] His charges sensed that. "No matter what was going on," one observed, "he was there. . . . No matter what you were doing you would see him there smiling. You'd see him there, so proud of his students."[26] "I don't have any friends on other campuses that have the kind of access to their university president that we do at Drew," said another.[27]

Once at Drew, Kean returned to a calling he had put aside when he entered public office: teaching. His course, "Governing an American State," became one of the most popular on campus. Typically, he would invite a guest to join him during the first hour of the weekly seminar. After a short break, after the guest departed, he led the discussion with a group of fifteen students on the assigned topic. As he had at St. Mark's, Kean hosted a dinner for his students upon the conclusion of the last class. Also as he had at St. Mark's, he participated in student activities. When an English teacher went on sabbatical, Kean agreed to serve as faculty coadvisor to That Medieval Thing, a student organization devoted to the Middle Ages. Occasionally, he would appear in costume as part of a human chessboard. He continued in the role of faculty adviser long after the professor returned.

To assist him in running the university, Kean brought with him a handful of veterans from his days in Trenton. Margaret ("Peggi") E. L. Howard, his former deputy chief of staff in Trenton, became his chief of staff at Drew. Michael McKitish, a twenty-year veteran of state government, who had most recently managed New Jersey's General Service Administration, came on board as Drew's vice president for finances. In charge of Drew's security operations, Kean placed Thomas W. Evans, a decorated officer in the New Jersey State Police. Barbara Grove, Kean's personal secretary and aide de camp from his days as a state legislator and at Realty Transfer, took up her old duties in new, and occasionally more relaxed, surroundings. Other old Kean hands would come and go, assisting with speechwriting, scheduling, fund-raising, and correspondence.

Early in Kean's tenure, McKitish discovered that for the preceding two years, Drew's budgets had been out of balance. Once again, Kean used bad news as an opportunity both to correct deficiencies and to plan for a brighter future. Rather than issue pronouncements from above, he granted the entire university community a role in developing and implementing a strategic plan for the university. He challenged each of Drew's three schools (undergraduate, graduate, and seminary) to decide how it would meet the six criteria established by a presidential planning committee.[28] He found ways to recognize and reward outstanding teaching. For example, at each commencement ceremony, he personally presented the President's Award to a faculty member who had distinguished himself or herself both in teaching and in advising students. Professors were free to use half of the ten-thousand-dollar stipend any way they wished, with the remainder spent in ways that benefited the university.

During his second year in office, Kean persuaded university trustees to commit to building a new state-of-the-art athletic facility. Nine months after breaking ground, he announced that two Morris County residents, former U.S. treasury secretary William E. Simon and his wife, Carol, provided the lead gift of $2.5 million to what would be an $11-million project. Opened in 1994, the Simon Forum, a 127,000-square-foot multipurpose facility, became the busiest place on campus. Kean referred to it as Drew's "new town square." In his time as Drew's president, he brought to campus, often to the Simon Forum, a parade of notables, including four American presidents (Ford, Clinton, and G.H.W. and G. W. Bush), former secretary of state Henry Kissinger, First Ladies Barbara Bush and Hillary Clinton, comedian Bill Cosby, actress Olympia Dukakis, historian David McCullough, journalist David Halberstam, and multiple others. On May 24, 1999, and April 17, 2005, Kean held reunions on the Drew campus for those who had served in his state administration. History was made on November 21, 2003, in the Simon Forum, when he convened the fourth public hearing of the National Commission on Terrorist Attacks upon the United States (9–11 Commission) in its gymnasium.

The Simon Forum was the first of several visible changes Kean brought to Drew. He allowed the New Jersey Shakespeare Festival, a privately incorporated nonprofit company that had been in residence at Drew since 1972, to build a new theater. He requested that it comply with several conditions: the walls of the structure that was being replaced would be incorporated into the new facility, the troupe would put on more performances, Drew students would have opportunities to participate in the company, and all the two-hundred-year-old maple and oak trees that surrounded the site would be left undisturbed. (While serving as governor, Kean had nixed a developer's plan to replace a small park next to the statehouse with a parking lot. On the grassy plot stood fifteen trees, one dating back to at least 1812.)[29] The New Jersey State Council on the Arts awarded to the new theater $2.5 million from the cultural bond issue that Kean had established while governor. Presumably at his behest, Drew donated $1 million. The F. M. Kirby Foundation awarded the $7.5-million facility its largest private-sector gift of $1.5 million.

Kean's legacy to Drew also included a new arts center. After Dorothy Young, a onetime Broadway celebrity who had became a painter, donated $12.5 million for a new facility for classrooms, studios, and a black-box theater, Kean and McKitish obtained an additional $5 million from the New Jersey Economic and Development Authority for a wing for musical performances. On Kean's seventieth birthday, April 21, 2005, the New Jersey Symphony officiated at the gala that marked the official opening of the new hall. When he arrived on campus in 1990, Kean said that he prayed that he might honor the memory of those who had come before him by "leading Drew to its brightest days."[30] When he stepped down as its president in 2005, universal opinion was that he had.

Extracurricular Activities

If Drew provided Kean with opportunities to return to teaching and education, the nature of the position he occupied allowed him time to remain active in public affairs, write a newspaper column, and serve on boards of directors of corporations, charities, foundations, and nonprofit organizations.[31] Just three weeks into his presidency of Drew, Kean, upon the invitation of President George H. W. Bush, headed the American delegation to the World Conference on Education for All in Jomtiem, Thailand. Under the auspices of UNESCO, the conference would eventually set a ten-year goal of universal primary education. As a member of the Basic Education Coalition, Kean lobbied Congress to target more foreign assistance to primary education. George H. W. Bush also tapped him to serve on the Points of Light Foundation, a public-private–sector partnership that recruited volunteers to help ameliorate social ills. He also designated Kean chairman of the President's New American Schools Development Corps, a privately funded concern charged with improving American students' performance.[32] During the elder Bush's time in office, the National Endowment for Democracy, a nonprofit entity established during the Reagan administration to support democratic movements around the world, elected Kean to its board.

In 1994, President Bill Clinton named Kean to a bipartisan commission on entitlement and tax reform. Headed by U.S. senators Bob Kerrey (D-NE) and John Danforth (R-MO), the group was tasked with assessing proposed alternatives to the tax structure and exploring ways to assure the solvency of entitlement programs such as Social Security and Medicare. In accepting his assignment, Kean suggested that the path to keeping these latter two programs solvent could be found either through one of four avenues or through a combination of them: (1) raising the retirement age, (2) taxing Social Security benefits like other income, (3) means testing, and (4) spending caps.[33] After the commission failed to achieve a consensus, Kean complained that its public hearings attracted only those with vested interests in then-prevailing practices.[34]

In spring 1995, at the invitation of President Bill Clinton, Kean journeyed to China as the vice chairman of the U.S. delegation to the Fourth United Nations Conference on Women. Kean joked about his minority status as one of the few males at the conclave and one of only two men in an American delegation that included First Lady Hillary Clinton, United Nations ambassador Madeleine Albright, and Health and Human Services secretary Donna Shalala. Afterward, he reassured conservatives that he had not succumbed to some radical feminist cabal. The women he had met, he assured them, only wanted what most men already had.[35]

The conference occurred at a time when relations between the United States and China were particularly strained because of an increase in the host nation's violations of human rights. Some commentators noted the irony of a conference on women's issues taking place in a country that practiced forced abortion. Attempting to minimize participants' contacts with Chinese nationals and the media, the Chinese government had the proceedings take place in Huairou, thirty-five miles outside Beijing. Expecting the press to show particular interest in a speech First Lady Hillary Clinton was scheduled to deliver in which she was expected to criticize the host country's human rights policies, Chinese officials tried to restrict media access. As the American delegation made its way into the hall to hear the first lady, Kean fended off Chinese security guards, who had tried to block NBC News correspondent Andrea Mitchell from gaining entry.[36] Kean returned home hopeful that the conference had directed world attention to the disparities in education between the sexes, officially sanctioned discrimination, and violence against women.[37]

After leaving public office, Kean continued his association with the Carnegie Corporation, serving on its board from 1991 to 1997 and as its chairman form 1997 to 2002. He rejoined the board in 2005. In his association with Carnegie, he continued his work to establish national standards for teacher certification, improve teacher training, and research early child development and a host of other challenges facing young children, adolescents, and women. Kean's enthusiasm for these subjects became evident both to his colleagues and to journalists covering his and Carnegie's activities.[38] Kean's Carnegie associates remembered him for his capacity to find consensus, his fair-mindedness, his eagerness to interact with staff as equals, his knowledge of the subject matter, and his readiness to break with established patterns and policies.[39]

At the request of Dr. David Hamburg, Carnegie's president, Kean agreed in 1996 to serve as the founding president of the National Campaign to Prevent Teen Pregnancy. Funded through private donations, the "campaign" traced the impetus for its founding to a challenge President Bill Clinton had issued in his 1995 State of the Union address for citizens to "join together in a national campaign against teen pregnancy." Kean agreed to serve as chair for only six months. He would remain in the post for more than a decade, never missing a meeting. He attributed his long tenure both to the organization's mission and to the entrepreneurial spirit of its founders, economist Isabel Sawhill and researcher Sarah Brown.

Kean advised the organization to keep itself from becoming embroiled in the abortion debate. That, he said, would tag it in the public's mind as a preserve "of the left."[40] He suggested that it forge a broad consensus around the need to reduce the number of teen pregnancies and not allow itself to become sidetracked into debating the best means. At a time when liberals favored improved and expanded sex education and easier access to contraception, and conservatives stressed abstinence, Sawhill and Brown worked with organizations attempting both approaches.[41] Kean liked that. At his urging, the campaign made a conscientious effort to reach out to Republicans and conservatives and invite them to join its board of directors.

"Only at a group such as ours," Brown said, "would you find a Catholic nun sitting next to the vice president of Planned Parenthood, flanked on either side by an officer from the Urban League and an official from MTV."[42] Such a setting was tailor-made for Tom Kean. Between 1995 and 2001, he devoted seven of his newspaper columns to the problem of teen pregnancy and to the solutions the campaign recommended. By 2004, the organization was on the verge of achieving its ten-year goal of reducing the number of teen pregnancies by one-third.[43] Pleased with the results, Kean took the news more as mixed than as good. "Yes, teen pregnancy is down," he would say, "but it is still higher than any place else in the industrialized world. We have quite a way still to go."[44]

Kean was forced to cut back temporarily on both his official and his extracurricular activities late in 1995. After complaining of chest pains, he was rushed to Morristown Memorial Hospital, where doctors performed an angioplasty to clear a clogged artery. Even before the ambulance carrying New Jersey's most famous patient reached the hospital, news of his illness traveled across the country and around the world. Briefing reporters on Kean's condition, attending physician William Tansey said that the "only people who can have a future worry are those who play tennis with him." Asked about Kean's spirits, Tansey explained that Kean had told his examiners that he thought he had indigestion, "that grin" flashing widely across his face.[45]

Shortly after his surgery, the hospital staff suggested that Kean, in spite their decree that he take no telephone calls, might want to take just one. Bill Clinton was on the line. Clinton inquired about Kean's condition. As the conversation progressed, the president, then in the midst of budgetary negotiations with the Republican Congress, sought Kean's advice. "What do you know about this fellow [House of Representatives Speaker] Newt Gingrich?" Clinton inquired.[46] Kean, not long out of surgery, feeling exhausted, beads of sweat pouring from his forehead, began to doze. Upon Kean's release from the hospital seven days later, Clinton called him a second time.[47] This time, both parties remained awake and conversant.

The President's Initiative on Race

In a commencement address at the University of California at San Diego, June 14, 1997, President Bill Clinton declared that he would lead the American people in a "great and unprecedented conversation about race." He envisioned this dialogue being part of the "Bridge to the Twenty-first Century" theme he had advanced in his reelection campaign of the previous year.[48] To advise him on policies he might pursue in order to reduce racial divides, Clinton named a seven-member panel. Its members included Kean, the historian John Hope Franklin (chair), attorney Angela E. Oh (vice chair), former Mississippi governor William F. Winter, AFL-CIO executive vice president Linda Chavez-Thompson, pastor Suzan Johnson Cook, and Nissan Motor Corporation chief executive Robert Thomas. The president gave the group fifteen months to report back to him.[49] In his speech, Clinton asked a couple of questions he hoped the entire nation would contemplate as the panel conducted its work: "Can we be an America respecting, even celebrating, our differences, but embracing even more what we have in common? Can we define what it means to be an American, not just in terms of the hyphen showing our ethnic origins, but in terms of our primary allegiances to the values America stands for and the values we really live by?" Answering his own questions, the president said, "Our hearts long to answer 'yes,' but our history reminds us that it will be hard."[50]

Kean joined the panel hopeful that Clinton's initiative would exert a lasting and a positive impact.[51] He saw a parallel between what Clinton hoped would take place across the country and the daylong "Dialogue on Diversity" in which he had participated at Drew.[52] His optimism began to wane after the panel held its first public session. When Oh suggested that the panel go beyond the "black-white paradigm" to include other groups, such as new immigrants from Asia and Latin America, Franklin replied that the United States "cut its eyeteeth on racism with black-white relations."[53] Sensing that the media would focus on the divergence of opinion between the chairman and the vice chairwoman, Kean tried to bridge their differences to achieve a consensus. Suggesting that some on the "far right" and on the "far left" would just as soon see the president's initiative fail, he urged the group to embrace a common theme. He also urged that it reach out to "a number of thoughtful Republicans."[54]

Drawing upon a *Washington Post* story, which omitted the words *far left* from Kean's admonition to his colleagues, the *Weekly Standard* interpreted Kean's reference to the "far right" and to "thoughtful Republicans" as evidence that he shared the view of many liberals and Democrats that most of his fellow partisans were racists, with himself and a handful of moderates the exceptions.[55] The magazine subsequently published a "letter to the editor" from Kean, noting that its author included most elected Republican officials under the "thoughtful" rubric. This misinterpretation of Kean's comments aside, many conservatives, disagreeing with Clinton that race was a problem of concern to most Americans decades after passage of monumental civil rights legislation, remained critical of the commission. For the conversation Clinton commenced to be meaningful, they argued, it had to consider the merits and effectiveness of affirmative action, school vouchers, and crime and drug prevention programs. Clinton, in previous statements ("mend it, don't end it") and actions, had taken at least affirmative action off the table.

Seeking to avoid a repeat of what had ensued at the panel's first meeting, White House aides set the agendas for its future public sessions. Rather than allow panelists to debate issues, they scheduled formal presentations by speakers.[56] Kean made no secret of his dis-

dain for this format: "We [were] placed on an elevated platform looking out at the audience. . . . The rest of the day was spent listening
to various professors expand on their surveys and theories. Some of
it was unusual, some of it was obvious, and some of it was a waste of
time."[57] Kean considered the manner in which it operated a barrier
to the panel's effectiveness. "Every time we meet," he said, "we find
ourselves sitting around facing each other with an audience of 500
and the cameras of CNN."[58] He reported that presidential advisers
had informed him that if the panel met in private or any of its members discussed its business with one or more colleagues, they would
be in violation of the Federal Advisory Committee Act. As a consequence, Kean and other panel members never had the opportunity to
get to know one another well enough as colleagues to be able to conduct among themselves the kind of dialogue that Clinton wanted the
entire nation to undertake.

In his first public appearance before the panel, Clinton lent voice
to what Oh had said at its first session. After Kean stated that the
United States was unique in its ethnic and racial makeup and noted
that 125 languages were spoken in Jersey City, the president recommended that the panel visit Fairfax County, Virginia, where a similar
phenomenon was much in evidence.[59] It followed his suggestion.
Upon learning that the White House failed to invite Congressman
Tom Davis (R-VA), who represented the area in which the session
would be held, Kean raised the omission with the White House. The
administration countered by inviting both Davis and Virginia Democratic senator Charles Robb to participate in "break-out" sessions over
lunch. On the list of presenters, it included former education secretary Bill Bennett, still a fan of Kean's, and Arizona state superintendent of schools Lisa Graham, a pioneer in the "charter schools"
movement. Kean expressed pleasure that people on the program had
not offered additional excuses for why children could not learn. He
praised Fairfax County for the quality of education it provided to children of diverse backgrounds.[60]

Kean urged that the panel hear from prominent conservatives,
especially black conservatives. Franklin maintained that he was not
certain what Ward Connerly, a prominent foe of affirmative action,
could contribute to the discussion.[61] With conservative criticism of the
president's race initiative on the rise after the panel held a closed-
door meeting in Texas with an audience that consisted exclusively of
African Americans, Clinton invited a delegation of prominent conservatives to the White House.[62] Kean was the only member of the president's race panel to attend. (Franklin stated afterward that he stayed
away because he "knew their [the conservatives'] line.")[63] Clinton partisans interpreted Ward Connerly's comment that "Clinton understood

race like no other president, living or dead" as a public relations victory for the president.[64]

Kean and several of the panel's critics considered its final report too timid. Its most prominent recommendation was that a permanent entity within the government be created to continue the dialogue on race. It urged that affirmative action be continued, government keep the public informed about racial issues, and that leaders of business, government, and youth leaders "make racial reconciliation a reality."[65] Kean lamented that the administration discouraged the panel from advocating bolder measures.[66] He suggested that senior officials, responsible for policy development, had not invested the time or resources necessary for the panel to be more productive. Judith A. Winston, general counsel for the U.S. Department of Education, who acted as its staff director, agreed with that assessment. Most of Clinton's senior advisers, she said, considered the panel nothing but a lose-lose situation.[67]

Within the White House, divisions arose between liberals and centrists over whether Clinton should propose new policy initiatives and, if so, what they should be. As they debated, those assigned to monitor the panel took pains to ensure that, unlike the Kerner Commission of the 1960s, it not "get too far ahead of the president."[68] One Clinton adviser described Kean's comportment amid such an atmosphere as that of someone "who knew so well how things could have been done better, but who carried himself with grace."[69] Whatever contributions Kean made to the final report he rendered in private conversations with White House aides or with Clinton. Much of what he recommended, including his hope that Clinton would address Congress on the subject of race, either did not make its way into the final report or was not acted upon.

Given that, on the very day the panel's report was due, independent counsel Kenneth Starr presented his findings of his investigation of the president to Congress, the race panel's suggestions, modest though they were, received little attention.

Out of Politics, But Nevertheless In

As his colleagues at Drew suspected, Kean did not entirely abandon politics after he took on his new responsibilities as its president. In 1990, his first year at Drew, Kean served as an unofficial adviser to Christine Todd Whitman when she challenged incumbent U.S. senator Bill Bradley for reelection. In 1992, Kean chaired President George H. W. Bush's reelection effort in New Jersey. With Bush under assault from conservative commentator Pat Buchanan in the primary, Kean lauded the president's record on education and foreign affairs. Revealing that he had not lost the capacity to play the partisan when called upon, Kean predicted that the Democrats' return to power would mean a disarmed America, a return to gas lines (of the Carter era), and a rise of interest rates back to double digits.[70] Kean angered his fellow moderates at the Republican National Convention when, in response to a direct appeal from Bush, he discouraged members of his delegation from joining in an effort to spark a floor fight over language in the platform that committed the party to the right-to-life position on abortion.

During the fall election, Kean astonished more New Jersey Republicans when he granted permission to Democratic presidential nominee Bill Clinton to hold a rally at Drew. Clinton was scheduled to attend two fund-raisers in the vicinity. Desiring a more public venue, a Clinton aide telephoned Kean to request permission for the candidate to appear at Drew. The staffer said that the campus was in close proximity to both fund-raising events as well as to Morristown airport, where Clinton would be arriving. Kean said it would be an honor for his campus to host any major party candidate for president.[71] Kean did not attend the event. After proclaiming himself delighted that Drew would be receiving Clinton, he departed for Newark to introduce Bush at a labor rally. Kean left behind a letter to be read at the Drew event in which he welcomed his "friend" Clinton to the university and invited him back.[72]

Kean's hand could be seen in Bush's remarks. As had Gerald Ford twelve years earlier, Bush tried to establish a connection in voters' minds between a Democratic presidential candidate and a Democratic governor who had raised taxes, this time Florio.[73] To reporters afterward, Kean further ruffled some Republican feathers when he proclaimed the presidential election a contest between "two decent people."[74] Years later, Clinton recalled that Kean's granting the Democrat permission to speak at Drew was the second favor Kean had rendered the Arkansan that year. Months earlier, when partisan attacks upon Clinton were at their fiercest, Kean told the press that "both parties nominated their best candidate." "He did not have to do that," Clinton said.[75] The day before the election, Kean was back at Bush's side when the president scheduled a last-minute appearance at Madison's town hall.

Kean's politicking in 1992 drew some rare criticism from the university's newspaper. "We have no delusions about Kean giving up his political life for that of a university administrator," it opined, "but we would like to think that during his tenure here, however brief, Kean would act more like a president and less like a governor."[76] "You can't expect someone to become a political eunuch just because he's president of a university," Kean replied. "You've got to take on controversy from time to time. You've got to do things that people disagree with."[77] Kean would appear with presidential contender Bob Dole at an event in Morristown in 1996, again serve as an adviser to Whitman in 1997, and allow George W. Bush to stage a rally at Drew in his only stop in New Jersey in 2000.[78]

After Bret Schundler emerged as the victor of a highly contested gubernatorial primary in 2001, Kean, who had endorsed Schundler's opponent, Representative Robert A. Franks, became honorary chairman of Schundler's campaign. He served in similar capacities for other candidates in subsequent statewide GOP campaigns. In addition to Franks, Kean broke his own rule against primary endorsements when he openly supported Morris County state senator Bob Martin against a conservative challenger. While professing his neutrality in the 2005 Republican gubernatorial primary, Kean wrote a three-thousand-dollar check to the campaign of Todd Caliguire, who had served as an assistant counsel when Kean was governor. Increasingly, Kean invested more of his time and energies advising and assisting his favorite candidate, Thomas H. Kean Jr., in his unsuccessful race for Congress and subsequent winning campaigns for the assembly and state senate.

In his years out of office, Kean frequently commented on state issues. He made no secret of his disdain for Florio's tax policies, urged caution when Governor Christine Todd Whitman abolished the Department of Higher Education, and praised Whitman's environmental policies. After Kean spoke in support of Governor James McGreevey's proposal to merge Rutgers University and the University of Medicine and Dentistry into one institution, McGreevey hinted that he intended to make Kean the new entity's first chancellor.[79]

Often, Kean would exert his influence through carefully timed comments to reporters. Gun control proved a case in point. Early in his term, Governor James Florio pushed through a Democratic legislature a bill that banned the sale and possession of semiautomatic assault weapons. After the Republicans captured control of the legislature in 1991, feeling pressure from the National Rifle Association, its leaders sought to repeal the legislation. Kean, while being interviewed on another subject, said that he didn't know "what lawful purpose could be [served] in owning an assault weapon." His remark proved sufficient to stiffen the resolve of some Republicans who were reluctant to override Florio's veto of an NRA-endorsed measure. "To have a leader of my party do that, it took off the heat," said one.[80]

In his newspaper columns for the *Bergen Record,* Kean followed an approach he had displayed in the *Saint Marker* decades earlier. Whether his topic was the decline of civility in public life, teenage pregnancy, or court decisions regarding state expenditures on education, he would often take a position that drew upon ideas and sentiments across the political spectrum. Typical of his approach was his account of what he experienced when he traveled to Iowa in 1994 to urge the politics of inclusion upon a Republican gathering. Observers estimated that self-identified members of the Christian right comprised about a third of his audience of 1,700. Kean recorded that he had gone to the meeting expecting to face a band of zealots. Instead, he recorded, he encountered "decent, everyday people" who cared about the political process and wanted to use it to effect change. He then recited areas in which moderates such as himself and members of the Christian Coalition could find common ground. All within the party, he said, wanted to lower the number of teen pregnancies, abortions, AIDS and drug abuse cases, violent crime, and failing schools and wanted to lower taxes, reduce regulation, and extend personal responsibility.[81]

The *Wall Street Journal* wrote afterward that Kean's depiction of his listeners "scarcely fit" the media's description of them.[82] It noted too that Kean had been expected to denounce the religious right's influence within the party. That Kean ventured into Iowa, the state that held the first presidential selection caucuses, suggested that at least until 1994, he had not abandoned thoughts that he might be able to straddle the ideological divide just enough to make his way onto a national ticket. "I always thought that if I ran for president, I could be competitive," Kean said years later.[83] While his praise of religious conservatives won Kean increased respect within some quarters, it did little to bring him closer to the center of gravity within the national GOP. His Iowa trip marked his last endeavor either to move the national party in his direction or to accommodate himself, in part, to that in which it was headed. He would confine whatever ambition for elective office he still harbored to the confines of New Jersey. On four occasions, Kean gave some weight to suggestions that he seek to further his vision for the country by running for the U.S. Senate.

Not to Be a Senator

Arguing that a race against U.S. senator Frank Lautenberg in the 1994 election would come too soon after he had taken on new responsibilities at Drew, Kean declined to run for the U.S. Senate that year. Assembly Speaker Chuck Haytaian lost to incumbent Frank Lautenberg by 60,000 votes in a year when the GOP regained control of Congress for the first time in forty years. Republicans picked up nine seats in the Senate and fifty-four in the House.

Kean passed up a second opportunity to run for the U.S. Senate in 1996, when incumbent Bill Bradley, after serving three terms, did not seek reelection. In a newspaper column published two weeks after Bradley announced his intentions, Kean publicly pondered the pros and cons of seeking Bradley's seat. He suggested that his moderate views placed him outside the prevailing opinion within much of the congressional wing of the national Republican Party. He questioned whether the stands he had taken on education, the environment, and urban affairs would cause party leaders to place him on a committee on which he could achieve little on these issues. He wrote that he did not want to be marginalized.[84] Kean also expressed distaste for the strident partisanship that characterized much of Washington with a Republican Congress and a Democratic president engaged in constant battle. "It's so mean spirited down there," he wrote, "that it makes it difficult to sit down and find compromises to get things done for the public, to bring people together."[85]

Kean's protestations read like those of a man trying to rationalize a decision he had already made, but not exclusively for the reasons he cited. Yes, on the environment, Kean favored a more interventionist approach than did most of the congressional leadership. On education, urban affairs, and taxes, however, his views were closer in line with theirs than he admitted. No lesser lights than Ronald Reagan, Newt Gingrich, Bill Bennett, and Jack Kemp had all praised Kean for work in these areas. As a U.S. senator, elected in either 1994 or 1996, Kean, given the cordial relations he enjoyed with both "New Democrat" Bill Clinton and "Opportunity Conservative" House Speaker Newt Gingrich, would have been perfectly poised to evoke the "third way" strategy that had served him so well in the past. He, along with like-minded senators of both parties, might have served as a bridge between the executive and legislative branches, thereby lessening the partisan divide he so abhorred. Clearly, Kean had reasons for not running for senator. Not all of them related to his stand on issues.

That he was reluctant to leave Drew, where he enjoyed his work with students, was beyond question. He also enjoyed the variety of activities his life as a college president allowed him to pursue, such as serving on corporate boards, nonprofit organizations, think tanks, and charitable institutions. "I found what I was doing satisfying," he said, "and I was not sure that I wanted to be one of a hundred [senators]."[86] Kean's wife's aversion to his reentering public life was well known. Less widely reported was Governor Christine Todd Whitman's opposition to Kean's running. In their discussions, Whitman made clear her preference for Representative Richard A. Zimmer as the Republican nominee for the U.S. Senate. Had he been intent on running, Kean, savvy politician that he was, would have found a way around each of these perceived obstacles.

Speculation arose anew that Kean would reenter the political fray in 2000 with the retirement of U.S. senator Frank Lautenberg and the unexpected withdrawal of Whitman, still the incumbent governor, from the race to succeed him. As in 1996, leading national Republicans pressed Kean to run. Polls showed him commanding an easy lead. That Kean took more time to make up his mind than he had on prior occasions fueled suspicions that he leaned toward running. So had comments he had made such as, "I've been through all this before, but the circumstances are so unusual this time and so totally unexpected, I've got to give it some serious consideration."[87] Such comments as these suggested that he had come to believe that he might actually be able to make a difference in Washington, missed the political arena, and recognized that this might be his last chance at the job. "This was probably the most difficult decision I ever made in my life," he said after he again declined to run. He added that the decision had been all the more difficult for him to make because he had "definitely wanted to be a Senator."[88] This was the first time he had made such an admission. Again, conventional wisdom held that Debby Kean opposed his running, an impression Kean did little to correct. "That's a big part of it," he said. "I have always put family first."[89]

Kean's latest refusal did not bring an end to what one reporter termed the New Jersey ritual of "getting Kean to run for the U.S. Senate."[90] Two years later, with incumbent Robert Torricelli plagued by a series of alleged ethical violations, speculation arose that Kean might declare for the seat. As he showed signs of demurring once again, one observer concluded that the former governor preferred "agonizing about possible races to actually running for office."[91] After each of his declinations to run, word would spread that Kean might accept an appointment to the cabinet. Both Presidents George H. W. Bush and Bill Clinton confirmed that they seriously considered asking him to serve in such a capacity.[92] Weeks after his first election as president, Clinton stated that he had offered a cabinet position to "one Republican who could not do it." A Clinton aide stated—and Kean denied—that the president-elect had been referring to the former New Jersey governor who was then president of Drew.[93]

Four years later, with Clinton said to be leaning toward naming at least one prominent Republican to his cabinet, Kean's name surfaced again. "I hadn't really thought very much about the second Clinton Administration," he wrote, "until the media decided I was in it."[94] Cordial though his relations with several presidents were, Kean, once in the cabinet, would have been a subordinate. Like those who headed departments in the "outer cabinet" (those other than State, Defense, Treasury, and Justice), he would have interacted on a daily basis more with White House aides than with the president. Having occupied for eight years one of the strongest governorships in the country, he would not have taken easily to instructions from staffers years, if not decades, his junior.

By Kean's own choice, he would remain in public life but on his own terms, speaking out on issues however and whenever he chose, accepting part-time and nonsalaried posts he considered to be in the national interest. He would also continue consulting with presidents, but as an equal. Otherwise, he would continue in the now familiar, comfortable routine he had set for himself. It would take a national tragedy to propel him into the post in which he would render his most valuable service to his country.

chapter 22

Chairing the 9–11 Commission

An Ordinary Day

September 11, 2001, started out as an ordinary day for Tom Kean. Sometime after 9:00 a.m., he telephoned his dentist to check on an appointment. The doctor told him to turn on the television. A commercial jet had flown into one of the towers of the World Trade Center. After another plane hit the second tower a few minutes later, the world discovered that this was no accident. It was the work of terrorists. A third plane would smash into the Pentagon, while a fourth, diverted from its target by the actions of its brave passengers, crashed onto a field in Shanksville, Pennsylvania.

Kean immediately drove to Drew. He asked his staff to send runners to each of the dormitories, instructing students to meet him in the auditorium of the Simon Forum, where he would speak to them. There, joined by more than twelve hundred students, he presided over a makeshift service. "It is a time to reflect," he told the gathering. "It is a time to comfort each other. It is a time to pray. It is a time to go on as a community and as a nation."[1] "We talked, we prayed and we sang," he said afterward, "but mostly we talked."[2]

Like many New Jersey residents, Kean knew several people who died in the attacks of September 11. He had been especially close to some. Among the passengers on Flight 93, the plane that crashed in Shanksville, Pennsylvania, was Don Peterson, a friend with whom Kean had played tennis nearly every Saturday for more than thirty years. Another friend, John Hartz, died at the World Trade Center. Kean knew the World Trade Center well. The structure had been built while he was serving in the state assembly. The Port Authority of New York and New Jersey maintained its headquarters there. Kean was personally acquainted with Neil Levin, its executive director, and with several other of the bi-state agency's personnel who died in the latest assault upon the twin towers.

Kean served on the board of Aramark, which managed the food court on top of 2 World Trade Center and several concessions in the building. He was also a director of Fiduciary Trust Company, which was based at the World Trade Center. Eighty-seven of its employees died in the attacks of September 11. On October 16, 2001, Kean delivered one of their eulogies at a special service at the Cathedral of St. John the Divine, Ralph Adam Cram's architectural masterpiece on Amsterdam Avenue. "September 11 stands alone in its horror," he told an assemblage that included an abundance of children and pregnant women. "We don't know what kind of world will emerge from its ashes," he went on to say. "But we know it will be a poorer place because it lacks our husbands, and our wives, and our sons, and our daughters, and our colleagues and our friends." "And yet," he continued, "even now, we dare to hope, to rebuild to go on." His thoughts still on the deceased, he quoted a favorite passage from J. M. Barrie, author of *Peter Pan:* "God gave us memory that we might have roses in December."[3] He would attend several other commemorations in less magnificent settings over the next several months. Little did he suspect, as he joined in the sense of loss that had fallen over much of the nation, that he would play a major role in piecing together the puzzle of how nineteen young and angry fanatics, more interested in fomenting destruction than with the preservation of their own lives, managed to circumvent all the defenses the strongest nation on Earth had assembled in the previous sixty years.

A Call from the White House

On Saturday evening, December 15, 2002, Kean received a telephone call from Karl Rove, President George W. Bush's principal political adviser. Rove told Kean that he was one of the individuals the president was considering appointing chairman of a commission that would investigate the attacks of September 11 and recommend ways to prevent such tragedies in the future. Rove wanted to know whether Kean would decline the post in the event the president wished to appoint him.

The White House was in a quandary. Former secretary of state Henry Kissinger, whom Bush had named chairman of the commission weeks earlier, had resigned the previous day, two days after its vice chairman, former Democratic senate majority leader George Mitchell, had done the same. Both had cited as their reason potential conflicts of interest between their work with the commission and their business dealings. Mitchell mentioned the possibility of having to sever ties to his law firm. Kissinger did not wish to divulge the names of clients his consulting firm advised, as congressionally imposed financial disclosure requirements mandated.

Bush's selection of Kissinger had aroused controversy even before the former secretary of state had declined to divulge his client list. The *New York Times* questioned in an editorial whether, knowing Kissinger's penchant for secrecy, the administration, in naming the former official, sought to "contain an investigation it long opposed."[4] White House lawyers argued that as a presidential appointee to a legislatively established commission, Kissinger did not have to meet the same disclosure requirements as the other members. A Congressional Research Service report concluded otherwise, and the commission's new vice chairman, Lee Hamilton, released a statement saying that all five Democratic members supported disclosure and would comply fully with congressional requirements.[5] Kissinger withdrew two days prior to the deadline the statute set for all commissioners to be in place.

The Kissinger controversies were the latest in a series that surrounded the yet-to-be-fully-constituted commission. In the aftermath of the September 11 attacks, victims' families began pressing for an independent investigation into all elements of the tragedy. In December 2001, Senators John McCain (R-AZ) and Joseph Lieberman (D-CT) introduced a bill to create a commission to do so. Bush opposed the idea on the grounds that such an inquiry would divert attention from the war on terrorism. The congressional Republican leadership took the same view. Stating that he did not wish to make things easier for Osama bin Laden (the Saudi-born mastermind of the attacks), House majority leader Tom DeLay (R-TX) said that to establish a commission during times of war was "ill-conceived and irresponsible"; Senate majority leader Trent Lott (R-MS) opined that a commission would serve no immediate good purpose.[6]

Revelations before a joint investigation by the House and Senate of intelligence conducted after September 11, 2001, touched on repeated failures of the CIA, FBI, and other agencies to share information prior to the attacks on what they knew about al Qaeda (bin Laden's terrorist army scattered across the world), bin Laden's intentions to harm Americans, and the activities and whereabouts of the nineteen hijackers. The press reported that Bush was briefed in a memorandum on August 6, 2002, that bin Laden planned to strike the United States and that he might seek to hijack airplanes.[7] Conflicting reports of what that document contained, coupled with the administration's reluctance to make it public, fueled demands both in Congress and among victims' families that an independent investigation be undertaken to find out what the government had known in advance of the attacks and what actions it had taken to prevent them.

To the surprise of the House Republican majority leadership, Representative Tim Roemer (D-IN), with support from twenty-five Republicans, steered through the House on July 25, 2002, an amendment to the 2003 Intelligence Authorization Bill establishing such a commission. It passed 219–188. In late September, the administration, reversing its position, agreed to the creation of a ten-member bipartisan panel that would investigate the September 11 attacks.[8] Four days later, the Senate—where the Democrats enjoyed a majority of one, as a result of the defection of Vermonter Jim Jeffords from the GOP fold—in a vote of 90 to 8, accepted an amendment to the Homeland Security Bill providing for an independent commission.[9]

With the two houses nearing agreement on the commission's mission, powers, and duration, the White House voiced objections to the manner in which it would operate.[10] Stephen Push, cofounder of Families of September 11, told the Associated Press that the administration had been doing everything it could to block the creation of the commission since day one.[11] With the administration's hand strengthened after the 2002 elections, with the Republicans picking up two seats in the Senate, which restored their majority status, and six in the House, Bush's team hinted that the president might create a commission by executive order if Congress did not meet his objections. It acceded to his demands, raising the number of votes necessary to issue subpoenas from five to six, shortening the commission's life from two years to eighteen months, and granting the president the right to designate its chairman.[12] Congressional leaders of both parties in each house would name eight of the other members, with House and Senate leaders of the party opposite to the president's selecting the vice chairman. By informal agreement, John McCain was allocated one of the Senate appointments.

Kean told Rove he would not decline the post outright, but that he wanted to think about it.[13] Among the things he wanted to weigh was how good a job he might do, given the history and controversies that surrounded the commission's creation, the fifty-fifty partisan split in its composition, and the manner in which its members had been appointed. The following day, White House chief of staff Andrew Card followed up on Rove's call. He told Kean that he was calling on behalf of Bush, who was running late for a family gathering. He then informed Kean that he was the president's choice for the post and asked whether he would accept. Kean agreed. Card then told him that Bush would be calling him in a day or so.

Of his decision, Kean explained afterward, "The way I was brought up, when the president asks you to do something, you say 'yes.'"[14] After the White House announced his appointment, Kean said at a press conference at Drew that when he learned of Bush's decision, he felt as though a ton of bricks had fallen on him.[15] What led Bush to settle on Kean remains unclear. While Kean had met Bush several times and their relationship had been cordial, they did not know each other well. Kean surmised that the president's father, George H. W. Bush, whom he knew far better, had recommended him.[16]

White House spokesman Ari Fleischer's comment that Kean's name, along with Kissinger's, was among those Bush considered several weeks prior to announcing his appointment may have contained a clue.[17] In late September 2002, while the White House was negotiating with congressional leaders about the scope and powers of a potential commission, Bush journeyed to New Jersey to campaign for U.S. senatorial hopeful Doug Forrester. Kean, then serving as honorary chairman of Forrester's campaign, was invited to ride with Bush and Forrester to the Trenton War Memorial, where all three were to speak. En route, Bush and Kean provided Forrester, a first-time statewide candidate, with pointers on how best to engage his opponent. Bush and Kean both had been considered underdogs when they first ran for governor of their respective states. (Bush opposed popular incumbent Ann Richards. Kean had to overcome a double-digit lead Congressman James Florio enjoyed in the polls.) As the two swapped stories, they developed a rapport. Their exchange may have remained on Bush's mind after he returned to Washington.

In announcing Kean's appointment, a White House press release described him as "a leader respected for his integrity, fairness, and good judgment."[18] Fleischer noted that Kean had a "very close relationship with the 9–11 families" and that their concerns were "close and near to [Kean's] heart."[19] One family member, whose wife, a Fiduciary executive who died in the attacks, agreed. "I know he experienced a closeness to this that many people don't have," he said, predicting that Kean would "do well on behalf of those of us who lost people."[20] Family activists who had pressed for the creation of the commission voiced confidence that Kean's independence and integrity would compensate for what he lacked in experience in intelligence work.[21]

Kean used his first public appearance as the commission's chairman to set the tone he hoped would guide the panel's deliberations. He promised a thorough and fair investigation. "I hope the president felt I could conduct this in a nonpartisan manner," Kean said, adding that he had been working with Democrats and Republicans all his life. In characteristic understatement, he said that, "like any member of the public," he did not hail from Washington and that he had not played a part in any of the political battles that had transpired in the nation's capital in recent years. That, he suggested, meant that he would approach the work before him with "no prior prejudices."[22] Asked whether he had any conflicts of interests, Kean declared that his only clients were his students.[23]

As he presented himself to the national media for the first time in his new role, Kean advanced certain themes to which he would return in his capacity as the principal public face of a commission charged with the most extensive investigation of the U.S. government in its history. First, he attributed the best motives and intentions to the Bush administration. He would never move away from this public posture, even when he and his colleagues grew frustrated at the slow pace with which they were granted access to materials they believed they needed in order to conduct their investigation. This was Kean's way of signaling to the White House that he did not want or expect the commission's relationship with it to be adversarial. His repeated public comments that he expected and anticipated cooperation kept public pressure on government officials to comply with the commission's requests.

Second, Kean stressed that he wanted the investigation to proceed in a nonpartisan manner. With the panel consisting of five Republicans and five Democrats, nine appointed by the congressional leadership of both parties in both houses of Congress, with the tenth appointed by the president, it could easily deadlock. As he would in all future public and private statements, Kean stated from the outset of his tenure that he hoped and expected that the commission would be unanimous in its findings and in its recommendations. He established early on a practice of not calling for votes unless absolutely necessary. From the commission's first meeting to its last, he worked to organize its staff and to conduct its investigation in a manner that would enhance unity and diminish the likelihood of a minority report. Such an occurrence, he felt, would undermine the credibility of the commission's findings and diminish support for its recommendations.

Kean acted to reassure Democrats, both on the commission and off, that he intended to conduct a complete and impartial investigation and Republicans that he did not intend to be party to a witch hunt. He cemented the commission's internal cohesion by defending its prerogatives, stressing its independence, and declaring that its mandate was sufficiently broad as to grant it access to materials that no other public body outside of the executive branch had ever seen. Finally, Kean, by repeating that he was "not from Washington," cast himself in the role he most savored, that of the "public citizen," who took on assignments of importance to the country and returned to private life upon completing them. In adopting this stance, Kean was able to tap into the public's well-known aversion to the partisanship, personal attacks, and ideological divides that characterized much of what transpired in the nation's capital.

Kean proved most effective when he feigned innocence of Washington's ways and befuddlement at "how they do things" in the nation's capital. Whether consciously or otherwise, Kean in press conferences, on television, and in print took on a role Jimmy Stewart played on the screen, Ronald Reagan perfected as president, and North Carolina ("I'm just a country lawyer") Democratic senator Sam Ervin presented to the nation during the Senate Watergate hearings. "There's a certain 'Mr. Smith comes to Washington' quality about Tom Kean, even though he grew up here," said Kean's fellow commissioner Richard Ben-Veniste. "He has an aw-shucks quality about him, but underneath, he's a very savvy guy."[24] Kean worked these attributes to his advantage. They would be among the tools he used to rally public opinion behind him, win access to people and documents, persuade the administration and Congress to give him sufficient time and resources to complete his task, and propel Congress and the White House to enact the commission's most important recommendations more quickly than they desired.

One prediction Kean made upon his acceptance of the commission's chairmanship—that he would devote a day a week to his new duties—proved inaccurate. While continuing his other activities, especially those at Drew, for the better part of two years Kean would be an all-but-constant presence in Washington, commuting back and forth to the nation's capital almost as frequently as he had as a child. When not in town, he would be on the telephone to commissioners, staff, or government officials or in his study preparing for the next round of meetings, hearings, negotiations, or interviews. A Drew student, attending Kean's press conference after his appointment was made public, offered a view of how he thought Kean would comport himself as chairman. "He had a way of making people feel comfortable," the student said.[25] In not too long a time, Kean's nine colleagues on the commission, government officials, victims' families, congressmen, senators, and tough Washington interviewers were all saying the same thing.

Forging Bonds with the Commissioners

Kean took as his first priorities as the commission's chairman getting to know his fellow commissioners and assembling a staff. He set out to build the strongest possible working relationship with the commission's vice chairman, Lee Hamilton. A moderate Democrat who commanded wide respect on both sides of the aisle, Hamilton had chaired the House International Relations Committee and its Permanent Select Committee on Intelligence. He had cochaired the congressional investigation of the Iran-Contra affair in 1986–87 and later served on the Hart-Rudman Commission on National Security in the Twenty-first Century. Upon his retirement from the House in 1999, after serving for thirty-four years, he became director of the Woodrow Wilson International Center for Scholars. During his early forays to Washington in his new capacity, Kean made Hamilton's office his home away from home. He recognized that Hamilton possessed a familiarity with the intricacies of intelligence and other matters the commission would be investigating that he, as an educator and former state official, lacked. Hamilton's knowledge of Congress and the ways of Washington left him perfectly positioned to play the consummate "insider" to Kean's "outsider."

These factors, in addition to the fifty-fifty partisan composition of the commission, prompted Kean to regard Hamilton not as his second in command but as his cochairman. Kean and Hamilton spoke on the commission's behalf jointly. Quotes from both appeared in all press releases and statements the commission issued. Both men's bylines appeared on articles explaining commission policies and objectives. The two routinely appeared together at press conferences and on public affairs broadcasts on television. Because of this practice of theirs, their colleague Slade Gorton took to referring to them as the "twins." Kean and Hamilton decided on personnel and procedure for the commission. They talked by telephone more than once a day and joked that they talked to each other more often during the day than they did to their wives.

As their friendship grew, Kean and Hamilton made it their practice, wherever possible, not to disagree with one another—at least not in front of other commissioners or in public. The one time their informal agreement broke down was when, having failed to confer beforehand, they wound up on opposite sides on a decision to subpoena a particular government agency. Hamilton wound up voting with several Republicans against issuing it, while Kean sided with the majority, which consisted mostly of Democrats. The way they divided in this one instance underscored the extent to which they were prepared to go to establish and preserve the spirit of bipartisanship they developed on the commission. In time, commentators took to referring to the "Kean-Hamilton model" as the counterpoint to the partisanship and stridency that characterized relations between leaders of opposite parties and committee chairs and ranking minority members in Congress. The *Washington Post*'s David Broder wrote of the tone the two had established: "In the storm of controversy over the antiterrorism records of the Bush and Clinton administrations, the one thing for which everyone can be grateful is the quality of the referee who is handling the fight. . . . The tone of seriousness and bipartisanship was established from the start by the character of the chairman and vice chairman, respectively, Tom Kean . . . and Lee Hamilton. . . . They came to their work with sterling reputations and will enhance them by their handling of the investigation. They are being ably seconded by commission members."[26]

While Kean and Hamilton enjoyed reputations as centrists within their respective parties, the other eight commissioners varied widely across the ideological spectrum. Former U.S. senator from Georgia Max Cleland and former Watergate prosecutor Richard Ben-Veniste came to the commission as appointees of Senate majority leader Tom Daschle. Former U.S. senator from Nebraska Bob Kerrey would replace Cleland, who accepted a full-time appointment to the board of the Export-Import Bank. Former Indiana representative Tim Roemer and former deputy attorney general Jamie Gorelick joined the commission as appointees of House minority leader Richard Gephardt (D-MO). House Speaker Dennis Hastert (R-IL) tapped former Illinois governor James Thompson and former counsel to President Ronald Reagan Fred Fielding, while Senate minority leader Trent Lott (R-MS) named former U.S. senator Slade Gorton and, upon consultation with McCain, John Lehman, former navy secretary under Ronald Reagan. Thompson was the only member of the group with whom Kean had a prior working relationship. (Both had served simultaneously as governors of their respective states.) Kean worked hard in his first months to establish close personal ties with each of the commission's other members. He built time into their deliberations so that his fellow commissioners could spend time together, before or after meetings, over dinner, or at get-togethers at members' homes.

Kean and Gorelick found that they shared many acquaintances. Their mutual colleague, Jim Johnson, former chief of staff to former vice president Walter Mondale, who had served with Gorelick on the board at Fannie Mae and with Kean on the United Hospital Health Care board of directors, told her that "when things get tough, Tom heads for the high ground."[27] She would find that out for herself several months later. After word of Kean's appointment began to circulate, members of Congress from both parties telephoned Roemer to assure him that he would enjoy serving with Kean.[28] Had Kissinger stayed on as chairman, Roemer later opined, the commission would have gone down in history as the "Kissinger Commission." Kean, he said, made it the "9–11 Commission."[29]

Kean asked each of his colleagues to cultivate whatever ties they had on Capitol Hill, in the administration, or elsewhere, to advance the commission's goals. Gorton became the commission's ambassador to Senate Republicans; Thompson, to Speaker Hastert; Roemer, to House Democrats; Fielding, to the White House; Lehman, to John McCain and other Senate Republicans; and Gorelick to congressional Democrats and certain journalists. By giving them assignments, Kean both enhanced the commission's ability to succeed and gave each commissioner a sense of full participation and ownership of its final product. Gorton, who had served on other commissions, contrasted Kean's style with those of other chairmen he had known, who retained tight personal control over formal and informal contacts with outside parties.[30] Kean's efforts to establish a mutuality of interests and common bonds among his colleagues proved beneficial when several commissioners came under attack from political operatives or the media. Activists in both parties speculated that, given the identities of the commissioners and their method of selection, most, if not all, would see it as their role to exonerate a president of their own party from blame for not doing more to prevent 9–11. This seemed a logical premise, given that all the commissioners came to their positions with backgrounds that could be classified as partisan. Republicans were particularly concerned about the past activities of some Democratic commissioners.

In her capacity as Attorney General Janet Reno's deputy, Gorelick had been at the receiving end of several congressional probes into the workings of the Justice Department and the White House during the Clinton administration. Ben-Veniste, after serving as a Watergate prosecutor became chief counsel to the Senate Democratic minority during the Senate's investigation of Whitewater, an Arkansas real estate investment in which Bill and Hillary Clinton had participated. Cleland, weeks prior to his appointment, had been defeated for reelection in a campaign in which Republicans had presented him as soft on terrorism because he differed with the administration as to how to structure the new Department of Homeland Security. Roemer, who sponsored the amendment in the House that established the commission, had been at loggerheads with administration representatives over the fate of his proposal at several junctures.

Early in his days as chairman, Kean, primarily through Fielding, passed word that he understood Republican concerns. Increasingly, Fielding functioned as Kean's go-between and back channel to the administration and all-around adviser as to how things worked in Washington. On those few occasions when Kean could not journey to Washington, he asked Fielding to represent him in meetings with administration officials. Sometimes, he designated Fielding as his personal representative to negotiate the commission's way through delicate matters with the White House counsel.

At meetings, Kean would refrain from expressing a point of view until after he sized up the sentiments of his colleagues. When he chose to express an opinion, he would begin with the question, "What do you suppose would happen if . . . ?" When opinions diverged after each commissioner spoke, Kean would attempt to summarize what they had said, seeking to achieve a consensus. "What I think I heard you both saying" became a familiar Kean refrain. His failure to dominate the meetings hardly meant that he was disengaged or that he held no strong views on subjects that were unfamiliar to him. His practice was to hold back until he had fully ascertained the sentiments in the room. Opinions he voiced were ones to which he and Hamilton had previously agreed.

Gorelick attributed Kean's capacity to forge a consensus to his inexhaustible patience. "Sometimes I could see that Lee was eager to work through the agenda, while Tom would stop to let us make another point. It is sometimes important to do that," she observed.[31] Hamilton agreed. "Had I been chairman instead of Tom Kean," he said, the commission would have completed its work in January instead of in July. The only difference would have been that there would have been ten reports instead of one."[32]

In language practically identical to that which Kean's children might use in describing how he sought to discipline them when they were young, Gorton spoke of the manner in which Kean tried to prod colleagues to come together on certain issues. "He had a way of making people unwilling to upset him," Gorton said. "He could look so hurt."[33] After a rare instance in which Kean could not get all his colleagues to agree, Roemer commented to a reporter that one of Kean's great strengths was that "you always feel welcome back at the table."[34] "You have no idea what it means after you have argued against something he [Kean] wanted to do to find him coming up to you afterward, all smiles, requesting your help on a completely different matter," Roemer said.[35] Kean would repeatedly caution his peers that there were only two things that might endanger the commission's capacity to succeed in its mission: the appearance of partisanship and leaks either about its deliberations or of classified materials. He managed to keep both to a minimum. The commission's executive director, Philip Zelikow, director of the Miller Center of Public Affairs at the University of Virginia, cited as Kean's greatest strength his ability to see beyond the day's crisis and his sense for rhythms and trends.[36]

In addition to the reading he was able to do at home, Kean would spend hours at the commission's undisclosed location pouring over classified documents and transcripts and notes from interviews and interrogations. He also read books on subjects the commission was investigating. Two he took to recommending to reporters were Steve Coll's *Ghost Wars: The Secret History of the CIA, Afghanistan, and Bin Laden from the Soviet Invasion to September 10, 2001* and George Crill's *Charlie Wilson's War: The Extraordinary Story of the Largest Covert Operation in History.*

Staffing the Commission

To ensure that the bipartisan tone they set among the commissioners extended throughout the staff, Kean and Hamilton decided that the bipartisan commission would retain a nonpartisan staff. Rather than assemble two partisan staffs, as do congressional committees, the commission's staff, whatever individual members' partisan sympathies, would report to the commission as a whole through the executive director. Individual commissioners would not have staff of their own. All requests for information from commissioners would flow through Zelikow. Zelikow, a historian, had served on the National Security Council under President George H. W. Bush and on the bipartisan National Commission on Federal Electoral Reform, which former presidents Gerald R. Ford and Jimmy Carter chaired. He came to Kean's and Hamilton's attention through Gorton, who had worked with him previously. "I had seen him manage some big names with big egos and figured he could handle this group," Gorton recalled.[37]

What most impressed Kean about Zelikow was the historian's determination to write the authoritative account of what transpired on September 11, 2001, as a historical narrative. "His ideas were my ideas," Kean said.[38] Because Zelikow had a prior working relationship with administration officials, having authored a book on the unification of Germany with National Security Adviser Condoleezza Rice, having served on the president's Foreign Intelligence Advisory Board, and having assisted with aspects of the Clinton-Bush transition that pertained to the National Security Council, Kean and Hamilton agreed that the deputy executive director would be a Democrat. In that capacity, they retained Chris Kojm, a former State Department official, who previously worked under Hamilton on the House International Relations Committee. After a number of false starts, they settled upon Daniel Marcus, a veteran of both the Carter and Clinton administrations, as counsel. The rest of the staff was organized into nine teams with four to nine persons each, researching policy areas the commission's enabling legislation made part of its mission.

On more than one occasion, victims' families, disappointed that the commission had not been as aggressive in its stance toward the administration as they had hoped, assumed that Zelikow, because of his past ties to administration officials, had dissuaded it from using the full powers at its disposal. On several occasions, they asserted that Zelikow had a conflict of interest and demanded that he resign.[39] Kean backed his director each time. He also responded to the executive director's critics' concerns. Asked upon the conclusion of a hearing how he would respond to those who insisted that Zelikow was too polite to press the administration for materials, Kean quipped, "Dr. Zelikow has many faults," he said, "but politeness is not one of them."[40]

As often proved the case, Kean intended his remarks for more than one audience. One was the victims' families, whom he wanted to reassure that the commission was "hanging tough." Another was the administration with which he was still negotiating. A third was Zelikow, whom Kean wanted to show greater sensitivity to families' concerns. Kean talked with family representatives regularly by telephone, retained two full-time staff members to serve as liaison to family organizations, and held frequent meetings with family members. One three-hour session he held with them at Drew became rather emotional, with people shouting at Kean, pounding tables, and demanding that he use the power that he had been given, all with a reporter listening behind closed doors.[41]

Shortly after Kean's appointment had been announced, I called to congratulate him and offered to be of whatever assistance I could to him in the historical undertaking he was about to lead. A few weeks later, he telephoned to ask if I was interested in joining the commission's staff. When I replied in the affirmative, he said, "Fine, but you will need to talk with the executive director. He has seen your résumé and is familiar with your writings." Kean also said that the final decision as to who would be on the staff would rest with Zelikow. "Were I the executive director, I would not want my chairman dictating who I would have working with me, and neither would you," Kean added. Zelikow suggested that I could be of assistance investigating how the White House responded to the attacks of 9–11.

In passing, I asked how the commission would be handling press inquiries. Informed that someone else had been selected to serve in that capacity, I began my initial assignment. Soon thereafter, Kojm called to say that the person the commission had in mind as its spokesman would not be relocating to Washington. He asked whether I had an interest in serving in the post. When I said yes, he told me that, while Kean had already signed off on the reassignment, I would need to talk with Hamilton. I began my new role March 12, nineteen days before the commission was scheduled to hold its first public hearing.

Public Posture

The decision to hold frequent public hearings had been primarily Kean's. He intended the hearings to be part of a multifaceted strategy to ensure that the commission, unlike so many of its predecessors, would see its recommendations adopted. Several past commissions, he explained, produced excellent reports and worthy recommendations, only to see their submissions relegated to a shelf. If the fate of the 9–11 Commission and what it recommended was to be any different, he insisted, "it was absolutely essential that it involve the public in its work." He repeatedly spoke of "bringing the public along" and allowing it to "observe the commission as it went about its business." He looked upon hearings as a way to enhance the public's awareness of the issues the commission confronted and the choices before it. (Most of what the commission learned, however, would come from the 1,200 interviews it would conduct in private sessions with present and past officials and the more than 2 million pages of documents it would review.) He also wanted to hold open public sessions because he shared the view of victims' families that high-ranking government officials should be questioned in public and under oath about their actions on or before September 11.

Not all Kean's associates shared his enthusiasm for public hearings. Some thought them a waste of time. Staff argued, with justification, that each hour of public testimony required six hours of staff preparation, time they would have to take away from the investigation. Typical of his management style, Kean, John Lehman recalled, never "laid down the law and said, 'We will have hearings.' He just kept making the case for them until the staff had bought in."[42] The first several hearings were informational in nature; policy analysts offered contrasting views on how the U.S. government should restructure itself in the aftermath of September 11. Beginning in January 2004, the nature of the hearings shifted to the specifics of the commission's investigation. By way of introduction, the staff would read statements it had prepared on what it had learned about the subject the hearing would cover as of the date of the hearing. The staff statements served as interim reports, setting the tone for the questioning that followed.

The public hearings also served as occasions when Kean and Hamilton could meet with reporters afterward to answer questions about information that had been presented, comment on the progress of the investigation, keep public attention focused on the commission, and create expectations that its report would strongly affect the future security of the nation. During and after the hearings, invitations for the chairman, the vice chairman, and other commissioners to appear on public affairs TV programs poured into my office in a deluge of voice mails and e-mails.

From the instant he picked up the commission's gavel, Kean expressed firm ideas about how he wanted the commission's final report released. So that it would instantly become a topic of national conversation with an engaged public pressing policy makers to adopt the commission's recommendations, Kean wanted the widest number of people over a short period of time to read it. That meant that, in addition to making the report available on the Internet and through the Government Printing Office, as most government documents were presented, the commission would have the report in book form and available in bookstores and at a price the average person could afford. W. W. Norton published an initial printing of six hundred thousand copies of the paperback version, priced at ten dollars per copy. The commercial publisher had the books ready for distribution the day the report was released, July 21, 2004. It would stay on the *New York Times* best-seller list for twenty-six weeks and be nominated for a National Book Award. Norton subsequently followed with a hardcover version, containing an index. With the report in the public domain as an official government document, other publishers quickly printed it as well.

The morning of the report's release, Kean and Hamilton presented copies of it to congressional leaders and the president, while other commissioners briefed opinion leaders and family members on the commission's findings and recommendations. Commissioners made themselves available to the media immediately after the report became available. To assist with the overflow of demands from national, regional, and local television and radio stations and print and Internet journalists, the commission retained the assistance of Edelman Communications, a public relations firm known for its ability to handle a large volume of media requests over a short period of time and for the bipartisan composition of its staff. Kean's comfort level with Edelman was enhanced through its participation in a consortium with a company chaired by his former chief of staff, Greg Stevens.

In drafting the report, Kean allowed ample time for each of the commissioners to comment on both its findings and its recommendations. Staff would prepare drafts of each chapter for commissioners to review. Commissioners would come to the next meeting armed with notations, insertions, and recommended language of chapters they had reviewed. Staff would then incorporate suggestions accepted by a majority of commissioners into subsequent drafts. The process was repeated three to six times per chapter. After the report had been published, Kean joked that he could not read a passage without hearing the voice of the commissioner who had suggested certain wording.

The public hearings, Kean's and Hamilton's press briefings, the commissioners' appearances (on television, radio, and in print), the ready availability of the commission's report, and the manner in which its findings and recommendations were presented established for the commission a positive public persona. This proved an important source of political capital as its members began persuading policy makers to enact the report's policy recommendations. Before any of that could happen, Kean had to steer the commission through a series of intricate and not always anticipated procedural maneuvers in order to obtain access to critical documents and individuals. The manner in which Kean and Hamilton responded to these challenges further enhanced the commission's public standing and its subsequent ability to influence the direction of public policy.

Struggles for Funds and Access to Documents

Insufficient funds was the first hurdle the 9–11 Commission had to overcome. The bill establishing the commission provided an initial allocation of $3 million. The commission's initial boosters thought this an oddity, given that the government had allocated $40 million to investigating why the *Columbia* shuttle had exploded, spent $60 million on the Whitewater investigation, and awarded $34 million to Independent Counsel Kenneth Starr's probe of Bill Clinton. Roemer was particularly outspoken. "We lost 3,000 people in the September 11th attacks," he said, "and we could lose more if the terrorists attack again. . . . Not going after the facts in this case could kill people."[43]

Advised that the existing budget was sufficient to fund the commission for but a few months, Kean requested an additional $11 million. Publicly, Kean expressed optimism that the funds would be forthcoming: "The White House has told me they support us being adequately funded, and I am confident that will be the case."[44] Privately, he suggested that his colleagues approach their contacts on Capitol Hill. Disinclined to include funds for the commission in the supplemental appropriation it was seeking to fund the war in Iraq, the administration offered to provide the commission with an additional $9 million from other accounts. Kean stated that through some savings, the commission could complete its task with what the administration was offering, but not for a cent less.[45] McCain and Lieberman would eventually produce for the commission all the funds it sought. Not for the last time, the stance the administration took with regard to the commission sent a barrage of adverse criticism its way.

Family spokesman Stephen Push saw the White House's action as an attempt to render the commission ineffective.[46] "Reasonable people might wonder if the White House, having failed in its attempt to have Henry Kissinger steer the investigation, may be resorting to budgetary starvation as a tactic to hobble any politically fearless inquiry," wrote the *New York Times*.[47]

Weeks later, Roemer sought to review transcripts of hearings in which he had participated while a member of the House-Senate joint inquiry into intelligence failures prior to the attacks on 9–11. He was denied permission to read the materials even though he had the necessary clearances and the legislation that established the commission provided that it have access to such documents and transcripts. With Kean's concurrence, Zelikow had agreed to a White House request for government officials to review the documents before the commissioners did. "There are times when we're going to have big arguments over very serious matters," Kean said. "I don't think five days to a week is much to argue about."[48] Beneath Kean's aura of politeness had been a warning. As he spoke, commission staff and administration lawyers were already engaged in a dispute over the commission's request for access to certain documents and persons. These were indeed serious matters over which both sides were prepared to engage in serious arguments.

Kean's guarded but optimistic remarks were part of an approach Kean and Hamilton had been encouraging the commission to take. They preferred a public posture that cast the commission in the role of cooperating with the administration rather than confronting it. Both took the view that once the commission exercised its subpoena powers, its relations with the White House would become adversarial. This, they felt, would make it unlikely that their opposites would honor subsequent requests, even the most routine in nature, in the absence of a court order. With increasing frequency, Kean made the case to impatient colleagues that the *threat* of a subpoena, through the public pressure it put on officials, could often be as potent a weapon as the actual issuance of a subpoena.

Through their own reading and from conversations with legal authorities, Kean and Hamilton were also concerned that if they had issued subpoenas and the White House resisted turning over materials subpoenaed, the courts might rule for the administration. Some legal analysts informed them that on cases that involved executive privilege, save for those involving criminality, the courts had increasingly tended to side with the executive. Even if they prevailed in court, Kean and Hamilton reasoned, they might not obtain access to the information they sought before the commission's life span, set by statute, had expired.

When the course they had settled on failed to produce the desired results in a timely fashion, creating tensions within the commission and attracting criticisms from victims' families and editorial boards that the commission was too timid, Kean and Hamilton began pressuring the administration publicly. On July 8, 2003, they released at a press conference what they called the commission's "first interim report." Written in the style of a report card, it assigned grades to departments according to the speed and thoroughness with which they had replied to the commission's requests for documents. They gave the lowest grades to the Departments of Defense and Justice. They also objected to the Justice Department's practice of having "minders" from host agencies present when officials were interviewed. In response to a question about the minders, Kean suggested that their presence during interviews could be a form of intimidation, adding that he only consented to their presence so that interviews might take place.[49] On this occasion, as on many subsequent ones, he described himself as a "non-Washingtonian," feigning befuddlement as to how things were done "in this town." Kean and Hamilton said that the administration had "made significant efforts" to assist the commission, adding that, in their view, it had underestimated the amount of staff-hours that complying with the commission's requests entailed.[50] They also said that the commission needed strong support from the White House in order to fulfill its mission in the time that remained to it.[51] They promised to report again in September on their progress in obtaining the documents they had requested. One experienced Kean watcher recorded that the former governor, pretending to be a political innocent, had won the first round.[52]

Toward the end of September 2003, Kean and Hamilton held their second briefing. They said that although there had been a speedup in the flow of materials from government agencies, the commission still did not have all it needed to conduct its investigation. Again they gave an accounting of which agencies had not complied with their requests. In an attempt to turn up the rhetorical heat on the administration, they promised to inform the public promptly if the commission did not receive the access it needed. Hamilton suggested "crunch time" would come in the next few weeks. When asked about the minders, Kean cocked his head and exclaimed, "Still got 'em, still don't like 'em." Again, he reminded his audience he was not all that familiar with the workings of Washington. When asked what effect the commission's interim report of July 8 had on some agencies, Kean, to the delight of his audience said, "Well, it may have been an accident, but an awful lot of documents came in."[53] The aw-shucks demeanor Ben-Veniste had detected in Kean was becoming the public face of the commission.

As the commission continued to press for materials, the number of congressional and editorial voices calling upon the administration to comply with its requests increased. On October 10, Kean and Hamilton released a statement in which they urged the prompt resolution of remaining issues regarding documents.[54] Five days later, the commission issued a subpoena to the Federal Aviation Administration. Although its action was long anticipated, one of Kean's colleagues termed it "a warning shot across the White House bow."[55] On October 17, in a free-ranging interview with the *New York Times,* Kean suggested that he had run out of patience. "Any document that has to do with this investigation cannot be beyond our reach," he stated, adding, uncharacteristically, "I won't stand for it." He said the commission "would use every tool" at its disposal to get hold of every document without delay.[56]

Kean's comments, which appeared on the first page of the newspaper's Sunday edition, reverberated across the country. In the ensuing days, commentators, columnists, and editorial writers were demanding that the administration do as Kean asked. The *Wall Street Journal, New York Post,* and *Washington Times* were among the few dissenters. *New York Post* columnist John Podhoretz, in a piece titled "The Kean Mutiny," suggested that Kean's comments bespoke a "self-righteousness" of an "anachronistic brand of liberal Republicanism."[57] He and Kean's other critics failed to note that Kean spoke not only for himself but for the entire commission. Some of his fellow Republicans, exasperated at the lengthy delays in obtaining documents, indicated a willingness to issue subpoenas, while Democrats, who long favored going this route, accepted for the moment that Kean was moving in their direction and held back.

What was most at issue between the commission and the White House behind the scenes was the commission's request for access to the President's Daily Briefs, memos the CIA presented the president each day containing its assessment of potential threats to American interests around the world. Of particular interest to the media, victims' families, and some members of Congress was a document of August 6, 2001, in which Bush purportedly was warned that al Qaeda planned an attack against the United States. The commission had determined that it needed to see not only this particular memorandum, but hundreds of others. White House negotiators resisted, insisting that were they to grant the commission access, they would set a precedent for other entities outside the executive branch, especially Congress, to review materials presidents historically shared only with their most intimate advisers. Allowing the Congress or any of its creations to review the documents, they said, would violate the separation of powers.

Asked what he thought of this, Kean addressed the precedent-setting argument, insisting that the commission was unique, just as the attacks of 9–11 were unique in American history. He maintained that this was sufficient to override administration concerns. "Besides," he said, "we go out of business on a certain date, while Congress, God willing, extends into perpetuity."[58] As the talks dragged on, on November 7, 2003, the commission issued a subpoena to the North American Aerospace Defense Command of the Department of Defense for the immediate production of previously requested documents.

Beset with increasing criticism in the press and in Congress, the White House offered to provide commissioners with an oral briefing on the documents' contents. All ten found the oral presentation highly unsatisfactory. When the commission pressed to review the written materials, the administration agreed to permit only Kean and Hamilton to inspect them. Kean countered with the suggestion that the commission also be allowed to have two additional people of its own choosing review them. "Lee and I did not want to assume the full responsibility," Kean later explained. "We felt the more people who saw them, the better."[59] After the White House agreed to Kean's proposal, he and Hamilton designated Gorelick and Zelikow as their fellow readers. Initially, the agreement was for two of the four to review only documents the White House deemed pertinent, with the other two perusing the rest to ascertain that they fell outside the scope of the commission's work. Eventually, the administration allowed all four to read the materials.

Kean's insistence on granting more people from the commission the right to peruse the documents and on designating the additional readers proved a major turning point for the commission in both its public standing and its future ability to extract further concessions from the White House. Although not all of Kean's colleagues approved of the compromise he negotiated, eight went along with it. Ben-Veniste told the press afterward that the deal Kean struck with the White House respected the integrity of the commission.[60] In their public dissents, Roemer and Cleland directed their criticisms not at Kean, who they maintained brought back the best deal he could get, but at the White House. Earlier in the process, while Kean was still threatening to use the commission's subpoena power, Cleland called the chairman the "quiet velvet hammer" that the commission needed.[61] Kean proclaimed his own handiwork "a real breakthrough."[62]

Sandbagged by CBS

With its long impasse with the White House apparently broken, an incident of neither the commission's nor the White House's making threatened to undermine the cooperative relationship the parties believed they had established and the image Kean had created for the commission as "reasonable, fair, and dispassionate." At the end of the commission's hearing on emergency preparedness, held at Drew University, Randall Pinkston of CBS News approached me and requested permission to spend a half-day with Kean at Drew. Pinkston said that he was doing a human-interest piece for the magazine-style television show *60 Minutes 2*. He explained that its focus would be on how a "tweedy, former governor-turned-college-president came to investigate the worst tragedy in American history." On December 5, 2003, Pinkston spent several hours with Kean on campus. On December 17, Pinkston called at 6:15 p.m. to inform me that the Kean interview would air in fifteen minutes.

"But *60 Minutes 2* is not on today," I said. "We decided to go with it as hard news," Pinkston replied. "We will be leading with it tonight on *The CBS Evening News with Dan Rather*." I suggested that since the piece contained out-of-date material, perhaps Rather or someone else should interview Kean live. The reporter said there was not enough time and ended the conversation. I did not know that the network had been hyping the Kean interview as a pending bombshell for the preceding several hours.

Rather introduced the broadcast and segued to Pinkston. The correspondent began his report with the sentence "For the first time the chairman of the commission investigating the September 11 attacks is saying publicly that 9–11 could have and should have been prevented." The next thing viewers saw was Kean saying, "As you read the report, you're going to have a pretty clear idea of what wasn't done and what should have been done. This was not something that had to happen." Nothing in that passage was particularly unusual or newsworthy. Kean had been saying similar things for months. The network's promised bombshell exploded in the next passage. In the event the audience might miss it, Pinkston stated, "Kean is now pointing fingers inside the administration and laying blame." The network then aired a part of the interview in which Kean said, in response to a question, "There are people that, if I was doing the job, would certainly not be in the position they were in at that time because they failed. They simply failed." He had not referred specifically to any specific individuals. As it played Kean's voice, CBS broke to footage of National Security Adviser Condoleezza Rice saying in the aftermath of the attacks that no one could have anticipated terrorists using planes as missiles. It followed with victims' relatives criticizing Bush officials.[63]

The notion that Kean, within days of obtaining access to the vaunted presidential documents, would have been able to reach definitive conclusions about the administration's culpability was preposterous. "I was sandbagged," he said afterward.[64] Within minutes of Pinkston's broadcast, reporters from all over the world began calling to invite Kean to repeat his "assertions." Others telephoned him to inquire whether he thought the national security adviser or secretary of defense should resign or be fired. Acquaintances of mine in and around the administration called to ask what message Kean intended to send them. Back-channel contacts called Kean as well. "They went nuts" was how he described their reaction to the press's coverage of the broadcast.[65] Fielding said afterward that "Kean was the administration's appointee. They had to ride it out with him."[66]

The next day, Kean went on ABC's *Nightline* live. "We have no evidence that anybody high in the Clinton administration or the Bush administration did anything wrong," Kean said.[67] He added that conclusions about the performance of high-level officials would have to await the completion of the investigation. He repeated his prior assertion that people had failed in the performance of their jobs prior to September 11. Subsequent hearings the commission held bore him out.[68] That late Friday evening broadcast, coming twenty-eight hours after Pinkston's segment aired, smoothed the administration's and others' feathers slightly. Throughout the holiday period I continued to get calls from producers eager to interview the Republican chairman who had "pointed fingers at his president." One wanted to put him on the night before Christmas Eve or on Christmas Eve itself. After I asked him whether such people had heard of reindeer, Burl Ives, or even Christmas, Kean let out a boisterous laugh. His reaction convinced me that the commission had weathered its latest storm. There would be others.

New Disputes with the White House

The early months of 2004 brought new procedural disputes between the commission and the White House. The first of these controversies concerned the commission's deadline. The legislation that established the commission required it to issue its report no later than eighteen months to the day after it came into being. That would have been May 27, 2004. By the turn of the year, Kean and his colleagues concluded that the prolonged negotiations over the commission's access to materials had cost it valuable time. Several doubted that they could do as thorough a job as they hoped in the time that remained to them. Kean and Hamilton said in late January that they would ask for the commission's life to be extended sixty days. Their announcement came after a particularly arduous and emotional hearing in which the events of 9–11 were vividly recalled. Press coverage had been extensive.

Senators John McCain and Joseph Lieberman, sponsors of the

legislation that established the commission, supported the request. The White House and the House leadership opposed it. Representatives of both President Bush and House Speaker Dennis Hastert stressed the need to act immediately on the commission's recommendations for enhancing national security as the reason their principals opposed the extension.[69] On February 4, the White House reversed itself. A "senior Republican official" was quoted the next day as saying that the administration went along with the commission's request after learning from commission sources that the report was likely to "have some criticism of the White House, but will not conclude that there was a failure by Bush himself." He added that there would be "very little direct ammunition aimed at the president himself."[70] Unnamed commission sources called that assessment premature.[71] Hastert, meanwhile, clung to his position. His spokesman said that the Speaker did not want the commission's report to become a political football in the midst of a presidential campaign.[72] McCain suggested that the Speaker's reservations be accommodated by extending the commission's deadline beyond the election.

Kean announced that in the event the commission's request was not granted, it would cut back on the number and scope of its public hearings. He remained hopeful that his request would be granted. He continually referred to Hastert as a "reasonable man." At the same time, he suggested that Congress's possible rejection of the commission's request would be a disappointment and a "disservice to the American people."[73]

Many of his listeners agreed. CNN anchor Aaron Brown, in a rare departure from his usual format, began his nightly television show with a hard-hitting editorial:

> We admit we don't do causes very well on the program. And I don't do outrage well at all, yet tonight, a cause and an outrage. The decision by the Speaker of the House to deny the independent commission investigating the 9–11 attack on America a 60-day extension—that's all, 60 days—to complete its work is unconscionable and indefensible. . . . The commission itself has gone about its work quietly. It's had to fight tooth and nail to get necessary information. And now this, an arbitrary decision to deny to the commission—that's the least of it but to deny the country the chance to know all of what happened, how it happened, and how to prevent it from happening again.

Brown ended his commentary by urging his viewers to e-mail and write the House leadership urging it to relent. "Do it for the victims and their families," he said. "Do it for the country that was attacked and for history."[74]

After a meeting the next day with Kean, Hamilton, and Thompson, Hastert relented. Some attributed his change of position to pressure from the White House. Once the administration gave the extension its blessing, a Republican Congress's failure to go along, many argued, would reflect poorly on Bush's leadership.[75] Others said Hastert acted as he had as a means of enticing McCain and Lieberman to lift a hold they had put on the release of highway funds the Speaker wanted spent.[76] Hastert's endorsement of the sixty-day extension meant that the commission's report would be due the day the Democratic National Convention was to convene.

As the extension matter was moving toward resolution, the commission worked to resolve three other issues with the White House: how the committee of four that had reviewed the President's Daily Briefs would share what they learned with their colleagues, whether Bush would submit to an interview by the commission, and whether National Security Adviser Condoleezza Rice would testify under oath in open public session. Although the four commission representatives were permitted to take notes while they read the President's Daily Briefs, they had not been allowed to share the notes with their colleagues. After the press speculated that the commission was on the verge of subpoenaing the notes, White House lawyers, working with Gorelick and Zelikow, prepared a seventeen-page summary of them for their fellow commissioners to read. The press reported afterward that three commissioners, dissatisfied with the agreement, voted to subpoena the notes. Of the agreement, Kean said, "Was it everything I wanted? No. But, it's certainly enough to do what we need to do."[77]

At first, Bush was noncommittal about granting the commission an interview. When Tim Russert put the question to him on the television program *Meet the Press,* all Bush said was "perhaps, perhaps."[78] After the commission rejected out of hand a White House suggestion that Bush might be willing to meet informally "over a cup of coffee" with Kean and Hamilton, the administration signaled that Bush accepted the commission's invitation in principle. It subsequently hinted that the president would only meet with Kean and Hamilton and only for one hour. "The invitation was to meet before the whole commission," Kean took to saying whenever asked to comment on the subject.[79]

For six weeks, Kean would give the same answer. He declined to say what the commission might do if the White House rejected his terms. He confided to his colleagues that he was content to sit back for a while and "let the press do its job."[80] In his public statements, he praised Bush for his willingness to go as far as to offer to sit down with at least some commissioners even though he hoped that the president would do more. "But you know, this is the first president who ever agreed to be interviewed by any commission," Kean would say as he reminded interrogators that Lyndon Johnson had not given the Warren Commission an interview. "He sent them a one-page letter and that was it."[81]

Kean's strategy of praising Bush in public, while holding firm, in public as well as in private, began to have an effect. On March 10, the White House said Bush would be available for more than one hour. "Nobody is watching the clock," his spokesman suggested.[82] Bush critics attributed the sudden flexibility in the president's schedule not only to the pressure the commission applied but also to a comment Bush's presumptive Democratic opponent John Kerry had made. Kerry observed that while Bush spent three hours with NASCAR racers, he could not find more than one hour for the commission.

Two Tendentious Hearings and a Secret Interview

Had the White House initially allowed Rice to accept the commission's invitation to appear before it in public and under oath, she would have been one in a sequence of present and past officials to testify at hearings the commission held on counterterrorism policies of the Clinton and Bush administration on March 23 and 24, 2004. Other witnesses were past and present secretaries of state Madeleine Albright and Colin Powell; prior and current secretaries of defense William Cohen and Donald Rumsfeld; CIA director George Tenet; Rice's immediate predecessor as director of the National Security Council, Sandy Berger; and former coordinator for counterterrorism Richard A. Clarke. The White House had based its previous decision not to allow Rice to testify in public on the same grounds as it had its refusal to allow the entire commission to inspect the President's Daily Briefs: executive privilege. It feared that by allowing a member of the president's staff, who unlike cabinet officers, had not been subject to Senate confirmation, to appear before a legislatively established commission, they risked setting a precedent for future congressional intrusions into how the executive branch conducted its internal affairs.

Feigning innocence of the constitutional principle involved, Kean suggested he wanted Rice to testify because she would make a "superb witness." He reiterated statements he had made regarding access to the PDBs (that the commission had a proscribed life span, whereas Congress did not). Trying another approach, Zelikow, in an attempt to convince the White House that precedent existed for Rice to testify, reportedly faxed a photocopy of a photograph the *New York Times* ran on November 22, 1945, of Admiral William D. Leahy, chief of staff to Presidents Franklin D. Roosevelt and Harry S. Truman, testifying before a congressional inquiry into the Japanese attack upon Pearl Harbor. Zelikow allegedly attached a note suggesting that the Leahy photograph "would be all over Washington within twenty-four hours."[83] "This is what happens when you hire historians," said Kean with a chuckle.[84]

Clarke's testimony and the events that preceded it changed the tenor of the March 24 hearing, as well as the three that followed it. They also caused the White House to reverse, yet again, a stand it had taken in opposition to a commission request. One columnist referred to what ensued as "the week the Richard Clarke circus came to town."[85] On March 21, three days before he was scheduled to testify before the commission, Clarke, on the CBS television program *60 Minutes*, sharply criticized Bush's record on counterterrorism. "I find it outrageous that the president is running for re-election on the grounds that he's done such great things about terrorism. . . . He ignored terrorism for months, when maybe we could have done something to stop 9–11," Clarke told a national television audience. In anticipation of Clarke's *60 Minutes* interview and his appearance before the commission, his publisher advanced publication of his book, *Against All Enemies*, so that it would be available on the day of his testimony.

In response to Clarke's criticisms, the administration put several officials on television, including Rice, to refute his charges. Rice's frequent, often around-the-clock, appearances before the media caused many on the commission and off to question why the only forum from which she absented herself, pleading a technicality, was the only body charged with writing the authoritative account of the attacks of September 11.

Clarke began his testimony with an emotional apology to the families of those who died on September 11. "Your government failed you. Those entrusted with protecting you failed and I failed you."[86] In his now much-anticipated testimony, Clarke charged that "the Bush administration, unlike its predecessor, saw terrorism policy as important, but not urgent, prior to 9–11."[87]

For the first time, viewers watching the commission's proceedings on television could distinguish the Republican commissioners from the Democrats by the nature and manner of their questioning of a leading witness. Fielding, Lehman, and Thompson picked away at Clarke's credibility, challenging him to reconcile what he had written in his book with statements he had made in briefings to the press when he was still in Bush's employ. Democrats castigated the absent Rice for her willingness to contradict Clarke on television, but not before the commission and under oath. The next day, the *Washington Post* reported that Bush's counsel had telephoned Republican commissioners, peppering them with questions and talking points.

Kean was nonplussed. "Anyone has a right to telephone any member of the commission to discuss whatever they wish," Kean told me. "Members of Congress and 9–11 family members call all the time. Why can't the White House?"

The nature of Clarke's charges, the way he began his testimony, the applause he received, and the manner in which his interrogators attempted to discredit him, dramatically raised the commission's profile. Within days, the White House concluded that it was in its best interest to allow Rice to testify before the commission in public. On March 30, it announced that she would be permitted to testify. Almost as an afterthought, it added to its statement that President Bush and Vice President Cheney would meet together with all ten commissioners. In response, the commission convened a special hearing on April 8, 2004, with Rice as the only witness. As if in anticipation of the kind of revelations that emerged during congressional investigations—particularly those of Watergate and Iran-Contra— the three network and major cable television channels, in addition to C–SPAN, covered the hearing live.[88]

As Kean predicted, Rice came across as a knowledgeable and credible witness. The portrait she presented of Bush—as a president fully engaged, who "understood the threat [of al Qaeda]" and who "moved to develop a new and comprehensive strategy" to eliminate its terrorist network—was quite different from the impression Clarke had given of the chief executive.[89] At no point did she cast aspersions on the president's antagonist. She even praised Clarke as a "fine counter-terrorism expert."[90] If not for the manner in which her interrogators questioned her, Rice's appearance might have been anticlimactic. Evening broadcasts focused on Richard Ben-Veniste's aggressive cross-examination of the witness and on Bob Kerrey's colorful line of questioning. For the second time, the commission stood accused of allowing partisanship to make its way into its proceedings.

Publicly, Kean dismissed such allegations. He suggested that Ben-Veniste's approach had been more in the "style of a prosecutor" than of a partisan.[91] Privately, he knew he had to do something to allay suspicions of administration supporters that the commission was biased against it. "We have got to find a way to speak to conservatives," Kean told me. Finding the appropriate vehicle proved a challenge, given that the *Wall Street Journal, New York Post,* most conservative periodicals, and right-leaning television and talk-radio hosts had already concluded that the commission was part of a Democratic-inspired public relations campaign to discredit the president. We decided on Fox's *The O'Reilly Factor.* When Kean and Hamilton appeared on that TV program, they made the same points they had the same day on PBS's *The*

News Hour with Jim Lehrer, but they did so on a network and on a program the conservatives watched. For a time, Kean's conservative critics, upon seeing him once again as the reasoned, dispassionate, public figure they had come to know, appeared willing, once again, to give him and the commission the benefit of the doubt.

All but overlooked in the media hype surrounding the Rice hearing was the White House's decision to declassify at Kean's request the President's Daily Brief of August 6, 2001. That document had been at the center of a controversy between Bush critics and defenders over what the president was told about al Qaeda's activities and intentions prior to September 11. Kean submitted his request immediately following Rice's testimony. The White House made the document public the next day. Commenting on its vagueness and lack of precise information, Kean proclaimed that the sheet and a half of paper contained no "smoking gun." Kean voiced his disappointment at the inferior quality of the intelligence two presidents had received. Not for the first time, he suggested that much of what he read in classified files he had already seen in the popular press. He joked that when he told this to one of his minders, the official replied, "Yes, but you did not know that it was true."

Kean's decision to hold firm in pressing for all ten commissioners to interview the president, like his previous insistence that the commission would decide who it would send to review the President's Daily Briefs, further cemented the internal cohesion within the commission, paving the way for the unanimity in its final report. In acceding to the administration's request that it interview Bush and Cheney together, Kean took the view that, while the joint interview was unusual and, perhaps, unprecedented, he saw no reason not to go ahead with it. When a questioner asked whether such a setting would allow for "Mr. Cheney to help Mr. Bush with the answers," thereby compromising the investigation, Kean replied: "Well, we recognize that Mr. Bush may help Mr. Cheney with some of the answers. But . . . it was the suggestion of the White House and it seemed to us, in exchange for getting all ten commissioners to be able to ask any questions, that we'd get the answers to the questions we needed to write the report."[92]

Hamilton later attributed the White House's decision to compromise with the commission on its requests for access to people and documents to the sense of trust he and Kean had established with their negotiating partners in multiple, lengthy sessions.[93] Historians may question whether, after accepting without hesitation the White House's offer to break the stalemate by allowing the president and vice president to meet jointly with the full commission, the commission, particularly its chairs, paid too little attention to the format the session would take and procedures to which it adhered.[94] As with the matter of access to the PDBs, the principal question before them was whether the agreement enhanced their ability to conduct the investigation. They concluded that the two compromises had.

One upside to the media's preoccupation with Rice's much-awaited public testimony was that it diverted public attention away from the private interview the commission had previously scheduled later that day with former president Bill Clinton. With the media preoccupied with audience reaction to Rice's testimony, the commissioners departed en masse to their next meeting. On the way, they joked among themselves that, unlike Bush, whom they expected to put a time limit on their encounter with him, Clinton might extend his session beyond their capacity for endurance. The Clinton interview exceeded four hours.

Acting on a leak, the media set up stakeouts at each of the exits to the nondescript government building where the Clinton interview took place. Mistaking the commission's chairman for the former president, one camerawoman shoved a camera into Kean's face as he entered a car, waiting to take him to a television studio. Meanwhile, Clinton, according to plan, made his exit from an underground garage. Once en route, Kean mused over how the woman could have mistaken him for Clinton.

By this point, the commission had been granted an extension, its internal committee had reviewed the President's Daily Briefs and was able to inform the other commissioners of their contents, Rice had testified, the PDB of August 6, 2001, had been made public, and Bush had agreed to meet with all ten commissioners. The commission had reason to believe it had overcome all the obstacles that stood in the way of its ability to write the authoritative account of the events of 9–11. That optimism proved short lived.

Putting Out Brushfires

On the morning of the hearing that the commission convened on April 13 to consider law enforcement and the intelligence community, the *New York Times* ran a story asserting that the "staff statement" that would be read at the hearing's commencement would characterize Attorney General John Ashcroft as having been uninterested in counterterrorism policy in the days preceding the attacks of September 11.[95] In his testimony, Ashcroft went on the offensive. He stated that the "single greatest structural cause for the September 11 problem was the wall that segregated or separated criminal investigators from intelligence agents."[96] He traced the existence of this "structural cause" to a 1995 memorandum instructing the FBI to develop procedures that separated counterintelligence investigations from criminal ones. Its author was Jamie Gorelick, now a member of the commission. Adding to the drama, Ashcroft also announced that he had declassified the memorandum that very day.

As the hearing was taking place, Representative F. James Sensenbrenner (R-WI), chairman of the House Judiciary Committee, issued a statement charging Gorelick with a conflict of interest. He demanded that she resign.[97] House majority leader Tom DeLay followed with an open letter to Kean, in which he condemned what he called the "camera-driven tone" of the hearings and their "gotcha-style questioning."[98] The House leader complained of what he termed the "circus atmosphere pyrotechnics" of the hearings. He called them an insult to the "troops now in harm's way, to say nothing of those who have already given their lives in this conflict."[99] The *New York Post* published DeLay's message in its entirety as an op-ed the next day. It subsequently denied the commission an equal amount of space in which to print Kean's reply. Following up on DeLay's actions as well as those of other House members, ten U.S. senators fired off a letter demanding that Gorelick testify in public about her previous role at the Justice Department. The name at the head of the list was that of Kit Bond (R-MO), Ashcroft's former colleague from the Show Me State.[100]

In actuality, rather than construct or even shore up the "wall" to which Ashcroft had referred in his testimony, Gorelick had tried through her memo to gain greater flexibility for the FBI under then-existing restrictions so that intelligence information could be shared with law enforcement officials in certain instances. Her memo was in conformity with court rulings dating as far back as 1978. In response to questioning by Slade Gorton, Ashcroft admitted that, upon taking office, his staff had reissued Gorelick's decree. Over the lunch break, Gorelick, eager to tell her side of the story, reached for the telephone. "What are you doing?" Kean asked her. "I am calling Tom Daschle," she replied. "Put the phone down," he told her. "Let us do it."[101]

In response to a question at a press conference after the hearing, Kean was conciliatory toward Ashcroft and firm in his defense of Gorelick. "We do not want to get into a fight with the Attorney General," he said, adding that he hoped that the attorney general "did not want to get into a fight with us."[102] He termed demands that Gorelick resign "silly." He called Gorelick one of the hardest-working members of the commission and lauded the bipartisan spirit she demonstrated in its deliberations.[103] Asked how he would respond to congressional calls for her to step down, Kean said that "people ought to stay out of our business."[104]

Kean's choice of words earned him the animus of some conservative commentators. Radio talk-show host Rush Limbaugh declared Kean an elitist.[105] In his answer to DeLay's open letter, Kean noted that while the commission's public exchanges had been pointed, the commission in its deliberations was devoid of the partisanship that characterized so many of the proceeding that took place in Congress. He added that, unlike the case in Congress, none of the commission's votes had been cast on a partisan basis.[106] With regard to the senators, Kean worked through back channels to reassure Bond, with whom he had enjoyed cordial relations when both had been governors, that the commission was conducting a fair and impartial investigation.

The attacks on Gorelick marked another turning point for the commission, further reinforcing its sense of unity and common purpose. Each of Kean's colleagues joined him in defending Gorelick. When John Lehman, considered by some to be the most conservative of the commission's members, was asked whether Gorelick should step down, he replied with a single word: "Baloney."[107]

After again demonstrating the bipartisan unity that by now had become the commission's trademark, Kean through his actions suggested that he had again taken to heart criticisms from outsiders about how some of his colleagues had comported themselves. Members of past commissions and former government officials charged that in airing their opinions in the press and on television about either the state of the investigation or antiterrorism policies they would recommend, some commissioners ran the risk of appearing to step out of their roles as impartial jurors, weighing evidence.[108] Kean and Hamilton told their colleagues that in the weeks preceding the commission's next hearing, they would not be granting interviews, barring some unforeseen event that required them to issue a statement. They requested that their colleagues do the same. Not wanting to disappoint Kean, most complied.

Attempting to lower the partisan temperatures that had risen in recent weeks, Kean reverted to the "third way" and "outsider" stances that had served him so well in the past. "Trying to do anything in Washington is very, very difficult because the atmosphere is so poisonous and there are rockets coming from the right and the left," he said. "But I believe we'll steer through the distractions and write a fair and balanced report."[109] By the end of April, the furor had quieted down. It rose again in May. At a hearing in New York, after the commission documented that failed communications systems impeded rescuers in their endeavors to assist victims after the attacks upon the World Trade Center, John Lehman suggested that the city's failure to correct the problem was a "scandal" and that its command-and-control system was "unworthy of the Boy Scouts." The city's tabloid press misconstrued the commissioner's remarks as intended criticism of the rescuers and first responders on 9–11.[110] Above a front-page photograph of a firefighter poised among the rubble at ground zero on September 11, 2001, the *New York Post* headline screamed, "INSULT: This Man Is a Hero, He Is Not a 'Boy Scout.'"[111] This time Kean was cast in the role of defending a Republican commissioner against barbs from the same newspaper that had recently savaged Gorelick.

The commission regained its balance during its final hearing in June, when it attempted to recapitulate the events of 9–11 as they unfolded, describing in detail how the U.S. government had responded to the largest attack in its history. Afterward, reporters appeared more interested in the differing interpretations Vice President Cheney and the commission placed on a phrase in a commission staff statement that discussed the nature of contacts the government of Iraq had with al Qaeda prior to September 11. Although it found that the two maintained contacts, the commission found no evidence of a "collaborative relationship." It subsequently inserted the word *operational* in front of the word *collaborative* after Cheney cited the passage in support of arguments that the two parties had provided mutual support to each other in planning the attacks.

At first Hamilton tried to smooth over differences in interpretation between the administration and the commission. "The vice president is saying, I think, that there were connections . . . we don't disagree with that," the vice chairman said. "[There is] just 'no credible evidence' of Iraqi cooperation in the 9–11 attack."[112] Kean, in trying to differentiate between an interim staff report and the final report of the commission, added to the confusion when he stated that "members [commissioners] do not get involved in staff reports."[113] After Cheney suggested that he might have had access to information the commission had not seen, the chairs released a statement, suggesting that the commission and Cheney had reviewed the same evidence.[114] With that last public relations flap behind them, the commission and its staff retreated from public view to review their findings for the final time and to decide what they would recommend to reduce the likelihood of future attacks of the kind that took place on September 11, 2001.

"Unity of Purpose; Unity of Effort"

On July 22, 2004, Kean, Hamilton, and their colleagues gathered in the Mellon Auditorium in Washington to present the commission's long-awaited findings and recommendations to the nation. Kean began by asking his listeners to recall how they felt on the day of the attacks. He asked them to recall the sense of grief and loss they experienced and the way in which Americans of all backgrounds put aside their differences to "come together as a nation." Anticipating criticism for its decision not to assign blame for what ensued on that day to particular government officials and individuals, he declared: "Our failure took place over many years and administrations. There is no single individual who is responsible for this failure. Yet individuals and institutions are not absolved of responsibility. Any person in a senior position within our government during this time bears some element of responsibility for the government's actions. It is not our purpose to assign blame. As we said at the outset, we look back so that we can look forward. Our goal is to prevent future attacks."[115]

Kean summarized the commission's findings, citing repeated instances in which government agencies failed to share information. He, like the 567-page report he introduced, attributed these failings both to structural defects in the manner in which intelligence gathering had been organized and to a "failure of imagination" on the part of policy makers. Hamilton then summarized the commission's forty-one recommendations. They fell into several categories: bringing the entire intelligence-gathering apparatus under a single head, transforming a bureaucratic culture that put a premium on the "need to know" into one that emphasized a "need to share" information, strengthening congressional oversight of intelligence and of homeland security, and establishing more effective public diplomacy.

Kean concluded by recalling that the commission had approached its task with a "unity of purpose." He proclaimed its greatest strength to be its unanimity, and its greatest achievement, its ability to come together. "We file no additional views," he said. "We have no dissents." He then announced that the commissioners agreed among themselves that they would play no active role in the presidential campaign. Instead, they would engage in a "unity of effort" to press for the enactment of their recommendations. "We believe that, in acting together, we can make a difference," he declared. "We can make our nation safer and more secure."[116] He then called upon those listening to him to join them. As he spoke, trucks began delivering the commission's report to bookstores across the country. Within hours, thousands of copies began flying off shelves.

Upon the conclusion of his remarks, Kean and his commissioners took to the airwaves and began fanning out across the country to explain their findings and recommendations. Unlike members of past commissions, they would not retreat from public view after they submitted their report. So that they could remain part of the policy process, Kean and his peers assembled a skeletal operation to assist in answering the public's questions about the report and its recommendations and to keep the public informed of progress they had made in getting them implemented. "We go out of business as a commission," Kean said, "but we do not go out of business as people."[117] They dubbed the new enterprise the "9–11 Public Discourse Project" and funded it with grants from private foundations and individuals. They agreed to reconvene in a year to report what recommendations had and had not been implemented.

Recommendations Become Law

In their reactions to the commission's report, policy makers were at first cautious. Congressional leaders, who only a few months earlier had opposed granting the commission a sixty-day extension on the grounds that they should lose no time in enacting the commission's recommendations, expressed doubt that Congress would be able to act upon its recommendations before it adjourned.[118] President Bush pronounced the commission's recommendations constructive, adding that he looked forward to studying them and to working with responsible parties within his administration to "move forward."[119] His opponent, Senator John Kerry (D-MA), endorsed the recommendations in their entirety. Suddenly, the upcoming presidential election, which many feared might politicize the commission's report, thereby

Fig 22.1. At the height of the 2004 presidential election, with much of the country falling into two distinct camps, "red states" and "blue states," both parties competed to be seen in conformity with the recommendations of the 9–11 Commission. The bipartisan nature of its deliberations brought the commission an influence all but unprecedented. Unlike so many previous commissions, it saw many of its recommendations adopted. (© 2004, The *Washington Post* Writers' Group. Reprinted with permission.)

impeding swift adoption of its recommendations, began to work in its favor as both candidates competed to be seen as more in line with what the commission proposed. Bush issued a series of executive orders, which he said would implement much of what the commission recommended.

With the commission's recommendations receiving wide coverage from the media and appearing to enjoy broad public support, House Speaker Dennis Hastert and Senate majority leader Bill Frist announced that both houses of Congress would hold hearings during the traditional August recess. Throughout August and much of September, Hamilton, Kean, and their colleagues appeared before twenty committees and subcommittees. Congressional observers doubted that any legislative action on the commission's proposals would ensue prior to the installation of the new Congress in January.[120] Opinions began to change after Democratic presidential nominee John Kerry suggested that Bush call Congress back into session during the election and John McCain urged that Congress go into special session immediately after the election to consider the commission's recommendations.

Although he endorsed the commission's proposal to create a director of national intelligence to oversee all of the nation's domestic, foreign, and nontactical military intelligence agencies and its recommendation that a counterterrorism center operate within this new apparatus, Bush initially opposed the suggestion that the new entity be granted complete budgetary and hiring and firing authority over the fifteen intelligence agencies the director would oversee.[121] By early September, he had adopted the commission's position.[122] In mid-October, both houses passed a version of a bill to restructure the nation's intelligence-gathering operation. While the Senate bill was closer in conformity to what the commission had recommended, Kean suggested that he and his colleagues remained open to ideas the House proposed. "We don't think we're Moses come down with the Ten Commandments," he said, insisting that his major concern was that the director of national intelligence be granted all the powers the commission proposed.[123]

As Congress prepared to adjourn for the fall elections, Kean publicly called upon Bush to press the House and Senate to resolve their differences: "I would certainly urge the president to do everything in his power to get a final bill to his desk before the election." He said that he believed Bush wanted a "strong bill" and had been told the president would be active in pushing for an agreement.[124] Within days, the White House sent a letter to House and Senate conferees, urging them to grant the national intelligence director "full budget authority" and "explicit authority" to transfer funds among agencies.[125] Negotiations came to a standstill when the chairman of the House Armed Services Committee, Duncan Hunter, released a letter he had received from the chairman of the Joint Chiefs of Staff, General Richard B. Myers, dated October 21, arguing that the bill would disrupt the military command structure.[126]

Speculation immediately arose as to how strongly, if at all, Bush wanted an intelligence bill, whether Myers had acted on his own, and whether he was empowered to speak for the administration.[127] After the election, negotiations resumed but did not advance. After a compromise appeared on the verge of passage during a rare weekend session prior to Thanksgiving, Speaker Hastert declined to allow the measure to go to the floor after Hunter and House judiciary chairman F. James Sensenbrenner Jr., both of them conferees, spoke against the measures in the House Republican Conference. Hastert maintained that he had been moved by Hunter's assertion that the bill might endanger troops in the field. Hastert made no mention of Sensenbrenner's objections in his statement. He would eventually promise to consider early in the next session the judiciary chairman's insistence that the bill include provisions that made it more difficult for illegal aliens to obtain drivers' licenses.

Between them, Hunter and Sensenbrenner were said to command sufficient votes to prevent the Republican majority from passing the bill on its own. That meant that if Hastert pressed ahead, the measure could only pass with Democratic support. While that outcome appeared likely, this was not a route that Hastert, who headed a narrow majority, wanted to travel. Some noted that Hastert's decision to "hold" the bill was consistent with his previously expressed disinclination to bring measures to the floor that did not command support from a majority of the majority party.[128] Kean, himself a former Speaker of a state legislature, maintained privately that had the measure been brought to a recorded vote, Hastert's unruly renegades, not wanting to incur the wrath of their constituents, would have recanted.

While many objected to Hastert's tactics, few questioned his commitment to seeing the legislation through. The Speaker asked conferees to keep working and stated that the House would not adjourn sine die. He also publicly requested that the president "get personally involved."[129] Days later, Kean, appearing with Hamilton on *Meet the Press*, seconded Hastert's request that Bush get more heavily involved. "The president's got to go to work," he said. Kean then proceeded to charm Bush into a corner: "This president is very successful when he's going to work on legislation. This president's for it. He said he's for it in the campaign. He said he's for it since. And I believe with his support and his help that this bill will pass."[130]

Bush had left himself open to Kean and Hastert's challenge. In his first press conference following his reelection, he had said that he had earned "political capital" during the campaign and that he intended to spend it. He had also stated that he placed winning the war against terror high on the list of priorities he intended to pursue.[131] The overlap between his goal and the commission's recommendations became readily apparent. Conservative commentator Robert Novak, considered friendly to the administration, summarized the president's predicament.

> Actually, the Bush team never dreamed it would have to cope with the intelligence bill once Congress recessed for the election. The president's men thought they had just dodged a bullet. . . . But non-passage of the bill was eclipsed by other events, especially Osama bin Laden's tape, before the election.
>
> It was not that the president was inactive after the election. He telephoned Sensenbrenner and sent Vice President Cheney to see him. But there was no full-court-press. "This should be a lesson for the president," a member of the House leadership told me. "Going half-way won't work." At least it won't work in the second term.[132]

For reporters, the intelligence bill became a symbol of Bush's resolve. His failure to deliver, many argued, boded poorly for his hopes to reform the tax structure and Social Security. Yet, days before Kean and Hamilton's appearance on *Meet the Press,* the intentions of the president and his team remained in doubt. One Republican official, claiming to have discussed the matter with West Wing officials, in summarizing the administration's attitude suggested to reporters that Bush's team "had to look like they're pushing the bill," but would cry no tears for its demise. "No one in this administration wants to be held hostage to an external power like the 9–11 commission or the so-called 9–11 families," he said.[133]

Reporters passed up no opportunity to ask the president his views on the stalled bill. "Let's see if I can say this as plainly as I can," an exasperated president said during a visit to Ottawa. "I am for the intelligence bill. I believe this bill is necessary and important and I hope we can get it done next week." He volunteered that he had spoken with all the key participants in Congress and would be speaking to congressional leaders once again.[134] At a press conference, flanked by seven other former 9–11 commissioners, Kean kept the pressure on both Bush and Hastert. "Our request to the nation's leaders today," he said, "is give us a vote." To an interviewer afterward, he said that he never "heard of a bill that had the strong support of the president, the vice president, the Speaker of the House, the Senate majority leader, the minority leaders of both houses and a large majority of the American people and that didn't pass."[135]

Kean's continued pressure began to have an effect. Vice President Cheney talked with Hunter. Senate Armed Services Committee chairman John Warner, after announcing that he shared Hunter's concerns, began seeking language to insert in the bill that would satisfy Hunter that the bill would not deprive troops on the ground access to intelligence from satellites or other sources, without changing the substance of the legislation.[136]

On December 17, 2004, in the Mellon Auditorium, the site where the commission had released its report five months earlier, two years and a day after Bush had announced Tom Kean's appointment as chairman of the 9–11 Commission, George W. Bush signed into law the first major overhaul of the American intelligence system since 1947. Days later, the *New York Times* began a story on post 9–11 American policymaking with the following lead: "Washington— Fresh from their role in overhauling the nation's intelligence agencies, members of the independent Sept. 11 commission say they will now lobby to restructure Congress and what the commission described in its final report as the lawmakers' dysfunctional oversight of the CIA, other spy agencies and the Department of Homeland Security."[137]

Having defied expectations, first that the commission would fail to achieve unanimity, and later that its most important recommendation would not be enacted for several months, if not years, Tom Kean was far from finished.

Epilogue

A Public Legacy

In each post Tom Kean occupied, he left behind sizable legacies. He helped transform an old, crusty, anachronistic state legislature into an effective institution, able to meet the demands of a growing and increasingly suburban population. He set an ethical standard against which New Jersey officials continue to be judged, however frequently and far they fall short of meeting it. Present at the creation of an active environmental movement, Kean authored and guided to passage laws that preserved open space, wetlands, and the coastline, safeguarded beaches, and protected the public health at a time when New Jersey was undergoing its greatest growth in both population and construction in its history. He devoted much of his time to these issues as governor.

In a state that was among the first to witness the dimensions of a festering urban crisis, Kean, while in the assembly, enacted the first urban aid package in New Jersey history and the first program to bring the benefits of a college education to its poorest citizens. As governor, he raised educational standards, reformed welfare, established enterprise zones, and made the state, its cities, and its universities more attractive to new industries. He rebuilt the state's infrastructure, reduced prison overcrowding, and found permanent solutions to recurring health emergencies. Because he established in the public mind the link between a good education and a high-paying job, Kean made the case for holding providers of services such as education accountable to the public and for the governor as the ultimate guarantor of that accountability.

As governor, Kean used the bully pulpit of his office to build a positive image of New Jersey in the minds of its residents. Like his family erstwhile nemesis, Franklin Delano Roosevelt, Kean showed a talent for motivating others. Whatever his target audience (disadvantaged youths; fellow legislators; party caucuses; state residents; governors of other states; college faculty, students, and administrators; a national commission evenly divided in partisan composition; or even presidents), he was a master at instilling a sense of pride and purpose. Institutions, he maintained, be they public or private, could not in themselves guarantee results but could "help dreams come true." In his nearly five decades in public service, Kean advanced many dreams and came to the rescue of many dreamers.

During bad economic times, Kean argued that the investments he wanted to make in the state's future would work to its benefit when the economy improved. He spoke so often about how, in deciding where to locate, businesses should consider the quality of a region's schools, transportation system, the state of the natural environment, and the quality of life—all high priorities for him—that job creators listened. In times of crisis, Kean became a reassuring force. Through his visible presence, his sharing of information, and his willingness to act, he demonstrated to residents that the state government he headed was both concerned for their welfare and acting to enhance their safety.

As he gave voice to the hopes and aspirations of nearly 8 million state residents, Kean developed a deep and personal relationship with disparate groups within the state population. He assembled his landslide reelection victory by winning substantial majorities within them all. Demonstrating his concern for causes they held dear, he signed legislation divesting the state's portfolio of investments in companies that maintained operations in apartheid South Africa, and used his access to Ronald Reagan to assist Russian refuseniks and to press the case for redress for Japanese Americans interned during World War II. As recently as 1985, when his party's candidates were scoring in single digits with African American voters, Kean won more than 60 percent of the votes they cast for governor of New Jersey. He kept conservatives in his corner, while pulling other traditionally Democratic voters into his camp. To his counterparts elsewhere seeking to replicate his success among minority voters, he shared his winning formula: "Establish first your commitment to civil rights and appeal to them in ways you do to other audiences." Although several followed his example, few made inroads comparable to Kean's.

At a time when the federal government was pulling back on its commitment to domestic programs, Kean was among the first governors to welcome the new responsibilities Washington had tossed his way. In devising innovative ways to meet new challenges, he and his counterparts across the country enhanced both their individual powers at home and their collective clout in Washington. This they used to bridge partisan and institutional divides on these issues between presidents and Congresses under the control of opposite political parties.

As chairman of the 9–11 Commission, Kean drew upon the "third way" style he had used to forge coalitions with legislators of both parties in New Jersey, his capacity to build and hold public support, and his preference for bipartisanship and pragmatism to produce what many thought impossible: a unanimous report together with recommendations that were quickly enacted.

Strengths

Kean's greatest strength as a leader was his capacity to motivate others. Before large groups, he acted as the major cheerleader for whatever cause he advocated. Working with peers (be they legislators, fellow governors, college administrators and faculty, or members of a national commission), he would lead from the sidelines, giving each of his colleagues a say. In the manner of a good coach, he would prod the group in the direction in which he wanted it to go, asking a question here, summarizing what he took to be a consensus, there, waiting—but not too long—for others to challenge his assessment. He also worked to create cohesion among whatever group he was part of, establishing a sense of common purpose, building a feeling of camaraderie.

Kean's second-greatest strength as a leader was his persistence. Able to take the long view, he could wear down would-be and actual adversaries. His determination as a freshman legislator to save Sunfish Pond, and his willingness to confront his adversaries in several forums, helped block a public works project that would have altered the character of his region and which the federal government, four state governments, big labor, and big business all supported. He proved just as tenacious as governor when he sought to reform teacher training, take over troubled schools, stop ocean dumping, finance infrastructure repairs, relieve prison overcrowding, and build a performing arts center in Newark.

Many an administration official in Washington, D.C., learned not to mistake Kean's gentle tone, good manners, and pleasant demeanor as chairman of the 9–11 Commission as signs of weakness. Through these qualities, he not only brought unity to a body many expected to deadlock, but broadened the scope of its investigation and won every procedural dispute over access to documents and individuals, money, and time.

In each of the positions he held, Kean applied what he had learned from past experience to new situations. He had seen as governor that by threatening to veto a bill while it was still before the legislature, he could craft it more to his liking. Sometimes such a warning proved just as effective as an actual veto. As chairman of the 9–11 Commission, Kean took a similar approach to the issuance of subpoenas. By threatening to invoke the commission's authority to issue them in well-timed statements to the press, he often gained access to materials he might not have obtained had the administration resisted his demands in court. Convinced that the race panel on which he sat failed to take on difficult issues because its members never got to know one another well enough to establish mutual trust, Kean set out early in his tenure on the 9–11 Commission to get to know each of his fellow commissioners as individuals. Having seen a federal entitlement commission on which he served bog down when members, pressured by outside interest groups, refused to put aside philosophical differences, he asked his fellow 9–11 commissioners to see if they could agree on the facts they were investigating before they began to debate what they would recommend.

Another characteristic that helped Kean succeed in his objectives was his nonjudgmental nature. Because he could accept people on their own terms, he was able to see situations from their point of view as well as from his own. That helped him enter into coalitions easily with people of divergent points of view and backgrounds. Kean could at the same time reach out to constituencies unaccustomed to voting for members of his party and to party conservatives, delivering the same message and attracting almost identical allegiance. As a legislator, Kean, the suburban moderate, staked out ground between rural-oriented conservative Republicans and urban-based liberal Democrats, shifting his stance accordingly as different issues came to the floor. He performed a similar balancing act as governor between a Democratic state legislature and a conservative national administration and between a Democratic Congress and a Republican president.

Weaknesses (Personal and Partisan)

Kean's preferred method of leading through consensus, often bipartisan, served him best when his partisan opposites were willing to work with him and to meet him at least halfway. In the assembly, he found Democratic leaders Christopher Jackman, Howard Woodson, David Friedland, and others amenable to working in such a fashion. Among the nation's governors, Kean encountered kindred spirits in Democrats Bill Clinton (AK), Bruce Babbitt (AZ), Charles Robb and Gerald Baliles (both VA), Michael Dukakis (MA), and many others. He did again on the 9–11 Commission, first with vice chairman Lee Hamilton and eventually with each of the commissioners.

Kean's most frustrating moments as governor came when opposition leaders in command of partisan majorities in either legislative chamber actively resisted him. During Kean's first term, Alan Karcher, while Speaker of the assembly, battled with Kean over the budget and spending priorities. Late in his second term, John Russo, as senate president, acted similarly, if to a lesser degree, to thwart Kean's endeavors to have the state move against failing schools. Although Kean often got much of what he wanted from both legislative leaders, and learned to maneuver around them, he sometimes yielded more than he intended when pressures to break legislative impasses were at their highest. Most observers believed Karcher won the budget battle the instant Kean agreed to an increase in the state income tax after repeatedly proclaiming such a course unacceptable. Kean came to agree with some critics that the concessions he made to Russo in order to pass the takeover bill weakened the statute's ultimate effectiveness. Before both matters were resolved, Kean compounded his difficulties by making, in moments of exasperation, threats that neither he nor his adversaries expected him to keep. (He never made good on his threats to cut programs when the legislature refused to raise the gasoline tax. Nor did he follow up on his suggestion that he would not campaign for Republican state senators who voted against the school takeover.)

At the root of Kean's reluctance to get tougher with his adversaries was his aversion to personal confrontations. This, coupled with his unwillingness to risk giving offense, impeded his effectiveness as a party leader. Unwilling to choose between two Republican aspirants for the U.S. Senate, both wanting to run for the seat of the disgraced Harrison A. Williams in 1982, he appointed a caretaker to fill the vacancy Williams's resignation created. His action ensured both a contested primary contest and a more difficult general election for the eventual nominee. With party fund-raisers coalescing around a candidate to oppose incumbent Senator Frank Lautenberg in 1988, Kean declined to throw his weight behind an African American member of his cabinet, whose candidacy would have demonstrated to the nation the validity of Kean's politics of inclusion.

That same year, Kean declined to endorse a candidate in the presidential primaries while the nomination remained in contention. Nor did he, after failing to groom a successor during his eight years in office, choose among several supporters contesting for the 1989 GOP gubernatorial nomination; he appeared in television commercials for several. Again, a contested primary ensued, compounding difficulties for the eventual nominee.

Had Kean succeeded in electing a Republican U.S. senator, especially in 1988, and/or a Republican successor as governor in 1989, he might have shown that the wide support he commanded, especially after his landslide reelection in 1985, extended beyond his personal appeal, thereby strengthening his argument that it was in the national Republican Party's interest to move in his direction.

Political Ambitions

To be complete, any biography of Tom Kean must consider why a public figure who entered public life relatively early, and who rose to the highest leadership positions in his state as a young man, did not seek public office again after he left the governorship at a relatively young age. From the instant he became a part of Bill Scranton's presidential campaign in 1964, Kean had both a cause and a calling. The cause was relieving the plight of the inner cities. The calling was elective office. He began participating in state politics as soon as he returned from the 1964 Republican National Convention. Three years later, at the age of thirty-two, he was a freshman assemblyman. Five years after that, he became its Speaker, the youngest in its history. A decade later, he was the state's forty-eighth governor and, again, among the youngest to have held the post. Along the way, Kean had sought and failed to advance his way up the state's political hierarchy by contesting two popular favorites of party elders in primaries.

At each of these junctures, Tom Kean appeared to possess ambition as well as talent. Part-time legislative leader, part-time maverick, he made his mark quickly and permanently on policy (education, the environment, consumerism, tenants' rights) and on the institution (written caucus rules, standing committees, conference committees, full-time partisan staff). Having shown his mettle early when he battled powerful interests to preserve a glacial lake, Kean the reformer proved capable of striking a political deal. Some said be made the "deal of deals" when he became Speaker through the intervention on his behalf of an ethically challenged, disaffected machine politician, who moved several votes Kean's way.

After waging a spirited and contentious campaign, Kean was elected governor in 1981 by the narrowest of margins—safeguarded, some insisted, by white vigilantes patrolling the very neighborhoods

Kean had entered the public arena to help. During the next eight years, he compiled a record presidential aspirants would envy (restored state pride, economic revitalization, education reform, infrastructure repairs, reduced crime, tax cuts, welfare reform, urban revitalization). These were clearly the actions and achievements of an ambitious man; ambitious for himself, ambitious to test the limits of what he might achieve through public service on behalf of his fellow citizens.

While denying any interest in a place on his party's national ticket in 1988, Kean spent much time speaking around the country, urging his party to embrace the very politics of inclusion that he had pursued in New Jersey. Whatever his protestations, he had clearly been testing his future viability in a national party that had in the years since he first participated in national politics veered steadily to the right ideologically and toward the Sunbelt geographically. His brand of inclusion and his record as governor proved insufficient to enable him to exert as powerful an influence on events within the national Republican Party as he had on New Jersey's. Kean made one last foray into national party politics in 1996 when he ventured into Iowa and attempted to find common ground with religious conservatives. While party conservatives praised Kean for his efforts, presidential nominee Bob Dole selected as his running mate Jack Kemp, whose message on inclusion was similar to Kean's, but who was right-to-life on abortion.

Kean gave serious thought to running for the one office that might allow him to exert the kind of impact on national policy many believed he sought, that of U.S. senator. Had he served in that role, Kean most assuredly would have once again carved out a "third way" path between a centrist Democratic president and a Republican Congress, or even between Republican moderates and Democrats in Congress and a conservative Republican president. However strong his inclinations might have been to try, two countervailing forces tugged him in the opposite direction: his ambivalence about abandoning a niche in which he felt comfortable, that of "statesman without portfolio," and his wife's aversion to seeing him back in the political fray, especially in an era in which personal attacks and negative campaigning had become the norm rather than the exception.

A Leader for All Seasons

The greatest irony of Kean's career came several months after he had said no to a Senate run for the last time. President George W. Bush tapped him for a role in which he would draw upon all the strengths he had shown in previous positions to enhance the security of the entire nation, that of chairman of the 9–11 Commission. This opportunity to render his nation a contribution of lasting value would be greater than that afforded to most U.S. senators and even some presidents. Tom Kean made the most of it. As was his way, he did it by mastering the material, working hard to motivate others, and by persisting.

What Kean said about how he accomplished as much as he had as governor equally applies to his manner of leading the 9–11 Commission. "One thing about being governor is that you have staying power. You try to convince. If you fail to prevail through one approach, you try another. And you keep coming back at it. Eventually you prevail."[1] Most of the time, he did it wearing a ready smile. Asked to assess Kean's most substantive achievement, former New York City mayor Edward I. Koch said that his colleague across the Hudson "demonstrated that nice guys can finish first."[2] Kean approached his greatest task like the professional he had become. Like professionals in other endeavors, especially sports, he made all he attempted look easy. Those familiar with his story know how difficult it was for him to achieve much of what he did.

Interviews

Note: All interviews were conducted by the author.

Albanese, George. Telephone. 10 June 2003.
Alexander, Lamar. Telephone. 15 April 2005.
Altman, Drew. Telephone. 1 August 2003.
Bennett, Bill. Telephone. 4 October 2004.
Berthelsen, Lee. Telephone. 27 February 2003.
Beveridge, Albert. Washington, D.C. 27 February 2003.
Bodman, Roger. Trenton, N.J. 24 July 2002.
Bradley, Bill. New York, N.Y. 21 November 2002.
Broonige, Tom. Telephone. 7 February 2005.
Brown, Sarah. Washington, D.C. 29 November 2004.
Burgio, Jane. West Caldwell, N.J. 13 August 2002.
Byrne, Brendan T. Roseland, N.J. 13 August 2002.
Canaday, Bob. Telephone. 17 February 2003.
Carter, Hodding. Telephone. 17 March 2003.
Castle, Michael. Washington, D.C. 13 April 2005.
Chambers, Raymond G. Morristown, N.J. 5 August 2002.
Cicatiello, Anthony. Plainfield, N.J. 4 August 2002.
Cino, Maria. Telephone. 26 June 2003.
Clinton, Hillary Rodham. Washington, D.C. 1 October 2002.
Clinton, William Jefferson. Telephone. 5 February 2003.
Coleman, Leonard S. Middletown, N.J. 27 September 2002.
Colgate, Bob. Telephone. 3 February 2003.
Coolidge, Linzee. Telephone. 2 February 2003.
Cooperman, Saul. Bernardsville, N.J. 4 October 2002.

Daggatt, Chris. Telephone. 26 August 2003.

Deming, Frederick W. Telephone. 15 February 2002, 22 February 2003.

Donaldson, Vicki. Telephone. 27 March 2003.

Duberstein, Ken. Washington, D.C. 16 October 2003.

Edley, Christopher. Telephone. 19 May 2005.

Edwards, Cary. Hawthorne. N.J. 13 August 2002.

Fenske, Helen Carner. Telephone. 25 May 2005.

Fenster, Saul. Telephone. 31 July 2002.

Fielding, Fred F. Washington, D.C. 29 November 2004.

Florio, James J. Newark, N.J. 12 August 2002.

Forbes, Steve. New York, N.Y. 21 November 2002.

Ford, Gerald R. Telephone. 28 May 2002.

Franks, Robert A. Washington, D.C. 8 August 2002.

Freeman, Peter. Telephone. 11 February 2003.

Gingrich, Newt. Telephone. 24 September 2002.

Golden, Carl. Florence, N.J. 4 August 2002.

Gonzales, Joseph. Trenton, N.J. 23 July 2002.

Gorelick, Jamie. Washington, D.C. 11 November 2004.

Gorton, Slade. Telephone. 9 December 2004.

Hamburg, David. Telephone. 1 December 2004.

Hamilton, Lee. Washington, D.C. 12 January 2005.

Hanson, John. Telephone. 3 October 2002.

Hausmann, C. Stewart. Telephone. 7 February 2003.

Hicks, Elizabeth Kean. Greenwich, Conn. 13 July 2002.

Hines, Jerome. Telephone. 14 December 2002.

Hodes, Harold. Telephone. 21 August 2002.

Holman, Frank. Telephone. 13 July 2005.

Horn, Geraldine. West Orange, N.J. 27 September 2002.

Horn, Michael. West Orange, N.J. 27 September 2002.

Howard, Peggi. Telephone. 29 November 2004.

Hsu, Ming. Telephone. 22 July 2002.

Hughey, Robert. Telephone. 23 November 2003.

Hyer, John L. Telephone. 2 June 2003.

Jenkins, James. Telephone. 11 February 2003.

Kaltenbacher, Philip. West Orange, N.J. 22 November 2002.

Katz, Joseph W. Princeton, N.J. 23 July 2002.

Kaufman, Luna. Telephone. 12 December 2002.

Kaufman, Ron. Washington, D.C. 3 September 2003.

Kean, Hamilton Fish II. New York, N.Y. 23 July 2002.

Kean, Reed. Telephone. 5 September 2004, 6 October 2004.

Kean, Robert W. Jr. Oldwyck, N.J. 15 October 2002.

Kean, Thomas H. Madison, N.J. 30 July 2001, 6 August 2001, 10 September 2001, 12 November 2001, 29 April 2002, 25 June 2002,

26 June 2002, 29 July 2002, 4 October 2002, 6 February 2003, 7 March 2003, 19 September 2003, 14 October 2003. Telephone. 8 August 2002, 26 August 2002, 12 November 2004, 29 June 2005.

Keene, David. Washington, D.C. 12 July 2005.

Kemp, Jack. Telephone. 17 March 2003.

Keybida, Andrew. Telephone. 20 May 2003.

Klagholz, Leo. Telephone. 26 June 2003.

Koch, Edward I. New York, N.Y. 12 July 2002.

Kolm, William. Telephone. 19 September 2002.

Kotok, David. Telephone. 15 January 2003.

Kuttner, Bernard A. Telephone. 27 January 2003.

Lansbury, Rose Kean. New York City, N.Y. 12 August 2002.

Lehman, John. Telephone. 30 December 2004.

Leo, Joseph. Telephone. 12 April 2003.

Leone, Richard C. Princeton, N.J. 23 July 2002.

Littell, Robert. Washington, D.C. 17 December 2003.

Littell, Virginia. Washington, D.C. 17 December 2003.

McGlynn, Edward. Point Pleasant, N.J. 27 September 2002.

McNany, Eugene. Telephone. 17 February 2003.

Marcus, Alan. Telephone. 15 March 2003, 26 August 2003.

Marcus, Dan. Washington, D.C. 7 January 2005.

Marshall, John. Telephone. 10 February 2003.

Merin, Ken. Telephone. 30 January 2003.

Merritt, Arthur. Telephone. 22 February 2002.

Miller, John J. Telephone. 8 February 2002.

Mills, Richard. Telephone. 20 June 2005.

Mitchell, Andrea. Telephone. 22 December 2004.

Morgenthau, Joan. Telephone. 29 November 2002.

Neff, Robert. Telephone. 20 February 2003.

Noble, Nick. Peterborough, N.H. 20 July 2003.

Odgen, Maureen. Telephone. 1 January 2003.

Pell, Edward. Washington, D.C. 17 June 2004.

Plechner, Richard. Telephone. 12 May 2003.

Price, Clement A. Telephone. 24 February 2003.

Reynolds, May. Telephone. 9 July 2002.

Roemer, Tim, Washington, D.C. 23 November 2004.

Roemmele, Herbert A. Telephone. 27 January 2003.

Roper, Richard. Telephone. 10 February 2003.

Shapiro, Peter. South Orange, N.J. 15 July 2002.

Sinsheimer, Warren. Telephone. 11 February 2003.

Sklaw, Harvey. Telephone. 18 February 2002.

Smith, Mary. Telephone. 22 October 2002.

Squier, Karla. Sunset Beach, N.C. 30 November 2002. Telephone. 14 March 2003.

Stein, Gary. Telephone. 1 January 2003.

Stevens, Greg. Telephone. 20 August 2002.

Stewart, Vivian. Telephone. 23 December 2004.

Stone, Roger. Telephone. 24 March 2005, 6 April 2005.

Strong, Alexandra Kean. Telephone. 9 October 2004, 11 October 2004.

Ujifusa, Grant. Telephone. 26 September 2003.

Yerkes, Peter. Washington, D.C. 30 March 2003.

Zelikow, Philip. Telephone. 15 February 2005.

Notes

Preface

1. See Walter Isaacson and Evan Thomas, *The Wise Men: Six Friends and the World They Made* (New York: Simon and Schuster, 1986).

Prologue

1. Terence Hunt, Associated Press, 9 April 2004.
2. Ibid.

1. The Early Years

1. Elizabeth Kean Hicks, interview by author, Greenwich, Conn., 13 July 2002.
2. Thomas H. Kean, interview by author, Madison, N.J., 4 October 2002.
3. Thomas H. Kean, *The Politics of Inclusion* (New York: Free Press, 1988).
4. Thomas H. Kean, interview by author, Madison, N.J., 30 July 2001.
5. "Doll[e]y Madison Delves into Howard-Kean Romance! Engagement of Elisabeth S. Howard and Robert W. Kean Comes as Surprise to Society—'Walk-ins' Coldly Treated at Miss Howard's Ball," *Evening Mail,* 7 July 1920.
6. John Winthrop (Mass.), John Winthrop (Conn.), Lewis Morris (New York, New Jersey), and Peter Stuyvesant (New York).
7. Susan was the daughter of Livingston's brother, Peter Van Brugh Livingston, of the New York branch of the famous family. John and Susan's son Peter married into the Morris family. Through this connection, the Keans' progeny became descendants of Lewis Morris, signer of the Declaration of Independence, and his great-grandfather, also Lewis Morris, a colonial governor of New Jersey. One of Peter's daughters married Hamilton Fish, governor of New York, U.S. senator, U. S. Grant's secretary of state, and father and

grandfather of two congressmen who carried his name. Peter's son John, Tom Kean's great-grandfather, had seven children, two of whom (John Kean and Hamilton Fish Kean) became U.S. senators.

8. "The Kean Family: A Long Tradition of Public Service," *West Essex Tribune*, 21 January 1982.

9. Robert W. Kean, *Four Score Years* (Privately published, 1974), 66.

10. Victor Kalman, "Robert Winthrop Kean: The Past . . . the Present . . . and the Future," *Newark Star-Ledger*, 26 November 1978.

11. Robert W. Kean, *Four Score Years,* ix.

12. "A Brief History of the Keane Family: Variants of the Name Keane, O'Keane, Kane, O'Kane, Kahane, O'Kaane, Cahan, O'Cahan, Cahane, Cane, Cain," Shannon Development Company and J. D. Williams, 1983. The researcher found the spelling *Kean* most common in Waterford.

13. Arthur K. Lenihan, "The Keans of New Jersey: A Proud Heritage Bestows Its Blessings and Burdens," *Newark Star-Ledger,* 12 September 1982; "Family, Tradition Cast the Mold of Jersey's Keans," *Newark Star-Ledger,* 13 September 1982; and "Cohesive Keans Retain a Sense of Family in Their Diverse Pursuits," *Newark Star-Ledger,* 14 September 1982.

14. Kean owed his military title to his years of service on the staff of Governor William Pennington.

15. Thomas H. Kean, *The Politics of Inclusion,* 131. Family lore holds that the more Webster drank that evening, the more in command he appeared to his audience.

16. "Doll[e]y Madison Delves into Howard-Kean Romance!"

17. Thomas H. Kean, interview by author, Madison, N.J., 6 August 2001. For an account of Sara Delano's personality that coincides with Elsa Kean's impressions, see Jan Pottker, *Sara and Eleanor: The Story of Sara Delano Roosevelt and Her Daughter-in-Law Eleanor Roosevelt* (New York: St. Martin's Press, 2004).

18. Robert W. Kean, *Four Score Years,* 46.

19. Rose Kean Lansbury, interview by author, New York, N.Y., 12 August 2002.

20. The family connection to the twenty-sixth president came through the marriage of Hamilton Fish Kean's oldest sister, Christine Griffin Kean, to Emlen Roosevelt, TR's first cousin and principal financial adviser.

21. Linda Donn, *The Roosevelt Cousins* (New York: Alfred A. Knopf, 2001), 163–199.

22. Robert W. Kean, *Four Score Years,* 14–15. U.S. senators would not be elected by the people until after passage of the Sixteenth Amendment to the U.S. Constitution in 1916. John Kean had endeared himself to New Jersey Republicans by placing seven thousand votes ahead of President Benjamin Harrison, who lost the state and nation to Grover Cleveland in 1892. Prior to his appointment to the Senate, Kean served two nonconsecutive terms in the House of Representatives.

23. Ibid. See also Joseph Benson Foraker, *From a Busy Life* (Cincinnati: Stewart and Kidd, 1916), 22. Aldrich was the grandfather of a powerful figure whose political fortunes would intersect with those of the Keans: Nelson Aldrich Rockefeller.

24. Robert W. Kean, oral history, New Jersey Historical Commission, 18 June 1979, 1; and Robert W. Kean, unpublished memoir. (Courtesy of Hamilton Fish Kean II.)

25. "America holds above her head the lamp of human liberty, welcom-

ing the oppressed of all nations that the world may see and follow. By the sacrifices of her people, she has grown in strength. She is at war not for conquest of nations or the spoils of cities, but for the right of humanity and human liberty. America was peopled by people who gave up home, country, and friends for liberty. I see that a German speaker calls us the 'scum of Europe,' but it requires more than ordinary bravery to be willing to give up home surroundings and traditions and to start a new life in a new world." *Elizabeth Daily Journal*, 4 June 1917.

26. Lansbury, interview, 12 August 2002.

27. Ibid.

28. Robert W. Kean, *Four Score Years*, 203–209.

29. McLean went on to serve in the House of Representatives from 1933 to 1945. Later in his career, he served on the New Jersey Superior Court.

30. Robert W. Kean, *Four Score Years*, 206–209; Robert W. Kean, oral history, New Jersey Historical Commission, 18 June 1979.

31. In his memoirs, Kean went out of his way to inform his readers that the bank had been named for *Theodore* Roosevelt. See Robert W. Kean, *Dear Marraine* (Privately published, 1969), ix.

32. Frank E. Vandiver, *Black Jack: The Life and Times of John J. Pershing* (College Station: Texas A& M University Press, 1977), 2:920.

33. Robert W. Kean, *Dear Marraine*, 198.

34. Hamilton Fish Kean lost the senatorial primary in 1924 to incumbent Walter E. Edge, won election to the Senate in 1928, and lost his bid for re-election to former governor A. Harry Moore in 1934.

35. Robert W. Kean, *Four Score Years*, 203–210; Robert W. Kean, unpublished memoir.

36. "Kean Cites Wilson in Plea for Tariff: Asks Adequate Protection from German Dye and Chemical Imports," *Newark Evening News*, 23 October 1929. At the time, the workforce at most New Jersey chemical companies consisted largely of German immigrants.

37. *New York Times*, 21, 29, 31 December 1931, 2 January 1932; and *Newark Evening News*, 21, 29, 31 December 1931.

38. "Mothers Thank Kean for Freeing Ocean of Filth," *Kean Action News* (campaign flyer, 1934).

39. *Newark Evening News*, 17 November 1933 and 22 April 1934. The site would eventually become part of the 26,000-acre Gateway National Recreational Area.

40. On May 11, 1928, while Hamilton Fish Kean was running for U.S. senator, the *Newark Evening News* published a letter from one of his African American supporters, Newark resident Asa Bryant. It read in part, "I recall how Mr. Kean fought for seating of the late Henry Lincoln Johnson, Georgia Negro delegate to the last National Republican Convention. If Johnson had been as white as a December snow he could not have had a more loyal supporter." For contemporaneous accounts of Kean's efforts on Johnson and his delegation's behalf, see *New York Times* and *Newark Evening News* for the month of July 1924.

41. In the 1920s, Leonides Dyer (R-MO) was the primary sponsor of antilynching legislation. After the Democrats took control of Congress in 1930, Dyer's bill was reintroduced by Democratic senators Edward Costigan (CO) and Robert F. Wagner (NY). Both efforts succumbed to Democratic filibusters in the Senate.

42. Once in command of the party structure, Hoover gave his support to

efforts to replace African American and integrated delegations at nominating conventions with ones that were "lily-white," a practice Kean had successfully worked to resist four years earlier. See Donald J. Lisio, *Hoover, Blacks, and Lilly Whites: A Study in Southern Strategies* (Chapel Hill: University of North Carolina Press, 1985).

43. Robert W. Kean, unpublished memoir.

44. Ibid.

45. Ibid.

46. Ibid.

47. A case in point was his relationship with Livingston farmer Whitehurst Carner, a World War I flying ace who had suffered a gas attack when his plane was shot down. Carner remained partially disabled for the rest of his life. When he fell on hard times during the Great Depression, Robert W. Kean, through his father, U.S. Senator Hamilton Fish Kean, arranged for Carner to be named Livingston town postmaster. Though an appointee of Herbert Hoover, Carner, through a combination of future representative Robert W. Kean's intervention and a change in the law that grandfathered incumbent postmasters after they had become part of the civil service, remained in his post during twenty years of Democratic rule under Presidents Franklin D. Roosevelt and Harry S. Truman. He retired during the Eisenhower administration. (Helen Carner Fenske, telephone interview by author, 25 May 2005.)

48. Ibid. It did Kean's cause no harm and much good that Little just happened to be married to Kean's brother John's mother-in law.

49. Ibid.

50. Ibid.

51. Thomas H. Kean, interview, 30 July 2001.

52. Ibid.

53. Thomas H. Kean, *The Politics of Inclusion*, 2.

54. Thomas H. Kean, interview, 6 August 2001.

55. Thomas H. Kean, interview, 30 July 2001.

56. Robert W. Kean, *Four Score Years*, 86, 104–105.

57. Hamilton Fish Kean 2nd, interview by author, New York, N.Y., 23 July 2002.

58. Thomas H. Kean, interview, 30 July 2001.

59. Linzee Coolidge, telephone interview by author, 2 February 2003.

60. Geoffrey C. Ward, *A First-Class Temperament: The Emergence of Franklin Roosevelt* (New York: Harper & Row, 1989), 211.

61. Hamilton Fish Kean II, interview, 2 February 2002.

62. Thomas H. Kean, interview, 30 July 2001.

63. During World War I, Elsa worked through the Junior League to tend to the welfare of soldiers and their families. "R. Winthrop Kean and Miss Howards Are to Be Married: Old New York Families to Be United by Their Wedding Next Autumn," *Sun and New York Herald*, 7 July 1920.

64. Thomas H. Kean, interview, 30 July 2001.

65. Lansbury, interview, 12 August 2002.

66. Hicks, interview, 13 July 2002.

67. Hamilton Fish Kean II, interview, 23 July 2002.

68. Thomas H. Kean, interview, 4 October 2002.

69. Hamilton Fish Kean II, interview, 23 July 2002; Hicks interview, 13 July 2002.

70. Thomas H. Kean, interview, 30 July 2001.

71. Ibid.

72. Ibid.

73. Lansbury, interview, 12 August 2002.

74. Hicks, interview, 13 July 2002.

75. For insight into Hoover's performance in this capacity, see Michael Dobbs, *The Nazi Raid on America* (New York: Alfred A. Knopf, 2004); and Richard Gid Powers, *Secrecy and Power: The Life of J. Edgar Hoover* (New York: Free Press, 1987).

76. Robert W. Kean, unpublished memoir.

77. For an assessment of how the implementation of the Social Security Act discriminated against African Americans, see Ira Katznelson, *When Affirmative Action Was White* (New York: Norton, 2005).

78. In 1955, U.S. Senator Clifford P. Case inserted into the *Congressional Record* an article from the magazine of the Fraternal Order of Eagles in which the organization hailed Representative Robert W. Kean as "Mr. Social Security." See *Congressional Record*, 8 July 1955. Representative Peter Rodino, in his eulogy to Robert W. Kean in 1980, referred to his former colleague as "Mr. Social Security." See *Congressional Record*, 24 September 1980.

79. Robert W. Kean, unpublished memoir.

80. Ibid.

81. Ibid.

82. Ibid.

83. *New York Times*, 17 November 1941.

84. Robert W. Kean, unpublished memoir.

85. Ibid.

86. *New York Times*, 12 March 1941 and 20 March 1941.

87. The New Jersey Supreme Court declared the statute unconstitutional on 5 December 1941, two days before the Japanese attacked Pearl Harbor.

88. For a fuller account of events mentioned in this paragraph, see Warren Grover, *Nazis in Newark* (New Brunswick, N.J.: Transaction, 2003). For a plausible fictional counter-history of this period, see Philip Roth, *The Plot against America* (Boston: Houghton Mifflin, 2004).

89. Gaulkin was a recognized leader of the Jewish community through his service as trustee of the Jewish Family Service Association. He served as Livingston Township attorney and assistant Essex County prosecutor before being appointed to the state superior court in 1958, rising to the appellate division. Gaulkin won considerable fame for his successful prosecution of four men in what became known as the "Newark milk scandal case."

90. "Edelstein Dies after House Talk: New Yorker Makes a Reply to Rankin's Charge on Jews and Collapses in Lobby," *New York Times*, 5 June 1941.

91. Robert W. Kean, unpublished memoir.

92. Ibid., and "Remark at Hearing Protested by Kean: Says Witness Criticizing Henderson Aims at Racial Antagonism," *Newark Evening News*, 11 October 1941; and "Kean Assails Move to Stir Racial Hate: Raps Georgia Official for Innuendo at Price Hearing," *Newark Star-Ledger*, 12 October 1941.

93. For a description of what Gore proposed, see Robert W. Kean, unpublished memoir; and Kyle Longley, *Senator Albert Gore, Sr.: Tennessee Maverick* (Baton Rouge: Louisiana State University Press, 1005), 49–55.

94. Thomas H. Kean, interview, 6 August 2001.

95. Robert W. Kean, unpublished memoir.

96. Thomas H. Kean, interview, 6 August 2001.

97. *Congressional Record-House*, 19 March 1943, 2240. The meeting Kean advocated took place a month later, not in Ottawa but in Bermuda. It recommended no additional rescue efforts. See David S. Wyman, *The Abandonment of the Jews: America and the Holocaust* (New York: New Press, 1988), chap. 6.

98. Wyman, *The Abandonment of the Jews*, 93–97.

99. For further discussion see Michael Beschloss, *The Conquerors: Roosevelt, Truman, and the Destruction of Hitler's Germany, 1941–1945* (New York: Simon and Schuster, 2002); Henry C. Feingold, *The Politics of Rescue* (New Brunswick, N.J.: Rutgers University Press, 1970); Arthur D. Morse, *While Six Million Died: A Chronicle of American Apathy* (New York: Overlook Press, 1998); Walter Laquer and Richard Breitman, *Breaking the Silence* (New York: Simon and Schuster, 1986); David S. Wyman and Raphael Medoff, *A Race against Death: Peter Bergson, America, and the Holocaust* (New York: New Press, 2002); and Wyman, *The Abandonment of the Jews*.

100. Wyman, *The Abandonment of the Jews*, 136; and Dr. Rafael Medoff, "Lobbying Against Genocide Then and Now," *Arutz Sheva*, 5 March 2004, www.ourjerusalem.com/opinion/story/opinion20040309.html.

101. See sections on Long in ibid. and Beschloss, *The Conquerors*.

102. Directed by Moss Hart and produced by Billy Rose, the play depicted thousands of years of Jewish history and featured prominent actors, including Edward G. Robinson, Sylvia Sydney, and Paul Muni. See Wyman and Medoff, *A Race against Death; Washington Evening Star*, 14 April 1943; and *Washington Post*, 14 April 1943. Kean's files contain an invitation to the event. Even if he did not witness the performance, he had to be aware of the Bergson group's efforts to publicize it, which included placing full-page advertisements in several newspapers, including the *New York Times*.

103. Kean's daughter Beth and Morgenthau's daughter Joan remained close friends for decades following their fathers' time in public service in Washington. Tom Kean remembered his parents pointing out the Morgenthau residence on Belmont Road, off Kalorama Road, on Sunday drives.

104. Robert W. Kean, "Address before the Long Branch, New Jersey Committee for the Celebration of the 10th Anniversary of the State of Israel, 1 June 1958," *Congressional Record-House*, 3 July 1958, 13028. (Submitted by Senator Clifford P. Case.)

105. Thomas H. Kean, interview, 30 July 2001.

106. Ibid.

107. Thomas H. Kean, *The Politics of Inclusion*, 2.

2. Kean Comes of Age

1. For a history of the school, see Edward Tuck Hall, *Saint Mark's School: A Centennial History* (Lunenburg, Vt.: Stinehour Press, 1967). Its rival school, St. Paul's, which Hamilton Fish Kean attended, was founded in 1856. Endicott Peabody established Groton, Franklin D. Roosevelt's alma mater, in 1885.

2. "Muscular Christianity" took as its goal the preparation of young men for a life of action, whether in sports competition, the field of battle, or public service. Those who sought to transplant the model of the English "public"

school to the United States no doubt agreed with the Duke of Wellington that the "Battle of Waterloo was won on the playing fields of Eton." They hoped that those they graduated would attain similar achievements in both war and peace. A curriculum that promoted muscular Christianity presumed that students, through strenuous physical exertion, would "sweat out evil." To achieve this end, headmasters often placed a higher priority on sports than on academics. Groton's founder, Endicott Peabody, once said that "the best thing for a boy is to work hard . . . to play hard . . . and then . . . to be so tired that he wants to go to bed and go to sleep." Muscular Christianity had reached its zenith by 1893, the year Robert W. Kean was born, when MIT president Francis Walker used the term in an address to Phi Beta Kappa. One of its leading exponents, future U.S. senator Henry Cabot Lodge Sr., saw among its virtues the subordinating of the individual to the group, through athletics, as a means of achieving national greatness or fulfilling high ideals. See Kim Townsend, *Manhood at Harvard: William James and Others* (New York: Norton, 1996), 97–120. See also Geoffrey Ward, *Before the Trumpet: The Emergence of Franklin Roosevelt, 1882–1905* (New York: Harper & Row, 1985), 171–179.

3. Hamilton Fish Kean II, interview, 23 July 2002.

4. Thomas H. Kean, *The Politcs of Inclusion* (New York: Free Press, 1988), 210–214; and Thomas H. Kean, interview, 30 July 2001.

5. *The Lion* (1953), 9. Tom was never paddled, a punishment most often administered for talking back to or insulting an upperclassman.

6. Thomas H. Kean, interview, 30 July 2001.

7. Ibid.

8. Hall, *Saint Mark's School,* 183.

9. Thomas H. Kean, interview, 30 July 2001.

10. Ibid.; and Matilda Cuomo, ed., *The Person Who Changed My Life: Prominent People Recall Their Mentors* (New York: Barnes and Noble Books, 1999), 107–109.

11. William Jefferson Clinton, telephone interview by author, 5 February 2003.

12. Thomas H. Kean, interview 30 July 2001.

13. Hall, *Saint Mark's School,* 190.

14. Thomas H. Kean, interview, 30 July 2001.

15. Ibid.

16. Robert W. Kean, *Four Score Years* (Privately published, 1974), 64.

17. Thomas H. Kean, interview, 30 July 2001.

18. Arthur K. Lenehan, "The Keans of New Jersey: Sense of Honor Is Wealthy Clan's Driving Force, Family Has Invested in Jersey's Future," *Newark Star-Ledger,* 12 September 1982.

19. Thomas H. Kean, interview, 30 July 2001.

20. Ibid. Roosevelt's contemporary critics expressed a view similar to Kean's of the Rough Rider's internal integrity. "Even in our hot bitterness over the Brownsville affair [an episode in which Roosevelt had disciplined an entire black regiment for the alleged misdeeds of a few], we knew that he [Roosevelt] believed he was right, and that he . . . had to act in accordance with his beliefs," opined the NAACP upon TR's death. See Kathleen Dalton, *Theodore Roosevelt: A Strenuous Life* (New York: Alfred A. Knopf, 2002), 524.

21. *The Lion* (1953).

22. Lee Berthelsen, telephone interview by author, 27 February 2003.

23. *The Lion* (1953), 63.

24. For an assessment of Robert W. Kean's relationship with Cohen, see

Edward D. Berkowitz, *Mr. Social Security* (Lawrence: University Press of Kansas, 1995), 75, 92, 99, 288, 339, and 344. Cohen routinely supplied Kean with questions and information the congressman would use at public hearings.

25. Robert W. Kean, unpublished memoir.

26. Robert W. Kean, oral history, New Jersey Historical Commission, 18 June, 1979, 19. For a discussion of the Kean Committee's work, see Henry Regnery, *Memoirs of a Dissident Publisher* (New York: Harcourt Brace Jovanovich, 1979), 134; and Jule Abels, *The Truman Scandals* (New York: Regnery, 1956).

27. Gerald R. Ford, telephone interview by author, 28 May 2002. Kean described a much revered colleague, Representative Dewey Short, in language similar to that which Ford had used when referring to R. W. Kean. "When it was known he was going to speak, the House would fill as the Members enjoyed listening to his eloquence." See Robert W. Kean, unpublished memoir; and Robert S. Wiley, *Dewey Short, Orator of the Ozarks* (Cassville, Miss.: Litho Printers and Bindery, 1985).

28. Kean did not specify whether he had proposed Ford for the vice presidential nomination in 1960 or in 1968. Kean had retired from the House in 1959, prior to both nominating conventions. Bolton remained an additional ten years. When I mentioned this to him, Ford confided that he had been totally unaware of R. W. Kean's support.

29. Robert W. Kean, oral history, 32.

30. Thomas H. Kean, interview, 30 July 2001.

31. Robert W. Kean, oral history, 28–29. Kean considered most other senators, who had to serve on more committees than House members, less informed than their House counterparts. For a description of the media attention Warren's daughters commanded at the convention and beyond, see Kevin Starr, *Embattled Dreams: California in War and Peace, 1940–1950* (New York: Oxford University Press, 2002).

32. Thomas H. Kean, "Sound and Fury: McCarthy, the Man and the Issue," *Saint Marker*, 3 October 1952.

33. Thomas H. Kean. "Sound and Fury: The Rosenbergs, Should They Die?" *Saint Marker*, 23 June 1953.

34. Thomas H. Kean, "Sound and Fury: Taft vs. Attlee," *Saint Marker*, 11 June 1953.

35. Thomas H. Kean, "Sound and Fury: The New Policy," *Saint Marker*, 20 February 1953.

36. "How can a fundamentally honest man such as Governor Stevenson sit back and listen to his supporters call Nixon a 'demagogue,'" Kean asked, "while the biggest demagogue of them all, Truman, goes up and down the country making charges and calling people names?" See Thomas H. Kean, "Sound and Fury: About Face," *Saint Marker*, 17 October 1952.

37. "Congressman Kean Gives Talk; Gives Views on Elections, Politics," *Saint Marker*, 21 November 1952.

38. *The Lion* (1953), 26.

39. Ward, *Before the Trumpet*, 192–193.

40. Robert W. Kean, *Four Score Years*, 168. While at Groton, Franklin Roosevelt joined an organization with a similar mission and an identical name. See Ward, *Before the Trumpet*, 192.

41. Hamilton Fish Kean II, interview, 23 July 2002.

42. Thomas H. Kean, interview, 30 July 2001. After becoming president of Drew University, Tom Kean would encounter people of his generation

who would tell him that they had only recently learned that his father had financed their education.

43. "Union Orders Halt on Pond Swimming: Kean's Property Closed to Bathers after Residents Lodge Protests," *Newark Evening News,* 29 June 1932; "Defends Swimming Hole: Senator Kean Acts to Preserve Pond on His Jersey Estate," *New York Times,* 26 June 1932; and "'Swimming Hole' Is Denied: Senator Kean Loses Fight for Young Bathers in Union," *New York Times,* 3 July 1932.

44. "Union Orders Halt on Pond Swimming."

45. Richard E. Noble, *Brantwood: A History* (N.p.: Trustees of Brantwood Camp, 1985), 1–2 and 19.

46. Thomas H. Kean, interview, 30 July 2001.

47. Letter from Dorothy B. Herrick to Peter B. Freeman, 3 June 1953, box 3, Brantwood Camp Collection, Peterborough Historical Society.

48. Thomas H. Kean to Peter B. Freeman, undated, box 3, Brantwood Camp Collection, Peterborough Historical Society.

49. Thomas H. Kean, interview, 30 July 2001.

50. John Marshall, telephone interview by author, 10 February 2003.

51. Thomas H. Kean, interview, 30 July 2001.

52. Marshall, interview, 10 February 2003.

53. Coolidge, interview, 10 February 2003.

54. Albert Beveridge, interview by author, Washington, D.C., 27 February 2003.

55. Thomas H. Kean, interview, 4 October 2002.

56. Ibid.

57. Coolidge, interview, 10 February 2003.

58. Marshall, interview, 10 February 2003.

59. Coolidge, interview, 10 February 2003.

60. Peter Freeman, telephone interview by author, 11 February 2003.

61. Quoted in Michael Norman, "Man in the News: A Reluctant Politician; Thomas Howard Kean," *New York Times,* 20 January 1982.

62. Quoted in Thomas H. Kean, *The Politics of Inclusion;* and Cuomo, ed., *The Person Who Changed My Life,* 108.

63. Quoted in Marshall, interview, 10 February 2003.

64. From cup itself and Noble, *Brantwood,* 147.

65. Thomas H. Kean, interview, 30 July 2001.

66. Alexander Leitch, *A Princeton Companion* (Princeton, N.J.: Princeton University Press, 1978).

67. Thomas H. Kean, interview, 30 July 2001.

68. Frederick W. Deming, telephone interview by author, 22 February 2003.

69. Beveridge, interview, 27 February 2003.

70. F. Scott Fitzgerald, *This Side of Paradise* (Ann Arbor, Mich.: Borers Classics, 2004), 39.

71. *Life,* 17 June 1957.

72. Thomas H. Kean, interview, 30 July 2001.

73. George F. Kennan, *Memoirs: 1925–1950* (Boston: Little, Brown, 1967), 9–15.

74. Thomas H. Kean, interview, 30 July 2001.

75. Arthur Merritt, telephone interview by author, 22 February 2002.

76. Thomas H. Kean, interview, 30 July 2001.

77. Berthelsen, interview, 27 February 2003.

78. Thomas H. Kean, interview, 30 July 2001.
79. Deming, interview, 22 February 2003.
80. Merritt, interview, 22 February 2002.
81. Beveridge, interview, 27 February 2003.
82. Thomas H. Kean, "Niemcewicz" (Senior thesis, Princeton University, 1957), preface.
83. Ibid., 32.
84. Ibid., 17–56.
85. The quotations in this paragraph are all from ibid., 10, 23.
86. Ibid., 80.
87. Ibid., bibliography.
88. R. R. Palmer, *The Age of Democratic Revolution: A Political History of Europe and America, 1760–1800* (Princeton, N.J.: Princeton University Press, 1959), vi.
89. Thomas H. Kean, interview, 30 July 2001.
90. Ibid.
91. Gary S. Stein, telephone interview by author, 1 January 2003.
92. Thomas H. Kean, interview, 30 July 2001.

3. In the Service of His Father

1. Thomas H. Kean, interview, 6 August 2001.
2. Robert W. Kean, unpublished memoir.
3. Moore, a close associate of Frank Hague, had been elected governor in 1925 and again in 1931. After defeating Kean, he resigned from the U.S. Senate in 1937, at Hague's behest, to return to his old post in Trenton. Prior to 1949, governors served terms of three years.
4. John O. Davies Jr., "Kean to Seek Senate Seat; Democrats' Field Increased: Representative Tells Goal," *Newark Evening News*, 30 January 1958.
5. John O. Davies Jr., "Kean Entry Gives Democrats Problems," *Newark Evening News*, 2 February 1958.
6. Thomas H. Kean, interview, 6 August 2001; and Herbert A. Roemmele, telephone interview by author, 27 January 2003.
7. Thomas H. Kean, interview, 6 August 2001.
8. Thomas H. Kean, interview, 30 July 2001.
9. Hicks, interview, 13 July 2003.
10. Hamilton Fish Kean II, interview, 23 July 2002.
11. Joseph W. Katz, "Kean Speaks for Tax Overhaul," *Newark Evening News*, 23 October 1958. (See other campaign stories by Katz and Davies.)
12. John O. Davies Jr., "Foe's Voting Role Draws Kean Fire," *Newark Evening News*, 15 October 1958.
13. Robert W. Kean, oral history, New Jersey Historical Commission, 18 June 1979.
14. *Newark Evening News*, 15 October 1958; and "Are You There?" editorial, *Newark Evening News*, 16 October 1958
15. During their conversation, after Mrs. Khalaf mentioned to Ike that her two sons, ages seven and nine, had wanted to stay home on the day of his call but had to go to school, the president promised to write the youngsters. For days, the press staked out her home in anticipation of the president's letter. After it arrived, Republican-leaning newspapers dutifully published its

contents. See "Letter from Ike: Two Maplewood Boys Are Happy," *Newark Evening News*, 17 October 1958.

16. Quoted in John O. Davies Jr., "No Need Seen for Ike, Nixon Visit," *Newark Evening News*, 29 October 1958.

17. John O. Davies Jr., "Eisenhower Endorses Kean," *Newark Evening News*, 28 October 1958.

18. Thomas H. Kean, interview, 6 August 2001.

19. Ibid.

20. Ibid.

21. Joseph W. Katz, "Senate Campaign Tempo Increases: Kean Notes ADA Help to Rival," *Newark Evening News*, 22 October 1958.

22. Quoted in Irvine White, "Report of New Jersey," *Newark Evening News*, 19 October 1958.

23. John O. Davies Jr., "Kean Hits Rival on Exodus of Jobs," *Newark Evening News*, 30 October 1958.

24. One exception was the *Newark Star-Ledger*, which, at the time, was prone to go in the opposite direction from its rival, the *Newark Evening News*.

25. William R. Clark, "Political Foreground: N.J. Senate Race Predictions 'Iffy': Essex Vote Seen Holding Key to Kean-Williams Outcome," *Newark Evening News*, 2 November 1958.

26. Katz, "Senate Campaign Tempo Increases."

27. Dawes Thompson, "N.J. Senate Candidates Appeal for Negro Votes," *Newark Evening News*, 28 September 1958.

28. *Newark Evening News*, 30 September 1958.

29. Clark, "Political Foreground."

30. Ted Hall, "Kean's District Was No Tip-off," *Newark Evening News*, 5 November 1958.

31. John O. Davies Jr., "Senate Hopefuls Sum Up Views: Kean Lays Stress on Experience," *Newark Evening News*, 2 November 1958.

32. John O. Davies Jr., "Williams by 85,000: House Is 9–5, Defeat of Kean Ends 22-Year GOP Hold," *Newark Evening News*, 5 November 1958.

33. Ibid.; and Clark, "Political Foreground."

34. Davies, "Senate Hopefuls Sum Up Views."

35. Roemmele, interview, 27 January 2003.

36. Hamilton Fish Kean II, interview, 23 July 2002.

37. "Kean Takes Cost Lead: Morris Is Second in Expenses, Grogan Ranks Third," *Newark Evening News*, 14 April 1958.

38. Robert W. Kean, oral history.

39. Thomas H. Kean, interview, 30 July 2001.

40. Robert W. Kean, unpublished memoir; and Robert W. Kean, *Four Score Years* (Privately published, 1974), 78–79.

41. Ibid.

42. *Newark Evening News*, "An Old Tale That Has a Sequel," 31 July 1928.

43. *Newark Evening News*, 31 July 1931.

44. Nelson Johnson, *Boardwalk Empire* (Medford, N.J.: Plexus, 2002), 96–97.

45. *Newark Evening News*, 16 and 17 May 1928.

46. "Jersey Primary Clean: Congress Inquiry Finds No Fraud in Senate Race," *New York Sun*, 2 February 1929.

47. *New York Times*, 5 June 1928.

48. *Newark Evening News*, 7 June 1928.

49. Ibid. One accuser made precisely such an allegation four years before Robert W. Kean declared his candidacy for the U.S. Senate. In a letter to his daughter, opened after his death in 1954, former governor Harold G. Hoffman wrote that when he ran for Congress in the 1920s, a certain wealthy elder candidate promised to finance his campaign. After the election, the man, Hoffman said, paid him $2,500 instead of the $17,000 he had promised him. Hoffman confessed to embezzling $300,000 to cover his debts and expenses. Harold G. Hoffman and Kean were both elected to federal office in 1928: Hoffman to his second term in the House of Representatives; Kean to the U.S. Senate. See *Newark Evening News*, 16 June 1954.

50. John O. Davies Jr., "Kean Hits Rival on Exodus of Jobs," *Newark Evening News*, 30 October 1958.

51. Thomas H. Kean, interview, 6 August 2001.

52. Leonard S. Coleman, "The Politics of Inclusion: The Black Perspective, Unfinished Business for the Republican Party," *New Jersey Reporter*, November 1989, 23.

53. For many years Mary Alice Kean served as regent of the Mount Vernon Ladies Association. She was the guiding force behind the conversion of Liberty Hall into a museum.

54. Robert W. Kean, *Four Score*, dedication page.

55. Thomas H. Kean, interview by author, Madison, N.J., 29 April 2002.

4. Kean Finds His Calling

1. Thomas H. Kean, interview, 6 August 2001.

2. Ibid.

3. Quoted by Thomas H. Kean, interview, 6 August 2001.

4. Ramsay Wood, "Profiles," *Saint Marker*, 29 January 1960, 2.

5. *The Lion* (1962), dedication.

6. Thomas H. Kean, interview, 6 August 2001.

7. *Saint Marker*, 5 May 1960, 4–5.

8. Ibid.

9. Thomas H. Kean, interview, 6 August 2001.

10. Ibid.

11. Thomas H. Kean, *The Politics of Inclusion* (New York: Free Press, 1988), 12.

12. Thomas H, Kean, interview, 6 August 2001.

13. Ibid.

14. Joseph W. Katz, "Nixon in State Drive: Experience Is Stressed, Matches Kennedy Crowd at Paterson in Start of Four-County Tour," *Newark Evening News*, 4 October 1960; and Joseph W. Katz, "Roaring Essex Crowd Hears Nixon Hit Foe's Farm Plan," *Newark Evening News*, 5 October 1960.

15. Katz, "Roaring Essex Crowd."

16. Ibid. Robert W. Kean's bringing Nixon to Newark was hardly a waste of the candidate's time. At the time, Kennedy and Nixon were competing heavily for the votes of African Americans, who were reported to have cast 60 percent of their votes for the Eisenhower-Nixon ticket four years earlier. Commentators on the election, as well as historians, attribute the support Kennedy received from African Americans (70 percent) to the widely publicized telephone call he placed to Mrs. Martin Luther King Jr. after her husband's arrest on 19 October, in Atlanta, Georgia, and subsequent sentence to

four months' hard labor. King's arrest came roughly three weeks after Nixon's visit to Newark. Though his support among African Americans dropped to half of what Eisenhower had polled four years earlier, or roughly 32 percent, Nixon's showing remains 20 percentage points higher than that any subsequent Republican presidential candidate has received. See Alvin S. Felzenberg, "Race and Republicans," *Weekly Standard*, 7 June 1999; Taylor Branch, *Parting the Waters: America in the King Years* (New York: Simon and Schuster, 1988), 374; and Theodore H. White, *The Making of the President, 1960* (New York: Atheneum, 1961), 315, 321–323.

17. *The Speeches, Remarks, Press Conferences, and Study Papers of Vice President Richard M. Nixon, August 1 through November 7, 1960, Final Report of the Committee on Commerce, United States Senate* (Washington, D.C.: Government Printing Office, 1961), 1169.

18. Kennedy placed ahead of Nixon in New Jersey by 22,324 votes. In Essex County, Robert W. Kean's counterpart, Democratic county chairman Dennis F. Carey, turned out a 50,000-vote plurality for Kennedy.

19. Thomas H. Kean, interview, 6 August 2001.

20. Ibid.

21. Ibid.

22. Ibid.

23. Ibid.

24. Ibid.

25. James Jenkins, telephone interview by author, 11 February 2003.

26. Quoted in Byron C. Hulsey, *Everett Dirksen and His Presidents* (Lawrence: University Press of Kansas, 2000), 196.

27. Rick Perlstein, *Before the Storm: Barry Goldwater and the Unmaking of the American Consensus* (New York: Hill and Wang, 2001), 364.

28. As evidence of the popularity of anti-integrationist sentiment in the North, political strategists pointed to Alabama segregationist Governor George C. Wallace's capture of 34 percent of the vote in Wisconsin's Democratic presidential primary in 1964 and 43 percent in Maryland's. See Perlstein, *Before the Storm*, 325–326, 342–343.

29. Theodore H. White, *The Making of the President, 1964* (New York: Atheneum, 1965), 90.

30. Thomas H. Kean, interview, 6 August 2001; Warren Sinsheimer, telephone interview by author, 11 February 2003. For an assessment of the strategy that won Willkie the nomination, see Steven Neal, *Dark Horse: A Biography of Wendell Willkie* (New York: Doubleday, 1984); and Charles Peters, *Five Days in Philadelphia: The Amazing "We Want Willkie" Convention of 1940 and How It Freed FDR to Save the Western World* (New York: Public Affairs, 2005).

31. Author's conversation with Gerald R. Ford, Philadelphia, 2 August 2000.

32. White, *The Making of the President, 1964*, 164.

33. Thomas H. Kean, interview, 6 August 2001.

34. Ibid.

35. Ibid.

36. Thomas H. Kean, *The Politics of Inclusion*, 10.

37. Ibid.

38. Perlstein, *Before the Storm*, 385.

39. Thomas H. Kean, interview, 6 August 2001.

40. Perlstein, *Before the Storm*, 447–451.

41. Thomas H. Kean, interview, 6 August 2001.
42. Richard O. Shafer, "Case Walks Out on Barry, Blasts Civil Rights Stand," *Newark Star-Ledger,* 17 July 1964; and Angelo Baglivo, "Case and Blau Reject Barry," *Newark Evening News,* 16 July 1964.
43. Richard O. Shafer, "Jersey Negro Delegate Leads Goldwater Boycott," *Newark Star-Ledger,* 17 July 1964.
44. Thomas H. Kean, interview, 6 August 2001.
45. Sinsheimer, interview, 11 February 2003.
46. Thomas H. Kean, interview, 6 August 2001.
47. Ibid.
48. For an examination of Todd's chairmanship, see Patricia Beard, *Growing Up Republican: Christine Todd Whitman, the Politics of Character* (New York: HarperCollins, 1996), 117–124.
49. Interpreting Todd's pledge of neutrality as an attempt to assist Nelson A. Rockefeller's challenge to Nixon for the 1968 nomination, Nixon entrusted both of his New Jersey campaigns to Bergen County chairman Nelson Gross, as well as the dispensing of patronage afterward.
50. Joseph Leo, telephone interview by author, 12 April 2003.
51. That political season would be memorable for the exchange the two gubernatorial candidates had over whether to dismiss from the state university a professor who, at an antiwar "teach-in," announced that he would welcome a Viet Cong victory. Republican gubernatorial nominee Wayne Dumont pledged to have the professor, Eugene Genovese, removed from the Rutgers faculty. Democratic governor Richard J. Hughes, seeking reelection, took the opposite view in the name of academic freedom, while making certain to assert his personal opposition to the professor's opinions. The election took on national overtones when Richard Nixon and Robert F. Kennedy both journeyed to the state to rally to the side of their fellow partisans. Hughes defeated Dumont by 363,572 votes, carrying in with him overwhelming Democratic majorities in both houses of the legislature.
52. Waller Waggoner, "Hearing on Finks Held in Newark: GOP Panel Told of Racist Songs, Denials Made," *New York Times,* 20 March 1966; and Robert Kohler, "A New Jersey Right-Wing Political Faction Adds a New Dimension to Group Singing: Anti-Semitism and Racism," *ADL Bulletin,* May 1966. Assisting Tomkins was Leonard J. Felzenberg, a second cousin of the author.
53. Ibid.
54. Ronald Sullivan, "Young G.O.P. Split at Jersey Parley," *New York Times,* 22 May 1966.
55. Grace Alselmo D'Amato, *Chance of a Lifetime: Nucky Johnson, Skinny D'Amato, and How Atlantic City Became the Naughty Queen of Resorts* (Harvey Cedars, N.J.: Down the Shore Publishing, 2001); Charles E. Funnell, *By the Beautiful Sea: The Rise and High Times of That Great American Resort City* (New Brunswick, N.J.: Rutgers University Press, 1983); Nelson Johnson, *Boardwalk Empire* (Medford, N.J.: Plexus, 2002); and Martin Paulsson, *The Social Anxieties of Progressive Reform: Atlantic City, 1854–1920* (New York: New York University Press, 1994).
56. Thomas H. Kean, interview, 6 August 2001.
57. Essex, Bergen, Passaic, Union, Sussex, and Hunterdon.
58. Thomas H. Kean, interview, 6 August 2001.
59. Quoted in Harvey Fisher, "Ex-Rat Fink for Judge: Kean Nominee has Strong Past," *Bergen Record,* 1 December 1988.
60. While the Constitution of 1947 transformed New Jersey's governor

from among the weakest in the country to one of the strongest—extending the governor's term from three to four years and permitting incumbents to seek reelection to one consecutive term, strengthening the veto by requiring a two-thirds legislative vote to override, and consolidating existing agencies, boards, and commissions into no more than twenty cabinet departments—it did nothing, by prior agreement, to alter the form or the structure of the legislature. A series of federal cases and their state counterparts, such as *Baker v. Carr* and *Reynolds v. Simms,* which decreed that districts be apportioned according to the "one man, one vote" principle, began a long and arduous process of legislative redistricting in the state.

61. Ronald Sullivan, "A Hughes Setback: Republican Majority Is 3 to 1," *New York Times,* 8 November 1967.

62. *Newark Evening News,* 10 September 1967.

63. Thomas H. Kean, interview, 6 August 2001.

64. Roemmele, interview, 27 January 2003.

65. One of Kaltenbacher's uncles, Philip Lowry, had been a Newark tax commissioner. Another, Mortimer Lowry, served in the assembly while Woodrow Wilson was governor.

66. The source for Kaltenbacher's background, as well as the quotation by him, is Philip Kaltenbacher, interview by author, West Orange, N.J., 22 November 2002.

67. Thomas H. Kean, interview, 6 August 2001.

68. Kaltenbacher, interview, 22 November 2002.

69. Thomas H. Kean, interview, 6 August 2001.

70. Freeman, interview, 11 February 2003.

71. Thomas H. Kean, interview, 6 August 2001.

72. Ibid.

73. Ibid.

74. Ibid.

75. Robert W. Kean, *Four Score Years* (Privately published, 1974), 76.

76. "Baird Declines Brandle Debate; Tells 10,000 Jersey War Vets He Will Continue Fight in 'Orderly' Fashion," *New York Times,* 5 October 1931.

77. "An Unlucky Barbecue," editorial, *New York Times,* 8 October 1931.

78. Robert W. Kean, *Four Score Years,* 68–69.

79. Ibid., 54. In 1987, Elsa and her children bequeathed the maquette to the New Jersey State Museum. Accepting it for the state was her son the governor.

80. Herbert A. Roemmele, interview, 27 January 2003.

81. Ibid.

82. Ibid.

83. Ibid.

84. Ibid.

85. C. Stewart Hausmann, telephone interview by author, 7 February 2003.

86. John J. Miller, telephone interview by author, 8 February 2003.

87. *Newark Evening News,* 1 November 1967.

88. *Newark Evening News,* 27 October 1967.

89. Angelo Baglivo, "Case, McNany Jolt Parties," *Newark Evening News,* 1 November 1967.

90. Ibid.

91. "Essex GOP Pair Complain McNany's Tactics Unfair," *Newark Evening News,* 2 November 1967.

92. *Irvington Herald*, 2 November 1967.

93. Ronald Sullivan, "Jersey GOP Captures Control of Legislature," *New York Times*, 8 November 1967.

94. Ibid.

5. The Precocious Freshman

1. For the tenor of the times, see Charles Kaiser, *1968 in America: Music, Politics, Counterculture, and the Shaping of a Generation* (New York: Grove Press, 1988); Mark Kurlansky, *1968: The Year That Rocked the World* (New York: Random House, 2005); and Theodore H. White, *The Making of the President, 1968* (New York: Atheneum, 1969).

2. Thomas H. Kean, interview, 6 August 2001.

3. Hausmann, interview, 7 February 2003.

4. William Jefferson Clinton, interview, 5 February 2003.

5. Thomas H. Kean, interview, 6 August 2001.

6. Ibid.

7. Thomas H. Kean, *The Politics of Inclusion* (New York: Free Press, 1988), 15.

8. Moraites acted as a bridge between the regimes of the former county leader, former state senator Walter Jones, and his successor, Nelson Gross.

9. Thomas H. Kean, interview, 6 August 2001.

10. Ibid.

11. *The Kerner Report: The 1968 Report of the National Advisory Commission on Civil Disorders* (New York: Pantheon Books, 1988), 1.

12. Peter Carter, "Battle Due on Community Affairs Bill," *Newark Evening News*, 22 March 1968; and Angelo Baglivo, "GOP Blushes, Bill Seems to Be Dead," *Newark Evening News*, 26 March 1968. Republican opposition to the department centered on Hughes's appointment of former Ford Foundation executive Paul Ylvisaker as the department's commissioner. Some feared that Ylvisaker would, as he had at the foundation, steer funds to community activists. For a glimpse into Ylvisaker's operating style, see Howard E. Covington and Marion A. Ellis, *Terry Sanford: Politics, Progress, and Outrageous Ambitions* (Durham, N.C.: Duke University Press, 1999), 294–352.

13. Peter Carter, "Essex GOP Assemblymen Push Welfare Bills Ahead," *Newark Evening News*, 2 April 1968.

14. Ernest Johnson Jr., "King Spends Day in Newark: Promotes D.C. March," *Newark Star-Ledger*, 28 March 1968.

15. Charles Q. Finley, "Negroes and Whites Side by Side: 25,000 Marchers Honor King in Newark," *Newark Star-Ledger*, 8 April 1968.

16. Ibid.; and Thomas H. Kean, interview, 6 August 2001.

17. Peter Carter, "Hughes Ghetto Aid Plan Will Cost $126 Million," *Newark Evening News*, 25 April 1968; Peter Carter, "GOP Vows City Aid; Wants Public Views," *Newark Evening News*, 26 April 1968; and Peter Carter, "How Much City Aid?" *Newark Evening News*, 18 April 1968.

18. "GOP Welfare Package Goes to the Governor," *Newark Star-Ledger*, 25 June 1968.

19. Peter Carter, "Hughes, GOP Reach Uneasy Bond Pact," *Newark Evening News*, 11 June 1968; and Peter Carter, "Hughes Fights Back," *Newark Evening News*, 16 June 1968.

20. Ibid.

21. *Newark Star-Ledger*, 18 February 1969.

22. Consistent with the pact the two county delegations had made, most of the urban bills proceeded to the floor under Bergen County sponsorship.

23. Thomas H. Kean, interview, 6 August 2001.

24. Ibid.

25. Ibid.

26. E-mail to author from Ralph A. Dungan, 5 April 2002.

27. Michael J. Hayes, "Rutgers Hall Held by Black Students," *Newark Evening News*, 24 February 1969; and Robert J. Braun, "Rutgers Officials Trying to Coax Students from Hall," *Newark Star-Ledger*, 25 February 1969.

28. Ibid.; Ladley K. Pearson, "Black Students Firm in Rutgers Seizure," *Newark Evening News*, 25 February 1969; and Ladley K. Pearson, "Sit-Ins Refuse to Leave," *Newark Evening News*, 26 February 1969.

29. Richard P. McCormick, *The Black Student Protest Movement at Rutgers* (New Brunswick, N.J.: Rutgers University Press, 1990), 40, 45, and illustrations.

30. Vicki Donaldson, telephone interview by author, 27 March 2003.

31. Frederick Kunlde and Nikita Stewart, "Anthony Imperiale Dies at 68," *Newark Star-Ledger*, 27 December 1999; David M. Halbfinger, "Anthony Imperiale, 68, Dies, Polarizing Force in Newark," *New York Times*, 28 December 1999.

32. Halbfinger, "Anthony Imperiale, 68, Dies."

33. Ladley K. Pearson, "Sit-in Ends at Rutgers," *Newark Evening News*, 12 December 1969.

34. Ladley K. Pearson, "Black Students Warn Rutgers Not to Modify Agreement," *Newark Evening News*, 6 March 1969.

35. "Dungan to Probe Incidents," *Newark Evening News*, 11 March 1969.

36. Donaldson, interview, 27 March 2003.

37. William Doolittle, "State Colleges: Negro Enrollment Lags," *Newark Evening News*, 1 April 1968; and William Doolittle, "Fewer Negro Students in New College Date," *Newark Evening News*, 24 April 1968. Surveys commissioned by Dungan revealed that Rutgers's Newark campus enrolled 60 African American students in a student body of 2,900.

38. Donaldson, interview, 27 March 2003. The commission Hughes had appointed to investigate the causes of the 1967 riots had cited the location of the medical school and the lack of community participation in the decision on where to situate it as contributing factors to the disturbances. For Dungan's role in settling the dispute surrounding the location of the medical school, see Connie Cedrone, "Medical School Will Be Settled Today: Dungan," *Newark Star-Ledger*, 1 March 1968; and Charles Q. Finley, "Basic Objections Resolved: Hughes Lauds Agreement on Med College," *Newark Star-Ledger*, 3 March 1968.

39. "Dungan to Probe Incidents."

40. Hayes, "Rutgers Hall Held by Black Students."

41. Thomas H. Kean, interview, 6 August 2001.

42. Ibid.

43. Ibid.

44. Donaldson, interview, 27 March 2003.

45. Ibid.

46. McCormick, *Black Student Protest Movement at Rutgers*, 67–77.

47. Ben St. John, "New Program: Rutgers Eases Entry," *Newark Evening News*, 15 March 1969; "Black Students Hail Eased Rutgers Entry," *Newark*

Evening News, 16 March 1969; Ladley K. Pearson, "New Rutgers Policy Bound to Cause Uproar," *Newark Evening News,* 16 March 1969; Peter Carter, "Legislators Hit Rutgers Plan," *Newark Evening News,* 16 March 1969; and William Doolittle, "Board Backs Rutgers Plan," *Newark Evening News,* 22 March 1969.

48. Peter Carter, "Legislators Avoid Floor Debate on Rutgers Admissions Policy," *Newark Evening News,* 18 March 1969.

49. "Plan Hearings on Rutgers," *Newark Evening News,* 13 May 1969.

50. "Legislators Avoid Floor Debate on Rutgers Admissions Policy."

51. "Plan Hearings on Rutgers."

52. Robert J. Braun, "Protests Build over Denial of More Aid for Rutgers," *Newark Star-Ledger,* 6 April 1969; Robert J. Braun, "Rutgers Turns Its Back on Commuter Students," *Newark Star-Ledger,* 13 April 1969; Robert J. Braun, "Rutgers-Newark Story: Campus Left Out in the Cold," 14 April 1969; and Robert J. Braun, "Middle Class in a Bind: Rutgers Policy May Increase Tensions," *Newark Star-Ledger,* 15 April 1969.

53. Michael J. Hayes, "Rutgers May Be Gubernatorial Issue," *Newark Evening News,* 15 March 1969.

54. "Rutgers Asks Urban Funds," *Newark Evening News,* 17 November 1969.

55. Peter Carter, "Assembly May End Rutgers Fund Ban," *Newark Evening News,* 14 April 1970; Peter Carter, "Vote Rutgers Fund Curb," *Newark Evening News,* 24 March 1970; and McCormick, *Black Student Protest Movement at Rutgers,* 81–90.

56. "The Ecologist Plea: 'Save Sunfish Pond,'" *New York Times,* 14 May 1972.

57. Ibid.

58. Thomas H. Kean, interview, 6 August 2001.

59. Quoted in ibid.

60. Charles J. Garrity, "Sunfish Pond Bill on Tap," *Newark Star-Ledger,* 12 April 1972.

61. "Assembly OK's Sunfish Pond Bill," *Newark Evening News,* 21 June 1968; "Assembly Votes Land Repurchase at Sunfish Pond," *Newark Star-Ledger,* 10 February 1970; Joseph A. Sullivan, "Assembly Votes to Reacquire 389 Acres near Sunfish Pond," *Newark Evening News,* 10 February 1970; Charles J. Garrity, "Sunfish Pond Bill on Tap," *Newark Star-Ledger,* 12 April 1972; Roger Witherspoon, "Utilities Spurned: Assembly Votes for Purchase of Sunfish Pond," *Newark Star-Ledger,* 13 April 1972; James M. Staples, "Sunfish Pond Measure Fails to Get Senate Approval," *Newark Evening News,* 19 May 1972; and Roger Witherspoon, "Sunfish Pond: Senate Balks at Buying Back Woodland Site," *Newark Star-Ledger,* 19 May 1972.

62. Thomas H. Kean, interview, 6 August 2001

63. "The Ecologist Plea: 'Save Sunfish Pond.'"

64. Thomas H. Kean, interviews by author, Madison, N.J., 6 August 2001 and 10 September 2001.

65. Ibid.

66. Ibid.

67. Ibid.

68. Ibid.

69. Thomas H. Kean, interview, New Jersey State Legislature Oral History Project, 3 October 2001.

70. Thomas H. Kean, interview, 6 August 2001.

71. Ibid.

72. James M. Staples, "Compromise in Works to Save Sunfish Pond," *Newark Evening News*, 7 July 1968; John J. Farmer, "Hughes Backs Tocks Switch," *Newark Evening News*, 9 July 1968; James M. Staples, "Kean to Reintroduce Sunfish Pond Bill," *Newark Evening News*, 12 January 1969; and Richard Harpster, "Case Buoys Hopes for Sunfish Pond," *Newark Evening News*, 27 May 1969. (Congressional approval was necessary for the pump storage system that was to be part of the Tocks Island Dam.)

73. "The Ecologist Plea: 'Save Sunfish Pond'"; and Thomas H. Kean, interviews, 6 August 2001 and 10 September 2001.

74. James M. Staples, "Tocks Power Project Approval Seen Sure," *Newark Evening News*, 20 March 1969.

75. Thomas H. Kean, interviews, 6 August 2001 and 10 September 2001.

76. Linda Lamendola, "Meyner Plunging into Pond Sale Squabble Today," *Newark Star-Ledger*, 24 July 1968; "Meyner and Dumont Tangle over Pond," *Newark Evening News*, 24 July 1968; and Staples, "Tocks Power Project Approval Seen Sure."

77. Gordon Bishop, "Cahill Rejects Tocks Plan as Fiscal, Ecological Mistake," *Newark Star-Ledger*, 14 September 1972.

78. Kean became alerted to the threat that agricultural runoff posed to the reservoir as he battled, unsuccessfully, to enact a bill to reduce the quantity of phosphates in detergents. Lobbyist Alan Marcus, working on behalf of the detergent industry, argued that the amount of pollution phosphates contributed to rivers and streams was minimal when compared to that produced by agricultural runoff, containing both pesticides and wastes. Alan Marcus, telephone interview by author, 15 March 2005.

79. Thomas H. Kean, interview, 10 September 2001.

80. Ibid.

81. Ibid. and Thomas H. Kean, oral history.

82. "Kean Questions Rutgers on Pesticides," *Newark Evening News*, 31 October 1969.

83. Thomas H. Kean, interview, 10 September 2001.

84. *Newark Evening News*, 8 August 1968.

85. For assessments of Bliss's brand of leadership, see John C. Green, ed., *Politics, Professionalism, and Power: Modern Party Organization and the Legacy of Ray C. Bliss* (Latham, Md.: University Press of America, 1994); and Sean J. Savage, *JFK, LBJ, and the Democratic Party* (Albany: SUNY Press, 2004), 191, 258, 279–280. In addition to workshops in such as those described in the text, Bliss invested party resources in such areas as College Republicans, Young Republicans, and minority outreach.

86. *Newark Evening News*, 8 August 1968.

87. Alan Marcus, interview, 15 March 2005.

88. Hausmann, interview, 7 February 2003.

89. Eyewitness account by author.

90. "Skirbst Urges Local Support of Hausmann, 2 Assemblymen," *Irvington Herald*, 30 October 1969.

91. "Officials Warned by Kean on State School Aid Plan," *Irvington Herald*, 25 December 1969.

92. *Irvington Herald*, 30 October 1969.

93. Jean Joyce, "Cahill Bids Essex GOP Grow Up," *Newark Evening News*,

10 April 1970. "I don't know of any county that did less and got more than Essex," Cahill joked from the dais, at a dinner at which he delivered an ultimatum to local leaders to end their fratricidal feuding.

94. Thomas H. Kean, interview, 10 September 2001.

95. Ibid.

96. Ibid.

97. Linda Lamendola, "Cahill Symbolically Signs Environment Agency Bill," *Newark Star-Ledger*, 23 April 1970; "Earth Day Draws Throngs," *Newark Evening News*, 23 April 1970; and "Environmental Bill Signed," *Newark Evening News*, 23 April 1970. When the assembly passed the measure a week earlier, Kean noted that his bill would not only bring several agencies under one roof but consolidate under its purview several functions he had been pressing the state to take on, including initiation of complaints, the regulation of pesticides, and registration and regular reporting by industrial polluters. See "Assembly Backs New Department for Environment," *Newark Star-Ledger*, 14 April 1970.

98. Angelo Baglivo, "Cahill Backs Law Curb on Former Governors," *Newark Evening News*, 3 October 1969.

99. Ibid.

100. Peter Carter, "Cahill Says Meyner Danced to Tune of Power Interests," *Newark Evening News*, 11 September 1969; and John T. McGowan, "Meyner Discusses Role in Sunfish Sale," *Newark Evening News*, 12 September 1969.

101. "Meyner Accused of Distortion," *Newark Evening News*, 27 July 1969.

102. Angelo Baglivo, "Hudson Voters Get Word: 'Pull B-1 for Bill Cahill,'" *Newark Evening News*, 23 October 1969; and Angelo Baglivo, "Hudson Hails Cahill in Hero's Welcome," *Newark Evening News*, 22 October 1969.

103. "Jockeying Begins for GOP Leaders Jobs," *Newark Evening News*, 13 November 1969.

104. Thomas H. Kean, interview, 6 August 2001.

105. The source for details and quotations in this paragraph is Linda Lamendola, "Assembly Post to Kean: Essex Wins a Leadership Role," *Newark Star-Ledger*, 25 November 1969.

6. The Institutional Reformer

1. For an assessment of Cahill's record as governor, see Richard J. Connors, "William T. Cahill (1970–1974)," in *The Governors of New Jersey: Biographical Essays, 1664–1974*, ed. Paul A. Stellhorn and Michael J. Birkner (Trenton, N.J.: New Jersey Historical Commission, 1982), 228–233; Richard C. Connors, "William T. Cahill," in *Encyclopedia of New Jersey*, ed. Maxine N. Lurie and Mark Mappen (New Brunswick, N.J.: Rutgers University Press, 2004), 111; and Alvin S. Felzenberg, "The Impact of Gubernatorial Style on Policy Outcomes: An In-Depth Study of Three New Jersey Governors" (Ph.D. diss., Princeton University, 1978).

2. Thomas H. Kean, interview, New Jersey State Legislature Oral History Project, 3 October 2001.

3. James M. Staples, "Our Environment: 3 Pollution Cures" (4th of 6 articles), *Newark Evening News*, 26 August 1970.

4. Thomas H. Kean, interview, 10 September 2001. Kean patterned the

bill after a Michigan statute enacted in 1969. He said he began researching the issue after learning that people who wanted to act against polluters had been denied legal standing in court. The concept of class-action suits in environmental matters was said to have originated with University of Michigan law professor Joseph A. Sax. Kean justified the measure on the grounds that every citizen had the "right to take action to protect the air we breathe and the water we drink." He voiced the hope that "if the polluter knows every citizen is empowered to act against him," he might think twice. See "Bill for Citizen Pollution Suits," *Newark Evening News*, 20 April 1970. Thirty years after introducing the legislation, Kean defended his action, arguing that citizens had no other alternatives open to them at the time. Few corporations and governmental entities maintained in-house environmental advocates to address community concerns. This, he recalled, was a time when rivers were catching on fire and clouds of pollution hung over the New York skyline, making their way into eastern New Jersey. By the time he had left elective office, Kean voiced the view that times had changed to the point where people sued too much.

5. Ibid.

6. See Alan Rosenthal, "Reform in State Legislatures," in *Encyclopedia of the American Legislative System: Studies of the Principal Structures, Processes, and Policies of Congress and the State Legislatures Since the Colonial Era*, ed. John H. Silbey (New York: Charles Scribner's Sons, 1994), 2:837–854.

7. Citizens Conference on State Legislatures, *The Sometimes Governments* (New York: Bantam Books, 1971).

8. Ibid., 49.

9. Thomas H. Kean, oral history, 3 October 2001.

10. Angelo Baglivo, "GOP Caucus: Rules in Writing," *Newark Evening News*, 15 February 1970; Charles Garrity, "Assembly Works on Changes: Caucus System's Future in Doubt," *Newark Star-Ledger*, 12 December 1970; and Linda Lamendola, "In the Open: Assembly Will Replace Caucus with Committees," *Newark Star-Ledger*, 10 January 1971.

11. Thomas H. Kean, interview, 10 September 2001.

12. Garrity, "Assembly Works on Changes"; Peter Carter, "GOP Out to Abolish Caucus in Assembly," *Newark Evening News*, 30 December 1970; and Lamendola, "In the Open."

13. Thomas H. Kean, interview, 10 September 2001; and Thomas H. Kean, oral history, 3 October 2001.

14. "Golden New Aide to GOP," *Newark Evening News*, 12 January 1970.

15. Carl Golden, interview by author, Florence, N.J., 4 August 2002.

16. Thomas H. Kean, interview, 10 September 2001.

17. Kaltenbacher, interview, 22 November 2002.

18. Jane Burgio, interview by author, North Caldwell, N.J., 13 August 2002.

19. John McLaughlin, "Mr. Kean, Tracer of Lost Millions," *New York Daily News*, 24 January 1977.

20. Ibid.

21. Linda Lamendola, "A Fractured Leg Won't Keep Kean from His Big Day," *Newark Star-Ledger*, 10 December 1971; and Angelo Baglivo, "Kean Takes GOP Post Despite Broken Leg," *Newark Evening News*, 12 January 1970.

22. Mary Smith, telephone interview by author, 22 October 2002.

23. *Newark Star-Ledger*, 3 November 1971.

24. Leonard J. Fisher, "Friedland, Two Suspended from Law Practice," *Newark Star-Ledger,* 28 July 1971.

25. Joseph Carragher, "Stewart Victory Triggers Race for Assembly Reins," *Newark Star-Ledger,* 30 November 1971.

26. Peter Carter, "To Withhold 5 Names in Brennan Inquiry," *Newark Evening News,* 2 January 1969; Peter Carter, "Probe Mulls 'Spanking,'" *Newark Evening News,* 12 January 1969; Herb Jaffe, "Ethics and the Legislature: Lawmakers Wink at 'Scandalous Conflicts,'" *Newark Star-Ledger,* 12 January 1969; John T. McGowan, "Would Curb Wiretap Use," *Newark Evening News,* 16 January 1969; Peter Carter, "Crime No Partisan Issue, Hughes Warns Republicans," *Newark Evening News,* 16 January 1969; and Peter Carter, "Legislators Cool to Move 'Clarifying' Beadleston Report," *Newark Evening News,* 22 January 1969.

27. Eyewitness observation by the author.

28. Roger Harris, "Friedland Hands Assembly to GOP: Defection Deal Elects Kean Speaker," *Newark Star-Ledger,* 12 January 1972.

29. Joseph Carragher, "Anatomy of a Deal: Lawmaker Accuses Leader of Breach of Trust," *Newark Star-Ledger,* 16 January 1972.

30. Alan Marcus, interview, 26 August 2003.

31. Harris, "Friedland Hands Assembly to GOP"; and Carragher, "Anatomy of a Deal."

32. Ibid.

33. Leonard J. Fisher, "Governor Says Hudson Won't Get Special Treatment," *Newark Star-Ledger,* 20 January 1972.

34. Charles J. Garrity and Joseph Carragher, "Hudson Dems Drum Out Friedland: 2 Other Defectors Bounced," *Newark Star-Ledger,* 13 January 1972; and James J. Florio, interview by author, Newark, N.J., 12 August 2002.

35. Ronald Sullivan, "4 Democrats Give GOP Jersey Assembly Control," *New York Times,* 12 January 1972.

36. Thomas H. Kean, *The Politics of Inclusion* (New York: Free Press, 1988), 22.

37. *Newark Star-Ledger,* 16 January 1972 and 23 January 1972.

38. Kean, *The Politics of Inclusion,* 22.

39. Franklin Gregory, "Legislature—Old Circus, New Clowns," *Newark Star-Ledger,* 16 January 1972.

40. Peter Yerkes, interview by author, Washington, D.C., 30 March 2003.

41. Kean, *The Politics of Inclusion,* 21; and Leonard J. Fisher, "Controversy Nothing New to Friedland," *Newark Star-Ledger,* 16 January 1972.

42. Joseph Gonzales, interview by author, Trenton, N.J., 23 July 2003; and Fisher, "Controversy Nothing New to Friedland."

43. Charles Garrity, "Kean: Deal Was Made for Benefit of Essex," *Newark Star-Ledger,* 23 January 1972.

44. Gregory Hewlett, "As I See It," *Maplewood-South Orange Record,* 20 January 1972.

45. Ibid.

46. Thomas H. Kean, interview, 10 September 2001.

47. Leonard J. Fisher, "Two Dem Camps Claim Victory on Committee Posts," *Newark Star-Ledger,* 22 January 1972.

48. Ibid.

49. Alvin S. Felzenberg, "New Jersey: Speaker Kean Challenges a Deadlock," *Ripon Forum,* March 1972.

50. Harvey Fisher, "The State House," *New Jersey Reporter*, February 1988.

51. Thomas H. Kean, oral history, 30 October 2001.

52. Eagleton Poll Archive, poll 002, questions 34 and 36, February 1972.

53. Thomas H. Kean, "Cahill Listened to His Conscience, Not to Polls," *Bergen Record*, 14 July 1996.

54. *New York Times*, 17 July 1972.

55. *Newark Star-Ledger*, 11 April 1972.

56. *Newark Star-Ledger*, 30 June 1972.

57. *Newark Star-Ledger*, 16 March 1972.

58. "Bill on Pollution Amended to Prohibit Private Suits: Kean Leads Debate to Strike Changes He Says Would 'Cripple' Measure—Passage in Assembly Indicated," *New York Times*, 23 January 1973.

59. Roger Witherspoon, "Busy Day: Assembly Faces Bank Rules, Rent Leveling, Open Burning," *Newark Star-Ledger*, 14 February 1973.

60. Dan Weissman, "Rent Leveling: Kean Proposal Detours Committee Bottleneck," *Newark Star-Ledger*, 30 January 1973.

61. Dan Weissman, "Rent-Leveling Measure Voted by the Assembly," *Newark Star-Ledger*, 14 February 1973.

62. Dan Weissman, "State Top Court Backs Local Rent Lids," *Newark Star-Ledger*, 5 April 1973.

63. Thomas H. Kean, "On Protecting Our Coastal Areas," *Irvington Herald*, 9 March 1972.

64. Roger Harris, "Senate Soundly Defeats Environmental Package," *Newark Star-Ledger*, 27 April 1973.

65. Dan Weissman, "Assembly Returns to Approve Coast Protection Compromise," *Newark Star-Ledger*, 8 June 1973.

66. Fred Hillman, "Byrne Quits Court for Governor Race," *Newark Star-Ledger*, 25 April 1973.

67. Kean, *The Politics of Inclusion*, 24.

68. Burgio, interview, 13 August 2002.

69. Joseph F. Sullivan, "'Outside Issues' Plaguing Kean," *New York Times*, 28 October 1973.

70. Leo Carney III, "Ozzard Accuses Kean of Conflict in PUC Bill," *Newark Star-Ledger*, 30 October 1973; and "Ozzard Battling Kean on P.O.C. Proposal," *New York Times*, 4 November 1973.

71. Ibid.

72. Harvey Fisher, "The Day Wimp Turned Whip," *New Jersey Reporter*, November 1983, 32.

73. Howard Cossell, *I Never Played the Game* (New York: William Morrow, 1985), 59–80.

74. *Newark Star-Ledger*, 21 November 1973 to 2 December 1973.

75. Herb Jaffe, "Byrne, Giants Work Out New Lease Pact: Governor-elect Will Now Support Moral Pledge," *Newark Star-Ledger*, 28 November 1973.

76. Herb Jaffe, "Assembly Clears Moral Pledge for Cahill Signature," *Newark Star-Ledger*, 4 December 1973.

77. Thomas H. Kean, interview by author, Madison, N.J., 25 June 2002.

78. Golden, interview, 4 August 2002.

79. Joseph Carragher, "GOP Staffers Survive Democratic Landslide," *Newark Star-Ledger*, 6 January 1974.

7. In the Minority But Not in the Wilderness

1. Daniel Hays, "GOP Green Acres Plan Could Force Byrne Hand," *Newark Star-Ledger*, 13 May 1974; and Daniel Hays, "Byrne Proposes a Unique Plan for Green Acres," *Newark Star-Ledger*, 17 May 1974.

2. "Kean Urges Byrne to Obstruct Tocks Dam," *Newark Star-Ledger*, 3 May 1974.

3. "Kean Presses Vet Loan Aid Bill," *Newark Star-Ledger*, 5 April 1974.

4. *Newark Star-Ledger*, 30 April 1974. After voters rejected a referendum to allow casino gambling in 1974, gaming proponents succeeded in putting the question on the ballot again in 1976. The measure, which passed, restricted casinos to Atlantic City and dedicated a portion of casino-generated taxes to subsidies for prescription drugs for senior citizens.

5. James McQueeny, "Amendments Called 'Crippling': 'Right to Sue' Measure Advances," *Newark Star-Ledger*, 30 April 1974.

6. Eyewitness observation by author.

7. Quoted in James McQueeny, "School-Funding Commission Is One Step Closer," *Newark Star-Ledger*, 23 April 1974.

8. For a discussion of perceptions of Byrne's reversal of position, see Alvin S. Felzenberg, "The Impact of Gubernatorial Style on Policy Outcomes: An In-Depth Study of Three New Jersey Governors" (Ph.D. diss., Princeton University, 1978).

9. Fred Hillman, "Dem Majority Is Operating in Name Only," *Newark Star-Ledger*, 12 May 1974. Though Hillman focused primarily on the state senate, his observations pertained to the assembly as well.

10. Thomas H. Kean, interview, 10 September 2001.

11. Fred Hillman, "Kean Declares His Candidacy in Fifth District," *Newark Star-Ledger*, 27 March 1974; Ronald Sullivan, "Jersey G.O.P. Assembly Leader Seeks Congressional Nomination," *New York Times*, 27 March 1974; and Tony Wilson, "Kean Will Seek Fifth District Seat," *Trentonian*, 26 March 1974.

12. Tony Wilson, "Mr. Clean vs. Mrs. Clean for Congressional Bid?" *Trentonian*, 6 April 1974.

13. See Amy Schapiro, *Millicent Fenwick: Her Way* (New Brunswick, N.J.: Rutgers University Press, 2003), 131–133.

14. Thomas H. Kean, interview, 10 September 2001.

15. Ibid.; Schapiro, *Fenwick*, 136.

16. Quoted in Schapiro, *Fenwick*, 136; and *New York Times*, 10 March 1974.

17. Schapiro, *Fenwick*, 137. The Churchill and Meir references are the eyewitness recollection of the author, who heard Fenwick refer to them while on the stump.

18. Thomas H. Kean, "Foreword," in Schapiro, *Fenwick*, ix.

19. Tony Wilson, "Kean: Nixon Follows History of White House Abuses," *Trentonian*, 28 March 1974.

20. *Can One Man Make a Difference?* Kean newsletter in author's possession.

21. State of New Jersey, results of the primary election held 4 June 1974.

22. Thomas H. Kean, *The Politics of Inclusion* (New York: Free Press, 1988), 25.

23. Thomas H. Kean, interview, 10 September 2001.

24. Anthony Cicatiello, interview by author, Plainfield, N.J., 4 August 2002.

25. Linda Lamendola, "Senate Approves Measure: Assembly Delays Road Bonds," *Newark Star-Ledger*, 20 September 1974.

26. Thomas H. Kean, interview, 10 September 2001.

27. Dan Weissman, "Factionalized Dems Get Little Done in Assembly," *Newark Star-Ledger*, 20 October 1974.

28. Quoted in Thomas H. Kean, oral history, 89.

29. Quoted in "GOP Stalls Decision on Parkway Directors," *Newark Star-Ledger*, 30 October 1974.

30. Daniel Hays, "Arm-twisting May Be Pinched," *Newark Star-Ledger*, 26 November 1974.

31. "New Elective Posts Urged," *New York Times*, 1 June 1975.

32. "Kean Assails Special Panels That Don't Meet," *Newark Star-Ledger*, 12 September 1975.

33. Dan Weissman, "Kean Extracts Vote Pledge on Governor Study," *Newark Star-Ledger*, 28 November 1974; and "Study of Governor Office Bumped by Broader Plan," *Newark Star-Ledger*, 24 January 1975.

34. Linda Lamendola, "Kean Demands Explanation of Byrne Trip Costs," *Newark Star-Ledger*, 29 October 1975.

35. "Dems Smother GOP Tactic," *Newark Star-Ledger*, 21 February 1975.

36. Ibid.

37. Daniel Hays, "Lawmakers' Ratings Follow Party Lines," *Newark Star-Ledger*, 10 August 1975.

38. Quoted in *Irvington Herald*, 30 October 1975.

39. Ronald Sullivan, "GOP in a Partial Accord on Splitting Dinner Funds: State Committee and Assembly Election Campaign to Share Money Raised at Presidential Affair on Oct. 4," *New York Times*, 12 September 1975.

40. Fred Hillman, "By-play Held More Interest than President," *Newark Star-Ledger*, 12 October 1975.

41. *New York Daily News*, 30 October 1975.

42. Quoted in *Newark Star-Ledger*, 6 November 1975.

43. Fred Hillman, "Assemblyman-Elect Criticizes 'One Man Rule': Kean Facing Challenge to GOP Leadership," *Newark Star-Ledger*, 16 November 1975.

44. Fred Hillman, "Kean Returned as GOP Leader in the Assembly," *Newark Star-Ledger*, 25 November 1975.

45. "Kean Appointed to Head Ford's New Jersey Campaign," *Newark Star-Ledger*, 17 November 1975; and "Kean Named Jersey Head of Ford's Election Drive," *New York Times*, 17 November 1975.

46. "Ford Committee Tactics Irking Jersey Republicans," *New York Times*, 23 November 1975.

47. Fred Hillman, "Old Rivals Use 'Super Bowl' to Even Score," *Newark Star-Ledger*, 6 June 1976.

48. David Keene, interview by author, Washington, D.C., 12 July 2005.

49. Fred Hillman, "Reagan Slate Persists without His Blessing," *Newark Star-Ledger*, 23 May 1976.

50. Thomas H. Kean, interview by author, Madison, N.J., 12 November 2001.

51. Karla Squier, interview by author, Sunset Beach, N.C., 30 November 2002.

52. *Newark Star-Ledger*, 7 June 1976. Remarks of President Gerald R. Ford, Paterson, N.J., 6 June 1976.

53. Joseph F. Sullivan, "Statewide Criteria for Public Schools Debated

in Jersey," *New York Times*, 22 April 1976; and Joseph F. Sullivan, "A Pupil-Performance Bill Is Opposed," *New York Times*, 12 May 1976.

54. The other Republicans were Walter Foran (Hunterdon), Karl Weidel (Mercer), Anthony Villane (Monmouth), and Robert Littell (Sussex).

55. Alfonso A. Navarez, "Jersey Legislators Seeking Tax Accord," *New York Times*, 19 June 1976.

56. The legislature would eventually provide such relief in the form of homestead rebates.

57. Arthur K. Lenehen and Robert Cohen, "Assembly GOP Challenges School Order," *Newark Star-Ledger*, 29 June 1976.

58. After Karl Weidel (R-Mercer) voted in the affirmative, Robert Littell (R-Sussex) provided the forty-first vote.

59. Robert Littell, interview with author, Washington, D.C., 17 December 2003.

60. Ronald Sullivan, "Ford's Jersey Leader Warns on Reagan," *New York Times*, 28 June 1976.

61. *Newark Star-Ledger*, 8 August 1976; and Thomas H. Kean, interview by author, 12 November 2001.

62. Craig Shirley, *Reagan's Revolution* (Nashville: Nelson Current, 2005), 211; and Thomas H. Kean, interview, 12 November 2001.

63. Fred Hillman, "Reagan-Schweiker Pitch Lands Four State Delegates," *Newark Star-Ledger*, 6 August 1976. Reagan's three delegates were Thomas Bruinooge and F. Walton Wanner, both of Bergen County, and Donald Katz of Middlesex. Joseph Yglesias, of Hudson, was the alternate.

64. Ibid.

65. *Newark Star-Ledger*, 16 August 1976.

66. Ibid.

67. Reagan had already done precisely that when he announced prior to the convention that his choice as running mate was U.S. Senator Richard Schweikert of Pennsylvania.

68. *Newark Star-Ledger*, 17 August 1976.

69. *Newark Star-Ledger*, 20 August 1976.

70. Thomas H. Kean, interview, 12 November 2001.

71. Quoted in Robert Maitlin, "Kean Picked to Direct Ford Jersey Campaign," *Newark Star-Ledger*, 2 September 1976.

72. Thomas H. Kean, interview, 12 November 2001.

73. Greg Stevens, telephone interview by author, 20 August 2002.

74. Fred Hillman, "Zigs and Zags in the Lineup for Governor's Race," *Newark Star-Ledger*, 3 September 1976.

75. Carter promised not to raise taxes on the middle class; Byrne had said that the state did not need an income tax.

76. Fred Hillman, "Ford Laces in to Carter on Jersey Tour: Crowds Are Larger and Friendly," *Newark Star-Ledger*, 14 October 1976.

77. Ibid.; and Fred Hillman, "Jersey Hands Ford a Peacock's Plume for Campaign Derby," *Newark Star-Ledger*, 17 October 1976.

78. Ford, interview, 28 May 2002.

79. James T. Harney Jr., "Ford Claims 'Momentum' during Final Jersey Swing," *Newark Star-Ledger*, 28 October 1976; and Thomas H. Kean, interview, 12 November 2001.

80. See David Smallen, "Betty Applauded in Shore Swing," *Newark Star-Ledger*, 29 October 1976; and photo of Jack Ford leading a parade in Kearny, N.J., *New York Times*, 1 November 1976.

81. Hillman, "Zigs and Zags in the Lineup for Governor's Race."

82. Greg Stevens, interview, 20 August 2002.

83. Fred Hillman, "Kean Tosses His Hat into Gubernatorial Ring: Says He'll Let Income Tax Die," *Newark Star-Ledger,* 14 January 1977; David A. Maraniss, "Kean Enters Governor Race," *Trenton Times,* 14 January 1977; and Joseph F. Sullivan, "Kean Opens Drive for Governor: Says He'll Let Income Tax Expire," 14 January 1977.

84. Thomas H. Kean, interview, 29 April 2002.

85. Fred Hillman, "Kean's New Suit, Like the Emperor's, Is Very Revealing," *Newark Star-Ledger,* 16 January 1977.

86. Alan Marcus, interview, 26 August 2003.

87. Ibid.

88. David A. Maraniss, "Kean's TV Move Sets Trend in N.J.," *Trenton Times,* 22 March 1977.

89. *Newark Star-Ledger,* 2 June 1977.

90. Robert W. Kean, oral history, New Jersey Historical Commission, 18 June 1979.

91. John McLaughlin, "The Difference," *Trenton Times,* 6 June 1977. The tactic Kean found so frustrating would, by the Clinton era, go by the name "triangulation." In his subsequent campaigns, Kean would prove a master at its use.

92. "Cahill Backs Bateman and Prompts Clash: Kean Aide Brands Move 'Predictable,'" *Newark Star-Ledger,* 24 May 1977. Paul Sherwin, Nelson Gross, and Anthony Statile had all been indicted for electoral-related improprieties. Noel Gross had not.

93. Quoted in ibid.

94. Fred Hillman, "Kean 'Regrets' Remark," *Newark Star-Ledger,* 25 May 1977; Fred Hillman, "Kean Damaged by Innuendo in Spite of Apology," *Newark Star-Ledger,* 29 May 1977; and Marc Morgenstern, "'Cahill Gang' Slur May Have Cost Kean," *Trenton Times,* 8 June 1977.

95. Kean, *The Politics of Inclusion,* 29–30.

96. Hillman, "Kean Damaged by Innuendo in Spite of Apology."

97. *Irvington Herald,* editorial, 2 June 1977.

98. Roger Bodman, interview by author, Trenton, N.J., 24 July 2002; Robert A. Franks, interview by author, Washington, D.C., 8 August 2002; Alfonso A. Navaraez, "Bateman Joined by Kean in Try to Oust Byrne," *New York Times,* 23 August 1977; and "Bateman Names Kean as Aide: Bergen County Troubleshooter," *Newark Star-Ledger,* 23 August 1977.

99. Thomas H. Kean, interview, 29 April 2002.

100. "Bontempo Leaves Highway Authority," *New York Times,* 18 December 1977.

101. Harold Hodes, telephone interview by author, 21 August 2002.

102. Remarks of President Ronald Reagan at a Republican fund-raiser in Whippany, N.J., 15 October 1981.

103. *West Essex Tribune,* 25 September 1980.

8. The Making of the Governor, 1981

1. For an overview of Pat Kramer's career, see Christopher Norwood, *About Paterson: The Making and Unmaking of an American City* (New York:

Saturday Review Press, E. P. Dutton, 1974); and "The New Jersey Handicap," editorial, *New York Times*, 20 May 1981.

2. Passaic, Bergen, Morris, Hudson, Warren, Cape May, and Cumberland.

3. The author was on the scene when Imperiale made these remarks.

4. Thomas H. Kean, *The Politics of Inclusion* (New York: Free Press, 1988), 42–43; and Roger Stone, telephone interview by author, 24 March 2005.

5. David Wald, "Kean Officially Joins Race," *Newark Star-Ledger*, 28 January 1981.

6. Ibid.

7. David Wald, "Courter Agrees to Lead New Kean Campaign," *Newark Star-Ledger*, 3 February 1981.

8. Kean, *The Politics of Inclusion*, 30.

9. Thomas H. Kean, interview, 4 October 2002. (Fenske is the daughter of Whitehurst Carner, an associate of Robert W. Kean. See chapter 1, note 47.)

10. Henry B. Bryan, "Kean Would Slash Sales Tax and Reduce State Programs," *Trenton Times*, 29 April 1981; and Tony Wilson, "Kean Standing Tall on Tax Plan," *Trentonian*, 13 May 1981. See also "A Litmus Test in New Jersey," *Newsweek*, 4 May 1981.

11. "A Litmus Test in New Jersey."

12. Rowland Evans and Robert Novak, "Tax Cut Unites Both GOP Wings," *New York Post*, 13 May 1981.

13. "Reagan 'Hovers' over His Flock in GOP Primary," *Newark Star-Ledger*, 24 May 1981.

14. Ibid.

15. "Sullivan Attacks Kean in TV Commercials," *Newark Star-Ledger*, 27 March 1981; and Joseph F. Sullivan, "If Gibes Hint Lead, Kean's Out Front," *New York Times*, 16 April 1981.

16. "Sullivan Attacks Kean in TV Commercials," *Newark Star-Ledger*, 27 March 1981.

17. *Newark Star-Ledger*, 17 May 1981.

18. Joseph F. Sullivan, "If Gibes Hint Lead, Kean's Out Front."

19. David Wald, "Sullivan Aims for Two-Man GOP Primary," *Newark Star-Ledger*, 29 March 1981.

20. David Wald, "Middlesex County Backs Kean," *Newark Star-Ledger*, 8 March 1981.

21. David Wald, "Union GOP Backs Sullivan for Governor: Essex Fells Hopeful Overcomes Kean Lead to Win on Fourth Ballot," *Newark Star-Ledger*, 15 March 1981.

22. "Ford Advocates Death Penalty for Gun Assaults," *Newark Star-Ledger*, 3 April 1981.

23. "Byrne Signs Open Primary Law," *Newark Star-Ledger*, 24 March 1981.

24. *Newark Star-Ledger*, 24 May 1981.

25. James J. Florio, interview, 12 August 2002.

26. "Republican Posts Comfortable Victory," *Newark Star-Ledger*, 3 June 1981.

27. Ibid.

28. Thomas H. Kean, interview, 4 October 2002; and Herb Jaffe, "It's Florio versus Kean for Governor; Republican Posts Comfortable Victory," *Newark Star-Ledger*, 3 June 1981.

29. Jaffe, "It's Florio versus Kean for Governor."

30. Eagleton Poll Archive, poll 044, question q 31, May 1981. Reagan's

ratings in New Jersey would not reach their lowest point until after the 1981 election. In March 1982, during Kean's second month in office and with the recession at it deepest point, Reagan's favorable ratings fell to 38 percent while his unfavorable ones rose to 59 percent. See Eagleton Poll Archive, poll 047, question 2, May 1982. These figures would not reverse themselves until the eve of the 1984 presidential election.

31. Henry B. Bryan, "Kean 'Appalled' by Actions of Interior's Watt," *Trenton Times,* 16 July 1981.

32. Richard S. Remington and David Wald, "Reagan Boosts Kean during Morris Address," *Newark Star-Ledger,* 16 October 1981.

33. Dan Weissman, "Kean Breaks with Reagan on Transit Subsidy," *Newark Star-Ledger,* 15 September 1981.

34. "Kean Attacks Moral Majority," *Bergen Record,* 15 October 1981.

35. Charles Q. Finley, "Rivals in Race for Governor: Kean Breaks the Old Mold," *Newark Star-Ledger,* 7 June 1981; and Joseph F. Sullivan, "Jersey Race to Test President's Policies," *New York Times,* 7 June 1981. For a surprisingly similar account of Ronald Reagan's own commitment to a "positive," if not activist, view of state government, see Louis Cannon, *Governor Reagan: His Rise to Power* (New York: Public Affairs, 2003).

36. Byrne's first state chairman was Hudson County state senator James Dugan. His second was Mercer County Democratic chairman Richard J. Coffee.

37. Kaltenbacher, interview, 22 November 2002. See also David Wald, "Kean Chooses a Former Legislator as GOP Chairman," *Newark Star-Ledger,* 10 June 1981

38. The source for this paragraph is Golden, interview, 4 August 2002.

39. David Wald, "Florio and Kean Run the Race at Different Speeds," *Newark Star-Ledger,* 25 October 1981.

40. Eagleton Poll Archive, Poll 043, question q 7, September 1981.

41. David Wald, "The Final Days All Come Down to a Question Mark," *Newark Star-Ledger,* 1 November 1981.

42. After he became governor in 1990, Florio broke with the NRA when he advanced legislation banning the possession and sale of semiautomatic weapons and "cop killer" bullets. Because of his actions, the John F. Kennedy Foundation presented him with its "profile in courage award" in 1993.

43. Finley, "Rivals in Race for Governor."

44. Peter Marks, "Rivals in Race for Governor: Florio Poised, Hard Driving," *Newark Star-Ledger,* 7 June 1981.

45. Sullivan, "Jersey Race to Test President's Policies."

46. "Florio Assails GOP on Social Meanness," *Newark Star-Ledger,* 15 October 1981.

47. Matthew Purdy, "Florio Accepts Kennedy Endorsement," *Trenton Times,* 23 October 1981; and John Raymond, "Kennedy's Support 'Surprise' to Florio," *Asbury Park Press,* 23 October 1981.

48. Raymond, "Kennedy's Support 'Surprise' to Florio."

49. The information and quotations in this paragraph come from Donald Warshaw and David Wald, "Florio Takes Aim at Disputed Senatorial Courtesy," *Newark Star-Ledger,* 15 September 1981.

50. David Wald, "Kean Launches Million-Dollar Television Blitz," *Newark Star-Ledger,* 28 August 1981.

51. Vincent R. Zarate, "Kean Visits Rival's Turf, Cites Camden 'Neglect,'" *Newark Star-Ledger,* 22 September 1981.

52. David Wald, "Kean and Florio Split Difference at First Debate," *Newark Star-Ledger,* 30 August 1981.

53. Accumulated accounts of the *Newark Star-Ledger, Asbury Park Press, Trenton Times, New York Times, Bergen Record,* 26 August 1981.

54. Eyewitness account by author; and David Schwab and David Wald, "Florio, Kean Clash on Economic Issues," *Newark Star-Ledger,* 26 August 1981.

55. Ibid.

56. Ibid.

57. Tony Wilson, "Kean Flogs Florio in First Debate," *Trentonian,* 31 August 1981.

58. See photograph in *Asbury Park Press* and *Newark Star-Ledger,* 26 August 1981.

59. David Wald, "Florio and Kean Run the Race at Different Speeds," *Newark Star-Ledger,* 25 October 1981.

60. Eyewitness account by author.

61. "Reagan Meets Kean at Airport," *Newark Star-Ledger,* 8 September 1981.

62. Eagleton Poll Archive, poll 045, question q 1, September 1981.

63. Roger Stone, "The Edge of Tom Kean," *Philadelphia Inquirer,* 21 April 2004. According to Stone, Labor Secretary Ray Donovan, who had chaired Reagan's effort in New Jersey the previous year and had favored Sullivan in the primary, was slow to warm to Kean's candidacy and resented Kean's periodic criticism of his fellow cabinet officer Watt. Armed with polls showing that Kean could win, Stone lobbied presidential chief of staff James Baker for greater assistance from Washington to Kean's campaign. Baker had high regard for the accuracy for which Kean's pollster Robert Teeter was known. He had also personally observed Kean's strengths as an organizer and on the stump in 1976, when Kean managed Gerald Ford's campaign in New Jersey and Ford, contrary to expectations, won the state.

64. David Wald, "Kean Blames Governor for 'Crisis' in Prisons," *Newark Star-Ledger,* 27 September 1981.

65. David Wald, "Kean Buys the Beer in Hudson Incursion," *Newark Star-Ledger,* 16 September 1981.

66. Richard S. Remington and David Wald, "Reagan Boosts Kean during Morris Address," *Newark Star-Ledger,* 16 October 1981.

67. Ibid.

68. Mark Quinlan, "Tom Kean and Tom Dunn Do It with Style," *Elizabeth Daily Journal,* 23 September 1981.

69. Frederick W. Byrd, "Kean, Florio Fault State Education System," *Newark Star-Ledger,* 20 September 1981.

70. The source for this paragraph is ibid.

71. Robert J. Braun, "SAT Slump Deepens in Jersey: Figures Contradict Gains Reported in Minimum Basic Skills Test," *Newark Star-Ledger,* 27 September 1981.

72. Ibid.; and Robert J. Braun, "Testing Controversy Raises Fundamental Education Issues," *Newark Star-Ledger,* 9 October 1981.

73. Robert J. Braun, "Probe Is Demanded in SAT Score Drop," *Newark Star-Ledger,* 30 September 1981.

74. Tim O'Brien, "Kean Cites SAT Drop as Proof of 'T & E' Failure," *Newark Star-Ledger,* 1 October 1981.

75. Robert J. Braun, "Kean Chides Burke amid Dem Defenders," *Newark Star-Ledger,* 3 October 1981.

76. The sources for this paragraph are Robert J. Braun, "Kean vs. Florio: Education," *Newark Star-Ledger*, 13 October 1981; and eyewitness account by author.

77. *Newark Star-Ledger*, 15 October 1981

78. *Newark Star-Ledger*, 16 October 1981.

79. "Reagan Visit Nets GOP $520,000," *Asbury Park Press,* 17 October 1981.

80. Bob De Sando, "TV Debate Crowd Boos Kean, Applauds Florio," *Asbury Park Press*, 19 October 1981; and Vincent R. Zarate, "Kean, Florio Debate on Dem's 'Home Turf,'" *Newark Star-Ledger*, 19 October 1981.

81. Eyewitness account by author.

82. Jon Shure, "Florio, Kean Get Last Licks In: Final Debate Marred by Heckling," *Bergen Record*, 19 October 1981.

83. Eyewitness observation by the author.

84. Shure, "Florio, Kean Get Last Licks In."

85. Thomas H. Kean, *The Politics of Inclusion*, 51–52.

86. *Newark Star-Ledger*, 30 October 1981.

87. Jon Hanson, Kean's designated chairman of the sports authority, recalled that at no time did Kean suggest that the authority rename the facility (Jon Hanson, telephone interview by author, 3 October 2002). Given the personal friendship Kean enjoyed with Byrne, this may have been the one promise Kean made that he had no intention of keeping. During the administration of Christine Todd Whitman, the arena was renamed Continental Arena in recognition of the corporation's contributions to its renovation.

88. *Newark Star-Ledger*, 1 November 1981.

89. When asked at a press conference his opinion of Vaughn Meader's impersonation of him on a best-selling recording, *The First Family,* Kennedy said that he thought the voice sounded "more like Teddy." When questioning the veracity of Democratic campaign promises, Reagan would depart from his remarks, look into the camera, and proclaim, "And they call *me* an actor."

90. "Kean Tours Camden," *Passaic Herald News*, 21 October 1981.

91. Editorial, *Bergen Record*, 25 October 1981.

92. "The Choice in the Region: Close Call in New Jersey," editorial, *New York Times*, 26 October 1981.

93. "Choice for Governor," editorial, *Newark Star-Ledger*, 25 October 1981.

94. *Newark Star-Ledger*, 3 November 1981.

95. Quoted in David Wald, "Jerseyans Vote Today for New Governor: Kean, Florio in Close Race; Polls Are Open until 8 p.m.," *Newark Star-Ledger*, 3 November 1981.

9. A Truncated Transition

1. Jonathan Friendly, "Jersey Election Posed Problems for TV News Units," *New York Times*, 5 November 1981.

2. Bodman, interview, 24 July 2002.

3. Friendly, "Jersey Election Posed Problems for TV News Units."

4. Thomas H. Kean, interview, 29 April 2002.

5. Bodman, interview, 24 July 2002; and Thomas H. Kean, interview, 29 April 2002.

6. Friendly, "Jersey Election Posed Problems for TV News Units."

7. Joseph F. Sullivan, "Florio and Kean in Tight Race," *New York Times*, 4 November 1981. Kean quoted in David Wald, "Kean, Florio in Dead Heat: Vote Tallies Still Inconclusive in One of Jersey's Closest Races," *Newark Star-Ledger*, 4 November 1981.

8. Quoted in Wald, "Kean, Florio in Dead Heat."

9. Peter Marks, "Byrne Is Quipster on the Morning After," *Newark Star-Ledger*, 5 November 1981.

10. Dan Weissman, "Florio Goes to a Flick Alone," *Newark Star-Ledger*, 5 November 1981.

11. The quotations from Kean's news conference are in Arthur K. Lenehan, "Kean Banters to Break the Strain of Waiting," *Newark Star-Ledger*, 5 November 1981.

12. David Wald, "Unofficial Count: Kean by 1,726 Votes," *Newark Star-Ledger*, 6 November 1981.

13. Richard J. Meislin, "Jersey's Ballots Impounded with Tiny Margin Wavering," *New York Times*, 5 November 1981.

14. Richard J. Meislin, "Kean and Florio Plan Court Fight: Race in New Jersey Still Undecided—Camps Trade Charges," *New York Times*, 6 November 1981. "All we want is an honest election," said Republican national chairman Richard Richards.

15. Richard J. Meislin, "Jersey Controversy Widens over G.O.P. Patrols at Polls," *New York Times*, 7 November 1981.

16. Robert W. Kean, unpublished memoir.

17. Meislin, "Kean and Florio Plan Court Fight."

18. Franks, interview, 8 August 2002.

19. Meislin, "Kean and Florio Plan Court Fight."

20. Meislin, "Jersey Controversy Widens over G.O.P. Patrols at Polls"; and Dan Weissman and James Benson, "Prosecutor Quizzes Ballot Force Chief, May Grill Imperiale," *Newark Star-Ledger*, 17 November 1981.

21. David Wald, "Kean Terms Ballot Force 'Insensitive' and 'Overzealous,'" *Newark Star-Ledger*, 3 December 1981.

22. Peter Marks, "State Disbands Voter Watchdog Unit after Logging 'Handful of Complaints,'" *Newark Star-Ledger*, 11 November 1981.

23. Meislin, "Jersey Controversy Widens over G.O.P. Patrols at Polls."

24. Richard J. Meislin, "Jersey Vote Controversy Moves Further in Courts," *New York Times*, 8 November 1981.

25. Selwyn Raab, "Queries Arise on Background of Ballot Task Force Official," *New York Times*, 11 November 1981.

26. Meislin, "Jersey Controversy Widens over G.O.P. Patrols at Polls."

27. Ibid.; and David Wald, "Kean Boards Air Force 1 as 'Winner,'" *Newark Star-Ledger*, 7 November 1981.

28. Meislin, "Jersey Controversy Widens over G.O.P. Patrols at Polls."

29. The photo ran in the *New York Times* on 7 November 1981.

30. Squier, interview, 14 March 2003.

31. Quoted in Wald, "Kean Boards Air Force 1 as 'Winner.'"

32. Cary Edwards, interview by author, Hawthorne, N.J., 13 August 2002.

33. *New Jersey Legislative Manual* (1982), 459.

34. Golden, interview, 4 August 2002.

35. David Wald, "Kean Proclaims Victory but Expects a Recount," *Newark Star-Ledger*, 11 November 1981.

36. Its other members included state chairman Philip Kaltenbacher; Congressman Jim Courter; former senate president Raymond Bateman; Leonard

Coleman, executive director of the Greater Newark Urban League; Kean financier and real estate investor Jon Hanson; William Tremayne, vice president of the Prudential Insurance Company; Kean's friend from the National Guard and Paramus attorney Gary Stein; Marie Garibaldi, president-elect of the New Jersey Bar Association; Joseph Rodriquez, former head of State Commission of Investigation; and Eugene McCaffrey, Gloucester County chairman and former head of Bush's 1980 New Jersey campaign. See ibid.

37. Ibid.

38. Ibid.

39. Finding himself in a similar situation when he and George W. Bush finished in a virtual tie in Florida, Democratic presidential nominee Al Gore took a different stance from Florio when he requested a recount only in counties where he had run ahead.

40. David Wald, "Two Voting Machines Are Seized at Kean's Headquarters in Union," *Newark Star-Ledger*, 17 November 1981.

41. Weissman and Benson, "Prosecutor Quizzes Ballot Force Chief; May Grill Imperiale."

42. Raab, "Queries Arise on Background of Ballot Task Force Official."

43. David Wald, "Kean Terms Ballot Force 'Insensitive' and 'Overzealous,'" *Newark Star-Ledger*, 3 December 1981.

44. Ibid.

45. Dan Weissman, "Kean Says Recount Is Impeding His 'Recruiting' of an Administrative Team," *Newark Star-Ledger*, 24 November 1981.

46. David Wald, "Florio Concedes Race to Kean," *Newark Star-Ledger*, 1 December 1981.

47. *New Jersey Legislative Manual* (1982).

48. Wald, "Florio Concedes Race to Kean."

49. Bodman, interview, 24 July 2002.

50. Edwards resigned from the assembly in order to accept the post.

51. Reagan had divided responsibilities among James Baker (chief of staff), Edwin Meese (counselor), and Michael Deaver (adviser).

52. Byrne's troika consisted of Lewis B. Kaden (counsel), Richard C. Leone (state treasurer), and Geraldine English (counselor). Byrne's first counselor was Robert Mulcahy. After Mulcahy became executive director of the New Jersey Sports and Exposition Authority, Byrne turned to Harold Hodes.

53. The term for this practice was *agency shopping*. Edwards, interview, 12 August 2002.

54. Ibid.

55. Charles Q. Finley, "Burgio Stresses Active Role for Women," *Newark Star-Ledger*, 17 January 1982.

56. Here, as in the case of the troika, Kean was also following in the footsteps of Reagan, who retained Pendleton James, a professional "headhunter," to assist him in filling major positions in his administration.

57. One of the firm's principals, William Hutchison, a Short Hills resident, was a close personal friend of Kean.

58. Neither Byrne nor Hughes had served in the legislature. Cahill served a single term in the assembly early in his career.

59. Kean maintained that while he would cap his own salary at the amount of Byrne's, he wanted the flexibility to offer incumbents of major departments more than the then-prevailing amount. Unlike other chief executives, he felt unbound by protocol that held that no state official should earn more than the governor.

60. Vincent R. Zarate, "Kean Favors Increase in Salary for Cabinet, Judges, and Himself," *Newark Star-Ledger,* 24 December 1981.

61. Brendan T. Byrne, interview by author, Roseland, N.J., 13 August 2002.

62. See *Newark Star-Ledger* coverage of Kean's preinaugural activities, 16–20 Januay 1982.

63. James C. Humes, *Confessions of a White House Ghostwriter* (Washington, D.C.: Regnery, 1997), 86.

64. Thomas H. Kean, inaugural address, *New Jersey Legislative Manual* (1983).

65. Ibid.

10. Kean Settles In

1. Thomas H. Kean, *The Politics of Inclusion* (New York: Free Press, 1988), 60–95.

2. Vincent R. Zarate, "Kean Maps Steps on Fiscal Squeeze: Hiring Freeze Planned to Cut $130 Million Shortfall," *Newark Star-Ledger,* 3 January 1982.

3. Upon learning of Jackman's defeat, Charles Marciante, president of the AFL-CIO, accused Democratic state chairman James Malone of intervening in what should have been a contest among legislators. The results, he said, meant that a "bunch of lawyers" would be "running the Democratic show." See Vincent R. Zarate, "Assembly Speaker Election Divides Dems, Angers Labor," *Newark Star-Ledger,* 25 December 1981.

4. Peter Shapiro, interview by author, South Orange, N.J., 15 July 2002. For a summary of Karcher's career see Jennifer Potash, "Alan Karcher Dies at 56, Former Speaker of the State Assembly," *Princeton Packet,* 27 July 1999.

5. Kean, *The Politics of Inclusion,* 84.

6. For an account of O'Neill's strategy and tactics, see John Aloysius Farrell, *Tip O'Neill and the Democratic Century* (Boston: Little Brown, 2001), 539–692 and Alvin S. Felzenberg, "Tipping Point: Tip O'Neill and the End of the Democratic Era," *Weekly Standard,* 11 June 2001.

7. Zarate, "Assembly Speaker Election Divides Dems, Angers Labor."

8. Dan Weissman, "Short 'Honeymoon': Democratic 'Retaliation' Upsets Kean Forces," *Newark Star-Ledger,* 24 January 1982.

9. "Karcher Triumphs over Jackman," *Newark Star-Ledger,* 8 December 1981.

10. In 1979, Orechio won reelection by nine hundred votes. The last thing he wanted to see was a Republican governor, who had carried the Democrat's hometown of Nutley, campaigning there against him in 1983.

11. Weissman, "Short 'Honeymoon.'"

12. The program was titled the "Governor's Management Improvement Program." Under its auspices, hundreds of corporate executives set up shop in state agencies, fine-tooth combing budgetary practices.

13. Vincent R. Zarate, "Kean Asks Tax Hike in $6.3 Million Budget," *Newark Star-Ledger,* 11 March 1982.

14. This would be in addition to the eight-cent-per-gallon tax the state already placed on gas and the four-cent federal tax.

15. Tom Johnson, "Kean Remains Optimistic on Economic Plan," *Newark Star-Ledger,* 4 July 1982.

16. Vincent R. Zarate, "Governor Scrambles for Gas Tax 'Clincher,'" *Newark Star-Ledger*, 22 June 1982.

17. Vincent R. Zarate, "Budget Gets Mixed Reviews from Divided Legislature," *Newark Star-Ledger*, 16 March1982.

18. Vincent R. Zarate, "Governor Defends Gas Tax Plan as Dem Budget Opposition Grows," *Newark Star-Ledger*, 12 March 1982.

19. Joseph F. Sullivan, "Kean's Rocky Honeymoon," *New York Times*, 4 July 1982.

20. Thomas H. Kean, interview by author, 29 April 2002.

21. Joseph F. Sullivan, "Legislature Survives a Stormy Session," *New York Times*, 1 August 1982. The four Republican senators who changed their votes from yes to no were Gerald Cardinale (Bergen), John Paolella (Bergen), John Dorsey (Morris), and James Vreeland (Morris).

22. Quoted in Sullivan, "Kean's Rocky Honeymoon."

23. Thomas H. Kean, *The Politics of Inclusion*, 88.

24. Johnson, "Kean Remains Optimistic on Economic Plan."

25. Ibid.

26. Vincent R. Zarate, "Budget Battle Shaping Up over Slash in Transit Aid," *Newark Star-Ledger*, 27 June 1982.

27. Sullivan, "Kean's Rocky Honeymoon."

28. Richard S. Remington, "Kean Calls Cuts 'Insensitive' on Funds for Bulging Prisons," *Newark Star-Ledger*, 7 July 1982.

29. Quoted in Joseph F. Sullivan, "Kean at Odds with Democrats over Prisons," *New York Times*, 11 July 1982.

30. Stein, interview, 1 January 2003.

31. Ibid.; and Remington, "Kean Calls Cuts 'Insensitive' on Funds for Bulging Prisons."

32. Richard S. Remington, "Prison Bonding: 'Heavyweights' Line Up for Referendum," *Newark Star-Ledger*, 28 September 1982.

33. Vincent R. Zarate, "Karcher Will Propose Bigger State Income Tax Bite for Higher Brackets," *Newark Star-Ledger*, 8 August 1982.

34. Ibid.

35. Dan Weissman, "Nine Towns Sue Kean in Utility Tax Share Rift," *Newark Star-Ledger*, 16 November 1982.

36. Joseph F. Sullivan, "Kean Finds a Split in Democrats' Unity," *New York Times*, 21 November 1982.

37. Joseph F. Sullivan, "Kean's 'Sounding Board' Picks Up Bad Vibes," *New York Times*, 28 November 1982.

38. Ibid.

39. Joseph F. Sullivan, "Kean Signs Bills Raising Two Taxes to Cut Budget Gap," *New York Times*, 1 January 1983; and Vincent R. Zarate, "Kean Gives Final Approval to Income, Sales Tax Hikes," *Newark Star-Ledger*, 1 January 1983.

40. Thomas H. Kean, interview with author, Madison, N.J., 29 July 2001.

41. Linda Lamendola, "Day-Care Center Cuts Will Be 'Re-examined,'" *Newark Star-Ledger*, 1 April 1982; and "Union Leader Lauds Kean as 'Understanding,'" *Newark Star-Ledger*, 25 April 1982.

42. Quoted in David Wald, "GOP Leaders Try to Grin and Bear the Tax Increase," *Newark Star-Ledger*, 9 January 1983.

43. James J. Florio, interview, 12 August 2002.

44. The author was present when Kean told this story to the press.

45. Many believed that Garry Trudeau, the creator of the *Doonesbury* comic strip, modeled one of his characters, the blue-blooded congresswoman Lacey Davenport, on Fenwick. See Amy Schapiro, *Millicent Fenwick: Her Way* (New Brunswick, N.J.: Rutgers University Press, 2003).

46. Robert Cohen, "Brady Submits Judgeship Nominees as Donovan Looks to Influence Pick," *Newark Star-Ledger*, 22 September 1982.

47. The Atlantic City Expressway, the Garden State Parkway, and the New Jersey Turnpike.

48. Guy T. Baehr, "P.A. Director Sees Merit in Finance Plan," *Newark Star-Ledger*, 1 October 1982.

49. Vincent R. Zarate, "Kean's Call for Infrastructure Bank Is Attracting Interest Nationwide," *Newark Star-Ledger*, 20 February 1983.

50. *Newark Star-Ledger*, 19 September 1983.

51. Vincent R. Zarate, "Legislators, Kean Square Off on Funds for 'Infrastructure Bank,'" *Newark Star-Ledger*, 15 May 1983.

52. Stein, interview, 1 January 2003.

53. Ibid.

54. Donald Warshaw, "Builders Make Christmas 'Wish List' Urging Kean to Seek Re-election," *Newark Star-Ledger*, 21 December 1984.

55. Ernest Robertson, "Kean Gearing State as High-Tech Haven," *Newark Star-Ledger*, 4 April 1982; "State Panel Takes Steps to Lure High-Tech Outfits," *Newark Star-Ledger*, 13 September 1982; and "Jersey Is Falling behind in High-Tech Recruiting: Panel Emphasizes Tax Incentives Needed to Lure Growing Industry," *Newark Star-Ledger*, 3 October 1982.

56. As it had in support of the Transportation Trust Fund, the *Star-Ledger* ran a multipart series assessing the status of high technology in New Jersey and describing the potential benefits of increased state investment.

57. Rutgers University and the University of Medicine and Dentistry in Piscataway would house a center for biotechnology; a consortium of the New Jersey Institute of Technology, Stevens Institute of Technology, and UMDNJ in Newark would pioneer a center for hazardous and toxic substance management; Rutgers would maintain a center for ceramics at its main campus, while its agricultural school based at Cook College would operate a center devoted to food processing and distribution. Other centers would be established focusing on plastic processing, optical fibers, aquaculture, telematics, and distribution management at these and other sites.

58. Quoted in Vincent R. Zarate, "Jersey Coalition Formed to Boost $90 Million 'High-Tech' Bond Issue," *Newark Star-Ledger*, 16 April 1984.

59. Kitty MacPherson, "Kean Boosts $90 Million Hope for High-Tech Era: Governor Signs Ballot-Query Authorization with Fanfare," *Newark Star-Ledger*, 26 July 1984.

60. Ibid.

61. Thomas H. Kean, interview, 29 July 2002.

62. Robert J. Braun, "Upward Bound: NJIT Moving to World Class Status," *Newark Star-Ledger*, 12 April 1987.

63. Thomas H. Kean, interview by author, Madison, N.J., 26 June 2002.

64. Ibid. Kean was particularly proud that among the new hires at Rutgers University was an Oxford-trained biologist. He delighted in relaying that New Jersey had been attacked on the floor of the United Nations for "raiding" the talent pool in Great Britain. Also retained at Rutgers under the

challenge grant program was David Levering Lewis, who won a Pulitzer prize for his biography of W.E.B. Du Bois.

11. Building New Jersey Pride

1. Eyewitness account by author.
2. Betty M. Liu, "4 Advertising Agencies Selected as Finalists in Jersey Promotional Campaign," *Newark Star-Ledger,* 26 September 1982.
3. Linda Lamendola, "Governor Promotes Lure of 'NJ & You,'" *Newark Star-Ledger,* 7 April 1983.
4. "States Turn to Tourism for New Funds and Jobs," *New York Times,* 16 August 1985.
5. Lamendola, "Governor Promotes Lure of 'NJ & You.'"
6. Linda Lamdendola, "Official Admits Telling Kean Aides of Ad Runover; Budget Panel Grills Commissioner on Overspent Tourism Commercials," *Newark Star-Ledger,* 23 April 1983.
7. *New Yorker,* 1 December 1986.
8. Jim Goodman, "Guv Breaks Bread in the Burg," *Trenton Times,* 3 May 1984.
9. Thomas H. Kean, interview, 25 June 2002.
10. "Jerseyans Like Their State," editorial, *Newark Star-Ledger,* 10 March 1983.
11. Thomas H. Kean, *The Politics of Inclusion* (New York: Free Press, 1988), 115.
12. Herb Jaffe, "Governor Woos GM on Saturn," *Newark Star-Ledger,* 16 February 1985.
13. David Wald, "Mondale Chides Hart for Remark on Jersey," *Newark Star-Ledger,* 28 May 1984.
14. Ibid.
15. Ibid.
16. Kean, *The Politics of Inclusion,* 115–116.
17. Michael Barone and Grant Ujifusa, *The Almanac of American Politics, 2000* (Washington, D.C.: National Journal, 1999), 1020.
18. Kean, *The Politics of Inclusion,* 116.
19. Michael Norman, "Small War between States Pits New York against Jersey: Citing New Economic Gains, Garden State Beckons Trade," *New York Times,* 27 March 1984.
20. Dan Weissman, "$500 Million Hoboken Port Plan Debuts: Kean Backs Proposal for Apartments, Offices, Hotel, Marina," *Newark Star-Ledger,* 23 September 1982.
21. Al Frank, "Kean Attends 'Bubbly' Launching of Jersey City Waterfront Project," *Newark Star-Ledger,* 6 April 1983.
22. The Staten Island project was expected to produce between seven and eight thousand civilian jobs.
23. Guy T. Baehr, "Kean Threatens Retaliation If Albany Stalls P.A. Project in Hoboken," *Newark Star-Ledger,* 15 September 1983.
24. Richard Goldensohn, "Kean Appeals for N.Y. Truce, Hints Countersuit," *Newark Star-Ledger,* 22 March 1984; and Joseph F. Sullivan, "Kean Calls for an End to New York–Jersey Feud on Federal Aid," *New York Times,* 22 March 1984.

25. Joseph F. Sullivan, "Kean Calls for an End to New York–Jersey Feud on Federal Aid." In a letter to the author, 30 March 1984, Lindsay wrote that Kean had "talked in high tones" about New York and New Jersey's "mutual problems" and "mutual strengths."

26. Goldensohn, "Kean Appeals for N.Y. Truce, Hints Countersuit"; William E. Geist, "Koch Asserts U.S. Aid Gives Rival Edge in Business Fight," *New York Times*, 27 March 1984.

27. Edward I. Koch, interview by author, New York, N.Y., 12 July 2002.

28. Geist, "Koch Asserts U.S. Aid Gives Rival Edge in Business Fight."

29. Harvey Fisher, "The New York Hustle," *New Jersey Reporter*, April 1985.

30. Frederick W. Byre, "Kean Lashes N.Y. PM Welfare 'Refugees': Shipping 1,000 to Jersey Called 'Callous and Irresponsible,'" *Newark Star-Ledger*, 14 July 1983.

31. Thomas H. Kean, interview by author, Madison, N.J., 25 June 2002.

32. "How am I doing?" became the quotation most associated with him.

33. Koch, interview, 12 July 2002.

34. Ibid.

35. Thomas H. Kean, "Border Wars on the River," *Bergen Record*, 31 May 1998.

36. John Herbers, "Study Sees States Moving to Achieve World Trade Ties: Governors Say U.S. Program Is Inadequate—President Backs Growing Efforts," *New York Times*, 5 August 1985.

37. Ming Hsu, telephone interview by author, 22 July 2002.

38. Thomas H. Kean, interview, 25 June 2002.

39. Quoted in Joseph F. Sullivan, "Kean, Seeking Business, Joins the Asian Parade," *New York Times*, 2 October 1987.

40. "Kean Defends Trade Missions," *Bergen Record*, 10 August 1988. See also Chris Mondics, "Kean's Trips: High Costs, Low Return," *Bergen Record*, 24 July 1988.

41. Maia Wechsler, "Foreign Firms Invest in N.J.," *Trenton Times*, 23 April 1989.

12. The Education Governor

1. *Newark Star-Ledger*, 3 June 1981.

2. Thomas H. Kean, *The Politics of Inclusion* (New York: Free Press, 1988), 208–239.

3. Ibid., 214.

4. Ibid.

5. Robert J. Braun, "Future State Teachers Score Lowest on Collegiate Skills, Entrance Tests," *Newark Star-Ledger*, 7 February 1982.

6. Sometimes he would vary his example, mentioning John Updike, when the subject under discussion was literature, and Isaac Stern, when it was music. See Kean, *The Politics of Inclusion*, 227.

7. For an accounting of the many problems that plagued Burke, see Robert J. Braun's coverage of Burke's final year in office in the *Newark Star-Ledger*, 1981–1982.

8. Robert J. Braun, "Nominee for Education Chief 'Cribbed' Part of Doctor Thesis," *Newark Star-Ledger*, 9 May 1982.

9. Saul Cooperman, interview by author, Bernardsville, N.J., 4 October 2002.

10. Ibid.

11. Ibid.

12. Dan Weissman, "Governor's School for Special Achievers," *Newark Star-Ledger*, 19 October 1982.

13. The National Commission on Excellence in Education, *A Nation at Risk: The Imperative for Educational Reform* (Washington, D.C., April 1983).

14. Alvin S. Felzenberg, ed., *The Keys to a Successful Presidency* (Washington, D.C.: Heritage Foundation, 2000), 140. The Gallup Poll reported a jump in Reagan's ratings from 41 to 54 percent between April and December of 1983. That was the period in which Reagan most vigorously drew attention to the warnings contained in *A Nation at Risk.*

15. Robert J. Braun, "Kean Education 'Blueprint' Calls for Higher Teacher Pay," *Newark Star-Ledger*, 7 September 1983.

16. Cooperman, interview, 4 October 2002.

17. Robert J. Braun, "Kean Urges New System for Licensing Teachers," *Newark Star-Ledger*, 8 September 1983.

18. Ibid.

19. Ibid.

20. Ibid.

21. Annelise Wamsley, "The New Route to Teaching: Alternate Program at Crossroads," *New Jersey Reporter*, March 1987, 16.

22. Robert J. Braun, "Top Grade: 'New Route' Teachers Making Gains," *Newark Star-Ledger*, 28 November 1988

23. "Alternate Route Success," editorial, *Trenton Times*, 1 February 1989.

24. Matthew Reilly, "Top British Officials Hope to Learn from New Jersey's Innovative Teacher Training: England Is Finding It Difficult to Bolster Ranks of Instructors," *Newark Star-Ledger*, 7 June 1988.

25. Robert J. Braun, "Lessons for Teachers: Governor Unveils Plans for an Academy to Improve Skills," *Newark Star-Ledger*, 20 March 1984.

26. Dan Weissman, "$5,000 Bonus Urged for 'Master Teachers,'" *Newark Star-Ledger*, 10 July 1984.

27. Joseph F. Sullivan, "Kean Offers Plan to Upgrade Education," *New York Times*, 7 September 1983.

28. Robert J. Braun, "Kean Poised for Battle on Master Teacher Plan," *Newark Star-Ledger*, 9 December 1984.

29. Ibid.

30. Thomas H. Kean, interview, 29 July 2002.

31. Cooperman, interview, 4 October 2002.

32. Remarks of Governor Thomas H. Kean before the College Board, New York City, 26 October 1986.

33. Robert J. Braun, "Kean Outlines His 'Initiative' for Urban Schools: Two-Part Program Aims to Improve Skills, Behavior in Selected Districts," *Newark Star-Ledger*, 7 March 1984; and "Better to Have Tried," editorial, *Newark Star-Ledger*, 12 March 1984.

34. Kean, *The Politics of Inclusion*, 221–222.

35. Robert J. Braun, "Kean to Head National Commission on Education Policy in the States," *Newark Star-Ledger*, 16 December 1984.

36. Diane Blair, *Arkansas Politics and Government: Do the People Rule?* (Lincoln: University of Nebraska Press, 1988), 259–262; and David Maranniss, *First in His Class: A Biography of Bill Clinton* (New York: Simon and Schuster, 1995), 409–454.

37. Thomas H. Kean, interview, 25 June 2002.

38. Clinton, interview, 5 February 2003.

39. Hillary Rodham Clinton, interview by author, Washington, D.C., 1 October 2002.

40. See "Excerpts from the Carnegie Report on Teaching" and "Proposals for Transforming Teaching from Occupation into a Profession," *New York Times,* 16 May 1986; and Robert J. Braun, "Kean Backs Radical Changes in Education Mapped by Blue-Ribbon Panel," *Newark Star-Ledger,* 18 May 1986.

41. Robert J. Braun, "Kean Warns School Takeover Foes on State Action If Legislation Stalls," *Newark Star-Ledger,* 18 November 1986.

42. After Kean left office, the resignations of two governors, with the resignations of Christine Todd Whitman and James McGreevey, and the elevation of two senate presidents as acting governor sparked renewed efforts to establish a lieutenant governor.

43. Thomas H. Kean, fifth annual message, *Manual of the Legislature of New Jersey* (Trenton, N.J., 1987).

44. Cooperman, interview, 4 October 2002.

45. "Hostile Takeover," editorial, *Wall Street Journal,* 6 June 1988.

46. Richard Servero, "Kenneth Clark, Who Helped End Segregation, Dies," *New York Times,* 2 May 2005.

47. Newt Gingrich, *To Renew America* (New York: HarperCollins, 1995), 82.

48. "Kean Blames Education Problems on School Boards That Are 'Political,'" *Newark Star-Ledger,* 14 December 1987.

49. Margaret Dolan, "State Takeover of a Local District in New Jersey: A Case Study," Consortium for Policy Research in Education, April 1992.

50. Robert J. Braun, "Kean Backs Plan for School Takeovers," *Newark Star-Ledger,* 18 June 1986.

51. Ibid.

52. Quoted in Lena Williams, "Kean Speech on Education Welcomed by Urban League," *New York Times,* 28 July 1986.

53. Quoted in Dan Weissman and Stanley E. Terrell, "Kean Champions the City School in Tough Urban League Address," *Newark Star-Ledger,* 23 July 1986.

54. The source for this paragraph, including the quotation by Keith Jones, is Stanley E. Terrell, "Kean Calls on NAACP to Make Schools Priority," *Newark Star-Ledger,* 7 July 1987.

55. Robert J. Braun, "Senate Rebuffs Kean-Backed Bill for Takeover of Ailing Schools," *Newark Star-Ledger,* 11 September 1987.

56. "No Winners on This One," editorial, *Trenton Times,* 14 September 1987.

57. Harvey Fisher and David Blomquist, "Kean to GOP: Don't Buck Me," *Bergen Record,* 15 September 1987; Dan Weissman, "Kean Vows Revenge on Failed School Bill," *Newark Star-Ledger,* 14 September 1987; and Dan Weissman, "GOP Fears Losing Senators over School Battle: Leaders Try to Soothe Tempers after Kean Vows to Punish Foes," *Newark Star-Ledger,* 16 September 1987.

58. David Wald, "GOP Scrambles to Mend Breach over Failed School Takeover Bill," *Newark Star-Ledger,* 20 September 1987.

59. Weissman, "Kean Vows Revenge on Failed School Bill."

60. David Wald, "Kean Stumps for Foes of School Takeover Bill," *Newark Star-Ledger,* 23 October 1987.

61. Quoted in David Wald, "Bennett Stumps in Hudson for School Takeover," *Newark Star-Ledger,* 28 October 1987.

62. William Bennett, telephone interview by author, 4 October 2004.

63. Dolan, "State Takeover of a Local District in New Jersey," 8. The administration's decision to allow both principals and teachers to retain tenure resulted more in the moving around of personnel than in replacements, as principals deemed incompetent asserted their rights to tenured teaching positions, therefore "bumping" incumbents of lesser seniority to other jobs.

64. Tom Johnson, "School Takeover Measure Suffers Senate Setback," *Newark Star-Ledger,* 11 December 1987.

65. Ibid.

66. Ibid.

67. Robert J. Braun, "Russo Lashes Back at Governor in Takeover Feud," *Newark Star-Ledger,* 16 December 1987.

68. Robert J. Braun, "Takeover Bill Path Has Been Long and Rocky," *Newark Star-Ledger,* 12 December 1987.

69. Robert J. Braun, "Kean Clears Takeovers, Sees 'Hope' for Schools," 14 January 1988.

70. Ibid.

71. Matthew Reilly, "Jersey City May Face Aid Cutoff: Kean Criticizes Efforts of Leaders to Prevent Proposed Takeover," *Newark Star-Ledger,* 23 August 1988.

72. Kinga Borondy and Robert J. Braun, "Law Judge Allows the State to Seize Jersey City Schools," *Newark Star-Ledger,* 27 June 1989.

73. Carl Rowen, "Jersey Comes to the Rescue of Its Children," *Newark Star-Ledger,* 1 June 1988.

74. William F. Buckley Jr., "A Jersey City Option One Could Vouch For," *Newark Star-Ledger,* 2 June 1988.

75. Cooperman, interview, 4 October 2002.

76. Ibid.

77. Jim Goodman, "Takeover Bill's Lessons Ready to Be Carried Out," *Trenton Times,* 20 December 1987.

78. Kean, *The Politics of Inclusion,* 223.

79. Thomas H. Kean, interview, 29 July 2002.

80. State courts had shown a tendency in recent years to side with the state executive against the legislative branch on matters pertaining to the budget, conditional vetoes, and executive orders. The state supreme court upheld Kean's line-item veto of legislation to reverse cutbacks he had made in the disbursal of gross-receipts revenues to municipalities (on the grounds that the chief executive, through his veto powers, was part of the legislative process). It also agreed that Kean could set spending priorities. It let stand his executive order that disallowed most development around freshwater wetlands.

81. Thomas H. Kean, interview, 29 July 2002.

82. Thomas H. Kean, interview, 25 June 2002.

83. President Ronald Reagan, State of the Union address, January 26, 1988.

84. William Kristol, "Talking Points on Education," 22 December 1987, file SP 230–88 582448, White House Subject File Case, on file in the Ronald Reagan Library, Simi Valley, Calif.

85. By this time, Kristol had gone on to become chief of staff to Vice President Dan Quayle. For George H. W. Bush's comments on alternate teacher certification, see Robert J. Braun, "Bush Visits Jersey, Pushes 'Freer' Schools," *Newark Star-Ledger,* 14 April 1989.

86. Thomas H. Kean to Ronald Reagan, January 26, 1986, White House Correspondence Tracking Sheet, SP 230–88; ID 542381, Ronald Reagan Library.

87. Ronald Reagan to Thomas H. Kean, handwriting file, White House Correspondence Tracking Sheet, SP 230–88, ID 542381, Ronald Reagan Library. For a published text of the letter, see Kiron K. Skinner, Annelise Anderson, and Martin Anderson, eds., *Reagan: A Life in Letters* (New York: Free Press, 2003), 696.

88. Remarks of President Ronald Reagan at the National Forum for Excellence in Education in Indianapolis, Indiana, 8 December 1983.

89. Radio address of President Ronald Reagan to the nation, 12 May 1984.

13. Kean and the Arts

1. Michael Redmond, "Symphony Makes Strides in Fund-Raising Effort: Long-Term Outlook Still Unresolved," *Newark Star-Ledger*, 11 February 1981.

2. For a review of the condition in which the New Jersey Symphony found itself on the eve of Kean's election, see Michael Redmond's four-part series on the subject in the *Newark Star-Ledger*, 8–11 February 1981.

3. Valerie Sudol, "National Endowment Chairman Applauds Kean Initiative on Funding for the Arts," *Newark Star-Ledger*, 28 March 1984.

4. Remarks of Governor Thomas H. Kean before the New Jersey Council on the Arts, 27 March 1984, printed in *Arts New Jersey*, June 1985.

5. *Newark Star-Ledger*, 30 January 1981.

6. Dan Weissman, "Byrne and Lan Staging Bitter Fight over Transfer of Arts Council," *Newark Star-Ledger*, 29 January 1981.

7. Dan Weissman, "Arts Chief Faces Axe in Misuse of $500," *Newark Star-Ledger*, 2 October 1982; and "Ethics and Arts in Trenton," *Newark Star-Ledger*, 31 October 1982.

8. Dan Weissman, "Arts Council 'Returned' to Department of State," *Newark Star-Ledger*, 28 January 1983.

9. The other was a bill establishing a commission to study the effects of Agent Orange.

10. "Kean Seeking Shift of Offices," *Newark Star-Ledger*, 2 February 1983.

11. For an overview of the festival, see Dan Weissman, "Smithsonian Puts Jersey in Spotlight," *Newark Star-Ledger*, 28 January 1983; Anne-Marie Cottone, "National Gala Offers Jersey Some Respect," *Newark Star-Ledger*, 27 February 1983; Edna M. Baily, "Kean Boosts Smithsonian's Jersey Exhibit," *Newark Star-Ledger*, 26 May 1983; Robert Cohen, "The Taste and Touch of Jersey in Washington . . . Garden State Shows Off Its Flair as Smithsonian Affair Opens Today," *Newark Star-Ledger*, 23 June 1983; J. Scott Orr, "Jersey's Opening-Day Act Proves a Smash on the Mall in D.C.," *Newark Star-Ledger*, 24 June 1983; and Michael Norman, "In Washington, a Garden of Jersey Delights," *New York Times*, 25 June 1983.

12. Mark Finston, "Princeton Hosts Birthday Bash for the Treaty of Paris' 200th," *Newark Star-Ledger*, 18 November 1983.

13. Ibid.

14. Dan Weissman, "Governor Wants Arts Council to Act on Judge's Ouster Ruling for Director," *Newark Star-Ledger*, 5 October 1982.

15. The New Jersey Symphony, McCarter Theatre, Crossroads Theater, New Jersey Chamber Music Society, Paper Mill Playhouse, WBGO-Radio, and the Newark and Montclair museums.

16. Jerome Hines, telephone interview by author, 14 December 2002.

17. Jim Goodman, "Arts Council Fight Seals End of Merlino Term," *Trenton Times,* 20 June 1984; Jim Goodman, "Stockman Crusades Unrealistic," *Trenton Times,* 24 June 1984; and Anthony Shannon, "Funding for Arts in Appointments Hassle," *Newark Star-Ledger,* 17 June 1984.

18. "Artful Dodge," editorial, *Newark Star-Ledger,* 24 June 1984 and accompanying cartoon, "Rembrandt He Ain't."

19. John L. Hyer, telephone interview by author, 2 June 2003.

20. Linda Lamendola, "Kean, Stars Lead Rally for Arts Council Funds," *Newark Star-Ledger,* 26 June 1984. For other coverage of the rally, see Nancy Freiberg, "Arts Rally Supports State Funds," *Princeton Packet,* 26 June 1984; Jim Goodman, "Art-Council Backers Give Stockman the Brush-off," *Trenton Times,* 26 June 1984; and the *Trentonian,* 26 June 1984.

21. Quoted in Dan Weissman, "Kean, Dems End Rift on Nominee Logjam," *Newark Star-Ledger,* 15 June 1984.

22. Valerie Sudol, "Arts Groups Urged to Plea for Share of State Surplus," *Newark Star-Ledger,* 24 October 1984.

23. Michael Redmond, "Arts Group Hopes Rally Can Pump New Life into Aging Halls, Theaters," *Newark Star-Ledger,* 3 May 1985.

24. Thomas H. Kean, interview, 4 October 2002.

25. Ed McGlynn, interview by author, Point Pleasant, N.J., 27 February 2002.

26. Andy Seiler, "Celebrities Join Cry for N.J. Arts Funds: Hundreds March on Trenton in Bid for $50 Million for Cultural Center," *New Brunswick Home News,* 7 June 1985.

27. Remarks of Governor Thomas H. Kean at a rally for the arts in front of Statehouse, Trenton, N.J., 6 June 1985.

28. Vincent R. Zarate, "Budget Buoys Governor," *Newark Star-Ledger,* 11 June 1985.

29. Dan Weissman, "Kean Proposes Development of a Performing Arts Mecca," *Newark Star-Ledger,* 28 December 1986; and "For Art's Sake," editorial, *Newark Star-Ledger,* 4 January 1987.

30. Valerie Sudol, "Bond Issue Proposed for Cultural Centers," *Newark Star-Ledger,* 25 March 1987; and Constance E. Beaumont, "Two States Push Right Buttons to Fund Historic Preservation," *Preservation News,* September–October 1995.

31. Dan Weissman, "Kean Clears Way for 'Quality-of-Life' Bond Referendum in November," *Newark Star-Ledger,* 11 September 1987.

32. Jim Goodman, "Kean Sets Terms on Memorial: State Would Restore, Then Run Auditorium," *Trenton Times,* 13 January 1988.

33. Dan Weissman, "World-Class Arts Complex Proposed for Newark Site," *Newark Star-Ledger,* 23 July 1987; Joseph F. Sullivan, "Kean Plans and Arts Center for Newark with 8,000 Seats," *New York Times,* 23 July 1987; and Valerie Sudol, "Newark Arts Center Hailed as 'Grand' Idea for the State: Cultural Mecca Wins Bravos On Stage and Off," *Newark Star-Ledger,* 26 July 1987.

34. Quoted in Sudol, "Newark Arts Center Hailed as 'Grand' Idea for the State."

35. "A Star for the State's Crown," editorial, *Bergen Record,* 30 July 1987.

36. Bruce Chadwick, "Newark Not Place for an Arts Center," *New York Daily News*, 24 July 1987.

37. "N.J. Doesn't Need a Lincoln Center," editorial, *Courier-News*, 6 February 1987; and Gordon A. MacInnnes, "N.J. Can't Afford 'Lincoln Center' in Newark," *Morristown Daily Record*, 11 March 1988.

38. Mary Kay Risi, "Million-Dollar Question: Will Business Back Arts Complex?" *New Brunswick Home News*, 27 July 1987.

39. Quoted in Monica Maske, "Catholics Reassured on Famed City Church," *Newark Star-Ledger*, 26 July 1987.

40. William Gordon, "A Bright Future Is Cast for Symphony Hall as It Undergoes Renovation," *Newark Star-Ledger*, 26 July 1987. See also Anthony F. Shannon, "Van Fossan Dead; Mutual Life Chief," *Newark Star-Ledger*, 30 October 1989. In addition to his other activities, Van Fossan founded "Renaissance Newark" in the aftermath of the 1967 riots and "Partnership New Jersey" in the 1980s. Old-timers knew Symphony Hall as "the Mosque," a reference to the Egyptian revival structure, built in the 1920s, to serve as a Masonic temple.

41. Sudol, "Newark Arts Center Hailed as 'Grand' Idea for the State."

42. Quoted in Frederick W. Byrd, "Land Sale Won't Delay Arts Center in Newark," *Newark Star-Ledger*, 3 May 1988; and Al Frank, "Arts Center Plan Stirs Development Dispute," *Newark Star-Ledger*, 8 May 1988.

43. Ibid.

44. Robert Caro, *The Power Broker* (New York: Vintage, 1974), 127–139.

45. Robert J. Braun, "Ensuring a Place for the Arts as a Political Priority," *Newark Star-Ledger*, 10 June 1988.

46. Robert J. Braun, "Kean's 'Stand' for the Kids Is Time Well Spent," *Newark Star-Ledger*, 5 June 1987.

47. Ellen Moodie, "Papp's Festival Latino Set for Liberty Park," *Jersey Journal*, 27 April 1988.

48. Robert Schwaneberg, "Key Legislator, Kean Aide at Odds on Arts Council Funding of N.Y. Groups: Weiss Says Law Strictly Stipulates Spending on Jersey Artists Only," *Newark Star-Ledger*, 30 April 1987.

49. Bob Campbell, "An Oscar Send-Off for Olympia Dukakis," *Newark Star-Ledger*, 11 April 1988.

50. Dan Weissman," Big Role for Olympia in Cousin's Campaign," *Newark Star-Ledger*, 3 May 1988.

51. Michael Redmond, "New Maestro: Symphony Selects a Director-Conductor," *Newark Star-Ledger*, 12 June 1985.

52. Michael Kimmelman, "New Jersey Orchestra on the Rise," *New York Times*, 8 May 1987.

53. Michael Redmond, "Hugh Wolff Orchestrates a Carnegie Hall Triumph," *Newark Star-Ledger*, 24 November 1987.

54. Ibid.

55. Raymond G. Chambers, interview by author, Morristown, N.J., 5 August 2002.

56. Joseph F. Sullivan, "Kean Proposes Concert Hall for Newark: Legislators May Resist $33 Million Budget Item," *New York Times*, 8 February 1989.

57. Quoted in ibid.

58. Al Frank, "New Arts Complex Plan: Concert Hall First Phase of Riverfront Project," *Newark Star-Ledger*, 8 February 1989.

59. Quoted in ibid.

60. Thomas H. Kean, interview, 29 July 2002. See also Sullivan, "Kean Proposes Concert Hall for Newark."

61. Dan Weissman, "Compromise Proposal Orchestrated on Financing of Newark Arts Center," *Newark Star-Ledger*, 23 June 1989.

62. Thomas H. Kean, interviews, 29 July 2002 and 26 August 2002.

14. Kean the Environmentalist

1. J. Scott Orr and Tom Johnson, "Jersey Heads Priority List on Toxic Sites," *Newark Star-Ledger*, 21 December 1982.

2. Susan J. Tolchin and Martin Tolchin, *Dismantling America: The Rush to Deregulate,* (Boston: Houghton Mifflin, 1983), 103.

3. Richard Goldensohn, Scott Orr, and Tom Johnson, "Bradley, Kean Lobby for Superfund Reform," *Newark Star-Ledger*, 2 September 1983.

4. Thomas H. Kean, *The Politics of Inclusion* (New York: Free Press, 1988), 104.

5. Robert Schwaneberg, "Kean Approves 2 'Get Tough' Laws on Chemical Execs, Dump Operators," *Newark Star-Ledger*, 2 September 1982.

6. Tom Johnson, "Kean Sues to Block Offshore Drilling at Sites Vital to State Fishing Industry," *Newark Star-Ledger*, 28 July 1982.

7. Dan Weissman, "Watt Rebuffs Kean on Offshore Drilling," *Newark Star-Ledger*, 10 August 1982.

8. J. Scott Orr, "Kean, Watt Reach 'Understanding' for Safeguards on Offshore Drilling," *Newark Star-Ledger*, 26 April 1983.

9. Dan Weissman, "Governors' Panel Backs Kean on Offshore Drilling," *Newark Star-Ledger*, 31 July 1084.

10. Quoted in Reginald Roberts, "Kean Tours Chemical Plant, Assures Belleville Residents," *Newark Star-Ledger*, 1 June 1983.

11. Quoted in ibid.

12. Tom Johnson, "Heavy Dioxin Levels Found at Closed Newark Factory," *Newark Star-Ledger*, 3 June 1983.

13. Ibid.

14. Douglas C. McGill, "Kean Tours Area Near Dioxin Site: Contamination Is Limited, He Tells Residents in Newark," *New York Times*, 5 June 1983.

15. Ibid.

16. Ibid.

17. Kean, *The Politics of Inclusion,* 124.

18. Golden, interview, 4 August 2002.

19. Harvey Fisher, "No Heavy Lifting," *New Jersey Reporter*, January 1985.

20. Tom Johnson, "'Right to Know' Goes on Books in Jersey," *Newark Star-Ledger*, 30 August 1983.

21. Ibid.; and Chapin Wright, "Business Calls Bill Enormous Setback," *Trenton Times*, 25 August 1983.

22. Dan Weissman, "Northeast Governors Move on Acid Rain," *Newark Star-Ledger*, 21 July 1984; and Gordon Bishop, "Governors Act to Stem the Threat of Acid Rain," *Newark Star-Ledger*, 6 December 1983.

23. Ibid.

24. Jane Perlez, "Governors and Reagan Talk about Acid Rain," *New York Times*, 21 January 1984.

25. Richard E. Cohen, *Washington at Work: Back Rooms and Clean Air* (New York: Macmillan, 1992), 45–63; and Patrick Jenkins, "Kean Opens Classes on Environment," *Newark Star-Ledger*, 13 July 1989.

26. Tom Johnson and Richard S. Remington, "Kean Vows to Veto Bill on Wetlands," *Newark Star-Ledger*, 25 March 1987.

27. Ibid.

28. Tom Johnson, "Governor Orders 'Freeze' in Wetlands," *Newark Star-Ledger*, 9 June 1987.

29. Ibid.

30. Robert Littell, interview by author, Washington, D.C., 17 December 2003.

31. Michael Rozsansky, Jerry Thomas, and Tom Johnson, "Radon Soil Going South," *Newark Star-Ledger*, 23 July 1987.

32. Quoted in Mark Finston, "A Peek at History: Kean in Awe as He Views 772-Year-Old Magna Carta," *Newark Star-Ledger*, 16 June 1987.

33. Tom Johnson, "Compromise Reached on Wetlands 'Freeze,'" *Newark Star-Ledger*, 26 June 1987.

34. Tom Johnson, "Kean Signs Wetlands Bill, Lifts Building Moratorium," *Newark Star-Ledger*, 2 July 1987.

35. Ibid.

36. Michael Piserchio and Robert Schwaneberg, "State Police Bunker Team Keep Emergencies from Becoming Disasters," *Newark Star-Ledger*, 29 September 1985.

37. Herb Jaffe, "N.Y. Agrees to Act on Shore Pollution," *Newark Star-Ledger*, 17 November 1987. President Franklin Delano Roosevelt had employed the word *infamy* to describe the significance of the Japanese attack on Pearl Harbor, December 7, 1941.

38. Deborah Coombe, "Garbage Slick off Shore Forces Ban on Swimming," *Newark Star-Ledger*, 15 August 1987; and "50 Miles of Garbage Closes Jersey Beaches," *New York Times*, 15 August 1987.

39. Dan Weissman and Donna Leusser, "Governor Posts Bounty of $5,000 for Those Who Caused Garbage Slick," *Newark Star-Ledger*, 26 August 1987.

40. Ibid.

41. Ibid.

42. Herb Jaffe, "N.Y. Agrees to Act on Shore Pollution," *Newark Star-Ledger*, 17 November 1987.

43. Bill Gannon, "Med Waste War: Kean and Cuomo Join for Emergency Action," *Newark Star-Ledger*, 11 August 1988.

44. Tom Johnson, "Kean Asks Millions to Safeguard Shore," *Newark Star-Ledger*, 18 November 1987; and "Kean Enacts Package to Fight Shore Pollution," *Newark Star-Ledger*, 12 July 1988.

45. Fenske, interview, 25 May 2005.

46. Thomas H. Kean, telephone interview by author, 26 August 2002.

47. See Tom Johnson, "Kean Asks Millions to Safeguard Shore," *Newark Star-Ledger*, 18 November 1987; Tom Johnson, "Kean Enacts Package to Fight Shore Pollution," *Newark Star-Ledger*, 12 July 1988; Matthew Reilly, "Kean Orders Development Limits; Stresses Need for Coastal Agency," *Newark Star-Ledger*, 4 October 1988; and Gordon Bishop, "Kean Launches End-of-Term

Drive for Major Environmental Safeguard," *Newark Star-Ledger*, 14 February 1988.

48. Quoted in Jenkins, "Kean Opens Classes on Environment."

15. The Politics of Inclusion

1. Thomas H. Kean, *The Politics of Inclusion* (New York: Free Press, 1988).

2. Thomas H. Kean, interview, 4 October 2002.

3. Richard Goldensohn, "Garibaldi Encourages Ethnics to Help Others," *Newark Star-Ledger*, 18 October 1982.

4. Eyewitness observation of the author.

5. Thomas H. Kean, interview, 29 July 2002.

6. Bill Bradley, *Time Present, Time Past: A Memoir* (New York: Knopf, 1996), 312.

7. David Kotok, telephone interview by author, 15 January 2003.

8. Branden Phillips, "Salute to Honor Men Who Freed Nazis' Prisoners," *New York Times*, 29 May 1983.

9. Ibid.

10. Eileen Watkins, "Trenton Exhibits Reflect on Holocaust," *Newark Star-Ledger*, 29 May 1983.

11. Quoted in Mitchell Seidel, "Dinner Funds Holocaust Statue," *Newark Star-Ledger*, 17 September 1984. The phenomenon of memorials to victims of the Holocaust was only beginning to take hold during Kean's time in office. The Holocaust Museum on the National Mall in Washington, D.C., would not open its doors until 1993.

12. Remarks of Governor Thomas H. Kean, Solidarity Day, Temple Beth Shalom, Manalapan Township, 4 November 1984. Thomas H. Kean personal papers.

13. Richard Goldensohn, "Anti-Semitism Meets Its Match in Group of Dedicated Children," *Newark Star-Ledger*, 5 November 1984; and Tracy Schroth, "3,000 Answer Manalapan's Solidarity Call," *Asbury Park Press*, 5 November 1984.

14. Remarks of Governor Thomas H. Kean to the Governor's School, Trenton State College, 17 July 1985. Thomas H. Kean personal papers.

15. Luna Kaufman, telephone interview by author, 12 December 2002.

16. Dan Weissman, "Kean Embarks on Journey to Israel with Memories of His Brave Father," *Newark Star-Ledger*, 17 March 1983.

17. Also in attendance was Prime Minister Menachim Begin, whose autobiography Kean had been reading. Impressed at the degree to which Kean had prepared for his trip to Israel, Begin arranged for Kean to meet with him in private on another day.

18. Thomas H. Kean to Uri V. Andropov, 22 April 1983, Thomas H. Kean personal papers.

19. Transcript of conversation between Thomas H. Kean and Boris Klotz, 10 April 1984, Thomas H. Kean personal papers; and Dan Weissman, "Kean Quietly Lobbies for a Soviet Dissident," *Newark Star-Ledger*, 11 April 1984.

20. Letter from Boris Klotz to Thomas H. Kean, 6 October 1986, Thomas H. Kean personal papers.

21. Martin Liebman to President Ronald Reagan, 31 January 1984, and Raymond F. Smith, Office of Soviet American Affairs, State Department, to Martin Liebman, 7 February 1984, ID 8403089, Ronald Reagan Library.

22. Boris Klotz to Thomas H. Kean, 6 October 1986, Thomas H. Kean personal papers.

23. Thomas H. Kean to Mikhail Gorbachev, 27 February 1987, Thomas H. Kean personal papers.

24. A. Zhavakin, vice consul, Embassy of the USSR, to Thomas H. Kean, 9 September 1987, Thomas H. Kean personal papers.

25. Smith, interview, 22 October 2002.

26. Dan Weissman, "Kean Track Record with Minorities Frequently Foiled by Bureaucrats," *Newark Star-Ledger,* 9 October 1983.

27. Ibid.

28. Richard S. Remington, "Kean Taps Black for P.A. Vacancy," *Newark Star-Ledger,* 30 June 1983.

29. Monica Maske, "Black Churchmen Laud Governor for 'Service,'" *Newark Star-Ledger,* 22 March 1984.

30. Jack Kemp, telephone interview by author, 17 March 2003.

31. Richard Remington, "Kean Ushers in 'Enterprise Zones' to Revitalize Newark and Camden," *Newark Star-Ledger,* 16 August 1983.

32. Leonard S. Coleman, "The Politics of Inclusion: The Black Perspective, Unfinished Business for the Republican Party," *New Jersey Reporter,* November 1989, 23–29.

33. Jeremy Olsham, "In Atlantic City, Mourners Bid Farewell to Former Mayor James Usry," *Atlantic City Press,* 3 February 2002.

34. Kirk Johnson, "James L. Usry, Atlantic City Mayor in 1980's, Dies at 79," *New York Times,* 26 January 2002.

35. Jim Goodman, "A.C. Mayor Ursy Arrested in Bribe: Bad News for GOP," *Trenton Times,* 28 July 1989; and Mark Tyler and Jeremy Olshan, "Former Atlantic City Mayor Usry Dies," *Atlantic City Press,* 26 January 2002.

36. The first was Edward W. Brooke of Massachusetts, also a Republican, who was elected in 1966.

37. Thomas H. Kean, interview by author, Madison, N.J., 19 September 2003.

38. Afterward, Coleman observed that, to his surprise, some party conservatives appeared more willing to support him than were many of their better-heeled, more progressive moderate counterparts. See Coleman, "The Politics of Inclusion."

39. James Benson, "Conferees Restore Rank of 'Lost' Black Historians: Forum Highlights Rutgers Events in Honor of Afro-American Legacy," *Newark Star-Ledger,* 20 February 1983.

40. Kean's remarks were recalled by Clement A. Price, in a telephone interview by author, 24 February 2003.

41. Ibid.

42. Kathy Barrett Carter, "Kean to Approve Pension Divestment," *Newark Star-Ledger,* 21 August 1885.

43. Ibid. See also Joseph F. Sullivan, "Kean Backs Halt in Investing Tied to South Africa: Governor Will Sign Bill to Sell $2 Billion in State Assets as Apartheid Protest," *New York Times,* 21 August 1985.

44. Hodding Carter, telephone interview by author, 17 March 2003. See also Robert Kinloch Massie, *Loosing the Bonds: The United States and South Africa in the Apartheid Years* (New York: Doubleday, 1997), 588. Named for a

Philadelphia minister, the Sullivan principles were a series of pledges that corporations active in South Africa made to their stockholders and the public in which they agreed to extend full civil rights to their employees at their places of business and to press for change in South African policies.

45. Carter, "Kean to Approve Pension Divestment."

46. Grant Ujifusa, telephone interview by author, 26 September 2003.

47. Thomas H. Kean, interview, 25 June 2003.

48. Grant Ujifusa to Thomas H. Kean, 24 November 1987, ID 544222, Ronald Reagan Library.

49. June Masuda Goto to President Ronald Reagan, 19 December 1987, ID 544222, Ronald Reagan Library.

50. Ibid.

51. Ujifusa, interview, 26 September 2003.

52. *Pacific Citizen*, 15 December 1945.

53. Remarks of President Ronald Reagan on signing the bill providing restitution for the wartime internment of Japanese American civilians.

54. Ujifusa recalled this incident in an interview, 26 September 2003.

55. Ibid.

16. The Administrator

1. Jim Goodman, "Kean Hires a $54,000 Image Man," *Trenton Times*, 1 January 1983.

2. "There's Always Room for an Old Pal," *Trentonian*, 1 January 1983.

3. Robert Schwaneberg, "Kean Responds to Movie Panel after Resignation," *Newark Star-Ledger*, 24 April 1983.

4. Kean's first choice as education commissioner withdrew from consideration after it was discovered that he had plagiarized portions of his doctoral dissertation. An assistant secretary of transportation resigned after a month in office after it became known that he did not hold a degree in engineering, as he had claimed. His designee to head the division on women asked that Kean not go ahead with her appointment when it was revealed that she had a mail-order Ph.D. See Linda Lamendola, "Kean Backs Nominee with 'Bought' Degree," *Newark Star-Ledger*, 29 September 1982; and Dan Weissman, "Kean Administration Isn't Doing Its Homework on Nominees," *Newark Star-Ledger*, 31 October 1982.

5. "Creative Patronage," editorial, *Newark Star-Ledger*, 6 May 1982.

6. "Appointment Troubles in Trenton," *New York Times*, 20 May 1983.

7. "Kean Defends Imperiale Action," *Newark Star-Ledger*, 7 May 1982.

8. Harvey Fisher, "No More Mr. Nice Guy," *New Jersey Reporter*, June 1983, 30.

9. David Wald, "GOP Invites Thousands to Join Governor's Club," *Newark Star-Ledger*, 20 January 1983.

10. David Wald, "Kean Staff Shuffle Buys Party Peace with 'Cosmetics,'" *Newark Star-Ledger*, 17 April 1983.

11. Samuel G. Freedman, "Kean's Town Meeting: Local Issues Stand Out," *New York Times*, 17 June 1983.

12. Linda Lamendola, "Kean Forgoes Mansion for Home, Sweet Home," *Newark Star-Ledger*, 27 June 1982.

13. Harvey Fisher, "The Empire Strikes Out," *New Jersey Reporter,* April 1983.

14. Thomas H. Kean, interview, 26 Jun3 2002.

15. Linda Lamendola, "Debby Kean Boosts Her Odds-On Favorite," *Newark Star-Ledger,* 13 October 1985.

16. Ibid.

17. Sharon Schlegel, "The Girl Tom Kean Married: Shunning Campaign Spotlight on Purpose," *Trenton Times,* 28 October 1981.

18. Koch, interview, New York City, N.Y., 12 July 2002.

19. Schlegel, "The Girl Tom Kean Married."

20. Robert D. McFadden, "Mansion Antiques Are Rejected by Mrs. Kean," *New York Times,* 24 January 1983.

21. Dan Weissman, "Kean Threatens to Drop Out of Northeast States Alliance," *Newark Star-Ledger,* 9 August 1982.

22. Thomas H. Kean, interview, 26 June 2002.

23. Joseph F. Sullivan, "Kean Says He Made Decision on Furnishings: Denies His Wife Ordered Removal of Antiques," *New York Times,* 25 January 1983.

24. "Dressing Up Drumthwacket," *Newark Star-Ledger,* 28 January 1983.

25. Linda Lamendola, "Estate of State: Drumthwacket Spurned for 'Common Good,'" *Newark Star-Ledger,* 1 February 1983.

26. Richard C. Halverson, "Licences at Sears to Be Provided by GOP Contributor," *Asbury Park Press,* 10 April 1985.

27. Mike Piserchia, "Governor Lashes Out for Lack of Candor on Photo License Fee," *Newark Star-Ledger,* 12 April 1985; and Pat R. Gilbert, "Kean: Snedeker Action 'Stupid,'" *Trenton Times,* 12 April 1985.

28. "The bottom line is whether this arrangement will serve the public, and everything I have seen so far indicates that it will," he said. See Gilbert, "Kean: Snedeker Action 'Stupid.'"

29. Mike Piserchia, "DMV Director Quits as Photo Deal Is Voided," *Newark Star-Ledger,* 23 April 1985.

30. Mike Piserchia, "Top Officials Talked of Photo Disclosure," *Newark Star-Ledger,* 3 May 1985; and "DMV Deleted GOP Backer's Name from Photo License Announcement," *Newark Star-Ledger,* 7 May 1985.

31. A former assemblyman, Snedeker was well liked among his colleagues in both parties. While Democrats criticized him in his capacity as a Kean administration official, they rallied to his defense after his resignation. Their complaints that their friend was being made a scapegoat triggered the SCI investigation.

32. Harvey Fisher, "A Cavalier Snow Job," *New Jersey Reporter,* June 1985.

33. Ibid.

34. Linda Lamendola, "Official Admits Telling Kean Aides of Ad Runover," *Newark Star-Ledger,* 23 April 1985.

35. McGlynn, interview, 27 September 2002.

36. Thomas H. Kean, interview, 4 October 2002.

37. Edwards, interview, 13 August 2002.

38. McGlynn, interview, 27 September 2002.

39. Reagan played George Gipp, the legendary football player at Notre Dame, in the movie *Knute Rockne—All American* (1940). After he entered politics, Reagan supporters and Reagan himself recycled a line used in the film, "Win one for the Gipper," to urge the election of Republican candidates.

40. J. Scott Orr, "Kean Advises 'Hands Off' on Defense Issues," *Newark Star-Ledger,* 1 March 1983.

41. Thomas H. Kean, interview, 25 June 2002.

42. Quoted in Dan Weissman, "Kean, Cuomo Say 'Nyet' to Top Soviet: Newark, N.Y. Airports Barred to Gromyko, Other Diplomats," *Newark Star-Ledger*, 16 September 1983.

43. Ken Duberstein, interview by author, Washington, D.C., 16 October 2003.

44. Richard S. Remington and Vincent R. Zarate, "Kean Cites Harshness of Reagan Budget," *Newark Star-Ledger*, 5 February 1985.

45. For an assessment of Reagan's governorship, see Cannon, *Governor Reagan*; Jordan Rau, Carl Ingram, and Robert Saladay, "The Reagan Legacy: A Seasoned Style, Green Record as Governor," *Los Angeles Times*, 7 June 2004; and George Skelton, "Ronald Wilson Reagan, An Environmentalist Who Raised Taxes When Needed," *Los Angeles Times*, 6 June 2004.

46. "I know it's hard for you young people to believe that any of the rest of us remember what it was like or know what you're thinking or feeling. . . . And you may not think about it now, but many of the things that you do now will affect how well you're going to be able to get around in later years, and whether you're going to be able to enjoy life as you're presently enjoying it. . . . I look out, and I see your bright, young faces, and I just want to say: Don't waste the health and the youth that God gave you. Don't take drugs." Remarks of President Ronald Reagan at River Dell High School in Oradell, New Jersey, 20 June 1984.

47. Remarks of President Ronald Reagan on signing a national minimum drinking age bill, 17 July 1984.

48. Remarks of President Ronald Reagan at a Reagan-Bush rally in Elizabeth, N.J., 26 July 1984.

49. Remarks of President Ronald Reagan at the St. Ann's Festival in Hoboken, N.J., 26 July 1984.

50. Ibid.

51. Francis X. Clines, "Reagan Courts Ethnic Voters by Assailing Foes," *New York Times*, 27 July 1984.

52. Guy Sterling and Lisa Peterson, "Hail to the Chief: Hoboken, Elizabeth Host Reagan Today," *Newark Star-Ledger*, 27 July 1984.

53. Remarks of Thomas H. Kean, introduction of President Ronald Reagan, spaghetti dinner fund-raiser, West Orange, N.J., October 12, 1988. Thomas H. Kean personal papers.

54. Remarks of President Ronald Reagan at a Reagan-Bush rally in Hammonton, N.J., 19 September 1984; and Patrick Jenkins, "Reagan Boosts Economy, Hails Rural Jersey Town," *Newark Star-Ledger*, 20 September 1984.

55. Remarks of President Ronald Reagan at a Reagan-Bush rally in Hackensack, N.J., 26 October 1984.

17. The Reelection of the Governor, 1985

1. "Mr. Kean's a Popular Fellow," editorial, *Trentonian*, 25 June 1985.

2. Vincent R. Zarate, "Budget Praised, Panned," *Newark Star-Ledger*, 31 January 1984.

3. Vincent R. Zarate, "Kean Wants Surplus Used as 'One-Shot' Tax Rebate," *Newark Star-Ledger*, 2 May 1984.

4. Robert Schwaneberg and Dan Weissman, "Dems See Proposal as 'Gimmickry,'" *Newark Star-Ledger*, 10 May 1985.

5. Dan Weissman, "Address Garners Plaudits," *Newark Star-Ledger*, 9 January 1985.

6. David Wald, "Kean Aides Consider Waging Re-election Campaign without Public Funding," *Newark Star-Ledger*, 18 November 1984; and "Kean Aides Hope to Push Florio Out of the Race," *Newark Star-Ledger*, 3 March 1985.

7. David Wald, "Kean Seeks Public Matching Funds for Unopposed GOP Primary Race," *Newark Star-Ledger*, 17 April 1985.

8. David Wald, "Kean Leaves Foes in a Dither over Campaign Dollars," *Newark Star-Ledger*, 3 April 1985.

9. Linda Lamendola, "Debby Kean Boosts Her Odds-On Favorite," *Newark Star-Ledger*, 13 October 1985.

10. Thomas H. Kean, interview, 6 June 2002; and Strong, interview, 9 October 2004.

11. David Wald, "Kean's Marathon Reveals Candidate Who Won't Flinch," *Newark Star-Ledger*, 7 April 1985.

12. Dan Weissman and Robert Misseck, "Kean Hails Jersey Upsurge, Launches Re-election Bid," *Newark Star-Ledger*, 3 April 1985.

13. Remarks of Governor Thomas H. Kean, 2 April 1985.

14. David Wald, "Kean, Shapiro Pledge Issues-Oriented Campaign," *Newark Star-Ledger*, 6 June 1982.

15. David Wald, "Democrats Say McCann's Loss Is Shapiro's Gain," *Newark Star-Ledger*, 13 June 1985.

16. Shapiro, interview, 15 July 2002.

17. Jane Perlez, "Democratic Victor in Jersey Prepares to Battle a Popular Incumbent," *New York Times*, 6 June 1985. The slogan in the movie was "McKay: The Better Way."

18. Shapiro, interview, 15 July 2002.

19. Herb Jaffe and Donald Warshaw, "Shapiro Takes Essex Race: Narrowly Beats Cryan," *Newark Star-Ledger*, 7 June 1978.

20. Quoted in Donna Leusner, "Kean Commends Shapiro as Exec Begins New Term," *Newark Star-Ledger*, 3 January 1983; and Alan C. Miller, "Kean and Shapiro: Political Pals, Friendly Foes," *Bergen Record*, 12 August 1985.

21. Ibid.

22. Eyewitness observation by author.

23. Remarks of President Ronald Reagan to the citizens of Bloomfield, N.J., 13 June 1985.

24. David Wald, "Kean Starts Fall with Massive Lead," *Newark Star-Ledger*, 1 September 1985; and "Shapiro Better Move Quick to Avert a Knockout," *Newark Star-Ledger*, 1 September 1985.

25. Donald Warshaw, "State AFL-CIO Supports Kean Campaign at Meeting of Its Delegates," *Newark Star-Ledger*, 17 September 1985.

26. Shapiro, interview, 15 July 2002.

27. "If Mondale Had Won, Would Reagan's Men Have Pulled Such Pranks?" *New Jersey Monthly*, September 1985.

28. Jim Goodman, "Bickering between Candidates Nearly Scuttled Debate," *Trenton Times*, 3 October 1985; Frank Herrick, "Kean and Shapiro Get Tough in Debate," *Trentonian*, 3 October 1985; and David Wald, "Exposure Gives Shapiro Victory in First Debate," *Newark Star-Ledger*, 6 October 1985.

29. Ibid.; and Al Frank and David Wald, "Kean Spars with Shapiro in Debate," *Newark Star-Ledger*, 3 October 1985.

30. Ibid.

31. Goodman, "Bickering between Candidates Nearly Scuttled Debate."

32. Ibid.

33. Remarks by President Ronald Reagan at a Republican fundraising luncheon in Parsippany, N.J., 4 October 1985.

34. David Wald, "Reagan Rallies Jersey's GOP," *Newark Star-Ledger*, 5 October 1985.

35. "Supporters Applaud Campaigning Governor," *Newark Star-Ledger*, 14 October 1985.

36. Ibid.

37. Dan Holly, "Governor Stumps for Big Turnout by Voters," *Newark Star-Ledger*, 21 October 1985.

38. David Wald, "Kean Holds 51-Point Lead over Shapiro," *Newark Star-Ledger*, 13 October 1985.

39. David Wald, "Waste Issue Isn't a Barrel of Laughs for the Underdog," *Newark Star-Ledger*, 20 October 1985.

40. David Wald, "Bush Sees Kean to Crest of GOP 'Tidal Wave,'" *Newark Star-Ledger*, 25 October 1985.

41. Robert Schwaneberg, "Coretta King Calls Kean a 'Warrior for Peace,'" *Newark Star-Ledger*, 26 October 1085.

42. Dan Weissman, "Shapiro Charge Spurs Heated Clash on Kean Efforts to Win Black Vote," *Newark Star-Ledger*, 28 October 1985.

43. Quoted in David Wald, "Shapiro Punches, Kean Parries in Uninspired 'Bout,'" *Newark Star-Ledger*, 27 October 1985.

44. David Wald, "Incumbent Maintains Big Lead," *Newark Star-Ledger*, 3 November 1985.

45. Audubon Park and Chesilhurst, two small Democratic hamlets in Camden County, and Roosevelt, a Monmouth County borough named for the New Deal president. In two of these three municipalities, the race had been close. In Audubon Park, Shapiro pulled ahead of Kean 159 to 132 and in Chesilhurst, 173 to 153. The Democrat's margin was wider in Roosevelt, where he received 220 to Kean's 185.

46. Quoted in David Wald, "Kean Wins in Landslide: Governor Chalks Up Largest Plurality and Takes All 21 Counties in the State," *Newark Star-Ledger*, 6 November 1985.

47. Ibid.

48. Quoted in David Wald, "'Street Smart' Shapiro Trying to Gain Ground," *Newark Star-Ledger*, 21 July 1985.

18. The Storm over the Wilentz Case

1. For an overview of Hughes's political and judicial career, see Alvin S. Felzenberg, "The Impact of Gubernatorial Style on Policy Outcomes: An In-Depth Study of Three New Jersey Governors" (Ph.D. diss., Princeton University, 1978), 180. The quotation comes from an interview the author conducted with Richard J. Hughes, 26 September 1975.

2. Ibid.

3. Ibid.

4. Ibid. The quotation comes from an interview the author conducted with Richard J. Hughes, 26 September 1975.

5. For an overview of Wilentz's overall judicial style, see Robert G. Seidenstein, "Governor Will Reappoint Wilentz," *Newark Star-Ledger*, 22 May

1986; Cathy Barrett Carter, "Wilentz Dies after Battle with Cancer," *Newark Star-Ledger*, 24 July 1996; and David Stout, "Robert Wilentz, 69, New Jersey Chief Justice, Dies; Court Aided Women and the Poor," *New York Times*, 24 July 1996.

6. Jim Goodman, "The Governor," *New Jersey Reporter*, February 1987.

7. "Doing It Kean's Way," editorial, *Newark Star-Ledger*, 8 December 1985.

8. Karen De Masters, "Chief Justice Renomination Shakes GOP," *Asbury Park Press*, 22 May 1986.

9. Ibid.

10. Karen De Masters, "Charges Forced Decision on Wilentz," *Asbury Park Press*, 23 May 1986.

11. Dan Weissman, "Defiant Governor Re-nominates a Chief Justice and Takes on a Tradition," *Newark Star-Ledger*, 25 May 1986.

12. Ibid.

13. Golden, interview, 4 August 2002.

14. De Masters, "Charges Forced Decision on Wilentz."

15. Robert G. Seidenstein, "Kean Quickly Renominates Wilentz as Chief Justice to Blunt Politicking," *Newark Star-Ledger*, 25 May 1986.

16. De Masters, "Chief Justice Renomination Shakes GOP."

17. Herb Jaffe, "Judiciary Chairman Warns Witnesses to Be 'Precise' at the Pressler Hearing," *Newark Star-Ledger*, 30 September 1983.

18. Kathy Barrett Carter, "Senate Stands Firm on Judgeship Denial," *Newark Star-Ledger*, 18 September 1983.

19. Robert G. Seidenstein, "Wilentz Confirmation Stalls on a Question of Residency," *Newark Star-Ledger*, 25 July 1986.

20. Robert G. Seidenstein, "Wilentz Residency Still at Issue," *Newark Star-Ledger*, 29 July 1986.

21. The five Democrats were Paul Contillo (Bergen), Catherine Costa (Burlington), Daniel Dalton (Camden), Frank Pallone (Monmouth), and Raymond Zane (Salem). The two Republicans were Wayne Dumont (Warren) and William Gormley (Atlantic).

22. Robert G. Seidenstein, "Wilentz Confirmed, 21–19, Following Kean Intervention," *Newark Star-Ledger*, 1 August 1986.

23. Ibid.

24. Ibid.

25. Quoted in Joseph F. Sullivan, "Man in the News; Uncompromising Jersey Chief Justice: Robert Nathan Wilentz," *New York Times*, 2 August 1986.

26. Richard J. Hughes to Thomas H. Kean, 13 August 1986, Thomas H. Kean personal papers.

27. Jim Goodman, "The Governor," *New Jersey Reporter*, February 1987.

28. Ibid. Wilentz remained on the court for an additional ten years. His enhanced tenure was marked by additional controversies. In 1990, acting in his administrative capacities, he refused to allow the Essex County Courthouse to be filmed in the movie *The Bonfire of the Vanities* because he disagreed with the manner in which African Americans were being presented. His action cost the county $250,000 it expected to receive from the producers. A federal judge reversed Wilentz's decree on the grounds that it violated free speech. Wilentz also reversed twenty-seven death sentence convictions that came under the reenacted death penalty statute Kean had signed into law in 1982, affirming three. See Stout, "Robert Wilentz, 69, New Jersey Chief Justice Dies."

19. Kean Reforms Welfare

1. Drew Altman, telephone interview by author, 1 August 2003.

2. Federal regulations allowed them to remain at home until their children reached the age of six.

3. "Governor Kean's 'Real Welfare Program,'" editorial, *New York Times*, 8 January 1987.

4. Ibid.

5. William K. Stevens, "The Welfare Consensus," *New York Times*, 22 June 1988.

6. Ibid.

7. Joseph F. Sullivan, "From Both Parties, Support for Jersey's 'Workfare,'" *New York Times*, 20 April 1987.

8. Linda Lamendola, "Kean Delivers Welfare Plan to White House," *Newark Star-Ledger*, 14 September 1986.

9. Altman interview; and Michael Rozansky, "Governor Gets Workfare Rolling, Says Federal Waivers Have Been Granted: REACH Under Way for Recipients in Bergen, Union, and Middlesex," *Newark Star-Ledger*, 9 October 1987.

10. Jim Goodman, "Will Bush Treat N.J. Better?" *Trenton Times*, 27 November 1988.

11. Quoted in Rozansky, "Governor Gets Workfare Rolling."

12. Remarks of President Ronald Reagan, at a luncheon hosted by the New Jersey Chamber of Commerce in Somerset, N.J., 13 October 1987.

13. President Ronald Reagan to Governor Thomas H. Kean, 6 February 1987. Thomas H. Kean personal papers.

14. J. Scott Orr, "Governors Endorse Welfare Reforms," *Newark Star-Ledger*, 25 February 1987.

15. David S. Broder, "Governors Endorse Welfare Overhaul; Speaker Wright Holds Out Hope for House Action This Spring," *Washington Post*, 25 February 1987; and William Raspbery, "Nobody Knows How to Fix Welfare," *Washington Post*, 27 February 1987.

16. Carol Matlack, "Clinton at Opening Press Conference in Washington," *Arkansas Gazette*, 2 February 1987.

17. William Jefferson Clinton, interview, 5 February 2003.

18. Lou Cannon, *Governor Reagan: His Rise to Power* (New York: Public Affairs, 2003).

19. Broder, "Governors Endorse Welfare Overhaul."

20. Orr, "Governors Endorse Welfare Reforms."

21. Quoted in ibid.

22. J. Scott Orr, "Welfare Moms Join Kean to Boost Jersey Reforms," *Newark Star-Ledger*, 23 February 1988.

23. William K. Stevens, "The Welfare Consensus," *New York Times*, 22 June 1988.

24. "Armed with President's Support, Governors Take Plan to Congress. Association, Lawmakers Agree 'Time Has Come' for Welfare Reform," *Arkansas Democrat*, 25 February 1987.

25. Quoted in J. Scott Orr, "Reagan, Kean Confer on Welfare Reforms," *Newark Star-Ledger*, 24 February 1987.

26. William Jefferson Clinton, interview, 5 February 2003.

27. Donna Leussner, "Official Fired in 'Shortfall," *Newark Star-Ledger*, 21 April 1989.

28. Jim Goodman, "Altman Was Easy Mark for Moore," *Trenton Times*, 30 April 1989.

29. Leusser, "Official Fired in 'Shortfall.'"

30. Altman, interview, 1 August 2003.

31. Ibid.

20. The Man with the Message

1. Thomas H. Kean, speech before the Heritage Foundation, 11 December 1985. Thomas H. Kean personal papers.

2. McGlynn, interview, 27 September 2002. See also Dan Weissman, "Citizen Kean Painstakingly Maps His Course of Manifest Destiny," *Newark Star-Ledger*, 16 March 1986.

3. David Wald, "Governor Assumes High National Profile, Low-Key Role at Home," *Newark Star-Ledger*, 7 December 1986.

4. Dan Weissman, "Kean Named Vice Chairman of Republican Governors, Predicts '86 Gains," *Newark Star-Ledger*, 11 December 1985.

5. Dan Weissman, "Guest Speaker Kean Is a Big Hit at New Hampshire GOP Dinner," *Newark Star-Ledger*, 10 March 1986.

6. Squier, interview, 30 November 2002.

7. Weissman, "Guest Speaker Kean Is a Big Hit at New Hampshire GOP Dinner."

8. Ibid.; and Jim Goodman, "Kean's Trips Haven't Built National Stature," *Trenton Times*, 26 October 1986.

9. David Broder, "Governors Put Congressmen to Shame," *Newark Star-Ledger*, 15 December 1985.

10. Weissman, "Guest Speaker Kean Is a Big Hit at New Hampshire GOP Dinner."

11. Joseph F. Sullivan, "Kean Tells the GOP to Widen," *New York Times*, 10 March 1986.

12. Weissman, "Guest Speaker Kean Is a Big Hit at New Hampshire GOP Dinner."

13. Quoted in Dan Weissman, "Kean Receives a Warm Welcome from Michigan Republicans," *Newark Star-Ledger*, 20 April 1986.

14. David Wald, "Kean Forming a Personal PAC to 'Speak Out on National Issues,'" *Newark Star-Ledger*, 22 April 1986. Among those for whom Kean campaigned were William Lucas, an African American running for governor of Michigan; Janet Rzewnicki, candidate for state treasurer in Delaware; William W. Scranton III, seeking the post his father once held as governor in Pennsylvania; and Robert A. Taft III, Ohio lieutenant governor hopeful.

15. Joseph F. Sullivan, "Kean Visits Midwest in Bid to Mold '88 Issues," *New York Times*, 19 October 1986; and Jim Goodman, "Kean Busy in Midwest: Speaks to Officials, Business Leaders," *Trenton Times*, 17 October 1986.

16. Dan Weissman, "Governor Stumps for GOP Candidates amid Speculation on His Own Plans," *Newark Star-Ledger*, 17 October 1986.

17. "Kean Set to Test His National Appeal," *Trentonian*, 10 September 1986.

18. "Razing Kean," *National Review*, 24 October 1986.

19. George F. Will, "GOP 'Sinner' Tom Kean Should Be a Candidate," *Trenton Times*, 10 October 1986.

20. Quoted in Dan Weissman, "Kean May Be Hinting at Ambition in Plea to GOP for 'Open Doors,'" *Newark Star-Ledger*, 13 July 1986.

21. Elected were Guy Hunt (Alabama), Evan Meacham (Arizona), John R.

McKernan (Maine), George Mickelson (South Dakota), Garrey Carruthers (New Mexico), Harry Bellmon (Oklahoma), Carroll A. Campbell Jr. (South Carolina), and Tommy G. Thompson (Wisconsin).

22. Quoted in Dan Weissman, "Kean Predicts Governors Will Utilize Election Triumphs as a Power Tool," *Newark Star-Ledger*, 9 November 1986; and J. Scott Orr, "Kean Tells GOP Leaders of the Steep Cost of Snubbing the Minority Vote: Shortsighted Strategy Blamed for Failure to Keep Senate Control," *Newark Star-Ledger*, 20 November 1986.

23. Fred Pieretti, "Bennett Lauds Governors for Efforts in Education, Extols Kean's Policies," *Newark Star-Ledger*, 10 December 1986.

24. Jim Goodman, "The Governor," *New Jersey Reporter*, January 1987.

25. Quoted in ibid.

26. Quoted in John J. Farmer, "D.C. Short-Circuits Statehouse Power," *Newark Star-Ledger*, 8 December 1986.

27. Quoted in Mary Kay Risi, "It's the Day of the Governors, and Kean Is Shining," *New Brunswick Home News*, 14 December 1986.

28. Ibid.

29. Joseph F. Sullivan, "GOP Governors' Post Gives Kean New Stage," *New York Times*, 10 December 1986.

30. Dan Weissman, "Not Even the 'Iran' Circus Could Sidetrack the GOP Governors' Big Show," *Newark Star-Ledger*, 14 December 1986.

31. Dan Weissman, "Focus on Governors: Kean Hosts Muscle-Flexer for GOP State Chiefs," *Newark Star-Ledger*, 7 December 1986.

32. Larry Eichel, "Nixon Says Critics Should Get Off Reagan's Back," *Philadelphia Inquirer*, 10 December 1986.

33. Thomas H. Kean, interview, 25 June 2002.

34. Robert Cohen, "Reagan Tells Governors of Finding 'Smoking Gun,'" *Newark Star-Ledger*, 10 December 1986. Kean confirmed after the meeting that "smoking gun" had been the expression Reagan had used.

35. Quoted in Thomas H. Kean, interview, 25 June 2002; and in Thomas H. Kean, *The Politics of Inclusion* (New York: Free Press, 1988), 71. In addition to Regan, Vice President George H. W. Bush and James Miller, the director of the Office of Management and Budget, were in attendance at the meeting. A former member of Congress and a rising party conservative, Campbell was said to have considerable standing with the Reagan White House.

36. Quoted in ibid.

37. Quoted in Cohen, "Reagan Tells Governors of Finding 'Smoking Gun.'"

38. Broder, "Governors Put Congressmen to Shame."

39. Quoted in Risi, "It's the Day of the Governors, and Kean Is Shining."

40. Ibid.

41. "The Statehouse: Action and Innovation: A New Breed of Governor Upstages Washington," *Newsweek*, 24 March 1986, 30–32.

42. See Larry Sabato, *Good-Bye to Good-Time Charlie: The American Governorship Transformed* (Washington, D.C.: CQ Press, 1983).

43. David Osborne, *Laboratories of Democracy: A New Breed of Governor Creates Models for National Growth* (Boston: Harvard Business School Press, 1988).

44. David Wessel, "Can-Do Capitals: States Enlarge Roles as Congress Is Unable to Solve Problems, Pragmatic Governors Offer Plans to Curb Pollution; Better Schools in Arkansas, Showing Where the Taxes Go," *Wall Street Journal*, 28 June 1988.

45. Ibid.

46. Susan Agrest, "A Patrician Who Makes New Jersey Work," *Newsweek*, 24 March 1986, 31.

47. Clinton's remarks were recalled by Thomas H. Kean, in an interview, 25 June 2002.

48. Joseph F. Sullivan, "Kean Seeks a Key Role in GOP: But Resists Pressure to Seek Presidency," *New York Times*, 9 March 1987. Dukakis's lieutenant governor was future U.S. senator John F. Kerry.

49. Joseph F. Sullivan, "Kean's Star Rising in G.O.P.," *New York Times*, 27 December 1987.

50. Family connections extended a further generation back. Kean's grandfather, Hamilton Fish Kean, and Bush's grandfather had been classmates at the Stevens Institute of Technology. Of all the public figures with whom she became acquainted, Debby Kean's favorite was George H. W. Bush. Kean jokingly referred to the forty-first president as his "main rival for [my] wife's attentions." Thomas H. Kean, interview, 25 June 2002.

51. Sullivan, "Kean's Star Rising in G.O.P."

52. Most who took sides went with Bush. Kean's present and past transportation secretaries, John Sheridan and Hazel Gluck, endorsed Dole. Leonard Coleman backed Kemp.

53. Kean, *The Politics of Inclusion*, 42.

54. Roger Stone, telephone interview by author, 24 March 2005.

55. Quoted in David Broder, "Sensible Governors Find It Easy to Stay Neutral," *Newark Star-Ledger*, 24 February 1988.

56. David Wald, "Bush Receives Kean Backing, Adopts Governor's Themes," *Newark Star-Ledger*, 22 March 1988; and Jim Goodman, "Kean Tries to Dash VP Rumors: GOP Leaders Hope Speech Gives Him No. 2 Spot," *Trenton Times*, 30 June 1988.

57. Joseph F. Sullivan, "Kean Gets Bipartisan Advice on Speech," *New York Times*, 30 June 1988.

58. Jim Goodman, "Governors Convene in Bipartisan Spirit," *Trenton Times*, 10 August 1988.

59. David Bloomquist, "Kean: Keynote Selection Should End VP Slot Talk," *Bergen Record*, 30 June 1988; and Goodman, "Kean Tries to Dash VP Rumors."

60. David Wald, "Kean as Keynoter: Hopes to Stress 'Inclusive GOP,'" *Newark Star-Ledger*, 30 June 1988.

61. Ibid.

62. "Walkout Threatened," *New York Times*, 30 June 1988.

63. "'Threat' to Keynote Countered by Kean," *New York Times*, 1 July 1988. Interestingly, Kean never referred to abortion in his keynote address.

64. Thomas H. Kean, interview, 26 June 2002.

65. In Cuomo's address, he sarcastically suggested that he would not ask Ronald Reagan, who purported to be a "family-values president," when he had last seen his grandchild.

66. Joseph F. Sullivan, "The Republicans in New Orleans: The Kean Way: Keynoter with Common Touch," *New York Times*, 16 April 1988.

67. "Kean as Keynoter: Address Suffered from Split Personality," editorial, *Asbury Park Press*, 18 August 1988.

68. Thomas H. Kean, interview, 26 June 2002.

69. Dukakis's admonition to Kean not to talk too long had been a reference to the lengthy speech Bill Clinton delivered at the Democratic convention weeks earlier when he nominated Dukakis. In a letter to Kean, Richard Nixon also admonished him not to repeat Clinton's mistake. "After

the stupidity of your colleague from Arkansas, I am sure you do not have to be reminded that . . . no speech in prime time should be more then twenty minutes," Nixon told him. Richard Nixon to Thomas H. Kean, 9 August 1988. Thomas H. Kean personal papers.

70. Governor Thomas H. Kean, "1988 Republican National Convention Keynote Address," 16 August 1988.

71. Ibid.

72. Ibid.; and Dan Cohen, *Undefeated: The Life of Hubert H. Humphrey* (Minneapolis: Lerner, 1978), 131.

73. Thomas H. Kean, interview, 26 June 2002.

74. Robinson had decades earlier been called before the House Un-American Activities Committee. Lewis Allen wrote the song's lyrics.

75. Thomas H. Kean, interview, 26 June 2002.

76. Dan Weissman, "Analysts Weigh Kean's National Prospects," *Newark Star-Ledger*, 21 August 1988.

77. Ibid.

78. Kemp, interview, 17 March 2003.

79. David Wald, "Kean Says He'll Endorse Gubernatorial Candidate," *Newark Star-Ledger*, 19 August 1988.

80. Representative Jim Courter chaired his 1981 primary and general election campaigns. Cary Edwards served as Kean's counsel during his first term and as attorney general during his second. Atlantic County state senator Bill Gormley was among Kean's most dependable allies in the legislature. Bo Sullivan, Kean's 1981 primary opponent, had become one of his staunchest fund-raisers. Assembly Speaker Chuck Hardwick shepherded many of the bills Kean supported through the lower house of the legislature.

81. The only primary endorsement he made as governor was that of James Courter over Rodney Frelinghuysen, in a congressional primary, in 1982. Courter had been Kean's campaign chairman in the previous year's gubernatorial primary.

82. Courter took a pro-life stand as a candidate. He announced a reversal in his position after losing the election to Florio.

83. Jim Goodman, "Kean Image Has Seen Its Prime," *Trenton Times*, 1 October 1989.

84. Quoted by Thomas H. Kean, interview by author, Madison, N.J., 25 June 2002.

85. Eagleton Poll Archive, poll 075, question 31, September 1981.

86. Author calculations based on statistics supplied by the U.S. Department of Labor.

87. Author calculations based on statistics supplied by the U.S. Department of Commerce, Bureau of the Census.

88. Ibid.

89. Author calculations based on statistics supplied by the Bureau of Economic Analysis.

90. Ibid.

21. Citizen Kean

1. The moniker, a reference to Orson Welles's famous movie *Citizen Kane*, said to be based on the life of newspaper publisher William Randolph Hearst, was first used by Kean himself to refer to his new role as a former

governor. For its first appearance in print, see Bill Gannon, "Soon-to-Be Citizen Kean, Governor Plans for Life Away from the Statehouse," *Newark Star-Ledger*, 26 November 1989.

2. John T. Cunningham, *University in the Forest: The Story of Drew University*, 3d ed. (Florham Park, N.J.: Afton, 2002), 285, 342.

3. Quoted in Anne-Marie Cottone, "Kean Courts the Scientific: Brightest of High School Students Urged to Stay in State," *Newark Star-Ledger*, 14 August 1985.

4. George H. W. Bush, e-mail to author, 3 February 2003.

5. "Farewell, President Kean and Fare Well, Freshman Class," editorial, *Acorn*, 3 September 2004.

6. Gloria Meikle, "Kean Prepares Exit after 15 Years as University President," *Acorn*, 3 September 2004.

7. Thomas H. Kean, interview by author, Madison, N.J., 14 October 2003.

8. Lawrence Hackett, "'The Perfect Match': Kean and Drew Pictured as Made for Each Other," *Newark Star-Ledger*, 12 February 1989.

9. Quoted in Lawrence Hackett, "Kean Will Assume Presidency of Drew University in 1990," *Newark Star-Ledger*, 11 February 1990.

10. Cunningham, *University in the Forest*, 340.

11. Quoted in Hackett, "Kean Will Assume Presidency of Drew University in 1990." Kean, while governor, used the word *jewel* to describe New Jersey's primary cultural treasures. He used the word to describe historic Waterloo Village in Stanhope, Liberty State Park in Jersey City, and Princeton University. In making these references, he consciously borrowed from Benjamin Disraeli's reference to India as the "jewel in the crown" of Britain's imperial monarch, Queen Victoria.

12. Peggi Howard, telephone interview by author, 29 November 2004.

13. Ibid.

14. Thomas H. Kean, interview, 14 October 2002.

15. Ibid.

16. Quoted in Tom Johnson, "Kean Ends Eight Years in Office with Mix of Sadness, Anticipation," *Newark Star-Ledger*, 17 January 1990.

17. Dory Devlin, "Pageantry at Drew: Crowd Glitters for Kean's Inaugural Gala," *Newark Star-Ledger*, 21 April 1990; and Cunningham, *University in the Forest*, 352–353.

18. Cunningham, *University in the Forest*, 352.

19. Robert L. Chapman, "A Tribute to the New President," insert into the inaugural program of Thomas H. Kean, 20 April 1990.

20. "Prepared Comments of Thomas H. Kean . . . on the Occasion of his Inauguration," Thomas H. Kean personal papers.

21. Dory Devlin, "Pageantry at Drew."

22. Cunningham, *University in the Forest*, 350.

23. Michael Meagher, "Growing to a Mighty Oak: President Thomas H. Kean Marks His First 10 Years at Drew University," *Drew Magazine*, Winter 2000, 25–32.

24. Thomas H. Kean, column, *Drew Magazine*, Summer 2002.

25. Meagher, "Growing to a Mighty Oak," 26; and ibid.

26. Ibid.

27. Kristen Alloway and Bill Swayze, "Kean Shows Staying Power at Drew: Former Governor Brings Distinction to Madison University," *Newark Star-Ledger*, 20 February 2000.

28. Cunningham, *University in the Forest*, 359–360. Overall university

priorities were excellence in liberal education, responsible stewardship of resources, improved community life and ethos, greater external recognition, promotion of international education, and incorporation of technology into the learning process.

29. Vincent Zarate, "Unkindest Cut: 177-Year-Old Statehouse Tree to Get the Ax," *Newark Star-Ledger*, 20 July 1989.

30. Meagher, "Growing to a Mighty Oak," 25; and Thomas H. Kean, "Prepared Comments . . . on the Occasion of His Inauguration."

31. Kean wrote a biweekly column for the *Bergen Record* from 1993 to 2001. Beginning in the mid-1990s he and his predecessor, Brendan Byrne, began holding joint interviews with the *Star-Ledger*, which printed their observations in the form of a column. After leaving the governorship, Kean served on the boards of Amerada Hess, Aramark, Bell Atlantic, CIT Group, Fiduciary Trust International, Pepsi Bottling Company, and the United Health Care Group. His nonprofit activities included service with the Carnegie Corporation, the Century Foundation, the Campaign to Prevent Teen Pregnancies, Big Hourglass Solutions, the National Council of the World Wildlife Fund, and the Robert Wood Johnson Foundation, among others. Upon his retirement from Drew in 2005, he became chairman of the Robert Wood Johnson Foundation, returned to the Carnegie Corporation board, and joined HealthpointCapital, LLC.

32. Patricia Cappon, "Kean to Lead Volunteer Drive," *Newark Star-Ledger*, 23 June 1989; and J. Scott Orr, "3 Top Jerseyans Head Effort to 'Retool' Nation's Schools," *Newark Star-Ledger*, 9 July 1991.

33. Thomas H. Kean, "Taking on the Enemy Within Our Fiscal Gates," *Bergen Record*, 19 June 1994.

34. Thomas H. Kean, "Entitlements: What a Mess," *Bergen Record*, 8 January 1995.

35. Thomas H. Kean, interview, 14 October 2004. The stated objective of the conference was "a new partnership between men and women, involving equal sharing of paid and unpaid work, and equal participation of women and men in civil, political, economic, social, and cultural life."

36. Andrea Mitchell, telephone interview by author, 22 December 2004.

37. Thomas H. Kean, "Report from Beijing: Thousands of Women Join at U.N. Forum in Fight for Justice," *Bergen Record*, 10 September 1995; and Thomas H. Kean, "Change Is in the Air for Women," *Bergen Record*, 24 September 1995.

38. David Hamburg, telephone interview by author, 1 December 2004.

39. Ibid.; and Vivian Stewart, telephone interview by author, 23 December 2004.

40. Sarah Brown, interview by author, Washington, D.C., 29 November 2004.

41. Betty McKay and Ann Carns, "As Teen Births Drop, Experts Are Asking Why," *Wall Street Journal*, 17 November 2004.

42. Brown, interview, 29 November 2004.

43. Tom Kean and Isabel Sawhill, "More Teens Just Say, 'No,'" *Washington Post*, 5 May 2000; Al Hunt, "Abstinence Only for Teenagers: A Pipe Dream," *Wall Street Journal*, 2 May 2002; and Al Hunt, "Beware the Moral Cops," *Wall Street Journal*, 2 December 2004.

44. Thomas H. Kean, interview, 14 October 2003.

45. "Kean Hospitalized with Blocked Artery: Ex-Governor Is Doing Well after Surgery," *Newark Star-Ledger*, 17 November 1995.

46. During the period in which Kean was convalescing, the federal government would twice shut down before Clinton and Congress reached agreement on the budget.

47. Judy Peet, "Kean's Holiday at Home: Ex-Governor Ends 7 Days in Hospital," *Newark Star-Ledger*, 14 November 1995.

48. According to the recollections of one of the program's architects, Christopher Edley, telephone interview by author, 19 May 2005.

49. Michael Fletcher, "Clinton Names Advisory Panel to Address U.S. Racial Divide," *Washington Post*, 13 June 1997.

50. Ibid.

51. Thomas H. Kean, "Americans Must Try Anew to Reach across Racial Divide," *Bergen Record*, 27 July 1997.

52. Thomas H. Kean, "Tackling Unfinished Business," *Drew Magazine*, Summer 1997, 3.

53. Peter Baker, "A Splinter on Race Advisory Board: First Meeting Yields Divergent Views on Finding 'One America,'" *Washington Post*, 15 July 1997.

54. The President's Initiative on Race, transcript, Washington, D.C., 14 July 1997.

55. Christopher Caldwell, "The Disgrace Commission: Clinton's Race Initiative Aims Mainly to Prop Up Affirmative Action," *Weekly Standard*, 8 December 1997. Kean explained that the "thoughtful Republican" phrase referred to elected officials in Congress, including its leadership, and at the state and local levels.

56. Steven A. Holmes, "President Nudges His Race Panel to Take Action," *New York Times*, 1 October 1997.

57. J. Scott Orr, "Kean's Insider Shot Prods Race Advisers: He Calls for More Candor and Viewpoints," *Newark Star-Ledger*, 3 December 1997.

58. Ibid.

59. Thomas H. Kean, "Closing the Race Gap: The Dialogue Begins," *Bergen Record*, 5 October 1997; Peter Baker, "Clinton Sees Fairfax as Racial Model for U.S.: President Wants Panel to Study County's Varied Population for Clues to the Future," *Washington Post*, 1 October 1997; and Michael A. Fletcher, "Initiative on Race Ends Short of Its Soaring Goals," *Washington Post*, 17 September 1998.

60. Ruth Larson, "Race Panelists Urge 'No More Excuses' in Education: Clinton's Board Meets amid Success of Diverse Fairfax," *Washington Times*, 18 December 1997.

61. Ibid. At the time, Connerly was spearheading a ballot initiative to end affirmative action in admissions at public universities in California.

62. The invitees were Elaine Chou, of the Heritage Foundation; former Howard University trustee Thaddeus Garrett Jr.; authors Stephan and Abigail Thernstrom; Florida Republican representative Charles T. Canady; former Reagan official Linda Chavez; University of California Board of Regents member Ward Connerly; former secretary of labor Lynn Martin; and Kean.

63. Manning Marable, "A Conversation with John Hope Franklin," *Souls*, Summer 1999.

64. "Clinton Debates 9 Conservatives on Racial Issues: A Wide-Ranging Meeting, Merits of Affirmative Action Dominate Discussion and Provoke a Few Sparks," *New York Times*, 20 December 1997.

65. Steven A. Holmes, "Clinton Panel on Race Urges Variety of Modest Measures," *New York Times*, 18 September 1998.

66. Ibid.; and Thomas H. Kean, "Now What," unpublished paper, 20 October 1998. Author's files.

67. Judith A. Winston, "Educational Equity and the President's Initiative on Race," paper presented at a conference, *"Brown v. Board of Education: Did It Make Any Difference?"* Woodrow Wilson International Center for Scholars, 9 January 2001.

68. Edley, interview, 19 May 2005.

69. Ibid.

70. Thomas H. Kean, "Who's Presidential? No Candidate Is Better than Bush," *New York Times,* 13 March 1992.

71. Thomas H. Kean, interview, 25 June 2002.

72. Dory Devlin, Patrick Sullivan, and David Wald, "Clinton Offers a Recovery Plan Spurred by Construction," *Newark Star-Ledger,* 1 October 1992.

73. David Schwar, "Bush Blasts Rival, Touts Record before Union Local in Newark," *Newark Star-Ledger,* 1 October 1992.

74. Ibid.

75. Clinton, interview, 5 February 2003.

76. Anthony De Palma, "Far from the Governor's Office, but Not from Politics," *New York Times,* 28 October 1992.

77. Quoted in ibid.

78. *Drew Magazine,* Winter 2001; and *Washington Post,* 9 October 1996.

79. Robert J. Braun, "Kean Urges 'Close Look': Ex-Governor Expresses Concern on Higher Ed Shakeup," *Newark Star-Ledger,* 27 March 1994; Laura Mansnerus, "University Merger Plan Has Support as Well as Concerns," *New York Times,* 16 October 2002; and "Good Citizen Kean," *Newark Star-Ledger,* 22 December 2002.

80. Michael Winerip, "Gun Juggernaut vs. Gentleman Named Kean," *New York Times,* 30 August 1992.

81. Thomas H. Kean, "Religious Right Can Be a Force Only If It Agrees to Disagree," *Bergen Record,* 3 July 1994.

82. "God and Prime Ministers," editorial, *Wall Street Journal,* 25 July 1994.

83. Thomas H. Kean, interview, 2 October 2002.

84. Joseph F. Sullivan, "Kean Rejects Senate Bid, Citing Rise in Meanness," *New York Times,* 1 September 1995; and Thomas H. Kean, "The Senate: To Run or Not to Run," *Bergen Record,* 27 August 1995.

85. Ibid.

86. Thomas H. Kean, interview, 29 July 2002.

87. Quoted in Gail Russell Chaddock, "New Jersey GOP Tilts toward a New Senate 'Savior': After Governor Drops Out, Citing Money, Popular Former Governor Considers Bid," *Christian Science Monitor,* 13 September 1999.

88. David Wald, "Kean Refuses Run for Senate: Decision Will Make GOP Race a Tossup," *Newark Star-Ledger,* 5 October 1999.

89. Ibid.

90. Chaddock, "New Jersey GOP Tilts toward a New Senate 'Savior.'"

91. David Von Drehle, "In N.J., GOP Seeks to Reclaim Lost Ground: But Senate Race Fails to Yield Strong Contender," *Washington Post,* 2 June 2002.

92. George H. W. Bush to author, 3 February 2003; and Clinton, interview, 5 February 2003.

93. Ibid.

94. Thomas H. Kean, "Advice for Clinton on His Cabinet," *Bergen Record,*

17 November 1996. See also Michael K. Frisby and James M. Perry, "Clinton's Cabinet May Be Big Enough for a Republican," *Wall Street Journal,* 8 November 1996.

22. Chairing the 9–11 Commission

1. Lorraine Ash, "Attack Creates Bond in Drew Community: Students, Faculty, Find Comfort in Gathering in Athletic Center," *Daily Record of Morris County,* 12 September 2001.

2. Thomas H. Kean, interview, 12 November 2004.

3. Video of the Fiduciary Trust International Service at the Cathedral of St. John the Divine, 16 October 2001. See also "Citizen Kean," editorial declaring Kean "Citizen of the Year," *Philadelphia Inquirer,* 2 January 2005.

4. *New York Times,* 29 November 2002.

5. Dan Eggen, "Kissinger Quits Post as Head of 9–11 Panel: Withdrawal a Setback for White House," *Washington Post,* 14 December 2002.

6. "Daschle Seeking a Special Inquiry on 9–11 Attack: GOP Criticizes the Plan," *New York Times,* 22 May 2002.

7. CBS, 15 May 2002; and *New York Times,* 5–22 May 2002.

8. David Firestone and James Risen, "White House in Shift, Backs Inquiry on 9–11, Broad Outside Study of Failures Is Planned," *New York Times,* 21 September 2002

9. *Washington Post,* 25 September 2002.

10. David Firestone, "White House Blocks Deal by Congress on 9–11 Panel," *New York Times,* 11 October 2002.

11. *New York Times,* 10 October 2002.

12. Subpoenas could also be issued by the concurrence of the chair and vice chair. In either instance, bipartisan cooperation would be required.

13. "Good Citizen Kean," interview, *Newark Star-Ledger,* 22 December 2002

14. Quoted in ibid.

15. Philip Shenon, "Bush Names Former New Jersey Governor to 9–11 Panel," *New York Times,* 17 December 2002. Kean's description of how he reacted to his appointment was surprisingly similar to how President Harry S. Truman described to reporters the day after Franklin Roosevelt's death the sensation he felt upon hearing the news. "I felt like the moon, the stars, and all the planets had fallen on me," Truman said. See www.whitehouse.gov/history/presidents/ht33.html.

16. Thomas H. Kean, interview, 14 October 2003.

17. Scott Lindlaw, Associated Press, 16 December 2002.

18. White House Office of the Press Secretary, 16 December 2002; and Robert Cohen, "Bush Names Kean to Head 9–11 Panel," *Newark Star-Ledger,* 17 December 2002.

19. Scott Lindlaw, "Former N.J. Governor to Head 9–11 Panel: Gov. Thomas H. Kean to Replace Henry Kissinger in Investigation," Associated Press, 16 December 2002.

20. Abbott Koloff, "Kean to Chair Sept. 11 Inquiry," *Morris Daily Record,* 17 December 2002.

21. Robert Cohen, "Bush Names Kean to Head 9–11 Panel"; and Philip Shenon, "Bush Names Former New Jersey Governor to 9–11 Panel," *New York Times,* 17 December 2002.

22. Ledyard King, Gannett News Service, 17 December 2002.

23. Koloff, "Kean to Chair Sept. 11 Inquiry." Arguing the contrary, some at both ends of the political spectrum cited Kean's presence on the board of Amerada Hess as a conflict. The company had formed a joint venture, Delta Oil, which participated in the construction of a proposed pipeline through Afghanistan. Delta Oil's two principals appeared on a United Nation's list of suspected al Qaeda financiers. One, Khalid bin Mahfouz, was a brother-in-law of bin Laden. The joint partnership dissolved prior to Kean's appointment. For a sampling of criticisms of Kean for his Amerada-Hess ties, see Michel Chossudovsky, "New Chairman of the 9–11 Commission Had Business Ties with Osama's Brother-in-Law," www.GlobalResearch.ca, 29 December 2002; and Paul Sperry, *Crude Politics: How Bush's Oil Cronies Hijacked the War on Terror* (Nashville: WND, 2003), 187–188.

24. Quoted in Siobhan Gorman, "Refusing to Fail," *National Journal,* 17 July 2004.

25. Quoted in Lawrence Ragonese, "Kean Pledges to Continue His Work as Drew President," *Newark Star-Ledger,* 17 December 2002.

26. David Broder, "A Very Thorough 9–11 Commission," *San Diego Union,* 4 April 2004.

27. Jamie Gorelick, interview by author, Washington, D.C., 11 November 2004.

28. Tim Roemer, interview by author, Washington, D.C., 23 November 2004.

29. Ibid.

30. Slade Gorton, telephone interview by author, 9 December 2004.

31. Gorelick, interview, 11 November 2004.

32. The author heard Hamilton pay this tribute to Kean during a meeting the two had with the editorial board of *USA Today.*

33. Gorton, interview, 9 December 2004.

34. Mike Kelly, "Kean Feels Weight of Past, Present, and Future Too," *Bergen Record,* 15 February 2002.

35. Roemer, interview, 23 November 2004.

36. Philip Zelikow, telephone interview by author, 15 February 2005.

37. Gorton, interview, 9 December 2004.

38. Thomas H. Kean, interview, 14 October 2004.

39. Philip Shenon, "Clinton Aides Plan to Tell Panel of Warning Bush Team on Qaeda," *New York Times,* 21 March 2004.

40. The author observed this exchange between Kean and reporters as the commission broke for lunch during one of its hearings.

41. Bob Braun, "Kean Feels the Wrath of Irate 9–11 Families; Panel Chairman Faces Hours of Questions," *Newark Star-Ledger,* 12 February 2004.

42. John F. Lehman, telephone interview by author, 30 December 2004.

43. Quoted in Dan Eggen, "Members of 9–11 Panel Warn of Funding Woe," *Washington Post,* 27 March 2003.

44. Quoted in ibid.

45. Dan Eggen, "9–11 Panel to Receive More Money: Negotiations Cut Commission's Request by $2 Million," *Washington Post,* 29 March 2003.

46. Ibid.

47. "Undercutting the 9–11 Inquiry," editorial, *New York Times,* 31 March 2003.

48. Quoted in Laurence Arnold, Associated Press, 26 April 2003.

49. *First Interim Report of the National Commission on Terrorist At-*

tacks upon the United States and press briefing, 8 July 2003. (See www.9–11 commission.gov.)

50. Ibid.

51. *Second Interim Report of the National Commission on Terrorist Attacks upon the United States* and press briefing, 23 September 2003.

52. Bob Braun, "In Measured Words, a Winning Strategy," *Newark Star-Ledger,* 9 July 2003.

53. Press briefing, National Commission on Terrorist Attacks upon the United States, 23 September 2003.

54. Statement by Thomas H. Kean and Lee H. Hamilton, National Commission on Terrorist Attacks upon the United States, 10 October 2003.

55. Mike Kelly, "Will Kean Get Tough?" *Bergen Record,* 2 November 2003.

56. Quoted in Philip Shenon, "9–11 Commission Could Subpoena Oval Office Files," *New York Times,* 26 October 2003.

57. John Podhoretz, "The Kean Mutiny," *New York Post,* 28 October 2003.

58. Quoted in ibid.

59. Thomas H. Kean, interview, 12 November 2004.

60. Philip Shenon, "Panel Reaches Deal on Access to 9–11 Papers," *New York Times,* 13 November 2003; and Dan Eggen, "9–11 Panel Reaches Deal on Access to Papers," *Washington Post,* 13 November 2003.

61. Kelly, "Will Kean Get Tough?"

62. Abbott Koloff, "Kean Ready to Discuss 9–11 Probe with Public," *Daily Record,* 19 November 2003.

63. "9–11 Chair: Attack Was Preventable," CBSNEWS.com, 17 December 2003; and Fran Wood, "Truth and Consequences," *Newark Star-Ledger,* 28 December 2003.

64. Quoted in ibid.

65. Thomas H. Kean, interview, 14 October 2003.

66. Fred F. Fielding, interview by author, Washington, D.C., 29 November 2004.

67. Quoted in "9–11 Chair: There's No Evidence to Blame Clinton or Bush," Newsmax.com, 18 December 2003.

68. The first would occur in January, when a customs agent explained how he had denied entrance into the United States to a man later suspected of having been recruited as the twentieth hijacker. Less attentive officials had obviously admitted the other nineteen.

69. Dan Eggen, "Panel Unlikely to Get Later Deadline," *Washington Post,* 17–19 January 2003; Dan Eggen, "Battle over 9–11 Panel's Deadline Intensifies," *Washington Post,* 29 January 2003; and Shaun Waterman, "9–11 Commission Eyes an Extension," United Press International, 21 January 2003.

70. Mike Allen and Dan Eggen, "Extension for 9/11 Probe Not Backed," *Washington Post,* 5 February 2004.

71. Ibid.

72. Philip Shenon, "Extension of the 9–11 Panel Is Said to Hinge on Speaker," *New York Times,* 27 February 2003.

73. *Newsnight with Aaron Brown,* CNN, transcript, 27 February 2004.

74. *Newsnight with Aaron Brown,* CNN, transcript, 26 February 2004.

75. John King, interview by Lou Dobbs, CNN, transcript, 27 February 2004.

76. Helen Dewar and Dan Eggen, "In Reversal, Hastert Endorses 9–11 Panel Deadline," *Washington Post,* 27 February 2004.

77. Quoted in Dan Eggen, "9–11 Panel to Accept Summary Briefings:

Legal Challenge Scrapped; Agreement Angers Some Members," *Washington Post,* 11 February 2004; Philip Shenon, "9–11 Panel Threatens to Issue Sub-poena for Bush's Briefings," *New York Times,* 10 February 2004; and Robert Cohen, "White House Papers No Help, Says Member of 9–11 Panel," *Newark Star-Ledger,* 13 February 2004.

78. *Meet the Press,* NBC News, transcript, 8 February 2004.

79. Scott J. Paltrow, "Bush Inaction Angers Some on 9–11 Panel," *Wall Street Journal,* 24 February 2004.

80. Roemer, interview, 23 November 2004.

81. *American Morning,* CNN, transcript, 27 February 2004.

82. Mike Allen and Dan Eggen, "Bush Backs Off Limit on 9–11 Question-ing," *Washington Post,* 10 March 2004.

83. *Newsweek,* 12 April 2004.

84. Quoted in ibid.

85. David Brooks, "See Dick Spin," *New York Times,* 27 March 2004.

86. Quoted in ibid.; and National Commission on Terrorist Attacks upon the United States, transcript of eighth public hearing, 24 March 2004.

87. National Commission on Terrorist Attacks upon the United States, transcript of eighth public hearing, 24 March 2004.

88. Peter Johnson, "Big 3 Tout Live Coverage of Rice," *USA Today,* 9 April 2004.

89. Philip Shenon, "Members of the 9–11 Commission Press Rice on Early Warnings," *New York Times,* 9 April 2004.

90. Ibid.

91. *The O'Reilly Factor,* Fox News, transcript, 8 April 2004.

92. Quoted in *Washington Post,* 2 April 2004

93. Lee Hamilton, interview by author, Washington, D.C., 12 January 2005.

94. Unlike in the cases of Clinton and Gore, who were interviewed separately and in the presence of several commission staff, the Bush-Cheney interview was not taped. Nor were transcripts produced. Zelikow was the only commission staff member present. Under procedures the com-mission had established, all witnesses were asked in advance whether they were willing to have their interviews taped and the commission abided by their wishes.

95. Philip Shenon and Lowell Bergman, "9–11 Panel Is Said to Offer Harsh Review of Ashcroft," *New York Times,* 13 April 2004.

96. National Commission on Terrorist Attacks upon the United States, transcript of tenth public hearing, 13 April 2004.

97. "Congressman Calls for 9–11 Panel Member to Step Down," Associ-ated Press, 9 August 2004.

98. "DeLay: 9–11 Panel Should Drop Mudslinging," Associated Press, 20 April 2004.

99. Tom DeLay's open letter to Thomas H. Kean was dated 16 April 2004.

100. Ed Henry, "Senate Republicans Call on Gorelick to Testify," CNN, 23 April 2004. Also signing it were Trent Loft (MI), Ted Stevens (AL), Saxby Chambliss (GA), Robert F. Bennett (UT), Conrad Burns (MO), Pete Domenici (NM), Norm Coleman (MN), Don Nickles (OK), and Mitch McConnell (KY).

101. Gorelick, interview, 11 November 2004.

102. Quoted in Dan Eggen and Walter Pincus, "House Member Seeks Gorelick's Resignation," *Washington Post,* 15 April 2004.

103. Quoted in ibid.

104. Quoted in "9–11 Commission Faults Intelligence," CNN, 19 May 2004.

105. Rush Limbaugh, "Elitist Kean Chairs Joke Commission," transcript, 15 April 2004.

106. "DeLay: 9–11 Panel Should Drop Mudslinging"; and "Republicans Clash over 9–11 Panel," Reuters, 17 April 2004.

107. Adam Nagourney and Eric Lichtblau, "Evaluating the 9–11 Hearings' Winners and Losers," *New York Times*, 18 April 2004.

108. For a sense of what critics said of the commission's visibility, see Jim Rutenberg, "9–11 Panel Comments Freely (Some Critics Say Too Freely)," *New York Times*, 15 April 2004; and Juliette Kayyem and Wayne Downing, "From One Commission to Another, Shut Up," *New York Times*, 16 April 2004.

109. Quoted in Hope Yen, "Kean Vows Lower Profile for 9–11 Panel," Associated Press, 20 April 2004.

110. Gersh Kuntzman, "Debate, American Style," *Newsweek*, 25 May 2004; and "INSULT: Memo to 9–11 Commission: This Man Is a Hero, He Is Not a 'Boy Scout,'" front-page headline, *New York Post*, 19 May 2004.

111. *New York Post*, 19 May 2004.

112. Quoted in William Safire, "The Zelikow Report," *New York Times*, 21 June 2004.

113. Quoted in ibid.

114. Statement by Thomas H. Kean, chair, and Lee H. Hamilton, vice chair, of the 9–11 Commission, 6 July 2004.

115. Public Statement upon the release of the 9–11 Commission report by Thomas H. Kean and Lee H. Hamilton, 22 July 2004.

116. Ibid.

117. Quoted in Scot Paltrow and Greg Hitt, "Final 9–11 Report Urges Changes and Avoids Blame," *Wall Street Journal*, 23 July 2004.

118. Brian Debose, "Lawmakers to Delay Action on 9–11 Report," *Washington Times*, 19 July 2004; Paltrow and Hitt, "Final 9–11 Report Urges Changes and Avoids Blame"; Dan Morgan, "Overhaul of Congressional Panels Urged," *Washington Post*, 23 July 2004.

119. Greg Miller, "9–11 Report Assails Failures," *Los Angeles Times*, 23 July 2004.

120. Paltrow and Hitt, "Final 9–11 Report Urges Changes and Avoids Blame"; and Mimi Hall, "Fix Terror Strategy, 9–11 Panel Says," *USA Today*, 23 July 2003.

121. Maura Reynolds, "Bush Supports 9–11 Panel But Not on Details," *Los Angeles Times*, 3 August 2004.

122. Elisabeth Bumiller and Philip Shenon, "Bush Now Backs Budget Powers in New Spy Post," *New York Times*, 9 September 2004; David S. Cloud and Greg Hitt, "Bush Endorses Budget Powers for Spy Chief; Move Gives Major Push to 9–11 Commission's Plan for Intelligence Overhaul," *Wall Street Journal*, 9 September 2004; Charles Babington, "House GOP Seeks Own Response to 9–11; DeLay, Hastert Stress Chamber's Expertise Rather than the Panel's Recommendations," *Washington Post*, 9 September 2004; and Adam Entous, "Bush Unveils Plan, Falls Short of 9–11 Panel," Reuters, 16 September 2004.

123. Quoted in Babington, "House GOP Seeks Own Response to 9–11."

124. Quoted in Philip Shenon, "Panel's Chief Wants Help from Bush," *New York Times*, 15 October 2004.

125. Philip Shenon, "White House Urges Quick Passage of 9–11 Bill," *New York Times*, 20 October 2004.

126. Philip Shenon, "Delays on 9–11 Bill Are Laid to Pentagon," *New York Times*, 26 October 2004; and William Branigan, "Rumsfeld Denies Lobbying against Intel Bill," *Washington Post*, 23 November 2004.

127. Walter Pincus, "Hope Fades for Intelligence Bill Compromise Soon: Sense of Urgency Disappears as Budget Powers of New Director Continue to be Sticking Point," *Washington Post*, 28 October 2004.

128. Charles Babington, "Hastert Launches a Partisan Policy," *Washington Post*, 27 November 2004.

129. Statement by Speaker Dennis Hastert, 20 November 2004.

130. *Meet the Press*, NBC News, transcript, 28 November 2004.

131. Press conference of President George W. Bush, transcript, 4 November 2004.

132. Robert Novak, "Bush Finding Out Ride Gets Bumpier in Second Term," *Chicago Sun Times*, 2 December 2004.

133. Quoted in Charles Babington and Mike Allen, "White House View of Stalled Bill in Doubt," *Washington Post*, 24 November 2004.

134. Quoted in Philip Shenon, "Bush Reaffirms Support for Intelligence Bill," *New York Times*, 1 December 2004.

135. Quoted in ibid.

136. Mary Curtius, "Bush Scores Intelligence Bill Victory," *Los Angeles Times*, 7 December 2004.

137. Philip Shenon and Eric Lipton, "9–11 Panel Looks to Revamp Congress: Offshoot Group Lobbying Campaign to Begin Next Month," *New York Times*, 21 December 2004.

Epilogue

1. Thomas H. Kean, telephone interview by author, 29 June 2005.

2. Koch, interview, 12 July 2002. See also Edward I. Koch, "Some of His Best Friends Are Republicans," *Wall Street Journal*, 8 August 1988.

Index

Winthrop, Robert, 6
Winthrop family, stories about, 30–31
wiretap bill, 137
Wirth, Conrad L., 102
Wise, Steven S., 24
Wlodychak, Steve, 160
Wolff, Hugh, 275
women: Burgio's appeal to, 128;
    employment concerns of, 117; U.N.
    conference on, 393; welfare reform
    and, 361, 362, 509n2
Woodbridge, lawsuit of, 291
Woodcock, Joseph A., 149
Woodruff, Connie, 307
Woodson, S. Howard, 119, 120, 131,
    447
workers: anticipated shortage of, 362;
    German immigrants, as chemical
    industry, 457n36; on infrastructure
    bank concept, 214–215; 1981 guber-
    natorial campaign and, 169; strike
    benefits for (S-400 law), 77, 85. *See
    also* economic development; jobs
    and job opportunities; labor unions
workfare concept, 360–362, 509n2
Works Progress Administration
    (WPA), 11, 19
World Conference of Soviet Jewry,
    299–300
World Conference on Education for
    All, 392
World Jewish Congress, 24
World Trade Center, 2, 213, 405–406.
    See also National Commission on

Terrorist Attacks upon the United
    States (9–11 Commission)
World War I, RWK in, 9–10
World War II: daily awareness of, 16;
    Pearl Harbor attack in, 22, 23, 290,
    500n37; redress for Japanese Amer-
    ican internment in, 309–311, 325;
    remembrances of, 324; U.S. isola-
    tionism in, 20–21. *See also* Holo-
    caust
World Wildlife Fund, 515n31
Worthington State Forest, 100–103

Yeomans, William F., 75, 78, 83, 108
Yglesias, Joseph, 480n63
Ylvisaker, Paul N., 470n12
Young, Dorothy, 392
Young Americans for Freedom (YAF),
    95
Young Republicans, 73–75, 128

Zacarelli, "Joe Bayonne," 118
Zane, Raymond, 508n21
Zelikow, Philip: as 9–11 Commission
    executive director, 416, 417, 421;
    President's Daily Briefings viewed
    by, 424, 428; on Rice's testimony,
    429–430; on THK's style, 415
Zhou Enlai, 230
Zimmer, Richard A., 402–403
zoning ordinances, Supreme Court
    decisions on, 351–352
Zwillman, Abner ("Longie"), 22

About the Author

Alvin S. Felzenberg served as the principal spokesman for the National Commission on Terrorist Attacks upon the United States (the 9–11 Commission) and for the 9–11 Public Discourse Project. More recently, he has been a fellow at the Institute of Politics at the John F. Kennedy School of Government at Harvard University. He has held senior staff positions with the majority party on two congressional committees, has assisted two presidential administrations, and served as New Jersey's assistant secretary of state in the 1980s. His writings have appeared in the *Washington Post*, the *Philadelphia Inquirer*, the *Boston Globe*, the *Weekly Standard*, and other publications. He is the editor of *Keys to a Successful Presidency* and the coeditor of *Evolution of the Modern Presidency: A Bibliographical Survey*. He has frequently appeared as a commentator on CNN, Fox News, National Public Radio, ABC, NBC, and CBS. Felzenberg holds an M.A. and Ph.D. in politics from Princeton University and a B.A. and M.A. from Rutgers University. He divides his time between Washington, D.C., where he makes his home, and New Jersey.